The American Indian and the United States

A Documentary History

WILCOMB E. WASHBURN is Director of the Office of American Studies at the Smithsonian Institution, Washington, D.C. He was awarded a Ph.D. from Harvard University in 1955. He is the author of *The Governor and the Rebel: A History of Bacon's Rebellion in Virginia* (1957), *Red Man's Land/White Man's Law* (1971), and editor of *The Indian and the White Man* (1964).

The American Indian and the United States

A Documentary History —Volume I

WILCOMB E. WASHBURN

Smithsonian Institution

Random House, New York

Reference Series Editors:
WILLIAM P. HANSEN
FRED L. ISRAEL

FIRST EDITION
BP 9 8 7 6 5 4 3 2 1

Manufactured in the United States of America

Library of Congress Cataloging in Publication Data

Washburn, Wilcomb E., comp.
  The American Indian and the United States.

  1. Indians of North America—Government relations. 2. Indians of North America—History. I. Title. E93.W27
970.5   72-10259   ISBN 0-394-47283-7

Foreword

March, 1973. The American people watched their television sets in disbelief. A trading post at Wounded Knee, South Dakota—a place made famous by the massacre of Big Foot's band by United States troops in 1890—had been captured by a group of renegade Indians and the occupants made hostages. The Indians, members of the American Indian Movement, demanded that the Government investigate the violation of Indian treaties, examine charges of mismanagement by the Bureau of Indian Affairs, and repudiate the existing tribal leadership on the Pine Ridge Reservation. The dramatic and symbolic action of the Indians highlighted the knotty problem of defining the relationship between the American Indian and the United States Government. Among the many racial groups composing the United States of America, the American Indians are unique in possessing a special legal status by virtue of their race. They are the only racial group having a bureau of government concerned exclusively with them. How that relationship evolved is the subject of the four volumes presented here.

I have drawn material from five principal sources for the study of this special relationship: reports of the commissioners of Indian affairs, congressional debates, judicial decisions, treaties, and acts of Congress. I have selected those reports, debates, cases, treaties, and acts that seemed to me to illustrate most effectively the evolution of that relationship. I have chosen to present the documents in chronological order within each of the major categories. While other forms of organization might have been chosen for the benefit of those concerned with specialized aspects of Indian-white relations, the form chosen is designed for more general use, whether for specific reference or casual reading. The spelling, grammar, and punctuation of the original documents have been retained. Of course, the sources from which the documents are drawn contain great numbers of additional documents that have not been reproduced here. What has been brought together, however, conveys what I believe to be the essence of the special relationship between the American Indian and the United States Government as it has evolved over time. A study of the history of that relationship will, hopefully, provide insights to those (both Indian and white) concerned with its further evolution.

CONTENTS

VOLUME I

VOLUME II

Congressional Debates on Indian Affairs

VOLUME III

Acts, Ordinances and Proclamations

Indian Treaties

VOLUME IV

Legal
Decisions

xiv

REPORTS *of the* COMMISSIONERS *of* INDIAN AFFAIRS

Introduction

THE MANAGEMENT of Indian affairs by the United States Government originated within the War Department, where its existence was formalized in 1834 by the establishment of an Indian office headed by a Commissioner of Indian Affairs. In 1849 the office was transferred to the Department of the Interior, where it has remained ever since. Prior to 1834 personnel within the War Department concerned with Indian matters received the general designation "Indian department." This department received the reports of special agents and superintendents sent among particular Indian groups (who normally reported through the territorial governors to the War Department), maintained the records of disbursements made to Indians, and took care of other Indian-related matters. The office of Superintendent of Indian Trade was established within the War Department in 1806 to carry out the provisions of the factory trading system authorized by Congress, but with the abolition of the system in 1822 this office—a potential Indian Bureau—lapsed. Two years later, however, on March 11, 1824, Secretary of War John C. Calhoun established on his own authority a Bureau of Indian Affairs within the War Department and appointed to head the bureau Thomas L. McKenney, Superintendent of Indian Trade from 1816 until the abolition of the office in 1822.

Although McKenney was given responsibility for handling correspondence and accounts of agents and superintendents dealing with Indian matters, for administering funds earmarked for Indian education and civilization, and for preparing reports requested by Congress of the Secretary of War, he was not given commensurate authority or power. Even minor matters had to be referred for decision to the Secretary of War. To expedite administrative procedures, McKenney drew up a bill, which was introduced in the House of Representatives in 1826, authorizing the appointment of a "General Superintendent of Indian Affairs," but the bill failed to pass. However, another bill reorganizing Indian affairs and authorizing the President to appoint a Commissioner of Indian Affairs under the Secretary of War, did become law in 1832, after McKenney had been removed from office. Though many members of Congress and military men advocated the return of the Bureau of Indian Affairs to War Department control during the turbulent 1850's and 1860's, no such retrocession was effected.

From 1832 to the present day the incumbent commissioner, through his required annual report, has been able to review the state of Indian affairs in the country and to make recommendations for change. The following excerpts from some of these annual reports have been selected to show the various levels of comprehension, concern, and commitment demonstrated by successive commissioners. The role of commissioner, by virtue of its

3

subordination to more powerful positions in the Cabinet, has inevitably been restricted in scope and authority. Nevertheless, this very restriction in power has often led to a greater effort to communicate with and persuade those to whom the report has been directed. That audience, though nominally the Secretary of War or the Secretary of the Interior, has more realistically been the Congress of the United States, and, secondarily, the American people. Although more recent annual reports have tended to be bland and non-controversial, earlier reports contain searing indictments of Government policy, honest expressions of moral outrage, and heartfelt recommendations for needed change. In addition, each year's report provides an invaluable official history of Indian-white relations for the preceding year. In earlier years these reports were buttressed with voluminous correspondence from agents in the field. More recently, statistical summaries of accomplishments in health, education, and the like have replaced the well-written historical and philosophical essays that graced the pages of the reports of many former commissioners.

Although the reports of the commissioners of Indian affairs consciously represent the official voice of the Government in its dealings with the Indians, in fact they frequently express the Indian point of view. Sometimes that point of view is cited to be refuted or ridiculed. But, as often as not, the Indian point of view is referred to factually or with sympathy. Thus, even though these reports tended to justify official policies which appear contradictory and wrongheaded when viewed in retrospect, they contain the most authoritative and most extensive information for an understanding of the history of Indian-white interaction. They provide, therefore, a view of the Indian unobtainable elsewhere.

Report of Commissioner of Indian Affairs Thomas L. McKenney November 20, 1826

(Annual Report of the Commissioner of Indian Affairs for the Year 1826, pp. 507-10)

The Office of Indian Affairs was established in 1824 as a branch of the War Department. Thomas L. McKenney was the first commissioner. McKenney's 1826 report to the Secretary of War is perceptive in recognizing the need for Government support for schools in which Indians could be educated in arts and letters. Such schooling, McKenney believed, would serve as a link between less educated Indians and the white people. Furthermore, it would be a preliminary step to Indian assimilation into the white man's economic way of life.

I HAD THE HONOR on the 4th instant, of furnishing the estimate in two papers, No. 1 & 2, of the amount which will be required to be appropriated for the current expenses of the Indian Department for the year 1827, to wit: $181,224. The demand for the increase over the amount appropriated for the last year, to wit: $25,124, arises out of new obligations incurred by treaty; and by an extension of our Indian relations, a reference to which I have had the honor more fully to make in my letter of the 4th instant.

The amount of money disbursed in the Indian Department for the three last quarters of the present year, that is, to the 30th of September, is: $820,080.00; and the amount for the settlement of which returns have been received within the same period, is $573,732.00, leaving to be accounted for $246,348.00. This deficiency, if it can be so called, is, however, only apparent. It arises in great part out of remittances which have been made to Superintendents and Commissioners, for certain objects which have not yet been fully accomplished; and out of the difference between the period in which, by the act of Congress amendatory of the act of 1802, approved May 6, 1822, the Agents are required to make their returns, which is to the 1st day of September in each year; and the period, to wit: the 30th of September, embraced by the call for a statement of the disbursements and receipts. The Agents making their returns up to the 1st of September in conformity to the act of Congress, they show only their disbursements up to that date; whilst they are charged with whatever they may have had remitted to them for application to the 30th of the month. The result is, an apparent balance against the Agent, and for just the amount which he may have on hand on the 1st of September, and which may be applicable to the objects for which it was remitted to the close of the third quarter of the year.

5

It is believed that of the entire amount disbursed, not a cent will be lost; and that as soon as the application of the money is made on account of the objects for which it has been remitted to the several Agents charged with its application, returns will be received for every dollar.

The amount of demands for this year against the provision of $10,000, on account of education of Indian children, as per act of 3d March, 1819, appropriating that sum for the civilization of the Indians, is $13,783.33 1/3.

This act went into operation before those to whom it was deemed best to entrust its humane provisions, were fully prepared to engage in their application. The sum consequently increased, and a surplus arose out of this state of things. This surplus in the first years after the passage of the act was considerable; but it had become reduced to the last year to $3,550.00; and now the whole of it is absorbed and every dollar of the appropriation is disposed of in the apportionments which have been made towards the support of the schools that are in operation under the regulations of the Department. It is to be regretted that the sum at the disposal of the Department for an object so beneficent, and which is in such exact conformity to the principles of our Government, should be so limited; and especially now when experience has demonstrated the utility of the plan, and that success is attending it whenever it has been put in operation. It is a lamentable fact, that hundreds of Indian children are turned away, annually, from those nurseries of kindness, for want of ability on the part of the Superintendents to receive them. Numerous applications for assistance, and from the most respectable societies are now on file in this office, to which it has not been possible to return any other answer than that the fund appropriated by the Congress is exhausted.

It is respectfully, but earnestly recommended, that the sum be increased. The personal inspection which I have been able to make during the last Summer of some of the schools, that, for example, at Michilimackinac, and that near Buffalo, in the State of New York, on the Seneca Reserve, has confirmed all my previous convictions of the vast benefits which the Indian children are deriving from these establishments; and which go further, in my opinion, towards securing our borders from bloodshed, and keeping the peace among the Indians themselves, and attaching them to us, than would the physical force of our Army, if employed exclusively towards the accomplishment of those objects.

It is respectfully suggested whether, after the Indian children shall have passed through a course of instruction, and made capable thereby of taking care of themselves, some suitable provision of another kind ought not to be made for them. If, after they shall have acquired a knowledge of letters, and of the arts, they are thrown back into uneducated Indian settlements, is it not to be apprehended that the labor of instructing them, and the expense attending it, will be lost? To make the plan effective, therefore, and to follow out its humane designs, it is respectfully recommended that, as these youths are qualified to enter upon a course of civilized life, sections of land be given to them, and a suitable present to commence with, of agricultural or other implements suited to the occupations in which they may be disposed, respectively, to engage. They will then have become, an "intermediate link between our own citizens, and our wandering neighbors, softening the shades of each, and enjoying the confidence of both." For a further illustration of this subject, I beg leave respectfully to refer to the report of the Commissioners which accompanies the treaty recently concluded at the Fond du Lac Superior.

The number of schools, their location, and number of teachers to each, and the number of pupils, are all shewn . . . . The reports from all of the schools are flattering, indeed, some of them remarkable, as indicating the extraordinary advances made by the children in all the branches of practical, and moral, and religious improvement.

In addition to the schools enumerated, there is one at Great Crossings, in Kentucky, at which are fifty-four children. This school was established by the Choctaws, and is supported out of their own resources, under the direction of the President of the United States. The Creeks, impressed with the important benefits of education, appropriated part of their means, arising out of the treaty of 22d April, 1826, for the education of some of their children at the same school. Thirty-five children have been added to the schools during the present year; and fifty-four received into the Chowtaw Academy. Last year the number was 1159; and this year 1248, making an increase of 89.

Provision was made at the last session of Congress for holding treaties with certain Indian tribes on Lake Superior, and at Green Bay; in Indiana and Mississippi. Commissioners were duly appointed for holding these treaties, and treaties have been entered into accordingly with the Chippewas of Lake Superior, and with the Miamies and Pottawatomies of Indiana. For reasons which will appear in the report of the Commissioners who negotiated the treaty on Lake Superior, no Council was held at Green Bay. A treaty was held, by the Commissioners appointed for that object, in Indiana, which, together with the treaty of Fond du Lac Superior, and the proceedings under both I have the honor to enclose herewith. No returns have yet been received from the Commissioners appointed to negotiate with the Choctaws and Chickasaws of the State of Mississippi.

Measures have been duly taken to carry into effect the act of Congress of 20th May, 1826, making appropriations for defraying the expense of negotiating and carrying into effect certain Indian treaties; the act of the same date, to aid certain Indians of the Creek nation in their removal West of the Mississippi; the act making appropriation to carry into effect a treaty concluded between the United States and the Creek nation, and ratified 22d April, 1826; and an act for the relief of the Florida Indians. The treaty with the Creeks has been carried into effect; the condition money paid, and in the mode prescribed by the Congress, and the returns made by the Agent, to the Department.

Information having been received by the Department of the hostile dispositions of the Osages and Delawares towards each other, and that a war of extermination was likely to be waged between those tribes and their allies, your instructions were complied with, in addressing letters to the Agents of the Department to interfere, and by their counsels, put a stop, if possible, to the threatened tragedy. Letters received from General Clark of the 12th ultimo, accompanied by a treaty of peace between those tribes, and which I have the honor to submit herewith, shew that a war, so fatal in its effects as that promised to be, has been, by the interference of that officer, happily avoided.

The Commissioners appointed under the act of 3d March, 1825, to mark out a road from the Western Frontier of Missouri, to the Confines of New Mexico, having been by the first article of that act authorized to hold treaties with the intervening tribes of Indians, to obtain their consent to the making of said road, and the undisturbed use thereof to the citizens of the United States, and of the Mexican Republic, have reported no treaties subsequent to those made with the Osages and Kanzas, and which were ratified the 3d of May last.

An informal treaty was entered into between the late Peter Wilson, Sub-agent on the Missouri, and the Assiniboins; informal only because he had no power to make it. The provisions are proper, and as these Indians are sometimes troublesome, it is respectfully suggested whether due powers should not be conferred on the successor of Mr. Wilson, with instructions to make a treaty upon the same basis. I have the honor to enclose the treaty, together with the letter from General Clark, which accompanied it, to the Department.

To that part of your order which forms the basis of this report, which directs me to add such remarks as I may think proper in relation to the administration of the Indian Department, I beg leave respectfully to refer to an act which was reported by the Committee of Indian Affairs, of the House of Representatives at the last session as embracing, in my opinion, all that will be required to give promptitude and efficiency to this branch of our Government relations.

Report of Commissioner of Indian Affairs Thomas L. McKenney November 1, 1828

(Excerpt from *Report for 1828*, pp. 95-96)

McKenney's earliest reports tended to be perfunctory and statistical. In 1828 he broke out of this framework and asked the vital question: "What are humanity and justice in reference to this unfortunate race?" What was Government policy toward these native Americans? Was it extermination? Preservation? Whatever the policy, McKenney noted, it should be considered and acted upon.

I DEEM IT UNNECESSARY to add any remarks in illustration of the absolute necessity of a new modification of this office; the subject having been repeatedly urged before, and the reasons for it submitted, not only in reports from this office, but by distinguished heads of the Department proper, whose views cannot but entitle it to the most respectful consideration. A simple law connecting the responsibility of this branch of the public service with the Congress, and upon precisely the same basis as rests the other branches of the Department of War, followed by a well digested system of regulations for the better government of the diversified subjects which have to be acted on, would ensure to the public, and the Indians, and the agents attached to the service, all that could be desired in the relations which exist between them.

Without such a system, and it being impossible to improve that which now exists, it being, in my opinion, although inadequate, as good as *the Executive* has the power to make it, things must, from necessity, continue in the future as they have been in the past; since no intelligence, however enlightened—nor industry, however untiring—nor experience, however universal, can remedy the evils complained of.

I forbear also to remark, except briefly, upon measures of general policy in regard to our Indians. The subject is growing in interest every day, and is surpassed only by the extreme delicacy of their situation, and of our relations with them. I refer especially to those whose territory is embraced by the limits of States. Every feeling of sympathy for their lot should be kept alive, and fostered; and no measures taken that could compromit the humanity and justice of the nation; and none, I am sure, will be. But the question occurs—*What are humanity and justice in reference to this unfortunate race?* Are these found to lie in a policy that would leave them to linger out a wretched and degraded existence, within districts of country already surrounded and pressed upon by a population whose anxiety and

9

efforts to get rid of them are not less restless and persevering, than is that law of nature immutable, which has decreed, that, under such circumstances, if continued in, *they must perish?* Or does it not rather consist in withdrawing them from this certain destruction, and placing them, though even at this late hour, in a situation where, by the adoption of a suitable system for their security, preservation, and improvement, and at no matter what cost, they may be saved and blest? What *the means* are which are best fitted to realize such a triumph of humanity, I leave to be determined upon by those who are more competent than I am to decide. But that something must be done, and done soon, to save these people, if saved at all, it requires no very deep research into the history of the past, or knowledge of their present condition, embracing especially their relation to the States, to see.

Report of Commissioner of
Indian Affairs Thomas L. McKenney
November 17, 1829

(Excerpt from *Report for 1829*, pp. 164-68)

Removal—the instant solution to the troublesome Indian problem—was easier enunciated than executed. Among the impediments to removal, Mc-Kenney cited the reluctance of the chiefs to countenance a diminution of their prestige (to which McKenney uncharitably attributed the reluctance of the Cherokee chiefs to accede to removal) and the concern of the general public over the suffering and anguish incident to such moves.

ON THE 30TH MAY last, General Carroll, of Tennessee, was appointed Commissioner, to go among the Cherokee and Creek Indians, and hold conferences with them on the subject of emigration. On the 8th July following, General Coffee was united in the same commission. . . .

Meanwhile, Col. Montgomery, the Agent for the Cherokees, was acting under instructions growing out of the provisions of the treaty of Washington, of 6th May, 1828, and the Creek Agent, Col. Crowell, under the act of Congress of 20th May, 1826, to aid certain Indians of the Creek nation in their removal West of the Mississippi, and a subsequent act of 9th May, 1828, appropriating $50,000 with a view to the same object.

Under the treaty of the 6th May, 1828, and with the means provided by Congress to carry the same into effect, Col. Montgomery has enrolled and sent off 510 souls, of whom 431 are Cherokees, and 79 blacks; and Col. Crowell has sent off 1200 Creeks. The evidence furnished the Department, as to the disposition of both those tribes to remove, is demonstrative of their willingness to go; but they are held in check by their chiefs and others, whose interest it is to keep them where they are. Among the Creeks, especially, the most severe punishments have been inflicted, by mutilating, and otherwise, those who had enrolled to go, and while in their camp, and where they supposed they would be protected. Such is the dread of these people of the violence of their chiefs, that they are afraid to express their wishes on this subject, except in whispers, and then only to those in whom they have entire confidence. It will be seen from Gen. Coffee's report . . . that a like terror is exercised over the Cherokees. It is by no means unnatural for the chiefs of those tribes to oppose the going away of their people. It would be unnatural if they did not. In proportion to the reduction of their numbers does their power decrease; and their love of power is not less strong than other people's. It confers distinctions, not only among themselves, but in relation, also, to neighboring tribes. And to this

11

feeling may be superadded the uncertainty which rests upon the future, drawn from the lessons of the past. But there are, I respectfully suggest, remedies for both, and the Federal Government has the power to apply them. The presence of an armed force would effectually relieve the first; and the adoption of a system for their security, and preservation, and future happiness, that should be as effective and ample as it ought to be permanent, would relieve the last. I would not be mistaken as to the use that should be made of the military. Its presence should be preceded by the solemn declaration that it was coming not to compel a single Indian to quit the place of his choice, but only to *protect* those who desire to better their condition, and in the exercise of their wish to do so. Humanity seems to require this, and, if this measure had been adopted sooner, many who now smart under the lash of their chiefs, and who are doomed to pass the remainder of their lives with mutilated bodies, would be free from the one, and not have to endure the suffering and disgrace of the other.

Surely when States, in the exercise of their sovereignty, are extending their laws over a people whose chiefs admit (I refer to the Cherokees) that such a measure would *"seal their destruction,"* and when every circumstance appears to have combined to render the great body of our Indians within the limits of States unhappy, and to impoverish and destroy them, something ought to be done for their relief. Justice demands it, and Humanity pleads for these people. The public sympathy is strongly excited.

The Florida Indians, there is little doubt, are willing to join the Creeks; and the dispositions of the Chickasaws are indicated by the extract herewith submitted, on the subject of their recent visit to seek a country. The Indians in Ohio, especially the Senecas and Delawares, seek to go. I submit a talk of the chiefs of the former, addressed to the President on this subject. The Agent, Col. M'Elvaine, is of opinion that, in five years, with the means to effect their removal, there will remain no Indians in Ohio.

A new difficulty has arisen in regard to the Cherokees and between them and the State of Georgia. It relates to boundary. The subject is amply discussed in your letter to His Excellency the Governor of Georgia. I accompany this with a copy of it. No report has been received from Gen. Coffee, who was appointed to collect and report all the facts touching the controversy. The Cherokees, however, have furnished the Department, through the Agents, with the grounds upon which they rest their claim to the boundary for which they contend. These documents are on file in this office.

In reference to emigration, and to the means necessary for its accomplishment, I beg leave respectfully to add, that, in lieu of the usual mode of *estimating,* for all the different branches of expenditure, upon the basis of numbers, for rations, transportation, &c., &c., which can never be done with certainty, (if not being possible to know beforehand how many will go,) a sum be appropriated and made applicable to emigration *generally,* and to compensation for improvements, and placed at the disposal of the Executive; and for this object I recommend the sum of $300,000. It is my opinion, also, that a great saving might be effected by changing the agencies for emigration from the local agents to contractors. I have seen nothing to induce a belief that the Agents employed among the Cherokees and Creeks have not been zealous; but it does appear to me that a saving of more than one-third of the cost of each emigrant could be realized upon contract. The Agents might be well employed, and usefully and abundantly, in cooperating, and especially in seeing that all the terms of the contracts in which the comfort, and health, &c., of the emigrants were concerned, were faithfully executed.

But it does appear to me as indispensable, that, as a first step in any great movement of the sort, the country on which it is proposed to place these people at rest, and forever, should be clearly defined, and nothing left unprovided for by the Government, that concerns either their security, preservation, or improvement. Nor should the emigrants be sent off to settle where and how they might list; but the whole business should, I respectfully submit, be conducted upon one regular and systematic plan; and what may be done in reference to the whole of it ought to be done with a view to their solid and lasting welfare.

With the exception of the rencontre between certain Indians in Missouri and some of the citizens of that State, which took place in Randolph county, peace has been preserved between the white and red men along our borders. This rencontre has not yet been fully reported upon. It is understood the parties charged with the killing of the whites are now undergoing an examination of St. Louis. Some of the Western tribes, the Sioux, Sacs, and Foxes, are at war with each other. But this is common to those tribes. Theirs are feuds of ancient origin. They will, it is presumed, fight on until some one or other of the tribes shall become too reduced and feeble to carry on the war, when it will be lost as a separate power. Meanwhile, however, Gen. Clark has been instructed to bring about a pacification, if he can. Humanity directs that these people, who sport so with each other's lives, should be counselled frequently, and led, if possible, to cherish the more agreeable state of peace and friendship. The great sufferers in general contests of this sort, next to the Indians, are the traders. The hunting parties are broken up by these wars, and there is a corresponding reduction in their returns, and of loss to the companies; for they furnish the Indians, upon credit, with their annual outfits. If they are killed, the traders lose finally; or, if they quit hunting and go to war, payment is delayed. I beg leave respectfully to refer, and no more, to the advantage which the British have over the American traders. The leading articles in the Indian trade, blankets and strouds, cannot be manufactured for the want of the proper kind of work in the United States; and the Indians of the North and Northwest will not trade in any other or inferior goods.

On the subject of the administration of this office, to which you have called my particular attention, I have to remark, that a new modification of it is indispensable to its efficiency. It is, although as well organized as, perhaps, it could be by a merely Executive arrangement—and it rests upon this only—too powerless to be effective, and too responsible for its feebleness. It should, I respectfully suggest, rest as the other branches in the Department do, upon Congressional enactments; and the responsibility should be to that body, through the head of the Department proper. It never was intended to remain as it was first established; and two Committees of the House of Representatives have, since its creation, unanimously reported a bill upon the basis I have suggested; which bills were twice read in the House, but were not acted on, because they could not be reached. A new organization has been esteemed to be important by every head of the Department of War, including the one under whose administration it was created, and recommended by them all. So pressing did this necessity grow, that Governor Cass and General Clark were called to Washington to digest a system. This was done. (See Doc. No. 117, 20th Congress, 2d Session.) I consider their report able and judicious, and the provisions of the bill which accompanies it, ample and apposite, with one exception: this relates to the mode of accounting. I esteem the mode of settling accounts partially, [or fictitiously] and then generally, [or finally,] and the taking from one head of the appropriation to give to another, to be fatal to the harmony and credit of the service, and one that ought not to be practised. In lieu of that mode, I would respectfully suggest, that in each Department, beginning with this, (and it should begin here, since all the estimates are prepared here,) accounts should be *opened* under each head of appropriation; and *settled* under each head. If an agent is deficient at all in his payments, or his vouchers, it will be seen under which head; and instead of closing his account by abstracting money from another branch of the service, to *close* not finally his account, it should be left open under each and every head, for which he had not accounted. There would than remain always the means to meet demands properly due from each head; and not, as has been, and as has been shewn at the commencement of this report, a diversion from one head of the appropriation, made to close a deficiency in another, to the *exclusion* of the legitimate demands against the head thus abstracted from—the demands having, meanwhile, to lie over until *other* and final returns come in, bringing the vouchers upon which a *counter warrant* is issued, to replace the amount to the credit of the fund from which it had been diverted.

To exemplify my meaning as to the mode, which I respectfully suggest ought to be adopted, and acted upon throughout the whole progress of the settlement of accounts, touching this branch of the service, I submit two forms, (No. 7 and 8,) one shewing the heads under which estimates are made, and another shewing a settlement of a set of returns under this form. The adoption of this mode of settling the accounts, with the report of Messrs. Cass and Clark, as referred to, will give to the Indian Department the efficiency it needs, and without which, it is not possible to maintain that accuracy and speed which should characterize a branch of the Government service, the importance of which may be estimated from the varied and multiplied and laborious character of its duties, and the immense sums of money that are annually involved in its operations.

Report of Commissioner of Indian Affairs Samuel S. Hamilton November 26, 1830

(Excerpt from *Report for 1830*, pp. 162-63)

Hamilton's report suggested administrative modification of the method used to regulate Indian affairs, and a redefinition of the boundary to the Indian country established in 1802.

A FEW REMARKS in reference to the existing laws relating to Indian affairs, with a view to some change or modification of the provisions of the same, will close this report.

The first act providing for Indian annuities, and which is still in force, was passed in 1796. Other acts for the same object have been since passed, from time to time, as they were required by new treaties, which are limited or permanent, according to the treaty stipulations for which they are intended to provide. A part of the provisions of some of them, though not directly repealed, has been superseded by treaties or acts of more recent date; hence it is difficult (except for persons who are familiar with these changes) to distinguish the provisions that are still in force from those that are not. There are now twenty-one acts under which Indian annuities are drawn, and they require as many accounts to be opened and kept on the books of the Treasury. If the same system be continued, every new treaty that stipulates for an annuity will necessarily increase the number of acts for that object, and, of course, the number of accounts. I, therefore, respectfully submit, whether it be not desirable to change the system, and adopt one which is more simple, and will require less time and labor to execute it. This, I humbly apprehend, may be attained by repealing all the existing acts of appropriation for annuities, and embodying the whole in one act, to be passed annually, on a statement to be laid before Congress at the commencement of every session, showing the annuities due, and to be provided for, in the ensuing year. This would keep Congress annually informed of the state of the Indian annuities, and the actual amount required from year to year to pay them. The appropriation might be made in one sum, equal to the whole amount of annuities due for the year to be provided for, or for the specific sums due, for such year, to each nation or tribe. In either case, it would never require more than one account to be opened on the books of the Treasury. . . .

The act to regulate trade and intercourse with the Indian tribes, and to preserve peace on the frontiers, passed in 1802, is the principal one that governs all our relations with the Indian tribes. Since this act was passed, many treaties have been concluded, which, with other causes, growing out of the increase of our population, and the consequent extension of our settlements, have contributed to produce changes in our Indian relations, which, it would seem, required corresponding changes in the laws governing them. It is believed that the line defined by the act of 1802 as the Indian boundary, and to which its provisions were intended particularly to apply, has long since ceased to be so. It is, therefore, respectfully submitted whether the public interest does not, also, require such a modification of the act of 1802 as would better adapt its provisions to the present state of our Indian relations. A judicious modification of this act, and others connected with it, (embracing some specific provision for the adjustment of the claims for depredations, &c., which are provided for by the 4th and 14th sections) would, no doubt, greatly facilitate and open the way for other improvements in the administration of the affairs of the Indian Department, of which the claims for depredations just mentioned form no unimportant or inconsiderable part. It may not be improper to add, that, should the foregoing propositions in regard to the laws relating to Indian affairs be deemed worthy of consideration, much useful and more detailed information may be obtained from the report which was made on this subject by Governor Cass and General Clark, and laid before Congress the session before last;for which, see State Papers, 2d session 20th Congress, vol. 3, Doc. No. 117.

Report of Commissioner of Indian Affairs Elbert Herring November 19, 1831

(Excerpt from *Report for 1831*, pp. 172-75)

Herring's account of the "humane policy" and "salutary principle" incorporated in the system of removal of Indians from the east to the west reflected the optimism (naivete?) of early nineteenth-century policy makers that such a move would facilitate the "civilization" and education of the Indian. That the policy was blind to Indian cultural traits and also concealed white economic motives became too soon apparent.

THE HUMANE POLICY, exemplified in the system adopted by the Government with respect to the Indian tribes residing within the limits of the United States, which is now in operation, is progressively developing its good effects; and, it is confidently trusted, will at no distant day, be crowned with complete success. Gradually diminishing in numbers and deteriorating in condition; incapable of coping with the superior intelligence of the white man, ready to fall into the vices, but unapt to appropriate the benefits of the social state; the increasing tide of white population threatened soon to engulf them, and finally to cause their total extinction. The progress is slow but sure; the cause is inherent in the nature of things; tribes numerous and powerful have disappeared from among us in a ratio of decrease, ominous to the existence of those that still remain, unless counteracted by the substitution of some principle sufficiently potent to check the tendencies to decay and dissolution. This salutary principle exists in the system of removal; of change of residence; of settlement in territories exclusively their own, and under the protection of the United States; connected with the benign influences of education and instruction in agriculture and the several mechanic arts, whereby social is distinguished from savage life.

In pursuance of this policy, the necessary measures have been taken for the execution of the Choctaw treaty ratified at the last session of Congress, and the Indians of that tribe are now in motion. It is presumed that about 5000 will emigrate west of the Mississippi before the winter sets in; and there are the best grounds for believing, that a much greater number will go over in the course of the ensuing year. Sanguine expectations may thus be indulged, that the whole nation will be moved within the time (three years) prescribed by the treaty.

The Chickasaw Indians who are disposed to follow their friends and neighbors, the Choctaws, and to reside near them, have not yet been provided with suitable lands. For the purpose of procuring such for their

18

accommodation, it became necessary to effect an arrangement with the Choctaws for a cession of a portion of their country in the west. Major John H. Eaton and General John Coffee have accordingly been constituted commissioners to treat with the Choctaws for this object. In the event of a successful issue of their negotiation, the removal of the Chickasaws will probably take place before the termination of another year.

The chiefs of the Cherokees have given, as yet, no evidence of a relinquishment of their determination not to accept the propositions of the Government, so cordially embraced by the tribes before-mentioned, for an exchange of lands and residence. The influence of the Indian chief is of a nature to overrule the general wish, which, if allowed to express itself freely, might be favorable to removal. Being induced to believe, from information to be relied on, that a number of the tribe would emigrate, if encouraged and aided by the Government, the department endeavored to revive emigration under the provisions of the treaty of 1828. The plan is in operation, but is of too recent date to admit of calculating the probability and extent of its success.

The Creek Indians are in the same predicament—their position having been unaltered through the past year. Involved in difficulties, they have shown no inclination to relieve themselves from the embarrassment of their situation, by accepting the liberal and often-repeated propositions of the Government. It is to be hoped that the time will shortly come, when better counsels will prevail, and a juster appreciation of the benefits submitted to their choice, open their eyes to a sense of their real interests.

In other quarters, more favorable issues have awaited our efforts. Colonel James B. Gardiner, who was appointed on the 31st March last Special Agent or Commissioner, to treat with the Indians in Ohio for an exchange of lands, and their removal west of the Mississippi, has successfully negotiated for these objects. Treaties have been concluded, and signed by him and the Indian Agent, Colonel McElvain, with the Shawneese, Ottawas, and the mixed band of Shawneese and Senecas of Lewistown. The Senecas had concluded a treaty for the same objects, during the past winter, which was ratified at the last session of Congress, and they are now on their way to their western domain. The only Indian possessions remaining in Ohio, are those of the Wyandots, with whom the preliminaries of a treaty have been agreed on, and will be finally concluded, in the event of a favorable report by the deputation sent out by them to look at the country of their proposed destination. The treaties above-mentioned are herewith communicated. By these arrangements, the entire Indian population of Ohio will, in all probability, have been removed, within the coming year, from the confines of the State, and will have formed new settlements under better auspices. The benefits of the measure will be still further enhanced, by the considerable quantity of valuable lands which, in consequence, will be thrown open to the enterprise of the citizens of the State.

A band of Sac Indians, headed by a warrior, called Black Hawk, continuing to reside on lands on Rock river, in Illinois, ceded by treaty to the United States, and evincing an obstinate purpose of remaining, associated with strong indications of hostility towards the citizens of that State, residing in the vicinity. Under such menacing circumstances, the Governor thought it expedient to order out a body of militia for their protection, and for the removal of the Indians. This timely movement, on the part of the executive of that State, with the cooperation of the troops of the United States, promptly afforded by the commanding General, (Gaines,) caused the Indians to yield their unjustifiable purpose, and to move off peaceably to their lands west of the Mississippi. The step was judicious—as it is presumable from the reports to this department—that this well-timed display of military force prevented resistance and bloodshed. . . .

It will always be a desideratum to repress the feuds, and lessen the occasions of strife between neighboring tribes. It is equally the dictate of humanity and prudence, and is a necessary emanation from the benevolent policy, before spoken of, towards the aboriginal race of the country. In reference thereto, a treaty of peace was effected in July, 1830, by General Clark and Colonel Morgan, at Prairie du Chien, between the Sacs and Foxes, and the Winnebagoes and Menomonies, and other tribes, by which it was hoped that hostility was provided against, if not merged in kinder dispositions, and tranquillity secured to our borders. But, contrary to every reasonble expectation, a year had hardly passed away, before the provisions of the treaty were grossly violated. In defiance of its obligations, and of the respect due to the flag of the United States, an atrocious act was committed on the 31st of July last, by a party of the Sacs and Foxes, near Fort Crawford, and within reach of its guns, by an attack in the night upon a Menomonie camp, in which twenty five of their number were killed, and many others wounded. Immediately on the intelligence of this most insulting and barbarous outrage, measures were taken by the department for the arrest and punishment of the offenders. Time has not, as yet, been allowed to learn their result. Meanwhile, the aggrieved party, the Menomonies, have been counselled to remain quiet, under an assurance that the Government will cause justice to be done, by punishment of the guilty, and ample satisfaction for the loss of their friends. . . .

Marauding parties, of the various tribes, will incessantly seek opportunities of rapine and violence. Their march is in the dead of night—their haunt is in the wilderness. Hence, it is difficult to restrain them, and their aggressions will sometimes escape merited retribution. It is, however, steadily inculcated on the agents of the Government, to interpose its authority to the utmost for the prevention of any acts tending to disturb the harmony, or endanger the security of person or property, among the Indian tribes under its protection.

During the last spring some difficulties took place, from the cause above alluded to, between the Osages, and Creeks and Cherokees, on account of depredations committed by the former on the latter tribes. These however have been happily settled by a conference between these Indians, called together by the authority of General Clark, at Cantonment Gibson, and at which treaties of peace and amity were concluded.

These are the only cases of disturbance of importance among the Indians that have come to the knowledge of this department during the year. Differences and contentions about matters wholly relating to themselves, will, and frequently do, occur among separate bands living near each other, sometimes accompanied by violence and bloodshed. These happening in the Indian country, cannot easily be provided against by the Government, but find impunity in remoteness of place, and in obscurity of circumstance touching the perpetration. And it must be expected under this view, that the sons of the forest will continue to seek occasions of disputing and fighting with each other, while the savage notion subsists in full force among them, that war furnishes for their young men the only road to distinction.

It is respectfully submitted, whether a salutary modification may not be effected in the existing laws relating to intercourse with the Indians, and the payment of their annuities.

There are more than twenty different acts of Congress, providing for the payment of Indian annuities, and they require an equal number of accounts to be opened and kept in the books of the Treasury; and some of the provisions of these acts have been repealed by treaties of more recent date. In accordance with this system, every new treaty, stipulating the payment of annuities, will increase the number of acts for that object, and consequently the number of accounts. The multiplication of these acts and accounts tends to confusion, and renders it difficult to distinguish existing provisions from those that have been virtually repealed.

It is apprehended, that an annual act, predicated on a statement to be laid before Congress, at the commencement of every session, shewing the annuities due, and to be provided for in the ensuing year, would simplify this branch of business, and render it at once much more intelligible, and much less laborious. Congress would be thereby annually informed of the actual state of the annuities, and of the precise amount required for their liquidation. Such a consolidating act would at once prevent unnecessary complication; and while it would lessen labor in the different offices, by reducing the number of accounts kept open in their books, would, at the same time, render plain and clear what, from numerous entries, is apparently intricate and obscure.

Our relations with the Indian tribes are mainly governed by the act of Congress passed in 1802, to regulate trade and intercourse with them, and to preserve peace on the frontiers. The boundary line, defined by that act, and to which its provisions were applicable, has been varied by subsequent treaties; and the increase of our population, and the extension of our settlements have effected changes calling for a revision of that act, that its provisions may be adapted to the present state of our Indian relations.

Report of Commissioner of Indian Affairs Elbert Herring November 22, 1832

(Excerpt from *Report for 1832*, pp. 160-64)

Herring's prose in his second year in charge of the Indian Department rose to literary heights that can be thought of 150 years later only in terms of parody. Here is the full panoply of Picts, Vandals, and Goths, reclaimed from a "heathenish darkness . . . irradiated by the light of knowledge and the sun of Christianity." From the "benign considerations" of the Government to protect the Indian "arose the generous policy of transferring their residence." "Founded in pure and disinterested motives, may it meet the approval of heaven, by the complete attainment of its beneficent ends!" It would be hard to find prose as remote from the reality of the frontier as from predictive accuracy.

THE CONTRIBUTIONS of the Government to the establishment and maintenance of Indian schools, grounded, as they are, on the most humane considerations, cannot fail to be followed by beneficial results. If there be any human means of directing the intelligence of the Indian from its narrow and contracted sphere, to enlarged and comprehensive views, it must exist in the cultivation of knowledge, operating to expand and improve the mental faculties. The lessons of early instruction rarely fail to carry their impress to after life. Indian children evince a facility of acquirement no wise inferior to those of European origin, and their rapid improvement under tuition, and the gratification they manifest in their progress, afford ample proof of the benefits of cultivating this benign source of amelioration of the savage condition. Influenced by so genial an incitement, and actuated by impulses honorable to humanity, numerous religious and benevolent associations have sent forth laborers in the field of improvement, or have rendered pecuniary aid towards forwarding the work, for the promotion of which Government furnishes liberal and steady assistance. Unrelaxing efforts may be expected to be crowned with eventual success. The benighted regions of other parts of the earth have become gradually enlightened by the prosecution of similar means, long continued; and the Picts of England, and Vandals and Goths of continental Europe, remain standing monuments of savage habits and heathenish darkness, subdued and irradiated by the light of knowledge and the sun of christianity.

Kindred benefits may be calculated on in the institution of the comprehensive scheme, adopted by the Government for the removal of the Indian tribes to territories in the west, now in actual and progressive operation.

Contiguity of white settlements had invariably tended to depreciate the Indian character. The evil was always without counterbalance of possible good, either present or in reversion, and was always accompanied by a demonstration of decreasing population. It was evident, that they must either be left to the fate that was gradually threatening their entire extinction, or that the Government, by some magnanimous act of interposition, should rescue them from approaching destruction, and devise a plan for their preservation and security. From such benign considerations arose the generous policy of transferring their residence, and congregating their tribes, in domains suited to their condition, and set apart for their use. In the consummation of this grand and sacred object rests the sole chance of averting Indian annihilation. Founded in pure and disinterested motives, may it meet the approval of heaven, by the complete attainment of its beneficent ends!

In pursuance of the policy embraced by the views thus detailed, measures have been taken for the execution of the treaties concluded with the Seneca, Shawnee, Ottoway, and Wyandot Indians, and ratified at the last session of Congress; and those tribes are now on their way to their western home, where it is presumable they will arrive previously to the ensuing winter.

Suitable steps have also been taken to carry into effect the treaty concluded with the Creek Indians at the last session of Congress. The liberal provision made by the Government for that tribe will, it is believed, greatly tend to the improvement of their condition, and, at the same time, be productive of much benefit to the State of Alabama, within whose confines their wide and extended possessions are situated.

The Seminole Indians having sustained much suffering for several preceding years, through the failure of crops, occasioned by the inundation of their lands, and from other causes, felt disposed, under the privations of the past winter, to seek a better fortune in a kinder soil. Colonel James Gadsden was accordingly commissioned to negotiate with them for the relinquishment of their title to land in Florida, and for their removal to the west of the Mississippi among their Creek kinsmen. A provisional treaty was consequently concluded with them, and will be obligatory, if the deputation of their chiefs, who have gone to examine their destined country, shall pronounce on it favorably for the future residence of the tribe. The treaty is herewith communicated.

Colonel Gadsden has also concluded a treaty with the principal band of the Appalachicola Indians in Florida, for the relinquishment of their land to the United States, and their removal to the west of the Mississippi river, and beyond the limits of the States and Territories of the United States. The state of the negotiation with the two remaining bands, warrants the belief that they will soon follow their kinsmen, and thereby relieve Florida of its entire Indian population. The treaty is herewith submitted.

The Cherokees have not, as yet, signified any determination to accept the generous overtures of the Government for their removal; but, from the increasing evils unavoidably connected with their present location, and a favorable change of sentiment in some of their chiefs, together with the obvious benefits that would result from their acceptance of the proffered terms, it is reasonable to suppose that their adverse feelings are fast subsiding, and will, at no distant day, give place to more favorable views. The chiefs opposed to the scheme, avail themselves of their arbitrary authority, and resort to menaces to keep the well disposed from emigrating. The Government has, in the meantime, encouraged their emigration under the provisions of the treaty of 1828, and about six hundred and thirty of their tribe proceeded, during the past summer, to the land allotted to them west of the Mississippi.

It was confidently expected that, before this period, an arrangement would have been made with the Choctaws for a portion of their land, for the future residence of their friends and former neighbors, the Chickasaws. The efforts of the Government to effect that object have been hitherto unavailing. Twenty-one millions of acres of land have been allotted to the Choctaws, being more than twelve hundred acres to each individual; and although this vast extent of territory is beyond any possible requirement for their use, they have continued to manifest a pertinacious unwillingness to dispose of any portion for the accommodation of the Chickasaws. Further exertions will be made for the attainment of the object, and it is confidently hoped that they will result in a successful issue. In the event of failure, other territory will be allotted to them. General Coffee, on the part of the United States, has recently concluded a treaty with them; and it is therein provided, that their lands in Alabama and Mississippi shall be surveyed and sold. That provision may be considered a recorded declaration of their intention, not merely to sell their territory, but also to cross the Mississippi, and seek a home in accordance with the policy instituted by the Government for the removal and concentration of the Indian tribes.

The public lands west of the Mississippi, yet unappropriated, far exceed, in quantity, what the comfort and welfare of the unprovided tribes may be possibly supposed to require. A sufficient territory will therefore be assigned to each individual tribe; and definite boundaries between the domains of the different tribes will be permanently established, to prevent dispute, and guard against collision on this head.

At the last session of Congress, acts were passed to extinguish the Indian title to land in Illinois, Indiana, Missouri, and the Territory of Michigan. Commissioners were accordingly appointed, and treaties have been concluded with the respective tribes claiming title, by which they have relinquished to the United States all their lands in Indiana, Missouri, and Illinois, with the exception of a few inconsiderable reservations; and by which the Potawatomies have also ceded to the United States all their land in the Territory of Michigan.

In compliance with the requisition of the 4th section of the act of May 5,

1832, to submit to Congress a general report of the proceedings under the act to provide the means of vaccinating the Indian tribes, as a preventive of the small pox, measures were immediately taken to carry the law into effect. Physicians were appointed for the purpose, vaccine matter was forwarded to them, and they were instructed to proceed, forthwith, in that humane employment, and to report their proceedings to the department. Their reports have been received, and a condensed statement, with extracts from them, is herewith submitted.

In the early part of last summer, a large body of Sac and Fox Indians, headed, and not improbably instigated, by the noted war-chief Black Hawk, assumed a hostile attitude, which was soon followed by depredation and atrocious outrage on our contiguous frontier. The United States' troops under the command of General Atkinson, supported by volunteer companies of citizens, and requisitions of militia by the executives of the adjoining States, were promptly ordered to the points most exposed to the inroads of the savages, for the protection and defence of the suffering inhabitants. Major General Scott was commissioned to take the command of the combined forces, and to subdue and punish the aggressors.

These prompt and vigorous measures speedily accomplished the desired object. The hostile Indians were defeated whenever they could be brought to action, and finally routed with great loss. Few escaped, most of them having been either killed or taken prisoners. Among the captives were Black Hawk himself, and many other principal chiefs, now in confinement at Jefferson barracks, as hostages for the future good conduct of their respective tribes. The chastisement of the aggressing Indians was prompt, decisive, and exemplary, and will have taught a lesson, long to be remembered, that similar offences cannot be practised with impunity. In the signal and merited retribution of these unprovoked hostilities, and in the distress in which they involved the assailants, will probably be found the lasting indemnity of our frontier settlements from similar perpetrations.

Major General Scott, and Governor Reynolds of Illinois, commissioners on the part of the United States, concluded a treaty with the Winnebago nation of Indians on the 15th day of September last; and, on the 21st day of the same month, the same commissioners concluded a treaty with the confederated tribes of Sac and Fox indians. The United States have acquired by those treaties a vast accession of valuable territory, and provided for their frontier citizens complete security. The abovementioned treaties are herewith communicated.

The particulars of a barbarous outrage on a camp of the Menomonies, by a party of Sac and Fox Indians, were detailed in the report of this bureau of the last year. The Government having demanded in vain, through its agents, the surrender of the aggressors in that case, a military detachment was ordered to enforce the demand; and, in failure of compliance, to seize and detain hostages until their delivery. Three of them have been given up, and the residue having fled, and joined in the late hostilities, have probably met with the just recompense of their wanton and unatoned barbarity.

Some of the Indian tribes have proceeded to hostile acts, in the course of the year past, against each other, and conflicts have ensued, in which blood has been spilt in defiance of the obligation imposed by the guarantee of the United States, for the preservation of peace and tranquillity among them. The instigators of such unwarrantable proceedings, as well as the chief actors in every instance of ascertained outrage, are justly considered responsible to the Government for the transgression, and are invariably required to be given up to its authority to answer for the offences.

It is difficult to restrain such aggressions, growing out of ancient feuds, prompted by an unchecked spirit of rapine, and a thirst for warlike distinction, and, particularly, when probable impunity furnishes an additional incentive. To prevent outrage is, however, far better than to punish the offenders; nor should the expense attendant on the remedy to be found in the employment of a sufficient body of mounted rangers preclude its exercise. A display of military force, and the certainty of speedy punishment, can alone prevent a ready resort to rapine and bloodshed on the part of those who recognize no restraint on plunder, no bounds to the gratification of revenge.

On the whole, it may be matter of serious doubt whether, even with the fostering care and assured protection of the United States, the preservation and perpetuity of the Indian race are at all attainable, under the form of government and rude civil regulations subsisting among them. These were perhaps well enough suited to their condition, when hunting was their only employment, and war gave birth to their strongest excitements. The unrestrained authority of their chiefs, and the irresponsible exercise of power, are of the simplest elements of despotic rule; while the absence of the *meum* and *tuum* in the general community of possessions, which is the grand conservative principle of the social state, is a perpetual operating cause of the *vis inertiae* of savage life. The stimulus of physical exertion and intellectual exercise, contained in this powerful principle, of which the Indian is almost entirely void, may not unjustly be considered the parent of all improvements, not merely in the arts, but in the profitable direction of labor among civilized nations. Among them it is the source of plenty; with the Indians, the absence of it is the cause of want, and consequently of decrease of numbers. Nor can proper notions of the social system be successfully inculcated, nor its benefits be rightly appreciated, so as to overcome the habits and prejudices incident to savage birth, and consequent associations of maturer years, except by the institution of separate and secure rights in the relations of property and person. It is therefore suggested, whether the formation of a code of laws on this basis, to be submitted for their adoption, together with certain modifications of the existing political system among them, may not be of very salutary effect, especially as co-operating with the influences derivable from the education of their youth, and the introduction of the doctrines of the christian religion; all centering in one grand object—the substitution of the social for the savage state.

Influenced by sentiments analogous to these views, Congress, at its last session, passed an act for the appointment of commissioners, in relation to this and various other subjects connected with the Indian system; and, under its provisions, commissioners have been appointed. The acknowledged talents and well known philanthropy of those gentlemen, guaranty the faithful and able execution of the important trusts committed to them by the Government. From their joint efforts, and united wisdom, may reasonably be anticipated the attainment of the ends which Congress had in view in establishing the commission. Results vastly important may grow out of this initiatory step, civilization receive an impetus hitherto unknown, and the welfare and prosperity of the aborigines of the country be settled on the imperishable basis of religion and law.

Report of Commissioner of Indian Affairs Elbert Herring
November 24, 1835

(Excerpt from *Report for 1835*, pp. 275-76)

The incident related by Commissioner Herring regarding Major Armstrong's attempt to force the Choctaws to abandon their custom of condemning witches to death is instructive of the peremptory approach taken by whites to Indian customs considered shocking to a "civilized" conscience. Under the threat of death to whomever should be instrumental in executing a witch, and the lash to whomever should accuse another of being a witch, the major succeeded in terminating this "superstitious custom."

MAJOR J. BROOKES has succeeded in concluding a treaty with the Caddo Indians, by which they cede their land in Louisiana to the United States, and agree to remove, at their own expense, beyond our territorial limits, never to return. This alternative may possibly save the small remains of the tribe from total extinction—a fate that seemed to be impending on a continued residence in their present location, surrounded by a population that operates on the children of the forest like miasma on constitutions unused to its baneful influence. The treaty and journal of proceedings are herewith communicated.

A treaty has also been concluded by Governor Stokes and General Arbuckle, with the Camanches and Hitchetas, two of the three nations of Indians of the great western prairie. It is confidently expected that the Kioways, the third nation, will also become parties to the treaty; and there are good grounds for believing that it will have a salutary tendency in repressing a long-indulged spirit for depredation, and in preserving peace among all the Indian tribes west of the Mississippi. The treaty and journal of proceedings are herewith transmitted.

Major Francis W. Armstrong was associated in the commission with the above-named gentlemen. He had left home to attend the council, but was suddenly arrested by disease, which ended in death, before he could reach his destination. By this unhappy event, the Government lost a meritorious and efficient officer, and the Choctaws were deprived of a faithful, able, and devoted agent. It affords me a melancholy opportunity of stating a matter highly creditable to the deceased, in which the good done will live after him, and consecrate his memory. In one of his communications to the Department, he informed that the Choctaws had then recently condemned to death, and actually executed, two of their tribe, on a charge of witchcraft. Such, it seems, had been the practice among them in preceding times, showing the unhallowed influence of the superstition, and its concomitant horrors. Immediately on being apprized of the shocking transaction, he convened the chiefs in council, and prevailed upon them to abolish the custom, under penalty of death for being instrumental thereafter in such execution, and of the lash on whoever should prefer a charge of witchcraft against any of their tribe. To his decision and firmness may be ascribed the termination of a superstitious custom, that triumphs in the weakness of human nature, gives a sort of legalized sanction to the most barbarous acts, and calls for the immolation of innocent victims, as an acknowledgment of its paramount authority.

There has been no intermission of exertion to induce the removal of the Cherokees to the west of the Mississippi, in conformity with the policy adopted by the Government in favor of the Indians, and to which they form almost the sole exception. There can be little doubt that bad advisement, and the intolerant control of chiefs adverse to the measure, have conduced to the disinclination of a large portion of the nation to emigrate, and avail themselves of the obvious benefit in the contemplated change. Another portion has viewed the measure in a more favorable light, and enlisted in its advocacy with much warmth. Such a diversity of sentiment could not fail to create collisions and animosity, and the effect has been, so far, a prevention of the requisite unanimity to bring the question to a favorable issue. In this state of things, a provisional treaty has been made with John Ridge and other influential members of the nation, favorable to the cause of removal, and by them submitted to their brethren in May last. No accounts of their final decision have yet been received. The provisions of the treaty are so liberal, and the disadvantages of continuing among the white population, that has entrenched itself on their borders, and even interspersed itself among them, are so glaring, that its cordial and speedy adoption might reasonably be anticipated. All proper efforts have been made by the Government to insure this result, under the conviction that its acceptance would lead to their tranquillity, prosperity, and happiness.

Indications of a contumacious and hostile spirit on the part of the Seminoles excited apprehension that they meditated resistance to the fulfilment of their late treaty, and that their removal could not be effected without compulsion. To intimidate the disaffected, and quell a spirit of turbulence, a military detachment was ordered to repair to their country; and they were expressly assured that a compliance with their treaty, made by them with much caution and deliberation, and after an exploring party of their chiefs had examined the land allotted for their residence in the West, and passed upon it their unqualified approbation, would be enforced by the Government. It is gratifying to add that they have subsequently seen their interest and obligation in a clear light, and that they are busily engaged in preparations to remove during the ensuing spring.

The Creek Indians are beginning to wake from their long-indulged lethargy, and a general spirit of emigration is manifesting itself among them. From recent communications, much confidence is entertained that a considerable portion will be in readiness to proceed to their western home in the course of a few weeks, and that they will be followed by the residue of the nation within the coming year.

It is respectfully suggested as a matter of extreme importance, that early appropriation should be made for the annuity money due to the different tribes, that the publication of proposals, in those cases where goods are to be furnished, may be issued in sufficient time to insure competition in the most eligible markets, and that thereby the most suitable articles may be procured on the most reasonable terms. In addition to this obvious advantage, much benefit would accrue to the Indians, and their convenience be materially promoted by the early transmission of their goods and money, so that distribution and payment might be made in the months of June and July, before the commencement of their sickly season, and avoiding the interference of a later period with their hunting campaign. Complaints have been repeatedly made by the different tribes of injury sustained by them through the long-delayed payment of their annuities, owing to protracted appropriation.

The year has passed without any marked event of a general character to communicate. The period has been a pacific one, with little of violence or bloodshed to record; and the Indian condition is decidedly on the improvement, so far as relates to their previous characteristic traits. The exclusion of ardent spirits, where it could be effected, has done much good; and on this exclusion, and the substitution of other pursuits for war and the chase, must depend their gradual growth and eventual proficiency in civilization—a consummation earnestly desired by every philanthropic mind.

Report of Commissioner of Indian Affairs T. Hartley Crawford November 25, 1838

(Excerpt from *Report for 1838*, pp. 410-14, 424-26)

Commissioner Crawford's report dealt primarily with the progress of the removal policy by which the Indians east of the Mississippi were to be sent west of the Great River, presumably out of the way of the advancing white settlements. The excuse that the Indian, separated from the corrupting influence of the white man, would be better able to maintain his character and virtue was entertained simultaneously with the unblushing assertion that the Indians' lands should be divided in severalty, since "common property and civilization cannot co-exist." Logic has never been the principal ingredient of white policy toward the American Indian.

THE MOST STRIKING feature of the peculiar relations that the Indians bear to the United States is their removal to the west side of the Mississippi—a change of residence effected under treaties, and with the utmost regard to their comfort that the circumstances of each admitted. The advance of white settlements, and the consuming effect of their approach to the red man's home, had long been observed by the humane with pain, as leading to the speedy extinction of the weaker party. But it is not believed that any suggestion of the policy now in a course of execution was authoritatively made prior to the commencement of the present century. Since, it has repeatedly, and at various intervals, received the sanction of the Chief Magistrates of the United States, and of one or the other House of Congress; without, however, any definite action, previous to the law passed eight years ago. Treaty engagements had been previously made for their removal West with several of the tribes; but the act referred to was a formal and general recognition of the measure, as desirable in regard of all the Indians within any State or Territory east of the Mississippi. Whatever apprehensions might have been honestly entertained of the results of this scheme, the arguments in favor of its adoption, deduced from observation, and the destructive effects of a continuance in their old positions, are so far strengthened by the success attendant upon its execution as to have convinced all, it is thought, of the humane and benevolent tendency of the measure.

Experience had shown that, however commendable the efforts to meliorate a savage surrounded by a white population, they were not compensated to any great extent by the gratification which is the best reward of doing good. A few individuals in a still smaller number of tribes have been educated, and profited by the opportunities afforded them to become civilized and highly respectable men; but the mass has retrograded, giving by the contrast greater prominency to their more wisely judging brethren. What can even the moral and educated Indian promise himself in a white settlement? Equality he does not and cannot possess, and the influence that is the just possession of his qualities in the ordinary social relations of life is denied him. Separated from deteriorating associations with white men, the reverse will be the fact. A fair and wide field will be open before him, in which he can cultivate the moral and intellectual virtues of the human beings around him, and aid in elevating them to the highest condition which they are capable of reaching. If these views are correct, the reflection is pleasant that is derived from the belief that a greater sacrifice of feeling is not made in their removal than falls to the lot of our fellow-citizens, in the numerous changes of residence that considerations of bettering their condition are daily producing. Indeed, it cannot be admitted to be so great; for, while the white man moves west or south, accompanied by his family only, the Indians go by tribes, carrying with them all the pleasures of ancient acquaintance, common habits, and common interests. It can scarcely be contended that they are more susceptible of suffering at the breaking up of local associations than we are; for, apart from their condition not favoring the indulgence of the finer feelings, fact proves that they sell a part of their possessions without reluctance, and leave their cabins, and burial-places, and the mounds and monuments which were the objects of their pride or affection, for a remote position in the same district. For whatever they have ceded to the United States they have been amply compensated. I speak not of former times, to which reference is not made, but of later days. The case of the Cherokees is a striking example of the liberality of the Government in all its branches. By the treaty, they had stipulated to remove west of the Mississippi within two years from its ratification, which took place on 23d May, 1836. The obligations of the United States, State rights, and acts by virtue of those rights, and in anticipation of Cherokee removal, made a compliance with this provision of the treaty indispensable at the time stipulated, or as soon thereafter as it was practicable without harshness. To ensure it, General Scott was despatched to their late country, and performed a delicate and difficult duty, embarrassed by circumstances over which there is no human control, with great judgment and humanity. Early in the past season several parties had been despatched to the West, under the direction of officers detailed for that duty, amounting, as is estimated, to six thousand, of whom muster-rolls have not yet been received at this office. The preparations for the removal of those who remained being in progress, John Ross and other chiefs, in virtue of a resolution by "the national committee and council and people of the Cherokee nation in general council assembled," proposed to the commanding general that the entire business of emigration should be confided to the nation; that the removal should commence at the time previously agreed on, to wit, when the sickly season had passed away, unless some cause, reasonable in the judgment of the general, should intervene to prevent it; that the expense should be calculated on the basis of one wagon and team and six riding-horses for fifteen persons; and that the Cherokees should select the physicians, and such other attendants as might be required for the safe and comfortable removal of the several detachments to their places of destination. This proposal was accepted on certain conditions by General Scott, in a communication to the chiefs, (with an exception of such of the treaty making party as might not choose to emigrate under the direction of John Ross and his associates,) on 25th July. To the conditions prescribed they acceded on the 27th, stipulating for the months of September and October to get all their people in motion, and transmitting a resolution of the Cherokee council, conferring on them authority to make the necessary arrangements. The application as to time was answered by saying that the emigration must re-commence on 1st September, and be completed on or before the 20th October, with a reservation in favor of the sick and superannuated, who might be unable to travel by land, if the waters continued too low for steamboat navigation, and with permission to such respectable Cherokees as might apply for the purpose to remove themselves on the first rise of the moon although it should be after the 20th October. An estimate was submitted by the Cherokee chiefs on the 31st July, which put the cost of the removal of 1,000 souls at $65,880. General Scott intimated that this estimate appeared to be high, and requested its re-consideration, when its reasonableness was affirmed, a trifling but indispensable sum added, and the estimate was thereupon approved. Of this disposition to conduct themselves with propriety, there is evidence in the letter of General Scott to yourself of 3d August, of which I herewith send an extract. Throughout their collection and emigration so far as this office is informed, the Cherokees have manifested proper temper, and an inclination to do whatever was required, with fewer exceptions than might have been expected, and these not of an important nature. It would seem that the cost of removal, according to the Indian estimate, is high; but, as their own fund pays it, and it was insisted on by their own confidential agents, it was thought it could not be rejected. The latest advices give assurances that the last of the Cherokees would be on the road early in November. It has been estimated that 12,000 will be removed by John Ross and the other chiefs, which, added to the number that had emigrated previously during the year, (believed to be about 6,000,) will give an aggregate of 18,000 Cherokees, who have ceased to live east of the Mississippi during the spring, summer, and autumn. It is thought that when muster-rolls of the emigrants come in, the number will be found to be somewhat larger; but, at present, the above is according to the information possessed. The last annual report of my predecessor made the number of East Cherokees 14,000; but when General Scott had collected the great body of the Indians for emigration, it was computed that there remained, after deducting those who had removed since the above report was made, 12,000. Those emigrants being reckoned, as before stated, at 6,000, would make the whole number 18,000 a year ago.

A retrospect of the last eight months, in reference to this numerous and more than ordinarily enlightened tribe, cannot fail to be refreshing to well-constituted mind. In and previous to May last, a large party, led by educated and intelligent chiefs, were dissatisfied and gloomy, discontented with the treaty of December, 1835, disinclined to emigration, and created by their conduct serious apprehensions for the consequences when the day of removal should arrive. It did come on the 23rd of May; but on the 18th, the privilege of wealth and strength to yield what they might withhold was exercised as an act of grace and beneficence by the executive branch of the Government. In answer to a communication from a delegation of the Cherokee nation, then in Washington, the Secretary of War on that day informed them that the best efforts of the United States would be put forth to prevail on the States interested in their removal to refrain from pressing them inconveniently, or so as to interfere with their comfortable emigration, and that he was quite sure the exertion would be successful, that the Cherokee agents should remove the nation, if desired, and he would so instruct the general in command in their country; and that he thought the expense of their emigration should be borne by the United States. He promised them an escort and protection while on the way west; and that as the sum heretofore set apart for the payment of reclamations of various kinds, and to defray the expenses of their removal, was deemed inadequate for these purposes, a further appropriation would be asked to meet them. This communication met the approbation of the President of the United States, who transmitted it to Congress, "that such measures may be adopted as are required to carry into effect the benevolent intentions of the Government towards the Cherokee nation, and which, it is hoped, will induce them to remove peaceably and contentedly to their new homes in the West." The fruit of this message was the law of 12th June, 1838, giving to the Cherokees the sum of $1,147,067. When it is considered that, by the treaty of December, 1835, the sum of $5,000,000 was stipulated to be paid them as the full value of their lands, after that amount was declared by the Senate of the United States to be an ample consideration for them, the spirit of this whole proceeding cannot be too much admired. The communication to the Cherokee delegation, submitted by the Chief Magistrate to Congress, addressing itself to feelings correspondent with those in which it originated, found in both Houses a ready and willing concurrence. By some, the measure may be regarded as just; by others, generous: it perhaps partook of both attributes. If it went farther than naked justice could have demanded, it did not stop short of what liberality approved. Thus was the foundation broadly laid for all that has since been constructed upon it. In compliance with his engagement, the Secretary, on the 23d of May, transmitted to General W. Scott a copy of the above communication, and authorized him "to enter into an agreement with the agents of the nation for the removal of their people"; which produced the arrangement with John Ross and others, already referred to. The natural results of granting so much to the means, to the feelings, and wishes of the Cherokees, followed. If our acts have been generous, they have not been less wise and politic. A large mass of men have been conciliated, the hazard of an effusion of human blood has been put by, good feeling has been preserved, and we have quietly and gently transported 18,000 friends to the west bank of the Mississippi.

The Pottawatomies of Indiana, the time for whose removal, by their treaty stipulations, had arrived for some, and approached for others, showed an indisposition to comply with their engagements. White men had settled upon the lands they had ceded, and collisions arose that threatened the peace of the country and the spilling of blood, which induced the agent, to whom the direction of their emigration was confided, on the application of the white settlers, to call upon the Governor of Indiana for a military force to repress any outbreak that might occur. The Governor authorized General John Tipton to accept the services of one hundred volunteers; who raised them, and used their services in the collection and removal of the Pottawatomies. A copy of his report to the Governor of Indiana is herewith submitted. By this operation, 768 Indians are now on their way to the West. There have emigrated within the year 151 Chippewas, Ottawas, and Pottawatomies; 177 Choctaws; 4,106 Creeks, being chiefly composed of the families of the warriors of that tribe who served in Florida, and who had left their homes prior to the last report, but arrived west since; 4,600 Chickasaws, and 1,651 Florida Indians; making an aggregate of 29,453; which, added to those who had previously occupied their new abode, makes 81,082 emigrant residents, of whom 31,343 are now subsisted at the expense of the United States, at a daily cost of $3,186.24. In the whole number of emigrants, of those for the year, and those living at the expense of the United States, are included the Cherokees and Pottawatomies, who, it is supposed, will have reached the end of their journey before this report is presented. There yet are east of the Mississippi 26,682 Indians. A tabular statement, which accompanies this communication, exhibits, in detail, the foregoing facts.

Information was received on the 6th of November from the agent employed in that service, by letter dated at Pensacola on the 28th October last, that all the Appalachicola Indians, and thirty-four Creeks, were embarked for the West. Recent communications are calculated to induce the belief that the Winnebagoes will remove quietly in the spring. They concluded a treaty at Washington on the 1st November, 1837, which was ratified on the 15th June, 1838, by which they covenanted to leave their present residences for the Neutral Ground, west of the Mississippi, within eight months after the ratification. The day will arrive in winter, and it is understood they wish to be indulged till spring, which seems to be not unreasonable, although the distance to be travelled is short; and I am sure they will be gratified. On the other hand, information of a different character has reached this office, stating that it is uncertain whether they will remove. In any event, I think the above request ought to be granted.

The number of Indians on this side of the Mississippi is comparatively small, and it cannot be that much time shall elapse before the entire east country will be relieved of their presence—an event desirable in all aspects of the subject. It is an expensive operation; but it is difficult to withhold any draught upon the public funds in reference to it. Our great purpose is their peaceable and comfortable translation; and in effecting it, the movement should have a liberal infusion of feeling and humanity, and not be misshaped by narrow rules.

The different treaties providing for their removal, and the act of 1830, entitle the Indians to receive patents for the lands allotted to them in the West. To so many of them as are there, would it not be just to give the evidence of title? They will look for it, and would be gratified by its receipt. Few surveys have been made; designation of boundary on the ground might prevent collisions, and is proper. This work should be attended to, I think.

* * *

There is one measure that, in my judgment, is of great importance: it has, heretofore, attracted the attention of Congress, and, I hope, will meet with favor. As any plan for the government of the Western tribes of Indians contemplates an interior police of their own in each community, and that their own laws shall prevail as between themselves, for which some of their treaties provide, this, as it seems to me, indispensable step to their advancement in civilization cannot be taken without their own consent. Unless some system is marked out by which there shall be a separate allotment of land to each individual whom the scheme shall entitle to it, you will look in vain for any general casting-off of savagism. Common property and civilization cannot co-exist. The few instances to be found in the United States and other countries of small abstracted communities, who draw their subsistence and whatever comforts they have from a common store, do not militate against this position. Under a show of equality, the mass work for two or three rulers or directors, who enjoy what they will, and distribute what they please. The members never rise beyond a certain point, (to which they had reached, generally, before they joined the society,) and never will, while they remain where they are. But if they should, these associations are so small and confined as to place their possessions in the class of individual estates. At the foundation of the whole social system lies individuality of property. It is, perhaps, nine times in ten, the stimulus that manhood first feels; it has produced the energy, industry, and enterprise that distinguish the civilized world, and contributes more largely to the good morals of men than those are willing to acknowledge who have not looked somewhat closely, at their fellow-beings. With it come all the delights that the word *home* expresses. The comforts that follow fixed settlements are in its train; and to them belong not only an anxiety to do right, that those gratifications may not be forfeited, but industry, that they may be increased. Social intercourse and a just appreciation of its pleasures result, when you have civilized and, for the most part, moral men. This process, it strikes me, the Indians must go through, before their habits can be materially changed; and they may, after what many of them have seen and know, do it very rapidly. If, on the other hand, the large tracts of land set apart for them shall continue to be joint property, the ordinary motive to industry (and the most powerful one) will be wanting. A bare subsistence is as much as they can promise themselves. A few acres of badly-cultivated corn about their cabins will be seen, instead of extensive fields, rich pastures, and valuable stock. The latter belong to him who is conscious that what he ploughs is his own, and will descend to those he loves—never to the man who does not know by what tenure he holds his miserable dwelling. Laziness and unthrift will be so general as not to be disgraceful; and if the produce of their labors should be thrown into common stock, the indolent and dishonest will subsist at the expense of the meritorious. Besides, there is a strong motive in reference to ourselves for encouraging individual ownership. The history of the world proves that distinct and separate possessions make those who hold them averse to change. The risk of losing the advantages they have, men do not readily encounter. By adopting and acting on the view suggested, a large body will be created whose interests would dispose them to keep things steady. They would be the ballast of the ship.

Plans have, at various times, been proposed for a confederation of the Indian tribes west of the Mississippi, embracing those who shall hereafter remove. I incline much to doubt the expedience of such a measure. It could only be executed with the consent of the tribes that might become members of it. The Choctaws have twice signified their disinclination to it. The treaty with the Cherokees of December, 1835, discourages it. The idea of such a bond between dependent communities is new. The league could only be for regulation among themselves, and not for mutual protection, which is the usual object of such combinations. They have no common property to secure, or common interest to advance. Any plan I have seen is based upon the power of the President to reject their articles of association, which exhibits, strikingly, their true position. They may be likened to colonies, among whom a confederation does not exist. They are governed, and their legislation, by each community for itself, is supervised and controlled, by the parent country. When they contemplate a different attitude, they confederate. A general council of the Indians might pass resolutions of a pacific character, or to arrest actual hostilities, and to regulate their intercourse with each other; but this could be done better by Congress, leaving to each tribe the management of its own internal concerns, not interfering with treaties or laws. There are inherent difficulties in the dissimilar conditions of the tribes. Some of them are semi-civilized, others as wild as the game they hunt. Some are rich, others poor. Some number but a few hundred souls, others more thousands. We cannot frame for them, much less could they do it, articles of confederation which would bring into council a just representation of the different tribes. If you allot so many representatives to a tribe, looking to its population, the smaller would be swallowed up in the larger. If you limit to a certain number, or within or between two numbers, you are unjust to the larger tribes, which a combination of the smaller, with fewer motives to rectitude, might control. A small proportion of all might come into the confederation, and these separated from each other by bands who would not join in the arrangement, and would not, on any principle, be bound by the resolves of the general council. We owe duties to ourselves. Cogent reasons for not giving to these neighboring communities more concentration than they have must be seen. While they are treated with all kindness, tenderness even, and liberality, prudential considerations would seem to require that they should be kept distinct from each other. Let them manage their internal police after their own views. One or more superintendents, and as many agencies as may be deemed proper, with such regulation of their intercourse with each other, and such guards for their protection as Congress shall think fit to prescribe, would, it appears to me, meet the emergence. Through the officers thus stationed among them, they could make their complaints known, and ask redress for grievances, which would be afforded when it was proper. It is not understood that the deliberations of the council could result in any act that would be valid, until approved by the Chief Magistrate, which does not lessen the force of what has been said.

It would, perhaps, be judicious not to pay a compliment at some hazard, especially where it would not be appreciated; but to assert directly, for general purposes, the authority which actually exists, and which must, upon any suggestion that may be adopted, be really felt and acknowledged. At some future period, if circumstances should be so changed as to call for a Territorial Government, or for any other alteration in the system, the United States can, in the guardian position they occupy, make such modification as sound judgment and an anxious desire to benefit the Indians shall dictate.

Report of Commissioner of Indian Affairs Orlando Brown
November 30, 1849

(Excerpt from *Report for 1849*, pp. 937-46)

During the 1840's, white expansion left the Mississippi River far behind, and with it the removal policy of the 1830's. A new removal policy, for those Indians west of the Mississippi, was now demanded. Commissioner Brown's report focused on this problem and raised questions that were to bedevil Indian relations for years to come: the extent to which the United States should be concerned with warfare between one Indian tribe and another, how to react to Texas' refusal to recognize any Indian rights in the lands within the new state's boundaries, and the like. Brown's report outlined the design of providing great corridors to the greater West through the Indian nations bordering on the existing settlements. This design, which dominated Indian policy for many years, provided for the removal and concentration elsewhere of Indians astride the corridors selected.

IN SUBMITTING a brief view of our Indian affairs and relations during the past year, I would respectfully refer to the accompanying documents for more detailed information, in many particulars, than can be embraced in a general report like this. Emanating from the several classes of local agents of the department having the immediate charge and supervision of the different tribes and their affairs, and from the devoted and zealous missionaries of various Christian denominations, who are actively and laboriously co-operating with the government in its efforts to improve the moral and intellectual condition of the red man, they embrace information not only of great practical value in the administration of our Indian affairs, but which must be of no ordinary interest to all who feel any concern in regard to the present condition and future destiny of the remaining aboriginal inhabitants of our country.

Among the border of tribes and others with whom we have defined and fixed relations, and maintain any immediate and regular intercourse, as great a degree of peace and tranquillity has prevailed as during the same length of time at any former period. They have generally conducted themselves peacefully towards our citizens, and towards each other. This circumstance speaks well for the vigilance and activity of our agents and of the military stationed in the Indian country, and attests the good effects of the policy pursued by the government in promptly repressing any symptoms of outbreak, and compelling tribes committing outrages upon others to make ample and suitable reparation for the injury, so far as, under present circumstances, these objects can be accomplished. Nor must we overlook the influence of the good example of some of our more civilized and orderly tribes, and the happy effects of the exertions of the many excellent persons who, animated by a truly philanthropic and Christian spirit, have voluntarily banished themselves beyond the confines of civilization and all its comforts and advantages, and gone to labor zealously and disinterestedly for the temporal and spiritual welfare of an unfortunate and semi-barbarous people. Both doubtless have, in some degree, aided in securing so desirable a result.

It is impossible, however, to prevent the occurrence of occasional difficulties among our more remote border tribes, who, from their position and other circumstances, have not, as yet, sufficiently felt the influence of the policy and measures of the government for the civilization and improvement of our Indians to be induced to give up their natural habits of war and the chase. From their disinclination for agricultural and other peaceful and more profitable pursuits of civilized life, they have ample time and opportunity for indulgence in those habits; and as it is in their hunting excursions—when they are beyond any supervision or control, and which bring them more or less into collisions—that difficulties most generally occur. There have been several cases of the kind, attended with bloodshed and loss of life, between some of the northwestern tribes, as will be seen from the reports of the agents in that quarter. As far as possible, measures have been adopted to compel the aggressors to make reparation for the injuries inflicted by them—those receiving annuities being required to make as satisfactory a compensation in money as the case admitted; and in order still further to teach them and others that the government will not overlook such acts of outrage, but will interpose to punish and put a stop to them, the more reckless and daring individuals concerned in, and who should in a great measure be held responsible for them, have been arrested, in cases where they could be identified, and will be held in confinement at some of the military posts until a salutary impression is made upon them and their brethren of the enormity of their conduct, and the displeasure it has given to the government.

So far as I am aware, it has not been the practice to interfere in cases of difficulty between different tribes, further than to interpose, by military force or otherwise, to put a stop to them; and even the practice of compelling satisfaction for outrages to be made out of annuities is one of recent adoption. The punishment of the guilty parties by arrest and confinement may therefore be regarded as an extreme measure; but there is ample authority and justification for it, arising out of the nature of the relations between the government and the Indians, as guardian and wards.

It is to tribal and intestine wars and difficulties, as much if not more than to any other causes, that the decline and misery of the Indian race are justly to be attributed. Enmity between them is hereditary and implacable, and no occasion is omitted to indulge it, by the destruction of life and other outrages: the retaliatory law of blood, which universally prevails among the uncivilized tribes, causes it to remain unappeased and unappeasable, whether existing between different tribes or between members of the same tribe. It is, therefore, no less the dictate of humanity, than it is a high moral duty on the part of the government, to interpose its strong arm, in the most effectual manner possible, to put a stop to its lamentable and dreadful consequences, if the feeling itself cannot be eradicated. Compelling compensation to be made out of annuities, and the mere imprisonment of offenders, are not sufficient for the accomplishment of this great object; while, by the former, the innocent are made to pay for the acts of the guilty, whose distributive shares of the annuities alone ought to be taken for such a purpose, unless the tribe generally should fail properly to exert themselves to prevent the commission of such outrages. But the only effectual remedy, and one which is loudly called for by humanity, as well as by sound policy, will be, for Congress to make provision for the trial of the offenders in such cases, in some appropriate manner, and for their punishment, by death, hard labor at the military posts, or otherwise, according to the nature and aggravated character of the offence. And I would go further, and recommend that authority also be given for taking cognizance of cases of theft or robbery, and of habitual or repeated intemperance among the members of a tribe; and to inflict some suitable kind of punishment as a corrective of these two evils, where they are taken notice of and properly punished by the tribe itself. They are among the greatest drawbacks to the civilization and improvement of our Indians. A well-disposed Indian, desirous of improving the condition, and to provide more permanently for the comfort, of himself and family, by resorting to agricultural pursuits, raising stock, or acquiring other species of property, is, in most instances, among the less civilized tribes, deterred from doing so, because of the disposition, especially among the idle and dissolute, to consider almost all kinds of property as common, and to which any one having the power to take it has as good a right as its possessor.

The baleful and lamentable effects of indulgence in ardent spirits by the Indians have been so often and so vividly portrayed in former reports, as to render unnecessary any extended remarks upon the subject on this occasion. All the laws passed by Congress, and the most strenuous efforts of the Indian agents and the military stationed in the Indian country, to put a stop to the inhuman traffic in this article, have in a great measure failed to effect that end. In consequence of the extent of the Indian frontier, and the impossibility of guarding it at every point, the fiend-like and mercenary wretches who engage in it, in defiance of all law, human and divine, find ample opportunities for introducing liquor into the Indian country, and to vend it to the Indians at profits so enormous as to stimulate them to encounter a considerable degree of risk in doing so. If, in addition to some proper and salutary punishment, in cases of continued or repeated intoxication, means were provided for suitably rewarding those Indians who might distinguish themselves by their zeal and efforts to prevent the introduction and use of ardent spirits among their brethren, it is confidently believed that in a few years an effectual check would be given to this great curse of the tribes on our borders.

If the foregoing suggestions be carried out, a stop will in a great measure be put to tribal wars and intestine broils and difficulties; the idea of individual property and its security will be promoted, which will lead to industry and thrift; intemperance, which paralyzes the benevolent efforts of the government, of Christian associations, and of individuals, will be banished from the Indian country; and, under the effects of the other beneficial measures of policy now in operation, there would be manifest in the condition and circumstances of another generation of many of our less civilized Indians evidences of moral and social improvement, and of advancement in all the substantial elements of tribal and individual prosperity and happiness, similar to those which, to the gratification and encouragement of the philanthropist and the Christian, are conspicuously evident among some of the semi-civilized tribes, such as the Cherokees, Choctaws, Chickasaws, and others. These people have regular forms of government, good and wholesome laws, with proper officers for their administration; and their affairs are conducted with a degree of wisdom, vigor, and impartiality, by which the vicious are restrained, crime punished, and justice dispensed, in a manner that would be creditable to many civilized communities. Among this class of our Indians, the exercise of such powers as those suggested would not, therefore, be necessary.

There is a portion of the Seminole tribe of Indians who did not emigrate with, and have never joined, their brethren west of the Mississippi river—they having been permitted to remain in Florida, under an arrangement made in 1842 by General Worth, then commanding the troops employed to subdue and remove the tribe, which had for some time been in a state of hostility. This arrangement was intended to be, and was, of a temporary character only, and could not have been otherwise, as the removal of the Indians was required by positive treaty stipulations, which it was the duty of the Executive to see carried into effect. They could not be induced to remove voluntarily, and, being limited in number it was easy for them, from the nature of the country, to elude the troops; so that their forcible removal could probably have been effected only by the continued employment of a large amount of military force, at a great expense, and after considerable delay, during which they would have continued to keep the frontier citizens in a state of constant alarm and danger. To put an end to this unpleasant state of things, it seems to have been deemed best to enter into an amicable arrangement for their remaining for the time being, on condition of their retiring to, and residing within, a district of country designated for the purpose in the southern portion of the peninsula of Florida, on the gulf side, and abstaining from hostilities or acts of annoyance against our citizens. The further to provide against collisions between them and the whites, a strip of land twenty miles wide was laid off and reserved, upon which it was the intention that neither should settle. These arrangements were all made through the military, in whose charge the Indians have been ever since—this department having had no agent over them, except for a short period during the present year, one having been appointed, in consequence of an application from the proper quarter, to relieve the military of the duty. Before, however, this agent could reach the country of the Indians and communicate with them, a small number, without any well-ascertained cause, again broke out into hostilities, and committed several murders, and destroyed the property of some of our citizens. At the time of these unfortunate occurrences, this department was engaged in maturing a plan for the emigration of these Indians, who had no right to remain permanently where they were, and could not much longer be permitted to do so, without preventing the settlement of a valuable portion of the State of Florida, and incurring the risk of collision between them and the whites who were settling in their neighborhood. And, considering their own future welfare and best interests, the sooner they were removed and permanently settled with their brethren in the west, the better. With the view of convincing them of this fact, and of using all possible means to induce them to emigrate peaceably—and thus to avoid the expense and possible blood-shed of a resort to coercive measures—it was determined to offer a gratuity to each individual who would do so, and to send to them a delegation of the western Seminoles, who had manifested much and commendable interest on the subject of their removal, and offered the services of a suitable number of their most intelligent men for the purpose, to satisfy them of the superiority of their position west, and the advantages of emigration. This plan was accordingly adopted to be carried out under the supervision of the Indian agent and the military.... On further consideration, however, it being believed that, under the changed state of things, the services of the Indian agent could be of very little if of any use, and that all the measures, of whatever character, necessary to effect the removal of the Indians, could best be conducted by the military alone, the appointment of the agent was revoked on the 28th of September last. The entire control having thus reverted back to the military, that department will, no doubt, report the result of the measures adopted for the removal of the Indians, so far as put in operation, as well as state what has been done towards punishing those concerned in the outrages referred to, and to prevent a repetition of such occurrences, so long as the Indians may remain in Florida. I may add, however, that, according to the latest information, there seems to be a fair prospect of effecting their emigration peaceably at an early day, in which the services of the delegation of their western brethren sent by this depart-ment will no doubt prove in no inconsiderable degree instrumental.

In the early part of the season, a serious outbreak took place on the part of some of the Indians in Texas, who, before they could be checked, ravaged an extensive frontier along the Rio Grande, nearly down to the gulf coast, committing a number of murders, making captive several women and children, and destroying and carrying off a considerable amount of property. This occurrence was wholly unexpected, and, so far as known, without any sufficient cause, other than the restless and predatory character of the Indians. Our only agent in that quarter had exerted himself with energy and success in settling slight difficulties which had previously occurred, and in keeping them quiet and peaceable; and from his reports there was every reason to believe that they would continue so disposed. The proper measures were taken by the military, with their usual promptitude, to extend protection to the settlements, and to prevent a recurrence of the outrage. The Indians were soon driven back into their own country, and, under the salutary effect of chastisement inflicted on some portions of them, have since remained quiet and peaceable. The Comanches, who are the largest, and generally the most troublesome, of the tribes, and who are supposed to have been principally concerned in the outbreak, have recently, on the occasion of filling the vacancy occasioned by the death of their principal chief, with the full concurrence of their new chief, manifested their sense of the folly and temerity of being guilty of acts that would bring them into collision with the government, as such a course was always followed by severe punishment, and would eventually terminate in their destruction. The new chief himself and another individual came in as delegates to the commanding officer of the troops in Texas, to inform him of their determination to abstain from hostilities, and, as far as possible, to prevent any members of their tribe from committing depredations upon our citizens; but, from the character and peculiar situation of the Indians in Texas, the entire want on the part of the general government of any jurisdiction or control over the country occupied by them, and from a proper supply of local agents to aid in the management of our Indian affairs in that State not having been authorized, this condition of things cannot, with any degree of certainty, be expected to continue for any length of time; and this department should not be held accountable for any disturbances or difficulties that may occur, unless new and more effective arrangements be soon made. The anomalous position of these Indians, and the necessity of our relations with them being placed upon a different footing, have been referred to and fully explained in preceding annual reports from this office; and I would earnestly, but respectfully, again invoke attention to the subject.

Texas, on coming into the Union, retained control and jurisdiction over all her public domain; so that none of the laws or regulations of our Indian system are in force within her limits. The department has, therefore, no power to prevent intrusions into the country occupied by the Indians, or any trade or intercourse with them, of however improper a character they may be, or however likely to excite jealousy on the part of the Indians, and collisions and difficulties between them and our citizens. Nor is it authorized to encourage the Indians to settle down in any particular section or sections of country, with a view to civilizing them and improving their condition.

Until a particular district or districts shall have been set apart for their permanent residence, within which the general government will have the same power to prevent intrusions, and to regulate trade and intercourse with them, as it has in regard to our other Indians on territory of the United States, and until a suitable number and description of agents shall have been authorized for them, the department should not be held at all responsible for the proper and efficient management of our Indian affairs in Texas. . . .

So far as information has reached this office, the Indians of the prairies, who infest the two routes to our possessions west of the Rocky mountains— the one by the Platte and the other by the Arkansas rivers—have been much less troublesome during the past season than heretofore. With the exception of one or two comparatively unimportant instances, they have abstained from attacks and depredations upon our emigrants, and in some cases, on the Arkansas route, have shown them acts of kindness. They have been influenced in their general good conduct, however, by the expectation of some reward from the government, and not from fear—as they have not as yet felt our power, and know nothing of our greatness and resources.

These Indians, who have so long roamed free and uncontrolled over the immense prairies extending westward to the Rocky mountains, and who consider the whole country as their own, have regarded with much jealousy the passing of so many of our people through it, without any recognition of their rights, or any compensation for the privilege. The great destruction of the buffalo by the emigrants has also caused much dissatisfaction among them, as it has more or less interfered with their success in the chase, and, if continued, must, at no late day, so far diminish this chief resource of their subsistence and trade, as not only to entail upon them great suffering, but it will bring different tribes into competition in their hunting expeditions, and lead to bloody collisions and exterminating wars between them, in which some of our border Indians will become more or less involved, and the peace and security of our frontier may thus be seriously disturbed. It is also much to be feared that the unfavorable feelings engendered by the circumstances named may, at an early period, break out into open hostilities on the part of the Indians, which would be attended with serious consequences to our emigrants, or compel the government, at an enormous expense, to afford them protection by the employment of a large military force on both routes. Under these circumstances, it has been deemed expedient and advisable to take measures to bring about a proper understanding with the Indians, which will secure their good will, and prevent collisions and strife among them, by obligating each tribe to remain as much as possible within their respective districts of country, and providing that, where disputes or difficulties occur, they shall be submitted to the government, and the Indians abide by its decision. Instructions have accordingly been given to hold a treaty with the different tribes, making provision for the accomplishment of these objects, and stipulating that, for the unrestricted right of way through their country, for their good conduct towards our emigrants, and for the destruction of game unavoidably committed by them, they shall be allowed a reasonable compensation annually, to consist principally of presents of goods, stock and agricultural implements, with assistance to instruct and aid them in cultivating the soil, and in other kindred pursuits, so that they may thus be enabled to sustain themselves when the buffalo and other game shall have so far disappeared as no longer to furnish them with an adequate means of subsistence. It is also intended to bring in a delegation from the different tribes, for the purpose of visiting some of the more populous portions of the country, in order that they may acquire some knowledge of our greatness and strength, which will make a salutary impression upon them, and through them upon their brethren, and which will no doubt tend, in no slight degree, to influence them to continue peaceful relations towards the government and our citizens. It was at first supposed that the negotiations might be held this fall, and the delegation be brought in early next spring; but more recent and better information has led to the conclusion that the Indians cannot be assembled for the purpose until some time next season.

Since the establishment of the new Territory of Minnesota, the attention of a large number of our enterprising citizens has been directed to that quarter, in consequence of the fine climate and the richness and fertility of the lands on the Mississippi and within a wide sweep on both sides of it, by the superabundant water power afforded by that river and some of its tributaries, and by the superior advantages offered by the extensive forests of pine, convenient to water transportation, for a large and lucrative trade in lumber. There has consequently been considerable emigration there during the past year; and it will, no doubt, go on increasing annually, so that in a very few years the population will be sufficient to justify a demand for admission into the Union as a State.

The Indian title has been extinguished to but a comparatively small portion of the country within the limits of the Territory—lying principally on the east side of the Mississippi; being bounded on the north by a line extending east, from opposite the mouth of the Crow-wing river, till it intersects the western boundary line of Wisconsin, at about 92° 15′ west longitude; on the east by that boundary, from the above point to the head waters of the St. Croix river, and down it to the Mississippi; and on the west and southwest by the latter river. The country above the northern boundary belongs to the Chippewa Indians of Lake Superior and the Mississippi, though many of those Indians still remain, by sufferance, on the lands south of it, which they ceded to the United States by treaties made with them in 1837 and 1842. They are under obligations to remove from them whenever required by the President, which should be at an early day, as their longer residence there is incompatible with the tranquillity and interests of our citizens, who suffer annoyance and loss from their depredations. And in view of the rapid spread of our population in that direction, and of the permanent welfare of the Indians, it may be expedient, at an early period, to renew the effort, unsuccessfully made in 1847, to purchase all their remaining lands east of the Mississippi up to our northern boundary, and provide for their removal and concentration west of that river—where, confined within narrower limits, they will be compelled, as the game becomes scarce, to give up the chase, and their wild and unsettled mode of life, and to resort to agriculture and other civilized pursuits. In such a situation, too, the government, aided by the zealous missionaries of our various religious denominations, would have a far better opportunity effectively to bring to bear upon them its policy and measures for the civilization of our Indian tribes, by means of manual-labor schools, and instruction and and aid in agriculture and mechanical arts.

The desirable portions of that part of Minnesota, east of the Mississippi, to which the Indian title has been extinguished, were already so far occupied by a white population as to seem to render it absolutely necessary to obtain, without delay, a cession from the Indians on the west side of that river, for the accommodation of our citizens emigrating to that quarter, a large portion of whom would probably be compelled to precipitate themselves on that side of the Mississippi, and on the Indians' lands, which would inevitably lead to collisions and bloodshed, unless the Indians were purchased out and removed. These lands are owned by the Sioux, who are a wild and untamable people, and whom, after years of unremitted efforts, and the expenditure of large sums of money, the government has not been able, to any beneficial extent, to induce to resort to agriculture, or to adopt any of the habits of civilized life. They are the most restless, reckless, and mischievous Indians of the Northwest; their passion for war and the chase seems unlimited and unassuageable; and so long as they remain where they are, they must be a source of constant annoyance and danger to our citizens, as well as to the Indians of our northern colony, between some of whom (the Chippewas) and themselves there exists a hereditary feud, frequently leading to collisions and bloodshed, which disturbs the peace and tranquillity of the frontier, and must greatly interfere with the welfare of the Indians of that colony, and with the efforts of the government to effect their civilization. The game having become scarce in that portion of their country desired, many are leaving it and emigrating westward, where the toils of the chase are better rewarded. It is, therefore, comparatively valueless to them, though much of it, on the Mississippi and Minnesota (or St. Peter's) rivers, is rich and fertile, and capable of sustaining a dense civilized population, and, when open to settlement, will soon be occupied.

In view of the facts and circumstances thus briefly detailed, it was deemed advisable, as soon as possible after the department became fully acquainted with them, to make an effort to obtain a cession of the lands referred to; and two commissioners were accordingly appointed for that purpose in August last—one of them, the excellent and efficient governor of the Territory, who is ex-officio superintendent of Indian affairs; and the other a distinguished citizen of ability, peculiarly fitted for the discharge of such a duty, from his having held a similar position as governor of the Territory of Iowa, and being consequently well acquainted with our Indian affairs in that quarter, and especially our relations with, and the character, habits and disposition of the Indians with whom the negotiations were to be held. . . .

On repairing to the Indian country, the commissioners found that most of the Indians had left for their fall hunt—in consequence of which, and other causes of difficulty, which may hereafter be obviated, they succeeded in effecting only a partial compliance with their instructions. Their efforts resulted in a treaty for the purchase, on reasonable terms, of a tract of country lying immediately on the west side of the Mississippi, and estimated to contain about three hundred and eighty-four thousand acres, which was set apart for the half-breeds of the tribe by the treaty of July 15, 1830. It is represented to be valuable for agricultural and other purposes, and will, no doubt, at once be occupied by a large influx of our hardy and enterprising emigrants. The necessity and importance of this purchase fully justify the expense that has been incurred; and the treaty will be laid before you, at the proper time, to be submitted to the President and the Senate for their consideration.

The situation of some of the smaller border tribes west of the Mississippi requires the attention of the government. Most if not all of them possess an extent of country which, however desirable originally, with reference to their maintaining themselves by the chase, now that game has become scarce, is not only of no use, but a positive disadvantage to them, as it has a tendency to keep them from concentrating and applying themselves with any regular or systematic effort to agriculture and other industrial pursuits. They are also thus thrown into detached and isolated positions, which renders them more liable to be attacked and plundered, as is too frequently the case, by larger and stronger tribes, and from which they would be safe if brought nearer together, so that they could aid and sustain one another, and protection could be more conveniently and promptly extended to them by the government. Another good result of their being more concentrated would be, that the good example and more prosperous state of those more advanced in civilization would exert a powerful influence upon those less so, and stimulate them to exert themselves to produce a like change in their condition and circumstances; while, at the same time, it would enable the government, without any enlargement in its scale of operations, or any increase of expenditure, to extend to a greater number the benefits of its policy and measures for their civilization and improvement.

Some of the tribes referred to have themselves become impressed with the disadvantages of their present position, and have made known to the government their desire to dispose of their surplus lands, and to unite themselves together—the amount to be allowed them for their lands to be held or used as a fund to be applied in various ways towards improving their condition; and a like arrangement could, no doubt, be made with most, if not all, the other tribes similarly situated. Some of them are very destitute, having no annuities or other means to encourage or enable them to endeavor to effect a change in their condition as hunters and vagabonds. And as the diminution of game within their reach has rendered the avails of the chase—the only means of sustaining themselves—very uncertain and precarious, they are frequently subjected to great hardship and suffering; while, both in their own country and in their hunting expeditions, they are exposed to much injury from attacks of other and larger tribes. In view of this state of things, I would respectfully recommend the adoption, at the earliest practicable period, of the proper measures for bringing them nearer together, in positions where they will be more safe, and which will afford greater inducements and facilities for effecting a radical and favorable change in their condition and circumstances. The dictates of humanity, and a wise and enlightened policy, alike call for the adoption of such a course; and I would, therefore, suggest that provision be made for the employment and expenses of commissioners to visit all the tribes so situated, with the view of entering into arrangements for the purpose.

A prominent feature in this course of policy should be the carrying out of an excellent suggestion in the annual report of my predecessor of last year, that the smaller tribes scattered along the frontier, above the Delawares and Kickapoos—embracing the Sacs and Foxes of the Missouri, the Iowas, the Omahas, the Ottoes and Missourias, the Poncas, and if possible the Pawnees—should be moved down among the tribes of our southern colony, where suitable situations may be found for them, in connexion with other Indians of kindred stock. Such an arrangement, in connexion with the change which must inevitably take place in the position of the Sioux, would, as remarked by my predecessor, open a wide sweep of country between our northern and southern Indian colonies for the expansion and egress of our white population westward, and thus save our colonized tribes from being injuriously pressed upon, if not eventually overrun and exterminated, before they are sufficiently advanced in civilization, and in the attainment of its resources and advantages, to be able to maintain themselves in close proximity with, or in the midst of, a white population.

Report of Commissioner
of Indian Affairs Luke Lea
November 27, 1851

(Excerpt from *Report for 1851*, pp. 265-74)

Commissioner Lea's report reflected the problems brought about by the enormous territorial expansion in the preceding decade. In discussing the Winnebagoes, for example, Lea noted that it was "one of the legionary cases arising out of our Indian relations, in which it is impossible for the department to ascertain with certainty what should be done." Lea concluded his report by quoting the remarks of former Attorney General Legaré, that "there is nothing in the whole compass of our laws so anomalous, so hard to bring within any precise definition, or any logical and scientific arrangement of principles, as the relation in which the Indians stand towards this government and those of the States."

THE LIMITS OF a report of this description will admit only of a very general and summary view of the condition of our Indian affairs, and the operations of this branch of the public service during the last twelve months. For detailed information reference must be had to the documents herewith, consisting of the reports of superintendents, agents, missionaries, and others, which contain a mass of facts and speculations, curious, interesting and important.

In the last annual report from this office, allusion was made to mutual aggressions on the part of the Sioux and Chippewas, attended by melancholy incidents of Indian barbarity and folly. In despite of all efforts to prevent it, similar occurrences have taken place within the last year, by which both tribes have suffered, more or less, from depredations upon their property, and in the murder of a number of their men, women and children. No treaty arrangements among themselves appear to be regarded, or are of sufficient force to prevent the deadly enmity which exists between the two tribes from manifesting itself, as often as opportunity offers, in the most shocking atrocities. With this exception, a gratifying degree of order has prevailed among all the tribes with whom we have defined and established relations, and who have felt the controlling influence of the government in directing their pursuits, and in the management of their affairs. Towards our own citizens all have been peaceful and friendly. Most of them have readily yielded to the policy and measures of the department for the improvement of their condition; and such are the advances many of them have made in civilization, that flattering encouragement is not only afforded for continued effort on the part of the government and its agents among

50

them, but on the part, also, of benevolent Christian missionaries, who, with commendable and self-sacrificing spirit have been engaged in imparting to the various tribes the divine truths of Christianity.

During the past summer treaties have been made with various bands of the Sioux Indians, by which they cede a large and valuable extent of country west of the Mississippi river, in the Territory of Minnesota and State of Iowa. To the treaties themselves, and the report of the commissioners on the part of the government by whom they were effected, you are respectfully referred for detailed information concerning these important negotiations. In view of the rapid spread of the white population in the State and Territory within which the lands acquired by these treaties are situated, the growing discontent among the warlike Indians from whom they are obtained, embroiled, as they often are, in difficulties with the Chippewas, and threatening more and more the peace of the frontier in that quarter, the extinguishment of their title to the lands now ceded has long been a subject of serious consideration and desire by the government.

A considerable number of the Chippewas who had continued to reside on the ceded lands east of the Mississippi, in Wisconsin and Minnesota, since the treaties of 1837 and 1842, have been removed during the present year. Indeed, with the exception of the Anse and Vieux Desert bands, together with a portion of the Pellican lake and Wisconsin river bands, an entire removal has been effected. The chiefs and about one-half of the two last-named bands have emigrated. The remainder, with the Vieux Desert band, were recently reported as suffering severely from small-pox and measles. This, with other causes, will prevent any attempt to remove them until the coming spring, when it is believed such of them as it may be expedient to remove can easily be induced to emigrate. The number removed this year is reported to be three thousand; and including the Anse band, it is supposed that only seven hundred remain on the ceded lands. Apprehensions, however, are entertained, that by reason of the proximity of those who have removed to their old hunting grounds, they will return in considerable numbers, and not only again molest our citizens, but be reduced to destitution and want, as in such event they will forfeit their annuities, and have to depend alone on the wild products of the country, which are now so nearly exhausted as not to afford them the means of subsistence. The same view of this subject induced me heretofore to recommend that efforts be made to concentrate them within proper limits west of the Mississippi, where, with additional means beyond those already provided, arrangements could be made to introduce among them a system of education, embracing the knowledge and practice of agriculture and the simpler mechanic arts. But as the country referred to was not the common property of the whole tribe, part of it belonging exclusively to particular bands who are not parties to any treaties, and who receive no annuities or material aid from the United States, it was also recommended that Congress be asked for an appropriation to defray the expense of negotiating with all the bands for the purpose of acquiring such portions of the country on the east side of the Mississippi as might be required to supply the wants of our white population; providing, also, that the whole of their remaining lands, together with their present and future means, should be the common property of the entire tribe; and that as large a proportion of their funds as practicable should be set apart and applied in such manner as best to secure their comfort, and most rapidly advance them in civilization and prosperity. No action was had upon this recommendation, owing mainly, it is believed, to the shortness of the session, and the pressure of business upon both Congress and the department. I now, therefore, renew the recommendation, satisfied that the policy thus briefly referred to is not only best calculated to promote the future welfare of this large and interesting tribe, but is necessary to save them from actual starvation, as the game on which they mainly depend for the means of living is fast disappearing, and cannot much longer afford them a support.

By permission of the President, the Menomonees still remain on the lands in Wisconsin ceded by them under the provisions of their treaty of 1848 with the United States. In that treaty it was stipulated that they were to be permitted to remain two years from the date thereof, and until they were notified by the President that the lands were wanted by the government. To induce them to remove to the country in Minnesota assigned to them by the treaty, it was also stipulated that it should be explored by a suitable delegation to be selected for that purpose. This exploration took place in the summer of 1850, but from representations made to the department, it appears that the Indians, previously dissatisfied with the treaty, are dissatisfied also with the country assigned to them, and manifest the greatest reluctance to remove. The fall of last year was the period fixed upon for their removal; but owing to their urgent appeals, and those of many of the whites in their immediate vicinity, and in consideration of their peaceful habits, the President granted them permission to remain until the 1st of June of the present year. At the expiration of this last-named period, it being known that they had made no arrangements, and were in no condition to emigrate, the President again, at their earnest solicitation, consented that they might remain a twelvemonth longer, on condition, however, that they should not interfere with the public surveys, and with the distinct understanding that this extension of time was to be considered an act of favor, they being still subject to removal at his discretion; and of this Superintendent Murray was instructed to take care that they should be fully advised. Of the nature of their alleged grievances the superintendent was also informed, and he was directed, by instructions from this department of the 4th June last, at as early a period as practicable, to acquaint himself thoroughly in regard to their condition, and to make a full report thereof. In order, too, that the President might act advisedly on their petition to occupy permanently a part of the ceded territory, the superintendent was also instructed to examine the country; to report all the facts bearing on this particular subject; and to furnish all other information necessary to a correct understanding of the course of policy proper to be pursued in regard to the future disposition and management of the tribe. In pursuance of these instructions, the superintendent has reported in favor of their being permitted to remain in Wisconsin, on a particular tract of limited extent more remote from the whites than that on which they now reside, and well adapted to their use, and which, from other reliable information, it is understood will not be required by our emigrating population for many years to come. The extreme poverty of this tribe, their harmless disposition and habits, and their inability to remove to the country assigned them without aid from the government, operate forcibly in inducing me to recommend that they be permitted to occupy the tract designated for their future residence by Superintendent Murray in his report. . . . Should this course be adopted, another treaty will be necessary, providing, among other things, for a relinquishment of their title to the lands in Minnesota set apart by the treaty of 1848 for their future home; which lands, it is to be remarked, in consequence of their proximity to the Mississippi river, will, in all probability, be more strongly desired for settlement by the whites than those on which it is proposed to allow them to remain. In the mean time, other important questions connected with this tribe, and which formed the subject of a special communication from this office . . . may be duly considered, and such provision made for the benefit of this people as the peculiar hardship of their condition and their future well being may appear to require.

A treaty was made with the Ottawas and Chippewas in 1836, by which they cede all their lands in the State of Michigan, reserving however, for their own use, certain tracts and sections therein particularly described. When the treaty came to be acted on by the Senate, it was so amended as to restrict their occupancy of said tracts and sections "for the term of five years from the ratification of the treaty, and no longer," without permission from the United States; in consideration of which it was provided that they should be paid, at the expiration of the five years, or when they surrendered their reservations, the sum of $200,000, and, until that time, the annual interest on that amount. The five years expired in 1841, but the annual payment of the interest on the $200,000 has been regularly continued up to the present time, although the Indians have not been required to surrender their reservations. Inasmuch, however, as some of the committees of the last Congress indicated a disposition to discontinue these payments of interest, Superintendent Murray was instructed to visit these Indians, and, with a view to the future policy of the government in reference to them, to report their general condition, the contiguity of their settlements to the whites, and the necessity, if any, for their removal in consequence of the emigration to that region. From the flattering account given by him and Agent Sprague of the present condition of these Indians, it appears that there is an unusual degree of improvement and prosperity prevailing among them. Their principal settlements are at Grand and Little Traverse, where they have purchased tracts of land which are well improved. A large share of the money recently paid to them they took to their homes to purchase more lands, and make still further improvements. Many individuals, for the purpose of securing homes for themselves and families, have left the reservations and located on lands in the vicinity, which they have purchased from the government. All this, and the willingness with which they devote themselves to the pursuits of civilized life, commend them to the continued favor and protection of the government. I would therefore recommend, that an appropriation be made by Congress for the purpose of enabling the Department to consummate such measures as are necessary for their permanent settlement in the country where they now reside.

The course of policy heretofore strongly urged by several of my predecessors and myself, in reference to a portion of the tribes located on the borders of the western States, is the only one competent, in my judgment, to save them from being swept away by the rapid and onward current of our white population. While there has been ample outlet at the southwest, below the most southern of our colonized tribes, another of a more northern latitude is required, leading towards our remote western possessions. The recent purchase made from the Sioux of a large portion of their country supplies this outlet in part, and will enable the government, by the removal of a few tribes between the Sioux territory and the Kanzas river, to throw open a wide extent of country for the spread of our population westward. This is the only practicable means of saving the border tribes from extinction. Without it, in a few years, they will be forced to abandon their present possessions to an emigrating population, and be driven forth to perish on the plains. All the arrangements necessary and proper to prevent so sad a catastrophe should be made ere it is too late, else an abiding reproach will rest upon our government and people. If timely measures are taken for the proper location and management of these tribes, they may, at no distant period, become an intelligent and Christian people, understanding the principles of our government, and participating in all its advantages. The necessity for an appropriation to carry these measures speedily into effect is the more apparent and imperious, in view of the already imposing demonstrations of public feeling in favor of the early organization of a territorial government over the territory on which these Indians reside.

In a communication addressed to you on the 28th of May last, a copy of which is herewith, I had the honor to recommend, for the reasons therein set forth at length, that the scrip issued for the benefit of the Choctaw Indians should no longer be withheld from those still remaining east of the Mississippi, but that it be paid over to them where they now reside. The superintendent of emigration reports that this and other measures, intended to stimulate their removal west, have had the desired effect, and that, consequently, a large number may be expected to emigrate during the present year. However this may be, I entirely concur in the opinion of the agent for the Choctaws west, that it will put an end to a long continued system of fraud and peculation upon the government. Were a law passed providing for the payment in money of the funded portion of the scrip, and payments were made west to those only who may be permanently settled in the Choctaw country, the States of Alabama, Mississippi and Louisiana, it is thought, would soon be relieved from the annoyance of an Indian population.

The Winnebagoes seem to be gradually becoming better satisfied with the country to which they have been removed, and, as their general condition is improving, it is hoped they will, ere long, become a thrifty and contented people. Abundant crops have been made at the agency the past season. The Indians assisted in ploughing, planting and harvesting, and displayed not only willingness but anxiety to work. The crops on the Mississippi were not so good, owing mainly to the lateness of the season in which they were planted. A number of log and two frame dwellings have been erected at the agency the past summer, and several more it is expected will be completed before the close of the year. These Indians express great desire to have dwellings, barns, stables, &c., and are fast abandoning their savage habits. A good grist and saw mill will also soon be ready for their use. The agent reports that there are now living within their own country some seventeen or eighteen hundred Winnebagoes. They are represented as being peaceable and well disposed.

The tribes of the Osage river agency, composed of the Weas, Piankeshaws, Peorias, Kaskaskias and Miamies are said to be doing well. They have generally abandoned the chase as a means of subsistence; many of them have engaged in agricultural pursuits; and, during the past season, they have made corn enough to supply them with bread for another year. The Weas, Piankeshaws, Peorias and Kaskaskias are, in fact, but a single tribe. By frequent intermarriages and adoptions, their distinctive characteristics, if any ever existed, have disappeared. They reside upon the same territory, speak the same language, are in constant social intercourse, have similar habits, and in all respects are so completely identified as not to admit of any practical discrimination. They are greatly in advance of the wilder tribes contiguous to them; and, but for the facility afforded them of procuring ardent spirits from the shops that are planted along the borders of the State, a thorough and early abandonment of all their vagrant habits might reasonably be expected. Recently, however, with but a few exceptions, they signed a pledge to abstain from the use of intoxicating drinks for the term of twelve months; and, among the Miamies, flattering evidences of a similar reform have been reported to this office.

The condition of the Iowas, Sacs and Foxes, of Missouri, and Kickapoos, is steadily improving. These tribes have made abundant crops the past season, particularly the Kickapoos, whose farms, the agent reports, will not suffer by comparison with those of their white neighbors.

In the early part of the last spring the Sacs and Foxes suffered severely from the small-pox. They lost about one-fifth of their tribe before a check was given to the further spread of the dreadful disease by a vaccination of the remainder. Prompt measures were adopted to prevent the pestilence from being communicated to other tribes, without which there would doubtless have been a wide spread mortality among them.

With the consent of, and encouraged by the Iowas, two bands of Winnebagoes, in number about three hundred, have settled on the lands of the former; principally near the Great Nemaha river, where they have this season made good crops of corn, and are in a fair way of bettering their condition. By reason of intermarriage and association with the Iowas, to whom these Winnebagoes seem much attached, the most friendly relations exist between them, and all seem anxious that their connexion shall not be disturbed. On the part of the Iowas much devotedness and generous feeling have been displayed, illustrating in a highly creditable manner the sincerity of their friendship for these sojourners of another tribe among them. On several occasions they have gone so far as to request the agent to allow the Winnebagoes to participate in their annuities equally with themselves. This rare evidence of disinterestedness and generosity is of itself sufficient to commend the wishes of these Indians to indulgent consideration on the part of the government; and, when it is considered that these Winnebagoes have manifested an unconquerable aversion to the country assigned to their tribe in Minnesota, it may well be doubted whether the interests of the government and the Indians will not be promoted by permitting them to remain where they are. But it is apprehended by some that serious difficulties may result from the adoption of this policy; while, on the other hand, it is certain that their removal to Minnesota cannot be effected without considerable expense and trouble. No little diversity of opinion exists in relation to this subject, and it presents one of the legionary cases arising out of our Indian relations, in which it is impossible for the department to ascertain with certainty what should be done.

The three commissioners appointed by authority of Congress to negotiate treaties with the Indian tribes in the Territory of Oregon entered upon the duties of their commission in February last. They report that the Indians on the Willamette and lower Columbia rivers are peaceably disposed, but that other tribes north and south of those rivers are wild and fierce. Six treaties have been negotiated by them with the various bands of Calapoogas and Morlal-les, allowing all the bands reservations on the west side of the Cascade mountains. The Indians refused to have any of their money set apart for agricultural and school purposes, except the Twallalty band, who consented to have a small portion of theirs appropriated for the purchase of agricultural implements. Many of them are good farm hands, and labor in that capacity for the citizens. They profess to be anxious to adopt the habits and customs of civilized life. The country ceded in these treaties comprises that part of Willamette valley, extending southward from Oregon city to Mary's river, and is represented to be the most valuable and thickly settled part of the district.

The commissioners, by whom the treaties referred to were negotiated, being informed by this office that their functions had been abrogated by a recent law of Congress, the commission was dissolved, and the duty of prosecuting negotiations with the Indians in Oregon was imposed on the regular officers of the Indian department in that Territory.

Superintendent Dart reports that he met a delegation from almost every tribe east of the Cascade mountains, and all, except the Snake and Rogue river Indians, were submissive to his authority; and he considers the Indians generally, in Oregon, as the most temperate, peaceful, and easily managed of all our wilder tribes. He has been successful in negotiating several important treaties with them, which are represented as highly advantageous to the government, but they have not yet been received at this office.

From our agents in California much interesting information has been received concerning the Indians in that State, but it is unfortunately of too desultory a character to be entirely satisfactory. A number of treaties have been made with these Indians, embracing from eighty to ninety tribes or bands; and although considerable opposition by citizens of California to the measures of the agents has been exhibited, yet there is reason to believe that much good has resulted from their efforts to put a stop to hostilities, and secure peace for the future between the whites and the Indians. Of the necessity or expediency of the particular measures adopted by them for this and other purposes, it is difficult, at this distance from the scene of operations, to judge with confidence, especially as there is on some points a difference of opinion among the agents themselves.

In the treaties negotiated with the Indians in California and Oregon there are novel provisions, the practical operation of which cannot be foreseen. Whether they shall be ratified as they stand, is a question which will, of course, be duly considered by those whose constitutional province it is to determine in what form they shall become a part of the supreme law of the land.

The means heretofore placed at the disposal of the department, applicable to Indian purposes in California, have been manifestly inadequate. It is quite evident that, without the expenditures of large sums of money, our Indian affairs in California and Oregon cannot be properly conducted; and in this connection I respectfully suggest the policy of passing a law establishing the office of Assistant Commissioner of Indian affairs for that State and Territory. A general and controlling power, more direct than it is possible for this office to bring to bear, is of the highest importance in the adjustment of our relations with the numerous tribes of Indians in those remove portions of our wide-spread domain.

It will be seen from the reports of the Governor and ex-officio Superintendent of Indian Affairs in New Mexico, that no material change has taken place in the condition of our Indian relations in that Territory since my last annual report. The apparently slow progress which has been made in the work of establishing friendly relations with such Indians of the Territory as

have been for years plundering and murdering the inhabitants without fear
or restraint, may be justly attributed to a combination of circumstances over
which the officers of this department have had no control. The country
itself, wild, desert and mountainous; the savage nature and untamed habits
of most of the Indians who roam over it; the lawlessness of many of its other
inhabitants, often more reckless than the Indians themselves; the scattered,
mixed, and heterogeneous character of its population in general—all tend to
produce a state of things so discreditable and deplorable, as to render its
acquisition a misfortune, and its possession a reproach to the government.
To remedy these evils, liberal appropriations of money, and a more vigorous and untrammelled exercise of authority by the civil officers of the
Territory, are indispensable.

The usefulness of the agents in New Mexico has been seriously impaired
by their failure to obtain from the military the usual facilities. Without the
means of transportation, and the escorts necessary to enable them to
penetrate the Indian country with safety, it has been impossible for them to
go where their presence was most needed, and the good of the service
required. It is always to be desired that the utmost harmony and concert of
action should prevail among the various officers and agents of the government in any way entrusted with the management of our Indian affairs; and
to this end it has been enjoined on the officers of the army and the agents of
this department in New Mexico, to consult together and co-operate in all
their movements. Unhappily, however, this desirable object has not been
fully secured; nor can it be, I apprehend, until the Governor of the
Territory shall be in fact, what he is in name, *Superintendent of Indian
Affairs*.

Pursuant to the provisions of a late act of Congress, an agent has been
appointed for the Indians in Utah; and that full justice should be done to
the people of that Territory, and our Indian relations therein be placed
upon a proper footing, the discretionary power vested by law in the
department has been exercised by the appointment, also, of two sub-agents
for said Indians. A delegation of the Shoshonees, or Snake Indians, a
disaffected and mischievous tribe, infesting one of the principal routes of
travel to Oregon and California, was conducted by the agent to the grand
council recently held at Fort Laramie with the wild tribes of the prairies.
These Indians were not considered by the superintendent as embraced in
his instructions, and were, consequently, not parties to the treaty negotiated
with the other tribes. The delegation, however, were kindly received,
suitable presents were bestowed upon them, and they returned to their
people with more friendly feelings towards the government and the whites.
No other information of any importance has been received at this office
concerning the Indians in Utah.

The treaties recently concluded by Superintendent Ramsey with the
Chippewas, at Pembina, and by Superintendent Mitchell and Agent Fitzpa-
trick with the wild tribes of the prairies at Fort Laramie, came to hand at so

late a period as to afford but little time for considering their provisions; but they are fully explained in the accompanying reports of the commissioners, who, doubtless, have discharged with fidelity and ability the arduous and important duties imposed upon them.

No material change has taken place in our relations with the Indians in Texas. They remain in the same embarrassed and perplexed condition that has characterized them for several years past; and they must continue so, until the anomalous position in which the government is placed in regard to them be essentially changed. In the last annual report it was recommended that commissioners be appointed to confer with the proper authorities of Texas on this subject, with a view to an arrangement for placing the Indian affairs in that State under the exclusive control of the general government. The recommendation is now earnestly renewed; for, until this measure is effected, it is in vain to expect that Indian affairs in that State can be placed on a satisfactory footing. The number of these Indians is far less than is generally supposed. A large extent of territory is not required for them. They are in such condition as to be compelled to starve or steal; and if Texas will not consent to the arrangement suggested, necessary as it is to the security of her frontier, and the very existence of the Indians, she can have no just cause to complain of depredations committed by famished aborigines of the country, who certainly have a right to live somewhere; and nowhere, more certainly, than on the lands which they and their fathers have occupied for countless generations.

The commissioners appointed for the purpose of negotiating treaties with the Indians on the borders of Mexico, and for other purposes, being instructed that their expenditures must not exceed the amount of funds which had been placed in their hands, and finding them insufficient to accomplish the objects of their appointment, deemed it proper to dissolve the commission. The instructions under which they acted in bringing their labors to a close, together with a condensed account of their proceedings while in service, will be found in the documents herewith submitted.

The Indians in Florida have long been the occasion of enormous expense to the government, and of annoyance to the people of the State, who, with great unanimity, are deeply anxious for their removal to the country provided for their tribe west of the Mississippi river. Recognizing the obligation of the government to persevere in its endeavors to accomplish this desirable object, and satisfied that other means than those heretofore employed were indispensable, the department has deemed it expedient to test the efficacy of individual enterprise, stimulated by the hope of gain contingent on success. This has been done by an arrangement entered into with General Luther Blake, of Alabama, the particulars of which are set forth in his letter of instructions, a copy of which accompanies this report. Many causes combine to render the removal of these Indians a work of extreme difficulty; not the least of which is the offer heretofore made by officers of the army to pay them individually large sums of money, ranging from one hundred to ten thousand dollars, in consequence of which they naturally expect that they will not be required to remove without the payment of equal, or larger amounts than they have already refused. I am by no means sanguine, therefore, that the plan for removing them, now in operation, will be attended with success, but it is worthy of a trial; if it fail, the loss to the government will be a mere trifle; if it succeed, the gratifying result will amply vindicate the wisdom of the experiment.

The *regular estimates* of the office for the present, exceed those of the last year $59,445. This excess is caused mainly by the increased number of agents and interpreters for New Mexico and Utah, authorized by the act of the 27th of February, 1851, reorganizing this department, and the transfer from the special to the regular estimates of the item, $43,600, required to pay the interest on Choctaw scrip. The difference between the amount *appropriated* by Congress at its last session on *special estimates,* and the amount of that class of estimates for the present year, is very large, being $884,954.66, exclusive of the interest on the appropriation of $725,603.37, to pay the Cherokees, amounting to $402,802.86. The entire amount appropriated at the last session on Indian account, exceeds the aggregate sum of the regular and special estimates now submitted, $1,228,312.52. It is proper to remark, however, that additional appropriations will be required, the estimates for which will be submitted as soon as the necessary *data* are in the possession of the office. The explanatory remarks accompanying the estimates, it is hoped, will be found satisfactory, as care has been taken to make them comformable to law.

The second volume of the work published by authority of Congress, under the direction of this bureau, containing information respecting the history, condition and prospects of the Indian tribes of the United States, is in press, and will shortly be ready for distribution. It will be found a worthy sequel to the preceding volume, which was received with so much general favor.

The civilization of the Indians within the territory of the United States is a cherished object of the government. It undoubtedly merits all the consideration bestowed upon it, and the employment of all the means necessary for its accomplishment. There are not wanting those, who, judging from the apparently little success which in some instances has attended the instrumentalities employed, doubt the practicability of the measure. It should be remembered, however, that to change a savage people from their barbarous habits to those of civilized life, is, in its nature, a work of time, and the results already attained, as evinced in the improved condition of several of our tribes, are sufficient to silence the most skeptical, and warrant the assurance that perseverance in the cause will achieve success.

The history of the Indian furnishes abundant proof that he possesses all the elements essential to his elevation; all the powers, instincts and sympathies which appertain to his white brother; and which only need the proper development and direction to enable him to tread with equal step and dignity the walks of civilized life. He is intellectual, proud, brave, generous; and in his devotion to his family, his country, and the graves of his fathers, it is clearly shown that the kind affections and the impulses of patriotism animate his heart. That his inferiority is a necessity of his nature, is neither taught by philosophy nor attested by experience. Prejudice against him, originating in error of opinion on this subject, has doubtless been a formidable obstacle in the way of his improvement; while, on the other hand, it is equally certain that his progress has been retarded by ill conceived and misdirected efforts to hasten his advance. It is even questionable whether the immense amounts paid to them in the way of annuities have not been, and are not now, all things considered, a curse to them rather than a blessing. Certain it is, there has not at all times been the most wise and beneficial application of their funds. To arouse the spirit of enterprise in the Indian, and bring him to realize the necessity of reliance upon himself, in some industrial pursuit, for his support and comfort, is, generally, if not universally, the initiative step to his civilization, which he is often prevented from taking by the debasing influence of the annuity system. But the system is fastened upon us, and its attendant evils must be endured.

On the general subject of the civilization of the Indians, many and diversified opinions have been put forth; but, unfortunately, like the race to which they relate, they are too wild to be of much utility. The great question, How shall the Indians be civilized? yet remains without a satisfactory answer. The magnitude of the subject, and the manifold difficulties inseparably connected with it, seem to have bewildered the minds of those who have attempted to give it the most thorough investigation. The remark of the late Attorney General Legaré, is not more striking than true, that "there is nothing in the whole compass of our laws so anomalous, so hard to bring within any precise definition, or any logical and scientific arrangement of principles, as the relation in which the Indians stand towards this government and those of the States." My own views are not sufficiently matured to justify me in undertaking to present them here. To do so would require elaborate detail, and swell this report beyond its proper limits. I therefore leave the subject for the present, remarking, only, that any plan for the civilization of our Indians will, in my judgment, be fatally defective, if it do not provide, in the most efficient manner, first, for their ultimate incorporation into the great body of our citizen population.

Report of Commissioner of
Indian Affairs George W. Manypenny
November 22, 1856

(Excerpt from *Report for 1856*, pp. 571–75)

In a brief passage in his annual report, Commissioner Manypenny recounted the extraordinary number of treaties—over 50—that the United States had made with the Indian tribes during the previous three years. One hundred and seventy-four million acres had been acquired in one of the greatest real estate transactions in history. Projecting the American advance westward, Manypenny called for consideration of the position of the Indian ten years later, when, he predicted, the advance of the white population would have blotted out of existence the natives unless timely and generous measures were taken to provide permanent and irrevocable homes for them. The example of Kansas did not provide a favorable omen. As Manypenny pointed out, while white Kansans had quarrelled about the rights of the Negro, they had "united upon the soil of Kansas in wrong doing toward the Indian."

SINCE THE 4TH of March, 1853, fifty-two treaties with various Indian tribes have been entered into. These treaties may, with but few exceptions of a specific character, be separated into three classes: first, treaties of peace and friendship; second, treaties of acquisition, with a view of colonizing the Indians on reservations; and third, treaties of acquisition, and providing for the permanent settlement of the individuals of the tribes, at once or in the future, on separate tracts of lands or homesteads, and for the gradual abolition of the tribal character. The quantity of land acquired by these treaties, either by the extinguishment of the original Indian title, or by the re-acquisition of lands granted to Indian tribes by former treaties, is about one hundred and seventy-four millions of acres. Thirty-two of these treaties have been ratified, and twenty are now before the Senate for its consideration and action. In no former equal period of our history have so many treaties been made, or such vast accessions of land been obtained. Within the same period the jurisdiction of this office and the operations of its agents have been extended over an additional area of from four to six thousand square miles of territory, embracing tribes about which, before that time, but little was known; and by authority of several acts of Congress thirteen new agencies and nine sub-agencies have been established. The increased labor which has been thus devolved on the Commissioner of Indian Affairs and the entire force of the bureau, as well as upon the superintendents and agents, has been very great, and has swelled the business connected with our Indian affairs to an extent almost incredible. The labor of this branch of the service has doubled since 1852, and yet with this extraordinary increase, the permanent clerical force of this office is the same now that it was on the 4th of March, 1853. The permanent force is now insufficient to promptly perform the labor of the bureau; and the classification and arrangement of the business of the office should be modified and improved, but this cannot be done thoroughly without a small permanent increase in the clerical force.

The existing laws for the protection of the persons and property of the Indian wards of the government are sadly defective. New and more stringent statutes are required. The relation which the federal government sustains towards the Indians, and the duties and obligations flowing from it, cannot be faithfully met and discharged without ample legal provisions, and the necessary power and means to enforce them. The rage for speculation and the wonderful desire to obtain choice lands, which seems to possess so many of those who go into our new territories, causes them to lose sight of and entirely overlook the rights of the aboriginal inhabitants. The most dishonorable expedients have, in many cases, been made use of to dispossess the Indian; demoralizing means employed to obtain his property; and, for the want of adequate laws, the department is now often perplexed and embarrassed, because of inability to afford prompt relief and apply the remedy in cases obviously requiring them.

The general disorder so long prevailing in Kansas Territory, and the consequent unsettled state of civil affairs there have been very injurious to the interests of many of the Indian tribes in that Territory. The state of affairs referred to, with the influx of lawless men and speculators incident and introductory thereto, has impeded the surveys and the selections for the homes of the Indians, and otherwise prevented the full establishment and proper efficiency of all the means for civilization and improvement within the scope of the several treaties with them. The schools have not been as fully attended, nor the school buildings, agency houses, and other improvements, as rapidly constructed as they might otherwise have been. Trespasses and depredations of every conceivable kind have been committed on the Indians. They have been personally maltreated, their property stolen, their timber destroyed, their possession encroached upon, and divers other wrongs and injuries done them. Notwithstanding all which they have afforded a praiseworthy example of good conduct, under the most trying circumstances. They have at no time, that I am aware of, attempted to redress their own wrongs, but have patiently submitted to injury, relying on the good faith and justice of the government to indemnify them. In the din and strife between the anti-slavery and pro-slavery parties with reference to the condition of the African race there, and in which the rights and interests of the red man have been completely overlooked and disregarded, the good conduct and patient submission of the latter contrasts favorably with the disorderly and lawless conduct of many of their white brethren, who, while they have quarrelled about the African, have united upon the soil of Kansas in wrong doing toward the Indian!

In relation to the emigrated and partially civilized tribes in Kansas, the circumstances under which they were transplanted to that country, and the pledges of this government that it should be to them and their posterity a permanent home forever; the distrust and doubt under which they assented to the sale of a portion of their respective tracts to the United States for the use and occupation of our own population, I have in former reports treated fully; and have likewise endeavored to impress upon the minds of all persons that the small tracts which these tribes have reserved in Kansas as their permanent homes must be so regarded. They cannot again be removed. They must meet their fate upon their present reservations in that Territory, and there be made a civilized people, or crushed and blotted out. Their condition is critical, simply because their rights and interests seem thus far to have been entirely lost sight of and disregarded by their new neighbors. They may be preserved and civilized, and will be if the guarantees and stipulations of their treaties are faithfully fulfilled and enforced, and the federal government discharges its obligations and redeems its pledged faith towards them. As peace and order seem now to be restored to the Territories, it is to be hoped that the good citizens thereof will make haste to repair the wrong and injury which the red men of Kansas have suffered by the acts of their white neighbors, and that hereafter they will not only treat the Indians fairly, but that all good citizens will set their faces against the conduct of any lawless men who may attempt to trespass upon the rights of, or otherwise injure, the Indian population there.

In reviewing the events of the past year with reference to the improvement of our Indian population, there appears within the reserves of several tribes such unmistakable manifestations of progress as to excite and stimulate our lawgivers and the benevolent and philanthropic of the land to a more lively and active interest in the present condition and future prospects of the race, and to invite an increased effort and energy in the cause of Indian civilization. That the red man can be transformed in his habits, domesticated, and civilized, and made a useful element in society, there is abundant evidence. With reference to his true character, erroneous opinions very generally prevail. He is, indeed, the victim of prejudice. He is only regarded as the irreclaimable, terrible savage, who in war spares neither age nor sex, but with heartless and cruel barbarity subjects the innocent and defenceless to inhuman tortures, committing with exultant delight the most horrible massacres. These are chronicled from year to year, and are, indeed, sad chapters in our annals. But the history of the sufferings of the Indian has never been written; the story of his wrongs never been told. Of these there is not, and never can be, an earthly record.

As a man he has his joys and his sorrows. His love for his offspring is intense. In his friendships he is steadfast and true, and will never be the first to break faith. His courage is undoubted, his perception quick, and his memory of the highest order. His judgment is defective, but by proper training and discipline his intellectual powers are susceptible of culture and can be elevated to a fair standard. He can be taught the arts of peace, and is by no means inapt in learning to handle agricultural and mechanical implements and applying them to their appropriate uses. With these qualities, although the weaker, he is eminently entitled to the kind consideration of the stronger race.

The wonderful emigration to our newly acquired States and Territories, and its effect upon the wild tribes inhabiting them and the plains and prairies, is well calculated at the present period to attract special attention. Not only are our settlements rapidly advancing westward from the Mississippi river towards the Pacific ocean, and from the shores of the Pacific eastward towards the Mississippi river, but large settlements have been made in Utah and New Mexico between the two. Already the settlements of Texas are extending up to El Paso and spreading into the Gadsden purchase, and those of California have reached into the great valley of the Colorado, whilst the settlers of Minnesota are building cities at the very head of Lake Superior and villages in the remote valley of the Red river of the north, on their way to Puget Sound. Railroads built and building, from the Atlantic and Gulf cities, not only reach the Mississippi river at about twenty different points, but are extending west across Louisiana, Arkansas, Missouri, and Iowa. Roads of that character have also been commenced in Texas, looking to El Paso, and in Iowa, looking for the great bend of the Minnesota river for a present and for Pembina for a future terminus. The railroad companies of Missouri and Iowa are even now seeking aid from Congress to enable them to extend their roads to New Mexico, Kansas, Nebraska, and Utah, and thence to California, Oregon, and Washington. California has actually commenced the construction of a railroad leading up the Sacramento valley toward Utah.

It is impossible to avoid the conclusion that in a few years, in a very few, the railroads of the east, from New Orleans to the extreme west end of Lake Superior, will be extended westwardly up towards the Rocky mountains, at least as far as good lands can be found, and that roads from the Pacific coast will be built as far east as good lands extend; and that in both cases an active population will keep up with the advance of the railroads—a population that will open farms, erect workshops, and build villages and cities.

When that time arrives, and it is at our very doors, ten years, if our country is favored with peace and prosperity, will witness the most of it; where will be the habitation and what the condition of the rapidly wasting Indian tribes of the plains, the prairies, and of our new States and Territories?

As sure as these great physical changes are impending, so sure will these poor denizens of the forest be blotted out of existence, and their dust be trampled under the foot of rapidly advancing civilization, unless our great nation shall generously determine that the necessary provision shall at once be made, and appropriate steps be taken to designate suitable tracts or reservations of land, in proper localities, for permanent homes for, and provide the means to colonize, them thereon. Such reservations should be selected with great care, and when determined upon and designated the assurances by which they are guarantied to the Indians should be irrevocable, and of such a character as to effectually protect them from encroachments of every kind.

Before bringing this annual report to a conclusion, I desire to repeat the statement made in the first one which I had the honor to submit, that, "There is no absolute necessity for the employment by Indian tribes of attorneys or agents to attend to their business at the seat of government," and to urge, in the most solemn manner, that "it is the duty of the government as their guardians to cause all matters of a business character with them to be so conducted as to preclude the necessity of the intervention of this class of persons." This recommendation was repeated in my second and third annual reports, and is again urged as the result of convictions strengthened by experience. I also desire again to urge all that I have presented in former reports, as well as in this one, with reference to the obnoxious and fatal policy of removing Indian tribes, and the absolute necessity of fixed habitations and permanent homes as indespensible to their preservation, domestication and civilization. To preserve the small reservations already made, and hereafter to be made, by tribes who have or may resolve to settle down and till the land, and to preserve to all Indians their annuities, I again urgently recommend such penal and other legislation as may be required to effect these objects. But any measure of protection short of this will fail to guard the Indians against the artful schemes of those bad men who, under more or less specious pretences, desire to obtain either their lands or their money, or both. Upon such protection depends the question of their future existence, for when stripped of their property alms would only rapidly sink, not permanently elevate and preserve them. Humanity, Christianity, national honor, unite in demanding the enactment of such laws as will not only protect the Indians, but as shall effectually put it out of the power of any public officer to allow these poor creatures to be despoiled of their lands and annuities by a swarm of hungry and audacious speculators, attorneys, and others, their instruments and coadjutors. And no officer should, for the want of such legislation, be compelled, during his whole official existence, either to allow the Indians to be plundered or else have to devote his whole energies to the maintenance of a conflict to sustain their rights against combinations of men whose chief and first efforts are always directed towards obtaining influence with the press, and with those supposed to be high in the confidence of the executive and legislative departments of the government. It is asking too much of a subordinate officer. It exposes him to unnecessary danger and unnecessary temptation; and it is grossly unjust to the Indians thus to expose him to such a danger and to such a temptation. The security of their rights should be made as little dependent upon the virtue of a public officer as possible.

To preserve their property and to give them the blessings of education and Christianity is indispensible to their continuing "long in the land" which God gave to their fathers and to them. I sincerely hope that our government will have the aid of all its good citizens in faithfully executing its high trust and discharging its obligations to the remnants of the Indian tribes now left to its oversight and guardianship, so that they shall be intelligently and generously protected and cared for in all that makes life useful and happy.

Report of Commissioner of Indian Affairs Charles E. Mix November 6, 1858

(Excerpt from *Report for 1858,* pp. 354-59)

Commissioner Mix, who presided over the Bureau of Indian Affairs during a period of consolidation after the rapid expansion of white settlement into Indian lands, pointed out some of the deleterious consequences of that unregulated advance. The principle of recognizing and respecting the right of the Indian to the possession of the land he occupied and to the enjoyment of its fruits—a right recognized from the earliest days of white settlement—had been ignored by whites rushing into the territories of Oregon and Washington. Indian resentment and opposition was not only expected but justified. Similarly, Indian relations in Texas and California were impeded by the insistence of those states on exercising jurisdiction over Indian reservations and Indian affairs within their borders to the exclusion of the Federal Government. Mix called for corrective action in the name of humanity and of efficiency.

FROM THE COMMENCEMENT of the settlement of this country, the principle has been recognised and acted on, that the Indian tribes possessed the occupant or usufruct right to the lands they occupied, and that they were entitled to the peaceful enjoyment of that right until they were fairly and justly divested of it. Hence the numerous treaties with the various tribes, by which, for a stipulated consideration their lands have, from time to time, been acquired, as our population increased.

Experience has demonstrated that at least three serious, and, to the Indians, fatal errors have, from the beginning, marked our policy towards them, viz: their removal from place to place as our population advanced: the assignment to them of too great an extent of country, to be held in common; and the allowance of large sums of money, as annuities, for the lands ceded by them. These errors, far more than the want of capacity on the part of the Indian, have been the cause of the very limited success of our constant efforts to domesticate and civilize him. By their frequent changes of position and the possession of large bodies of land in common, they have been kept in an unsettled condition and prevented from acquiring a knowledge of separate and individual property, while their large annuities, upon which they have relied for a support, have not only tended to foster habits of indolence and profligacy, but constantly made them the victims of the lawless and inhuman sharper and speculator. The very material and marked difference between the northern Indians and those of the principal southern tribes, may be accounted for by the simple fact that the latter were permitted, for long periods, to remain undisturbed in their original locations; where, surrounded by, or in close proximity with a white population, they, to a considerable extent, acquired settled habits and a knowledge of and taste for civilized occupations and pursuits. Our present policy, as you are aware, is entirely the reverse of that heretofore pursued in the three particulars mentioned. It is to permanently locate the different tribes on reservations embracing only sufficient land for their actual occupancy; to divide this among them in severalty, and require them to live upon and cultivate the tracts assigned to them; and in lieu of money annuities, to furnish them with stock animals, agricultural implements, mechanic-shops, tools and materials, and manual labor schools for the industrial and mental education of their youth. Most of the older treaties, however, provide for annuities in money, and the department has, therefore, no authority to commute them even in cases where the Indians may desire, or could be influenced to agree to such a change. In view of this fact, and the better to enable the department to carry out its present and really more benevolent policy, I would respectfully recommend and urge that a law be enacted by Congress, empowering and requiring the department, in all cases where money annuities are provided for by existing treaties, and the assent of the Indians can be obtained, to commute them for objects and purposes of a beneficial character.

The principle of recognising and respecting the usufruct right of the Indians to the lands occupied by them, has not been so strictly adhered to in the case of the tribes in the Territories of Oregon and Washington. When a territorial government was first provided for Oregon, which then embraced the present Territory of Washington, strong inducements were held out to our people to emigrate and settle there, without the usual arrangements being made, in advance, for the extinguishment of the title of the Indians who occupied and claimed the lands. Intruded upon, ousted of their homes and possessions without any compensation, and deprived, in most cases, of their accustomed means of support, without any arrangement having been made to enable them to establish and maintain themselves in other locations, it is not a matter of surprise that they have committed many depredations upon our citizens, and been exasperated to frequent acts of hostility.

The Indians in Oregon and Washington number about 42,000 and are divided into 35 tribes and bands. The only treaties in force with any of them, are with those who inhabited the valuable sections of country embraced in the Rogue river, Umpqua and Willamette valleys. After repeated acts of hostility and continued depredations upon the white settlers, the Indians in Oregon were removed to, and are now living upon the reservations, one on the western and the other on the eastern side of the coast range of mountains; and the country to which their title was extinguished has rapidly filled up with an enterprising and thrifty population. In the year 1855, treaties were also entered into by the superintendent of Indian affairs for Oregon, and by Governor Stevens, *ex officio* superintendent for Washington Territory, with various other tribes and bands, for the purpose of extinguishing their title to large tracts of country, which were needed for the extension of our settlements, and to provide homes for the Indians in other and more suitable locations, where they could be controlled and domesticated. These treaties not having been ratified, the Indians were sorely disappointed in consequence of the expectations they were led to entertain of benefits and advantages to be derived from them not being realized. Moreover, the whites have gone on to occupy their country without regard to their rights, which has led the Indians to believe that they were to be dispossessed of it without compensation or any provision being made for them. This state of things has naturally had a tendency to exasperate them; and, in the opinion of well informed persons, has been the cause of their recent acts of hostility. The belief is confidently entertained, that, had the treaties referred to been ratified and put in course of execution, the difficulties that have occurred would not have taken place; and there can be but little if any doubt, that the cost of the military operations to subdue the Indians, and the losses sustained by our citizens from their depredations and hostilities, will amount to a far greater sum than would have been required to extinguish their title and establish and maintain them, for the necessary period, on properly selected reservations, had that policy in respect to them been sanctioned and timely measures taken to carry it out.

It cannot be expected that Indians situated like those in Oregon and Washington, occupying extensive sections of country, where, from the game and otherwise, they derive a comfortable support, will quietly and peaceably submit, without any equivalent, to be deprived of their homes and possessions, and to be driven off to some other locality where they cannot find their usual means of subsistence. Such a proceeding is not only contrary to our policy hitherto, but is repugnant alike to the dictates of humanity and the principles of natural justice. In all cases where the necessities of our rapidly increasing population have compelled us to displace the Indian, we have ever regarded it as a sacred and binding obligation to provide him with a home elsewhere, and to contribute liberally to his support until he could re-establish and maintain himself in his new place of residence. The policy, it is true, has been a costly one, but we have been amply repaid its expense by the revenue obtained from the sale of the lands acquired from the Indians, and by the rapid extension of our settlements and the corresponding increase in the resources and prosperity of our country.

One of the difficulties attending the management of Indian affairs in Oregon and Washington, is the insufficiency of one superintendent for the great extent of country, and the numerous tribes and large number of Indians in the two territories. The superintendent reiterates his former representations respecting the necessity for two additional superintendencies, and your attention is respectfully recalled to the subject, as presented in the report from this office on the 6th of May last.

The superintendent again represents the necessity for the employment of a small war steamer for the protection of our settlements and the friendly Indians along Puget's Sound and the waters of Admiralty Inlet, from the hostile and predatory visits of the warlike Indians from Vancouver's Island and the neighboring British and Russian possessions, who move so swiftly in their large boats that it is impossible to overtake or cut them off except by means of such a vessel.

The policy of concentrating the Indians on small reservations of land, and of sustaining them there for a limited period, until they can be induced to make the necessary exertions to support themselves, was commenced in 1853, with those in California. It is, in fact, the only course compatible with the obligations of justice and humanity, left to be pursued in regard to all those with which our advancing settlements render new and permanent arrangements necessary. We have no longer distant and extensive sections of country which we can assign them, abounding in game, from which they could derive a ready and comfortable support; a resource which has, in a great measure, failed them where they are, and in consequence of which they must, at times, be subjected to the pangs of hunger, if not actual starvation, or obtain a subsistence by depredations upon our frontier settlements. If it were practicable to prevent such depredations, the alternative to providing for the Indians in the manner indicated, would be to leave them to starve; but as it is impossible, in consequence of the very great extent of our frontier, and our limited military force, to adequately guard against such occurrences, the only alternative, in fact, to making such provision for them, is to exterminate them.

Five reservations have been established in California, on which, according to the reports of the agents, 11,239 Indians have been located; two in Oregon, with 3,200 Indians; and two in Texas, with 1,483. The whole amount expended in carrying out this sytem, thus far, has been $1,173,000 in California, and $301,833.73 in Texas. The exact sum which has been expended on account of the reservations in Oregon, has not yet been ascertained, but the whole amount disbursed for Indian purposes in that, and the territory of Washington since 1852, up to the 1st of July last, is $1,323,000. The amount disbursed in New Mexico for the same period and purpose, $212,506, and in Utah, from 1853 to the 1st of July last, $172,000.

The operations thus far, in carrying out the reservation system, can properly be regarded as only experimental. Time and experience were required to develop any defects connected with it, and to demonstrate the proper remedies therefor. From a careful examination of the subject, and the best information in the possession of the department in regard to it, I am satisfied that serious errors have been committed; that a much larger amount has been expended than was necessary, and with but limited and insufficient results.

From what is stated by the superintendent for Oregon and Washington . . . in regard to the two reservations in Oregon, it is apprehended that a great mistake was made in their location, the lands not appearing to be such as will afford the Indians a comfortable support by their cultivation, and that, consequently, so long as they are kept there they must be entirely sustained, at an enormous expense, by the government.

From accompanying reports, it would seem that in California a greater number of reservations have been established and a much heavier expense incurred than the condition and circumstances of the Indians required, as has probably been the case in respect of all the reservations or Indian colonies that have been commenced. In the outset it was the confident expectation that the heavy expense attending these colonies would rapidly diminish, from year to year, and that, after the third year at furthest, they would require but little if any outlay on the part of the government, the Indians in the meantime being taught to support themselves by their own exertions. This expectation has not been realized; neither have the expenses been diminished nor the Indians been materially improved. The fault has not, however, it is believed, been in the system, but in the manner in which it has been carried out. Too many persons have been employed to control, assist, and work for the Indians, and too much has been done for them in other respects. They have not been sufficiently thrown upon their own resources, and hence the colonies have not become any more competent to sustain themselves than they were when they first commenced. Time and experience having developed errors in the administration of the system, the proper reforms are now being introduced.

No more reservations should be established than are absolutely necessary for such Indians as have been, or it may be necessary to displace, in consequence of the extension of our settlements, and whose resources have thereby been cut off or so diminished that they cannot sustain themselves in their accustomed manner. Great care should be taken in the selection of the reservations, so as to isolate the Indians for a time from contact and interference from the whites. They should embrace good lands, which will well repay the efforts to cultivate them. No white persons should be suffered to go upon the reservations, and after the first year the lands should be divided and assigned to the Indians in severalty, every one being required to remain on his own tract and to cultivate it, no persons being employed for them except the requisite mechanics to keep their tools and implements in repair, and such as may be necessary, for a time, to teach them how to conduct their agricultural operations and to take care of their stock. They should also have the advantage of well conducted manual labor schools for the education of their youth in letters, habits of industry, and a knowledge of agriculture and the simpler mechanic arts. By the adoption of this course, it is believed that the colonies can very soon be made to sustain themselves, or so nearly so that the government will be subjected to but a comparatively trifling annual expense on account of them. But it is essential to the success of the system that there should be a sufficient military force in the vicinity of the reservations to prevent the intrusion of improper persons upon them, to afford protection to the agents, and to aid in controlling the Indians and keeping them within the limits assigned to them.

It would materially aid the department in its efforts to carry out the system successfully, in respect to the Indians in California, if that State would, like Texas, so far relinquish to the general government her jurisdiction over the reservations to be permanently retained there, as to admit of the trade and intercourse laws being put in force within their limits, so as to secure the Indians against improper interference and intercourse, and to prevent the traffic with them in ardent spirits. Much good could also probably be accomplished by the introduction of a judicious system of apprenticeship, by which the orphans and other children of both sexes, could be bound out for a term of years, to upright and humane persons, to be taught suitable trades and occupations: provided the necessary State laws were enacted to authorize and regulate such a system. I would suggest the propriety of an application being made to the proper authorities of California for the requisite State legislation on both these subjects.

Report of Commissioner of
Indian Affairs William P. Dole
November 27, 1861

(Excerpt from *Report for 1861*, pp. 639-43)

The problems of the Indians of the West Coast, particularly in California, confronted the Federal Government during the trying years of the Civil War. Commissioner Dole's account of the "perversion of power" illustrated in the so-called "Indian wars" of California touches on one of the black stains of American history.

OWING TO THE remoteness of California and the length of time necessarily employed in transmitting communications to and from the same, the department is compelled in a great measure to rely upon the sagacity and integrity of the superintending agents located there, and for the same reason those agents are often under the necessity of assuming grave responsibilities, as to await instructions would be, in many instances, to allow the opportunity to prevent flagrant wrongs, correct existing abuses, and secure valuable ends to pass unimproved.

I desire to call especial attention to the reports of the superintending agents of the two districts, (northern and southern,) into which, for Indian purposes, the State has been divided. From those reports it will be seen that a complete change in the management of our Indian relations is demanded. A change involving the breaking up of some of the existing reservations; the correction of gross and palpable wrongs upon others; the re-establishment of new reservations, as I trust will be the case, upon a far more ample scope than any heretofore established; the furnishing of an almost entirely new outfit of tools and other necessary articles to those established and to be established; and a thorough investigation, and, if possible, a correction of outrageous wrongs perpetrated, under color of law, against not only the property but also the persons and liberty of the Indians. To effect this change will require time, a considerable expenditure of money, and the exercise, on the part of all persons connected therewith, of great care, patience, and circumspection.

The remarks made under the head of the superintendency of New Mexico upon the subject of Indian reservations, and the methods by which they should be established, apply to California with peculiar force. Within the southern district of the State not a single reservation exists that is not claimed or owned by the whites, nor is there one that is at all adequate in extent to the wants of the Indians. They appear to be simply farms, a few hundred acres in extent, about and upon which the Indians are expected by hundreds, and, in some instances, by thousands to congregate, and from which a small proportion of their wants are supplied. These farms, in several instances, are in the midst of regions thickly inhabited by whites, to whom the Indians prove a constant source of annoyance, and by whom they are prevented from wandering over large tracts of country, as they are by nature and long habit so strongly inclined to do. Thus the chief objects for which reservations are desirable is frustrated. Instead of being a retreat from the encroachments of the whites upon which they may concentrate and gradually become accustomed to a settled mode of life, while *learning* the arts and advantages of civilization, and which at a proper time is to be subdivided and allotted to them in severalty, and thus a home furnished to each of them, around which shall cluster all those fond associations and endearments so highly prized by all civilized people, and they in a condition to appreciate the same, the reservation is a place where a scanty subsistence is doled out to them from year to year, they become accustomed to rely upon charity rather than their own exertions, are hemmed in by people by whom they are detested, and whose arts and customs they have neither the power nor inclination to acquire, and thus they become vagrants and vagabonds, accomplishing for themselves no desirable end, and are a nuisance to their white neighbors.

Within the northern district the reservations are owned by government, but with the exception, perhaps, of that of Round valley, they, too, are insufficient in size, and in consequence of their occupation under one pretext or another, by whites, are of no more real utility to the Indians than those of the southern district. At Nome Lake reservation there were at one time between two and three thousand Indians, but owing to encroachments of whites upon the reservation, their settlement around its borders—the evils which invariably attend immediate attack of the two races—a pernicious system of indenturing the Indians to the whites, and the further fact that the farm has been suffered to fall into decay, and the buildings to become dilapidated, there are now not exceeding two hundred in all, the remainder having wandered off because it was no longer possible to remain. This reservation, judging by the report of the superintending agent, ought to be abandoned, for the reason that it has not the natural facilities to adapt it to the purpose intended, inasmuch as there is no fishery, and the timber is twelve miles distant, objections which at the time of its establishment were not so insuperable as now, because at that time all the adjacent region was not occupied by whites. I have mentioned this reservation particularly, because it combines objections which, to some extent and in greater or less degree, exist with reference to all the others, and is a forcible illustration of the necessity that all Indian reservations should be large in area, and so located as not to be liable to come in immediate contact with white settlements, which contact is seldom or never beneficial, and in many instances causes an actual degradation of the Indians.

There are, as I am informed, many unsettled claims for expenditures made in behalf of the Indian service in California, which require immediate attention. Measures must also be taken to cause the removal of whites from such reservations as it is deemed advisable to retain, and to provide for the payment of such improvements thereon as are of utility to the Indians.

Under a law recently passed by the State legislature, large numbers of Indians have been nominally "indentured" for long terms of years to white masters. This "indenturing," if my information as to the character of the law and its practical operation is correct, is but another name for enslaving those who are so unfortunate as to become its objects, since, by its operation, Indians of any age under thirty, and of either sex, without their consent, or, if they be minors, that of their parents, are "indentured" to white masters, who thereupon become entitled to "the care, control, custody, and earnings" of those thus "indentured," whom, in consideration thereof, they undertake to "feed, clothe, care for, and protect," but no security is required that this undertaking shall be performed, nor are any penalties prescribed for its violation. A law like this is subject to enormous and outrageous abuse, and may be made the means by which the most wicked oppression may be perpetrated, and I cannot believe that it was enacted with due consideration and deliberation, or that its provisions will not, at the earliest practicable moment, be so amended as to prevent its conversion by wicked and unscrupulous men to the purposes of a cruel oppression, disgraceful alike to a community in which it is permitted, and a State under color of whose authority it is perpetrated. I wish, however, to be understood as not objecting to a law for the "indenturing" of Indian youths to discreet and respectable whites, with such safeguards incorporated therein as will secure for the Indian apprentice the same benefits and advantages as are deemed indispensable in the case of white children. The law to which I have alluded is (if my information is correct) grossly deficient in this respect, and all proper remedies should at once be restored to rescue those who, under color of its provisions, have become victims of the avarice of base and designing men.

The statement, as made by Superintending Agent Hansen, of the causes which led to the employment of United States and volunteer forces against the Indians in the frontier portions of Humboldt and Mendocino counties, and of the crimes that are committed in the wake, and, as seems to be the case, under the *quasi* protection of those forces, presents a picture of the perversion of power and of cruel wrong, from which humanity instinctively recoils. This so-called "Indian war" appears to be a war in which the whites alone are engaged. The Indians are hunted like wild and dangerous beasts of prey; the parents are "murdered," and the children "kidnapped." Surely some plan may be devised whereby the Indians may cease to be the victims of such inhumanity, and the recurrence of scenes so disgraceful rendered impossible.

Representations as to the causes of and manner in which this "Indian war" is being prosecuted, as also in relation to various other alleged abuses in the Indian service in California, Oregon, and the Territory of Washington, induced me, with your approbation, and at the urgent request and upon the recommendation of several prominent public and private citizens, to appoint, in August last, Dr. Elijah White, represented to be a gentleman of large experience in Indian affairs, as special agent, to visit those places and investigate the various subjects of complaint, and I am anxiously awaiting his report in the hope that his mission may be productive of good results.

From what has been stated in relation to the condition of the Indians in California, and from the papers herewith relating to that subject, will be seen how great is the necessity that the subject should receive the earnest consideration of the approaching Congress, to which I trust it will be commended, and its wisdom and liberality earnestly invoked in behalf of the Indians, so that adequate remedies may be provided to cure the deplorable evils by which they are surrounded.

Indian affairs in Oregon continue to be discouraging in some respects, and gratifying in others. The incompleteness of the arrangements of some of the reservations, and the dilapidated condition in which the buildings and other improvements have been suffered to fall, have furnished evil-disposed persons with a plausible pretext to assert to the Indians that the government of their "Great Father" is destroyed, and that no more annuities will be paid them. The consequence of this is that the Rogue River Indians have abandoned their reservation, and that the Indians of other reservations are threatening to follow their bad example. Measures, which it is hoped will prove successful, have been taken to compel the return of such as have wandered away, and, so far as possible, counteract the effects of the wicked representations by which the trouble has been caused. With the exception of a series of robberies and murders committed in the neighborhood of the Dalles, by some Indians of the Warm Springs reservation, who were promptly surrendered by the tribe to be dealt with according to law, the affairs of that reservation are progressing with quiet and regularity. On the Umatilla reservation a remarkable degree of industry and consequent prosperity is noticeable, which is to be credited principally to the Cayuses, and secondarily to the Umatillas. Although the Cayuses number *less* than 400 souls, they own property valued at exceeding one hundred thousand dollars. They are justly considered the most advanced of all the tribes in Oregon. On this reservation, besides the two bands already named, there is a band of Walla-Wallas, less industrious and provident than the others. These bands unitedly exceed one thousand in number, and would be much benefited by the establishment of a school among them. The discovery of gold in this region has the unwelcome effect of bringing to it many vicious men of the white race, whose trade in spirituous liquors is highly prejudicial to the Indians. They establish themselves just outside the reservations, and present a case on the Pacific coast similar to that already noticed in the northern superintendency, as requiring additional legislation by Congress, or the State government, or both. On the Siletz reservation agricultural operations are quite extensive. More than 1,200 acres are under tillage, of which nearly one-half was this year devoted to an oat crop, about one-fourth to wheat, and most of the remainder to potatoes. There is a school on this reservation, but difficulty is experienced in securing the attendance of the children. Though more than two thousand Indians are now collected on this reservation, only two hundred and fifty-nine of them are under confirmed treaty relations. This circumstance was regretfully alluded to by the agent in his report for last year, and reference to it is repeated in his present report. It was thought best by the late superintendent, with whom the present concurs, that the treaty of August 11, 1855, should not be ratified, and he was likewise of opinion that the formality of a new treaty is unnecessary, although he earnestly commended to the justice of Congress the case of those 1,766 Coast Indians, who had, in good faith and reliance upon the government, relinquished their native haunts and removed to the reservation. He suggested that annuities should be extended to them sufficient to purchase such articles and procure such comforts as are enjoyed by the small minority under treaty. My views upon this subject have been elsewhere expressed. There are several tribes of Indians in Oregon of formidable power, with some of whom we have negotiated no treaties, and with the others our treaties are not sufficiently comprehensive.

The Shoshones, or Snakes, and the Flatheads, are wealthy and powerful, and can cause their hostility to the remoter settlements and the overland emigration to be severely felt. Hence the pressing necessity of some speedy arrangement with them, which with the Snakes it is suggested should be (as a temporary measure) a treaty granting annuities in consideration of a right of way across their country.

For the Flatheads, who give expression of something like jealousy that they have not received the attention of our government, it would be well to gather a council, in which a more definite knowledge of their wishes and expectations could be arrived at, and stipulations looking to the safety of emigrants and miners agreed upon.

The Indian affairs in the distant Territory of Washington have not as yet assumed that degree of regularity and system which is desirable. The recent organization of the country, the ruggedness of its surface, and its paucity of white inhabitants, are impediments to the rapid development of our Indian policy, which will require no little time and patience. It is probably for this reason that the treaties of January 1, 1855, with Makah tribe, located in the extreme northwest corner of the Territory, and that of January 25, 1856, with the Qui-nai-elts and Quil-leh-utes, have not been carried into execution. Much dissatisfaction exists on the part of these tribes on account of the prolonged delay, and they are beginning to lose confidence in the good faith of the government; but I am assured by the late superintendent that so soon as we shall have executed the stipulations on our part of said treaties, for which arrangements are now completed, there will be no difficulty in the way of a speedy and full restoration of confidence and content. Goods have, this year, for the first time been distributed to the D'Wamish, Suquamish, and Skallams tribes, which tribes, it is represented, are mainly located upon their reservation, and, so soon as agency buildings can be erected, will be fairly under our protection and control, and it is to be hoped in a condition favorable to their welfare and improvement. A comparison of their own condition with that of the tribes who are living upon reservations under treaties with the government, has induced a change in the views of the Chihalis, Cowlitz, and Chinook Indians, who in 1855 refused to enter into treaty relations. They now desire to come under the care and protection of government, and to be located upon a reservation. Should their desires be gratified, a tract of land on the Chihalis river, at the mouth of Black river, which has been surveyed, is deemed a suitable reservation for the Upper Chihalis and Cowlitz bands; and it is believed that the Lower Chihalis and the Chinooks may, without difficulty, be associated with the Qui-nai-elts and Quil-leh-utes upon their reservation.

Several of the tribes in this Territory are making fair progress in agricultural pursuits, amongst whom may be mentioned the Yakamas. This tribe has a school, under the direction of Mr. Wilbur, which is highly spoken of. Upon the Tulelip reservation there is also a school, under the care of the Rev. E. C. Chirouc, which it is reported is doing much good.

The whole number of Indians in Washington Territory with whom treaties have been negotiated and confirmed is estimated at about fourteen thousand. Besides these, there are many tribes and bands with whom treaties should be negotiated as early as practicable, and it is believed that the most of them may be associated with the Indians of existing reservations, with whom they are known to possess strong affinities.

The rush of white persons, probably to the number of ten thousand, into the country of the Nez Percés, in search of gold, of which it is reported that valuable discoveries have been made, will require on the part of our agents great vigilance and care in order that collisions of the two races may be prevented, and it will probably be necessary to negotiate an additional treaty with that tribe, in order to adapt the location of their reservation to the circumstances now surrounding them, and so widely differing from those in existence at the time their present treaty was negotiated. Up to the present time no difficulties have occurred so far as I am informed. In my comments upon the Washington superintendency, I have mainly relied for facts upon the report of the late superintendent, that of the present incumbent not having yet been received.

Report of Commissioner of Indian Affairs William P. Dole November 26, 1862

(Excerpt from *Report for 1862*, pp. 169-85)

Commissioner Dole's report for 1862 discussed the problems in the Northern Superintendency caused by the depredations of the Sioux, who had been goaded to an outbreak by an insensitive Government. The tribulations of the loyal Southern Indians of the Indian Territory, overrun by Confederate troops, were likewise discussed by the commissioner, who praised their gallantry and steadfastness in what seemed to be a losing cause.

I HAVE THE HONOR to submit my annual report for the current year. The details of the present condition of most of the Indian nations and tribes within our borders, their wants, prospects, and the advancement made by them in civilization, as also of the operations of the various superintendents, agents, and employés located among them, may be learned from the accompanying papers.

Having in my last annual report treated, at considerable length, of the location, condition, and wants of the various superintendencies, I shall, upon this occasion, confine myself chiefly to those which, in my judgment, demand special consideration.

Another year has but served to strengthen my conviction that the policy, recently adopted, of confining the Indians to reservations, and, from time to time, as they are gradually taught and become accustomed to the idea of individual property, allotting to them lands to be held in severalty, is the best method yet devised for their reclamation and advancement in civilization. The successful working of this policy is not, however, unattended with difficulties and embarrassments, arising chiefly from the contact of the red and white races. This is especially the case in relation to Indians whose reservations are located within the limits of States.

In very many instances the reservation is entirely surrounded by white settlements, and however much the fact is to be regretted, it is nevertheless, almost invariably true that the tracts of land still remaining in the possession of the Indians, small and insignificant as they are when compared with the broad domain of which they were once the undisputed masters, are the objects of the cupidity of their white neighbors; they are regarded as intruders, and are subject to wrongs, insults, and petty annoyances, which, though they may be trifling in detail, are, in the aggregate, exceedingly onerous and hard to be borne.

They find themselves in the pathway of a race they are wholly unable to stay, and on whose sense of justice they can alone rely for a redress of their real or imaginary grievances. Surrounded by this race, compelled by inevitable necessity to abandon all their former modes of gaining a livelihood, and starting out in pursuits which to them are new and untried experiments, they are brought in active competition with their superiors in intelligence and those acquirements which we consider so essential to success. In addition to these disadvantages, they find themselves amenable to a system of local and federal laws, as well as their treaty stipulations, all of which are to the vast majority of them wholly unintelligible. If a white man does them an injury, redress is often beyond their reach; or, if obtained, is only had after delays and vexations which are themselves cruel injustice. If one of their number commits a crime, punishment is sure and swift, and oftentimes is visited upon the whole tribe. Under these circumstances, it is not surprising that very many of them regard their future prospects as utterly hopeless, and consequently cannot be induced to abandon their vicious and idle habits. It is gratifying that so many of them are steadily and successfully acquiring the arts of civilization, and becoming useful members and, in some instances, ornaments of society.

Very much of the evil attendant upon the location of Indians within the limits of States might be obviated, if some plan could be devised whereby a more hearty co-operation with government on the part of the States might be secured. It being a demonstrated fact that Indians are capable of attaining a high degree of civilization, it follows that the time will arrive, as in the case of some of the tribes it has doubtless now arrived, when the peculiar relations existing between them and the federal government may cease, without detriment to their interests or those of the community or State in which they are located; in other words, that the time will come when, in justice to them and to ourselves, their relations to the general government should be identical with those of the citizens of the various States. In this view, a more generous legislation on the part of most of the States within whose limits Indians are located, looking to a gradual removal of the disabilities under which they labor, and their ultimate admission to all the rights of citizenship, as from time to time the improvement and advancement made by a given tribe may warrant, is earnestly to be desired, and would, I doubt not, prove a powerful incentive to exertion on the part of the Indians themselves.

Having premised this much, I will now present such information and suggestions, in relation to the various superintendencies, as are deemed important.

NORTHERN SUPERINTENDENCY

The condition of Indian affairs within this superintendency is most deplorable and unfortunate. As is generally known, it has been the scene of the most atrocious and horrible outbreaks to be found in the annals of Indian history. The events are of too recent occurrence to justify me in an attempt to elucidate and explain all the causes which led to the disastrous state of affairs now existing; and unfortunately I have not as yet received the annual report of Mr. Galbraith, the agent in charge of the Sioux, (by whom the most formidable outrages were perpetrated,) and can glean but little definite information from the report of Superintendent Thompson.

For several years it has been known that much ill feeling existed towards the whites on the part of portions of the different bands of Sioux who were parties to the treaty of 1851. They are divided into two classes: the Farmer and the Blanket Indians. The former have heretofore been quiet and peaceable, disposed to acquire the arts of civilization, and, in many instances, have adopted our costume and methods of gaining a livelihood. The latter are wild and turbulent, pertinacious in adhering to their savage customs, and have committed many depredations upon the whites in their vicinity.

The payment of claims arising in consequence of these depredations has, under the law, been made from the annuities of the tribe, which have thereby been diminished to the same extent. The disaffected could not, or would not, understand why the amount of their annuities was diminished, and each annual payment has only served to add to the disaffection, which, during several of the past years, has been so great as to require the presence of troops at the time of payment in order to preserve the peace and prevent an open rupture. So violent was the demeanor of the disaffected Indians at the last annual payment, and so threatening the attitude they had since assumed, that, upon the earnest representation and solicitation of Superintendent Thompson, it was deemed absolutely essential to the preservation of peace that the full amount of their annuities, without any deduction on account of depredation claims, which had been paid therefrom, should be paid them during the past season; and for this purpose it was necessary to use a portion of the appropriation made for their use during the fiscal year ending June 30, 1863, and to postpone the usual time of payment until that appropriation became available.

About the usual time of the annual payment, the Sisseton and Wahpeton bands, and a few lodges of the Yanctonnais, assembled at the agency, without previous notice from the agent of his readiness to make the payment, (which notice it has been the uniform practice to give,) and in a threatening manner demanded their annuities. It was with the greatest difficulty, and not until a detachment of troops had arrived from the neighboring Fort Ridgely, and the agent had given the most positive assurances that payment should soon be made, that they were finally induced to refrain from violence, and agreed to return to their homes and there remain until notified by the agent of his readiness to make their payment.

Affairs remained in this position until Sunday, the 17th of August last, when five persons were murdered at Acton, in Meeker county, at least thirty miles distant from the agency. This act, according to a report made by

Lieutenant Governor Donnelly to Governor Ramsey, (which I have taken the liberty to incorporate among the accompanying papers,) was probably "one of those accidental outrages at any time to be anticipated on the remote frontier. It fell, however, like a spark of fire, upon a mass of discontent, long accumulated and ready for it." And now followed a series of cruel murders, characterized by every species of savage atrocity and barbarity known to Indian warfare. Neither age, sex, nor condition was spared. It is estimated that from eight hundred to one thousand quiet, inoffensive, and unarmed settlers fell victims to savage fury ere the bloody work of death was stayed. The thriving town of New Ulm, containing from 1,500 to 2,000 inhabitants, was almost destroyed. Fort Ridgely was attacked and closely besieged for several days, and was only saved by the most heroic and unfaltering bravery on the part of its little band of defenders until it was relieved by troops raised, armed, and sent forward to their relief. Meantime the utmost consternation and alarm prevailed throughout the entire community. Thousands of happy homes were abandoned, the whole frontier was given up to be plundered and burned by the remorseless savage, and every avenue leading to the more densely populated portions of the State was crowded with the now homeless and impoverished fugitives. While the terrible excitement occasioned by this unexpected outbreak on the part of the Sioux, in the western part of the State, was still at its height, it was still further increased by the most startling reports from the Chippewas, who reside in the northern portion thereof. From these reports it became the universal belief that a preconcerted and general uprising of all the Indians of the State was at hand, and that the State, already drained by the calls of the government of a large portion of its able-bodied citizens, and without any preparation, was to become the arena of a most formidable Indian war.

Having been in the midst of the Chippewa difficulties, and taken an active part in the measures which led to their adjustment, I am the better prepared to make a detailed and more satisfactory statement in relation thereto, and for this reason must be excused if I appear to give an undue prominence to the less prominent difficulties.

An appropriation was made at the last session of Congress for the purpose of negotiating a treaty with the Chippewas of Red Lake and Red River of the North, in order to secure to the people of the United States the free and safe navigation of that river. Superintendent Thompson and myself having been designated by you to effect this negotiation, I left this city in August last, in company with A. S. H. White, esq., of the Interior Department, and proceeded to St. Paul, in Minnesota: at which point it had been prearranged that we should meet Superintendent Thompson. On arriving at St. Paul we found everything in readiness for our contemplated journey to the Red river country. We accordingly proceeded, and arrived at St. Cloud on the 19th day of August. At this point we met Sergeant Tracy, who had been despatched to St. Paul by Captain Hall, the commandant at Fort Ripley, to procure troops to strengthen the fort and protect the settlements in its vicinity from an apprehended attack by the Chippewas of the Mississippi, under the lead of their chief, Hole-in-the-day.

I learned from Sergeant Tracy that the Indians, instigated by Hole-in-the-day, had commenced depredations by stealing and killing the cattle belonging to their agency, and by making several persons prisoners; that in consequence of this demonstration, and threats against his life, Agent Walker had sent a messenger to Fort Ripley for troops to protect the agency and its employes; that, in compliance with this request, some twenty-five troops had been sent from the fort to Crow Wing, where they met Agent Walker, who requested them to arrest the chief, as a necessary measure to prevent a general outbreak; and that in endeavoring to comply with this request, the troops had been discovered by Hole-in-the-day, who immediately fled to his house, situated upon the river some two miles above, and embarking with his wives in canoes, had well nigh gained the opposite bank before the arrival of the troops. He refused to comply with their demand that he should return, and on gaining the opposite shore turned and fired upon them. This fire was promptly returned, but with no other effect than to exasperate Hole-in-the-day. Ample evidence is in my possession showing that he immediately sent runners to all the bands of the Chippewas, advising them that war had begun, that their chief had been fired upon by United States troops, and that they must at once kill all the whites upon the various reservations, seize the property of the traders and others, and join him at his camp at Gull lake. At this juncture Sergeant Tracy had been despatched from Fort Ripley to Governor Ramsey for troops.

Upon receiving this information, I determined to send a messenger to the agency, distant from St. Cloud about sixty-five miles, that I might learn the full extent of the difficulty. The messenger was met by Agent Walker and his family, who were fleeing from the agency. The agent was so much excited that upon his arrival at St. Cloud I could obtain no reliable information from him as to the cause of the outbreak. His fears for the safety of his family and self had evidently affected his mind. He believed that there was a general and preconcerted rising of all the Indians of the country; which belief was strengthened by hearing of the outrages then being committed by the Sioux. Fully persuaded that we were surrounded by Indians, he started from St. Cloud for St. Paul, warning the people along his route to flee from the country; and a few days afterwards was found dead some distance from the road. He had evidently become deranged and committed suicide.

About this time a messenger reached us from Fort Ridgely, *via* St. Paul, who had been sent forward to warn us of the terrible outbreak of the Sioux, and that a party of them had started across the country to intercept us and, as they said, recover their money, with which they professed to believe we intended to make a treaty with their ancient enemies; and also intending to dispossess themselves of the goods and provisions with our train. Senator Wilkinson and Mr. Nicolay, secretary to the President, had joined our party at St. Paul. Upon consultation with them and others of the party, it was thought best to return to St. Paul to advise with the governor, and, if possible, assist in putting an end to the Sioux massacres, and also obtain from him an escort sufficiently strong to enable us safely to proceed upon our mission to the Red river, which up to this time had not been abandoned. Directions were immediately sent to the parties in charge of the goods, provisions, and cattle to proceed to Fort Abercrombie, and there await a reasonable time for further orders, which failing to receive, they were directed to deliver the property in their charge to the commandant of the fort. A letter was also despatched to Mr. Kittson, directing him to notify the Indians assembled at the treaty ground on Red river that we should probably be detained some two weeks.

These arrangements completed, we returned to St. Paul, where we learned that the Sioux outbreak was much more formidable than we had supposed, and that all hopes of an amicable adjustment had ended. Troops were being promptly forwarded for the protection of the frontier settlements and the relief of Fort Ridgely. Believing now that the danger of further trouble with the Chippewas was imminent, I requested Governor Ramsey to send two additional companies of infantry (one being already *en route*) to Fort Ripley. This request was at once complied with, and two companies, one under Captain Burt, the other under Captain Libby, were placed under my command. Meantime I received a message from Hole-in-the-day, through Mr. Sweet, of Sank Rapids, to the effect that he desired an interview. I also learned from Mr. Sweet, of Sank Rapids, to the effect that he desired an interview. I also learned from Mr. Sweet, who had visited the Chippewa camp at Gull lake, that Hole-in-the-day had there assembled about three hundred armed warriors and was ready to attack the settlements, but would wait three days for an interview with me, that, if possible, the existing troubles might be settled by negotiation. The two companies placed under my command had but just arrived at Fort Snelling; one of them was that day mustered into service; neither had received arms, tents, clothing, or camp equipage; and yet so efficient were the services of Mr. Chute, who had been appointed by the governor as quartermaster to the expedition, and so prompt were the officers and men, that one company started the day the order was issued and the other early the next morning, and both arrived at Fort Ripley in several hours less than three days, having marched a distance of one hundred and thirty miles.

On arriving at the fort, twelve miles distant from the agency, I notified Hole-in-the-day, that I was ready to hold a council with him and the chiefs who were with him, and to hear their complaints. I was promised an answer the following day. I found at the fort "Bad Boy," a chief of the Mississippi band of Chippewas, and his family; also Mr. Johnson, an educated Indian minister. These Indians, having refused to participate in the wicked schemes of Hole-in-the-day, had been compelled to flee for their lives. I also found at the fort several of the agency employés, who, after being robbed, had been driven from the reservations. From these Indians and employés I learned that the Pillager and Otter-tail Lake bands had promptly repaired to the camp of Hole-in-the-day upon receiving his summons. The Pillagers had made prisoners of the whites and some half-breed employés upon their reservation. The Otter-tails had driven all the whites from the settlement, destroyed the land office, breaking open the safe, and scattering the papers to the winds, and both bands had seized everything they could find, robbing stores, shops, dwellings, and schools, and destroying everything they could not use. The prisoners, after being taken to the camp at Gull lake, had been liberated through the influence of the chiefs of the Pillagers. There were, at the camp at Gull lake, at least three hundred warriors, who were being supplied with provisions from the agency, and who pretended that they were waiting for the commissioner, and only demanded that charges preferred against their late agent should be investigated.

I also learned while at the fort, that the Mille Lac, and, perhaps, the Sandy Lake and Pokagema bands, had not yet joined Hole-in-the-day. With a view to detach these bands from his interest, Messrs. Whitehead and Howard were despatched with a message to them, advising them of my presence in the country, and that I desired to hold a council with them at the fort. This message had the desired effect, and resulted in a council with the chiefs and some fifty or sixty of the headmen of the Mille Lac band. At this council the entire strength of these bands was alienated from Hole-in-the-day, and their friendship and good will secured. I feel confident that this diversion of nearly one-half the followers upon whom Hole-in-the-day doubtless relied, went far in enabling us finally to effect a settlement of the Chippewa difficulties without a resort to arms.

The day following my message to Hole-in-the-day, he sent me word that he would not meet me at the fort; and, upon being requested by Mr. Morrill, (whom I had appointed special agent, in consequence of the death of late Agent Walker,) to name a time and place of meeting, refused to reply. Judge Cooper, of St. Paul, a special friend and attorney of Hole-in-the-day, was in the vicinity at his request. I requested him to visit the Indian camp, hoping that, through his intimacy with the chief, I might be able to effect a council and settlement without further difficulty. The judge had preceded me to the reserve, had met the chief in consultation, and I was led by him to believe that the Indians were very penitent, and anxious for an adjustment of the difficulties. He was permitted to pass freely to and from the Indian camp during eight days, but effected no meeting, although several were appointed. That it was a mistake to allow any one, except the officers of the government, to visit the Indian camp, I have very little doubt. After Judge Cooper left for home, Superintendent Thompson, who had all along rendered me efficient aid, visited the hostile camp and met Hole-in-the-day, who informed him that they cared nothing about the investigation spoken of, but that they wanted another treaty, providing for their removal from the vicinity of the whites, and that he, the chiefs with him, and a few others, not exceeding thirty or forty in number, would meet me in council at Crow Wing the next day. To this I assented. I had previously placed one company of the troops at my disposal at the agency and another at Crow Wing. The other was stationed at the fort.

Some days prior to the proposed meeting at Crow Wing Hole-in-the-day had moved his camp to a point about two miles distant from that place, on the road leading to the agency. Soon after arriving at Crow Wing next morning, more than double the number of Indians that it had been agreed should visit the council ground were seen coming very slowly down the bank of the river, in order, as it afterwards appeared, that some two hundred of their number, who had crossed the river above, might come around through the brush, and thus surround us. When it was discovered that the entire body of Indians were thus posted, and that they were all armed and painted for war, it became evident that Hole-in-the-day was acting treacherously. The Indians had taken possession of the road leading into the town, and had made prisoners of two citizens. Hole-in-the-day now approached the council ground, with about eighty of his followers. Of course no good results could be expected from a council held under these threatening circumstances; but to gain time I resolved to proceed. Captain Libby's company, which was stationed at this point, was cautiously put under arms. The citizens of the town and other whites in attendance were on the alert and well armed. If the council could be prolonged until the middle of the afternoon, troops would arrive from the fort, (for which we sent a messenger in disguise through the Indian lines,) and we would thus be able to make a fair show for successful resistance, in case of an attack. I first demanded of Hole-in-the-day the release of the prisoners, the opening of the road, and that he should withdraw his warriors from the brush surrounding the town. After considerable parley, he consented to the release of the prisoners, and that citizens, and none others, might pass along the road. We then proceeded with the council, but arrived at no satisfactory result. Hole-in-the-day made no charges against the government or its agents. He complained that troops had been sent against him, that he had been fired upon, and stated that for this reason his people had taken arms. During the council he was insolent, defiant, and disrespectful. At its close he stated that it would require several days to settle the difficulty; and thereupon it was agreed that we should again meet for council on the following day. The Indians were then withdrawn from around us, and we returned to the fort, meeting our re-enforcements on the way. It is perhaps fortunate that they did not arrive before the conclusion of the council.

Being satisfied that the troops at my disposal were not sufficient to guard the fort, the agency, and settlements, should hostilities commence, a messenger was at once sent to Governor Ramsey, with a statement of our proceedings and a request or additional forces. The next day—having meantime taken the precaution to guard against being again surrounded—we repaired to Crow Wing, according to agreement. A messenger that I had that morning sent to the agency was seized on his return by the Indians, robbed of his horse, and compelled to return on foot. I also learned that the Indians still held as prisoner the wife of one of the government employes. I then sent a note to Hole-in-the-day, demanding the release of the prisoner and the return of the horse previous to the holding of any further communications. This demand was peremptorily refused. After another unsuccessful effort to procure a council, we returned to the fort. That day I learned, as I have reason to believe by the procurement of Hole-in-the-day, that he would accept ten thousand dollars' worth of goods, which he believed to be at my disposal, as a condition of laying down his arms and agreeing to maintain the peace. Of course no such proposition could be entertained; but it satisfied me that, whatever might have been the original intention of Hole-in-the-day, it was now simply an attempt to levy black-mail. That all hopes of success in this project might be at once abandoned, it was deemed best that I should return to St. Paul. I accordingly turned over to Captain Hall the command of the troops; gave the necessary instructions to Agent Morrill; and sent a letter to Hole-in-the-day, informing him of my intended departure, and that no further attempt would be made to negotiate with him or his people. I also notified him that if his camp was immediately broken up, and the stolen goods restored, and his warriors peaceably and quietly dispersed to their homes, rations would issued to those living at a distance, and that if this proposition was not accepted unconditionally, military force would be employed against him.

On the 12th day of September I left for St. Paul. Along the route as far as St. Cloud I found the utmost excitement in consequence of an apprehended attack. Farms, crops, houses, and furniture were in many instances abandoned; the villages were fortified, and every preparation being made for defence. We did all in our power to reassure the people, informing them of the measures taken for defence at the fort and adjacent settlements, and of the change of purpose which we believed had been made by Hole-in-the-day, and, further, that we had but little doubt that when he should learn of my departure, and that consequently no hope remained that he could extort from the government payment for good behavior, he would either submit unconditionally or be compelled thereto by his people. The sequel proved that we were entirely correct.

The message that I had left for Hole-in-the-day was that day delivered to him, and the other chiefs assembled in council, by Agent Morrill. That night the Indians must determine the question of peace or war. Until that time rations had been issued to them to prevent them from robbing settlers. These rations would now be stopped, unless they at once disbanded. The council was long and stormy. Hole-in-the-day advised an attack upon the agency. Big Dog and Buffalo, old chiefs of the Pillagers, counselled peace. The council ended without an agreement; and in the night a majority of the Indians abandoned Hole-in-the-day, came to the agency, surrendered the stolen property in their possession, received the promised rations, and started to their homes. The next day Hole-in-the-day, finding himself abandoned by a majority of his people, came humbly to the agency and surrendered the stolen property in his possession. Thus the entire and unconditional submission of the Indians was obtained. And it would have been well if this satisfactory condition of affairs had been suffered to remain unmolested. Unfortunately, however, as I believe, Governor Ramsey thought proper to refer my letter to the legislature for its action, instead of sending forward troops, as I had requested. The legislature appointed a commission to proceed to the Chippewa agency to *negotiate* a peace. This action, as I have no doubt, was induced by misrepresentations, made by parties for interested motives.

On our return we met this commission, accompanied by the governor, at Anoka. They were advised that it was believed that the Indians had already submitted; that it was deemed important that no further attempt at nego-tiation should be made, except through the medium of the agent, and that no good would result from again assembling the Indians. I informed the commissioners that I would consent to no terms other than unconditional submission to the existing laws and treaties, and that I believed any other settlement with Hole-in-the-day was only preparing the way for future raids and further efforts on his part to extort money from the government. I withheld permission for the commissioners to go upon the reserve, for the reason that the attorney of Hole-in-the-day was at its head; but in consider-ation of the terrible excitement, and fearing that the least future outbreak on the part of the Chippewas would result in the depopulation of the northern part of the State, I authorized the governor to hold a council with the Indians, promising to co-operate with him in any measures calculated to secure peace.

The governor and commissioners were met, between St. Cloud and Fort Ripley, by a messenger bringing the glad tidings that the Indians had sub-mitted and were *en route* for their homes. On arriving at the fort, Captain Hall informed them that he had been present at the councils with the agent; that the Indians had disbanded, and exhibited to them the war-club of Hole-in-the-day, which had been surrendered to him by the chief as an evidence of his submission. I can conceive of no reason for disturbing this state of affairs. Runners, however, were despatched at midnight, and the Indians recalled. A council was held and the form of a treaty (to be found with the accompanying papers) negotiated. It is evident that the terms of this negotiation cannot be accepted by the government, and that, in its present form, it ought not to be ratified. The first article provides that the leaders of this outbreak shall be exonerated from punishment. To this I do not strenuously object, as their punishment is, perhaps, in this instance, not necessary to secure future peace. The second article is grossly unjust to the white settlers, who, in many instances, have, by these depredations, lost all their possessions. The third article contains provisions wholly at variance with precedent and law, inasmuch as it provides for an investigation of the depredations committed by the Indians, and of their complaints against the government, by a commission entirely independent of the Interior Department, either in its appointment or in a supervision and concurrence in its finding. That the government is prepared thus to surrender its legitimate and constitutional control of Indian affairs, I am unprepared to believe. For my views as to the extent to which I consider this treaty binding upon this department, I respectfully refer to my letter to General Pope, to be found among the accompanying papers.

These troubles, which I feel that I have very imperfectly described, (and more especially so as to the Sioux,) have naturally produced the most intense excitement in the minds of the people of Minnesota, which, it is to be feared, will add much to the difficulty of a proper adjustment. No language can describe the enormity of the crimes committed by the Sioux; and no one will deny that swift and condign punishment should be meted out to the wicked perpetrators of those crimes, and the most ample security provided against their repetition. Happily we have now within the State ample means to enforce any line of policy we may choose to adopt. For the time the management of the Sioux is confided to the military authorities under the direction of the War Department. I have already called your attention to the decision of a court-martial, convened by General Pope, to try a large number of the warriors engaged in the massacres, who have voluntarily, as I understand, surrendered, by which over three hundred of the number have been condemned to death. I cannot refrain from the expression of an opinion that the execution of this sentence would partake more of the character of revenge than of punishment. It must not be forgotten that these savages, still red with the blood of our slaughtered kinsmen, have voluntarily surrendered as prisoners, and that we shall never be justified in judging them by our standard of morals. They are savages, far beneath us in both moral and intellectual culture. Their chiefs and head men wield an influence over them which it is difficult for us to understand or appreciate. Upon their leaders rests the burden of their guilt, and upon those leaders the weight of punishment should fall. I cannot but believe that the death penalty, visited upon the fiends who instigated and procured the commission of these dark and bloody crimes, and a milder form of punishment for those who, it may be, were their willing tools, will be found as effectual in preventing their repetition, and far more in accordance with the demands of justice and the spirit of the age in which we live.

I find that I have already extended my remarks in relation to this superintendency to a much greater length than I had intended, and shall close with a very brief allusion to the other Indians within its limits.

The Chippewas of Lake Superior, although intimately related with those of the Mississippi, and very much under the influence of Hole-in-the-day, I am gratified to state, have maintained their usual quiet and friendly relations, and have made a commendable degree of improvement during the past year. It was at one time greatly feared that they would join in the wicked schemes of Hole-in-the-day; but by the influence of Agent Webb, and others, in whom they have confidence, and especially of Senators Rice and Wade, who were fortunately in their neighborhood at the time of the apprehended danger, they were restrained.

For reasons already stated, the attempt to negotiate a treaty with the Chippewas of Pembina and Red Lake failed. The Indians assembled at the point agreed upon for the purpose of negotiating a treaty, and there remained until they had consumed all the provisions they had brought with them, and all they could procure. They then seized about $25,000 worth of goods, mostly the property, it is said, of British subjects, with which Mr. Kittson, already mentioned, happened to be passing through the country. They stated, at the time of this seizure, that they still desired to treat with the United States, and were willing to pay for the goods they had appropriated whenever a treaty was made. I am satisfied that the temper of these Indians is such that travel through their country will no longer be safe until a treaty is negotiated, or a line of forts established along the Red River of the North, with forces sufficient for the protection of the adjacent country. Superintendent Thompson recommends that their chiefs and head men be summoned to this city for the purpose of making a treaty. In this recommendation I entirely concur.

The condition of the Winnebagoes is peculiar. I am fully satisfied that, while it may be true that a few of their number were engaged in the atrocities of the Sioux, the tribe, as such, is no more justly responsible for their acts than our government would be for those of a pirate who might happen to have been born upon our territory. Notwithstanding this, from all I can learn, the exasperation of the people of Minnesota appears to be nearly as great towards these Indians as towards the Sioux. They demand that the Winnebagoes as well as the Sioux shall be removed from the limits of the State. The Winnebagoes are unwilling to remove. So exasperated are the people that they only leave their reservation at the imminent risk of their lives. The lands which, under their treaty, are to be sold to procure means to supply agricultural implements, have been withheld from market on account of the financial difficulties of the country. Hence they have not been supplied with the necessary implements, and have not been able to engage in agricultural pursuits, and to a very great extent must rely upon the chase for food. Game upon their reservation is well nigh exhausted, their arms have been taken from them, and, unless their wants are supplied, they must suffer for food. The least depredation on the part of any one of their number, it is feared, would expose the whole tribe to an assault from the whites, which would be inevitably attended with deplorable results. Under these circumstances measures must be taken to provide for their subsistence, until some line of policy can be adopted which will be alike just to them and to the whites.

It would have been fortunate if some territory had been reserved in the northwest, as is the case in the southwest, upon which these and all other tribes of that State could be congregated. There is, however, no unorganized territory remaining, and it is to be feared that the removal of the Indians to any of the organized territories will only serve to postpone a difficulty which must at last be met, and will entail upon some future State the same troubles now existing in Minnesota.

I trust that, when time shall have elapsed sufficient for full consideration of the subject, some policy will be devised whereby all conflicting interests may be reconciled, and shall always be found ready to co-operate in any measures which promise to secure the peace and prosperity of our fellow-citizens of Minnesota, and which are just towards the Indians.

I should be derelict in duty if I failed to close this part of my report without urging the immediate and pressing necessity for action in behalf of those persons who have suffered in consequence of the depredations committed by the Indians of this superintendency. We may not compensate the loss of parents, children, husbands, wives, and friends; the breaking up of happy homes and the instant destruction of life, long hopes and aspirations, but the little remaining in our power should therefore be the more promptly and cheerfully done.

An investigation of the claims of the surviving sufferers should be instituted with the least possible delay. Many of them have been reduced from circumstances of comfort and plenty to abject want. To all of this class delay in paying their just demands is an injustice.

That the Sioux have clearly forfeited all claims upon government under their treaties is unquestionable. I therefore recommend that their available annuities, so far as applicable after the payment of the legitimate claims of the agency, shall be diverted to the payment of these claims. This fund will, however, be wholly inadequate; and in behalf of the sufferers I desire to make an earnest appeal to Congress for a prompt appropriation of an amount sufficient to compensate all pecuniary losses.

Central Superintendency

Every variety of Indian life, from that of the wild and untutored savage to that of the most civilized and intelligent of their race, is to be found within this superintendency. This diversity is exhibited in the comparative wealth of the tribes, in their costumes and pursuits, in their habitations, their provisions for the education and religious culture of their youth, and, in short, in everything that distinguishes civilized from savage life.

During the past year most of the tribes have made very considerable improvement. Health has been good, and those of them engaged in agricultural pursuits have generally been rewarded for their labor by bountiful crops, which, with their annuities, will amply supply the wants of the coming winter. With the exception of some difficulties of a hostile character between the Pawnees and Sioux, which, at the time, produced great consternation among the frontier settlements, the tribes have been at peace, and their universal loyalty and devotion to the cause of the government is very gratifying. As an instance of their loyalty I will mention this fact: Of two hundred and one Delawares, between the ages of eighteen and forty-five, one hundred and seventy have volunteered, and are now in the military service of the United States. It is doubtful if any community can show a larger proportion of volunteers than this. Other tribes have likewise shown a commendable zeal in furnishing volunteers, and I have no doubt that, if necessary, several thousand excellent soldiers could be added, without difficulty, to the Union army from the Indians of this superintendency. Several of the tribes have manual labor schools in successful operation, of which those of the Pottawatomies and Delawares deserve especial mention. It cannot be doubted that these schools are exerting a powerful influence, and will prove most efficient auxiliaries in advancing the best interests of the Indians.

Since my first annual report lands have been allotted in severalty to the Sacs and Foxes, and to the Kaws, as provided by their respective treaties. The allotment to the Delawares has also been completed. A treaty has been concluded with the Pottawatomies and Ottawas, providing for a similar allotment to such members of those tribes as may desire it. The necessary preliminary surveys are nearly completed, and steps have been taken to secure an early allotment of the lands. Thus, one by one, the tribes are abandoning the custom of holding their lands in common, and are becoming individual owners of the soil—a step which I regard as the most important in their progress towards civilization. A treaty has also been negotiated with the Kickapoos, providing for an allotment to the members of that tribe, and is awaiting the constitutional action of the Senate. I desire, also, to call your attention to treaties negotiated with the Iowas, and the Sacs and Foxes of the Missouri, and also with the Sacs and Foxes of the Mississippi, now pending before the Senate, in the hope that the attention of that body will be directed to the subject, and its early and favorable consideration had in the premises.

A fruitful source of difficulty, and one which detracts very much from the success of our Indian policy, is found in the fact that most of the reservations within this superintendency are surrounded by white settlements; and it has heretofore been found impossible to prevent the pernicious effects arising from the intercourse of vicious whites with the Indians. To remedy this it has been suggested that the various tribes should be removed to the Indian country immediately south of Kansas. This suggestion is heartily approved by the whites and by many of the Indians, and, under favorable circumstances, I should have no hesitation in recommending its adoption. It cannot be doubted that most, if not all, of the tribes of the Indian country have, in a greater or less degree, compromised their rights under existing treaties, and that upon the restoration of our authority their treaty relations will require readjustment, not only to provide for the punishment of those who have aided the rebellion, but also to secure the rights of those who have remained loyal. This will present a favorable opportunity for providing homes for such of the tribes and portions of tribes of the central superintendency as may desire to emigrate to that country. I do not wish to be misunderstood upon this point, either as to the action which should be had in relation to the tribes of the central or those of the southern superintendency. Those of the central superintendency who desire to remain there should be permitted to do so, without molestation in any form whatever. Most, if not all, of them hold their lands by the most indisputable of titles and by the most solemn forms, and upon every proper occasion have received the plighted faith of our people that they shall remain forever unmolested in their possession. For these possessions they have surrendered rights elsewhere, which we have always acknowledged to have been justly theirs, and a full and fair equivalent for all they have received. Any action therefore on our part which does not leave them perfectly free to elect whether they will remain where they now are or seek new homes, and that does not secure to them ample remuneration for their present possessions, and the quiet and peaceable possession of their new homes, in the event that they shall elect to emigrate, will be a wanton and disgraceful breach of their physical inability to resist any policy we may seek to force upon them.

With the tribes of the southern superintendency the circumstances are different. They occupy one of the most desirable portions of the American continent, sufficiently ample in extent to afford a home and country, not only for them, but also for all those tribes who will probably desire to share it with them. Besides this, no considerable number of whites are now there. Here, then, is a country which, by judicious, just, and forbearing action on our part, may be made a happy home for a large portion of our Indians, and where we have reason to believe they may successfully solve the problem of Indian civilization. As above remarked, most, if not all, of the tribes now there have, in a greater or less degree, compromised their rights under existing treaties. To a greater or less extent, they have participated in the great rebellion with which we are now struggling. When the rebellion is subdued it will be no easy task to re-adjust our relations with this people. In doing this two prominent facts must be borne in mind; first, that at the commencement of the rebellion all our forces were withdrawn from them, and many of them, doubtless, forced to join hands with the rebels; and, secondly, that thousands of them have been driven into exile, and endured untold sufferings, because of their unwavering loyalty to us and their fidelity to their treaty stipulations. To restore these fugitives to their homes, to reinstate them in their former possessions, is plainly our duty. To devise a policy which shall discriminate between those who are willingly traitors and those made so by circumstances will require careful thought and deliberation. I invoke for the whole subject the careful consideration of Congress, and the adoption of such measures as, in its wisdom, it may seem to demand.

Southern Superintendency

Referring to my last annual report, it will be seen that, at that date, we were in possession of but little accurate information in relation to the Indians of this superintendency.

Owing to the rebellion, neither the superintendent nor any of the agents (excepting the agent for the Neosho agency) had been able to repair to their respective posts of duty. It was believed, however, that a strong Union sentiment existed amongst the various tribes, which only needed military force sufficient to protect the loyal to secure its development. What was then believed has since been demonstrated in the strongest possible manner. In no part of the country have the sufferings and privations endured, and the sacrifices made by loyal citizens, on account of their fidelity to their country, exceeded those of the loyal Indians of this superintendency.

Among the earliest efforts of the seceded States was an endeavor to sever that allegiance of the Indians to the government, and secure their co-operation. The fact that the agents first appointed by the present administration to reside with them all proved traitors to their trust rendered this effort partially successful. Every species of fraud and deception was resorted to mislead them. They were gravely told that the government was at an end; that they would never be paid their annuities; that this city had been captured; that the United States government was overthrown; and, in short, that their only hope for the security resulting from a firm and stable government lay in joining their fortunes with the so-called Southern Confederacy.

The withdrawal of our troops from their country, the complete interruption of communication, and the assurances made by traitorous agents, gave an air of plausibility to these ridiculous stories, and resulted in the formation of a powerful secession party in their midst. As has been the case in all other localities so it was here: the secessionists were violent and aggressive, and hesitated not in resorting to cruel and forcible means to crush out every sentiment of loyalty. For many months the loyal party steadily resisted the tide of treason setting in upon them, and at length were compelled to resort to arms in defence of their persons and property. In December last, I learned that a very considerable force of Indian warriors, composed of Creeks, Seminoles, and a few members of all the other tribes, except, perhaps, the Choctaws and Chickasaws, had twice met in battle and defeated the rebel forces, who are represented to have greatly exceeded them in numbers and in military equipments. About this time, in compliance with repeated suggestions from this office, it was determined by the War Department to organize and send into the Indian country a force, composed in part of 4,000 volunteers, to be raised from amongst the loyal Indians of the central superintendency, to protect the loyal Indians, and enforce the authority of the United States government in the Indian territory; and orders were accordingly issued to that effect to Major General Hunter, then in command of the military department embracing that country. In compliance with instructions received from you I repaired to Kansas, in January last, for the purpose of rendering General Hunter such assistance in the execution of the orders above mentioned as might be in my power. On arriving in Kansas I learned from General Hunter that the rebels, being largely re-enforced by troops from Texas, had fought a third battle with the loyal Indians, resulting in the defeat and complete overthrow of the latter, who, with their old men, women, and children, had been compelled to flee for their lives from the country, and to the number of from 6,000 to 8,000, under the lead of O-poth-lo-yo-ho-lo, a very aged and influential Creek, had taken refuge near the southern border of Kansas, and were being fed from stores provided for the army of General Hunter, who, upon learning their disastrous condition, instantly detailed officers to go to their assistance, and was doing everything in his power to alleviate their sufferings. It would be impossible to give an adequate description of the suffering endured by these people during their flight, and for several weeks after their arrival. When it is remembered that they were collected for the journey, with scarcely a moment for preparation, amid the confusion and dismay of an overwhelming defeat; that their enemies were close upon them, flushed with victory, maddened by recent defeats, and under their well known code of warfare would spare neither age nor sex, it may well be believed that their preparations for the journey were wholly inadequate. It was in the dead of winter, the ground covered with ice and snow, and the weather most intensely cold. Without shelter, without adequate clothing, and almost destitute of food, a famishing, freezing multitude of fugitives, they arrived in Kansas entirely unexpectedly and where not the slightest preparation had been made to alleviate their sufferings or provide for their wants. Within two months after their arrival two hundred and forty of the Creeks alone died, in consequence of their exposure and want. Over a hundred frosted limbs were amputated within a like period of time. From these facts some idea may be formed of the intensity of their sufferings.

On the 6th of February I was informed by General Hunter that he could not furnish provisions for these people beyond the 15th of that month, and that it was beyond his power to furnish them even a moderate supply of tents and clothing. About the same time I also learned by telegraph from you that the military expedition to the Indian country had been postponed. There was no money at my disposal legitimately applicable to providing for the wants of these suffering people. There could be no delay. I must act, and that at once. With your approbation, I determined to purchase, upon credit, such supplies as their most pressing necessities seemed to require, and for that purpose appointed a special agent, charged with the duty of making the necessary purchases for food, clothing, and shelter, and delivering the same to Superintendent Coffin, who, with the agents of his superintendency, had, with commendable alacrity, repaired to the assistance of the fugitives. Congress at once authorized the annuities due to several of the tribes of the southern superintendency to be applied to the purpose of defraying the expenses thus incurred; and from the funds thus provided the fugitives have continued to be subsisted.

The military expedition already mentioned was not entirely abandoned. It was deemed a matter of great importance that these fugitives should be returned to their homes, and there protected, in time to raise crops during the past season, and no effort on the part of this office was omitted to accomplish that result. An order was procured from the War Department directing General Halleck, then in command of the western military department, to detail two regiments of white troops, who, together with two thousand armed Indians, were intended as a force to accomplish the purpose above indicated. The arms, with suitable ammunition, were obtained from the War Department, and delivered to Superintendent Coffin, for the use of the Indians, as early as the 16th of April last, but in consequence of various delays (the cause of which is not fully understood) the expedition was not prepared to march until near the 1st of July last. About this time the expedition started, and penetrated the country as far as Talequah. I am not in possession of information sufficiently accurate to attempt a detailed account of its operations. It is understood that, in consequence of unfortunate difficulties amongst the officers of the accompanying white troops, a retreat became necessary. For such information as I have in relation to this whole subject I refer to the accompanying papers relating thereto.

As was anticipated, a strong Union sentiment was found to exist among the Indians remaining in the Indian country. This was promptly manifested by the accession of an entire regiment of Cherokees to our forces. These volunteers are still in the service of the United States, having accompanied their brethren on the retreat just mentioned. By the withdrawal of the troops, accompanied by so many of their warriors and braves, the Union families would be left at the mercy of their inveterate foes, who would not be slow to wreak vengeance upon them for their loyalty, and thus a second flight of destitute men, women, and children became necessary from that unfortunate country, and has added nearly two thousand to the number now being fed and cared for in the south of Kansas. This retreat was, in all respects, unfortunate, and its necessity most keenly regretted and deplored by the loyal Indians.

It is due to the men composing the Indian regiments of this expedition to state that all accounts concur in awarding the highest praise to their soldierly bearing in battles, in camp, and upon the march. They are represented as obedient, hardy, and brave, and an honor to their race.

A second campaign into the Indian country is in progress, and there is every reason to believe that it will prove more successful than the former, and will result in the restoration of the national authority, and in enabling these distressed fugitives to return very shortly to their homes. It may, however, be found best that they should remain in their present location until spring on account of the difficulty of transporting provisions so great a distance during the winter, and the suspension of river navigation, it being understood that in consequence of a severe drought in that country, the crops of last season were very short, and that the country has been desolated by the ravages of the rebels, so that after their return they will require assistance until they should have had time to provide for their wants.

The expense incurred in aiding the refugees has thus far amounted to about one hundred and ninety-three thousand dollars, which, as elsewhere stated, has been paid from the annuities withheld from southern tribes, on account of their participation in the rebellion. As this fund is not common to the tribes, some of them having no interest therein, and inasmuch as, by the respective treaties under which it accrues, (which, so far as the loyal Indians are concerned, must remain practicably valid,) it is not applicable to the purpose of subsistence, this account, upon the restoration of order, will require careful scrutiny, and additional legislation will probably be necessary to secure a just settlement of the same as between the different tribes.

In concluding this subject I feel that my duty would be very imperfectly done should I fail to ask for these loyal, suffering, and destitute Indians the most generous and ample legislation on the part of Congress. In view of their unhesitating loyalty, the unparalleled sufferings they have endured, and the immense sacrifices they have made, it cannot be doubted that Congress will, upon proper representations, authorize the negotiation of such new treaties with them as will reinstate them in their homes, and, so far as practicable, restore them their possessions, and at the same time provide for the punishment of those of their race who shall be found guilty of instigating and promoting treason.

DAKOTA SUPERINTENDENCY

With the exception of the Sioux our relations with the Indians of this superintendency remain friendly. The principal tribes within its limits are the Sioux, Poncas, Gros Ventres, Mandans, Arickarees, Assinaboins, Blackfeet, and Crows. The only tribes with which we have treaties, other than of amity, are the Blackfeet, the Yancton Sioux, and the Poncas, each of which are located upon reservations. Under the efficient management of Agents Burleigh and Hoffman, the Yanctons and Poncas are rapidly improving their condition. Each of the seven bands composing the Yanctons have now a good farm under cultivation, upon which good crops have been raised during the past season, mainly by Indian labor. These Indians are fast learning to appreciate the importance of agriculture as a means of subsistence, and there can be but little doubt that within a few years, by judicious management, they will be prepared to receive and hold their lands in severalty, and thenceforth need but little of the supervisory care of the government.

Upon the Poncas reservation some five hundred acres of land are in cultivation, a fair crop has been raised during the past season, the Indians have been successful in their hunts, and ample preparations have been made to supply their wants during the coming winter. Very considerable additions have been made to the agency buildings; the chiefs have comfortable houses; many of the Indians are beginning to build; their school building will soon be completed and their school in operation; so that, upon the whole, the affairs of the tribe were never in a more promising condition.

The reports of Agents Latta and Reed, to be found among the accompanying papers, present, in detail, much interesting information concerning all the other tribes of the superintendency. It will be seen that, with the exception of various bands of Sioux, the time has fully arrived when it is not only practicable but very desirable that treaties should be made with these various tribes of Indians. They are an intelligent and friendly people, well disposed toward the white man, anxious to enter into more intimate relations with the government, and affording great evidence of their capacity to rapidly attain a respectable knowledge of aspects of civilization. When it is remembered that the Yanctons and Poncas have been upon their reservations but three years, prior to which their condition was similar to that of the other tribes of Dakota, and their present is contrasted with their former condition, the great advantages of the reservation system are at once apparent. I feel well assured that, with the exception of the Sioux, treaties might easily be negotiated with all the tribes of this superintendency, which could be alike beneficial to the Indians and the white settlers. The Territory is but recently organized and as yet but sparsely settled. At present, suitable reservations upon which to concentrate the Indians may easily be obtained. A few years hence the presence of settlers will render it more difficult. By acting promptly we may not only obtain locations best adapted to the wants of the Indians, but shall also avoid the vexations and trouble always attendant upon an attempt to appropriate to Indian purposes any part of the public domain upon which our own people have settled.

The Sioux of Dakota, who must not be confounded with those of Minnesota, number some thirteen thousand. They are among the most warlike and powerful of the tribes of the continent. They abound in everything which constitutes the wealth of wild Indians; have an abundance of horses; are expert riders; and if once engaged in actual hostilities with the whites would be found capable of inflicting an immense amount of damage upon the frontier settlements, and in a country like theirs exceedingly troublesome to subdue.

The defiant and independent attitude they have assumed during the past season towards the whites, and especially towards their agent, warns us that not a moment should be lost in making preparation to prevent, and, if need be, resist and punish any hostile demonstration they may make. They have totally repudiated their treaty obligations, and, in my judgment, there is an abundance of reason to apprehend that they will engage in hostilities next spring. Like the southern rebels, these savage secessionists tolerate no opposition in their unfriendly attitude toward the whites. Last spring Agent Latta found between two and three thousand of these people, being portions of seven different bands, assembled at St. Pierre to meet him. When it was ascertained that he was unaccompanied by military force, Big Head, a chief of the Yanctons, and his party refused to hold council with the agent.

The chiefs and head men of the other portions of bands, after much hesitation, consented to hold a "talk." Notwithstanding the fact that Agent Latta's entire report is among the accompanying papers, I deem it proper to here insert an extract therefrom, giving the substance of this talk on the part of the Indians, that, so far as is in my power, I may obtain for it that attention which its importance seems to demand. The following is the extract:

"They stated that they regretted to see me without a military force to protect them from that portion of their several bands who were hostile to the government, and to them who were friends to the white man and desired to live in friendly relations with this government, and fulfil their treaty stipulations; that General Harney, at Pierre, in 1856, had promised them aid; that they were greatly in the minority; that that portion of their people opposed to the government were more hostile than ever before; that they had, year after year, been promised the fulfilment of this pledge; but since none had come they must now break off their friendly relations and rejoin their respective bands, as they could hold out no longer; that their lives and property were threatened in case they accepted any more goods from the government; that the small amount of annuities given them did not give satisfaction; it created discord rather than harmony, nor would it justify them to come so far to receive it; that they had been friends to the government and to all the white men; had lived up to their pledges made at Laramie in 1851, as far as was possible under the circumstances, and still desired to do so, but must henceforth be excused, unless their 'Great Father' would air them. They requested me to bring no more goods under the Fort Laramie treaty, nor would they receive those present." With the exception of the chief, Bear's Rib, they actually refused to receive the presents with which Agent Latta was provided, and which he then offered them. After much parley, Bear's Rib consented to receive that portion of the goods designed for his people, stating at the same time that he thereby endangered not only his own life, but also the lives of all his followers, and requesting that no more goods be brought unless they could have protection. A few days after this the event justified the caution of the other chiefs, and proved that the apprehensions of Bear's Rib were not unfounded. A party of Sioux came in from the prairies, assaulted and killed Bear's Rib and several of his followers, compelling the others, some two hundred and fifty in number, to scatter and flee for their lives. Not content with thus repressing every manifestation among their own people of friendly feeling towards the government, these savages have also become the terror and scourge of all the lesser tribes of the upper Missouri who dare to remain on friendly terms with the United States. All these lesser tribes represent to our agents that, because of their adherence to their treaty stipulations, they have made themselves obnoxious to the Sioux, and are in extreme danger. Many of them dare not resort to their common hunting grounds, and are hence deprived of their usual supplies and must suffer much for want of food.

These tribes all unite in an earnest appeal for that protection to which, under their treaties, they are entitled, and I am not without apprehension that, in case protection is much longer withheld, they may be compelled, in order to save their lives, to repudiate their allegiance to the United States, as, under similar circumstances, some of our citizens have been compelled to do in other parts of the country.

Governor Jayne, who is *ex officio* superintendent of Indian affairs for the Territory, all our agents, all the friendly tribes, and all the Sioux who remain friendly, unite in representing the danger of hostilities in the spring. Being thus warned, from so many sources, of the impending danger, I trust that the necessary measures will be taken to avert from Dakota the enactment of such bloody scenes as have recently been witnessed in the neighboring State of Minnesota; and am the most solicitous that ample and seasonable preparations may be made to meet the danger because I believe by such preparation the probability is that hostilities will be prevented, and our authority over the hostile Indians of Dakota re-established without a resort to actual force.

As a possible indication of the cause of our difficulties with the Sioux of Dakota, I desire to call your attention to a communication from the Hon. J. R. Giddings to the Secretary of State, and to one from the Reverend Father De Smidt to this department, both of which are among the accompanying papers.

Report of Commissioner of
Indian Affairs William P. Dole
October 31, 1863

(Excerpt from *Report for 1863*, pp. 133-46)

Commissioner Dole's reports on the Indians of the West and of the Northern and Southern superintendencies updated the sad story discussed in his 1862 report. He noted that American actions toward the California Indians had been taken "in utter disregard" of their rights and by "precisely the same means as those employed towards the wild beasts of the country." Dole's report on the loyal Indians of the Southern Superintendency occupied by the Confederate forces concluded that "no portion of our people have suffered greater calamities, have met with more overwhelming disasters, or have more heroically battled for the common interests of the country, than have the loyal Indians within its limits."

CALIFORNIA SUPERINTENDENCY

THE CONDITION of Indian affairs within this superintendency is to me far from satisfactory, and I am fully satisfied that it can be materially improved as well in regard to economy as in promoting the welfare of the Indians and ridding the whites of the inconvenience and annoyance inseparable from the present system, or rather want of system, in organization.

The State is divided into two districts, the northern and southern, involving the necessity of two superintending agents, both of whom reside at San Francisco, and both requiring offices and clerks. This, as I conceive, nearly, if not quite, doubles the expense of the service performed.

The duties of a superintendent in California, who should perform all the labor incident to that position for the entire State, would not, in my opinion, prove more onerous than are those of the respective superintendents of several of the superintendencies, and would certainly be far less so than are those of the central and southern. I see no good reason, then, why the government should be burdened with the expense of two superintendents.

Within the northern district there are four Indian reservations owned by the government, viz: Klamath, Mendocino, Nome Lacke, and Round Valley. The first three of these are almost worthless as reserves. The buildings and improvements have been suffered to fall into decay, the adjacent country is occupied and owned by whites, and many settlers, under one pretext or another, by permission of agents and without permission, have gone upon the reservations; and the result has been, that they are almost entirely

102

abandoned by the Indians, who prefer to gain a precarious living as best they may, rather than submit to those vexations and aggressions incident to so close a proximity to the whites, and often leading to arson, robberies and murder, as well on the part of the whites as the Indians. Whether the whites or the Indians are the more blamable for this state of affairs, it is very evident that these three reservations are no longer desirable for the purposes for which they were established. Were it possible to rid them of the presence of white settlers, I should still favor their abandonment, for the reason that the country immediately adjacent is occupied by whites. The constant collisions that have occurred between the two races since the settlement of the State by the whites, and the measures of retaliation adopted by each, have engendered such a feeling of hostility and vindictiveness as to render it in the highest degree improbable that the Indians would be permitted to live in peace upon these reservations, however much they might be disposed so to do.

In obedience to a resolution passed at the second session of the thirty-seventh Congress, inquiries were instituted as to the propriety of reducing the number of Indian reservations within this State, the proper locations for such as might be retained, &c. The result of this investigation was such as to induce me in making my last annual report to strongly recommend the enlargement of the Round Valley reservation, and the establishment of another at Smith's river. The reservation at Round Valley, could it be enlarged in the manner then recommended, and all the white settlers removed therefrom, would in my opinion become by far the most eligible location for Indian purposes within the limits of the northern district. It is in the interior of the State; it is not adjacent to the mineral regions. Enlarged in the manner proposed, it would be so completely shut in by mountains as to be almost inaccessible; its area would be ample for the accommodation of all the Indians in the interior and northern portions of the State. Its climate is delightful and healthy. It has some six or eight thousand acres of arable land; is well watered and timbered. The three forks of Eel river would supply an abundance of fish, and the adjacent mountainous regions would furnish the "hunting grounds" so essential to the wants of the Indian while uncivilized. The only objection to the immediate enlargement of this reservation and its occupation by the Indians is the presence of white settlers, many of whom have doubtless just and equitable titles to the homes they have acquired. From information derived through late Superintending Agent Hanson, I have no doubt that such of the settlers as have just titles to their claims could be induced to sell the same to the government upon fair terms; nor have I any doubts that the purchase of these claims, the enlargement of this reservation as suggested, and the removal therefrom of all whites, except such as are required to conduct the official business of the government with the Indians, is a part of the only feasible plan which has yet been suggested for reducing our relations with the Indians of California to an economical and satisfactory system.

I regard it as essential to a proper location of the Indians of the northern district that there should be two reservations, one to be located in the interior, and the other upon the Pacific coast. It is said to be a fact, notorious to all observers, that Indians reared in the interior, and accustomed from childhood to its products, cannot be induced to remain upon the coast; and that those raised on the coast, and accustomed to sea-fish and weed, cannot be induced to remain in the interior. For the former, Round valley is a suitable home; and for the latter, Smith River valley, or some other location, should be had.

Smith River valley is in the extreme northwest corner of the State; on its north and east encompassed by mountains, so that no whites are likely to settle within twenty or thirty miles in those directions; on the south and west is the Pacific. The only entrance to the valley is in the southeast, and this is extremely narrow, rendering it practicable to almost wholly isolate the Indians, and secure them from the pernicious results which so invariably follow a contact with the whites. In addition to this valuable consideration, to which, in my judgment, too much importance cannot be attached, the valley is well watered and timbered, and has a suitable amount of arable land, while the adjacent mountains furnish an abundance of game, and the Pacific the best of fisheries. Government is now paying rent for the cultivated land of this valley at the rate of five dollars per acre, a price enormously disproportioned to the value of the improved land, all of which can be purchased, as I am informed, at rates averaging a little less than twelve dollars per acre. I know of no way to avoid these exorbitant charges for rent, except by the purchase of the land, or the establishment of a reservation at some other point upon the coast.

I have no doubt that, by timely action, we may yet secure for these people a home in the land of their birth, and feel that I should illy discharge my duty if I failed to urge upon you, and through you upon Congress, the importance of immediate action. Unless a tract of country is soon set apart for the use of the Indians, and its title secured to them, every available portion will be occupied by whites, and the Indians driven, by inevitable necessity, into a life of vagabondage and crime, resulting in constant annoyance and vexation to the whites, in frequent collisions between the two races, and, I fear, at last in the extinction of the red race.

On the 13th of January last I submitted for your consideration a communication from Superintending Agent Wentworth, informing me that hostilities had, to some extent, commenced with the Indians inhabiting that part of California known as the Owen's River valley, and expressing, in the strongest manner, his apprehensions that a general war would ensue with those Indians unless immediate measures should be adopted by Congress, having for their object the pacification of the Indians, and the securing to them of some portion of the home of their ancestors, where they could live unmolested by the whites. I regret to say that the apprehensions of Superintending Agent Wentworth have since been fully realized. The course of events in this valley is a forcible illustration of the wisdom and importance of entering into treaty relations with the wild Indians of our territories, prior to the occupation of their country. Here was a country extending from the eastern slope of the Sierra Nevada to the great desert, inhabited by several thousands of wild and warlike Indians, with whom we have hitherto failed to establish amicable relations, or, indeed, to hold any official intercourse whatever. The country had been in the unmolested possession of this people for generations, and was ample for their sustenance and support. In an evil day for them, it is discovered that their mountain gulches and ravines abound in the precious metals, and forthwith, in utter disregard of the rights of the Indians, and by resorting to precisely the same means as those employed towards the wild beasts of the country, a tide of emigration sets in upon them and begins to despoil them of their homes, the graves of their ancestors, and the means of supplying their rude and simple wants. Surely, it could not be supposed that all this could be accomplished without any manifestations of opposition and hostility on the part of the Indians; and it cannot be doubted that, aside from the humanitarian and moral aspects of the subject, it would have been far more economical had we treated with these Indians; obtained from them by fair purchase such portions of their country as are desirable for our people; secured to the Indians a location where they could live in peace, and where we could gradually subject them to those influences which would, in the end, reclaim them from their wild and barbarous modes of life. All this, I fully believe, might have been done if we had been prompt to recognize the rights of the Indians, and to prepare them for the occupation of their country. The opportunity has now passed, and it is probably not an overestimate to say that, besides the valuable lives of our own citizens as well as the lives of the Indians that have already been sacrificed, we have already expended and incurred liabilities in our military operations against these Indians more than double the amount that would have been required to establish relations with them upon the basis of a firm and lasting friendship.

I have no doubt that hostilities may yet be terminated in this region much more speedily by negotiation than by military power, and that thousands of treasure and many valuable lives may be saved. I trust that the subject will receive from Congress the consideration its importance demands, and that such legislation may be had as will not only result in a speedy termination of these troubles, but will also harmonize the conflicting interests of the whites and Indians throughout the State, and produce in the conduct of our Indian relations that order and system which is so imperatively demanded.

New Mexico

The principal tribes of this superintendency are the Navajoes, the Apaches, and the Utahs. The Navajoes occupy the western portion of the Territory, and are the most powerful and hostile tribe within its limits. But little progress has been made in reducing them to submission to the authority of our government, and they prove themselves a source of constant vexation and alarm to all our exposed settlements. The nature of the country and the character of their organization is such that it has hitherto been found impossible, with the forces sent against them, to produce any permanent and decisive results. Their country abounds in mountain fastnesses, rendering it extremely difficult for any adequate military force to pursue them to their retreats, or inflict upon them a blow which has any considerable effect in breaking their power.

They are represented as an ingenious and skilful people in manufacturing blankets and other fabrics, in the cultivation of wheat and corn, and as being in all other respects far in advance of all other tribes within the Territory.

The Apaches consist of three bands, viz: Jicarillas, occupying the northeastern portion of the Territory; the Mescaleros, occupying the southeastern portion, and the Gila Apaches the extreme southwest. With the exception of some four hundred of the Mescaleros, who are located at Bosque Rodondo, under charge of Agent Labadi, these Indians are also hostile, and constantly engaging in the commission of depredations against the whites. The four hundred above mentioned have, during the past season, under the immediate supervision of their agent, cultivated some two hundred acres of land, and at last accounts had a prospect of an abundant harvest, the result mainly of their own labor.

The Utahs of this superintendency are also divided into three bands, one located in the northeastern part of the Territory, and the other two in the northwestern. They are a powerful and warlike race, are expert hunters, and manifest but little disposition to abandon their ancient customs and modes of life. A few of them have, however, manifested a disposition to engage in agricultural pursuits.

The Indians known as Pueblos are an agricultural people, possessing many excellent traits of character. They are unwavering in their loyalty and devotion to the government, and have proven of inestimable service in protecting the frontier settlements.

In my former annual reports I have called attention to the imperative necessity of concentrating the powerful and warlike Indians of this superintendency upon suitable reservations. It is now fifteen years since we acquired possession of the Territory, and, so far as I can judge, the security and protection afforded by government to the lives and property of our citizens is but little if any better than at the outset. Hitherto there seems to have been no systematic policy pursued in the government and control of the Indians. They have been permitted to roam almost at will throughout the Territory, and have engaged in the commission of innumerable depredations upon the property, liberty, and lives of the white inhabitants. Doubtless many of their acts of hostility have resulted from wanton attacks upon them on the part of the whites, but many more have resulted from the occupation of their country by whites who have driven out the game upon which, to a great extent, they were accustomed to rely for subsistence, thus reducing them to want, and impelling them to resort to plunder, and this in its turn leading to measures of retaliation. Occasionally, outrages of unusual enormity are perpetrated, and these are followed by military expeditions against the Indians, which usually result in nothing more than the killing or capture of a few Indians, and the destruction of some of their villages, leaving the power of the Indians almost unimpaired, and the general insecurity as great as before.

Superintendent Steck asserts, and he claims to have reliable authority for the statement, that not less than three millions of dollars have been annually expended since our acquisition of the Territory in maintaining its military organizations, which, with the exception of repelling the Texas invasion of last year, have done nothing aside from these occasional expeditions against the Indians. It is also estimated that during the past three years not less than five hundred thousand sheep, and five thousand cattle, mules, and horses have been killed or stolen by the Indians. To this large account must also be added the lives of our citizens that have been sacrificed, the sufferings of others who have been carried into captivity, and the general insecurity which prevails throughout the Territory to such an extent that it is said there is not a single county that is absolutely secure. Surely a policy, or, I should rather say, a want of policy, which is so enormously expensive as this, so fruitless of good results, and which promises so little for the future, either in improving the condition of our own people or that of the Indians, ought to be abandoned at once and forever, and some system adopted from which better results may be reasonably anticipated.

I have heretofore urged the propriety of recognizing the right of the Indians to a qualified ownership of the soil, and treating with them for its extinction in such portions as may be required for the purposes of settlement, thereby providing a fund from which the Indians may derive such assistance as may be necessary, while acquiring a sufficient knowledge of the arts of civilization, to enable them to provide for their wants. I am still of the opinion that this is much the best policy to pursue towards the Indians in providing for their wants when located upon reservations, for, in the first place, it is attended with the same expense whether we assign them a tract of land, and then, by direct appropriations, provide for their necessities, or treating with them for their claim to the territory we extinguish their title to such portions as we desire, they retaining the same tract that would otherwise be assigned to them, and receiving for the lands surrendered the moneys which must otherwise be appropriated to enable them to live; and, secondly, it would preserve in the Indian his native pride and independence, since, instead of feeling that his freedom to roam at will had been restrained by arbitrary and resistless power, and he compelled to relinquish the homes and customs of his ancestors, he would realize that the change had been wrought by fair negotiations to which he was a party, and that, for the rights and privileges surrendered, he had received a fair equivalent. Whether the one method or the other shall be preferred, I think it perfectly evident that we shall be guilty of little less than criminal neglect if we longer delay the adoption of such measures as will result in the concentration of the Indians upon suitable reservations, and to this end I earnestly invite your cooperation in an endeavor to procure the passage of a joint resolution by Congress, at its approaching session, authorizing either the negotiation of treaties having for their object the establishing of the Indians upon three suitable reservations, of which one for the Utahs shall be in the northern or northwestern portion of the Territory, one for the Apaches in the southeastern, and one for the Navajoes in the western, or empowering the President, by proclamation, to set apart suitable tracts for such reservations, and vesting the title to the same in the respective tribes for which they are designed. As to the Pueblos, I believe they may safely be left, with temporary appropriations for their benefit, to the operation of the present Territorial and future State laws.

If action such as or similar to that I have indicated can be had from Congress, I have the fullest confidence that in a very few years it will prove of inestimable value alike to the Indians and the whites of New Mexico.

COLORADO

Considerable excitement has existed at various times during the past year on account of apprehended outbreaks on the part of the Indians of this Territory, caused mainly by reports of depredations committed by them in various parts of the superintendency, but upon pursuit of the marauders by the military it was ascertained, in every instance, that the depredations were committed by small bands of roving Indians, for which no tribe, as such, could be justly held accountable.

It appears from the report of Governor Evans, who is ex officio superintendent of Indian affairs for the Territory, that most of the Indians within its limits are divided into small bands, who lead a nomadic or wandering life in quest of the means of subsistence, and that although the tribes are numerous, and if closely united would be exceedingly formidable, there is not that unity of action and purpose as between the different bands composing a tribe that is elsewhere observed among Indians. This peculiarity is especially true of the Cheyennes and Arapahoes. It was, doubtless, in a great measure, owing to this that numbers of the bands were not included in the negotiations attending the treaty concluded with them at Fort Wise, whence arises the claim they so persistently urge that their right to roam at will throughout a country at least a thousand miles in extent has never been relinquished. An attempt was made, during the past season, to convene a general council of the disaffected bands with a view to obtaining their assent to the treaty, but, notwithstanding the most persevering efforts on the part of Governor Evans and the various agents, it failed, the various bands upon one pretext or another failing to attend the council. Measures have now been taken to accomplish the same object, by securing the assent, from time to time, of the several bands, and it is hoped that in this manner we may be able finally to induce all to concentrate upon the reservation, and become subject to the provisions of the treaty.

The Cheyennes and Arapahoes, who are parties to the treaty of 1861, are located upon the reservation bearing their name, and are under charge of Agent Colley. Their surveys have been completed; preparations are also made for the irrigation of their lands, and the construction of other improvements required by their treaty, and we have reason to believe that the reservation will soon be in successful operation. In addition to the Indians of this reservation, there are also under charge of Agent Colley several hundred Caddoes, who are refugees driven from the Indian Territory on account of their loyalty, and for whom a location has been selected on the Arkansas river, near the crossing of the Santa Fe route, and arrangements are being made to enable them to engage in agricultural pursuits. The good character of these Indians, and the progress they have made in the knowledge of industrial pursuits, are such that their example cannot fail to prove beneficial to the Indians in their vicinity.

The Kiowas and Comanches are likewise under charge of Agent Colley. They reside in the southeastern portion of the Territory, and for many years have been extremely troublesome to, and have committed many outrages and depradations upon, the emigrant routes leading through their country. During the past summer a delegation of their chiefs and headmen visited this city, and a treaty was concluded with them by which the right to establish mail stations at the rate of one for each twenty miles of the routes leading through their country, and the safe transit of emigrants, is secured, and the Indians agree to refrain from camping along such routes, and to protect the same so far as may be in their power from the depredations of other Indians. This treaty will in due time be laid before you for transmission to the President and Senate.

In consequence of the great extent of the country occupied by the numerous small bands of Indians in the eastern and southeastern portions of this superintendency, it is exceedingly difficult for the agent now in charge to attend promptly to the exigencies of the service, which, from time to time, require his attention at different and remote points. For this reason I respectfully recommend that Congress be requested by you to authorize the appointment of another agent to be stationed at or near Fort Larned, and to have under his charge the Indians of that vicinity.

A valuable and very interesting report from John G. Nicolay, esq., private secretary to the President, who was appointed as secretary to the commissioners selected to attempt a negotiation of a treaty with the Utahs of Colorado, New Mexico, and Utah, will be found among the accompanying papers. It will be seen that by the treaty negotiated with the Tabequache band of Utahs, as above stated, the Indian title is extinguished to one among the largest and most valuable tracts of land ever ceded to the United States. It includes nearly all the important settlements thus far made in Colorado, and all the valuable mining districts discovered up to this time. Its importance in establishing friendly relations with these intelligent, powerful, and warlike Indians, in securing the lives and property of our settlers, and in promoting the peace and prosperity of the Territory, cannot be overestimated. I invite especial attention to the remarks of Mr. Nicolay upon the importance of an early ratification of the treaty, and promptness in carrying its provisions into effect. The treaty will be duly laid before you for transmission to the President and Senate, and will, I trust, receive that early and favorable consideration to which, in my judgment, it is entitled, as well on account of the intrinsic justness of its provisions as of the magnitude of the interests involved.

Dakota Superintendency

The condition of affairs in this superintendency is very far from satisfactory, whether it be regarded with reference to those tribes with which treaty relations have been established, or those with which no treaties other than of amity have been negotiated.

Of the former class are the Poncas, Yancton Sioux, Blackfeet, Sioux of Minnesota, and Winnebagoes; of the latter are the Sioux, Gros Ventres, Mandans, Arickarees, Assinaboines, and Crows. It will be remembered that at the date of my last annual report, the condition of the Poncas was never more flattering. Their crops of the preceding season had been abundant, their hunting had proven unusually successful; during the season quite a number of comfortable houses had been built, and these, together with their annuities, enabled them to pass the winter with a greater degree of comfort than ever before. With this practical demonstration of the advantages resulting from the change in their former mode of life, the Poncas last spring entered upon the labor of raising a new crop with increased confidence. Their grounds were ploughed, and their seeds planted in due season and in good order, but unfortunately a drought set in in the midst of the planting season, which in its severity and duration has been unexampled for many years, and has resulted in an utter prostration of their high hopes. Their crops being planted, they started at the usual season upon their summer hunt, in which they were unsuccessful, and from which they returned to find their crops withered and dried, and almost nothing at the reservation to relieve their pressing necessities. The agent has done all in his power with the means at his command for their relief. His means, however, were wholly inadequate to supply the unusual and unexpected demand, and the condition of the Indians is now pitiable in the extreme. Should their fall hunt prove unsuccessful, they will seek assistance at the hands of the Omahas, and such measures will be taken by this department for their relief as may be found practicable.

The conduct of the Poncas, as well in the times of their prosperity as in the midst of the severe privations which have come upon them, has been unexceptionable; they are unwavering in their fidelity to their treaty, and deserve at our hands the kindest consideration.

Amicable relations have also been maintained with the Yancton Sioux during the past year. They number over two thousand, and being a portion of the great Sioux nation, some apprehensions were felt that they might join with the remainder of their people in waging war upon the whites and the friendly Indians of the Territory. These apprehensions have thus far proven groundless, which, with the younger and more restless portion of the tribe, is doubtless owing to the military forces stationed at Fort Randall, in the immediate vicinity of their reservation. During the summer a detachment of soldiers was sent from the fort in pursuit of a party of hostile savages, who had come into the settlements and stolen a number of horses. Unfortunately the soldiers came up with a party of Indians who were out hunting, and were mistaken for the Indians of whom the soldiers were in pursuit. The Indians were at once made prisoners, and while endeavoring to escape seven of them were killed. It afterwards appeared that the whole party was composed of friendly Indians, some of whom were Yanctons, the others of the Two Kettles band of Sioux. The circumstance naturally created great excitement among these friendly Indians, but the mistake being promptly explained, and such reparation made as was practicable, the excitement subsided without a hostile outbreak, and it is believed that, notwithstanding the hostile attitude of other Indians within the Territory, peace will be maintained. The Yanctons, like their neighbors the Poncas, were very successful in their farming operations of last year, and, like them, have suffered severely from the drought of the past summer, but being more wealthy, and having had good success in their hunts, it is believed that with the supplies already provided by their agent they will be enabled to pass the winter without any great amount of suffering.

The Sioux and Winnebagoes, removed from Minnesota under the act of Congress passed at its last session, although within the limits of this superintendency, are included in that portion of this report which relates to the northern superintendency, they being still under the charge of Superintendent Thompson.

In regard to the friendly Indians of the Upper Missouri and Blackfeet agencies, I am able to give you but little information, for the reason that the agents, as hereafter stated, were unable to reach and remain at their posts.

Referring to my last annual report, it will be seen that at that date we were warned by Governor Jayne, then ex officio superintendent of Indian affairs for Dakota, by each of our agents, and by all the friendly Indians, that the danger of hostilities on the part of the Sioux was imminent, and that nothing but the most prompt action on our part would be efficient in averting so great a calamity. These various warnings were, however, suffered to pass unheeded, and no measures adopted looking to an effort to adjust the disturbed relations between this powerful and disaffected nation and the general government. Since that time, the Sioux, driven from Minnesota in consequence of the horrible atrocities perpetrated by them in that State during the autumn of last year, have taken refuge among their brethren of

Dakota, and neither expecting nor deserving forbearance at our hands until they have received the chastisement their crimes have merited, they have doubtless done all in their power, and it would appear with success, to induce their brethren to make common cause with them in an endeavor to exterminate or drive all whites from the Territory.

A very large proportion of the Sioux of Dakota were already hostile, or at least far from friendly, and the remainder or friendly portion being deprived of that protection to which under the provisions of the Fort Laramie treaty of 1851 they were entitled, and being in the minority, have now doubtless yielded to the various influences brought to bear upon them, and we now have upon our hands, in addition to the great rebellion, an Indian war of no mean proportions.

In January last, and again in March, I forwarded to you copies of communications received at this office, representing in the strongest manner the urgent necessity for the immediate establishing of military posts upon the Upper Missouri. These communications were by you laid before the War Department, from which I learned through you, on the 26th of March last, that the subject had been referred to the commander of that military department for the necessary action. What action was had I am uninformed, but certain it is that the posts were not established, nor were Agents Latta and Reed enabled to obtain an escort to accompany them to their respective agencies.

It is understood that the expedition under Brigadier General Sully, in consequence of the extreme drought, and the burning of the prairies by the retreating Indians, was only able to proceed to a point about sixty miles above Fort Pierre, and was therefore prevented from inflicting any considerable damage upon or crippling the power of the hostile Indians; nor can I learn that the campaign under General Sibley has been productive of any very favorable results, the probability being that another campaign will be indispensable.

No military posts have been established upon the Upper Missouri, the friendly Indians and the few whites are left without protection, and it is to be feared that many thousands of the Indians, who under other circumstances would have continued faithful to their amicable relations, will be compelled to side with those in hostility, to escape the consequences of their well-known policy of treating as enemies all who are not identified with them.

The boat conveying the annuity goods was unable to ascend the Missouri beyond Fort Union, in consequence of the extremely low water, so that the goods designed for the Blackfeet agency were necessarily stored at that point, and cannot be distributed before spring. Most of the goods designed for the Indians, under charge of Agent Latta, were distributed, but with the characteristic perfidy of Indians in hostility, it is believed that a majority of the Indians receiving them were afterwards engaged in an attack upon the boat with the design of murdering the crew and passengers, and capturing the goods designed for the Blackfeet agency.

It will thus be seen that the failure to establish military posts upon the Upper Missouri, together with the severe and almost unexampled drought, have resulted in an almost complete loss of the controlling influence we have heretofore held upon the Indians of that country, and that as a consequence the important and most direct route of the emigration setting in upon Idaho, by reason of the newly discovered and immense gold-bearing districts of that Territory, is cut off.

I am not without hope that the immense sacrifices of life and treasure which will result from a general war with the numerous and powerful tribes of that country may yet be averted by timely and peaceful negotiation, and am confident that at least the proportions of the struggle may be very materially reduced; and to this end I respectfully recommend to you, and through you to Congress and the War Department, the importance of establishing military posts along the Missouri, from the western limits of the State up to and including Fort Benton, at the earliest practicable moment, and that adequate measures be adopted to enable this department in the early spring to effect such negotiations with the tribes in hostility as may be found practicable and consistent with a just and honorable peace.

SOUTHERN SUPERINTENDENCY

This is by far the most important of our various superintendencies, whether it be considered with reference to its numbers, wealth, geographical position, or to the present condition of the Indians within its limits, their wants, their future prospects, and the careful consideration required in adopting a policy which shall at the same time prove just, generous, and humane towards those who have remained firm in their loyalty and allegiance to the federal government and to their treaty stipulations, and shall mete out the punishment their treason deserves to those who, unmindful of either, have taken arms against our authority.

The reports of the superintendent, the agents, and employes of this superintendency, to be found among the accompanying papers, possess an unusual degree of interest. A careful perusal of these reports, and those made during the existence of the present rebellion, will, I think, demonstrate that no portion of our people have suffered greater calamities, have met with more overwhelming disasters, or have more heroically battled for the common interests of the country, than have the loyal Indians within its limits. Possessing one of the most beautiful, fertile, and desirable portions of our country, and almost completely removed from the baneful effects so often attendant upon close proximity to white settlements, many of them were, prior to the rebellion, in the quiet enjoyment of most of the comforts and conveniences of civilized life; the various tribes were at peace with each other, and the whole people were presenting unmistakable evidences of improvement, thrift, and prosperity. During the vicissitudes of the war they have been visited by its direst calamities. They have been robbed, plundered, and murdered, their homes burned, their fields laid waste, their property seized and destroyed; they have been compelled to flee from their country, and from a condition of plenty and independence they have been reduced to the most abject poverty, suffering, and distress. Nor, as before intimated, have they tamely submitted to these calamities. From the outset they have battled, and are still battling, in defence of their homes, and for a restoration of the authority of our government, with a courage and zeal that entitles them not only to our sympathy, but to the most generous consideration in the readjustment of our relations with them, which have been so wantonly disturbed, and which must be had when the present rebellion is subdued, and the blessings of peace are once more restored.

As you are aware, the most of the refugees from the "Indian country" are now located in Kansas and the country immediately south, where the old men, women, and children—all, or nearly so, of the able-bodied males being in the federal armies—are being subsisted from the funds held in trust for several of the southern tribes by the government. The formidable front elsewhere presented by the rebellion has hitherto prevented the organization of a military force sufficient to drive the rebels from the Indian country and return the Indians to their homes. It is to be hoped, now that the Mississippi has been opened, and the power of the rebels in the west and southwest seems irretrievably broken and hastening to its final overthrow, that a military expedition, adequate to "take, hold, and possess" the country, may be speedily sent thither, and the loyal Indians reinstated in the enjoyment of their possessions.

The various tribes of the superintendency are the Osages, the Quapaws, Senecas and Shawnees, the Cherokees, Creeks, Seminoles, Choctaws, Chickasaws, and the Wichitas, and other affiliated bands.

The Osages, Quapaws, Senecas, and Shawnees are under the care of Agent Elder. The Osages, with the exception of Black Dog's band, have remained loyal throughout the rebellion. In June last they captured and destroyed a party of nineteen rebels who were passing through their country, and who, by the instructions and papers found upon their persons, were fully proven to have been commissioned by the rebel authorities to enrol and organize the disloyal in Arizona and Dakota. Occupying, as they do, a position between the white settlements in the southern portion of Kansas and the region in possession of the rebels, their fidelity to the government has been of inestimable value in protecting the frontier from the incursions of rebel guerillas.

As already mentioned, a new treaty has been negotiated with the Osages, and is awaiting the action of the President and Senate. By this treaty a tract of country 30 by 50 miles in extent has been ceded to the United States, to be occupied by Indians, now resident in Kansas, who may be induced to remove to and reside upon the same. Another tract, 20 miles in width, and extending from the western boundary of the cession just named along the entire length of their northern boundary, is also ceded for settlement by whites. Very liberal provisions are also made for educational, agricultural, and other beneficial purposes. I trust this treaty will be ratified, and have no doubt that it will result in good to the Indians as well as to ourselves.

The Osages have made very considerable progress in agriculture, and are not indifferent to the subject of education. For their improvement they are greatly indebted to the zealous and humane efforts of Rev. John Shoemaker, who has established a manual labor school among them, and has devoted the best years of his life to their service.

The Quapaws are a small tribe, owning a reservation immediately south of the Osages. They justly take pride in the fact that not one of their numbers has joined with the rebels. In the spring of 1862 they were driven from their homes, and since that time they have been subsisted as other refugee Indians.

The Senecas and Shawnees, residing still further south, were, at the outset of the rebellion, forced by the rebels into an unwilling alliance, and for a time were under treaty stipulations with them, from whom they received one instalment of their stipulated annuities. At the first appearance, however, of the federal forces, they threw off the authority of the rebels and returned to their allegiance. They, as well as the Quapaws, are now temporarily located upon the lands of the Ottawas, in Kansas, and no doubts are entertained as to their fidelity and future loyalty.

The Seminoles, at the last reliable census, numbered something over two thousand two hundred. This was prior to the breaking out of the rebellion. There are now in camp near Neosho Falls, under the charge of Agent Snow, six hundred and seventy-two, mostly women and children, the able-bodied men having joined the Union forces. It is estimated that about two-thirds of the tribe have remained loyal.

The Wichitas, and other bands affiliated with them, numbering about nineteen hundred souls, are now encamped near Belmont, Kansas, and are under charge of Agent Carruth. One of these bands, viz: the Tonkawas, under the leadership of a former United States agent, joined with the rebels at an early day, and endeavored to draw with them all the other bands. These machinations at length resulted in a battle, at which their former agent, with the entire rebel band, were exterminated, with the single exception of one old woman rescued by a Shawnee chief.

The Cherokees, prior to the rebellion, were the most numerous, intelligent, wealthy, and influential tribe of this superintendency. For many months they steadily resisted the efforts made by the rebels to induce them to abandon their allegiance to the federal government, but being wholly unprotected, and without the means of resistance, they were finally compelled to enter into treaty stipulations with the rebel authorities. This connexion was, however, of short duration, for upon the first appearance of United States forces in their country an entire regiment of Indian troops, raised ostensibly for service in the rebel army, deserted and came over to us, and have ever since been under our command, and upon all occasions have proven themselves faithful and efficient soldiers.

In February last the national council of the Cherokees was convened at Cowskin Prairie, and the following important bills were passed:

1. Abrogating the treaty with the "Confederate States," and calling a general convention of the people to approve the act.

2. The appointment of a delegation, with suitable powers and instructions to represent the Cherokee nation before the United States government, consisting of John Ross, principal chief; Lieutenant Colonel Downing, Captain James McDaniel, and Rev. Evan Jones.

3. Authorizing a general Indian council, to be called at such time and place as the principal chief may designate.

4. Deposing all officers of the nation disloyal to the government.

5. Approving the purchase of supplies made by the treasurer, and directing their distribution.

6. An act providing for the abolition of slavery in the Cherokee nation.

An official communication, informing me of these important acts on the part of the Cherokee authorities, will be found among the accompanying papers. Their importance, as affecting the Status of the only part of the nation whose rights have not been clearly forfeited by treason, will be generally appreciated when I mention the fact that for many years the Cherokees have had a regularly organized government, a printed code of laws, and have conducted their political affairs with a good degree of the order and system of civilized communities.

Until the autumn of 1862 only about three hundred of the Cherokees, and they mostly women and children, had taken refuge in Kansas. In the early part of that season from fifteen hundred to two thousand others, also in the main women and children, and claiming our protection, made their way to a point on the Cherokee neutral lands, about twelve miles south of Fort Scott, Kansas. Like all the other refugees, they were almost entirely destitute of all the necessaries of life, and required immediate assistance. Arrangements were immediately made by Superintendent Coffin to provide for their wants during the ensuing winter, so far as the limited means at his command would permit. These arrangements were scarcely completed when, without consultation with this department, or, so far as I am informed, authority from other sources, the military authorities assumed the control of the Indians, and late in the fall, or early part of the winter, removed them to Neosho, Missouri. This movement was unfortunate in conception and execution, the ostensible object being to return the fugitives to their homes. It not only failed in its object but has added immensely to the already heavy expense of subsisting the Indians. Assurances were given that two armies—one to move from Springfield, Missouri, under command of General Blunt, the other from Scott's Mills, under command of Colonel Phillips—were about to march through the Cherokee country on their way to the southwest. Relying upon promises that the Indians should not only be safely conducted to their country, but that a sufficient force should be stationed there for their protection while raising their crops, the Indians, under charge of Agent Harlan, were furnished with agricultural implements and seeds, and in March last proceeded to Talequah, reaching that point at the same time with the military expedition under Colonel Phillips.

They immediately scattered throughout the country, planted their crops, and had but fairly commenced their cultivation when the rebels made their appearance in such force that they, as well as the troops under Colonel Phillips, were compelled to take refuge at Fort Gibson. Their numbers were now increased to some six thousand by the addition of others, who, until then had remained at their homes, but were now compelled to flee, as the rebels overran the entire country, seizing everything of value that could be found, and destroying everything they could not convert to their own use. Thus this ill-advised and most unfortunate expedition terminated, leaving the Indians still more destitute than before their high hopes again prostrated, and they compelled to spend another season in want and idleness. They were now far removed from their source of supplies, which could only be furnished by transportation through a country so infested by guerrillas and bushwhackers that nothing could reach them without an escort of troops. This has more than doubled the expense of their subsistence and has exhausted the means at my disposal applicable to that purpose. Unless a liberal appropriation shall be made for their relief at an early date by Congress at its approaching session, their sufferings during the coming winter will be beyond the power of description, and many of them must perish of exposure and starvation. I trust that the urgent appeals in their behalf of their agent and the superintendent, to which I invite your especial attention, will not pass unheeded.

Something over three thousand of the Creek nation are now at the Sac and Fox reservation, in Kansas. As with the other refugees, so it is with these. Their numbers are almost exclusively composed of women and children, nearly every able-bodied man being in the Union army. In addition to the refugees at this point, there are very considerable numbers at Fort Gibson, who, at the memorable and terrible flight of these people in the winter of 1861–'62, were left behind, and afterwards took refuge in the country of the Cherokees, and with them were subsequently compelled to flee for protection to Fort Gibson.

These people, prior to the rebellion, were second to no community west of the Mississippi in point of wealth. They held large numbers of slaves, and many of them owned droves of cattle numbered by thousands. Their country is considered one of the finest agricultural and grazing regions within our borders, and has proven to the rebels a source of immense supplies for their armies.

Since my last annual report their old chief, O-poth-la-ya-ho-la, has deceased. During the last half century the influence of this chief has been second to no other among the southern tribes. He was ever the firm and unwavering friend of the whites, and to his influence, as much as that of any other man, is due the fact that so great a proportion of his people have never hesitated in their loyalty.

Believing that the treaty recently negotiated with the Creeks is just in its provisions, and imbodies a policy which, so far as practicable, should be adopted by the United States in readjusting its relations with the tribes of this superintendency, I bespeak for it a careful consideration. Its main features are as follows:

First. Perpetual peace between the contracting parties, and between the Creeks and other Indians, the United States stipulating that all necessary protection shall be furnished to secure the Creeks from hostilities on the part of other Indians.

Second. The "necessity, justice, and humanity" of the emancipation proclamation of January 1, 1863, is expressly recognized, and the Creeks solemnly covenant that henceforth slavery in their midst shall cease, and agree to set apart a suitable portion of their country for the occupation of the freed men, and all others of the African race who shall be permitted to settle among them.

Third. A cession of about seven hundred square miles of their territory for the use and occupation of such other tribes now resident in the States and territories as may hereafter be agreed upon, for which the United States agree to pay them five percent per annum on the sum of two hundred thousand dollars in money, or such mechanical or other useful articles as may be determined upon by the Secretary of the Interior, and to guarantee them the quiet possession of the remainder of their country.

Fourth. A provision for an equitable compensation of the loyal, and none other, for such losses of property (*other than slaves*) as they have sustained in consequence of the rebellion, and our failure to comply with former treaty stipulations.

Fifth. The utter exclusion of all persons who have engaged in the rebellion from all offices of profit and trust in the nation.

The Chickasaws and Choctaws, until recently, have been supposed to be almost unanimously in favor of the rebellion, only about three hundred of the latter having come within our lines. These are now upon the Sac and Fox reservation, under charge of Agent Coleman. With them, as with all the other refugees, the change from the comfortable houses, the abundant supply of fruits, vegetables, fresh meats, and, indeed, all other necessaries of life which they enjoyed in their own country, to their present mode of life, has been productive of much sickness and mortality. I am, happy, however, to state that their health has been much improved during the past season.

Recent information from refugees and other sources, believed by Colonel Phillips and others to be entirely reliable, indicates that a strong Union element exists among the Chickasaws and Choctaws; that Union leagues are formed in their midst, and that a very considerable portion of the people are prepared to throw off the authority of the rebels as soon as a Union force shall appear. It is said that even now the rebel authorities are obliged to keep a battalion of troops constantly stationed in their country to watch the movements of our friends.

I have now, so far as I can from the information in my possession, presented the present condition of the various tribes of this superintendency, and in closing this portion of my report desire to invite your attention to the singular unanimity with which the agents and superintendent join in urging the importance of the prompt return to and protection of the loyal Indians in the possession of their homes. No one who has not visited and conversed with these destitute people can fully appreciate their intense desire and longing for a return to the country from which they have been driven. The indescribable sufferings and privations they have endured, the sacrifices they have made, the patience with which they have submitted to the dire evils which have come upon them, and, above all, the heroism, fidelity, and zeal with which nearly every able-bodied man among them has fought for our common cause, fully demonstrate their loyalty and devotion to the government, and justly entitle them to the most generous consideration. The present indications are that the power of this most unrighteous rebellion is broken, and that it is fast hastening to its complete and final overthrow. I must trust that no delay will be permitted, or effort spared, in an endeavor to wrest the homes of these people from the hands of their spoilers, and, so far as may be in our power, restore them to the comforts of their former possessions.

Report of Commissioner
of Indian Affairs D. N. Cooley
October 31, 1865

(Excerpt from *Report for 1865*, pp. 200-10)

Cooley assumed the duties of commissioner only a few months before submitting his first annual report, yet his account of the Indians of the Southern Superintendency showed great insight and understanding. The ravages of war in the Indian Territory and the divisive struggles between the loyal and disloyal factions of the Five Civilized Tribes were clearly outlined. The uncertain obligation of the United States to the Indians— to those who fought for the Union and against it—was also discussed.

SOUTHERN SUPERINTENDENCY

AT THE PERIOD of the last annual report from this office, affairs in this superintendency, comprising what is known as the "Indian country," south of Kansas, together with the Osages along the southern border of that State, were still in the confused and discouraging condition which necessarily resulted from the war. Portions of the country about Forts Gibson and Smith, and the travelled route for government trains from the north to those posts, were held by United States troops; and a portion of the Indians, who had remained loyal to the government, were attempting to subsist themselves in the neighborhood of the above forts. Many of the able-bodied men of the loyal sections of the tribes were in the United States service as soldiers, but many thousands of the people were, in Kansas and portions of the Indian country, subsisted at the expense of the funds which, if the tribes had remained steadfast to the Union, would have gone to them as annuities. Serious complaints were being made to the department that stock owned by Indians, and necessary for their subsistence, and the small crops of corn raised by those who had been able to till the ground, were being taken from them by unprincipled speculators. Some of the military officers had laid the blame for this state of things upon the Indian agents, but an investigation of these charges showed them to be without foundation. The most stringent rules and regulations in regard to the sale of stock from the Indian country were adopted and issued, but it is apparent that the practice of running stock out of the country has continued, the keenness of the speculators enabling them to elude the vigilance of the officers, and it is believed that an immense amount of such stolen stock has been purchased at large prices by the government. The information obtained by Superintendent Sells, as given in his report, furnishes some idea of the enormous extent as well as profit of the business, where contractors obtain ready sale for the plunder at such rates as they have received from the government. The reports of Agents Harlan and Reynolds throw further light upon the subject, and it is gratifying to know that by their efforts, aided in good earnest by the military force put at their disposal by Major General Mitchell, who has shown every disposition to assist them, much has been done towards breaking up this nefarious traffic. It is manifest, however, that something more is needed in the form of legislation. Superintendent Sells informs us that the system of plunder is thoroughly organized, having its grade, of agents and participants, from the reckless and daring scouts and drivers, who are well acquainted with the country, and who steal and run off the cattle to the Kansas line, up through the agents of the contractors, who receive and arrange fraudulent bills of sale for them, to men of higher position in the social scale, who, incited by avarice, have seized with avidity this disgraceful means of gain. In fact, it appears as if an obliquity of conscience had affected the whole community on the border, for the great majority of the people seemed to favor the speculation, or regard it with indifference.

In confirmation of the estimate made by the superintendent as to the extent of this traffic, the position and influence, civil and military, of the persons engaged in it, the difficulty of preventing its continuance and of punishing its operators, I here subjoin brief extracts from a report which has just been received from Lieutenant George Williams, who was some time since detailed by the War Department to investigate these matters, under instructions from this office.

After alluding to the large number of persons who have made independent fortunes in the business, he says:

"Not content with having this odium attached to their own names, having carried it on so successfully and without interruption from those in authority, who knew of the whole transaction in this line, but who were too deeply interested themselves to try any measures to put a stop to it, they have induced men by the hundred to go down into the Indian territory and steal and drive out cattle," &c.

Again: "The military force sent into this State for the protection of these Indians have been the agents through whom a great portion of the stealing has been accomplished," &c.

After giving the names of some thirty or forty prominent men, merchants, military officers, Indian agents, traders and others, whom he charges directly with being implicated in this traffic in one way or another, Lieutenant Williams says:

"The above-mentioned parties and their allies, the cattle thieves, have been engaged in the business since 1862, and I have evidence against most of them in my possession, but there is scarcely if any use to attempt to prosecute them before any court in Kansas, because they openly make their boasts that they can buy men enough to swear anything they want them to, and I know they speak the truth from experience."

As to the extent of the business: "In my opinion, during the past four years there have been at least 300,000 head of cattle stolen from the Indian territory, a country at one time rich in their cattle possessions, and now scarcely a head can be seen in a ride of 200 miles."

The very late arrival of Lieutenant Williams's report, just as I am about closing this paper, makes it impossible for me to give it, with the voluminous accompanying testimony, sufficient examination to enable me to form a judgment as to whether the testimony fully supports the sweeping charges made by him, but I do not therefore feel at liberty to incorporate his report and testimony among the documents to be published with this report, but submit the papers for your information, and for such directions as you may see proper to communicate after having given them examination. I will only remark, that so far as the charges implicate any of the agents or employés of this bureau, every possible effort will be made to ascertain their truth, and bring to justice any that are found guilty.

The law enacted by the last Congress on this subject provides only for the punishment of those who actually drive or remove "any cattle, horses, or other stock from the Indian territory for the purpose of trade or commerce." This does not seem to reach the case of those who deal in the stolen property, and it is to be hoped that the wisdom of the next Congress will provide a more stringent act, reaching all concerned in the transaction, and making the possession of Indian cattle *prima facie* evidence of their larceny; or in some other manner provide a more effectual remedy for this great evil, by insuring severe and certain punishment to the guilty parties.

Hopes have been entertained that, when the war was ended, such arrangements could be made with the tribes occupying the Indian territory as would enable the department to find room within its ample bounds for many of the tribes in Kansas, or such portions of them as did not choose to abandon their tribal relations and become citizens, and that affairs in that country might be reorganized in such a manner as to render such an arrangement highly advantageous both to the Indians and the government. It was therefore with great satisfaction that I learned, through your department, early in July, that a council had been held on the 24th of May, by the tribes of the southwest, lately allied with the rebellion, at which delegates had been appointed from each of them to visit this city for a conference with the government.

It was at first contemplated to allow these delegates to come to Washington, but subsequent correspondence resulted in the designation of a board of commissioners to proceed to the Indian country, and meet them at Fort Smith, Arkansas, and the President appointed a commission comprising the following persons: D. N. Cooley, Commissioner of Indian Affairs; Hon. Elijah Sells, superintendent southern superintendency; Thomas Wistar, a leading member of the society of Friends; Brigadier General W. S. Harney, United States army; and Colonel Ely S. Parker, of General Grant's staff. As a prominent part of the history of Indian affairs during the past year I have included the report and official record of the proceedings of this commission, which was continued for thirteen days, among the documents accompanying this report, and need only notice briefly here the results which are more fully detailed in those papers.

The council assembled at Fort Smith, September 8, and delegates were present in the course of the sittings (though not all in attendance at first) representing the Creeks, Choctaws, Chickasaws, Cherokees, Seminoles, Osages, Senecas, Shawnees, Quapaws, Wyandotts, Wichitas, and Comanches. Immediately upon the opening of proceedings, the tribes were informed generally of the object for which the commission had come to them; that they for the most part, as tribes, had, by violating their treaties—by making treaties with the so-called Confederate States, forfeited all *rights* under them, and must be considered as at the mercy of the government; but that there was every disposition to treat them leniently, and above all a determination to recognize in a signal manner the loyalty of those who had fought upon the side of the government, and endured great sufferings on its behalf. On the next day the delegates were informed that the commissioners were empowered to enter into treaties with the several tribes, upon the basis of the following propositions:

1st. That each tribe must enter into a treaty for permanent peace and amity among themselves, each other as tribes, and with the United States.

2d. The tribes settled in the "Indian country" to bind themselves, at the call of the United States authorities, to assist in compelling the wild tribes of the plains to keep the peace.

3d. Slavery to be abolished, and measures to be taken to incorporate the slaves into the tribes, with their rights guaranteed.

4th. A general stipulation as to final abolition of slavery.

5th. A part of the Indian country to be set apart, to be purchased for the use of such Indians, from Kansas or elsewhere, as the government may desire to colonize therein.

6th. That the policy of the government to unite all the Indian tribes of this region into one consolidated government should be accepted.

7th. That no white persons, except government employés, or officers or employés of internal improvement companies authorized by government, will be permitted to reside in the country, unless incorporated with the several nations.

Printed copies of the address of the commissioners involving the above propositions were placed in the hands of the agents, and of members of the tribes, many of whom were educated men.

On the third day the delegates from the loyal Chickasaws, Chocataws, Senecas, Osages, and Cherokees, principally occupied the time with replies to the address and propositions of the commissioners, the object being partly to express a willingness to accept those propositions, with some modifications, if they had been clothed with sufficient power by their people, but chiefly in explanation of the manner in which their nations became involved with the late confederacy. The address of the Cherokees was especially noteworthy, inasmuch as they attempted to charge the causes of their secession upon the United States, as having violated its treaty obligations, in failing to give the tribe protection, so that it was *compelled* to enter into relations with the confederacy. The next day the loyal Seminoles expressed their willingness to accede to the policy of the government, and to make peace with those of their people who had aided the rebellion. The president of the commission then read a reply to the address of the loyal Cherokees above referred to, showing, from original and official documents, that, *as a tribe,* by the action of their constituted authorities, John Ross being then, as at the time of the council, their head, they had, at the very opening of the rebellion, entered into alliance with it, and raised troops for it, and urged the other tribes to go with them, and that they could not now, under the facts proven, deny their original participation in the rebellion. (The documents establishing the bad faith of John Ross had but recently come into possession of the department. They are very interesting, and taken in connexion with his course at Fort Smith in keeping aloof from the council, but exercising his powerful influence to prevent an amicable settlement with the hitherto disloyal part of the nation, will be found fully to justify the course taken by the commission in refusing to recognize him in any manner as chief of the Cherokees.)

The loyal Creeks on this day presented their address of explanation, setting forth the manner in which their nation, by the unauthorized action of its chief, entered into treaty relations with the confederacy, and the terrible sufferings which the loyal Creeks endured in battle and on the march to Kansas seeking protection from the United States, and asking "to be considered not guilty."

It being certain that no final treaties could be now concluded with the tribes represented, for the reason that, until the differences between the loyal and disloyal portions were healed, there could be no satisfactory representation of most of them, it was determined to prepare for signature by the commission, and by the delegates representing all factions and opinions, a preliminary treaty, pledging anew, on behalf of the Indians, allegiance to the United States, and repudiating all treaties with other parties; and on the part of the United States agreeing to re-establish peace and friendship with them. This was considered essential as preliminary to the main business of the commission, to wit: to make peace between the several tribes, and negotiations as to purchasing lands, territorial government, &c. This work was diligently pursued until, on the breaking up of the commission on the 13th day, all of the delegates representing the following tribes and sections of tribes, in the order given, had signed treaties, (some of them holding out for several days until they could agree among themselves:) Senecas, Senecas and Shawnees, Quapaws, loyal Seminoles, loyal Chickasaws, loyal Creeks, Kansas, Shawnees (uncalled for, but asking to be permitted again to testify their allegiance,) loyal Osages, tribes of the

Wichita agency, loyal Cherokees, disloyal Seminoles, disloyal Creeks, disloyal Cherokees, disloyal Osages, Comanches, disloyal Choctaws, and Chickasaws.

Friendly relations were established between the members of the various tribes hitherto at variance, except in the case of the Cherokees. The ancient feuds among this people are remembered still, and the Ross, Ridge, and Boudinot difficulties have never been healed. This portion of the nation was ably represented in council by Boudinot and others, and having learned from the action of those representing the loyal party that if they came back it must be as beggars and outlaws, asked the protection and good offices of the commission. Efforts were then made on the part of the commission to effect a reconciliation, but all that could be brought about was a promise upon the part of those representing the loyal party to present the question to their council, which is now in session, and I entertain the hope that soon I shall be able to furnish you a report of their proceedings, in which they offer fair and honorable terms of adjustment. If, however, I should be disappointed in this reasonable expectation, I trust the government will take the matter in hand, and, by a just and equitable division of their property, make a final settlement of all their difficulties.

When the majority of this nation returned to their allegiance to the government, in 1863, action was taken by their council, under direction of John Ross, confiscating the property of those who still continued in the service of the confederacy, thus cutting off about five thousand five hundred of the nation, leaving them homeless and houseless. This destitute portion of the tribe are still refugees on the Red river, suffering from the want of every necessary of life, and existing only upon the charity of the humane people of northeastern Texas. The department has, however, sent a special agent to look into the wants of these refugees, and must rely upon Congress for the necessary means to relieve their necessities.

The commission did not adjourn without having made valuable progress towards the consummation of treaty arrangements with several of the most important tribes. With the Osages a treaty was made, signed by the lately disloyal party at the council, and by the loyal chiefs afterwards at their agency, by which they cede to the United States a very large area of valuable land, which may be used for colonization of other tribes if it shall be needed for the purpose, or sold for their benefit. That treaty has just reached this office by the hand of Superintendent Sells, and will be submitted to you with his report.

The terms of a treaty were agreed upon with both parties of the Creeks, whereby they cede to the United States, for the use of the friendly Indians from Kansas or elsewhere, all of their lands north of the Arkansas river, and one-half of the remainder lying south of that river, on terms which I trust will meet the approval of the government. This treaty is to be signed in this city by delegates properly accredited by the united Creek nation.

With the Choctaws and Chickasaws a treaty was agreed upon, upon the basis of the seven propositions heretofore stated, and in addition to which those tribes agreed to a thorough and friendly union among their own people, and forgetfulness of past differences; to the opening of the "leased lands" to the settlement of any tribes whom the government of the United States may desire to place thereon; and to the cession of one-third of their remaining area for the same purpose; the United States to restore these tribes to their rights forfeited by the rebellion. This treaty, after its approval by the councils of the Choctaws and Chickasaws, is to be signed in this city by three delegates from each nation sent here for that purpose.

It is not intended to hold any general council in this city, but it was understood that delegates would, if necessary, visit Washington on behalf of any of the tribes owning lands in the Indian country which the government might desire to purchase for the use of other Indians, so that, by properly accredited delegates, all necessary arrangements with the several tribes might be made.

It became sufficiently evident, in the course of the council, that one great object in view by the government, the colonization of such of the tribes or portions of tribes from further north as should desire a permanent home in the Indian country, would be secured when the policy of the government in regard to them was fully understood; and it was gratifying to notice that the subject of the organization of an Indian territory, with provisions securing a certain degree of individuality to the various tribes—indeed, based upon the admirable form of government of the United States, and with a representative delegate in Congress—although at first distasteful to the leading spirits among the Indians, gradually increased in favor by the study of the few copies at hand of the bill proposed by yourself in the Senate last winter, until, near the close of the council, Mr. Boudinot, a man of education and ability, speaking on behalf of the Cherokees and others who had taken part in the rebellion, (his remarks being assented to by all present,) declared in a speech, a note of which is preserved among the records of the council herewith, that the plan was eminently satisfactory, and would entitle its projectors to the everlasting gratitude of the Indians. We may, then, reasonably hope to see this admirable project carried into operation at no distant day.

From the able and elaborate report of Superintendent Sells, and the several agents in charge of the tribes within this superintendency, we obtain much valuable information as to their present condition, in reference to both the loyal portions of them, who have been refugees from their homes during the war; and the disloyal, who made treaties and engaged actively with the late "southern confederacy." The contrast between their condition now and before the war, whether we refer to either loyal or disloyal, is sad indeed. Most of these tribes had advanced far in civilization, and their country was well provided with good schools and academies. Many of their leading men are to-day thoroughly educated men, of statesmanlike views, fully able to express those views in our language, in a manner which can be excelled in few of our deliberative assemblies. Their people were rich in real and personal property, living in the enjoyment of everything needed for their comfort; and considerable wealth had accumulated in the hands of some of them—the slaveholders—so that they lived in a style of luxury to which our thriving northern villages are most unaccustomed. Their crops were abundant, but their chief element of prosperity was stock-raising, and vast herds of cattle were in their hands as a means of wealth. The change is pitiful. Their land has been desolated by the demon of war till it lies bare and scathed, with only ruins to show that men have ever dwelt there. A perusal of the reports herewith will satisfy you that these remarks are no exaggeration, particularly as to the Cherokee, Quapaw, and part of the Creek bands; the condition of affairs in the Choctaw and Chickasaw country is not so serious, for the reason that those tribes went almost unanimously with the rebellion, and of course had no object in destroying their own property; though even there the effects of the war are distinctly visible. But in the Cherokee country, where the contending armies have moved to and fro—where their foraging parties have gone at will, sparing neither friend nor foe—where the disloyal Cherokees, in the service of the rebel government, were determined that no trace of the homesteads of their loyal brethren should remain for their return, and where the swindling cattle-thieves have made their ill-gotten gains for two years past, the scene is one of utter desolation. Of course, the loyal portions of all of these tribes have suffered most; for they became refugees from their homes, leaving them in the hands of their enemies, and everything that they left was destroyed. A large number of the loyal Indians of all the tribes entered the service of the United States, and many of them sealed their fidelity with their life-blood, while many others are maimed for life. Now that the war is over, the survivors of these loyal bands claim the sympathy and aid of the government. They are anxious to return to their country, but they have no homes there, and no subsistence. They are utterly destitute, and entirely dependent upon the government for food and clothing. In another season, if timely assistance in the way of agricultural implements and other aid is afforded them, they may become self-sustaining by tilling the ground; but for the present, at least, they must be dependent upon the government.

Let us glance at the condition of the several tribes as portrayed in the report of the superintendent and agents:

The Seminoles numbered before the war nearly 2,500, of whom more than half came out with the loyal Creeks and took refuge in Kansas, their able-bodied men joining the United States army. There are about 2,000 of the tribe left. Some 500 of them were furnished with seed and a few agricultural implements last spring, and upon land near Fort Gibson, in the Cherokee country, labored diligently and with some degree of success for the means of subsistence, having raised produce to the value of $2,500. The records of their old agency have been preserved through the war, and are safe at Fort Washita. They are anxious to go to their own country south and west of the Creek region, but matters there are not sufficiently settled as yet, and the agent thinks that they should be removed to some point among the Creeks and subsisted there, to be near their own lands at the opening of spring. About 1,000 of them are now drawing rations from government. They are very poor and destitute, and must be fed and clothed, or suffer and starve. Agent Reynolds says that they wish to settle upon individual lands, where they can own and enjoy the fruit of their own labors. As they are closely allied to the Creeks, and speak that language, they might perhaps be consolidated with them; or, if not, it is thought that they would be glad to dispose of the western portion of their lands, to be used for a home for other Indians, and thus procure the means for establishing themselves again in a condition to become self-supporting, and educate their children.

Agent Reynolds has been especially active in efforts to stop the plundering of Indian stock, and thinks that his efforts have been successful.

Of the Cherokees, all of the nation at first joined the rebels, including all factions, of full and mixed blood. Regiments were raised by the order of the party in power, then and now the majority, called the Ross party, which regiments fought against the Union forces at Pea Ridge and on other occasions. All seem to have agreed as to their course of action down to the fall of 1862, when a portion of the troops, under Colonel Downing, 2d chief, and a majority of the nation, abandoned the rebel cause and came within our lines. About 6,500 of the more wealthy portion still continued to co-operate with the south till the close of the war; and about 9,000, early and late, came back to their allegiance.

Two regiments of these people, numbering 2,200 men, deserted the rebel cause as above stated, and since that time, to the end of the war, have fought on the side of the Union. The total population of the nation is now estimated at about 14,000.

Bad as is the condition of all these southern Indians, that of the Cherokees is much worse than the remainder of the tribes. They have a domestic feud, of long standing, which prevents them from coming together for mutual aid and support in their manifold troubles. In 1863 a portion of them had gone back to their country, expecting to be protected by the United States troops in raising a crop for their support; but they were driven from their fields by rebel parties; and while their former brothers were plundering them from one direction, their white *friends* from Kansas were stripping the country of their stock from the other. The account given by Agent Harlan of the *modus operandi* of the cattle-thieving business would be amusing, if the thing described were not outrageously criminal. Some idea of the extent of this business may be obtained when it is seen that the agent estimates the losses of the Cherokees in stock alone at *two millions* ($2,000,000,) while Superintendent Sells thinks that the losses of *all* the tribes have amounted to full *four millions.*

About 9,000 Cherokees are now receiving rations from the government, and a large portion of those lately disloyal are suffering greatly for the necessaries of life. They need food, clothing, tools, everything in fact, to begin life again; and their condition must be that of extreme destitution until they can again realize the fruits of their labor upon their own soil. The Cherokees own a tract of 800,000 acres in the southeast corner of Kansas, which should be made available for their benefit; and have, besides, a vast tract of land below the Kansas line, very largely beyond their possible wants. All beyond those wants should be purchased by government, and the avails used for the benefit of the whole people. Superintendent Sells doubts whether the loyal and disloyal Cherokees can ever live in friendship together, and suggests that in case this proves to be impossible, the latter can easily make terms with the Chickasaws to join with them. I have already alluded to the condition in which this southern portion of the nation is left by the action of the party in power, and will only add here, that the sweeping act of confiscation passed by the council takes from them every acre of land, and all their improvements; and that by the hasty action taken under the law, everything has been sold for the most trivial consideration, improvements which were worth thousands selling often as low as five dollars; and when the repentant rebel party, no more guilty at first than the Ross party, came back and proposed to submit and live in peace and harmony with them again, they were told that they might all return, except their leaders, and go upon new lands and begin the world again; but no hope was held out to them of any restoration of property. They are thus left entirely dependent, being stripped of everything by the act referred to.

The Creeks were nearly divided in sentiment at the opening of the war; about 6,500 having gone with the rebellion, while the remainder, under the lead of the brave old chief Opothleyoholo, resisted all temptations of the rebel agents and of leading men, like John Ross, among the Indians, and fought their way out of the country northward, in the winter, tracked by their bloody feet upon the frozen ground. They lost everything—houses, homes, stock, everything that they possessed. Many joined the United States army. A large number have been constantly subsisted, often with scanty rations, by government. A part having gone this year to the Indian country, have raised some crops under many difficulties, and about one half of those who thus went south again will have enough corn to carry them through the winter; the others must be subsisted by government, while 5,000 are now receiving rations. A large number of the southern Creeks are in the same deplorable state. The aggregate number of the tribe is now stated at 14,396. Agent Dunn says that the buildings of the old Creek agency are in ruins, but the valuable mission buildings are standing, though badly injured. He thinks that a new location should be selected for the agency, at a point where there is water and timber; but as there may be other arrangements as to the final settlement of the tribe, he suggests that such temporary shelter for the agency as is necessary should now be provided.

The Choctaws and Chickasaws, who now number respectively about 12,500 and 4,500, or 17,000 in all, are supposed to have had a population of

25,000 at the beginning of the war, including 5,000 slaves. They have regularly organized governments and legislatures, written laws, and a regular judiciary system. They possessed admirable schools, and education had made great progress among them. Nearly the whole of these tribes proved disloyal, under the various influences brought to bear upon them. Agent Coleman ascribes their disloyalty, in a great degree, to the influence of the whites living among them, some of whom have had the assurance to apply for licenses to remain in the country as traders; but I am entirely satisfied, as the result of my inquiries when lately in the Indian country, that the disloyal action of these tribes is mostly, if not altogether, to be ascribed to the influence of the then superintendent, Mr. Rector, and the agents appointed by the United States government. The tribes are educated to respect the authority and be guided by the directions of these representatives of the government; and when, in the spring of 1861, these men, appointed under President Buchanan, came back from Washington and told the Indians that there was no longer a United States government to protect them, that its organization was broken up, and that they must join with the new government, (which by its location and its slaveholding basis would be in sympathy with them,) or be ground to powder, they readily acceded. They now see their error. No men were ever more penitent; and since they learned at the Fort Smith council the wishes of the government, their own council has met and taken prompt action upon the proposition submitted to them, and appointed a delegation to visit Washington to sign a final treaty. This appears more fully in the despatch from General Hunt, commanding at Fort Smith, dated October 24, communicating a letter from Governor Colbert, of the Chickasaw nation, which despatch will be found among the accompanying documents.

Only 212 persons belonging to these tribes are known to have remained loyal to the government. The disloyal portion need some help to get through the winter without suffering, but their country having been held by the rebels all the time during the war, and not traversed by the contending armies, and rations having been issued to them till last March, they have not suffered as much as the other tribes. Two thousand of both tribes are now receiving government rations. I have elsewhere referred to the propositions in regard to a cession of a portion of the Choctaw and Chickasaw lands.

Agent Snow has in charge the Neosho agency, comprising the Osages, and the small bands known as the Quapaws, Senecas, and Senecas and Shawnees.

The Osage lands are in Kansas, and comprise about 4,000,000 acres. In 1859 they had a population of 3,500; the agent thinks that their number does not now exceed 2,800. About 1,000 of the tribe joined the rebellion. Some two hundred and forty of their warriors were at one time in the service of the United States, but left from some difficulty with their officers, and cannot understand the propriety of the rule by which they have forfeited their pay. The report of Superintendent Sells is very full in its information as to the habits and mode of life of this tribe, which is entirely nomadic in its character, using the bow and arrow in the chase, and hunting the buffalo in the ranges southwest of their country. Their special home is near where the Verdigris river crosses the Kansas line. The sad example of the whites, who steal their stock, leads them to retaliate, and frequent collisions and difficulties with the settlers are the consequence. By the recent treaty with this tribe, their factions have become reconciled; and by the cession to the United States of a large body of land, it will be open to settlement, and they obtain from its avails the means of becoming civilized. In view of their nomadic habits, however, Agent Snow suggests their entire removal from Kansas and the neighborhood of the whites, and settlement upon lands in the western part of the Indian country, near the buffalo range; which suggestion I approve, and trust that within a few months their country will be so far at the disposal of the government, through the operation of the treaties now in progress, as the result of the recent council, that these and all of the other Kansas Indians who do not elect to become citizens may be removed into the Indian country.

The Quapaws and other small tribes of this agency, numbering only 670 in all, never showed any sympathy with the rebellion, but came north, abandoning their homes, and continued as refugees upon the Ottawa reservation until last spring, when they were removed to a point eighty miles further south, where they have raised some small supply of vegetables this year. An exploration of their former reservations, just below the Kansas line, exhibited the usual desolation of war; and everything must be provided anew for them. They had attained a fair degree of civilization, and were prosperous and comfortable before the war; and they, like the other loyal Indians, think that the government for which they suffered the loss of everything should in some degree compensate them for such loss. These people all receive rations at present from the United States.

The Catholic mission school at the Neosho agency has been continued in operation, though under great difficulties. On the occasion of the recent visit of Superintendent Sells to the agency, the school had in attendance sixty-five Osage and Quapaw boys, and fifty girls. The Indians regard this school with great favor.

The Wichita agency (Agent Gookins in charge) comprises 500 Shawnees, absentees from their tribes in Kansas, and who, it is probable, will not return to that State to remain permanently, but who are now in Osage county, Kansas; and the Wichitas and fragments of the Caddoes, Comanches, and others, amounting to about 1,800. These last were, before the war, settled upon lands leased from the Choctaws. They have never had much attention given them by the government, and were driven from Texas by the greed of white men. Thus they have not for years had a settled home. About 1,000 of them are now near Fort Washita, having done but little towards subsisting themselves, a flood having destroyed most of their crops. They are very poor and miserable, and must have help; and they ask to be placed somewhere, where they can feel that they have a permanent home, and go to work in earnest next spring. Rations are issued to 1,400 of the Indians belonging to this agency.

After a careful consideration of the facts set forth in these reports, and from my information obtained while in the Indian country, I am prepared to recommend prompt and liberal action on the part of the government in providing food, and necessary clothing, and shelter, and the materials for commencing early next spring the labor of getting in the crops which must feed them. In regard to food and clothing, the demand is immediate and pressing; as to the other, it must be provided in good time, and the sooner and better it is done, the sooner will the people relieve the government of the necessity of feeding them. It needs no argument—the bare suggestion is enough—to show the duty of the government towards the loyal and friendly portions of these tribes, who have sealed their devotion with their blood; but the necessity is none the less pressing on the part of many of the others. They *must be* fed and clothed, or their sufferings will surely lead them to steal; and difficulties will at once arise, out of which will come the necessity of stationing several regiments of troops in the country, with their concomitants of contractors, supply trains, &c., &c., the cost of which would amount to double what is needed to take care of these Indians till they can be re-established. The principle that it is cheaper to feed than to fight Indians is illustrated daily, and the cost of sustaining a small army in the far west in a campaign against the Indians, or even at posts where no speck of war ever appears on the horizon, is greater than the whole annual expenditure of the Indian department. On every account, then, of patriotism, humanity, and economy, I trust that there may be quick and liberal action in reference to the wants of these Indians.

In regard to the question of compensation of the loyal portion of these southern tribes for their untold losses and sufferings, I do not feel it necessary to use many words. A great many white people have endured severe losses, and undergone great sufferings, by reason of the rebellion; and many thousands of white people in the south have been abused and outraged, and driven from their homes by the demon of civil discord and war; and government has not yet made provisions for compensation in those cases; but our government was under obligations by solemn treaties to defend and protect these Indians; and without discussing the extent of this obligation, it can do no less now than to aid those who are actually suffering for the simplest necessities of life. This is only the dictate of humanity.

For the rest, the Indians must await their time; but when that time comes, their claim will be very strong, and must be heard. If the government will but act promptly in furnishing them liberally with the ordinary necessities of life now, and with means to make themselves and their families comfortable till they can raise a crop, it will go far to satisfy them that they have not suffered for a government which, in their distress and poverty, the result of their devotion to its cause, and faith in its protecting care, has *forgotten them.*

Whenever, in the progress towards a final settlement of the questions remaining open in regard to the reorganization of the Indian country, the proper time shall come, it will be advisable to provide for the construction of internal improvements in that region calculated to develop its magnificent resources. With a territorial government organized and in operation, its feuds healed, the scars of war gone from view, a judicious educational system in operation, the missionary establishments which have done so much for the people in the past reopened, and the industry of the country in full process of development, will have come a time when railroads must traverse the country, binding its several parts together, and all to one common Union, and giving a choice of markets and depots for exchange and shipment of produce, either on the Gulf of Mexico, say at Galveston, or northward, to connect with the great central converging points of railroads in Kansas. Whatever can properly be done by the government of the United States in paving the way for these improvements should, in my judgment, be done now, and thus avoid difficulties which may arise in the future.

Indian Peace Commission
Report to President Andrew Johnson
January 7, 1868

(Report of the Secretary of the Interior for 1868, pp. 486-510)

The commissioners, appointed by an act of Congress in 1867 to establish peace with certain hostile Indian tribes, made a report which illuminated the conditions under which Indian–white relations were managed, or mismanaged, much more brightly than did the reports of the Commissioner of Indian Affairs. The commission included hard-bitten generals like William Tecumseh Sherman, as well as humanitarians such as S. F. Tappan. Their report pointed out the poor communications, misunderstandings, and bad motives that had led to heavy loss of life and treasure—Indian and white—on the Great Plains. The commission was particularly eloquent in discussing the events leading up to Colonel Chivington's massacre of unoffending Indians in Colorado. The commissioners produced a report that is valuable not only for its historical account of important events in the history of Indian–white relations, but also for its administrative recommendations, which included the suggestion that Indian affairs be committed to an independent bureau or department.

THE UNDERSIGNED, commissioners appointed under the act of Congress approved July 20, 1867, "to establish peace with certain hostile Indian tribes," were authorized by said act to call together the chiefs and headmen of such bands of Indians as were then waging war, for the purpose of ascertaining their reasons for hostility, and, if thought advisable, to make treaties with them having in view the following objects, viz:

1st. To remove, if possible, the causes of war;

2d. To secure, as far as practicable, our frontier settlements and the safe building of our railroads looking to the Pacific; and

3d. To suggest or inaugurate some plan for the civilization of the Indians.

Congress, in the passage of the law, seemed to indicate the policy of collecting at some early day all the Indians east of the Rocky mountains on one or more reservations, and with that view it was made our duty to examine and select "a district or districts of country having sufficient area to receive all the Indian tribes occupying territory east of the said mountains not now peacefully residing on permanent reservations under treaty stipulations," &c. It was required that these reservations should have sufficient arable or grazing lands to enable the tribes placed on them to support themselves, and that they should be so located as not to interfere with

134

established highways of travel and the contemplated railroads to the Pacific ocean. The subsequent action and approval of Congress will be necessary, however, to dedicate the district or districts so selected to the purposes of exclusive Indian settlement.

When the act was passed, war was being openly waged by several hostile tribes, and great diversity of opinion existed among the officials of the government, and no less diversity among our people, as to the means best adapted to meet it. Some thought peaceful negotiation would succeed, while others had no hope of peace until the Indians were thoroughly subdued by force of arms. As a concession to this latter sentiment, so largely prevailing, as well as to meet the possible contingency of failure by the commission, it was, perhaps, wisely provided, that in case peace could not be obtained by treaty, or should the Indians fail to comply with the stipulations they might make for going on their reservations, the President might call out four regiments of mounted troops for the purpose of conquering the desired peace.

On the sixth day of August we met at St. Louis, Missouri, and organized by selecting N. G. Taylor president and A. S. H. White secretary.

The first difficulty presenting itself was to secure an interview with the chiefs and leading warriors of these hostile tribes. They were roaming over an immense country thousands of miles in extent, and much of it unknown even to hunters and trappers of the white race. Small war parties emerging from this vast extent of unexplored country would suddenly strike the border settlements, killing the men and carrying off into captivity the women and children. Companies of workmen on the railroads, at points hundreds of miles from each other, would be attacked on the same day, perhaps in the same hour. Overland mail coaches could not be run without military escort, and railroad and mail stations unguarded by soldiery were in perpetual danger. All safe transit across the plains had ceased. To go without soldiers was hazardous in the extreme; to go with them forbade reasonable hope of securing peaceful interviews with the enemy. When the Indian goes to war he enters upon its dreadful work with earnestness and determination. He goes on an errand of vengeance, and no amount of blood satisfies him. It may be because, with him, all wrongs have to be redressed by war. In our intercourse with him we have failed, in a large measure, to provide peaceful means of redress, and he knows no law except that of retaliation. He wages war with the same pertinacity, and indeed in the same spirit, with which a party litigant in full conviction of the right prosecutes his suit in court. His only compromise is to have his rights, real or fancied, fully conceded. To force he yields nothing. In battle he never surrenders, and it is the more expendable, therefore, that he never accepts capitulation at the hands of others. In war he does not ask or accept mercy. He is then the more consistent that he does not grant mercy.

So little accustomed to kindness from others, it may not be strange that he often hesitates to confide. Proud himself, and yet conscious of the contempt of the white man, when suddenly aroused by some new wrong, the remembrance of old ones still stinging his soul, he seems to become, as expressed by himself, blind with rage. If he fails to see the olive branch or flag of truce in the hands of the peace commissioner, and in savage ferocity adds one more to his victims, we should remember that for two and a half centuries he has been driven back from civilization, where his passions might have been subjected to the influences of education and softened by the lessons of Christian charity.

This difficulty, meeting us at the very threshold of our duties, had to be overcome before anything of a practical character could be accomplished. Fortunately, we had on the commission a combination of the civil and military power necessary to give strength and efficiency to our operations. Through the orders of Lieutenant General Sherman to the commanders of posts, and those of Commissioner Taylor to superintendents and agents under his charge, in the proper districts, a perfect concert of action was secured, and according to our instructions the hostile Indians of western Dakota were notified that we would meet them at Fort Laramie on the 13th day of September; and those then south of the Arkansas, including the Cheyennes, the Kiowas, Comanches, Arapahoes, and Apaches, that we would meet them for consultation at some point near Fort Larned, on or about the 13th day of October.

Whilst runners were being employed and sent out to notify them of our pacific intentions and our desire to meet them at the time and places stated, the commission resolved to occupy the time intervening before the first meeting in examing the country on the upper Missouri river. The steamer St. John was chartered, and such goods purchased as were thought suitable as presents to the Indians.

On the 13th of August we met at Fort Leavenworth and took the statements of Major General Hancock, Governor Crawford, of Kansas, Father DeSmet, and others. Thence we proceeded to Omaha, Nebraska, and took the statements of Major General Augur and others. At Yancton we met Governor Faulk, of Dakota, and took his evidence on the subjects embraced in our duties. Governor Faulk, at our request, accompanied the commission up the river, and was present at the subsequent interviews with the Indians of his superintendency.

Owing to the low stage of water, our progress up the river was much retarded, and we failed to reach Fort Rice as we had intended. On the 30th of August a point twelve miles above the mouth of the Big Cheyenne river was reached, when it was found necessary to turn back in order to fill our several engagements made with the Indians on the river as we went up, and then reach Fort Laramie by the 13th of September.

On the return trip councils were held with various bands of the Sioux or Dakota Indians at Forts Sully and Thompson, and also at the Yancton, Ponca, and Santee Sioux reservations, full reports of which will be found in the appendix. Although these Indians along the Missouri river are not hostile, and do not, therefore, legitimately come within the scope of duties assigned us, yet it was thought quite important, in determining whether the country itself was fit for an Indian reservation, to examine into the condition of those now there, and especially those who are endeavoring to live by agriculture.

The time given us was too short to make anything like a personal inspection of so large a district of undulated country as that which lies north of Nebraska between the Missouri river on the east and the Black Hills on the west, and to which public attempts is now being very generally directed as a home for the more northern tribes. We took evidence of those who had traversed this region in reference to the soil, climate, and productions, which evidence will be found in the appendix. To this subject we shall again allude when we come to speak of reservations for Indian settlement.

In this connection, however, before returning to the thread of our narrative, it is our duty to remark that the condition of these tribes demands prompt and serious attention. The treaty stipulations with many of them are altogether inappropriate. They seem to have been made in total ignorance of their numbers and disposition, and in utter disregard of their wants. Some of the agents now among them should be removed, and men appointed who will, by honesty, fair dealing, and unselfish devotion to duty, secure their respect and confidence. Where the present treaties fail to designate a particular place as a home for the tribe, they should be changed.

Returning to Omaha on the 11th of September, the steamer was discharged, and we immediately proceeded to North Platte, on the Pacific railroad, where we found a considerable number of the Sioux and northern Cheyennes, some of whom had long been friendly, while others had but recently been engaged in war. A council was held with them, which at one time threatened to result in no good; but finally a full and perfect understanding was arrived at, which though not then, nor even yet, reduced to writing, we have every reason to believe has been faithfully kept by them.

It was at this council that the hitherto untried policy in connection with Indians, of endeavoring to conquer by kindness, was inaugurated.

Swift Bear, a Brulé chief, then and now a faithful friend to the whites, had interested himself to induce the hostile bands to come in to this council, and had promised them, if peace were made, that ammunition should be given them to kill game for the winter. This promise was not authorized by the commissioners, but we were assured that it had been made not only by him, but by others of our runners, and that nothing less would have brought them in. These Indians are very poor and needy. The game in this section is fast disappearing, and the bow and arrow are scarcely sufficient to provide them food. To give one of these Indians powder and ball is to give him meat. To refuse it, in his judgment, dooms him to starvation; and worse than this, he looks upon the refusal, especially after a profession of friendship on his part, as an imputation upon his truthfulness and fidelity. If an Indian is to be trusted at all, he must be trusted to the full extent of his work. If you betray symptoms of distrust, he discovers it with nature's intuition, and at once condemns the falsehood that would blend friendship and suspicion together. Whatever our people may choose to say of the insincerity or duplicity of the Indian would fail to express the estimate entertained by many Indians of the white man's character in this respect. Promises have been so often broken by those with whom they usually come in contact, cupidity has so long plied its work deaf to their cries of suffering, and heartless cruelty has so frequently sought them in the garb of charity, that to obtain their confidence our promises must be scrupulously fulfilled and our professions of friendship divested of all appearance of selfishness and duplicity.

We are now satisfied, whatever the criticisms of our conduct at the time—and they were very severe both by the ignorant and the corrupt—that had we refused the ammunition demanded at this council, the war on their part would have continued, and possibly ere this have resulted in great loss of life and property. As it is, they at once proceeded to their fall hunt on the Republican river, where they killed game enough to subsist themselves for a large part of the winter, and no act of hostility or wrong has been perpetrated by them since.

The statement of this fact, if it proves nothing else, may serve to indicate that the Indian, though barbarous, is yet a man, susceptible to those feelings which ordinarily respond to the exercise of magnanimity and kindness. If it should suggest to civilization that the injunction to "do good to them that hate us" is not confined to race, but broad as humanity itself, it may do some good, even to ourselves. It will at least, for the practical man honestly seeking a solution of these troubles, serve a better purpose than whole pages of theorizing upon Indian character.

At this point we were informed by our scouts that the northern Sioux, who were waging war on the Powder river, would not be able to meet us at Fort Laramie at the time indicated; whereupon we adjourned the meeting until the 1st day of November, and requested them if possible to secure a delegation to meet us on our return. We then left the valley of the Platte and proceeded up the Kansas river and its tributaries to Fort Harker, and thence by the way of Fort Larned to a point 80 miles south of the Arkansas river, where we met the Kiowas, Comanches, Arapahoes, and Apaches, on a stream called Medicine Lodge creek. It should be stated at this point that when we arrived at St. Louis, on our way hither, we found that Lieutenant General Sherman had been summoned to Washington city by the President, and his place on the commission supplied by the appointment of Brevet Major General C. C. Augur, who joined the other members at Fort Larned and participated in all our subsequent proceedings. At our first councils at Medicine Lodge the larger body of the hostile Cheyennes remained off at a distance of 40 miles.

These latter Indians were evidently suspicious of the motives which had prompted us to visit them. Since the preceding April they had committed many depredations. They had been unceasingly on the warpath, engaged in indiscriminate murder and plunder. They knew that our troops had but recently been hunting them over the plains, killing them wherever they would find them. They could not, therefore, appreciate this sudden change of policy. For two weeks they kept themselves at a distance, sending in small parties to discover if possible our true intentions.

Before the arrival of the Cheyennes we concluded treaties with the Kiowas, Comanches, and Apaches, and after their arrival we concluded a joint treaty with the Cheyennes and Arapahoes, all of which we herewith submit and earnestly recommend for ratification.

Before these agreements were perfected we had many interviews or "talks" with the several tribes, some of which were exceedingly interesting as illustrative of their character, habits, and wishes. Being provided with an efficient short-hand reporter, we were enabled to preserve the full proceedings of these councils, and to them we especially call your attention.

After giving to these tribes their annuities, which had been detained at the military posts since last spring, on account of their alleged hostility, and after distributing among them some presents, the commission returned to Omaha, and thence by North Platte to Fort Laramie, to fill our second engagement with the hostile Sioux and Cheyennes of the north.

On arriving at Fort Laramie we found awaiting us a delegation of Crows, with whom a council was held and their statements taken. Red Cloud, the formidable chief of the Sioux, did not come to this council. The Crows, as a tribe, have not been hostile. Some of their young men, no doubt, have united themselves with the hostile forces of Ogallalla and Brulé Sioux and northern Cheyennes, who, since July, 1866, under the leadership of Red Cloud, have spread terror throughout this entire region of country.

We greatly regret the failure to procure a council with this chief and his leading warriors. If an interview could have been obtained, we do not for a moment doubt that a just and honorable peace could have been secured. Several causes operated to prevent his meeting us. The first, perhaps, was a doubt of our motives; the second results from a prevalent belief among these Indians that we have resolved on their extermination; and third, the meeting was so late in the season that it could not be attended in this cold and inhospitable country without great suffering. He sent us word, however, that his war against the whites was to save the valley of the Powder river, the only hunting ground left to his nation, from our intrusion. He assured us that whenever the military garrisons at Fort Phil. Kearney and Fort C. F. Smith were withdrawn, the war on his part would cease. As we could not then, for several reasons, make any such agreement, and as the garrisons could not have been safely removed so late in the season, the commission adjourned, to meet in Washington on the 9th day of December. Before adjourning we took the promise of the Crows to meet us early next summer, and sent word to Red Cloud and his followers to meet us at the same council, to be held either at Fort Rice, on the Missouri river, or at Fort Phil. Kearney, in the mountains, as they might prefer. We also asked a truce or cessation of hostilities until the council could be held.

Returning then by way of North Platte, we received new assurances of peace and friendship from the Indians there assembled. They will give us no further trouble at present. They are the same to whom we gave the ammunition.

Since arriving here we are gratified to be informed that Red Cloud has accepted our proposition to discontinue hostilities and meet us in council next spring or summer. And now, with anything like prudence and good conduct on the part of our own people in the future, we believe the Indian war east of the Rocky mountains is substantially closed.

Our first duty under the act, it will be remembered, was to secure a conference with the Indians. Having obtained that conference, our second duty was to ascertain from themselves the reasons inducing them to go to war. These reasons may be gathered from the speeches and testimony of the chiefs and warriors hereto appended. The limits of this paper will not permit more than a brief summary of these reasons. The testimony satisfied us that since October, 1865, the Kiowas, Comanches, and Apaches have substantially complied with their treaty stipulations entered into at that time at the mouth of the Little Arkansas. The only flagrant violation we were able to discover consisted in the killing of James Box and the capture of his family in western Texas about the 15th of August, 1866. The alleged excuse for this act is, that they supposed an attack on Texas people would be no violation of a treaty with the United States; that as we ourselves had been at war with the people of Texas, an act of hostility on their part would not be disagreeable to us.

We are aware that various other charges were made against the Kiowas and Comanches, but the evidence taken will pretty clearly demonstrate that these charges were almost wholly without foundation. The charges against the Arapahoes amounted to but little.

The story of the Cheyennes dates far back, and contains many points of deep and thrilling interest. We will barely allude to some of them and then pass on.

In 1851, a short time after the discovery of gold in California, when a vast stream of emigration was flowing over the western plains, which up to that period had been admitted by treaty and by law to be Indian territory, it was thought expedient to call together all the tribes east of the Rocky mountains for the purpose of securing the right of peaceful transit over their lands, and also fixing the boundaries between the different tribes themselves. A council was convened at Fort Laramie on the 17th day of September of that year, at which the Cheyennes, Arapahoes, Crows, Assinaboines, Gros-Ventres, Mandans, and Arickarees were represented. To each of these tribes boundaries were assigned. To the Cheyennes and Arapahoes were given a district of country "commencing at the Red Butte, or the place where the road leaves the north fork of the Platte river; thence up the north fork of the Platte river to its source; thence along the main ridge of the Rocky mountains to the headwaters of the Arkansas river; thence down the Arkansas river to the crossing of the Santa Fé road; thence in a northwesterly direction to the forks of the Platte river; thence up the Platte river to the place of beginning." It was further provided in this treaty that the rights or claims of any one of the nations should not be prejudiced by this recognition of title in the others; and "further, that they do not surrender the privilege of hunting, fishing, or passing over any of the tracts of country hereinbefore described." The Indians granted us the right to establish roads and military and other posts within their respective territories, in consideration of which we agreed to pay the Indians $50,000 per annum for 50 years, to be distributed to them in proportion to the population of the respective tribes. When this treaty reached the Senate, "50 years" was stricken out and "ten years" substituted, with the authority of the President to continue the annuities for a period of five years longer, if he saw fit.

It will be observed that the boundaries of the Cheyenne and Arapahoe land, as fixed by this treaty, include the larger portion of the Territory of Colorado and most of the western part of Kansas.

Some years after this gold and silver were discovered in the mountains of Colorado, and thousands of fortune-seekers, who possessed nothing more than the right of transit over these lands, took possession of them for the purpose of mining, and, against the protests of the Indians, founded cities, established farms, and opened roads. Before 1861 the Cheyennes and Arapahoes had been driven from the mountain regions down upon the waters of the Arkansas, and were becoming sullen and discontented because of this violation of their rights. The third article of the treaty of 1851 contained the following language: "The United States bind themselves to protect the aforesaid Indian nations against the commission of all depredations by the people of the United States after the ratification of this treaty." The Indians, however ignorant, did not believe that the obligations of this treaty had been complied with.

If the lands of the white man are taken, civilization justified him in resisting the invader. Civilization does more than this: it brands him as a coward and a slave if he submits to the wrong. Here civilization made its contract and guaranteed the rights of the weaker party. It did not stand by the guarantee. The treaty was broken, but not by the savage. If the savage resists, civilization, with the ten commandments in one hand and the sword in the other, demands his immediate extermination.

We do not contest the ever ready argument that civilization must not be arrested in its progress by a handful of savages. We earnestly desire the speedy settlement of all our territories. None are more anxious than we to see their agricultural and mineral wealth developed by an industrious, thrifty, and enlightened population. And we fully recognize the fact that the Indian must not stand in the way of this result. We would only be understood as doubting the purity and genuineness of that civilization which reaches its ends by falsehood and violence, and dispenses blessings that spring from violated rights.

These Indians saw their former homes and hunting grounds overrun by a greedy population, thirsting for gold. They saw their game driven east to the plains, and soon found themselves the objects of jealously and hatred. They too must go. The presence of the injured is too often painful to the wrong-doer, and innocence offensive to the eyes of guilt. It now became apparent that what had been taken by force must be retained by the ravisher, and nothing was left for the Indian but to ratify a treaty consecrating the act.

On the 18th day of February, 1861, this was done at Fort Wise, in Kansas. These tribes ceded their magnificent possessions, enough to constitute two great States of the Union, retaining only a small district for themselves, "beginning at the mouth of the Sandy Fork of the Arkansas river and extending westwardly along said river to the mouth of the Purgatory river; thence along up the west bank of the Purgatory river to the northern boundary of the Territory of New Mexico; thence west along said boundary to a point where a line drawn due south from a point on the Arkansas river five miles east of the mouth of the Huerfano river would intersect said northern boundary of New Mexico; thence due north from that point on said boundary to the Sandy Fork to the place of beginning." By examining the map, it will be seen that this reservation lies on both sides of the Arkansas river, and includes the country around Fort Lyon. In consideration of this concession, the United States entered into new obligations. Not being able to protect them in the larger reservation, the nation resolved that it would protect them "in the quiet and peaceable possession" of the smaller tract. Second, "to pay each tribe $30,000 per annum for 15 years;" and third, that houses should be built, lands broken up and fenced, and stock animals and agricultural implements furnished. In addition to this, mills were to be built, and engineers, farmers, and mechanics sent among them. These obligations, like the obligations of 1851, furnished glittering evidences of humanity to the reader of the treaty. Unfortunately, the evidence stops at that point.

In considering this treaty, it will occur to the reader that the 11th article demonstrates the amicable relations between the Indians and their white friends up to that time. It provides as follows: "In consideration of the kind treatment of the Arapahoes and Cheyennes by the citizens of Denver City and the adjacent towns, they respectfully request that the proprietors of said city and adjacent towns be admitted by the United States government to enter a sufficient quantity of land to include said city and towns at the minimum price of $1.25 per acre."

Large and flourishing cities had been built on the Indian lands, in open violation of our treaty. Town lots were being sold, not by the acre, but by the front foot. Rich mines had been opened in the mountains, and through the streets of these young cities poured the streams of golden wealth. This had once been Indian property. If the white man in taking it was "kind" to the savage, this at least carried with it some honor, and deserves to be remembered. By some it may be thought that a more substantial return might well have been made. By others it may be imagined that the property of the Indians and the amiable courtesies of the whites were just equivalents. But "kind treatment" here was estimated at more than the Indians could give. It was thought to deserve something additional at the hands of the government, and the sites of cities at $1.25 per acre was perhaps as reasonable as could be expected. If the absolute donation of cities already built would secure justice, much less kindness to the red man, the government could make the gift and save its millions of treasure.

When the treaty came to the Senate, the 11th article was stricken out: but it would be unjust to suppose that this action was permitted to influence in the least future treatment by the whites. From this time until the 12th of April, 1864, these Indians were confessedly at peace. On that day a man by the name of Ripley, a ranchman, came into Camp Sanborn, on the South Platte, and stated that the Indians had taken his stock; he did not know what tribe. He asked and obtained of Captain Sanborn, the commander of the post, troops for the purpose of pursuit. Lieutenant Dunn, with 40 men, were put under the guide of this man Ripley with instructions to disarm the Indians found in possession of Ripley's stock. Who or what Ripley was we know not. That he owned stock we have his own word—the word of no one else. During the day Indians were found. Ripley claimed some of the horses. Lieutenant Dunn ordered the soldiers to stop the herd, and ordered the Indians to come forward and talk with him. Several of them rode forward, and when within six or eight feet Dunn ordered his men to dismount and disarm the Indians. The Indians of course resisted, and a fight ensured. What Indians they were he knew not; from bows and arrows found, he judged them to be Cheyennes.

Dunn getting the worst of the fight, returned to camp, obtained a guide and a remount, and next morning started again. In May following, Major Downing, of the 1st Colorado cavalry, went to Denver and asked Colonel Chivington to give him a force to move against the Indians, for what purpose we do not know. Chivington gave him the men, and the following are Downing's own words: "I captured an Indian and required him to go to the village or I would kill him. This was about the middle of May. We started about 11 o'clock in the day, travelled all day and all that night; about daylight I succeeded in surprising the Cheyenne village of Cedar Bluffs, in a small cañon about 60 miles north of the South Platte river. We commenced shooting. I ordered the men to commence killing them. They lost, as I am informed, some 26 killed and 30 wounded. My own loss was one killed and one wounded. I burnt up their lodges and everything I could get hold of. I took no prisoners. We got out of ammunition and could not pursue them."

In this camp the Indians had their women and children. He captured 100 ponies, which, the officer says, "were distributed among the boys, for the reason that they had been marching almost constantly day and night for nearly three weeks." This was done because such conduct "was usual," he said, "in New Mexico." About the same time Lieutenant Ayres, of the Colorado troops, had a difficulty, in which an Indian chief under a flag of truce was murdered. During the summer and fall occurrences of this character were frequent. Some time during the fall, Black Kettle and other prominent chiefs of the Cheyenne and Arapahoe nations sent word to the commander at Fort Lyon that the war had been forced upon them and they desired peace. They were then upon their own reservation. The officer in command, Major E. W. Wynkoop, 1st Colorado cavalry, did not feel authorized to conclude a treaty with them, but gave them a pledge of military protection until an interview could be procured with the governor of Colorado, who was superintendent of Indian affairs. He then proceeded to Denver with seven of the leading chiefs to see the governor. Colonel Chivington was present at the interview. Major Wynkoop, in his sworn testimony before a previous commission, thus relates the action of the governor when he communicated the presence of the chiefs seeking peace: "He (the governor) intimated that he was sorry I had brought them; that he considered he had nothing to do with them; that they had declared war against the United States, and he considered them in the hands of the military authorities; that he did not think it was policy anyhow to make peace with them until they were properly punished, for the reason that the United States would be acknowledging themselves whipped." Wynkoop further states that the governor said the 3d regiment of Colorado troops had been raised on his representations at Washington, to kill Indians, and Indians they must kill." Wynkoop then ordered the Indians to move their villages nearer to the fort, and bring their women and children, which was done. In November this officer was removed, and Major Anthony, of the 1st Colorado cavalry, ordered to take command of the fort. He too assured the Indians of safety. They numbered about 500, men, women, and children. It was here, under the pledge of protection, that they were slaughtered by the 3d Colorado and a batallion of the 1st Colorado cavalry under command of Colonel Chivington. He marched from Denver to Fort Lyon, and about daylight in the morning of the 29th of November surrounded the Indian camp and commenced an indiscriminate slaughter. The particulars of this massacre are too well known to be repeated here with all its heartrending scenes. It is enough to say that it scarcely has its parallel in the records of Indian barbarity. Fleeing women, holding up their hands and praying for mercy, were brutally shot down; infants were killed and scalped in derision; men were tortured and multilated in a manner that would put to shame the savage ingenuity of interior Africa.

No one will be astonished that a war ensued which cost the government $30,000,000, and carried conflagration and death to the border settlements.

During the spring and summer of 1865 no less than 8,000 troops were withdrawn from the effective force engaged in suppressing the rebellion to meet this Indian war. The result of the year's campaign satisfied all reasonable men that war with Indians was useless and expensive. Fifteen or twenty Indians had been killed, at an expense of more than a million dollars apiece, while hundreds of our soldiers had lost their lives, many of our border settlers had been butchered, and much property destroyed. To those who reflected on the subject, knowing the facts, the war was something more than useless and expensive; it was dishonorable to the nation, and disgraceful to those who had originated it.

When the utter futility of *conquering* a peace was made manifest to every one, and the true cause of the war began to be developed, the country demanded that peaceful agencies should be resorted to. Generals Harney, Sanborn, and others were selected as commissioners to procure a council of the hostile tribes, and in October, 1865, they succeeded in doing so at the mouth of the Little Arkansas. At this council the Cheyennes and Arapahoes were induced to relinquish their reservation on the upper Arkansas and accept a reservation partly in southern Kansas and partly in the Indian territory, lying immediately south of Forts Larned and Zarah. The object was to remove them from the vicinity of Colorado.

By the third article of the treaty it was agreed that until the Indians were removed to their new reservation they were "expressly permitted to reside upon and range at pleasure throughout the unsettled portions of that part of the country they claim as originally theirs, which lies between the Arkansas and the Platte rivers." This hunting ground reserved is the same which is described in the treaty of 1851, and on which they yet claim the right to hunt as long as the game shall last. When this treaty came to the Senate for ratification it was so amended as to require the President to designate for said tribes a reservation outside of the State of Kansas, and not within any Indian reservation except upon consent of the tribes interested. As the reservation fixed was entirely within the State of Kansas and the Cherokee country, this provision deprived them of any home at all, except the hunting privilege reserved by the treaty. This statement, if not illustrative of the manner in which Indian rights are secured by our legislators, may at least call for greater vigilance in the future. Agreements were made at the same time with the Kiowas, Comanches, and Apaches.

So soon as these treaties were signed, the war which had been waged for nearly two years instantly ceased. Travel was again secure on the plains. What 8,000 troops had failed to give, this simple agreement, rendered nugatory by the Senate, and bearing nothing but a pledge of friendship, obtained. During the summer, fall, and winter of 1866, comparative peace prevailed. General Sherman, during this time, travelled without escort to the most distant posts of his command, and yet with a feeling of perfect security.

To say that no outrages were committed by the Indians would be claiming for more than can be justly claimed for the most moral and religious communities. Many bad men are found among the whites; they commit outrages despite all social restraints; they frequently, too, escape punishment. Is it to be wondered at that Indians are no better than we? Let us go to our best cities, where churches and schoolhouses adorn every square; yet unfortunately we must keep a policeman at every corner, and scarcely a night passes but, in spite of refinement, religion, and law, crime is committed. How often, too, it is found impossible to discover the criminal. If, in consequence of these things, war should be waged against these cities, they too would have to share the fate of Indian villages.

The Sioux war on the Powder river, to which we shall hereafter allude, commenced in July, 1866. When it commenced General St. George Cook, in command at Omaha, forbade within the limits of his command the sale of arms and ammunition to Indians. The mere existence of an Indian war on the north Platte aroused apprehensions of danger on the Arkansas. The Cheyennes of the north and south are related, and, though living far apart, they frequently visit each other. Many of the northern Sioux, desiring to be peaceable, (as they allege,) on the breaking out of hostilities in the north, came south, some to the vicinity of the Republican, and others as far south as Fort Larned. Their appearance here excited more or less fear among the traders and freighters on the plains. These fears extended to the settlements, from which they were reflected back to the military posts. The commanders became jealous and watchful. Trifles, which under ordinary circumstances would have passed unnoticed, were received as conclusive of the hostile purposes of these tribes. Finally, in December, Fetterman's party were killed at Fort Phil. Kearney, and the whole country became thrilled with horror. It is thus that the Indian in war loses the sympathy of mankind. That he goes to war is not astonishing; he is often compelled to do so. Wrongs are borne by him in silence that never fail to drive civilized men to deeds of violence. When he is your friend he will sometimes sacrifice himself in your defence. When he is your enemy he pushes his enmity to the excess of barbarity. This shocks the moral sense and leaves him without defenders.

When the news of this terrible calamity reached the Arkansas posts, the traders here too were prohibited from selling the Indians arms. Major Douglas, of the 3d infantry, as early as the 13th of January, 1867, communicated his fears to Major General Hancock. He pointed to no single act of hostility, but gave the statement of Kicking Bird, a rival chief of Satanta among the Kiowas, that Satanta talked of war and said he would commence when the grass grew in the spring.

On the 16th of February Captain Smith, of the 19th infantry, in command of Fort Arbuckle, reports to General Ord at Little Rock, which is at once forwarded to the department of the Missouri, that a negro child and some stock had been taken off by the Indians before he took command. His informant was one Jones, an interpreter. In this letter he uses the following significant language: "I have the honor to state further, that several other tribes than the Comanches have lately been noticed on the war path, having been seen in their progress in unusual numbers, and without their squaws and children, a fact to which much significance is attached by those conversant with Indian usages. It is thought by many white residents of the territory that some of these tribes may be acting in concert, and that plundering incursions are at least in contemplation."

After enumerating other reports of wrongs, (coming perhaps from Jones,) and drawing inferences therefrom, he closes by saying that he has deferred to the views of white persons who, from long residence among the Indians, "are competent to advise him," and that his communication "is more particularly the embodiment of their views." As it embodied the views of others, it may not be surprising that a re-enforcement of ten additional companies was asked for his post.

Captain Asbury, at Fort Larned, also reported that a small party of Cheyennes had compelled a ranchman named Parker, near that post, to cook supper for them, and then threatened to kill him because he had no sugar. He escaped, however, to tell the tale. Finally, on the 9th of February, one F. F. Jones, a Kiowa interpreter, files with Major Douglas, at Fort Dodge, an affidavit that he had recently visited the Kiowa camp in company with Major Page and John E. Tappan, on a trading expedition. That the Indians took from them flour, sugar, rice, and apples. That they threatened to shoot Major Page because he was a soldier, and tried to kill Tappan. That they shot at him (Jones) and missed him, (which in the sequel may be regarded as a great misfortune.) He stated that the Indians took their mules, and that Satanta requested him to say to Major Douglas that he demanded the troops and military posts should at once be removed from the country, and also that the railroads and mail-stages must be immediately stopped. Satanta requested him to tell Douglas that his own stock was getting poor, and hoped the government stock at the post would be well fed, as he would be over in a few days to get it. But the most startling of all the statements communicated by Jones on this occasion was that a war party came in, while he was at the camp, bringing with them 200 horses and the scalps of 17 negro soldiers and 1 white man. This important information was promptly despatched to General Hancock at Fort Leavenworth, and a short time thereafter he commenced to organize the expedition which subsequently marched to Pawnee Fork and burned the Cheyenne village.

On the 11th of March following, General Hancock addressed a letter to Wynkoop, the agent of the Cheyenne and Arapahoes, that "he had about completed arrangements for moving a force to the plains." He stated that his object was to show the Indians that he was "able to chastise any tribes who may molest people travelling across the plains." Against the Cheyennes he complained, first, that they had not delivered the Indian who killed a New Mexican at Fort Zarah, and, second, he believed he had "evidence sufficient to fix upon the different bands of that tribe, whose chiefs are known, several of the outrages committed on the Smoky Hill last summer." He requested the agent to tell them he came "prepared for peace or war," and that hereafter he would "insist upon their keeping off the main lines of travel, where their presence is calculated to bring about collisions with the whites." This, it will be remembered, was their hunting ground, secured by treaty. On the same day he forwarded a similar communication to J. H. Leavenworth, agent for the Kiowas and Comanches. The complaints he alleges against them are precisely the same contained in the affidavit and statement of Jones and the letter of Captain Asbury.

The expedition left Fort Larned on the 13th of April, and proceeded up the Pawnee fork of the Arkansas, in the direction of a village of 1,000 or 1,500 Cheyennes and Sioux. When he came near their camp the chiefs visited him, as they had already done at Larned, and requested him not to approach the camp with his troops, for the women and children, having the remembrance of Sand creek, would certainly abandon the village. On the 14th he resumed his march with cavalry, infantry, and artillery, and, when about ten miles from their village, he was again met by the headman, who stated that they would treat with him there or elsewhere, but they could not, as requested by him, keep their women and children in camp if he approached with soldiers. He informed them that he would march up to within a mile of the village, and treat with them that evening. As he proceeded the women fled, leaving the village with all their property. The chiefs and a part of the young men remained. To some of these, visiting the camp of General Hancock, horses were furnished to bring back the women. The horses were returned, with word that the women and children could not be collected. It was then night. Orders were then given to surround the village and capture the Indians remaining. The order was obeyed, but the chiefs and warriors had departed. The only persons found were an old Sioux and an idiotic girl of eight or nine years of age. It afterwards appeared that the person of this girl had been violated, from which she soon died. The Indians were gone, and the report spread that she had been a captive among them, and they had committed this outrage before leaving. The Indians say that she was an idiotic Cheyenne girl, forgotten in the confusion of flight, and if violated, it was not by them.

The next morning General Custer, under orders, started in pursuit of the Indians with his cavalry, and performed a campaign of great labor and suffering, passing over a vast extent of country, but seeing no hostile Indians. With the fleeing Indians reached the Smoky Hill they destroyed a station and killed several men. A courier having brought this intelligence to General Hancock, he at once ordered the Indian village, of about 300 lodges, together with the entire property of the tribes, to be burned.

The Indian now became an outlaw, not only the Cheyennes and Sioux, but all the tribes on the plains. The superintendent of an express company, Cottrell, issued a circular order to the agents and employés of the company in the following language: "You will hold no communications with Indians whatever. If Indians come within shooting distance, shoot them. Show them no mercy, for they will show you none." This was in the Indian country. He closes by saying: "General Hancock will protect you and our property."

Whether war existed previous to that time seems to have been a matter of doubt even with General Hancock himself. From that day forward no doubt on the subject was entertained by anybody. The Indians were then fully aroused, and no more determined war has ever been waged by them. The evidence taken tends to show that we have lost many soldiers, besides a large number of settlers, on the frontier. The most valuable trains belonging to individuals, as well as to government, among which was a government train of ammunition, were captured by these wild horsemen. Stations were destroyed. Hundreds of horses and mules were taken, and found in their possession when we met them in council; while we are forced to believe that their entire loss since the burning of their village consists of six men killed.

The Kiowas and Comanches, it will be seen, deny the statement of Jones in every particular. They say that no war party came in at the time stated, or at any other time, after the treaty of 1865. They deny that they killed any negro soldiers, and positively assert that no Indian was ever known to scalp a negro. In the latter statement they are corroborated by all tribes and by persons who know their habits; and the records of the adjutant general's office fail to show the loss of the 17 negro soldiers, or any soldiers at all. They deny having robbed Jones or insulted Page or Tappan. Tappan's testimony was taken, in which he brands the whole statement of Jones as false, and declares that both he and Page so informed Major Douglas within a few days after Jones made his affidavit. We took the testimony of Major Douglas, in which he admits the correctness of Tappan's statement, but, for some reason unexplained, he failed to communicate the correction to General Hancock. The threats to take the horses and attack the posts on the Arkansas were made in a vein of jocular bravado, and not understood by any one present at the time to possess the least importance. The case of the Box family has already been explained, and this completes the case against the Kiowas and Comanches, who are exculpated by the united testimony of all the tribes from any share in the late troubles.

The Cheyennes admit that one of their young men in a private quarrel, both parties being drunk, killed a New Mexican at Fort Zarah. Such occurrences are so frequent among the whites on the plains that ignorant Indians might be pardoned for participating, if it be done merely to evidence their advance in civilization. The Indians claim that the Spaniard was in fault, and further protest that no demand was ever made for the delivery of the Indian.

The Arapahoes admit that a party of their young men, with three young warriors of the Cheyennes, returning from an excursion against the Utes, attacked the train of Mr. Weddell, of New Mexico, during the month of March, and they were gathering up the stock when the war commenced.

Though this recital should prove tedious, it was thought necessary to guard the future against the errors of the past. We would not blunt the vigilance of military men in the Indian country, but we would warn them against the acts of the selfish and unprincipled, who need to be watched as well as the Indian. The origin and progress of this war are repeated in nearly all Indian wars. The history of one will suffice for many.

Nor would we be understood as conveying a censure of General Hancock for organizing this expedition. He had just come to the department, and circumstances were ingeniously woven to deceive him. His distinguished services in another field of patriotic duty had left him but little time to become acquainted with the remote or immediate causes producing these troubles. If he erred, he can very well roll a part of the responsibility on others; not alone on subordinate commanders, who were themselves deceived by others, but on those who were able to guard against the error and yet failed to do it. We have hundreds of treaties with the Indians and military posts are situated everywhere on their reservations. Since 1837 these treaties have not been compiled, and no provision is made, when a treaty is proclaimed, to furnish it to the commanders of posts, departments, or divisions. This is the fault of Congress.

As early as November, 1866, and long before the late war commenced, Lieutenant General Sherman, in his annual report to General Grant, indicated an Indian policy for the plains. He proposed, with the consent of the Secretary of War and the Secretary of the Interior, to restrict the Sioux north of the Platte, and east and west of certain lines, and "to deal summarily" with all found outside of those lines without a military pass. He then proceeds to say, "In like manner I would restrict the Arapahoes, Cheyennes, Comanches, Kiowas, Apaches, and Navajoes south of the Arkansas and east of Fort Union. This will leave for our people exclusively the use of the wide belt east and west, between the Platte and the Arkansas, in which lie the two great railroads over which passes the bulk of the travel to the mountain territories." He further says: "I beg you will submit this proposition to the honorable Secretary of the Interior, that we may know we do not violate some one of the solemn treaties made with these Indians, who are very captious, and claim to the very letter the execution on our part of those treaties, the obligations of which they seem to comprehend perfectly." On the 15th of January this suggestion was communicated by General Grant to the Secretary of War, with the following remarks: "I approve this proposition of General Sherman, provided it does not conflict with our treaty obligations with the Indians now between the Platte and Arkansas."

We have already shown that such a proposition was directly in the face of our treaty with the Cheyennes, Arapahoes, and Apaches. It is true that a communication of the then Commissioner of Indian Affairs on the subject to the Secretary of the Interior, dated January 15, 1867, was forwarded to the Senate and published by that body; but if any response was ever sent to General Sherman, informing him of existing treaty rights, we are not advised of it. Here, then, the responsibility attaches to the cabinet. A question of such vital importance should have been examined, and a prompt answer communicated to the officer asking the information. When officers are thus left to move in the dark, blunders are not theirs alone.

A few words only can be given to the origin of the Powder River war. This is partly in the country conceded to the Crows, and partly in that conceded to the Sioux by the treaty of 1851. The Sioux have gradually driven the Crows back upon the headwaters of the Yellowstone, in Montana, and claim as a conquest almost the entire country traversed by what is called the Powder River route to Montana. It will be recollected that the treaty of 1851 ceased to be operative in 1866. The annuities had been distributed, or rather appropriations therefor had been made for the last five years of the term, under the amendment of the Senate heretofore referred to.

The Indians were apprised, of course, that after that year they must look to their own exertions for subsistence. Since 1851, they had seen Colorado settled on the south, and Montana rapidly filling up to the north, leaving them no valuable hunting grounds of their ancient domain, except along Powder river and other tributaries of the Yellowstone. While the luxuriant growth of grass in this region made it desirable as an Indian in hunting ground, it also rendered it inviting to the gold hunter as a route to the new mines of Montana.

These Indians have never founded the title to their lands upon the treaty of 1851. They have looked upon that treaty as a mere acknowledgment of a previously existing right in themselves. The assignment of boundaries, they supposed, was merely to fix rights among the tribes—to make certain what was uncertain before. It is true, that by said treaty they "recognized" the right of the United States to establish roads and military posts. But it is equally true that in lieu of this privilege the United States was to pay them $50,000 per annum for 50 years. The Senate reduced the term to 10 years, and the Indians never having ratified the amendment, they have some right to claim, when the annuities are stopped at the end of 15 years a release from their obligations in this behalf.

The proper plan would have been to show some respect to their claims— call them pretentions, if you please—as also some regard for their wants, by entering into new relations with them. This, however, was not done. The Indian, who had stood by and seen the stream of population pouring over his lands to California, Utah, Oregon, and Montana, for so many years, began now, when thrown back by the government upon his own resources, to seek some place where he might be secure from intrusion.

But just at this moment, the war of the rebellion being over, thousands of our people turned their faces toward the treasures of Montana. The stories in regard to its mines eclipsed those fabulous tales that frenzied the Spaniard in Mexico. The Indian was forgotten. His rights were lost sight of in the general rush to these fountains of wealth. It seemed not to occur to any one that this poor despised red man was the original discoverer, and the sole occupant for many centuries, of every mountain seamed with quartz, and of every stream whose yellow sands glistened in the noonday sun. These mountains and streams, where gold is found, had all been taken from him. He asked to retain only a secluded spot, where the buffalo and the elk could live, and that spot he would make his home.

This could not be granted him. It lay on the route to these quartz mountains and Pactolian streams. The truth is, no place was left for him. Every inch of the land "belongs to the saints, and we are the saints."

On the 10th of March, 1866, General Pope, then commanding the department of the Missouri, issued an order to establish military posts "near the base of Big Horn mountain," and "on or near the upper Yellowstone," on the new route to Montana. On the 23rd of June, orders were issued from headquarters department of the Platte, directing a part of the 18th infantry to garrison Forts Reno, Phil. Kearney, and C. F. Smith. Colonel Carrington was placed in command of this new organization, called the "mountain district."

Phil. Kearney was established July 15th, and C. F. Smith August 3d. The Indians notified the troops that the occupation of their country would be resisted. The warning was unheeded.

An attempt was made during that summer, by the Interior Department, to stop the threatened war by negotiation. The Indians, in counsel demanded the evacuation of the country before treating. This could not be granted because the civil and military department of our governments cannot or will not understand each other. Some of the chiefs reluctantly submitted and signed the treaty, but Red Cloud retired from the council placing his hand upon his rifle saying, "In this and the Great Spirit I trust for the right."

As the fires of war blazed along the entire length of this new route, far from securing emigrant travel, the forts themselves were besieged; the mountains swarmed with Indian warriors, the valleys seemed to be covered by them. Wood and hay were only procured at the end of a battle. Matters grew worse until the 21st of December, when a wood party being attacked, a re-enforcement under Lieutenant Colonel Fetterman was sent out, and a fight ensued in which every man of our forces was killed. This is called the massacre of Fort Phil. Kearney.

As we have already stated, the Indians yet demand the surrender of this country to them. But they have agreed to suspend hostilities and meet commissioners next spring to treat of their alleged rights, without insisting on the previous withdrawal of the garrisons. Whether they will then insist on the abandonment of the route we cannot say. Of one thing we are satisfied—that so long as the war lasts the road is entirely useless to emigrants. It is worse than that; it renders other routes insecure, and endangers territorial settlements. It is said that a road to Montana, leaving the Pacific railroad further west and passing down the valley west of the Big Horn mountains, is preferable to the present route. The Indians present no objection to such a road, but assure us that we may travel it in peace.

If it be said that the savages are unreasonable, we answer, that if civilized they might be reasonable. At least they would not be dependent on the buffalo and the elk; they would no longer want a country exclusively for game, and the presence of the white man would become desirable. If it be said that because they are savages they should be exterminated, we answer that, aside from the humanity of the suggestion, it will prove exceedingly difficult, and if money considerations are permitted to weigh, it costs less to civilize than to kill.

In making treaties it was enjoined on us to remove, if possible, the causes of complaint on the part of the Indians. This would be no easy task. We have done the best we could under the circumstances, but it is now rather late in the day to think of obliterating from the minds of the present generation the remembrance of wrong. Among civilized men war usually springs from a sense of injustice. The best possible way then to avoid war is to do no act of injustice. When we learn that the same rule holds good with Indians, the chief difficulty is removed. But it is said our wars with them have been almost constant. Have we been uniformly unjust? We answer unhesitatingly, yes. We are aware that the masses of our people have felt kindly toward them, and the legislation of Congress has always been conceived in the best intentions, but it has been erroneous in fact or perverted in execution. Nobody pays any attention to Indian matters. This is a deplorable fact. Members of Congress understand the negro question, and talk learnedly of finance and other problems of political economy, but when the progress of settlement reaches the Indian's home, the only question considered is, "how best to get his lands." When they are obtained, the Indian is lost sight of. While our missionary societies and benevolent associations have annually collected thousands of dollars from the charitable, to be sent to Asia and Africa for the purposes of civilization scarcely a dollar is expended or a thought bestowed on the civilization of Indians at our very doors. Is it because the Indians are not worth the effort at civilization? Or is it because our people, who have grown rich in the occupation of their former lands—too often taken by force or by fraud —will not contribute? It would be harsh to insinuate that covetous eyes have possibly been set on their remaining possessions, and extermination harbored as a means of accomplishing it. They have known that our legislators and nine tenths of our people are actuated by no such spirit. Would it not be well to so regulate our future conduct in this matter as to include the possibility of so unfavorable an inference?

We are aware that it is an easy task to condemn the errors of former times, as well as a very thankless one to criticise those of the present; but the past policy of the government has been so much at variance with our ideas of treating this important subject, that we hope to be indulged in a short allusion to it.

The wave of our population has been from the east to the west. The Indian was found on the Atlantic seaboard, and thence to the Rocky mountains lived numerous distinct tribes, each speaking a language as incomprehensible to the other as was our language to any of them. As our settlements penetrated the interior, the border came in contact with some Indian tribe. The white and Indian must mingle together and jointly occupy the country, or one of them must abandon it. If they could have lived together, the Indian by this contact would soon have become civilized and war would have been impossible. All admit this would have been beneficial to the Indian. Even if we thought it would not have been hurtful to the white man, we would not venture on such an assertion, for we know too well his pride of race. But suppose it had proved a little inconvenient as well as detrimental, it is questionable whether the policy adopted has not been more injurious. What prevented their living together? First. The antipathy of race. Second. The difference of customs and manners arising from their tribal or clannish organizations. Third. The difference in language, which in a great measure barred intercourse and a proper understanding each of the other's motives and intentions.

Now, by educating the children of these tribes in the English language these differences would have disappeared and civilization would have followed at once. Nothing then would have been left but the antipathy of race, and that too is always softened in the beams of a higher civilization.

Naturally, the Indian has many noble qualities. He is the very embodiment of courage. Indeed, at times he seems insensible of fear. If he is cruel and revengeful, it is because he is outlawed and his companion is the wild beast. Let civilized man be his companion, and the association warms into life virtues of the rarest worth. Civilization has driven him back from the home he loved; it has often tortured and killed him, but it never could make him a slave. As we have had so little respect for those we did enslave, to be consistent, this element of Indian character should challenge some admiration.

But suppose, when civilized, our pride had still rejected his association, we could at least have removed the causes of war by giving him a home to himself, where he might, with his own race, have cultivated the arts of peace. Through sameness of language is produced sameness of sentiment and thought; customs and habits are moulded and assimilated in the same way, and thus in process of time the differences producing trouble would have been gradually obliterated. By civilizing one tribe others would have followed. Indians of different tribes associate with each other on terms of equality; they have not the Bible, but their religion, which we call superstition, teaches them that the Great Spirit made us all. In the difference of language today lies two-thirds of our trouble.

Instead of adopting the plan indicated, when the contact came the Indian had to be removed. He always objected, and went with a sadder heart. His hunting grounds are as dear to him as is the home of his childhood to the civilized man. He too loves the streams and mountains of his youth; to be forced to leave them breaks those tender chords of the heart which vibrate to the softer sensibilities of human nature, and dries up the fountains of benevolence and kindly feeling, without which there is no civilization.

It is useless to go over the history of Indian removals. If it had been done but once, the record would be less revolting; from the eastern to the middle States, from there to Illinois and Wisconsin, thence to Missouri and Iowa, thence to Kansas, Dakota, and the plains; whither now we cannot tell. Surely the policy was not designed to perpetuate barbarism, but such has been its effect. The motives prompting these removals are too well known to be noticed by us. If the Indians were now in a fertile region of country the difficulty would be less; they would not have to be removed again. But many of them are beyond the region of agriculture, where the chase is a necessity. So long as they have to subsist in this way civilization is almost out of the question. If they could now be brought back into the midst of civilization instead of being pushed west, with all its inconveniences, it might settle the problem sooner than in any other way; but were we prepared to recommend such a scheme, the country is not prepared to receive it, nor would the Indians themselves accept it.

But one thing then remains to be done with honor to the nation, and that is to select a district or districts of country, as indicated by Congress, on which all the tribes east of the Rocky mountains may be gathered. For each district let a territorial government be established, with powers adapted to the ends designed. The governor should be a man of unquestioned integrity and purity of character; he should be paid such salary as to place him above temptation; such police or military force should be authorized as would enable him to command respect and keep the peace; agriculture and manufactures should be introduced among them as rapidly as possible; schools should be established which children should be required to attend; their barbarous dialects should be blotted out and the English language substituted. Congress may from time to time establish courts and other institutions of government suited to the condition of the people. At first it may be a strong military government; let it be so if thought proper, and let offenders be tried by military law until civil courts would answer a better purpose. Let farmers and mechanics, millers and engineers be employed and sent among them for purposes of instruction; then let us invite our benevolent societies and missionary associations to this field of philanthropy nearer home. The object of greatest solicitude should be to break down the prejudices of tribe among the Indians; to blot out the boundary lines which divide them into distinct nations, and fuse them into one homogeneous mass. Uniformity of language will do this—nothing else will. As this work advances each head of a family should be encouraged to select and improve a homestead. Let the women be taught to weave, to sew, and to knit. Let polygamy be punished. Encourage the building of dwellings, and the gathering there of those comforts which endear the home.

The annuities should consist exclusively of domestic animals, agricultural and mechanical implements, clothing, and such subsistence only as is absolutely necessary to support them in the earliest stages of the enterprise. Money annuities, here and elsewhere, should be abolished forever. These more than anything else have corrupted the Indian service, and brought into disgrace officials connected with it. In the course of a few years, the clothing and provision annuities also may be dispensed with. Mechanics and artisans will spring up among them, and the whole organization, under the management of a few honest men, will become self-sustaining.

The older Indians at first will be unwilling to confine themselves to these districts. They are inured to the chase and they will not leave it. The work may be of slow progress, but it must be done. If our ancestors had done it, it would not have to be done now; but they did not, and we must meet it. Aside from extermination, this is the only alternative now left us. We must take the savage as we find him, or rather as we have made him. We have spent 200 years in creating the present state of things. If we can civilize in 25 years, it will be a vast improvement on the operations of the past. If we attempt to force the older Indians from the chase, it will involve us in war. The younger ones will follow them into hostility, and another generation of savages will succeed. When the buffalo is gone the Indians will cease to hunt. A few years of peace and the game will have disappeared. In the meantime, by the plan suggested we will have formed a nucleus of civilization among the young that will restrain the old and furnish them a home and subsistence when the game is gone.

The appeal of these old Indians is irresistible. They say, "We know nothing about agriculture. We have lived on game from infancy. We love the chase. Here are the wide plains over which the vast herds of buffalo roam. In the spring they pass from south to north, and in the fall return, traversing thousands of miles. Where they go you have no settlements; and if you had, there is room enough for us both. Why limit us to certain boundaries, beyond which we shall not follow the game? If you want the lands for settlement, come and settle them. We will not disturb you. You may farm and we will hunt. You love the one, we love the other. If you want game we will share it with you. If we want bread, and you have it to spare, give it to us; but do not spurn us from your doors. Be kind to us and we will be kind to you. If we want ammunition, give or sell it to us. We will not use it to hurt you, but pledge you all we have, our word, that at the risk of our own we will defend your lives."

If Congress should adopt these suggestions, the only question remaining is, whether there shall be one or two territories. Under all the circumstances we would recommend the selection of two, and locate them as follows, viz.:

First, the territory bounded north by Kansas, east by Arkansas and Missouri, south by Texas, and west by the 100th or 101st meridian.

In this territory the Cherokees, Creeks, Choctaws, and others of the civilized tribes already reside. In process of time others might gradually be brought in, and in the course of a few years we might safely calculate on concentrating there the following tribes, to wit:

Cherokees	14,000
Creeks	14,396
Choctaws	12,500
Chickasaws	4,500
Seminoles	2,000
Osages	3,000
Wichitas, (various tribes)	3,508
Kiowas and Comanches	14,800
Cheyennes, Arapahoes, and Apaches	4,000
Pottawatomies	1,992
Kansas Indians (various tribes)	4,029
Navajoes of New Mexico	7,700
Total	86,425

It will be seen that we include in this estimate the Kansas Indians and number them at their full population. We learn that treaties are now pending before the Senate for the removal of all the Indians in that State. Among these Indians are many upright, moral, and enlightened men, and our policy, as already indicated, would be to have them take lands in severalty on their present reservations, selling the remainder, and becoming incorporated among the citizens of the State.

The second district might be located as follows, viz.: the territory bounded north by the 46th parallel, east by the Missouri river, south by Nebraska, and west by the 104th meridian.

If the hostile Sioux cannot be induced to remove from the Powder river, a hunting privilege may be extended to them for a time, while the nucleus of settlement may be forming on the Missouri, the White Earth, or Cheyenne river. To prevent war, if insisted on by the Sioux, the western boundary might be extended to the 106th or even the 107th meridian for the present.

The following tribes might in a reasonable time be concentrated on this reservation, to wit:

Yancton Sioux	2,530
Poncas	980
Lower Brulés	1,200
Lower Yanctonais	2,100
Two Kettles	1,200
Blackfeet	1,320
Minneconjoux	2,220
Unepapas	1,800

Ogallallas	2,100
Upper Yanctonais	2,400
Sans Arcs	1,680
Arickarees	1,500
Gros-Ventres	400
Mandans	400
Assinaboines	2,640
Flatheads	558
Upper Pend d'Oreilles	918
Kootenays	287
Blackfeet	2,450
Piegans	1,870
Bloods	2,150
Gros-Ventres	1,500
Crows	3,900
Winnebagoes	1,750
Omahas	998
Ottoes	511
Brulé and Ogallalla Sioux	7,865
Northern Cheyennes	1,800
Northern Arapahoes	750
Santee Sioux	1,350
Total	54,127

It may be advisable to let the Winnebagoes, Omahas, Ottoes, Santos, Sioux, and perhaps others, remain where they are, and finally, become incorporated with the citizens of Nebraska, as suggested in regard to the Kansas tribes.

The next injunction upon us was to make secure our frontier settlements and the building of our railroads to the Pacific. If peace is maintained with the Indian, every obstacle to the spread of our settlements and the rapid construction of the railroads will be removed. To maintain peace with the Indian, let the frontier settler treat him with humanity, and railroad directors see to it that he is not shot down by employés in wanton cruelty. In short, if settlers and railroad men will treat Indians as they would treat whites under similar circumstances, we apprehend but little trouble will exist. They must acquaint themselves with the treaty obligations of the government, and respect them as the highest law of the land. Instead of regarding the Indian as an enemy, let them regard him as a friend, and they will almost surely receive his friendship and esteem. If they will look upon him. as an unfortunate human being, deserving their sympathy and care, instead of a wild beast to be feared and detested, then their own hearts have removed the chief danger.

We were also required to suggest some plan for the civilization of

Indians. In our judgment, to civilize is to remove the causes of war, and under that head we suggested a plan for civilizing those east of the mountains. But as it is impracticable to bring within the two districts named all the Indians under our jurisdiction, we beg the privilege to make some general suggestions, which may prove beneficial to the service.

1. We recommend that the intercourse laws with the Indian tribes be thoroughly revised. They were adopted when the Indian bureau was connected with the War Department. Since that time the jurisdiction has been transferred to the Interior Department. This was done by simply declaring that the authority over this subject, once exercised by the Secretary of War, should now be exercised by the Secretary of the Interior. Some of the duties enjoined by these laws are intimately connected with the War Department, and it is questionable whether they were intended to be transferred to the Secretary of the Interior. If they were so transferred, the military officers insist that the command of the army is, *pro tanto,* withdrawn from them. If not transferred, the Indian department insists that its powers are insufficient for its own protection in the administration of its affairs. Hence the necessity of clearly defining the line separating the rights and duties of the two departments.

2. This brings us to consider the much mooted question whether the bureau should belong to the civil or military department of the government. To determine this properly we must first know what is to be the future treatment of the Indians. If we intend to have war with them, the bureau should go to the Secretary of War. If we intend to have peace, it should be in the civil department. In our judgment, such wars are wholly unnecessary, and hoping that the government and the country will agree with us, we cannot now advise the change. It is possible, however, that, despite our efforts to maintain peace, war may be forced on us by some tribe or tribes of Indians. In the event of such occurrence it may be well to provide, in the revision of the intercourse laws or elsewhere, at what time the civil jurisdiction shall cease and the military jurisdiction begin, if thought advisable, also Congress may authorize the President to turn over to the military the exclusive control of the tribes as may be continually hostile or unmanageable. Under the plan which we have suggested the chief duties of the bureau will be to educate and instruct in the peaceful arts—in other words, to civilize the Indians. The military arm of the government is not the most admirably adapted to discharge duties of this character. We have the highest possible appreciation of the officers of the army, and fully recognize their proverbial integrity and honor; but we are satisfied that not one in a thousand would like to teach Indian children to read and write, or Indian men to sow and reap. These are emphatically civil, and not military, occupations. But it is insisted that the present Indian service is corrupt, and this change should be made to get rid of the dishonest. That there are many bad men connected with the service cannot be denied. The records are abundant to show that agents have pocketed the

funds appropriated by the government and driven the Indians to starvation. It cannot be doubted that Indian wars have originated from this cause. The Sioux war, in Minnesota, is supposed to have been produced in this way. For a long time these officers have been selected from partisan ranks, not so much on account of honesty and qualification as for devotion to party interests, and their willingness to apply the money of the Indian to promote the selfish schemes of local politicians. We do not doubt that some such men may be in the service of the bureau now, and this leads us to suggest:

3. That Congress pass an act fixing a day (not later than the 1st of February, 1869) when the offices of all superintendents, agents, and special agents shall be vacated. Such persons as have proved themselves competent and faithful may be reappointed. Those who have proved unfit will find themselves removed without an opportunity to divert attention from their own unworthiness by professions of party zeal.

4. We believe the Indian question to be one of such momentous importance as it respects both the honor and interest of the nation, as to require for its proper solution an undivided responsibility. The vast and complicated duties now devolved upon the Secretary of the Interior leave him too little time to examine and determine the multiplicity of questions necessarily connected with the government and civilization of a race. The same may be said of the Secretary of War. As things now are, it is difficult to fix responsibility. When errors are committed, the civil department blames the military; the military retort by the charge of inefficiency or corruption against the officers of the bureau. The Commissioner of Indian Affairs escapes responsibility by pointing to the Secretary of the Interior, while the Secretary may well respond that, though in theory he may be responsible, practically he is governed by the head of the bureau. We, therefore, recommend that Indian affairs be committed to an independent bureau or department. Whether the head of the department should be made a member of the President's cabinet is a matter for the discretion of Congress and yourself, and may be as well settled without any suggestions from us.

5. We cannot close this report without alluding to another matter calling for the special attention of Congress. Governors of Territories are now *ex officio* superintendents of Indian affairs within their respective jurisdictions. The settlements in the new Territory are generally made on Indian lands before the extinguishment of the Indian title. If difficulties ensue between the whites and Indians, the governor too frequently neglects the rights of the red man, and yields to the demand of those who have votes to promote his political aspirations in the organization of the forthcoming State. Lest any acting governor may suppose himself alluded to, we take occasion to disclaim such intention. We might cite instances of gross outrage in the past, but we prefer to base the recommendation upon general principles, which can be readily understood.

And in this connection we deem it of the highest importance that—

6. No governor or legislature of States or Territories be permitted to call out and equip troops for the purpose of carrying on war against Indians. It was Colorado troops that involved us in the war of 1864-'65 with the Cheyennes. It was a regiment of hundred day men that perpetrated the butchery at Sand creek, and took from the treasury millions of money. A regiment of Montana troops, last September, would have involved us in an almost interminable war with the Crows but for the timely intervention of the military authorities. If we must have Indian wars, let them be carried on by the regular army, whose officers are generally actuated by the loftiest principles of humanity, and the honor of whose profession requires them to respect the rules of civilized warfare.

7. In reviewing the intercourse laws it would be well to prescribe anew the conditions upon which persons may be authorized to trade. At present every one trades with or without the authority of the bureau officers on giving a bond approved by a judge of one of the district courts. Corrupt and dangerous men thus find their way among the Indians, who cheat them in trade and sow the seeds of dissension and trouble.

8. New provisions should be made, authorizing and positively directing the military authorities to remove white persons who persist in trespassing on Indian reservations and unceded Indian lands.

9. The Navajo Indians in New Mexico were for several years held as prisoners of war at the Bosque Redondo, at a very great expense to the government. They have now been turned over to the Interior Department, and must be subsisted as long as they remain there. We propose that a treaty be made with them, or their consent in some way obtained, to remove at an early day to the southern district selected by us, where they may soon be made self-supporting.

10. We suggest that the President may, at times, appoint some person or persons in the distant Territories, either civilians or military men, to make inspection of Indian affairs, and report to him.

11. A new commission should be appointed, or the present one be authorized to meet the Sioux next spring, according to your agreement, and also to arrange with the Navajoes for their removal. It might be well, also, in case our suggestions are adopted in regard to selecting Indian territories, to extend the powers of the commission, so as to enable us to conclude treaties or agreements with tribes confessedly at peace, looking to their concentration upon the reservations indicated.

In the course of a short time the Union Pacific railroad will have reached the country claimed by the Snakes, Bannocks, and other tribes, and in order to preserve peace with them the commission should be required to see them and make with them satisfactory arrangements.

Appended hereto will be found—

1. The journal of our meetings, and councils held.

2. The detailed mass of evidence taken and reports collected, illustrative of the objects embraced in the act creating the commission.

3. The treaty made and concluded with the Kiowas and Comanches.

4. The supplementary treaty made and concluded with the Apaches of the plains.

5. The treaty of peace made and concluded with the Cheyennes and Arapahoes.

6. The account current of all moneys received and disbursed by authority of the commission.

In conclusion, we beg permission to return our thanks to the officers of the military posts everywhere within the limits of our operations, for their uniform courtesy and kindness. The officers of the railroad companies on the plains especially are entitled to our thanks for kind cooperation in the objects of our mission, and attention to our convenience and comfort.

> N. G. TAYLOR, *President,*
> J. B. HENDERSON,
> W. T. SHERMAN, *Lieut. Gen.,*
> WM. S. HARNEY, *Bvt. Maj. Gen.,*
> JOHN B. SANBORN,
> ALFRED H. TERRY *Bvt. Maj. Gen.,*
> S. F. TAPPAN,
> C. C. AUGUR, *Bvt. Maj. Gen. U. S. A.,*
> *Commissioners.*

WASHINGTON, *November 26, 1868.*

DEAR SIR: I have read your remarks on the subject of transferring Indian affairs from the Interior to the War Department. I fully concur with you that such change ought not to be made. I do not know of any stronger proofs in support of your views on this subject than the facts I will here briefly state as the result of my own experience, which has not been very limited, as you will see by perusing the copy herewith, taken from the Congressional Globe.

In 1850 I was solicited to take the office of superintendent of Indian affairs in Oregon, which then contained also Washington and Idaho Territories, in which there were about 25,000 Indians. I declined the office unless the military force in that country could first be removed; there were six military posts there. In 1851 the troops were all removed from Oregon to California. I had charge of Indian affairs on that coast for three years, and during that whole time there was no trouble with the Indians, and not one dollar was the government called upon to pay to quell any Indian disturbances during that time. But it was said that that peaceful state of things brought no money to Oregon, and "Dart must be removed and the troops must come back." So in 1853 Dart was removed by President Pierce, and the troops brought back. The troubles that followed you know; the wars of 1854 and 1855, in Oregon, I believe have cost the government more than $8,000,000. I am sure there was no good reason for having trouble with any of the Oregon Indians.

I had a serious matter to settle, which grew out of the indiscretion of the officer in command of the last of the troops that were leaving Oregon. While passing the Rogue River country the officer was called upon to chastise the Indians in that neighborhood for some wrongs they were said to have committed; (chastising Indians only means killing them.) Word came to me that the troops on their way to California had killed 17 of the Rogue River Indians without any just cause. Upon a full investigation of that affair I found that the Indians were innocent of the charges laid against them. You can imagine that such an outrage was not easily settled.

When I first went to Oregon, no white man ventured to go into the upper country east of the Cascade mountains since the Cayuse war of 1848. I sent for the chief of the Cayuses to meet me at the Dalles of the Columbia. They refused to meet me until assured that I had no *bluecoats* with me. So I have in all my travels in the Indian country found the Indians to dislike the military; besides, I believe that ten per cent of the cost of the army management of the Indians will pay every expense necessary to keep them quiet and friendly in every part of our Indian country. But, sir, to do this, none but honest and tried men should be placed in care of the Indians. General Grant, I know, is for peace and economy in all parts of the United States. But if the management of the Indians is turned over to the War Department, can we expect peace and economy to follow such a move? Besides, you know there is a very strong Quaker spirit in our country that is uncompromisingly opposed to sending the army among the Indians. Should serious Indian wars, and an expense of many millions grow out of this proposed change, (as will surely be the case,) I should seriously fear its effect upon the incoming administration as very disastrous.

I have the honor to be your obedient servant,

ANSON DART.

[Editor's note: both the Indian Peace Commission Report of January 7, 1868, and the letter from Anson Dart are appendices to N. G. Taylor's Report of November 23, 1868.]

Report of Commissioner of Indian Affairs N. G. Taylor November 23, 1868

(Excerpt from *Report for 1868*, pp. 467-75)

Commissioner Taylor discussed the question of the transfer of the Indian Bureau to the War Department, a proposal frequently heard at the time. After stating his "admiration and love of the gallant officers and soldiers of our army," Taylor proceeded to lay the blame for most of the past failures of American Indian policy to the rashness and inefficiency of the U.S. Army. With rhetoric that might be envied by the bitterest foe of the Government today, Taylor recounted the sad record of Army mismanagement in the Indian field, whether in peace or in war. Sadly enough, Taylor's indictment rings true, though it is no more palatable to some today than it was 100 years ago.

THE QUESTION OF THE TRANSFER OF THE INDIAN BUREAU TO THE WAR DEPARTMENT

IT WILL BE SEEN, by referring to the proceedings of the peace commission at its late meeting at Chicago, that a resolution was adopted recommending to Congress the transfer of the Indian Bureau to the War Department. In view of probable action upon that recommendation, and impelled by solemn convictions of duty, I feel called upon to offer some facts and arguments, for the consideration of Congress, in opposition to the proposed transfer, and to give some views, suggested by nearly two years' intimate official connection with the Indian service, with regard to the best method for the future conduct of Indian affairs.

In 1849, Congress, upon the creation of the Department of the Interior, incorporated the Bureau of Indian Affairs in that department, giving to its head the supervisory and appellate powers theretofore exercised over Indian affairs by the Secretary of War. It is now proposed to re-transfer the bureau to the War Office.

It is presumed the question for legislative solution will be three-fold: Shall the bureau be transferred to the War Department; or shall it remain under the direction of the Secretary of the Interior; or shall it be erected into an independent department, upon an equal footing in all respects with the other departments, as recommended, unanimously, by the peace commission in their report to the President of 7th January last.

I shall endeavor to present some reasons against the transfer. These I proceed to offer, assuming all the time that the transfer means that in the future all our Indian affairs are to be administered by the army, under the direction of the War Office.

My reasons in opposition are—

1. *That the prompt, efficient, and successful management and direction of our Indian affairs is too large, onerous, and important a burden to be added to the existing duties of the Secretary of War.*

There is a limit to human capacity and endurance, and when either is taxed beyond that limit, it must fail in the performance of its functions, and the result must be disappointment, and most probably disaster, to the service.

The business of the War Department, in all its varied and complex ramifications, is sufficient already, if properly transacted, to employ all the faculties of the most accomplished head, even with all the aids he may summon to his assistance; and there are few men living, if any, who can give the requisite attention to its demands, and at the same time discharge properly and with requisite promptness the delicate, important, and numerous duties the care of Indian affairs would superadd.

None can deny that the safe and successful management of the military affairs of a republic of 40,000,000 of people, demands the constant and exclusive exercise of all the powers of an accomplished and experienced statesman.

A little investigation, and even a superficial knowledge and a little reflection, will convince every candid mind that there is no branch of the public service more intricate and difficult, and involving more varied and larger public and private interests, than our "Indian affairs;" none requiring in their control and direction a larger brain, or a more sensitive and charitable heart.

If these things be true, the conclusion is irresistible that the proposed "transfer" is unreasonable and wrong.

If the argument applies as well to the Interior as to the War Department, let it be so; its force is not abated by the admission.

2. *The "transfer," in my judgment, will create a necessity for maintaining a large standing army in the field.*

I yield to none in admiration and love of the gallant officers and soldiers of our army. They are the hope of the nation in times of public danger, when the honor, integrity, or the existence of the republic is threatened by foreign or domestic foes. But "there is a time for all things," and I submit that a time of peace is *not* the time for a large standing army. In time of war, the army is our wall of defence. In peace, large armies exhaust the national resources without advantage to the country. The safety of the country in peace is not to be sought in a magnificent array of bayonets; but in the virtue, intelligence, industry, and patriotism of the citizens. With the restoration of all the States to their peaceful relations to the federal government, and the return of their population to industrial avocations and prosperity, if peace is maintained, as at the present, with all foreign powers, our military establishment should soon be reduced to a peace footing, its material returned to industrial and producing employments, and the people, to the extent of many millions of dollars, annually relieved of taxes now expended in the support and pay of the army.

Surely Congress is not prepared to transfer the Indian Bureau to the War Department merely to create a necessity to keep up the army, and with it the taxes.

3. *Our true policy towards the Indian tribes is peace, and the proposed transfer is tantamount, in my judgment, to perpetual war.*

Everybody knows that the presence of troops, with the avowed purpose of regulating affairs by force, arouses feelings of hostility and begets sentiments of resistance and war even in the most civilized and peaceful communities. How much more intense and bitter are the feelings of hostility engendered in the bosoms of barbarians and semicivilized Indians by the presence of soldiers, who they know are sent to force them into subjection and keep them so. To their ears the sounds of the camp and the boom of the morning and evening gun are the infallible signs of oppression and war; and the very sight of armed and uniformed soldiers in their haunts and hunting grounds provokes and inflames the profoundest feelings of hostility and hate.

If a chronic war, with additional annual expenses of $50,000,000 to $150,000,000 annually on account of Indian affairs, is desired, the transfer, it seems to me, is a logical way to the result.

More than half the period in which this bureau was under the control of the War Office was spent in the prosecution of costly and unprofitable as well as unjust wars against the Seminoles and the Sacs and Foxes, and in vexations and expensive troubles with the Creeks and Cherokees. It should not be forgotten, in this connection, that almost all the Indian wars which have depleted the treasury and desolated our frontiers ever since the bureau was given to the Interior Department, had their origin in the precipitate and ill-considered action of the military stationed in the Indian country. As examples, I respectfully refer to the Sioux war of 1852–4, which, as I am informed, originated in this wise: An immigrant Mormon train abandoned a cow. A lieutenant and squad went to the camp of the Indians who had found and eaten her, and demanded the man who had killed her. The Indians refused to surrender the man, but offered to pay for the cow. The lieutenant and his squad fired upon them, killing and wounding a number, when they were surrounded and massacred. The Sioux war ensued, costing us $20,000,000 to $40,000,000 and several hundred lives, besides much private and public property.

In April, 1864, a ranchman named Ripley went to Camp Sanborn, on South Platte, and charged the Indians with stealing his stock. A Lieutenant Dunn proceeded to search for, but could not find it. Falling in with a company of Cheyennes, an attempt was made to disarm the latter. In the melee one soldier was killed and some others wounded. Then followed the

Cheyenne war, culminating in the massacre at Sand Creek of 120 friendly Indians, mostly women and children, resting in their own hunting grounds under the protection of our flag. This affair is known as the Chivington massacre.

This war cost the treasury probably not less than $40,000,000, an immense amount of valuable property, and no one can tell how many lives, involving, as it did, not only the Cheyennes and Apaches, but the Arapahoes, Kiowas, and Comanches, and many bands of the Sioux, and was ended by the treaty of 1865, at the mouth of the Little Arkansas.

In 1866 the military took possession of the Powder river country in Dakota, within the acknowledged territory of the Sioux, and planted military posts Phil. Kearney, Reno, and C. F. Smith, without the consent of the Indian proprietors, and in direct violation of treaty stipulations. A fierce and bloody war ensued, costing us many millions of dollars, several hundred lives, including those killed at the Fort Kearney massacre, and much valuable property.

On the 19th of April, 1867, a military command burned the peaceful village of the Cheyennes on Pawnee Fork, western Kansas, who had been at peace with us since the treaty of 1865, on the Arkansas, and were then on lands assigned them by the treaty. The Cheyennes flew to arms, and the war of 1867 followed, in which we lost over 300 soldiers and citizens, several millions of dollars in expenses, and an immense amount of public and private property, and killed, it is believed, six Indians, and no more.

The pretext for our celebrated Navajo war in New Mexico, it is understood, was the shooting of a negro servant boy of a military officer by an Indian, and the refusal to surrender the slayer on the part of the Navajoes, who, nevertheless, proposed to make the amend, after the Indian fashion, by pecuniary satisfaction for the offence.

Four campaigns against the Navajoes resulted, in three of which our army failed of either success or glory. In the fourth the Indians succumbed to the superior strategy of the renowned Kit Carson, and were compelled, by hunger, to surrender.

This war cost the treasury many millions of dollars, and the people the loss of many lives and valuable property.

On the Pacific coast the indiscretions of our military, I am informed, produced similar unfortunate results, and nearly all our troubles with the Indians there, marring our history with cruel massacres, and in some instances with the extermination of whole bands, had their origin in the presence and unwise action of our military. In evidence of this statement I refer to the letter of Mr. Anson Dart, ex-superintendent of Indian affairs for Oregon and Washington Territory, to be found herewith.

Now if, as I think, I have shown military interference has been prolific of war, even since the bureau has been in civil control, what of peace and tranquillity can be expected if it be placed entirely in military hands?

4. *Military management of Indian affairs has been tried for seventeen*

years and has proved a failure, and must, in my judgment, in the very nature of things, always prove a failure.

Soldiers are educated and trained in the science of war and in the arts of arms. Civilians are taught in the sciences and arts of peaceful civilization. In lifting up races from the degradation of savage barbarism and leading them into the sunlight of a higher life, in unveiling to their benighted vision the benefits of civilization and the blessings of a peaceful Christianity, I cannot for the life of me perceive the propriety or the efficacy of employing the military instead of the civil departments, unless it is intended to adopt the Mohammedan motto, and proclaim to these people "Death or the Koran."

If the mass of our people desire peaceful relations with our Indian tribes, mean to continue to recognize their natural rights, as our fathers have done, and do not desire their violent extermination, then I submit the peaceful and therefore the civil and not the military agencies of the government are better adapted to secure the desired ends.

Blight follows the sword as surely as desolation sits in the track of the hurricane or the conflagration.

Has not military management essentially failed in civilizing the Indians? When and where did it turn their minds from war and the chase and fix them upon agriculture or pastoral life? When and where did it reduce the cost of Indian affairs? It has only succeeded in illuminating our Indian history with bloody pictures, in surcharging the hearts of our tribes with hatred and revenge, and spending the money of the people by the fifty million dollars, oft repeated.

This war office management, now proposed, may look to the peace that follows extermination as the great desideratum of the service and the panacea for Indian troubles, but such peace is far in the distance if it is to depend upon extermination by arms. If we fought five or six hundred warriors on the little pent-up peninsula of Florida seven years, with the regular army with many thousand volunteer soldiers, and the navy thrown in, at a cost of 1,500 lives on our part, and fifty millions of dollars and more in treasure, leaving at last several hundred Seminoles in the everglades, who still claim to be free, how long will it require and at what expense of treasure and blood to exterminate (not merely subjugate) our 300,000 Indians now occupying and roaming over the plains and mountains of the interior, an area of more than 200,000 square miles? It would seem that the cost price of Indians slain in the Florida war, in the Sioux war, and in the late Cheyenne war, has been on a fair average about a million of dollars each; and if our Indian troubles are to be ended by exterminating the race, it is evident, at the present rate of one Indian killed per month, that the achievement will be completed at the end of exactly 25,000 years; and if each dead Indian is to cost the same hereafter as heretofore, the precise sum total we will have to expend is $300,000,000,000 to complete the extermination. But besides the cost to the treasury, it is found by actual comparison, approximating closely the truth, that the slaying of every Indian costs us the lives of 25 whites, so that the extermination process must bring about the slaughter of 7,500,000 of our people. Extermination by arms is simply an absurdity, unless we could get the Indians under the protection of the flag in large masses, surround and butcher them as at Sand Creek. But admitting, for the argument, they deserve extermination without mercy, and that we might achieve the grand consummation, it seems to me that the glory of the result would bear no proportion to the fearful sum of the cost.

5. *It is inhuman and unchristian, in my opinion, leaving the question of economy out of view, to destroy a whole race by such demoralization and disease as military government is sure to entail upon our tribes.*

I know no exception to the rule that the presence of military posts in the Indian country is speedily subversive of even the sternest ideas of Indian domestic morals. Female chastity, the abandonment of which in some tribes is punished with death, yields to bribery or fear; marital rights are generally disregarded, and shameless concubinage, with its disgusting concomitants, spreads its pestiferous stench through camp and lodge. The most loathsome, lingering, and fatal diseases, which reach many generations in their ruinous effects, are spread broadcast, and the seeds of moral and physical death are planted among the miserable creatures.

If you wish to see some of the results of establishing military posts in the Indian country, I call your attention to the 600 or 800 half-breeds till recently loafing around Fort Laramie; to the posts along the Missouri; to Fort Sumner in New Mexico, before the Navajoe exodus, and *to all our military posts in the Indian country, with no known exception.* If you wish to exterminate the race, pursue them with the ball and blade; if you please, massacre them wholesale, as we sometimes have done; or, to make it cheap, call them to a peaceful feast, and feed them on beef salted with wolf bane; but, for humanity's sake, save them from the lingering syphilitic poisons, so sure to be contracted about military posts.

6. *The conduct of Indian affairs is, in my judgment, incompatible with the nature and objects of the military department.*

The policy of our government has always been to secure and maintain peaceful and friendly relations with all the Indian tribes, and to advance their interests, by offering them inducements to abandon nomadic habits and the chase, and to learn to adopt the habits and methods of civilized life. To carry this benevolent and humane policy into practical effect, we have stipulated to settle them upon ample reserves of good land, adapted to pastoral and agricultural pursuits; to subsist them as long as requisite; to supply them with all necessary stock and implements, and teachers to instruct them in letters, in the arts of civilization, and in our holy religion. But all these things pertain properly, as all will admit, to civil affairs, not military. Military officers will doubtless display wonderful skill in the erection of forts; in the handling of arms and armies, and in the management of campaigns, but who would not prefer a practical civilian in the erection of corn cribs or hay racks; in the manoeuvering of ox teams, and the successful management of reapers and mowers? A well-trained lieutenant will doubtless perform admirably in drilling a squad in the manual of arms, but I doubt his capacity, as well as inclination, to teach Indians the profitable and efficient use of the hoe or the mattock, or to successfully instruct naked young Indian ideas how to shoot in a mechanical, literary, or scientific direction. You wish to make your son a farmer, a mechanic, a minister; you do not send him to be educated at West Point, but somewhere else to be taught as a civilian. Will you send professional soldiers, sword in one hand, musket in the other, and tactics on the brain, to teach the wards of the nation agriculture, the mechanic arts, theology, and peace? You would civilize the Indian! Will you send him the sword? You would inspire him with the peaceful principles of Christianity! Is the bayonet their symbol? You would invite him to the sanctuary! Will you herald his approach with the clangor of arms and the thunder of artillery?

The nation thinks of the War Department as the channel through which the chief executive directs the movements of our armies and manages all the military business and interests of the nation, not as the overseer, guardian, teacher, and missionary of the Indian tribes; it regards our officers and soldiers as its sword to repel and punish its enemies in war, to guard and secure its honor and interests, whenever necessary, in peace; but not as its superintendents, agents, agricultural and mechanical teachers of peaceful Indian tribes.

7. *The transfer to the War Office will be offensive to the Indians, and in the same proportion injurious to the whites.*

Let it be remembered that the demoralization resulting from the presence of military posts is not confined to the Indian, but reacts, with accumulated power, upon the soldier.

The nature and objects of the War Department, as indicated by its very name, WAR, are essentially military, while the nature of our relations with the Indians ought to be, and the objects aimed at in their conduct are, essentially civil.

I have met many tribes within twelve months, and consulted with their chiefs and warriors, publicly and privately, and, without exception, they have declared their unwillingness to have the military among them. It is of paramount importance to the interests of peace and to prevent wars, that respect should be paid to the wishes of these people in this matter. I believe there should be no soldier in the Indian country in time of peace. Who can wonder that these people do not wish to be placed under the control of our military authorities? What have they ever done to conciliate them? Is it to be supposed they can desire to be governed by those who have visited upon their race most of the woes they have experienced? Can they forget who have been employed to drive them from the Atlantic to the plains, and who still pursue them in their mountains and valleys, and persecute them even unto death? Can they ever forget the insignia of those who shot down, by military orders, their old men, women, and children, under the white flag and under our own banner, at Sand creek? Will they forget that our military sometimes burn their homes, as at the Pawnee Fork, and turn their women and children unsheltered into the wilderness?

As a rule, with rare exceptions, if any, Indian tribes never break the peace without powerful provocation or actual wrong perpetrated against them first; if they are properly treated, their rights regarded, and our promises faithfully kept to them, our treaty engagements promptly fulfilled, and their wants of subsistence liberally supplied, there is seldom, if ever, the slightest danger of a breach of the peace on their part.

If for want of appropriations the Indians now at war had not had their supplies of subsistence unfortunately stopped this spring, in my judgment the Cheyennes and their allies would have been at peace with us to-day. Respect then their wishes; keep them well fed, and there will be no need of armies among them. But violate our pledges; postpone, neglect, or refuse the fulfilment of our treaty engagements with them; permit them to get hungry and half-starved, and the presence of armies will not restrain them from war.

8. *In the report, 7th January last, of the peace commission, after full examination of the whole question, the commission unanimously recommended that the Indian affairs should be placed, not in the War Office, but upon the footing of an independent department or bureau.*

Then their facts were correct, their reasoning and conclusion sound, and to go back now upon that report and repudiate their own deliberate and unanimous recommendation, it seems to me, will subject the commission to severe criticism.

I have no reflections to cast upon those gentlemen of the commission who have changed front, for reasons doubtless satisfactory to themselves; but as no such reasons have addressed themselves to my mind, I adhere to the unanimous recommendation of our January report.

I think I can readily understand, however, why my colleagues of the army might desire the transfer. It is but natural they should desire it. It is the history of power to seek more power, and the dispensation of patronage is power. Besides, it is but natural that gentlemen educated to arms, and of the army, should desire to see the aggrandizement of the army.

9. *The methods of military management are utterly irreconcilable with the relation of guardian and ward.*

The self-assumed guardianship of our government over these unlettered children of the wilderness carries with it all the obligations that grow out of that relation. These can neither be shaken off nor disregarded without national crime as well as disgrace.

Guardianship is a most sacred and responsible trust, and as a nation we must answer to the God of nations for its faithful administration.

The paramount duty growing out of the trust is to teach, to enlighten, to civilize our wards. If teaching means the instruction given to the Aztecs by Cortez and Pizarro; if enlightening signifies the conflagration of Indian villages; if civilization means peace, and peace means massacre *à la* Sand creek, then by all means let us have the transfer. To every unprejudiced mind the mere mention of the military in connection with the relation of guardian and ward discloses the absurdity of the association.

10. *The transfer will in my opinion entail upon the treasury a large increase of annual expenditure.*

It is clearly demonstrable that the war policy in conducting our Indian affairs is infinitely more expensive than the peace policy; and if the transfer is made, as a matter of course the former will prevail. If so, it seems to me, our legislators would do well to investigate the question of comparative cost. It will not surprise me if an examination will show that in the last 40 years the war policy and management of Indian affairs have cost the nation little if any less than $500,000,000, and also that the civil management or peace policy has cost less than $60,000,000, including annuities, presents, payments for immense bodies of land, and everything else.

If it be objected that the war management does not necessarily involve war, I answer that Indian management by the military does involve the expense of a large standing army in the Indian country, and will cost the country all war costs except the destruction of property, and that the army can be far better dispensed with than not, under proper civil management, and its cost saved to the treasury. But whether war be a necessary result or not, it always happens that it does result and brings with it all its train of horrors and penalties. If it be alleged that many of our wars have occurred under the civil administration, and are therefore chargeable to it, I answer that while the fact is admitted the conclusion is false, for it has already been abundantly shown that nearly all our Indian wars since the bureau has been in civil hands had their origin in the rashness or imprudence of our military.

If economy is desirable in our present financial situation, the proposed transfer will, in my judgment, be disastrous.

11. *The presence in peaceful times of a large military establishment in a republic always endangers the supremacy of civil authority and the liberties of the people.*

History is so replete with striking illustrations of the truth of this proposition that argument to sustain it would be simply attempting to prove an axiom. I therefore close the argument by merely announcing it.

This brings me to the question, *whether the bureau ought not to be erected into an independent department?*

In whatever management Indian affairs are placed, there should be division of neither duties, powers nor responsibilities, but these should all, by all means, be concentrated in the same hands.

But I have already shown that the War Department should not be intrusted with these affairs, and I am of the opinion that the Interior Department should not have charge of them except in the alternative between the two; if for no other reason, from the fact that the head of that department, like the Secretary of War, has already as many duties as he can perform well without superadding the all-important business of Indian affairs.

I reach the conclusion, therefore, that the only wise and proper answer to the question is that Congress ought immediately to create a department exclusively for the management of Indian affairs.

If, however, Congress should think differently and make the transfer, it seems to me in that event the transfer should consist in a change of jurisdiction from the Interior Secretary to the Secretary of War, while all the functions of the bureau should still be performed by civilians.

If the management of Indian affairs by the bureau under the department of war was a failure, and if, as is admitted, it has been not fully satisfactory under the Interior, it is clear that the mere transfer of the bureau from the one to the other will leave the management still a failure.

Why talk of the transfer as if the simple turning over of a bureau from one department to another would magically cure all the defects of this branch of the public service. To me the proposition seems absurd. What is the "transfer?" Only a change, and, in my opinion, from bad enough to worse—that's all. The War Office operated the bureau 17 years and it did not give satisfaction. In 1849 it was transferred to the Interior Department, where it has remained ever since, and still its conduct of affairs is assailed. Each department in turn, with ample time for trial, has failed to manage Indian affairs with popular approbation. If either department is to blame, both are, for both in the public mind have failed. What is the remedy? To know this we must first ascertain the cause. In my judgment, the cause lies on the surface and is simply this: there is too much cargo for the capacity of the vessel, and too much vessel and freight for the power of the machinery. We have crammed into a bureau, which under the supervisory and appellate power is a mere clerkship, all the large, complex, difficult and delicate affairs that ought to employ every function of a first-class department. Now, with the cause of failure before our eyes, what is the remedy? Surely not merely to put the old bureau under another crew and commander! Why, such a transfer can give neither more capacity to the vessel nor more strength to the machinery. There is but one reasonable answer, and that is: If you would have all prosperous and safe in any sea and any weather, adapt your vessel to her cargo, and your machinery to your vessel and tonnage. In other words, launch a new Department of Indian Affairs, freight it with the vast and complicated reciprocal interests of both races, and the experiment must, I believe, prove a grand success.

Can it be that the civil departments of this great government have become so degenerate and weak, or the military so exalted and so potent, that the functions of the one are to be laid at the feet of the other, and the congenial sway of the republican statesman to be replaced by the mailed hand of the military tribune?

I believe there is ingenuity and wisdom enough in the American Congress to devise civil remedies for supposed bureau mismanagement: to strengthen where there is weakness; to purge and purify if there is rottenness; to punish if there is crime; to concentrate power for promptness and efficiency; and to make responsibility answerable in proportion to power, without transferring the functions of civil government to the military organization. If such a transfer of one bureau be necessary for successful administration, why not upon the same principle of others! And if of the bureau, why not of co-ordinate departments? The argument is cumulative with the increase of power, and the appetite which now yearns for a bureau may require at last, to satiate its hunger, the transfer of a department. The grasp for power always strengthens and enlarges with every concession of power, and after a while every vestige of civil authority may yield to its demands, and the liberties of the nation and the glories of the republic may wither together under the blighting sceptre of military despotism.

In the management of this great branch of the public service, involving the varied interests and relations of the government and people with so many distinct and dissimilar tribes and nations of men, occupying so many gradations in development, it seems to me there should be but one head to control, govern, and direct. In his hands ought to be placed all the power necessary for the prompt, vigorous, and efficient discharge of the duties imposed upon him by law in the conduct of all Indian affairs. All the agents through whom he operates, and upon whose action depends the success or failure of his administration, should be nominated by him to the President for confirmation by the Senate, and ought to continue in office during good behavior. He and they should be allowed adequate salaries, to place them beyond the temptations of want. The funds applicable to the service ought, under proper restrictions, to be subject to his direction; and always appropriated at least one year in advance of their probable use. I think he ought to be a cabinet minister, with all the influence with the President and Congress of any other head of department; and have under his control an efficient corps of clerks, sufficient in number to transact the business of the department with promptness and despatch, to hold their places during good behavior. Connected with this department, and subject only to the orders of its head, there should be a police force of officers and men sufficient in number to perform such duty as the exigencies of the Indian service might demand; re-enforced, if necessary, from time to time from the regular army or by volunteers, or diminished, as the Secretary might advise; to be stationed not in but on the borders of the several reservations, as deemed necessary by the Secretary of Indian Affairs. With such an organization, having a competent head, well versed in Indian character and the history of our Indian affairs, holding in his own hands all necessary powers for prompt and vigorous action, the nation might confidently expect peace and prosperity on our borders; the rapid and undisturbed settlement and development of our valuable mineral territories; the early and peaceful settlement of all our Indians on their several reservations; their easy transit from nomadic life and the chase to agriculture and pastoral pursuits; their localization in permanent habitations; their reception of ideas of property in things; their instruction in letters and education in the arts and sciences of civilization; and their adoption of the truths of our holy religion; in short, the country would inevitably soon realize a satisfactory solution of the Indian problem. But if our management of Indian affairs, conducted nominally by the bureau under the present mixed jurisdiction of two departments, civil and military, is considered a failure; and if, for 17 years, it was more and worse than a failure under military management, I venture the prediction that it will continue to be a failure under both or either; and that it never can and never will be a success unless conducted upon an independent basis, concentrating all necessary powers in a competent head, and holding him responsible for their faithful and proper exercise.

In urging these suggestions I am fortified fully by the report of the peace commission of January last, presented herewith.

Report of Commissioner of
Indian Affairs Francis A. Walker
November 1, 1872

(Excerpt from *Report for 1872*, pp. 391-403)

Commissioner Walker sought to explain why the Government's Indian policy seemed to reward those tribes hostile to the United States while it ignored and neglected those tribes whose loyalty to the Government was clear. Walker explained it simply: "With wild men, as with wild beasts, the question whether in a given situation one shall fight, coax, or run, is a question merely of what is easiest and safest." The powerful, hostile tribes could do the most harm to American citizens. Hence it was necessary to conciliate them most of all. Those who could do the United States no harm could safely be ignored, even if it meant they must suffer and go hungry. Indeed, Walker looked forward to the time "when, in fact, the last hostile tribe becomes reduced to the condition of suppliants for charity." Walker foresaw that eventuality even for the Sioux, who would soon be trapped between two transcontinental railway lines. However bitter their fate might seem to themselves, to Walker the reduction of the Indians to suppliants for charity was the "only hope for the aborigines of the continent."

I HAVE THE honor, in conformity with law, to render the annual report on the Indian affairs of the country, and in so doing beg leave to make it somewhat less formal, and considerably more general and liberal in scope and tone, than would be expected in a simple account of the operations of a bureau for a single year. It has seemed desirable, in recognition of the wide popular interest taken in the dealings of the Government with the Indians, and of the frankly admitted ignorance of the special subject on the part even of those most sincerely interested, to present at this time a pretty full statement of the situation of Indian affairs, and of the policy of the Government in view of that situation. I have, therefore, without attempting anything like a scientific contribution to the history or ethnology of the Indians of this continent, thrown together as much information as possible relating to their present condition, habits, and temper, giving especial prominence to those facts of the situation which may properly go to determine the judgment of the legislator and the private citizen upon the practical questions: What shall be done with the Indian as an obstacle to the progress of settlement and industry? What shall be done with him as a dependent and pensioner on our civilization, when, and so far as, he ceases to oppose or obstruct the extension of railways and of settlement?

The Indian Policy

The Indian policy, so called, of the Government, is a policy, and it is not a policy, or rather it consists of two policies, entirely distinct, seeming, indeed, to be mutually inconsistent and to reflect each upon the other: the one regulating the treatment of the tribes which are potentially hostile, that is, whose hostility is only repressed just so long as, and so far as, they are supported in idleness by the Government; the other regulating the treatment of those tribes which, from traditional friendship, from numerical weakness, or by the force of their location, are either indisposed toward, or incapable of, resistance to the demands of the Government. The treatment of the feeble Poncas, and of the friendly Arrickarees, Mandans, and Gros Ventres of the north is an example of the latter; while the treatment of their insolent and semihostile neighbors, the Sioux, furnishes an example of the former. In the same way at the south, the treatment of the well-intentioned Papagoes of Arizona contrasts just as strongly with the dealings of the Government by their traditional enemies, the treacherous and vindictive Apaches. This want of completeness and consistency in the treatment of the Indian tribes by the Government has been made the occasion of much ridicule and partisan abuse; and it is indeed calculated to provoke criticism and to afford scope for satire; but it is none the less compatible with the highest expediency of the situation. It is, of course, hopelessly illogical that the expenditures of the Government should be proportioned not to the good but to the ill desert of the several tribes; that large bodies of Indians should be supported in entire indolence by the bounty of the Government simply because they are audacious and insolent, while well-disposed Indians are only assisted to self-maintenance, since it is known they will not fight. It is hardly less than absurd, on the first view of it, that delegations from tribes that have frequently defied our authority and fought our troops, and have never yielded more than a partial and grudging obedience to the most reasonable requirements of the Government, should be entertained at the national capital, feasted, and loaded with presents. There could be no better subject for the lively paragraphist in his best estate, or for the heavy editorial writer on a dull news day, than such a course on the part of the Government. These things can be made to appear vastly amusing, and the unreflecting are undoubtedly influenced in a great degree to the prejudice of the Indian policy by the incessant small-arms fire of squibs and epigrams, even more perhaps than by the ponderous artillery of argument and invective directed against it. And yet, for all this, the Government is right and its critics wrong; and the "Indian policy" is sound, sensible, and beneficent, because it reduces to the minimum the loss of life and property upon our frontier, and allows the freest development of our settlements and railways possible under the circumstances.

The mistake of those who oppose the present Indian policy is not in erroneously applying to the course of the Government the standard they have taken, but in taking an altogether false standard for the purpose. It is not a whit more unreasonable that the Government should do much for hostile Indians and little for friendly Indians than it is that a private citizen should, to save his life, surrender all the contents of his purse to a highwayman; while on another occasion, to a distressed and deserving applicant for charity, he would measure his contribution by his means and disposition at the time. There is precisely the same justification for the course of the Government in feeding saucy and mischievous Indians to repletion, while permitting more tractable and peaceful tribes to gather a bare subsistence by hard work, or what to an Indian is hard work. It is not, of course, to be understood that the Government of the United States is at the mercy of Indians; but thousands of its citizens are, even thousands of families. Their exposed situation on the extreme verge of settlement affords a sufficient justification to the Government for buying off the hostility of the savages, excited and exasperated as they are, and most naturally so, by the invasion of their hunting-grounds and the threatened extinction of game. It would require one hundred thousand troops at least to form a *cordon* behind which our settlements could advance with the extent of range, the unrestrained choice of location, the security of feeling, and the freedom of movement which have characterized the growth of the past three or four years. Indeed, the presence of no military force could give that confidence to pioneer enterprise which the general cessation of Indian hostilities has engendered. Men of an adventurous cast will live and work behind a line of troops with, it is possible, some exhilaration of feeling on that account; but, as a rule, men will not place women and children in situations of even possible peril, nor will they put money into permanent improvements under such circumstances. Especially has the absence of Indian hostilities been of the highest value, within the last few years, in directing and determining to the extreme frontier the immigrants arriving in such vast numbers on our shores. Americans habituated to the contemplation of this species of danger as one of the features of pioneer life, will scarcely comprehend the reluctance with which men accustomed to the absolute security of person and property in the settled countries of Europe expose themselves and their families to perils of this kind. I was informed by the late president of the Northern Pacific Railroad that it was found almost impossible to hire Swedes and Norwegians to work upon the line of that road, then under construction from the Red River to the Missouri, on account of the vague apprehension of Indian attack which prevailed in connection with the progress of the road through the past summer. As a matter of fact, no well informed person believed that the savages would undertake any offensive operations whatever until after the Missouri had been crossed and passed at least one hundred miles. But these people, unaccustomed to regard possible torture and murder as one of the conditions of a contract to labor, would refuse high wages rather than subject themselves to the slightest risk. The fact that Americans are more daring and adventurous in the presence of a danger more familiar to them, only constitutes a stronger reason for maintaining the immunity which has, for three years now, been secured by the feeding system. There are innumerable little rifts of agricultural or mining settlements all over the western country which, if unmolested, will in a few years become self-protecting communities, but which, in the event of a general Indian war occurring at the present time, would utterly and instantly disappear, either by abandonment or massacre. The first month of hostilities would see fifty valleys, up which population is now slowly but steadily creeping under cover of the feeding system, swept bare by the horrid atrocities of Indian warfare, or deserted by their affrighted inhabitants, hastily driving before them what of their stock could be gathered at a moment's notice, and bearing away what of their household goods could be carried in their single wagons. Such would be the result even with the most favorable issue of military operations. It is right that those who criticise the policy of the Government toward the Indians, and ridicule it as undignified in its concessions and unstatesman-like in its temporizing with a recognized evil, should fairly face the one alternative which is presented. There is no question of national dignity, be it remembered, involved in the treatment of savages by a civilized power. With wild men, as with wild beasts, the question whether in a given situation one shall fight, coax, or run, is a question merely of what is easiest and safest.

The Use of the Military Arm

The system now pursued in dealing with the roving tribes dangerous to our frontier population and obstructing our industrial progress, is entirely consistent with, and, indeed, requires the occasional use of the military arm, in restraining or chastising refractory individuals and bands. Such a use of the military constitutes no abandonment of the "peace policy" and involves no disparagement of it. It was not to be expected—it was not in the nature of things—that the entire body of wild Indians should submit to be restrained in their Ishmaelitish proclivities without a struggle on the part of the more audacious to maintain their traditional freedom. In the first announcement made of the reservation system, it was expressly declared that the Indians should be made as comfortable on, and as uncomfortable off, their reservations as it was in the power of the Government to make them; that such of them as went right should be protected and fed, and such as went wrong should be harassed and scourged without intermission. It was not anticipated that the first proclamation of this policy to the tribes concerned would effect the entire cessation of existing evils; but it was believed that persistence in the course marked out would steadily reduce the number of the refractory, both by the losses sustained in actual conflict and by the desertion of individuals as they should become weary of a profitless and hopeless struggle, until, in the near result, the system adopted should apply without exception to all the then roving and hostile tribes. Such a use of the strong arm of the Government is not war, but discipline. Yet it would seem impossible for many persons to apprehend any distinction between a state of general Indian war, and the occasional use of the regular military force of the country in enforcing the reservation policy, or punishing sporadic acts of outrage on the part of disaffected individuals or bands. Such persons appear to think that the smallest degree of Indian hostilities is equivalent to the largest degree of such hostilities, or at least to hold that if we are to have any Indian troubles whatever—if everything in the conduct of Indian affairs is not to be as calm and serene as a summer day—we might just as well have all the Indians of the continent on our hands at once. Upon the other side, many persons zealously and painfully intent on securing justice to the aborigines of the country, bewail the slightest use of the military in carrying out the reservation system and repressing depredations, as in effect a making of war upon the Indians and a resort to the bloody methods of the past. This misunderstanding in regard to the occasional use of force in making effective and universal the policy of peace, has led no small portion of the press of the country to treat the more vigorous application of the scourge to refractory Indians which has characterized the operations of the last three months as an abandonment of the peace policy itself, whereas it is, in fact, a legitimate and essential part of the original scheme which the Government has been endeavoring to carry out, with prospects of success never more bright and hopeful than to-day.

It will be sufficient, perhaps, to mark the distinction, to say that a general Indian war could not be carried on with the present military force of the United States, or anything like it. Regiments would be needed where now are only companies, and long lines of posts would have to be established for the protection of regions which, under the safeguard of the feeding system, are now left wholly uncovered. On the other hand, by the reservation system and the feeding system combined, the occasions for collision are so reduced by lessening the points of contact, and the number of Indians available for hostile expeditions involving exposure, hardship, and danger is so diminished through the appeal made to their indolence and self-indulgence, that the Army in its present force is able to deal effectively with the few marauding bands which refuse to accept the terms of the Government.

The Forbearance of the Government

It is unquestionably true that the Government has seemed somewhat tardy in proceeding under the second half of the reservation policy, and in applying the scourge to individuals and bands leaving their prescribed limits without authority, or for hostile purposes. This has been partly from a legitimate deference to the conviction of the great body of citizens that the Indians have been in the past unjustly and cruelly treated, and that great patience and long forbearance ought to be exercised in bringing them around to submission to the present reasonable requirements of the Government, and partly from the knowledge on the part of the officers of the Government charged with administering Indian affairs, that, from the natural jealousy of these people, their sense of wrongs suffered in the past, and their suspiciousness arising from repeated acts of treachery on the part of the whites; from the great distance of many bands and individuals from points of personal communication with the agents of the Government, and the absence of all means of written communication with them; from the efforts of abandoned and degraded whites, living among the Indians and exerting much influence over them, to misrepresent the policy of the Government, and to keep alive the hostility and suspicion of the savages; and, lastly, from the extreme untrustworthiness of many of the interpreters on whom the Government is obliged to rely for bringing its intentions to the knowledge of the Indians: that by the joint effect of all these obstacles, many tribes and bands could come very slowly to hear, comprehend, and trust the professions and promises of the Government.

Such being the sentiment of the general community, that forbearance was due to the Indians on account of past wrongs; and such the knowledge on the part of the Government of difficulties to be encountered in fully acquainting these people with its benevolent intentions, all the resources of expostulation and conciliation have been exhausted before the aid of the military arm has been invoked. It is not a matter for wonder or blame that communities which suffer, meanwhile, from the continuance of the evil should complain bitterly and accuse the Government of inaction, without inquiring very closely whether the evil is not the result of a previous wrong on the part of those to whose evil as to whose good things they succeed alike, or whether their present troubles are not the waves of a storm that is over and past. But it is the duty of the Government to act in the premises with a somewhat broader view and more philosophical temper than is to be expected of those who are actually smarting in their families and their property from the scourge of Indian depredations.

The patience and forbearance exercised have been fully justified in their fruits. The main body of the roving Indians have, with good grace or with ill grace, submitted to the reservation system. Of those who still remain away from the assigned limits, by far the greater part are careful to do so with as little offense as possible; and when their range is such as for the present not to bring them into annoying or dangerous contact with the whites, this Office has, from motives of economy, generally been disposed to allow them to pick up their own living still by hunting and fishing, in preference to tying them up at agencies where they would require to be fed mainly or wholly at the expense of the Government.

THE IMPLACABLES

There is a residue whose disposition and behavior certainly give little encouragement to further forbearance. The numbers of the actually hostile and depredating bands of to-day probably do not exceed in the aggregate eight thousand. Among these are several bands of Apaches in Arizona, principally the Tonto Apaches, the Quahada Comanches, and their confederates of the Staked Plains, west of the Indian Country, and the greater portion of the Kiowa nation. It would be impossible, from the large number of tribes, great and small, known to the annals of the country, to select three which have so little in the way of past wrongs to justify present hostility as these three tribes, which commit, practically, all the outrages properly to be charged against Indians. The depredating Kiowas and the Quahada Comanches are utterly without excuse. They are compelled to go back as far as 1847 to find a single substantial grievance of which to complain. Since that time the United States have given them a noble reservation, and have provided amply for all their wants. No white man has gone upon their lands to injure them; the Government has failed in no particular of its duty toward them; yet, they have persisted in leaving their reservation, and marauding in Texas. They have not done this through any misapprehension of the intentions of the Government, from the pressure of want, or under the smart of any real or fancied wrong. I am disposed to think that the messages recently delivered to them by their agent and by the special commission sent to them the last summer; the unequivocal declarations made to their chiefs on the occasion of a recent visit to Washington; and, especially, the chastisement inflicted on the Quahada Comanches at McClellan's Creek, in October, by Colonel Mackenzie, have fully convinced these tribes that the Government is in earnest, and that a continuance in their present course will involve, as it ought, their extirpation. This may be enough; but, if it proves otherwise, they should be signally punished. An example made here would do much to strengthen the policy of peace, both with other Indians and with the country at large, as well as free the borders of Texas from a scourge that has become intolerable.

The Policy a Policy of Temporizing

It is saying nothing against the course of the Government toward the semi-hostile tribes, to allege, as is often done, that it is merely temporizing with an evil. Temporizing as an expedient in government may be either a sign of weakness and folly, or it may be a proof of the highest wisdom. When an evil is manifestly on the increase, and tends to go from bad to worse, to temporize with it is cowardly and mischievous. Even when an evil cannot be said to be on the increase, yet when, not being self-limited or self-destructive, and having, therefore, no tendency to expire of inherent vices, it cannot be shown to be transient, the part of prudence and of courage is to meet and grapple with it without hesitation and without procrastination. But when an evil is in its nature self-limited, and tends to expire by the very conditions of its existence; when time itself fights against it, and the whole progress of the physical, social, and industrial order by steady degrees circumscribes its field, reduces its dimensions, and saps its strength, then temporizing may be the highest statesmanship.

Such an evil is that which the United States Government at present encounters in the resistance, more or less suppressed, of the Indian tribes of this continent to the progress of railways and settlements, growing out of the reasonable apprehension that their own existence as nations, and even their own individual means of subsistence within the duration of their own lives, will be destroyed thereby. This case differs from others recorded in history only in this—that never was an evil so gigantic environed, invaded, devoured by forces so tremendous, so appalling in the celerity and the certainty of their advance.

The Beginning of the End

It belongs not to a sanguine, but to a sober view of the situation, that three years will see the alternative of war eliminated from the Indian question, and the most powerful and hostile bands of to-day thrown in entire helplessness on the mercy of the Government. Indeed, the progress of two years more, if not of another summer, on the Northern Pacific Railroad will of itself completely solve the great Sioux problem, and leave the ninety thousand Indians ranging between the two transcontinental lines as incapable of resisting the Government as are the Indians of New York or Massachusetts. Columns moving north from the Union Pacific, and south from the Northern Pacific, would crush the Sioux and their confederates as between the upper and the nether millstone; while the rapid movement of troops along the northern line would prevent the escape of the savages, when hard pressed, into the British Possessions, which have heretofore afforded a convenient refuge on the approach of a military expedition.

Toward the south the day of deliverance from the fear of Indian hostility is more distant, yet it is not too much to expect that three summers of peaceful progress will forever put it out of the power of the tribes and bands which at present disturb Colorado, Utah, Arizona, and New Mexico to claim consideration of the country in any other attitude than as pensioners upon the national bounty. The railroads now under construction, or projected with a reasonable assurance of early completion, will multiply fourfold the striking force of the Army in that section; the little rifts of mining settlement, now found all through the mountains of the southern Territories will have become self-protecting communities; the feeble, wavering line of agricultural occupation, now sensitive to the faintest breath of Indian hostility, will then have grown to be the powerful "reserve" to lines still more closely advanced upon the last range of the intractable tribes.

Submission the Only Hope of the Indians

No one certainly will rejoice more heartily than the present Commissioner when the Indians of this country cease to be in a position to dictate, in any form or degree, to the Government; when, in fact, the last hostile tribe becomes reduced to the condition of suppliants for charity. This is, indeed, the only hope of salvation for the aborigines of the continent. If they stand up against the progress of civilization and industry, they must be relentlessly crushed. The westward course of population is neither to be denied nor delayed for the sake of all the Indians that ever called this country their home. They must yield or perish; and there is something that savors of providential mercy in the rapidity with which their fate advances upon them, leaving them scarcely the chance to resist before they shall be surrounded and disarmed. It is not feebly and futilely to attempt to stay this tide, whose depth and strength can hardly be measured, but to snatch the remnants of the Indian race from destruction from before it, that the friends of humanity should exert themselves in this juncture, and lose no time. And it is because the present system allows the freest extension of settlement and industry possible under the circumstances, while affording space and time for humane endeavors to rescue the Indian tribes from a position altogether barbarous and incompatible with civilization and social progress, that this system must be approved by all enlightened citizens.

Whenever the time shall come that the roving tribes are reduced to a condition of complete dependence and submission, the plan to be adopted in dealing with them must be substantially that which is now being pursued in the case of the more tractable and friendly Indians, as described in the portions of the report which follow. This is the true permanent Indian policy of the Government.

The Claims of the Indian

The people of the United States can never without dishonor refuse to respect these two considerations: 1st. That this continent was originally owned and occupied by the Indians, who have on this account a claim somewhat larger than the privilege of one hundred and sixty acres of land, and to "find himself" in tools and stock, which is granted as a matter of course to any newly-arrived foreigner who declares his intention to become a citizen; that something in the nature of an endowment, either capitalized or in the form of annual expenditures for a series of years for the benefit of the Indians, though at the discretion of the Government as to the specific objects, should be provided for every tribe or band which is deprived of its roaming privilege and continued to a diminished reservation; such an endowment being not in the nature of a gratuity, but in common honesty the right of the Indian on account of his original interest in the soil. 2d. That inasmuch as the progress of our industrial enterprise has cut these people off from modes of livelihood entirely sufficient for their wants, and for which they were qualified, in a degree which has been the wonder of more civilized races, by inherited aptitudes and by long pursuit, and has left them utterly without resource, they have a claim on this account again to temporary support and to such assistance as may be necessary to place them in a position to obtain a livelihood by means which shall be compatible with civilization.

Had the settlements of the United States not been extended beyond the frontier of 1867, all the Indians of the continent would to the end of time have found upon the plains an inexhaustible supply of food and clothing. Were the westward course of population to be stayed at the barriers of to-day, notwithstanding the tremendous inroads made upon their hunting-grounds since 1867, the Indians would still have hope of life. But another such five years will see the Indians of Dakota and Montana as poor as the Indians of Nevada and Southern California; that is, reduced to an habitual condition of suffering from want of food.

The freedom of expansion which is working these results is to us of incalculable value. To the Indian it is of incalculable cost. Every year's advance of our frontier takes in a territory as large as some of the kingdoms of Europe. We are richer by hundreds of millions; the Indian is poorer by a large part of the little that he has. This growth is bringing imperial greatness to the nation; to the Indian it brings wretchedness, destitution, beggary. Surely there is obligation found in considerations like these, requiring us in some way, and in the best way, to make good to these original owners of the soil the loss by which we so greatly gain.

Can any principle of national morality be clearer than that, when the expansion and development of a civilized race involve the rapid destruction of the only means of subsistence possessed by the members of a less fortunate race, the higher is bound as of simple right to provide for the lower some substitute for the means of subsistence which it has destroyed? That substitute is, of course, best realized, not by systematic gratuities of food and clothing continued beyond a present emergency, but by directing these people to new pursuits which shall be consistent with the progress of civilization upon the continent; helping them over the first rough places on "the white man's road," and, meanwhile, supplying such subsistence as is absolutely necessary during the period of initiation and experiment.

A Legalized Reformatory Control Necessary

The assistance due to the Indians from the Government in the discharge of those obligations which have been adverted to should not much longer be irrespective of their own efforts. Just so soon as these tribes cease to be formidable, they should be brought distinctly to the realization of the law that if they would eat they must also work. Nor should it be left to their own choices how miserably they will live, in order that they may escape work as much as possible. The Government should extend over them a rigid reformatory discipline, to save them from falling hopelessly into the condition of pauperism and petty crime. Merely to disarm the savages, and to surround them by forces which it is hopeless in them to resist, without exercising over them for a series of years a system of paternal control, requiring them to learn and practice the arts of industry at least until one generation has been fairly started on a course of self-improvement, is to make it pretty much a matter of certainty that by far the larger part of the now roving Indians will become simply vagabonds in the midst of civilization, forming little camps here and there over the face of the Western States, which will be festering sores on the communities near which they are located; the men resorting for a living to basket-making and hog-stealing; the women to fortune-telling and harlotry. No one who looks about him and observes the numbers of our own race who, despite our strong constitutional disposition to labor, the general example of industry, the possession of all the arts and applicances which diminish effort while they multiply results, and the large rewards offered in the constitution of modern society for success in industrial effort, yet sink to the most abject condition from indolence or from vice, can greatly doubt that, unless prompt and vigorous measures are taken by the Government, something like what has been described is to be the fate of the now roving Indians, when they shall be surrounded and disarmed by the extension of our settlements, and deprived of their traditional means of subsistence through the extinction of game. Unused to manual labor, and physically disqualified for it by the habits of the chase, unprovided with tools and implements, without forethought and without self-control, singularly susceptible to evil influences, with strong animal appetites and no intellectual tastes or aspirations to hold those appetites in check, it would be to assume more than would be taken for granted of any white race under the same conditions, to expect that the wild Indians will became industrious and frugal except through a severe course of industrial instruction and exercise, under restraint. The reservation system affords the place for thus dealing with tribes and bands, without the access of influences inimical to peace and virtue. It is only necessary that Federal laws, judiciously framed to meet all the facts of the case, and enacted in season, before the Indians begin to scatter, shall place all the members of this race under a strict reformatory control by the agents of the Government. Especially is it essential that the right of the Government to keep Indians upon the reservations assigned to them, and to arrest and return them whenever they wander away, should be placed beyond dispute. Without this, whenever these people become restive under compulsion to labor, they will break away in their old roving spirit, and stray off in small bands to neighboring communities, upon which they will prey in a petty fashion, by begging and stealing, until they have made themselves so much of a nuisance that the law is invoked against them, or their apprehensions of violence become excited, when they will pass on, to become the pests of other and more distant communities. In a word, in the two hundred and seventy-five thousand Indians west of the Mississippi, the United States have all the elements of a large gypsy population, which will inevitably become a sore, a well-nigh intolerable, affliction to all that region, unless the Government shall provide for their instruction in the arts of life, which can only be done effectually under a pressure not to be resisted or evaded. The right of the Government to do this cannot be seriously questioned. Expressly excluded by the Constitution from citizenship, the Government is only bound in its treatment of them by considerations of present policy and justice.

Even were the constitutional incapacity of these people not what it is, and were there nothing in the history of the dealings of the United States with them to form a precedent for their being placed under arbitrary control, still, the manifest necessity of self-protection would amply justify the Government in any and all measures required to prevent the miserable conclusion I have indicated.

THE PRACTICAL SIDE OF THE INDIAN QUESTION

I have purposely divested these remarks of what is commonly known as "sentiment," and have refrained from appealing to the higher considerations of human and Christian charity, not because I have not respect for such considerations, nor because sentiment is out of place in dealing with such a question, but because I believe that the Indian policy of the Government, past and prospective, can be fully justified before the country by arguments addressed solely to self-interest, and because it has appeared to me that a certain class of the community have become a little wearied of appeals, in behalf of the Indians, to sentiments which are, perhaps, rather too fine for popular daily use. Nothing that the Government is doing toward the Indians but can be vindicated on grounds of practical usefulness and economy as completely as the expenditures of our American communities for the education of the young.

I know of no stronger proof that could be offered for the satisfaction of the country that the Indian policy of the Government, notwithstanding so much about it that appears whimsical and contradictory, is really to be justified on common-sense principles, than the fact that for several years bills making appropriations for the necessarily heavy expenditures involved, have run the gauntlet of the appropriation committees of both House and Senate, without losing a single original feature of value. No one who understands the constitution of those committees, and knows their readiness to slaughter any provision for any service which cannot give an unmistakable reason for itself, will need stronger assurance that when the details of the Indian policy come to be explained, point by point, to men versed in public affairs and in the methods of business, they are found to be based upon good practical reasons, and not upon theories or sentiments.

THE ENDOWMENT OF INDIAN TRIBES

I cannot admit that there is any reason for the apprehensions which many persons feel, that when the Indians cease to be formidable, they will be neglected. It is certainly desirable on all grounds, not merely to avoid the possibility of an occasional failure in the provision for their wants, but also for the sake of securing comprehensiveness and consistency in the treatment of the subject, that the endowments for the several tribes and bands be capitalized, and placed in trust for their benefit, out of the reach of accident or caprice. The proceeds arising from sales, as their reservations are from time to time diminished by authority of law, for the sake of securing a higher culture of the portions remaining, ought, if the Indians are honestly treated in the transaction, to be sufficient to provide for all ordinary beneficial expenditures in behalf of tribes and bands having lands secured to them by treaty.

The reservations granted heretofore have generally been proportioned, and rightly so, to the needs of the Indians in a roving state, with hunting and fishing as their chief means of subsistence, which condition implies the occupation of a territory far exceeding what could possibly be cultivated. As they change to agriculture, however rude and primitive at first, they tend to contract the limits of actual occupation. With proper administrative management the portions thus rendered available for cession or sale can be so thrown together as in no way to impair the integrity of the reservation. Where this change has taken place, there can be no question of the expediency of such sale or cession. The Indian Office has always favored this course, and notwithstanding the somewhat questionable character of some of the resulting transactions, arising especially out of violent or fraudulent combinations to prevent a fair sale, it can be confidently affirmed that the advantage of the Indians has generally been subserved thereby.

For those tribes and bands which have no reservations secured to them by treaty, from which they can hope in the course of time to realize a civilization and improvement fund, provision will still require to be made by law. Their right to endowment is none the less clear than the right of other tribes whose fortune it was to deal with the United States by treaty, before Congress put an end to the treaty system, with its many abuses and absurdities. We have received the soil from them, and we have extinguished their only means of subsistence. Nothing in the history of the United States justifies the belief that either Congress or the country will be wanting in justice or generosity in dealing with the necessities of a people who have been impoverished that we might be rich. Our national charity has sought the objects of its benefactions at the ends of the earth: Americans will never be wanting in simple justice to helpless dependents at home. I have, therefore, no fear for the future of the Indians of this continent when once the arms of their resistance are laid down, and Indian outrages are no longer reported to inflame the hostility of the border States, and to mingle doubt and misgivings with the philanthropic intentions of the charitable and humane.

The Present Situation and Condition of the Indians

With these remarks I respectfully submit the following detailed account of the numbers, the location, and the present condition of each tribe and important band within the administrative control of the Indian Office. This account, whether statistical or descriptive, has been carefully studied, with a view to securing the highest degree of exactness consistent with the nature of the subject. No unpleasant feature of the situation has been softened. No suppression has been permitted with any thought of relieving the service from odium thereby. On the other hand, the more agreeable aspects have been presented, if not in a skeptical, at least not in a sanguine spirit, for it is known and painfully appreciated how obstinate are the faults of character with which those who would improve the condition of the Indian have to deal; how delusive is oftentimes the appearance of improvement; and how easy the relapse to indolence and vice. Within the past year the Indian Office has seen the habits of industry of two important tribes, which had made a progress really commendable and even admirable toward self-support and independence, terribly shaken by the catastrophe of a total loss of crops from drought, and the ravages of grasshoppers; the progress of the people completely arrested thereby; and large numbers driven off to hunting and fishing, from which they will not easily or speedily be recalled. Such calamities are apt enough to discourage and demoralize communities that have made large accumulations, and, having been long in habits of industry, are not easily moved from them. But to a people just emerging from barbarism, making their first painful efforts at agriculture, ignorant and superstitious, with no resource and no reserve, it could hardly be a subject of wonder or blame if such a calamity as the utter destruction of their crop should undo the beneficial work of years and throw them back in complete discouragement upon courses which it was hoped they had abandoned forever. It is always a weary work to lift any man or people from degradation to self-respect, self-restraint, and self-reliance; while with the Indian of this continent we have the exceptional difficulty of a nature singularly trivial, and habits singularly incompatible with civilized forms of life and industry.

But such considerations as these afford reason for moderating anticipations, not for relaxing effort. Even were it hopeless to rescue the men and the women of a single tribe now under the control of the Government from the life and the death of savages, it would still be the interest and the duty of the nation to organize and maintain an increasing service for the instruction of these people in the arts of industry and life, in the hope and reasonable expectation that another generation may be saved from becoming a pest and a scourge to themselves and to the larger community upon which they are to be thrown, their traditional morality unlearned, their tribal and social bonds dissolved, all that there was of good in their native character and condition completely lost, and with only such substitute for all this as we shall now give them.

A Few Generalizations

The Indians within the limits of the United States, exclusive of those in Alaska, number, approximately, 300,000.

(*a*) They may be divided according to their geographical location, or range, into five grand divisions, as follows: In Minnesota and States east of the Mississippi River, about 32,500; in Nebraska, Kansas, and the Indian Territory, 70,650; in the Territories of Dakota, Montana, Wyoming, and Idaho, 65,000; in Nevada and the Territories of Colorado, New Mexico, Utah, and Arizona, 84,000; and on the Pacific slope, 48,000.

(*b*) In respect to the three lines of railroads—built or projected— Between the States and the Pacific Ocean, viz., the northern, central, and southern routes, they may be divided, excluding those residing east of Minnesota and of the Missouri River, south of Dakota, as follows: Between the proposed northern route and the British possessions, about 36,000; between the northern and central routes, 92,000; between the central and the proposed southern routes, 61,000; and between the Southern route and Mexico, 85,000, making a total of 274,000.

(*c*) As regards their means of support and methods of subsistence they may be divided as follows: Those who support themselves upon their own reservations, receiving nothing from the Government, except interest on their own moneys, or annuities granted them in consideration of the cession of their lands to the United States, number about 130,000; those who are entirely subsisted by the Government, about 31,000; those in part subsisted, 84,000—together about 115,000; those who subsist by hunting and fishing, upon roots, nuts, berries, &c., or by begging and stealing, about 55,000.

(*d*) They may be divided again, with respect to their connection with the Government, as follows: There are about 150,000 who may be said to remain constantly upon their reservations, and are under the complete control of agents appointed by the Government; 95,000 who at times visit their agencies either for food or for gossip, or for both, but are generally roaming either on or off their reservations, engaged in hunting or fishing; and 55,000 who never visit an agency, and over whom the Government as yet exercises practically no control, but most of whom are inoffensive, and commit no acts of hostility against the Government.

(*e*) Again, it may be said that of the 300,000 Indians of the country about 180,000 have treaties with the Government; 40,000 have no treaties with the United States, but have reservations set apart by Executive order or otherwise for their occupancy, and are in charge of agents appointed by the Government; 25,000 have no reservations, but are more or less under the control of agents appointed for them, and receive more or less assistance from the Government, the remainder consisting of the same 55,000 already twice described, over whom the Government exercises, practically, no control, and for whom there are no treaty or other provisions.

(*f*) As to civilization, they may, though with no great degree of assurance be divided, according to a standard taken with reasonable reference to what might fairly be expected of a race with such antecedents and traditions, as follows: Civilized, 97,000; semi-civilized, 125,000; wholly barbarous, 78,000.

Report of Commissioner of Indian Affairs Edward P. Smith November 1, 1873

(Excerpt from *Report for 1873*, pp. 380-82)

Commissioner Smith's description of the causes which led to the Modoc War make it clear that, had the issue been handled more prudently, hostilities could have been averted.

OCTOBER 14, 1864, a treaty was concluded with the Klamath and Modoc tribes and Yahooskin band of Snake Indians in Oregon, by the first article of which said Indians ceded to the United States all their right, title, and claim to all the country claimed by them, and accepted a reservation described in said article by natural boundaries, upon which they agreed and bound themselves to locate immediately after the ratification of the treaty.

The ratification of this treaty was advised and consented to by the Senate, July 2, 1866, and the same was proclaimed by the President February 17, 1870. At the date of proclamation the Modocs were found on their reservation, where they remained until April, 1870, and then left for their camp on Lost River.

There is evidence that Captain Jack and his band were prepared at this time to remain upon the reservation and settle down in the way of civilization, if there had been ordinary encouragement and assistance, and if the Klamaths, who largely outnumbered Captain Jack's band, and who were their hereditary enemies, had allowed them so to do. This band began to split rails for their farms, and in other ways to adopt civilized habits; but the Klamaths demanded tribute from them for the land they were occupying, which the Modocs were obliged to render. Captain Jack then removed to another part of the reservation, and began again to try to live by cultivating the ground. But he was followed by the same spirit of hostility by the Klamaths, from which he does not seem to have been protected by the agent. The issue of rations seems also to have been suspended for want of funds, and for these reasons Captain Jack and his band returned to their old home on Lost River, where they became a serious annoyance to the whites, who had in the meanwhile settled on their ceded lands.

This annoyance led to serious apprehensions on the part of the military authorities, and under date of the 19th of March, 1872, the honorable Secretary of War transmitted to this Department copies of correspondence between the military in regard to the matter. A copy of this correspondence was sent to Superintendent Odeneal by the Indian Office, April 12, 1872, with directions to have the Modocs removed, if practicable, to their reservation; and if removed, to see that they were properly protected from the Klamaths.

The superintendent was then instructed, in case they could not be removed, to report the practicability of locating them at some other point. The superintendent reported on the 17th June that their reservation was the best place for them to be located, but that he did not believe it practicable to remove them without using the military for that purpose, and that if they should resist, he doubted whether there was force enough in the country to compel them to go. In reply, the superintendent was directed, July 6, 1872, to remove them to the Klamath reservation. The attempt to execute this order resulted in a conflict between the Modocs and the troops and the white settlers. For the purpose of examining into the same, and, if possible, to procure a peaceable solution of the difficulties, a commission was appointed by the Secretary of the Interior in January last. This commission, as finally composed, consisted of A. B. Meacham, late superintendent of Indian affairs for Oregon, L. S. Dyar, agent for the Klamath agency, and Rev. E. Thomas, and by direction of the Secretary of the Interior, under date of March 22, 1873, they were put under the direction of General Canby. While engaged in a conference with Captain Jack, chief of the Modocs, and other representative men of the tribe, on the 11th of April, General Canby and Dr. Thomas were brutally murdered by these Indians, and Mr. Meacham severely wounded.

Thus ended the negotiations with the Modocs, who, after seven months' fighting, were subdued by the military, and Captain Jack and three of his principal men were tried by court-martial and executed. The remnant of this Modoc band has been transferred to the Indian Territory, and located for the present on the Quapaw Indian reservation, where they have gladly availed themselves of the privilege of putting their children in school, and have entered upon industrial life with such readiness and good will as to warrant the conclusion that if these Indians could have had this opportunity of gaining their support out of soil upon which an ordinary white man could get a living, and had received just treatment, there would have been no cause of trouble with them.

Report of Commissioner of Indian Affairs Edward P. Smith
November 1, 1874

(Excerpt from *Report for 1874*, pp. 324-27)

Commissioner Smith asserted that the trade and intercourse laws of 1834, under which Indian affairs were regulated, were entirely outmoded and that the Congress should adopt a new code of laws. Under the 1834 acts, each Indian nation was regarded as a sovereign unit, able to manage its own affairs. Smith professed to see the failure of past American Indian policy as "largely attributable to this fundamental failure to recognize and treat the Indian as a man capable of civilization, and, therefore, a proper subject of the Government and amenable to its laws." In his recommendations to Congress, Smith called for measures that were successively enacted into laws during the following two decades.

FREQUENT MENTION has been made in this report of the necessity for additional legislation on behalf of the Indians. This necessity is apparent from the fact that the only statutes under which Indians are managed and controlled are substantially those enacted in 1834, known as the trade and intercourse laws, whose main purpose was to regulate traffic in furs, and prevent sale of ammunition and intoxicating drinks, and intrusion upon an Indian reservation. This meager legislation was in accord with the theory then prevailing, that the Indian tribes were related to the American Government only as sovereignties who naturally would provide their own laws; and that the red men, being a people essentially wild and untamable, needed only to be kept as remotely as possible from all settlements, to be assisted as hunters, to be forcibly precluded from an undue supply of gunpowder and rum, and to be made as peaceable as possible by the presence of an agent and the distribution of a few annuities in cash and blankets.

In my judgment, whatever of failure has attended the management of Indian affairs in the past has been largely attributable to this fundamental failure to recognize and treat the Indian as a man capable of civilization, and, therefore, a proper subject of the Government and amenable to its laws. A judge in Idaho, who is also a United States commissioner, has decided that he had no jurisdiction, either as a territorial or Federal officer, in a case where one Indian had killed another, though the murder was committed in his own county and outside of any reserve. Thus it has come to pass that we have within our borders at the present time 75,000 wild Indians who need legislation appropriate to a people passing rapidly out

193

from a savage tribal government into a degree of control by the United States Government; and 200,000 other Indians who might be readily brought within the protection and restraint of ordinary law, and yet are practically without the benefit of any suitable government, a majority of them being property-holders, living upon their farms, having their schools and churches, and scarcely differing in their mode of life from the pioneer settlers of the country.

The damage which is inevitable to the Indians from this anomalous state of things, will be more apparent if we keep in mind that no officer of the Government has authority by law for punishing an Indian for crime, or restraining him in any degree; that the only means of enforcing law and order among the tribes is found in the use of the bayonet by the military, or such arbitrary force as the agent may have at command. Among the Indians themselves, all tribal government has been virtually broken down by their contact with the Government. The chiefs hold a nominal headship, depending for its continuance on the consent of the most turbulent and factious portion of the tribe. If a white man commits depredations upon the Indians in their own country no penalty is provided beyond that of putting him out of the country, a penalty which he readily takes upon himself when escaping with his booty.

Neither is there any provision of law by which an Indian can begin to live for himself as an American citizen. Being by the fiction of sovereignty, which has come into our Indian relations, citizens of a "domestic dependent nation," contrary to the American doctrine upon this subject he is not allowed to change his nationality at will, but required first to obtain consent of both parties to his tribal treaty. As a result of this restriction, many Indians are kept with the mass of their tribe who otherwise would strike out for themselves. The case of the Flandreaus, a small band of Sioux in Dakota, hereafter detailed, who availed themselves of a special provision to this effect in their treaty, is interesting as illustrating the advantage of a privilege which should be provided for all Indians.

Neither is there any provision under existing law by which an Indian desiring to continue his relations with his tribe is allowed to receive an allotment of his portion of the land owned in common; thus individual enterprise and self-support are materially repressed.

Many of the appropriations, in accordance with treaty stipulations, provide that annuities should be paid cash in hand, or in goods distributed per capita, to be accounted for to the Government on the receipts of the chief. All bounty of the Government bestowed in this form is worse than wasted, tending to perpetual poverty by providing for idleness and unthrift.

Qualified Citizenship

I therefore respectfully recommend that the attention of Congress be called to this subject, and that such legislation be requested as will secure—

First. A suitable government of Indians:

(1.) By providing that the criminal laws of the United States shall be in force upon Indian reservations, and shall apply to all offenses, including offenses of Indians against Indians, and extending the jurisdiction of the United States courts to enforce the same.

(2.) By declaring Indians amenable to the police laws of the State or Territory for any act committed outside a reservation.

(3.) By conferring upon the President authority, at his discretion, to extend the jurisdiction of the State courts, or any portion of them, to any reservation, whenever, in his judgment, any tribe is prepared for such control.

(4.) By providing a sufficient force of deputy marshals to enforce law and order both among and in behalf of Indians.

(5.) By giving authority to the Secretary of the Interior to prescribe for all tribes prepared, in his judgment, to adopt the same, an elective government, through which shall be administered all necessary police regulations of a reservation.

(6.) By providing a distinct territorial government, or United States court, wherever Indians are in numbers sufficient to justify it.

Second. Legislation for the encouragement of individual improvement:

(1.) By providing a way into citizenship for such as desire it.

(2.) By providing for holding lands in severalty by allotment for occupation, and for patents with an ultimate fee, but unalienable for a term of years.

(3.) By providing that wherever per capita distribution provided by treaty has proved injurious or without benefit to its recipients, a distribution of the same may, in the discretion of the President, be made only in return for labor of some sort.

In concluding these general statements respecting the Indian service, I desire to reiterate my conviction of the entire feasibility of Indian civilization, and that the difficulty of its problem is not so inherent in the race-character and disposition of the Indian—great as these obstacles are—as in his anomalous relation to the Government, and in his surroundings affected by the influence and interest of the white people. The main difficulty, so far as the Government is concerned, lies in the fact that the Indian's deepest need is that which the Government, through its political organization and operations, cannot well bestow. The first help which a man in barbarism requires is not that which can be afforded through a political party, but that which is offered by a fellow-man, wiser than himself, coming personally and extending a hand of sympathy and truth. No amount of appropriations and no governmental machinery can do much toward lifting an ignorant and degraded people, except as it works through the willing hands of men made strong and constant by their love for their fellow-men.

If, therefore, it shall be possible to continue the sympathy and aid of the religious people of the land in this work, and to rally for its prosecution the enthusiasm and zeal which belong to religion, and also if it shall be possible to procure the enactment of such laws as will recognize the essential manhood and consequent capabilities and necessities of the Indian, and to provide reasonably adequate appropriations which shall be expended both honestly and wisely for their benefit, and to hold steadily to well-defined and carefully prepared methods of treatment, every year will witness a steady decrease of barbarism and its consequent danger and annoyance, and a constant accession to the number of peaceful and intelligent Indians who shall take their place and part as subjects of the United States. Surely this cannot be too much to ask and expect of the people of the great republic. The record of the past cannot be rewritten, and it is not pleasant to recall. Much of administrative mistake, neglect, and injustice is beyond repair. But for Indians now living much of protection and elevation and salvation is still not only possible, but feasible and highly promising; and well will it be if we are wise enough to make the most of the opportunity left to deal justly and humanely with these remnants of the first American people.

Report of Commissioner of
Indian Affairs Edward P. Smith
November 1, 1875

(Excerpt from *Report for 1875*, pp. 506-14, 525-31)

Commissioner Smith's report discussed the reversal in Government policy relative to the Sioux and to the California Indians. The dramatic change in the relationship with the Sioux was noted by Smith who, after reporting how white miners had overrun the gold fields of the Black Hills despite the efforts of the military, noted that "only seven years ago the United States was willing to make any promise to the wild Sioux, whom we did not wish to fight, if they would allow us to push a railway across their plains toward the Pacific coast." The sad fate of the California Indians, dispossessed by legal sleight of hand from lands to which they thought they had title from the time of the Spanish missions, was also recounted.

IN MY LAST ANNUAL report I ventured the statement that "except under extraordinary provocation, or in circumstances not at all to be apprehended, it is not probable that as many as five hundred Indian warriors will ever again be mustered at one point for a fight; and with the conflicting interests of the different tribes, and the occupation of the intervening country by advancing settlements, such an event as a general Indian war can never again occur in the United States."

During the year passing in review there has been less conflict with Indians than for many previous years. With the exception of the Cheyennes and Comanches, who at the close of the period covered by my last report had still refused to surrender to the military, there has been no hostile engagement with the United States troops, and complaint of marauding has been much less than usual. This fact is significant. According to all experience in the management of Indians, this year should have been marked for bloody conflicts. White settlements have been brought nearer to wild Indians than ever before; many disturbing questions have arisen, and with the most warlike and powerful of all the tribes there has been a constant series of irritations which in any previous year would have raised the war-cry along a large exposed section of the frontier.

The Sioux have been many times represented as about to go out on the war-path; at other times they have been reported as disaffected by bad management of bad agents and goaded by desperation of hunger and cold to an outbreak. Nothing shows the utter want of truth in all these reports more clearly than the fact that when they were brought cheerfully to relinquish a cherished hunting and roaming privilege they requested that

197

nearly all the $25,000 received in compensation for this relinquishment should be expended in cows, horses, harness, and wagons. Such use of money indicates anything but a hostile intent on the part of the Red Cloud and Spotted Tail Sioux.

It will probably be found necessary to compel the northern non-treaty-Sioux, under the leadership of Sitting Bull, who have never yet in any way recognized the United States Government except by snatching rations occasionally at an agency, and such outlaws from the several agencies as have attached themselves to these same hostiles, to cease marauding and settle down, as the other Sioux have done, at some designated point. This may occasion conflict between this band of Indians and the soldiers. There is also a possibility that the Utes in Northern New Mexico, who are without a home, unsettled and insolent, and transiently fed at Cimarron and Abiquiu, may before long require coercion by force of arms. But neither of these bands can bring three hundred men into the field. I am led not only to repeat with increased confidence the statement made last year that a general Indian war is never to occur in the United States, but also to the opinion that conflict with separate tribes will hereafter be of rare occurrence, and only in the nature of skirmishing.

Relinquishment of Hunting-Privilege in Nebraska and Kansas

By the treaty of 1868 the Sioux retained for themselves the right to hunt in Nebraska on any lands north of the North Platte and on the Republican Fork of the Smoky Hill River. By act of Congress, March 3, 1874, $25,000 was appropriated for the purchase from the Sioux of the right to hunt in Nebraska. The negotiations for this purchase, undertaken by a special commission in 1874, having failed to obtain the consent of the Indians, were renewed during the visit of the Sioux delegation to Washington in May last, and resulted in an agreement signed by the chiefs and headmen in the presence of their tribe, a copy of which is herewith.

The treaty of 1868 also stipulated that "the country north of the North Platte River, in Nebraska, and east of the summits of the Big Horn Mountains, in Wyoming, should be held and considered unceded Indian territory, and that no white person or persons should be permitted to settle upon or occupy any portion of the same, nor, without the consent of the Indians first had or obtained, should pass through the same."

The distinction between the country assigned for a permanent reserve and that described as neutral territory seems never to have been clear to the Sioux minds and when the northern boundary line of Nebraska was surveyed, which by their treaty is made the dividing-line between their permanent reserve and the neutral country, they were surprised and troubled to find it running north of their present agencies and of the country which they have always regarded and intended to retain as their own; and they demanded that the surveyor's stakes should be taken up and moved south of the Niobrara River. The negotiations for the cession of this neutral country, in addition to that of the hunting rights, was thus found to be involved in unexpected difficulty. The Indians attached large value to the rights they were surrendering, and declined to accept the sum appropriated by Congress, except upon the condition that the Department would present their claim to Congress for the additional sum of $25,000. This pledge was given to them by the Secretary of the Interior when they entered into the agreement above named, reference to which will show that the attempt to procure the relinquishment of all the neutral country resulted in a compromise, by which the Sioux stipulate for themselves the right of occupation of that portion of Nebraska lying west of the 100th meridian and north of the south divide of the Niobrara River. Good faith with the Indians will therefore make it necessary to lay this matter before Congress and ask for an appropriation in the sum of $25,000.

THE SIOUX PROBLEM

It affords me no small gratification to find the observation and conclusions reached at that time upon this subject fully confirmed by the report of the Red Cloud investigating commission, after many weeks spent in the Sioux country in careful inquiry into the conditions and prospects of these Indians. The problem for these people has not approached a solution during the year, unless it shall be found that the discussion arising from the Black Hills excitement and the investigation at Red Cloud agency have so awakened the public attention to the present necessities and pitiable condition of the Sioux as to lead to immediate, appropriate, and vigorous measures for their relief, to remove the Indians at the Red Cloud and Spotted Tail Agencies to the Missouri River, by drawing out the squaw men who infest the Indian country and by compelling labor as a return for rations. These three essential undertakings will require for success three things: (1) Largely increased appropriations for the Sioux during the next two years which may thereafter be steadily diminished and then cease altogether; (2) the most efficient and hearty co-operation of the War Department; (3) in order to afford a suitable location for Red Cloud and his people, the removal of the Poncas from their present reservation which has marked their Sioux country and their consolidation with the Omahas of Nebraska.

Sooner or later those or other radical measures must be adopted, the only alternative being to continue to ration and clothe the Indians as idle and insolent vagrants and paupers. I do not believe it possible to subsist the Sioux many years longer upon the appropriations which Congress can be induced to take for feeding purposes only. The whole spirit of our people and of American institutions revolts against any process that tends to pauperism or taxation for the support of idlers. The bringing of these wild Sioux under such wholesome restraint would also be of a material aid to the process of civilization now progressing among other bands of the nation along the Missouri River upon whom it has as yet been impossible to enforce proper discipline of the requirement of labor for rations, because of the proximity and example of Red Cloud and Spotted Tail agencies.

But the reports of agencies along the river, with the possible exception of Standing Rock, show that it is entirely feasible to civilize the Sioux, provided a suitable country can be found for their occupation and the Government and its agents are capable of continuance in well-doing. At Cheyenne River, bands of Sioux who three years ago were as intractable, as impatient of labor, and in other respects as far from the first steps of civilization as Spotted Tail's immediate followers are to-day, have been induced to erect log houses and open farms to such an extent that the agency is able to report 240 Indian families, living in houses, 240 *male* Indians who labor in civilized pursuits with their own hands, and 138 children in school.

The report of the Crow Creek agent, as an account of a first successful year's effort in civilization, is equally encouraging. The reports of the Yankton and Santee Sioux are still more hopeful. Among the latter civilization is an accomplished fact, and if the Yanktons could plant crops with ordinary certainty of a harvest, they would shortly provide their own subsistance. Such progress indicates unmistakably that the difficulty of the Sioux problem does not inhere principally in the Sioux nature, but in the barrenness of their country and the absence of necessary control.

THE BLACK HILLS

The public excitement mentioned in my last report, occasioned by the discovery of gold in that portion of the Sioux reservation known as the Black Hills country, increased to such a degree in the opening of the spring season as to require action looking toward the purchase of this country from the Sioux proprietors and the opening up of the Big Horn Mountain country for settlement and building. For this purpose as well as for completing the negotiations for this relinquishment by the Sioux of their hunting rights in Nebraska and Kansas, a large delegation of this tribe, composed of representatives from those agencies, was brought to Washington in May last for an interview with the President. It was not expected that this interview would conclude the purchase, but that it would prove a preliminary step by which the Sioux tribe would become acquainted with the wishes of the Government and its purposes relative to their own necessities and interests. Accordingly, at the request of the delegation, the President sent a commission, of which Hon. W. B. Allison, of the United States Senate, was made chairman, to negotiate at a general council of the tribe in their own country. The commission has not yet submitted its report, but I am informed that the negotiations have failed on account of a wide disagreement as to the value of the rights to be relinquished by the Sioux. Meanwhile, notwithstanding the stringent prohibitory orders by the military authorities and in the size of the large military force which has been on duty in and around the Hills during the summer, probably not less than a thousand miners, with the number rapidly increasing, have made their way into the Sioux country. A mining association has been organized, laws and regulations have been adopted for mutual protection, and individual claims staked out, in the right to which they expect hereafter either to be protected by the Government or to protect themselves.

In this serious complication there seems to be but one alternative for the Government, either to so increase the military force and adopt such summary means as will insure a strict observance of the treaty rights of the Sioux by preventing all intrusion, or to renew the effort of negotiation. However unwilling we may be to confess it, the experience of the past summer proves either the inefficiency of the large military force under the command of such officers as Generals Sheridan, Terry, and Crook, or the utter impracticability of keeping Americans out of a country where gold is known to exist by any fear of orders or of United States cavalry, or by an consideration of the rights of others.

The occupation and possession of the Black Hills by white men seems now inevitable, but no reason exists for making this inevitability an occasion of wrong or lasting injury to the Sioux. If an Indian can be possessed of rights of country, either natural or required, this country belongs for occupation to the Soux; and if they were an independent, self-supporting people, able to claim that hereafter the United States Government should leave them entirely alone, in yearly receipt of such annuities only as the treaty of 1868 guarantees, they would be in a position to demand to be left in undisturbed possession of their country, and the moral sense of mankind would sustain the demand; but unfortunately the facts are otherwise. They are not now capable of self-support; they are absolute pensioners of the Government in the sum of a million and a quarter of dollars annually above all amounts specified in treaty-stipulations. A failure to receive Government rations for a single season would reduce them to starvation. They cannot, therefore, demand to be left alone, and the Government, granting the large help which the Sioux are obliged to ask, is entitled to ask something of them in return. On this basis of mutual benefit the purchase of the Black Hills should proceed. If, therefore, all attempts at negotiation have failed on the plan of going first to the Indians, I would respectfully recommend that legislation be now sought from Congress, offering a fair and full equivalent for the country lying between the North and South Forks of the Cheyenne River, in Dakota, a portion of which equivalent should be made to take the place of the free rations now granted.

SURVEY OF THE BLACK HILLS—THEIR VALUE TO THE INDIANS

In order to provide for the question of a fair equivalent for this country, by direction of the President, a topographical and geological survey of the

Black Hills was ordered, the preliminary report of which, by Walter P. Jenney, mining engineer in charge, will be found herewith. It furnishes many interesting and important facts respecting a region hitherto almost unknown. Professor Jenney and his assistants are entitled to large credit for the conscientious diligence and thoroughness, which are apparent at every point in their work. The aid rendered by the War Department, by the courtesy of the General of the Army, and by Col. R. I. Dodge, commanding the escort, has been invaluable to the success of the survey. Without such aid, no satisfactory results could have been obtained, on account of the limited funds available for this purpose. The report confirms, in a large degree, the statements of travelers and explorers and the reports of General Custer's military expedition of last year, and shows a gold-field with an area of eight hundred square miles, and around this gold region, principally to the north, an additional area within the Black Hills country of three thousand square miles of arable lands, and this latter embracing along its streams an area equal to two hundred square miles finely adapted to agriculture, while the hill-sides and elevations contiguous thereto are equally adapted to purposes of grazing, making the whole area of three thousand square miles of timber, grazing, and arable land of great value for agricultural purposes.

According to the findings of this report, if there were no gold in this country to attract the white man, and the Indians could be left to undisturbed occupation of the Black Hills, this region, naturally suited to agriculture and herding, is the one of all others within the boundaries of the Sioux reservation best adapted to their immediate and paramount necessities. I doubt whether any land not remaining in the possession of the General Government offers equal advantages; but it will be found impracticable to utilize the country for the Sioux. So long as gold exists in the same region, the agricultural country surrounding the gold-fields will be largely required to support the miners, and to attempt to bring the wild Sioux into proximity to the settlers and miners would be to invite provocations and bloody hostility.

These facts respecting the country which the Sioux seem about to be compelled to surrender, for the sake of promoting the mining and agricultural interests of white men, have an important bearing upon the question of compensation which shall be allowed for their lands; for it must be borne in mind that unless the Sioux Nation becomes extinct, of which there is no probability, the time is close upon them when they must have just such an opportunity for self-support as that which is now known to be offered in the Black Hills; and if, for the want of another such country, they are obliged to begin civilization under increased disabilities, humanity as well as equity demands that such disability shall be compensated by increased aid from the Government; and to avoid the perils of future legislation, or want of legislation, the compensation should be provided for and fixed at the time when we are taking away their valuable lands.

The fact that these Indians are making but little if any use of the Black Hills has no bearing upon the question of what is a fair equivalent for the surrender of these rare facilities for farming and grazing. They are children, utterly unable to comprehend their own great necessities just ahead; they cannot, therefore, see that the country which now only furnishes them lodge-poles and a few antelope has abundant resources for their future wants, when they shall cease to be barbarous pensioners upon the Government and begin to provide for their own living. Their ignorance of themselves and of true values makes the stronger appeal to our sense of what is right and fair.

The true equivalent to be offered the Sioux, as helpless wards of the Government, for the Black Hills will be found by estimating what eight hundred square miles of gold-fields are worth to us, and what three thousand square miles of timber, agricultural, and grazing lands are worth to them.

The Mission Indians of Southern California

These Indians have heretofore been the subject of much inquiry and effort for relief by the Department. In 1873 Special Commissioner Rev. John G. Ames made thorough inquiry into their condition and necessities, and made full report of the same. The measures suggested in that report and recommended to Congress for adoption not meeting with approval, Commissioner C. A. Wetmore, of California, made further inquiries as to the feasibility of a different plan for relieving their disabilities, and submitted his report in December, 1874. These reports furnished valuable information to the Office, from which, together with previous reports of superintendents and agents, the following facts respecting these Indians are compiled.

They have received the name of Mission Indians from their relation to the early Catholic missions on the Pacific coast, the first of which was established at San Diego in 1769, others following until 1804, at which time there were nine missions at different points lying along the coast between San Diego and San Francisco. The missionaries having a semi-religious and semi-political recognition by the authority of Spain and Mexico assumed control of the entire coast, and by degrees brought the Indians under subjection and gathered them in settlements around their missions, where they were instructed in agriculture and a low form of civilized life, and put to labor in cultivating large tracts of fertile lands, which they were allowed to occupy in common, under the direction and control of the padres. The original idea on which these missions were maintained seems to have been that so soon as these Indians should be brought, as converts of the church, into a condition for self-support, the lands which they were occupying and cultivating should be allotted as their own. But the profitableness of the peonage and the docility of the Indians made any haste in the direction of

individual rights unnecessary if not undesirable on the part of the missionaries. They were therefore continued in peonage and without recognition of
their individual rights up to the date of the secularization act of 1833. At
this time the Indian missions were the centers of industry and of wealth and
of social attraction for the Pacific coast country. In 1826, they were reported
at twenty-one missions as numbering 25,000 and possessed of 365,000 head
of cattle, sheep and horses, and harvesting 75,000 bushels of grain. The
"law of secularization" passed in the Mexican Congress treated all these Mexican lands, with their improvements, flocks, and herds, as the property of
the church, and divided them up among a few Spanish and Mexican families. The Indians were scattered over the country, principally along the coast,
upon the fertile, watered, and then unoccupied tracts, and procured their
living by herding wild cattle and horses, cultivating small patches of
ground, and receiving employment from the surrounding whites, whom
they accepted virtually as their masters.

In this way they gradually came into possession, and some have continued
to occupy the best portions of the country without inquiry as to whether
their homes were embraced in the boundary-lines of a Mexican grant or
liable at any moment to be entered at the land-office in the name of some
settler.

When the tide of trade and the gold emigration swept over the State of
California, these Indians were found practically without protection by law
in their rights to the land on which they were living, and by suits of
ejectment and cost of contingent fees it was comparatively easy for the
incoming American to dispossess all the Indians of Northern and Middle
California. Thus made homeless wanderers, the process of vice and destitution
by which they were carried away is fitly described as extermination. For the
4,000 or 5,000 who remained in the southern portion of Lower California,
this doom seems to have been postponed by the delay in the settlement of
the country. Gradually, however, for the past eight years, Southern California has been filling up by emigration; Spanish and Mexican grants have
been "determined" in such a way as to cover choice tracts wherever found;
large ranches have been cut up and the desirable portions of public domain
pre-empted; and thus all available agricultural lands have been seized or
occupied by individual owners who, in conformity to law, have become
possessed of the lands on which the remnants of a few thousand Mission Indians are making their homes in San Diego and San Bernardino
Counties. So long as the pre-emptors and purchasers did not require their
lands for use or sale, the Indians were allowed to remain undisturbed and in
blissful ignorance of the fact that the place they called home had by law
passed to the ownership of another. Of late, under the increasing demands
for these lands, writs of ejectment are being procured by which the Indians
are forcibly dispossessed and turn adrift in poverty and wretchedness.

The Indians living on the tract of land known as Temecula, in the county
of San Diego, have within the past two months been thus dispossessed. The

Temecula ranch was confirmed by the district court of the United States for the southern district of California to Louis Vigues in 1855. No steps were taken to disturb the Indians until 1873, when a judgment was recovered in the city of San Francisco against these Indians, who were at that time living 500 miles away, all unconscious that any person was seeking their possessions; and on the 17th of August last the owners, under Vigues, procured a writ from the court in San Francisco for ejectment of Indians and for the satisfaction of the costs by the personal property of the Indians. The execution of this writ has not only deprived the Indians of their homes and of their crops just maturing for harvest, but has taken their little personal property in satisfaction of cost of judgment. It is easy to understand the exasperation and despair produced among the Indians by such an order enforced by the authority of the State. Their remonstrance and threats under the provocation were interpreted to mean violence, and the aid of the United States military was evoked against them. Their forbearance and peaceful disposition were, however, soon manifest, and the fears of white citizens allayed. The agent has been instructed to procure, if possible, a suitable ranch which may be leased temporarily, with privilege of purchase; but the embarrassments under which the Department has labored for the past two years in its efforts to rescue these Indians from their present condition still continue. There are no adequate funds for their relief, either in purchasing small tracts of country, or leasing ranches, or for furnishing rations in adequate amount.

In 1870, on the representation of the agent, Lieut. A. P. Greene, United States Army, indorsed by the superintendent, B. C. Whiting, six townships were set apart for the permanent homes of these Indians, and the lands, by Executive order, were withdrawn from public sale. At that time a few settlers had made improvements of comparatively small value within these six townships. This tract of country, known as the Pala and San Pasqual reservations, was adapted to the Indians' wants, and contained lands sufficient to furnish homes for all the Indians in California who were liable to be dispossessed of the homes they were occupying. But the setting apart of these reservations received the most strenuous, united, and persistent opposition of the citizens and press of California. The proceeding was represented as an enormous swindle upon the Government and a hardship and outrage upon the Indians, and numerous petitions and remonstrances, signed by leading citizens, were forwarded to the President. And the Indians themselves, for whose benefit alone the reservations had been created, were induced to ask not to be sent thither, but to be "let alone" upon the lands they were then occupying, and which they were left to believe would remain permanently their homes.

In accordance with this demand of public opinion in California, Commissioner Parker suggested to the Department the propriety of restoring the Pala and San Pasqual reserves to the public domain, which was accordingly done by Executive order of February 17, 1871, and this last opportunity of furnishing these Indians with homes by substituting public land in California for those in the title to which the Government had failed to protect them was lost. A resistance to the public demand in strict conformity with justice to the Indians would have enabled the Government then at slight cost to assist the Mission Indians. . . . The necessary appropriation asked for this purpose not being granted, attention was again called during the last session of Congress to the same subject, and an appropriation of $100,000 asked for the Indian service in California, by which great relief would have been brought to these Indians; but that estimate was reduced in the bill to the usual amount granted for the other Indians of that State, leaving but a small amount which could in any case be used for the Mission Indians.

In my judgment, the best method of meeting the necessities of these Indians will be to secure to them by withdrawal from sale all the public lands upon which they are now living. Under directions from the Office, the agent has employed a surveyor to indicate such boundaries as will enable the President to issue an Executive order making the proper withdrawal. This course, however, will provide for but very few of the Indians, from the fact that nearly all of the arable lands in that section of the country have been sought for and are covered by Mexican land grants or entries in the United States Land Office. For the remainder, it will be necessary to purchase small tracts of land at different points upon which the Indians may locate permanent homes and where they will be in the vicinity of the planters and ranchmen, who will give them profitable employment as laborers. For the purchase of these tracts and of the improvements which may be found within other tracts desirable for small reservations, an appropriation of not less than $150,000 will be required, and I respectfully suggest that the attention of Congress be again called to the importance of this subject.

* * *

INDIAN CIVILIZATION

The question of Indian civilization is deeper and broader than is to be found in the inquiry and answer as to whether an Indian can be civilized. The question in that form has been long since answered, and the only form remaining, which is of practical interest to the American people, relates to the methods which are essential to any extended and successful effort for that end. I believe that the present unsatisfactory condition in which Indians of this country are still found, notwithstanding the large and increasing outlays of money which the Government has been making for a half-century, is due to the fact that by far the largest portion of the expenditures have been made with no practical reference to the question of civilization. An annuity in money or blankets, or bacon and beef, may have a tendency to draw the Indians within the reach of the Government, and prepare them for the beginning of a work of civilization, and also to render them disinclined to take up arms and go upon the war-path. But with any tribe a few years of this treatment is sufficient for the purpose, and after this end has been gained, a continuation of the feeding and clothing, without a reference to further improvement on the part of the Indians, is simply a waste of expenditure. This has been the case with a large portion of the money spent upon Indians during the last fifty years. It is true that the letter of treaties may have been complied with by such expenditures, and thus the credit of the nation saved in form. But the spirit of the treaties, which uniformly looked toward the civilization of the Indians, has been disregarded, in that no reasonable methods have been devised and adopted for promoting civilization. This is manifest from the fact that the question has not been raised as to whether an Indian should be subjected to a system of enforced industry, and no plan has been devised looking toward his elevation, by bringing to bear upon him the ordinary motive of industry which are found in the responsibilities that attack to self-support and individual manhood.

This negligence or long continued disregard of the main question relative to Indians has largely resulted from the history adopted from the beginning as to the political status of Indians. They have been treated as if capable of acting for themselves in the capacity of a nation, whereas all history shows no record of a tribe, within our republic, able to assume and continue the character and relations of a sovereign people. There may have been a reason in the weakness of the early colonies, and far superior numbers of their Indian foes, for recognizing this condition of Indian sovereignty. But that has long since passed away, and there is no longer any occasion for recognizing the tribes who remain with us as foreigners. Their own interests, more strongly even than those of the Government, require that they should be recognized and treated for what they are, an ignorant and helpless people, who have a large moral claim upon the United States—a debt which cannot be discharged by gifts of blankets and bacon, or any routine official care for their protection or relief. These are trifles compared with the one boon—civilization—which every consideration of humanity requires that we should give them. We have taken from them the possibility of living in their way, and are bound in return to give them the possibility of living in our way—an obligation we do not begin to discharge when we merely attempt to supply their wants for food and clothing. They need to be taught to take care of themselves. If any demonstration of the feasibility of this teaching is required, there are very few Indian agents now in the service who cannot, each out of his own experience and observation, furnish facts remarkably conclusive on this subject. An Indian is subject to like passions with the rest of us. So long as he can be subsisted by rations or by the chase, he will not labor; so long as he declines to labor, he cannot take the first step in civilization. The call to labor must come to him, not through memorials or treaties, councils or presents, but through his necessities. He must be driven to toil by cold and the pangs of hunger. Then, when he has taken this first step toward self-support, his wants, which at the beginning were registered only in his stomach, take on multiplied forms, and urge to increased industry. Naturally, when a man begins to toil for that which he receives, he begins to learn the value of personal-property rights, and thus takes the first step in separating from his tribe, and toward individual manhood.

Congress, at its last session, recognizing the propriety that Indians, like other people, should toil for what they have, directed that all annuities should hereafter be paid only in return for some form of labor, giving, however, to the Secretary of the Interior discretion which allows the exemption of certain tribes from the operation of this restriction. This eminently wise legislation has been of great avail to the Bureau during the year in enforcing industry. While in some cases it has excited hostility and produced slight disturbance, it has on the whole worked with eminent satisfaction.

The question has been raised by the Indians, and sometimes by their friends, as to the right of the Government to compel them to labor as a condition antecedent to receiving that which the Government has promised to give them, and without any such restriction being named in the promise. But when it is recollected that the Indian actually receives that which the Government has promised him, and enjoys beside the benefit of all the labor he performs, not only in its moral effect in promoting habits of industry, but also in the improvements made and crops raised, there can be no hesitation as to the positive benefit conferred upon the Indian by holding him to this restriction in the enjoyment of his funds; and when it is remembered that the Government has upon its hands the care and support of these Indians, not only for the brief period covered by their treaties, but until they shall be able to care for themselves, it will be seen that the interests of the Government, as well as those of the Indian, require that whatever expenditure is made in his behalf shall be so made as will tend most rapidly and certainly to his civilization. For this reason I would most respectfully recommend that the restrictions placed upon appropriations for annuities for Indians by the last Congress be hereafter continued, and that the discretion of the Department as to releasing any tribe from its operations be reduced to the minimum which the proper handling of wild Indians who cannot be at once reduced to labor will allow; and also that authority be given to expend a necessary portion of annuities in preparing the ground for Indian labor and the purchasing of seeds and implements and stock cattle. There have been several instances where an agent has been unable to put his Indians to labor because they had no land plowed and nothing but their hands to work with, and yet they would not consent that any of their cash annuity should be expended in these means of labor.

All attempts to require labor as a condition of receiving annuities will meet with much opposition. The Indians will resist it from their constitutional disrelish for toil. They will also be incited to such resistance by halfbreeds and squaw-men, traders, and other interested parties, who always turn up as champions for the rights of an Indian whenever any measure is proposed which threatens to disturb their peculiar relation as his next friend, and entitled to hold his money and divide his annuity goods.

As the means of enforcing civilization become more available, and the necessity arises to compel Indians, through the moral suasion of hunger, to do that which they dislike, it will be found necessary in many instances to rid agencies of the interference of this low class of whites by expelling them from the reservation. There is no reason why the Government should continue to clothe and feed any class of men who are able to shift for themselves, and especially does such obligation cease toward men who persist in making the terms of a treaty their pretext for thwarting the purposes of the Government and retarding the civilization of its wards. A law providing for their summary ejection and punishment for their subsequent return would relieve many a reservation from great embarrassment.

ECONOMY OF CIVILIZATION

But the adoption of these methods does not by any means secure civilization. It merely prepares the way for a rational effort in that direction. Three essential conditions still require to be met.

First, that the Indians should be placed or allowed to remain in a country affording water, timber, grass, and a soil upon which a white man could make a living. In the warm and dry climates, ordinary facilities for irrigation are sufficient.

Second, the necessary funds must be provided to carry the untaught barbarian through the period of his childhood in civilization. This childish ignorance requires much patient and expensive teaching. The farmer or mechanic who is to be his instructor, needs to be more than an ordinary man of that calling, and must receive suitable compensation. No view can be more short-sighted than that any common laborer will make a profitable employe upon an Indian reservation. But under the best of teaching there will necessarily be large expenditures in the fields of agriculture or herding. Awkwardness is wasteful. No man learns to take responsibility and care except by experience and this with an Indian comes at high rates. The first cow or yoke of oxen intrusted to his care will quite likely be rendered valueless by mismanagement, or eaten in stress of hunger, and you may be obliged to repeat the aid in several forms before you will have an Indian farmer capable of providing for his stock. There were purchased seven years since for the Winnebago Indians in Nebraska 307 cattle. For three years they were kept by the Government at large expense, under the care of farmers and herders, when it was decided to issue them to the Indians, and thus save at least the expense of keeping, which amounted annually to the value of the cattle. But few of these cattle are now remaining among the Winnebagoes. They have died for want of care, or have been eaten by their owners; but in this process, expensive as it has been, the Indians have learned the value and care of cattle, and are now receiving a new supply, purchased by their own money, and are giving them the treatment requisite for protection and increase. In the erection of houses upon a reservation, it will be more expensive to attempt to utilize the rough labor of an Indian than to hire white labor, but the house is worth tenfold more to him, not only for the increased interest with which he will always regard it as the work of his own hands, but for the lesson of labor which its erection has afforded him. In the same manner a plow or wagon broken in the Indian's experiment of his first useful exercise of muscle, is a costly expenditure, and yet experiments which involve these and more serious outlays, are in the end highly economical.

For this comparatively brief training-period larger annual appropriation will be required than if the Indian were allowed to continue his life of vagrancy and barbarism. The cost of furnishing school-houses and teachers in a commonwealth will be considerably greater in any five years than to allow the children to run in idleness and ignorance during that period. But before that generation of children has come to manhood, the cost for police and punishment will be many times greater than the sum required for their proper education. In like manner a discussion of the question of comparative economy in the civilization of Indians must not fail to count the cost of the alternative. When settlements approach an Indian country, this uncivilized class comes into new relations with the Government. If they are allowed longer to roam, they will be a heavy expense either to the people, by marauding, or to the Government, by the maintenance of a sufficient military force to prevent or punish such marauding. The Territory of Arizona presents a striking illustration of the economy of civilization. By the combined efforts of the War Department and the Interior, the fierce, bloody Apaches, who three years ago were the terror of that Territory, making a twenty-mile ride out from its capital unsafe without a guard, are now in quiet upon their reservations, and, with the exception of a small number, followers of Cochise, who as yet occupy the Dragoon Mountains, are digging ditches for crops, and making adobe dwellings. Meanwhile, the country is freed from hostile incursions, and the Government is enabled to reduce the military force hitherto required for peace and safety in Arizona. The cost of maintaining this half of the military in Arizona for a single year exceeds all the expenditures by the Indian Bureau for all the Apaches in that Territory for four years past, and from this time the expenditure will annually decrease until the Apaches become entirely self-supporting.

Third. The agents who stand for the Government in close contact with the Indians must be competent for the business in hand. They must be able to comprehend how far it reaches beyond the mere attempt to gratify the

Indians or to keep them quiet. They must be men who have faith in their fellow-men, who believe that the lowest creature God has made is capable of coming up higher. They must be not only strong in integrity and able to resist the plots and machinations by which greedy and unscrupulous men will seek to use them, but they must also possess such administrative ability as will enable them to bring all their personal and official power to bear in restraining and curing vicious habits and inspiring high motives and aiding feeble beginners in a better life. Men of this character are not to be found in the ordinary way of political appointment. Their selection must be made on no other ground than that of fitness for their peculiar duties. A mistake here is fatal to the whole effort. For this reason the mode adopted for the last few years, of procuring nominations of agents through the several religious bodies of the country, has worked most admirably. Not that the best men have always been selected by those bodies, but that the proportion of true, devoted, capable agents furnished in this way has been far greater than it would have been by any other method of appointment. When these agents thus selected have reached their distant fields of duty, they find, in the relations which they bear to the Christian people whom they represent, a constant inspiration to fidelity. Any man fit to receive such an appointment must constantly recognize the duty upon him to be true, not only to the Government, but to his own religious convictions, and to those in whose name he has been sent to engage in the work of lifting men out of barbarism. And it is exactly this element of enthusiasm which comes from living for an idea, from the purpose and consciousness of living for others, which is most essential to the effort of civilization among Indians. For this reason I most devoutly trust that the Government will still be inclined to call upon the religious bodies of the country to name the proper men for Indian agents.

With these three essential conditions, suitable country, reasonable appropriations and proper agents, supplied and continued for a reasonable length of time, there is not a shade of doubt, in my mind, that the Indians of this country can be reclaimed from barbarism and fitted for citizenship, and that every year, from the time of its adoption till its consummation, will give increased demonstration of the wisdom and ultimate success of the plan. But it must be borne in mind that all these conditions, namely, men, country, and funds, relatively important in the order named, are absolutely essential. If one of them is lacking, the highest excellence of the other two cannot repair the loss. You cannot civilize the Sioux on the alkali plains of Dakota with any amount of funds and the best of agents. You cannot civilize the Otoes on the best soil in Nebraska, with their large per capita annuity, without an agent capable of his high trust. You cannot civilize the Lac Court Oreille Chippewas in Wisconsin, on their fine reservation, and with all the encouragements which a competent subagent can give, without the means necessary to provide for their first steps in civilized labor.

It surely is not too much to expect that a work of such magnitude, involving, as it does, the welfare of so many poor who in all their history have stood in such peculiar relations to the American people, and who are now attracting the increasing interest of philanthropists and scholars and the commiseration of all classes, shall obtain such recognition by the Congress of the United States as will remove the difficulties which have heretofore been experienced in procuring the enactment of laws and the necessary appropriations by their training in civilization.

The following table shows the annual appropriations including deficiency and special appropriations, of each year since 1870, and the disbursements for the corresponding years, together with the funds derived from interest on Indian stocks and sales of bonds and lands and turned over to the Indians or expended for their benefit. This table shows the largest amount to have been expended in 1873, which was the uncertain period as to the number of the Sioux and the year in which the Apaches and other wild tribes were being gathered upon reservations in Arizona and New Mexico.

The expenditures of the year 1875, exclusive of expenditures of funds derived from interest of Indian stocks, and sales of bonds and lands, as compared with those of 1873, show a decrease of $1,002,947.19. The appropriations for 1876 are $5,435,627, and from present prospects it is confidently expected that the deficiency for this year will not exceed $200,000, making a total of $5,635,627, and a diminution of $1,524,446.46 against the cost of 1873. This reduction of expense has occurred partly by increased cheapness of supplies and decreased cost of transportation; but mainly by the definiteness with which numbers and wants of Indians have been ascertained, whereby waste and overissue of supplies have been in a degree prevented.

The cost of maintaining all the Indians, except the wilder tribes, like the Sioux, Utes, Crows, and Arickarees, will steadily decrease from this time on until they cease to be any burden to the Government; and this not through any process of extinction, but because of their increasing self-support in a civilized mode of life.

It is not improbable, however, that such additional expenditure will be required for bringing the wilder tribes through the transition from a state of almost complete barbarism into the beginning of civilization as will make the totals of appropriations for three or four years to come equal to those of the last three years, and perhaps greater.

The problem of the Sioux, as discussed elsewhere, involves even larger outlays for at least three years than are now required for the feeding process. The Sioux on the Upper Missouri, with the Piegans and Blackfeet, who are now procuring much the larger portion of their subsistence by hunting, will, before long, be compelled by scarcity of game to depend upon Government rations. When this necessity comes to them, and to the Crows and Utes, the change from a nomadic to an agricultural life, which must necessarily follow, will bring the temporary necessity of a corresponding increase of appropriations. These are the exigencies or the crises which come in the history of all tribes; and the fact that the cost of maintaining Indians is growing less, notwithstanding there are more of them upon reservations and under the immediate care of the Government to-day than ever before, is most instructive as well as encouraging. And if it were possible to show in figures the increased advantages which have been derived from the comparative quiet upon the border, and exemption from pillage and marauding, and the very marked decrease in expenditures incurred in campaigning against the Indians, a most gratifying exhibit could be made of economical results already accomplished.

A sum equal to the cost of fighting only a small portion of the Sioux, in 1862, if funded at 7 per cent., would yield an annual interest sufficient, even on the present unsatisfactory plan, to care for the whole Sioux people for all time.

It should also be remembered that we might naturally have expected an increase instead of a diminution in disturbance and depredation on the part of the Indians, with a correspondingly increased cost for police and restraint by the Army, on account of the growing settlements which have pushed their way on every side, up to the border, and sometimes into the very heart, of the Indian country.

Before yielding to any despondency or doubt as to the future, even of the most hopeless tribe, it is well to recall the fact that only seven years ago the United States was willing to make any promise to the wild Sioux, whom we did not wish to fight, if they would allow us to push a railway across their plains toward the Pacific coast. Five of the wisest and bravest leading generals of the Army did not consider it derogatory to the dignity of the Government to solemnly stipulate, in order to gain this end, that the larger part of Dakota, Nebraska, and Wyoming, claimed by the savages, should never be trodden by a white man's foot; that military forts and roads should be dismantled and abandoned; that no man wearing the United States uniform should ever be seen within their reservation; the Indians should receive large supplies of rations and clothing, and that these stipulations should never be altered by a subsequent treaty except on the written assent of three-fourths of the male members of the nation.

The trains on the Union Pacific roads have been running daily undisturbed; the surrounding country has been occupied, while Indian depredations have greatly decreased. The lands in Nebraska are now being occupied by settlers, the Indians having withdrawn their claim; soldiers are to be found in every part of the Sioux reservation, and the present season has witnessed thousands of miners and "pilgrims" swarming over the Sioux country, and digging into their sacred hills for gold. Yet there has been no fighting, under all this provocation, which, five years ago, would have brought ten thousand painted savages into the field for a war which would not have cost less than fifty millions. And with any kind and firm treatment, which bears resemblance to justice, there will be no serious contention with this powerful tribe hereafter. The results have therefore fully justified the negotiations of 1868, and have demonstrated most completely that it is far better to feed and temporize and parley with a wild, unreasoning savage, until you have brought him within authority and proper requirements, so that he may be assured, from experience, that the Government on the one hand desires only his good, and on the other is able to compel submission to law.

Report of Commissioner of Indian Affairs J. Q. Smith
October 30, 1876

(Excerpt from *Report for 1876*, pp. 384-91)

No more insensitive report of an Indian commissioner is on record than the 1876 report of Commissioner Smith. In suggesting a policy to be pursued, Smith rode roughshod over the desires of the Indians, existing treaties, and common humanity. Concentration of Indians on several large reservations was the first plank in Smith's program. Although the Indian Territory had been designated as one such area, Smith asserted that strict observance of the treaties setting aside such a reserve exclusively for Indians was "in many instances at variance both with their own best interests and with sound public policy." Smith further advocated that the laws of the United States should be extended over the Indians in the Indian country. Finally, Smith advocated a general law—not realized under 1887—"not only permitting, but requiring, the head of each Indian family to accept the allotment of a reasonable amount of land, to be the property of himself and his lawful heirs, in lieu of any interest in any common tribal possession." Under the hammer blows of such a policy the fate of the Indian who still maintained the traditions of his race could not long survive. An all-out campaign was in effect declared against the Indian view, the Indian tradition, and the Indian will.

THE POLICY TO BE PURSUED

IN ORDER TO FORM any wise opinion as to the best method of dealing hereafter with our Indians, a clear conception of their actual condition, and of our present relations with them, is necessary.

From the first settlement of the country by white men until a comparatively recent period, the Indians have been constantly driven westward from the Atlantic. A zigzag, ever-varying line, more or less definitely marked, extending from Canada to the Gulf of Mexico, and always slowly moving west, has been known as the "frontier" or "border." Along this border has been an almost incessant struggle, the Indians to retain and the whites to get possession; the war being broken by periods of occasional and temporary peace, which usually followed treaties whereby the Indians agreed to surrender large tracts of their lands. This peace would continue until the lands surrendered had been occupied by whites, when the pressure of emigration would again break over the border, and the Indian, by force or treaty, be compelled to surrender another portion of his cherished hunting-grounds.

So long as the illimitable West offered to the Indian fresh hunting-grounds, he was unwilling to exchange his wild freedom and indolent existence for the restraints and toil of the rude and imperfect civilization to which it was possible for him in only one life-time to attain. If any tribe of Indians in this country had made the effort to abandon their savage mode of life and undertake self-support by labor, it is at least doubtful whether for many years the change would not have rendered them more miserable and wretched. Their lack of means, of knowledge, and of previous training would, in all probability, have made such an attempt a conspicuous failure. If individual Indians had succeeded in acquiring property, they would probably have been swindled out of it by unscrupulous white men. The natural and the easiest course was to remove west and continue to hunt.

Toward the close of the first half of this century the tide of emigration and adventure swept even the frontier away and rushed across the continent. Throughout the vast regions of the West the adventurous, grasping Anglo-Saxon race is dominant and in possession of the fairest and richest portions of the land. Except in the Indian Territory and perhaps Dakota, the white exceeds the Indian population. No new hunting-grounds remain, and the civilization or the utter destruction of the Indians is inevitable. The next twenty-five years are to determine the fate of a race. If they cannot be taught, and taught very soon, to accept the necessities of their situation and begin in earnest to provide for their own wants by labor in civilized pursuits, they are destined to speedy extinction.

From the fact that for so long a period Indian civilization has been retarded, it must not be concluded that some inherent characteristic in the race disqualifies it for civilized life. It may well be doubted whether this be true of any race of men. Surely it cannot be true of a race, any portion of which has made the actual progress realized by some of our Indians. They can and do learn to labor; they can and do learn to read. Many thousands to-day are engaged in civilized occupations. But the road out of barbarism is a long and difficult one. Even in enlightened Europe there are millions of people whose ancestors a few generations ago were as ignorant and poor and degraded as our most advanced Indian tribes now are. Civilization is a vague, indefinite, comparative term. Our children's grandchildren may look upon our civilization as very rude and imperfect. It is not my wish to give any rose-colored view of the present condition of our Indians. Many of them are as miserable and degraded as men can be; but it cannot be denied that others are making reasonably satisfactory progress.

Within a few years the Government has undertaken somewhat systematically to bring them into civilized life. The "peace policy" has sought to throw around them healthful associations; to place at the several agencies agents and employés of good moral and Christian character and of active sympathies; and an earnest effort has been made to teach Indians to labor and to read. It is too soon, perhaps, to assert that this effort has proved a success, but the accompanying reports of agents abundantly show that, notwithstanding all surrounding difficulties, much has been accomplished toward establishing and maintaining peace, toward protecting Indians from evil influences, and toward awakening in them the desire for a better mode of life. The success of some of our agents, who have labored under reasonably favorable circumstances, deserves all praise, and has fully equaled the fondest hopes of the friends of the peace policy. Certainly enough improvement has been made to justify the continuance of the present benevolent efforts.

In considering whether modifications of existing methods may not be desirable, I have arrived at the conviction that the welfare and progress of the Indians require the adoption of three principles of policy:

First. Concentration of all Indians on a few reservations.

Second. Allotment to them of lands in severalty.

Third. Extension over them of United States law and the jurisdiction of United States courts.

CONSOLIDATION OF RESERVATIONS

The reservations upon which, in my opinion, the Indians should be consolidated, are the Indian Territory, the White Earth reservation in Northern Minnesota, and a reservation in the southern part of Washington Territory, probably the Yakama reservation. If it should be found impracticable to remove the Indians of Colorado, Utah, New Mexico, and Arizona, to the Indian Territory, they might be concentrated on some suitable reservation either in Colorado or Arizona.

I am well aware that it will take a long time, much patient effort, and considerable expense, to effect this proposed consolidation; but after consulting with many gentlemen thoroughly acquainted with Indian questions and Indian character, I am satisfied that the undertaking can be accomplished. If legislation were secured giving the President authority to remove any tribe or band, or any portion of a tribe or band, whenever in his judgment it was practicable, to any one of the reservations named, and if Congress would appropriate, from year to year, a sum sufficient to enable him to take advantage of every favorable opportunity to make such removals, I am confident that a few years' trial would conclusively demonstrate the entire feasibility of the plan. I believe that all the Indians in Kansas, Nebraska, and Dakota, and a part at least of those in Wyoming and Montana, could be induced to remove to the Indian Territory. There is also ground for the belief that the Colorado, Arizona, and New Mexico Indians, and a part if not all of those in Nevada, could also be taken to that Territory.

Many of these Indians are now located on lands utterly unfit for cultivation, where starvation or perpetual support by the Government are the only alternatives. It is doubtful whether even white people could cultivate profitably the greater part of the Sioux reservation in Dakota. In the Indian

Territory, on the other hand, are fertile land, a genial climate, and room for more Indians than there are in the whole Union.

That the Indian sentiment is opposed to such removal is true. Difficulties were experienced in bringing to the Territory its present inhabitants from east of the Mississippi; but the obstacles were overcome, and experience shows that there the race can thrive. With a fair degree of persistence the removal thither of other Indians can also be secured. The Pawnees have recently gone there, and seem content with their new home. The Poncas, and even the Red Cloud and Spotted Tail Sioux, give evidence that they are ready for the change; and if Congress will make a liberal appropriation to effect the removal of these Sioux, it is quite likely that within a year or two, other bands now on the Missouri River may also be induced to remove. If the Sioux are given a suitable reservation in that Territory for a permanent home, and are aided by the Government for a few years in their efforts at agriculture and stock-raising, I know of no reason why they may not, in one generation, become as far advanced as are the Cherokees and Choctaws now.

It is to be regretted that all the Indians in the United States cannot be removed to the Indian Territory; but it is doubtful whether, at least for many years, it will be best to attempt to remove Indians thither from the region of the great lakes or from the Pacific coast. I would therefore suggest that, for the tribes of Wisconsin and Minnesota, and the wandering Pembinas in Dakota, the White Earth reservation is best adapted as a permanent home. Containing thirty-six townships of well-watered timber and wheat lands, it offers far better agricultural facilities than do other reservations in those States, and is in about the same latitude with them.

My information in regard to the proper reservation for the Indians on the Pacific coast is less definite, and I have suggested the Yakama reservation, mainly because it is well known that the Indians there, under the direction of Agent Wilbur, have made remarkable progress. A commission now visiting the Indians in that region has been requested to make such suggestions on the subject as they may deem wise.

The importance of reducing the number of reservations is shown by the following considerations:

Many of the present reserves are almost worthless for agricultural purposes; others are rich in soil, mineral wealth, and timber. Nearly all are too small to subsist the Indians by hunting, and too large for them to occupy in agricultural and civilized pursuits. Many are so remote and difficult of access, that needed supplies can be furnished only at great expense. Nearly all are surrounded by white settlers, more or less numerous. Wherever an Indian reservation has on it good land, or timber, or minerals, the cupidity of the white man is excited, and a constant struggle is inaugurated to dispossess the Indian, in which the avarice and determination of the white man usually prevails. The length of the boundary-line between the reservations and the contiguous white settlements amounts in the aggregate to thousands of miles, every mile being a point of contact and difficulty. This aggregate boundary is so extensive as to render almost impossible the prevention of illicit trade in arms and whisky. As now constituted, these reservations are a refuge to the most lawless and desperate white men in America. There the vagabonds, the outcasts, the criminals, the most immoral and licentious of the population of the western portion of the country take up their abode, because there they are practically beyond the reach and operation of law, and can live lives of crime and debauchery with impunity and without reproach. Such men seriously obstruct, if they do not render nugatory, every effort to give assistance to the Indians.

By the concentration of Indians on a few reservations, it is obvious that much of the difficulty now surrounding the Indian question will vanish. Many agencies now conducted at large expense could be abolished. The aggregate boundary-lines between the reservations and country occupied by white people would be greatly reduced, and the danger of violence, bloodshed, and mutual wrong materially lessened. The sale of liquors and arms could be more effectually prevented; bad white men could more easily be kept out of the Indian country; necessary supplies could be more cheaply furnished; a far smaller military force would be required to keep the peace; and generally, the Indians, being more compact, could be more efficiently aided and controlled by the officers of the Government. Moreover, large bodies of land would be thrown open to settlement, proceeds of whose sale would be ample to defray all expense of the removals.

Allotments in Severalty

It is doubtful whether any high degree of civilization is possible without individual ownership of land. The records of the past and the experience of the present testify that the soil should be made secure to the individual by all the guarantees which law can devise, and that nothing less will induce men to put forth their best exertions. No general law exists which provides that Indians shall select allotments in severalty, and it seems to me a matter of great moment that provision should be made not only permitting, but requiring, the head of each Indian family to accept the allotment of a reasonable amount of land, to be the property of himself and his lawful heirs, in lieu of any interest in any common tribal possession. Such allotments should be inalienable for at least twenty, perhaps fifty years, and if situated in a permanent Indian reservation, should be transferable only among Indians.

I am not unaware that this proposition will meet with strenuous opposition from the Indians themselves. Like the whites, they have ambitious men, who will resist to the utmost of their power any change tending to reduce the authority which they have acquired by personal effort or by inheritance; but it is essential that these men and their claims should be pushed aside and that each individual should feel that his home is his own;

that he owes no allegiance to any great man or to any faction; that he has a direct personal interest in the soil on which he lives, and that that interest will be faithfully protected for him and for his children by the Government.

LAW FOR INDIANS

My predecessors have frequently called attention to the startling fact that we have within our midst 275,000 people, the least intelligent portion of our population, for whom we provide no law, either for their protection or for the punishment of crime committed among themselves. Civilization even among white men could not long exist without the guarantees which law alone affords; yet our Indians are remitted by a great civilized government to the control, if control it can be called, of the rude regulations of petty, ignorant tribes. Year after year we expend millions of dollars for these people in the faint hope that, without law, we can civilize them. That hope has been, to a great degree, a long disappointment; and year after year we repeat the folly of the past. That the benevolent efforts and purposes of the Government have proved so largely fruitless, is, in my judgment, due more to its failure to make these people amenable to our laws than to any other cause, or to all other causes combined.

I believe it to be the duty of Congress at once to extend over Indian reservations the jurisdiction of United States courts, and to declare that each Indian in the United States shall occupy the same relation to law that a white man does. An Indian should be given to understand that no ancient custom, no tribal regulation, will shield him from just punishment for crime; and also that he will be effectually protected, by the authority and power of the Government, in his life, liberty, property, and character, as certainly as if he were a white man. There can be no doubt of the power of Congress to do this, and surely the intelligent Committees on Indian Affairs of the Senate and House can readily propose legislation which will accomplish this most desirable result. I regard this suggestion as by far the most important which I have to make in this report.

Since our Government was organized two questions, or rather two classes of questions, have transcended all others in importance and difficulty, viz, the relations of the Government and the white people to the negroes and to the Indians. The negro question has doubtless absorbed more of public attention, aroused more intense feeling, and cost our people more blood and treasure than any other question, if not all others combined. That question, it is to be hoped, is settled forever in the only way in which its settlement was possible—by the full admission of the negro to all the rights and privileges of citizenship. Next in importance comes the Indian question, and there can be no doubt that our Indian wars have cost us more than all the foreign wars in which our Government has been engaged. It is time that some solution of this whole Indian problem, decisive, satisfactory, just, and final, should be found. In my judgment it can be reached only be a process similar to that pursued with the negroes.

In the three propositions above stated, will, I believe, be found the true and final settlement of this perplexing subject. However efficient may be the administration of the Indian Office, and however faithful the labors of its agents and their subordinates, I have little hope of any marked degree of success until the above suggestions are substantially adopted as a permanent Indian policy. If Congress concludes to act on these suggestions, laws should be passed at the coming session to extend the jurisdiction of the courts over all Indians, and to provide for the allotment of lands in severalty in the Indian Territory, and on such other reservations as may be selected as permanent; and an appropriation should be made with which to begin the removal of Indians to their permanent homes.

I trust I may be pardoned for stating that it appears to me that the fundamental difficulty in our relations hitherto with Indians has been the want of a well-defined, clearly understood, persistent purpose on the part of the Government. Indian affairs have heretofore been managed largely by the application of mere temporary expedients in a fragmentary and disjointed manner. For a hundred years the United States has been wrestling with the "Indian question," but has never had an Indian policy. The only thing yet done by the Government in regard to the Indians which seems to have been permanent and far-reaching in its scope and purpose, is the dedication of the Indian Territory as the final home for the race. Surely it is time that a policy should be determined on, which shall be fully understood by the Government, the people, and the Indians. We cannot afford to allow this race to perish without making an honest effort to save it. We cannot afford to keep them in our midst as vagabonds and paupers.

I appeal to the statesmen of the country to give to this subject their earnest attention; the sooner it is settled on some wise and comprehensive principle the better for all concerned. We have despoiled the Indians of their rich hunting-grounds, thereby depriving them of their ancient means of support. Ought we not and shall we not give them at least a secure home, and the cheap but priceless benefit of just and equitable laws?

THE INDIAN TERRITORY

Affairs in the Indian Territory are both complicated and embarrassing. By treaty the Government has ceded to the so-called civilized tribes, the Cherokees, Choctaws, Chickasaws, Creeks, and Seminoles, a section of country altogether disproportionate in amount to their needs. The Cherokees number about 13,000, and own 5,031,351 acres, or 279½ acres to each person. The 16,000 Choctaws have an average of 418 acres to each person; the 6,000 Chickasaws, an average of 775 acres; the 13,000 Creeks, an average of 247 acres, and the 2,438 Seminoles, an average of 82 acres. In the aggregate, for a population of 55,438 persons there are set apart 20,784,309 acres, or an average of 375 acres for each individual—an area nearly equal to the area of the State of Indiana for a population not much greater than that of many agricultural counties in the Eastern or Middle States.

No doubt a considerable portion of land in each reservation is unsuitable for tillage, but most of it is valuable for grazing, and the amount susceptible of cultivation must be many fold greater than can ever be cultivated by the labor of the Indians. But the Indians claim, it is understood, that they hold their lands by sanctions so solemn that it would be a gross breach of faith on the part of the Government to take away any portion thereof without their consent; and that consent they apparently propose to withhold. The question is thus directly raised whether an extensive section of fertile country is to be allowed to remain for an indefinite period practically an uncultivated waste, or whether the Government shall determine to reduce the size of the reservations.

The question is plainly a difficult one, and should be considered with calmness, and a full purpose to do no injustice to the Indians. Any opinion thereon is ventured with hesitancy on my part; but I cannot but believe that public policy will soon require the disposal of a large portion of these lands to the Government, for the occupancy either of other tribes of Indians or of white people. There is a very general and growing opinion that observance of the strict letter of treaties with Indians is in many cases at variance both with their own best interests and with sound public policy. Public necessity must ultimately become supreme law; and in my opinion their highest good will require these people to take ample allotments of lands in severalty, (to be inalienable for at least twenty years, and then only among Indians,) and to surrender the remainder of their lands to the United States Government for a fair equivalent. Upon the lands thus surrendered, other Indians should be located as rapidly as possible, and should be given allotments under the same restrictions.

From the recommendation above made, it must not be understood to be either the policy or purpose of this office to in any way encourage the spirit of rapacity which demands the throwing open of the Indian Territory to white settlement. That country was set apart, half a century ago, as the home of the Indians. The eastern and better portion contains sufficient room for all the Indians now there, and all who will ever remove thither. The true way to secure its perpetual occupancy by Indians is to fill it up with other Indians, to give them lands in severalty, and to provide a government strong and intelligent enough to protect them effectually from any and all encroachments on the part of the whites.

GOVERNMENT FOR THE INDIAN TERRITORY

The anomalous form of government, if government it can be called, at present existing in the Indian Territory must soon be changed. In some shape or other those Indians must be brought under law and the jurisdiction of the courts. The idea that that Territory is to consist forever of a collection of little independent or semi-independent nationalities is preposterous. If thirty or fifty thousand white men remove and settle in any part of the West, the United States extends over them its law and establishes a territorial government, preparatory to its admission into the Union as a State; and it can be neither a hardship nor an injustice to the tribes in the Indian Territory, if, recognizing their right to ample compensation for the surrender of lands which they do not need, we place them on a par with white men before the law.

Any such change would undoubtedly be resisted by many among the Indians themselves. In the so-called "nations" are a number of educated, intelligent, ambitious men, who under the present system are leaders of their people, controlling their affairs and the expenditure of their revenue. They very naturally deprecate any change which will endanger such power. They argue with great earnestness that the adoption of a territorial form of government would be followed by an influx of white men into the Territory, and that the ultimate result to the Indians would be dispossession of homes, and pauperism. Such a possibility could, however, be averted by an allotment of land to each Indian, made inalienable to white men, and by providing that no white man should become a citizen of the Territory, or own or lease any real estate therein.

As to the particular form of government for the Indian Territory, I am inclined to think that no better system can be devised than that suggested by my predecessor in the last annual report of this office, as follows:

"The need of this Territory to-day is a government of the simplest form possible; and, in my judgment, a government similar to that provided for 'the territory of the United States northwest of the river Ohio,' (Stat. at L., vol. 1, page 51,) preliminary to the organization of a general assembly, would, I think, be the best adapted for the Indian Territory at present, both on account of its simplicity and of its economy. It consisted of a governor, a secretary, and judges, who had power to adopt and publish in the Territory such laws of the United States, criminal and civil, as were found necessary and best suited to the circumstances of the Territory, said laws to be reported to Congress from time to time, and to be in force in said Territory unless disapproved by that body; the governor also to have power to appoint magistrates and other necessary civil officers.

"The anomalous state of social and political affairs in this Territory renders some such form of government as above set forth much better adapted to the circumstances and necessities of the case than an elective and representative government could possibly be for several years. Of the seventy-one thousand, all but seven thousand have attained to such a degree of civilization as to be capable of appreciating and profiting by a government of this character, and the remainder being the wilder and wholly uneducated tribes could be readily brought to feel its force in restraint and education. On the other hand an elective government for these people would bring together representatives from thirty-five different tribes, and any legislation or any discussion to be made intelligible must be translated into as many different tongues. But a more serious and I think more fatal objection would be found in the sectional and tribal jealousies, which have their strength in proportion to the ignorance of a people, and among these thirty-five tribes would render most if not all the enactments of such a representative body practically of no avail to govern its people or enforce its laws.

"I believe the simple form of government above suggested can be made strong and effective, and will prevent the experiment of a confederated self-government, for which the Indians are not prepared, and which would be sure to result in anarchy and strife.

"Great care should be taken, however, that this government be so restricted in its powers that its sole function shall be to make and administer law for the prevention of intrusion, the protection of the rights and interests of the Indians as against all outside parties, and to define the rights and enforce the obligations of the Indians as among themselves; and this government should be strictly prohibited from any attempt to confer rights or privileges upon any corporation whatever, or upon any individual other than the lawful members of the Indian tribes. By this method I deem it entirely feasible by appropriate legislation to provide an efficient government for the Territory, to the great benefit of the people governed, without encroaching upon the rights and privileges of individuals.

"If, however, it shall be deemed inexpedient to provide such a government on account of treaty stipulations that each separate tribe shall govern itself, then I would respectfully recommend the establishment of a United States court within the boundary of the Territory, with such a force of marshals as shall be sufficient for the execution of the process of court without calling for troops to act as posse.

"These Indians occupy a most interesting and important position in the history of the country. They ought not to be left the prey of the worst influence which can be brought to them in the life and example of the meanest white men. They deserve such guardianship and care on the part of the United States as will secure for them the powerful aid to elevation which comes from the presence of law."

I recommend this subject to the consideration of the honorable Secretary, with the hope that he will invite the serious attention of Congress to the grave questions involved.

Report of Commissioner
of Indian Affairs E. A. Hayt
November 1, 1878

(Excerpt from *Report for 1878*, pp. 442-45, 464-65)

Commissioner Hayt's report for the year recounted the sad fate of those Indians who had received title to lands in severalty. Almost invariably, the commissioner reported, the Indian had lost his land to white landsharks by deception or ignorance. The record made Hayt cautious about urging that citizenship be extended to the Indians. "The experience of the past," he noted, "has shown us that to make them citizens hastily is to make them paupers." Hayt's report contained the unusual proposal to create an auxiliary force of Indian cavalry to aid the Army in suppression of Indian disturbances. Although the historical record had demonstrated that the success of white arms against the red man was greatest when supported by such red auxiliaries, the military was reluctant to trust its Indian auxiliaries to any great degree. Hayt's account of the outbreak of the Bannocks, with detailed message traffic between the agent, the commissioner, and the various Army officers involved, provides an instructive insight into the methods customarily employed by these representatives of the Government in dealing with Indian problems. Finally, an excerpt from Hayt's report told of his travels with Chief Joseph to find land satisfactory to the exiled Nez Percé leader.

THE QUESTION of greatest importance to the present and future welfare of the Indians is that of a uniform and perfect title to their lands. The constant removals incident to the former land policy of the Indian service have been freighted with evil consequences to the Indians. Even when placed upon reservations they have come to consider, notwithstanding the most solemn guarantees from the United States that the same should be kept sacred and remain theirs forever, that the title to their land is without permanency, and that they are subject to be removed whenever the pressure of white settlers upon them may create a demand for their lands either before Congress or the department. So fixed has this opinion become among the more civilized tribes, that in the main they decline to make any improvements upon their lands, even after an allotment in severalty has been made, until they have received their patents for the same.

But after the issue of patents, the difficulties surrounding them do not cease. A few, it is true, hold to their land and make rapid and encouraging progress in agricultural pursuits. The major portion of them, however, yielding to the pressure surrounding them, fall victims to the greed of

225

unscrupulous white men, and, one by one, part with or are defrauded of their lands. Every means that human ingenuity can devise, legal or illegal, has been resorted to for the purpose of obtaining possession of Indian lands.

The question which now presents itself is, shall tenure of title to the land in the various reservations remain as now, or shall a new system be adopted, which shall protect them against all interference with their lands by whatever authority.

Before proceeding to consider the best means to be adopted for the protection of the Indians in this regard, it it perhaps best to show the method heretofore pursued, with a brief statement of the results which have followed. The older and more common Indian title has been title by occupancy. This title has from time to time been extinguished by treaty stipulation. Of the lands thus acquired, there have been at various times certain tracts set apart for the several tribes by treaties ratified by the Senate, in which possession in common has been guaranteed to them forever. These reservations have in general been established far beyond the limits of white settlement. As the settlements incident to the rapid growth of the country have approached the boundaries of the reservations, the pressure has in many cases become so great that the Indians have been compelled, as a matter of self-protection, to ask for a new reservation, or their lands have been seized by the settlers, and they have been ousted from possession of the same. War in defense of their rights has generally resulted in such cases, which it has been the duty of the government to suppress. Many of our Indian wars have arisen either from the bad faith of the government in the observance of treaties with regard to Indian land, or from the seizure of the same by its citizens, in violation of expressed treaty stipulations granting the reservation to the Indians in perpetuity.

In some cases title in severalty in fee simple has been given to the individual members of the tribes for a certain quantity of the lands embraced in the reservation. Experience has shown that even the most advanced and civilized of our Indians are not capable of defending their lands when title in fee is once vested in them. The reservations in such cases are at once infested by a class of land-sharks who do not hesitate to resort to any measure, however iniquitous, to defraud the Indians of their lands. Whiskey is given them, and while they are under its influence they are made to sign deeds of conveyance, without consideration. They are often induced to sign what they are informed is a contract of sale for a few trees growing on their land, with a receipt for the consideration paid; or some party goes to them claiming to be an agent of the State or county, distributing funds to the poor. This party will pay the Indian five or ten dollars, and procure his signature to a pretended receipt for the same, when in reality the paper signed is a warranty deed, which is recorded, and generally the land is sold to a third and innocent party before the Indian discovers the fraud which has been practiced upon him.

In other cases the Indians complain, and, as it appears, not without cause, that they are subjected to unequal and unjust taxation which they are unable to meet, and are thus divested of the title to their lands.

Again they are induced to mortgage their lands for small sums which they are told will enable them to make money and improve their farms as their white neighbors have done. These mortgages are made payable generally at a time when the Indians are likely to have no money; an attorney fee of seventy-five or one hundred dollars is inserted. At maturity if the mortgage is not satisfied, which generally happens, foreclosure is had, the land is sold, and the Indian is left homeless and hopeless, a pauper for the community to support.

Out of 1,735 Indians to whom patents were issued about the year 1871 on the Chippewa Reservation of Isabella County, Michigan, fully five-sixths have sold, or in some manner have been cheated out of, their lands. A few of them have sold at something near a fair consideration. Many have been defrauded of their lands by some of the measures above named or other equally nefarious practices, while others, in large numbers, sold their lands before the selections were approved or patents issued, receiving only a nominal price (about twenty-five cents per acre) for lands worth from $5 to $25 per acre. One of these selections was purchased for $15, and the party who purchased the same has been offered $4,000 for it but refused to sell.

All the circumstances connected with these sales point directly to collusion between the agent and the parties purchasing in the execution of these unmitigated frauds.

So well have the Indians of Isabella County, Michigan, become convinced of their entire inability to protect their lands, that at a recent council with them, held by a special agent of this office, at which a number of allotments were made, they unanimously requested that the patents for the lands allotted be issued to them without the power of alienation. These Indians are citizens and voters, and a few of them hold office in the towns where they reside. The investigations heretofore made show that the most intelligent of them have been victims of some of the practices above enumerated.

Under numbers of the treaties with the different tribes, patents have been issued restricting the right of sale, except upon the approval of the Secretary of the Interior and the President. In cases of this character, where the guards against fraud would appear to be sufficient to insure the most perfect good faith and to prevent a sale by a party not entirely competent to transact his own business, the records of this office show that frauds have been committed. Instances of this character will be found in the history of the Shawnee, Miami, Sac and Fox, Pottawatomie and other Indians of Kansas, to whom patents in fee or otherwise were issued, and who have been despoiled of their lands, and to whom the government has since been compelled to afford an asylum in the Indian Territory.

It has been strongly urged that citizenship should be extended to all of the so-called civilized Indians. Such citizenship, if conferred indiscriminately, would, in my judgment, while the Indians are in their present transition state, be of incalculable damage to them. We should move slowly in the process of making Indians citizens, until they are prepared to assume intelligently the duties and obligations of citizens. The experience of the past has shown us that to make them citizens hastily is to make them paupers. Indians of full age are infants in law; and in fact they need a long tutelage before launching them into the world to manage their own affairs. Entire civilization, with education, a knowledge of the English language, and experience in business forms and matters, especially such as relate to the conveyance of lands, should precede citizenship if it is the intention of the government to save the Indians from pauperism and extermination.

The progress made in Indian civilization, the history of each tribe, the reports of this office, and of each and every officer who has intelligently investigated this question, all go to show the necessity for a permanent home for the Indians with an indefeasible title to the same. If this desired reformation in the management of their affairs can be effected, I am assured that the progress of the Indians will be rapid and permanent, and that all cause for the maintenance of an armed force to restrain the Indians and secure peace in the Indian country will be at an end. They will then fall readily within the jurisdiction of the laws, and their future status as a peaceable and law-abiding people will be fixed.

After a careful consideration of this important question I have come to the conclusion that as fast as the Indians are consolidated upon reservations, as recommended in another part of this report, or in cases where they are now located on good agricultural lands, where it is deemed best that they should remain, the Secretary of the Interior should be authorized by a law applicable to all the tribes to allot the lands in such reservations among the Indians belonging thereon, in tracts not exceeding 160 acres to each head of a family, or 80 acres to each single person over 21 years of age, and to issue patents therefor without the right to sell, mortgage, lease, or otherwise alienate the same for the term of twenty-five years from the date of the patent, after which time the same may be alienated under such rules and regulations as the Secretary of the Interior, for the time being, may see fit to impose; said lands so patented to be exempt from taxation and from levy or sale under process of any court for a like term of years; all property acquired by the Indians, aside from the lands received from the government as above suggested, and the annuity or other tribal funds derived under any treaty with the government, to be subject in all respects to the laws of the State or Territory in which the party may reside. This may be accomplished by retaining the reservation intact for all purposes connected with the title to these lands.

Such an act would, I am satisfied, afford to the Indians the degree of protection necessary to their civilization and lead them gradually to a full comprehension of the rights, privileges, duties, and responsibilities of American citizenship, which I shall hope to see accorded to them whenever in the future they may become fully competent. A bill embracing the material points above indicated will be prepared for submission at the coming session of Congress.

INDIAN AUXILIARIES

The scattering of seventy-four Indian agencies over a wide extent of territory has apparently necessitated the establishment of a greater number of detached military posts. The dividing of the Army into so many small detachments tends to deprive it of the strength needed for the suppression of a sudden outbreak. For the past year it has been almost impossible to obtain even an escort of cavalry or infantry, inasmuch as the number of men at each military post has been sufficient only to furnish it a respectable garrison. The history of the past three years has proven conclusively that this attenuation of the Army renders it impossible to administer even a homeopathic dose of coercion until after a lapse of considerable time. This weakness emboldens the savages, so that a mere handful, like the 87 warriors, with their 200 women and children, under Dull Knife, can cut through a military department and spread terror and slaughter for a month with impunity.

The consolidation of Indian tribes upon fewer reservations, as recommended elsewhere, would enable the Army to concentrate and become more effective. There is, however, another remedy for the evil indicated, which, in my judgment, can be and should be quickly adopted to save the loss of life and property consequent on Indian outbreaks, and the great expense now entailed on the government by Indian wars. An auxiliary force of Indian cavalry should be organized, enlisted from the young men of the most warlike tribes, and placed under the command of Army officers of experience. Such a force should be held ready for effective service at a moment's warning. The mere fact of its existence would serve to check the tendency to outbreaks, and by enlisting the young and warlike from the various tribes, the element of strife that is now chafing for the excitement of the war-path would find legitimate occupation that would tend to repress the natural disposition for indiscriminate war and bloodshed.

Another consideration which calls for the organization of such a force is the fact that our Indians are among the best, perhaps are the very best, horsemen in the world; and it is no disparagement to white soldiers, whose bravery is deservedly held in high esteem, to admit that Indians are their superiors in following the trail of a foe. They will not stand up in the open field and fight like our white soldiers, but mounted and set upon a trail they will follow it with a persistent speed that no white man can equal.

Such an auxiliary force, not exceeding 3,000 men, could be so placed as to be brought rapidly into action, in case of any threatened outbreak. It should be held in large bodies, to be effective, and not divided up infinitesimally, as would be the case with ordinary army scouts; and it would put an effectual stop to raids running a course of from 700 to 1,800 miles. Of its feasibility there need be no question, for there can be no truer friend or braver man than the American Indian of the better type, and his loyalty to the government, when once enlisted in its service, is beyond any reasonable doubt. If the English Government can trust the sepoys of India, we can place full confidence in our Indian allies.

I would urge the speedy organization and equipment of this auxiliary force, to which the objections raised by many to the increase of the Army would not apply, because it could be used only to suppress, prevent, or shorten the duration of any Indian disturbance. Added to the Army, it would entail very little expense, and detract nothing from the productive resources of the country. Moreover, the utilizing of a portion of our population which we are now obliged to feed, and often to fight, would be an act of public economy. Under proper officers, this corps might even become a valuable training school, in which, when not in active service, the education of those enlisted could be greatly advanced. In the light of past experience, this would seem to be the only weapon with which to terminate this perpetual warfare without largely increasing the Army, and thereby drawing from the effective industry of the country.

It should be distinctly understood that the Indian auxiliaries would be entirely under control of the War Department, and that such an organization should not subtract one man from the number of enlisted men in the Army as at present provided by law. In view of the necessity of protecting white men from hostile Indians, the Army is insufficient in numbers. An addition of three thousand Indian auxiliaries would give it only the support it greatly needs, and enable it to cope successfully with the enemies of our peace.

The Outbreak of the Bannocks

The delay in carrying out the provisions of the treaty of July 3, 1868, for lack of any sufficient appropriation of money, and the small quantity of supplies furnished to the Bannocks by the government, have forced these Indians to continue their nomadic life to the present time.

It is not possible for them to settle upon the reservation which has been set apart for them until such time as sufficient funds are appropriated by Congress to subsist them while doing the first year's farm work. If they stop hunting and commence farming they must be fed until their crops are gathered. No appropriation has ever been made for them sufficient for this purpose. Each successive year they have been less successful in finding game when on the hunt, and during the war with the Nez Percés they were forced to remain upon their reservation and accept the scant allowance of food which the government had furnished for them.

Excited by what they heard of the war, irritated by what they esteemed to be bad faith in the issuance to them of scant rations, annoyed by the encroachments of the whites upon their reservation, and cherishing a chronic dislike for the Shoshones, with whom they were associated at Fort Hall Agency (the friendly and peaceable character of the latter rather aggravating their hostility to them), they became more and more restless until, during the summer of 1877, a Bannock Indian under the influence of whiskey and war-paint started out from the agency, armed with Winchester rifle and revolver, and shot and seriously wounded two unoffending teamsters who were passing the agency. On the 23d of November the perpetrator of this deed was arrested and handed over to the civil authorities through the instrumentality of the agent, without resistance or opposition. On the same day, as an outcome of the excitement and bitter feeling resulting from this arrest, another Bannock, a friend of the prisoner, shot and killed the agency butcher, Alexander Rhodan.

Troops were immediately called for. On the 20th of December, Colonel Smith, of the Fourteenth Infantry, arrived at the agency, and on the 9th of January, 1878, the murderer of Rhodan was arrested by the military at a point some sixty miles distant from the agency; subsequently he was tried and hanged.

The excitement and threatening demonstrations on the part of the Bannocks consequent upon this arrest were such that Colonel Smith, reenforced by cavalry, on the 16th of January surrounded two Bannock villages at the agency and captured 53 warriors with 32 guns and about 300 ponies. The prisoners, except the father and two brothers of the murderer, were released, after admonition by Colonel Smith, and were suffered to return to their people, and in April the captured ponies, being of but little value, were returned to them. The arms, although worthless, were retained. Their best arms had been secreted and their valuable ponies moved to places of safety before the military surrounded their camp. The failure of this attempt to disarm and dismount the Bannocks served to arouse and exasperate the Indians, and was followed, as the agent predicted that it would be, by retaliation as soon as the grass was in condition to feed the Indian ponies.

Meantime the cavalry, on the 18th of January, returned to Fort D. A. Russel, and on the 5th of May the infantry also left, with the exception of one officer and twenty-two men, entirely too small a force to restrain or intimidate the malcontents.

The situation of affairs at the Fort Hall Agency, between the time of the arrest of the Indian who shot the two teamsters and the commencement of the Bannock war, may be learned by the following telegrams:

HEADQUARTERS OF THE ARMY,
ADJUTANT-GENERAL'S OFFICE,
WASHINGTON, *November 27, 1877.*

LIEUT. GEN. SHERIDAN, *Chicago, Ill.:*

Indian agent at Ross Fork, near Fort Hall, Idaho, has reported to Secretary of Interior that, since shooting of Alexander Rhodan, Bannocks have been very bold and threatening, and that there is danger of outbreak at any time. Beef contractor unable to hire men to deliver beef at agency. Commanding officer at Hall has furnished seven (7) men, all he can spare.

Secretary of War has referred matter, with request that one hundred (100) troops be sent immediately, and General of the Army desires you to send that force at earliest practicable moment.

Please acknowledge receipt.

THOMAS M. VINCENT,
Assistant Adjutant-General.

ROSS FORK, IDAHO, *November 28, 1877.*
COMMISSIONERS OF INDIAN AFFAIRS,
Washington:

Bannock camp moved to Cedars, seven miles from agency. Satisfied they are purchasing ammunition at settlement north of us, and otherwise preparing for war. No further depredations committed. Cold weather in our favor.

DANILSON, *Agent.*

CHICAGO, *November 29, 1877.*
GENERAL THOMAS M. VINCENT,
Assistant Adjutant/General, Washington, D. C.:

Your telegram of this date received. Information from commanding officer at Fort Hall, forwarded to Washington yesterday's mail, led me to believe the Bannock agent is stampeded. Re-enforcements from Camp Douglas left by rail for Fort Hall yesterday morning. Should arrive to-day. It seems to me the agent should consult with the commanding officer about disturbances, which he neglected to do.

P. H. SHERIDAN,
Lieutenant-General.

OMAHA, NEBR., *November 28, 1877.*
GENERAL P. H. SHERIDAN,
Commanding Division, Chicago:

The following dispatch from Captain Bainbridge, dated 27th instant, received this morning:

"Your telegram received. I was at the agency two days ago, and returned to my post with the impression that there would be no outbreak. Did not consider the matter of sufficient importance to put government to the expense of a telegram, and made a written report of affairs at agency to department headquarters.

"From report of agent last night and this morning, think it possible an outbreak may occur. Mail-carrier, a soldier, reports this evening nothing unusual at agency. Indians trading at store as usual, and everything quiet. Inasmuch as this garrison is here for protection of agency, think it strange agent did not apply to me for troops. Did not know he had made the application. Think re-enforcement unnecessarily large." "BAINBRIDGE."

Subsequent to the dispatch to you of yesterday, a dispatch was received from Captain Bainbridge stating that there was danger of an outbreak. The above dispatch, which is a later one, is in reply to that sent him from these headquarters, and gives, I think, the true state of affairs.

Commanding officer at Camp Douglas reports that 104 men under Major Bryant left Douglas this morning for Hall.

GEO. CROOK,
Brigadier-General.

[First indorsement.]

HEADQUARTERS MILITARY DIVISION OF THE MISSOURI,
Chicago, November 28, 1877.

Respectfully forwarded to the Adjutant-General of the Army.

P. H. SHERIDAN,
Lieutenant-General, Commanding.

WAR DEPARTMENT,
WASHINGTON CITY, *December 6, 1877.*

TO THE HONORABLE SECRETARY OF THE INTERIOR.

SIR: I have the honor to transmit, for your information, a copy of a telegram from General Crook, communicating a report of Captain Bainbridge relative to an anticipated outbreak of the Bannock Indians at Fort Hall Agency.

Very respectfully, your obedient servant,

GEORGE W. McCRARY,
Secretary of War.

FORT HALL AGENCY,
IDAHO, *December 15, 1877.*

Hon. COMMISSIONER OF INDIAN AFFAIRS,
Washington, D. C.

SIR: I have the honor to transmit herewith, for your official action, a petition from the resident citizens of this vicinity praying that a sufficient number of mounted troops be stationed here to protect them from the Bannock Indians; also affidavits of Fred. S. Stevens, Joseph Warren, Albert T. Stout, and Charles W. Cline, relative to the hostility of the Bannocks.

Since the murder of Alex. Rhodan, on the 23rd ultimo, of which report has been made, the conduct of the Bannocks has been very bad. Demands have been made upon them by myself and the military for the murderer, but up to this time they have failed to make the arrest, stating he had escaped from the reservation, when they well knew he was in their camp, receiving aid and comfort from them. The military post of Fort Hall is located fifteen miles from the agency, from which it is separated by a range of mountains that are almost impassable during the winter months. The troops being stationed at such a remote distance are no restraint upon the Indians, or protection to the agency or settlers. The post should be near the agency, where troops could render assistance at short notice, and should be garrisoned by either cavalry or mounted infantry.

Very respectfully, your obedient servant,

W. H. DANILSON,
United States Indian Agent.

Ross Fork, *January 13, 1878.*

Commissioner Indian Affairs, *Washington:*

The murderer of Rhodan was captured by the military sixty miles north of agency, on the 9th instant. Is it best to disarm and dismount the Bannocks, to punish them for not giving up the murderer, leaving them here exasperated, taking chances of their depredating the country to make good their loss, and expose the citizens to further loss of life, or let the matter drop until measures can be taken to move them entirely, which I respectfully recommend, General Smith recommends also, and the military are ready to act upon your reply.

DANILSON.

Office of Indian Affairs,
Washington, *January 15, 1878.*

Danilson, *Ross Fork, Idaho:*

To what place do you propose to move the Indians? Can they be moved without creating disturbance and bloodshed? Give your opinion and that of the commanding officer.

E. A. HAYT,
Commissioner.

Ross Fork, Idaho, *January 16, 1878.*

Commissioner of Indian Affairs,
Washington, D. C.:

Bannock camp surrounded this morning; thirty-two guns and three hundred ponies captured without disturbance; their best guns, ponies, and no pistols could be found. The three companies cavalry from Fort D. A. Russell return on the eighteenth. I recommend that the Bannocks be sent with them, and held there until you decide what to do with them. Unless removed, a sufficient military force will be required to keep them in subjection.

DANILSON.

Office of Indian Affairs,
Washington, *January 17, 1878.*

Danilson, *Ross Fork, Idaho:*

Let Bannock prisoners be sent with military to the fort; will arrange with War Department for their subsistence.

E. A. HAYT,
Commissioner.

Ross Fork, Idaho, *January 25, 1878.*

Commissioner of Indian Affairs,
Washington, D. C. :

What disposition will you make of the ponies captured from Bannocks? They are in charge of the military and should be disposed of. Recommend they be sold and proceeds invested in stock-cattle for benefit of Bannock tribe.

DANILSON.

OFFICE OF INDIAN AFFAIRS,
WASHINGTON, *January 25, 1878.*

DANILSON, *Ross Fork, Idaho:*

Telegram of yesterday received. Wait until you receive further advice from this office about disposing of ponies.

E. A. HAYT,
Commissioner.

CHICAGO, ILL., *February 23, 1878.*

GEN. E. D. TOWNSEND, *Washington, D. C.:*

The following dispatch is respectfully forwarded.

R. C. DRUM,
Assistant Adjutant-General.

OMAHA, *February 23.*

ASSISTANT ADJUTANT-GENERAL,
Military Division Missouri:

I would request that information be furnished me as soon as possible as to disposal of Indian ponies at Fort Hall, which have to be fed there at heavy expense.

GEORGE CROOK,
Brigadier-General, Commanding.

CHICAGO, ILL., *February 25, 1878.*

GEN. W. T. SHERMAN,
Washington, D. C.:

It will save much expense and complication if you will allow General Crook to sell the Bannock ponies in accordance with the counsel of the Indian Department, and, after deducting the cost of keeping them, purchase young cattle with the remainder of the money. The Indian interest in cattle is beginning to develop satisfactorily.

P. H. SHERIDAN,
Lieutenant-General.

HEADQUARTERS ARMY OF THE UNITED STATES,
WASHINGTON, D. C., *February 26, 1878.*

GENERAL P. H. SHERIDAN,
Commanding Division, Chicago, Ill.:

General Whipple has arrived. Your dispatch about the Shoshone ponies is given to the Secretary of War, who will see the Secretary of the Interior and determine who shall sell the ponies and invest proceeds, of which you shall have prompt notice.

W. T. SHERMAN,
General.

Ross Fork, Idaho, *March 2, 1878.*

Commissioner of Indian Affairs,
Washington, D. C.:

Officer in command of troops here has orders to have an officer and twenty-five men report to commanding officer at Fort Hall, sixteen miles distant from agency, and balance of command to return to Salt Lake at once. This will leave agency entirely without protection at a time when the presence of troops is very necessary, as the Bannocks, upon realizing that their ponies are to be driven away and sold, will be more exasperated than ever. They have only been kept under subjection through fear of troops kept at the agency. Employes believe they will be in danger of their lives, and will leave to a man if troops are withdrawn. This is also the feeling of the settlers in the community. I respectfully request that a company of at least fifty men be left at the agency. Prompt and decided action necessary. Answer.

DANILSON.

Office of Indian Affairs.
March 3, 1878.

Danilson, Agent.
Ross Fork, Idaho:

War Department has been requested to leave at least fifty soldiers at your agency.

E. A. HAYT,
Commissioner.

Ross Fork, Idaho, *March 4, 1878.*

Commissioner of Indian Affairs,
Washington, D. C.:

Has War Department ordered troops to remain at the agency? The troops expect to leave in the morning. Unless one company is ordered to remain here the agency will be abandoned. Answer.

DANILSON.

War Department, *March 5, 1878.*

Commissioner Indian Affairs:

All troops at Fort Hall have been ordered to remain there until further orders, and until we can hear further as to the state of affairs at the post.

GEO. W. McCRARY,
Secretary of War.

Ross Fork, Idaho, *March 25, 1878.*

Commissioner Indian Affairs,
Washington, D. C.:

Military here and myself recommend that the order to sell Bannock ponies be revoked, and ponies returned to them. Number captured does not cripple them for offensive operations, and tends to make disaffected ones more troublesome. Twenty-five families have commenced farming. All of them have lost ponies. One man who came in last fall, and not implicated in the shooting, loses twenty head. Expenses of driving and selling will leave scarcely anything to invest.

DANILSON

OFFICE OF INDIAN AFFAIRS,
WASHINGTON, *March 26, 1878.*

DANILSON, AGENT,
Ross Fork, Idaho:

Military commander consenting, the ponies can be returned, provided Indians will do more farming than they would without them.

E. A. HAYT,
Commissioner.

OFFICE OF INDIAN AFFAIRS,
WASHINGTON, *April 1, 1878.*

AGENT DANILSON, *Ross Fork, Idaho:*

Have ponies been distributed? General Crook thinks that Salt Lake troops are no longer needed. Report immediately.

WM M. LEEDS,
Acting Commissioner.

ROSS FORK, IDAHO, *April 2, 1878.*

LIEUTENANT-GENERAL P. H. SHERIDAN,
Chicago, Ill.:

After a talk with the agent, the military officers, and principal men of the Indians, I have come to the conclusion that it would be best to return to the Indians the ponies lately taken from them in the surround. The greater part of them got away with their animals, leaving in our hands not enough to cripple them in case of hostilities, and these the property of our friends.

The arms taken do not amount to much, as the tribe seems to be well supplied. I am satisfied there will be no trouble, and that very good feeling exists; and would therefore recommend that the additional troops lately sent here be now returned to Salt Lake. I leave here to-day, and expect to reach Franklin to-morrow.

GEORGE CROOK,
Brigadier-General.

HEADQUARTERS MILITARY DIVISION MISSOURI,
CHICAGO, *April 3, 1878.*

GENERAL GEORGE CROOK, *Ogden, Utah:*

Your telegram of yesterday received. If you think it best you can return the ponies to the Indians, and in a day or two I will arrange for the return of the troops to Salt Lake.

P. H. SHERIDAN,
Lieutenant-General.

CHICAGO, ILL., *April 3, 1878.*

GENERAL E. D. TOWNSEND, *Washington, D. C.:*

General Crook reports such a good condition of affairs among the Fort Hall Indians as to induce me to ask the return of the Salt Lake troops. They were stopped some time ago while *en route* to Camp Douglas by direction of the General of the Army.

P. H. SHERIDAN,
Lieutenant-General.

[First indorsement.]

HEADQUARTERS OF THE ARMY,
WASHINGTON, *April 3, 1878.*

Official copy respectfully referred to the honorable Commissioner of Indian Affairs for an expression of opinion in regard to this request, asking immediate attention.

I think the agent at the Shoshone Agency, near Fort Hall, unduly scared.

W. T. SHERMAN, *General.*

FRANKLIN, IDAHO, *April 4, 1878.*

COMMISSIONER INDIAN AFFAIRS, *Washington, D. C.:*

Ponies have not been delivered. It is absolutely necessary to keep one company troops at agency. General Crook cannot know of his own personal knowledge that troops are not needed. Military prefer the luxuries of Salt Lake, and are making every effort to get ordered back.

DANILSON.

HEADQUARTERS DEPARTMENT OF PLATTE,
IN THE FIELD, FRANKLIN, IDAHO, *April 3, 1878.*

ADJUTANT-GENERAL MILITARY DIVISION MISSOURI,
Chicago, Ill.

COLONEL: I have the honor to report that on the 2d instant I reached the Shoshone and Bannock Agency at Ross Fork, Idaho, and immediately had a conference with the military officers temporarily stationed at the agency, Captain Bainbridge, Fourteenth Infantry, commanding Fort Hall, Mr. Danilson, the agent, and the principal men of the Bannocks and Shoshones. This conference satisfied me of the peaceable intentions of the Indians, and their determination to remain on good terms with our people.

The murder committed last summer was an individual act and not one with which any portion of the tribe sympathized. The disarming and dismounting of the tribe under these circumstances appears to have been unnecessary, especially since such of them as were the least disposed to be friendly had time to learn of the move contemplated and to conceal their animals and guns, leaving the burden of the punishment to fall upon our best friends and those upon whom we should have to rely in case of any trouble.

The tribe would not feel the loss inflicted, which was probably not one-fourth the total number of ponies, and its remembrance will only survive as an irritant. Although the loss of their ponies would not cripple these Indians in the event of hostilities, it will seriously interfere with their farming, for which purpose they are beginning to use them. The return of these animals would be good policy, as would also be that of the arms, which are almost entirely old-fashioned pieces, of very little account except for shooting such small game as can be found near the agency, while their retention will be dwelt upon as a grievance.

While there seems to have been some occasion for alarm in the fact of the murder referred to, the spirit of the Indians in general was not properly represented and the condition of affairs was unduly exaggerated. The tribe have no intention of going to war, and manifest most friendly feelings. In my conversation with Mr. Danilson, and from the complaints of the Indians, I learned that the rations issued at this agency are entirely inadequate. Hitherto it has been the practice to permit the young men to hunt the buffalo in the Big Horn and Yellowstone country, but the rapid settling up of that region, as well as of the country around this agency, makes any such dependence for the future most precarious, and I therefore urgently recommend an increase to the amount now allowed the Sioux and other Indians.

The maintenance of troops at the agency is in my opinion no longer necessary, and they can now be returned to their proper stations at Salt Lake.

GEORGE CROOK,
Brigadier-General.

[First indorsement.]

HEADQUARTERS MILITARY DIVISION Missouri,
CHICAGO, *April 10, 1878.*
Respectfully forwarded to the Adjutant-General of the Army.

P. H. SHERIDAN,
Lieutenant-General Commanding.

WAR DEPARTMENT,
WASHINGTON CITY, *April 16, 1878.*
THE HON. SECRETARY OF THE INTERIOR.

SIR: I have the honor to transmit for your information a copy of General Crook's report, dated April 3, 1878, of the result of his conference and observations at the Shoshone and Bannock Agency, and stating that the disarming and dismounting these Indians was unnecessary, and recommending that their rations be increased.

Very respectfully, your obedient servant,

GEO. McCRARY,
Secretary of War.

WAR DEPARTMENT,
WASHINGTON CITY, *April 11, 1878.*
THE HON. SECRETARY OF INTERIOR.

SIR: I have the honor to transmit for your information a copy of a telegram from General Crook, stating that the Indian ponies lately taken from the Indians at Fort Hall Agency should be returned to them; he also reports in regard to the additional troops sent to Ross Fork, Idaho, and recommends their return to Salt Lake.

Very respectfully, your obedient servant,

GEO. W. McCRARY,
Secretary of War.

HEADQUARTERS DEPARTMENT OF THE PLATTE,
OMAHA, NEBRASKA, *April 23, 1878.*
[General Orders No. 34—Extract.]

* * *

2. Companies D, E, and G, Fourteenth Infantry, are relieved from duty at Fort Hall Agency, Idaho, and will return without delay to their proper station, Camp Douglas, Utah. The commanding officer of the battalion will detail a commissioned officer and twenty-five enlisted men to remain at the agency, and the officer thus detailed will report to the commanding officer Fort Hall, Idaho.

* * *

By command of Brigadier-General Crook.

ROBERT WILLIAMS,
Assistant Adjutant-General.

OFFICE OF INDIAN AFFAIRS,
WASHINGTON, *June 5, 1878.*

DANILSON, *Agent, Ross Fork, Idaho:*

Telegraph immediately full report of the situation of your Indians. Nothing has been heard from you, and the papers are filled with rumors.

E. A. HAYT,
Commissioner.

Ross Fork, IDAHO, *June 6, 1878.*

COMMISSIONER OF INDIAN AFFAIRS, *Washington, D. C.:*

Nine hundred and eighty Indians here, mostly Shoshones, engaged in farming. Most of the Bannocks have left the agency. Have seen by papers they are committing depredations in Camas Prairie and vicinity, one hundred and fifty miles west of agency. A Shoshone has just come in from them and confirms newspaper reports. Indians here are very much excited. One officer and twenty-five soldiers here; need more troops. Will keep you advised of situation.

DANILSON, *Agent.*

ROSS FORK, IDAHO, *June 10, 1878.*

COMMISSIONER OF INDIAN AFFAIRS, *Washington, D. C.:*

Could not keep roaming Bannocks here when the amount of supplies was scarcely enough to feed Indians engaged in farming. See your dispatches of April 3d and 9th. All quiet at agency.

DANILSON.

In the light of succeeding events it is evident that neither the military officers at Fort Hall, nor General Crook, who made a visit to Fort Hall for the purpose of ascertaining whether the troops ought to remain there or not, nor General Sherman, who thought unfavorably of the agent because he wanted troops to remain at the agency, had a true appreciation of the effect which the unsuccessful attempt to capture arms and ponies would have upon the Indians. Notwithstanding the fact that against their will one officer and twenty-five men were left at the agency, the Indians broke out in hostilities, as the agent said that they would, as soon as the grass was in good condition for their ponies to travel. The long chase after these Indians is a matter of record, and as, with the history of the war, it more properly belongs to the War Department to set it forth, suffice it to say that under the vigorous campaign of General O. O. Howard the war begun in June was ended by the last of August, and the survivors of the hostile bands, either by capture or surrender, were held as prisoners of war. General Howard reports their number, in men, women, and children, to be about 1,000. In this connection the following letter, which was referred to this office by the honorable the Secretary of the Interior, will shed some light upon the difficulties with which General Howard had to contend:

UNITED STATES MARSHALL'S OFFICE,
BOISÉ CITY, IDAHO, *August 8, 1878.*

HON. CARL SCHURZ
Secretary of the Interior.

SIR: I wish to call your attention to the inclosed copy of a letter just received from Department commander, Brig. Gen. O. O. Howard. I have sent the letter above referred to to the Hon. Charles Devens, Attorney-General of the United States, in order that he may know the facts and give me such instructions as to him may seem proper.

It is a notorious fact here that the present hostile Indians could not keep the field but for the constant supply of arms and ammunition received from white men. There are four suspected localities, to wit, Malad City, Silver City, a post near Lewiston, and a post near Great Camas, on the overland route. The only mode of detection that to my mind promises success would be to employ detectives at the suspected points, and in time either the practice would be broken up or the guilty parties brought to justice.

I trust you will confer with the honorable the Attorney-General, and devise some means that will be effective to destroy this infamous practice.

E. S. CHASE,
*United States Marshal for the
District of Idaho Territory.*

CHICAGO, *September 9, 1878.*

E. D. TOWNSEND, *Washington, D. C.:*

Following dispatch just received, and forwarded for the information of the General of the Army.

P. H. SHERIDAN.
Lieutenant-General.

OMAHA, NEBR., *September 9, 1878.*

Major Upham, commanding Camp Brown, telegraphs as follows:

Dick Washaki's son, just in from Clark's Fork, brings account of a successful fight of a detachment of infantry and Crow Indians with about twenty lodges of hostile Bannocks. Fight occurred on the morning of the 5th instant, on Clark's Fork, the troops killing a good many horses—mostly stolen Americans—and all the squaws and children. One non-commissioned officer, one citizen, and one Crow killed, and one soldier wounded. Ploqua, Bannock chief, among the captured.

R. WILLIAMS.

In his report to headquarters from Fort Hall Agency, under date of December 25, 1877, General Smith said: "It is the opinion of the agent and others that the Bannocks will cause trouble in the spring." The dispatches cited prove conclusively that the agent was not unduly scared, and that the military were truly and well informed by the Indian agent and others of the actual state of affairs at Fort Hall Agency in time to be prepared for hostilities. They were on the spot, and could not have had any more favorable situation or opportunity for the control of the discontented and disaffected Bannocks and the forcible prevention of an impending outbreak than was actually in their possession.

Respecting the complaints of a lack of sufficient rations having been furnished the Bannocks of Fort Hall Agency, there were no specific quantities of subsistence supplies agreed to be furnished to them by the treaty of July 3, 1868. There are 1,507 Indians at the Fort Hall Agency more or less dependent for their support upon the government and treaty funds. For the fiscal year 1877 only $14,000 was appropriated for their subsistence. For the fiscal year 1878, $29,000 was appropriated, but as the Indians were prevented from hunting during the Nez Percé war the sum appropriated was entirely insufficient for their support, and they became discontented and restless until bloodshed and murder were followed by open war. For the present fiscal year only $24,000, which is less than 4½ cents per day per capita, has been appropriated; but it is to be hoped that the $15,000 additional, which was asked for by this office at the last session of Congress, will be granted during the coming session. The Indians at Fort Hall Agency have received as great a quantity of subsistence as the funds appropriated by Congress has enabled the Indian Office to purchase for them. This office cannot be held responsible for a discontent which was mainly caused by late and scant appropriations.

* * *

CHIEF JOSEPH

On the surrender of Joseph and his band of Nez Percés, General Miles recommended that they be kept on the Tongue River until the question of their final disposition could be definitely determined. The Lieutenant-

General of the Army strongly objected to this, on account of the expense attendant on furnishing them with supplies, and an order was issued by the War Department, in November, 1877, to send all the Nez Percé prisoners to the Missouri River, to Fort Lincoln or Fort Riley; on the 20th of the same month another order was issued to have them forwarded to Fort Leavenworth, instead of keeping them at either of the points named. November 27, 1877, the Lieutenant-General notified the Secretary of War of their arrival at the latter fort, and recommended that this bureau be requested to take charge of them at the earliest practicable date. The number of prisoners reported by the War Department, December 4 last, was as follows: 79 men, 178 women, and 174 children, making a total of 431. A few scattered members of the band were subsequently taken by the military and also sent to Fort Leavenworth.

The necessary provision having been made by Congress just before the close of the last session for the settlement of these Indians in the Indian Territory, this office, on the 9th of July last, recommended that the War Department be requested to cause the necessary orders to be issued to the commandant at Fort Leavenworth to deliver the prisoners to an agent, who would be designated by this bureau to receive them. Accordingly, on the 21st of the same month they were delivered to United States Indian Inspector McNeil and United States Indian Agent H. W. Jones, who without military escort conducted them to the location selected for them in the Indian Territory. The number reported to have been turned over to the inspector and agent was 410, three of whom—children—died on the route.

Inspector McNeil reported that the camping place selected by the commandant for these Indians, and where he found them, was in the Missouri River bottom, about two miles above the fort, "between a lagoon and the river, the worst possible place that could have been selected; and the sanitary condition of the Indians proved it." The physician in charge said that "one-half could be said to be sick, and all were affected by the poisonous malaria of the camp."' After the arrival of Joseph and his band in the Indian Territory, the bad effect of their location at Fort Leavenworth manifested itself in the prostration by sickness at one time of 260 out of the 410, and within a few months they have lost by death more than one-quarter of the entire number. A little care in the selection of a wholesome location near Fort Leavenworth would have saved very much sickness and many lives.

Since the location of these Indians in the Indian Territory, others belonging to the band have been arrested in Idaho, and with the approval of the department, United States Indian Agent Monteith, of the Nez Percé Agency, has recently received instructions to take charge of and conduct them to the Indian Territory.

On the 15th of October last, I visited the Nez Percé Indians at their camp, about three miles from Seneca, Mo., on the Quapaw Reservation. I found the sickness that had prevailed since their arrival in the Territory rapidly abating. Joseph had two causes of dissatisfaction, which he presented to notice in plain, unmistakable terms. He complained that his surrender to General Miles was a conditional surrender, with a distinct promise that he should go back to Idaho in the spring. The other complaint was that the land selected for him on the Quapaw Reservation was not fertile, and that water was exceedingly scarce on it; that two wells had been dug to a depth of 60 to 70 feet without reaching water; and that he did not like the country. He thought it unhealthy, and a very hard place for an Indian to earn his living by tilling the soil. He was pointed to the Modocs, who are his neighbors, and shown that they were actively engaged on their farms, and that they were prospering and getting ahead in the world.

After reflecting on the matter, and with the view of meeting his expectations, if it were possible to do so, with your consent I took him, with his interpreter and chief Husescruyt (Bald-Head), with me about 250 miles. I traveled with him in Kansas and the Indian Territory for nearly a week and found him to be one of the most gentlemanly and well-behaved Indians that I ever met. He is bright and intelligent, and is anxious for the welfare of his people. The only location that seemed to please him is situated a few miles west of the Ponca Agency, where the Shaskaskia empties into Salt Creek. The land is fertile and the country is a beautiful one, with sufficient timber for all practical purposes. When he gives up the hope of returning to Idaho, I think he will choose the location I have named.

The Nez Percés are very much superior to the Osages and Pawnees in the Indian Territory; they are even brighter than the Poncas, and care should be taken to place them where they will thrive. The extinction of Joseph's title to the lands he held in Idaho will be a matter of great gain to the white settlers in that vicinity, and a reasonable compensation should be made to him for their surrender. It will be borne in mind that Joseph has never made a treaty with the United States, and that he has never surrendered to the government the lands he claimed to own in Idaho. On that account he should be liberally treated upon his final settlement in the Indian Territory. Sooner or later the remnant of the tribe that went to Canada will return, and it will be proper and expedient to place them with Joseph's band.

The present unhappy condition of these Indians appeals to the sympathy of a very large portion of the American people. I had occasion in my last annual report to say that "Joseph and his followers have shown themselves to be brave men and skillful soldiers, who, with one exception, have observed the rules of civilized warfare, and have not mutilated their dead enemies." These Indians were encroached upon by white settlers on soil they believed to be their own, and when these encroachments became intolerable they were compelled, in their own estimation, to take up arms. Joseph now says that the greatest want of the Indians is a system of law by which controversies between Indians, and between Indians and white men, can be settled without appealing to physical force. He says that the want of law is the great source of disorder among Indians. They understand the operation of laws, and if there were any statutes the Indians would be perfectly content to place themselves in the hands of a proper tribunal, and would not take the righting of their wrongs into their own hands, or retaliate, as they now do, without the law. In dealing with such people it is the duty, and I think it will be the pleasure, of the department to see that the fostering hand of the government is extended toward them, and that it gives them not only lands on which to live and implements of agriculture, but also wholesome laws for their government.

Report of Commissioner
of Indian Affairs E. A. Hayt
November 1, 1879

(Excerpt from *Report for 1879*, pp. 71-77, 82-98, 103-07)

Commissioner Hayt's report is of special interest for its account of the so-called Meeker massacre, in which a Bureau of Indian Affairs agent to the Utes, by insensitive and peremptory treatment of "his" charges, caused a totally unnecessary little war. The insensitivity was not limited to Meeker the agent. Hayt the commissioner, as though to demonstrate his prescience, proudly quoted from his 1877 report recommending that all the Indians in Colorado and Arizona be shipped to the Indian Territory because their presence, in the face of unauthorized and illegal invasion of their reservations by miners, "will be sure to lead to strife, contention, and war." Hayt had supported his petty agent in his campaign of harassment against the Utes by ordering him "to adopt, without delay, decisive measures to put a stop to these roaming habits of your Indians." Small wonder that the conditions proved unbearable to the hitherto peaceful Utes. In other parts of Hayt's report there is evidence that the bureau was doing some things right, even if it did not know why such measures were working. Thus, the policy to give to the Indians the responsibility for and profit from freighting by wagon the annuity goods from the railheads to the reservation depots, and the policy to furnish Indians with cattle for stock-raising, proved highly successful, much to the surprise of the bureau.

IN FORMER YEARS when Indians committed serious crimes it was customary to inflict punishment therefor by sending them to Saint Augustine, Fla., to be kept in close confinement at Fort Marion. They were thus deprived of their liberty until they were believed to be in a fit frame of mind to be permitted to go back to their tribes, with a reasonable prospect of their remaining quiet in the future. Of late years the military, who have acted as custodians of these captive Indians, have objected to keeping them, on account of the expense of feeding them from the Army appropriation, and for the last two years it has been a difficult matter to cause Indian criminals to be held in custody beyond a very brief period of time, although the Army appropriation bill makes special provision for the support of Indian prisoners.

A penal settlement for the confinement and reformation of the more turbulent and troublesome individuals among the various Indian tribes is a pressing want, and immediate action should be taken for the establishment of such a settlement. For the worst class of refractory Indians, one settlement should be in Florida, which is far enough away from Indian reservations to make any attempt at escape hopeless. Another settlement should be established in the Northwest, at some point where a considerable quantity of arable land can be found, so that Indians who are thus restricted in their liberty may be taught to work for their support.

It is impossible to properly govern a barbarous people like our wilder Indians without being able to inflict some punishment for wrong-doing that shall be a real punishment to the offender. At the present time the military are called upon to suppress insurrections, and to chastise, by the penalties and losses of war, those who rebel against the government. These are temporary evils to the Indians, and unless the punishment inflicted is unusually severe the lesson is soon forgotten. Moreover, in such cases chastisement often falls heavily on innocent parties instead of the guilty. If the Indian Office had a penal settlement where turbulent individuals among the tribes could be placed, they could be taken from their homes to the place of punishment without disturbing the general peace, and the prompt infliction of a punishment of this kind would tend to curb the evil-disposed and prevent them from stirring up outbreaks. In fact there is nothing the Indian would dread more than to be deprived of his liberty.

Such a settlement should be guarded by a sufficient force to exercise perfect discipline, and such prisoners should be taught trades as well as agriculture. A school of correction of this kind would be of inestimable value to the Indian service, and it would exercise a reformatory influence that could not be obtained by simple confinement. Useful occupation provided for the captives, with some encouragement to industry, would in most cases enable them to be returned to their homes in an advanced condition of civilization.

SALE OF ARMS TO INDIANS

During the last two years the sale of arms and ammunition by Indian traders has been strictly forbidden and no case is known where the prohibition has been violated. Such vigilance has been exercised by the Indian Office in this matter that trader's licenses have been revoked whenever there was the slightest suspicion of the existence of this contraband trade. Nevertheless, outside of Indian reservations, men are everywhere found driving a thrifty business in selling breechloading arms and fixed ammunition to non-civilized Indians, and the sales thus made are limited in amount only by the ability of the Indians to purchase.

Previous to the late Ute outbreak the Indians were amply supplied with Winchester and Spencer rifles and fixed ammunition obtained from traders outside of their reservation. Game was abundant on or near their reserve, and for some time the Utes had been making sales of peltries to a large amount, and were thus enabled to provide themselves with such arms and ammunition as they desired. Their largely increased purchases of arms just before the outbreak might have served as a notice to these unscrupulous traders that an outbreak was impending in which the lives of innocent people would be sacrificed. There is no offense against the commonwealth showing greater moral turpitude than the crime of those persons who recklessly place in the hands of savages all the improved patterns of arms, which they know will be used to destroy the lives of innocent white citizens.

There is no statute against this crime, and the only semblance of prohibition is contained in the following joint resolution and proclamation, viz:

EXECUTIVE MANSION,
November 23, 1876.

A Joint Resolution adopted by Congress August 5, 1876, declares that—

Whereas it is ascertained that the hostile Indians of the Northwest are largely equipped with arms which require special metallic cartridges, and that such special ammunition is in large part supplied to such hostile Indians, directly or indirectly, through traders and others in the Indian country: Therefore,

Resolved by the Senate and House of Representatives in Congress assembled, That the President of the United States is hereby authorized and requested to take such measures as, in his judgment, may be necessary to prevent such metallic ammunition being conveyed to such hostile Indians, and is further authorized to declare the same contraband of war in such district of country as he may designate during the continuance of hostilities.

To carry into effect the above-cited resolution, the sale of fixed ammunition or metallic cartridges by any trader or other person in any district of the Indian country occupied by hostile Indians, or over which they roam, is hereby prohibited; and all such ammunition or cartridges introduced into said country by traders or other persons, and that are liable in any way or manner, directly or indirectly, to be received by such hostile Indians, shall be deemed contraband of war, seized by any military officer and confiscated; and the district or country to which this prohibition shall apply during the continuance of hostilities is hereby designated as that which embraces all Indian country, or country occupied by Indians, or subject to their visits, lying within the Territories of Montana, Dakota, and Wyoming, and the States of Nebraska and Colorado.

U. S. GRANT.

The foregoing resolution, is, at best, only a specimen of very loose legislation. In lieu thereof a well-considered penal statute should have been enacted forbidding such sales not only in the Northwest, but wherever there are non-civilized Indians, whether on or off reservations. The danger always is that such trading will be carried on just outside reservation limits, where all sorts of contraband sales are effected and where Indian agents are powerless.

Again, the joint resolution prohibits the sale of "metallic ammunition" only, and not of arms as well. The right of purchasing arms *ad libitum* is the evil complained of. Without arms, ammunition would be of no use, and the latter can be traded in to any extent with little danger of detection, since it can be easily carried concealed about the person. The sale of arms, on the other hand, could be readily detected and exposed; and it is against such sales that legislation should especially be directed. It would almost seem as if the very men engaged in this murderous traffic had framed the above resolution to protect their guild and to enable them to ply their trade with impunity. When it is considered how many lives have been lost during the time which has elapsed since the passage of this resolution (which virtually permits this unhallowed trade in the implements of death), it is strange that no adequate legislation has been had for the protection of human life. A law by Congress prohibiting under severe penalty the sale of both fire-arms and fixed ammunition to non-civilized Indians, is the only common-sense and practicable method of putting an end to this dangerous traffic.

INDIAN EDUCATION

The work of promoting Indian education is the most agreeable part of the labor performed by the Indian Bureau. Indian children are as bright and teachable as average white children of the same ages; and while the progress in the work of civilizing adult Indians who have had no educational advantages is a slow process at best, the progress of the youths trained in our schools is of the most hopeful character. During the current year the capacity of our school edifices has been largely increased, and some additional schools have been opened. The following tables will show the increase of school facilities during the year:

	1879	1878
Number of children, exclusive of the five civilized tribes, who can be accommodated in boarding-schools	3,461	2,589
Number of children who can be accommodated in day schools	5,970	5,082
Number of boarding-schools	52	49
Number of day schools	107	119
Number of children attending school one or more months during the year, male, 3,965, female, 3,228	7,193	6,229
Number of children among the five civilized tribes attending school during the year	6,250	5,993

In the last report of the Indian Office an account was given of the plan of Indian education initiated at Hampton, Va. The progress of the children sent to Hampton last year has been very satisfactory. They have learned as readily as could have been expected, and the success attending the experiment has led to the establishment of a training school of the same kind at Carlisle Barracks, Carlisle, Pa., under the immediate charge of Lieut. R. H. Pratt, U.S.A. He has now in full operation a school consisting of 158 Indian children of both sexes, three-fourths of whom are boys. These children have been taken in large numbers from the Sioux at Rosebud, Pine Ridge and other agencies on the Missouri River, and from all the tribes in the Indian Territory except the civilized Indians.

Carlisle is pleasantly situated in the Cumberland Valley. The soil is fertile and the climate healthy, and not at all subject to malaria. In the grounds surrounding the barracks a large amount of gardening can be done advantageously. The buildings are comparatively new brick buildings, in a good state of preservation, and furnish pleasant and commodious quarters for those already there, with a capacity to provide accommodations for at least four hundred more children. It is hoped that Congress will make further provision by which the number of pupils at this school may be largely increased.

These children have been very carefully selected, having undergone the same sort of examination by a surgeon to which apprentices for the Navy are subjected, and only healthy ones have been accepted. The pupils will not only be taught the ordinary branches of an English education, but will also be instructed in all the useful arts essential in providing for the every-day wants of man. The civilizing influence of these schools established at the East is very much greater than that of like schools in the Indian country. All the children are expected to write weekly to their homes, and the interest of the parents in the progress and welfare of the children under the care of the government is at least equal to the interest that white people take in their children.

In addition to the scholars at the Carlisle training school, the number during the coming year at Hampton will be increased to about sixty-five. Benevolent persons all over the country are taking a deep interest in both of these schools, and are contributing money to promote the improvement of the pupils, by furnishing articles that cannot be supplied and paid for under government regulations.

From the statements herein made it will be seen that the work of education among Indians has been largely increased, and the facilities now enjoyed will tend very materially to promote the work of Indian civilization. The interest of the Indian chiefs and ruling men in these educational movements is very great. They have already expressed a desire to send school committees from their tribes to see and report upon the progress and treatment of their children in the government schools, and permission to come east for that purpose will be granted to a limited number. The older Indians, and those experienced in the affairs of the tribes, feel keenly the want of education, and as a rule have favored all endeavors to educate their children, and it is a rare thing to find an Indian so benighted as not to desire to have his children taught to read and write in the English language.

Arrangements are now in progress for opening a school similar to the Carlisle school at Forest Grove, Oregon, for the education of Indian children on the Pacific coast.

INDIAN FREIGHTING

In the month of July, 1877, it was proposed to the Sioux chiefs Spotted Tail and Red Cloud, in a council held with them at their old agencies in

Dakota, that they should begin the work of their own civilization by hauling their annuity goods and supplies from the Missouri River to the new locations to which they were about to remove, distant respectively 90 and 183 miles westward from the river. The Indians promised that, whenever the government should furnish them with the means of transportation, they would willingly embark in the enterprise. Owing to the impending removal of the Indians and the lateness of the season, it was decided, after due deliberation, to defer putting the plan into execution until after the removal should have been accomplished and sufficient supplies should have been transported to the new locations to carry the Indians through the first winter. The department did not wish to incur the risk of making a trial of what was looked upon as an experiment, when any failure might deprive the Indians of sufficient food and shelter to enable them to withstand the rigors of a Dakota winter.

As related in my last report, a serious combination was made by contractors to take advantage of what was supposed to be the necessities of the government in the hope of thereby extorting exorbitant rates for the carrying of supplies from the Missouri to the two agencies. After advertising twice successively for bids for transportation without obtaining reasonable proposals, it was determined to purchase four hundred and twelve wagons and six hundred sets of double harness, and to hire the Indians with their four-pony teams to remove nearly 4,000,000 pounds of freight an average distance of nearly 150 miles. Even the boldest and most progressive agents pronounced the undertaking a novel and doubtful experiment and others declared it to be impossible, expressing the opinion that Indian ponies were too weak and unreliable to be depended upon for business of such serious importance. To add to the difficulties of the situation malicious white men burned the grass between the agency and the Missouri River for a space 40 by 60 miles in extent.

Under difficulties like these the task of teaching wild Indians to haul supplies with their unbroken ponies began October 11, 1878, and before January 1, 1879, their ability to perform the work had been successfully demonstrated, and 13,000 Indians were comfortably fed and clothed on supplies and annuity goods hauled by themselves without loss or waste.

In past years, when wagon transportation was performed by white contractors, the loss and waste were very considerable. Employés and teamsters lived on the flour, sugar, bacon, and coffee transported by them. The Indians, however, invariably carry their freight through intact. They have become expert drivers of four-pony teams, and now manage them with the skill of an experienced stage-driver.

The result of the experiment with the Sioux Indians has led to the purchase of enough transportation material to enable all our Indians, except the tribes in Colorado, New Mexico and Arizona, to haul their own supplies. One thousand three hundred and sixty-nine wagons and two thousand five hundred sets of double harness are now employed in the service with excellent results in all cases.

The influence of this industry upon the tribes in which it has been introduced has been marvelous. In the past all drudgery and much of the real work devolved upon the Indian women, while they laughed at and ridiculed any man who was disposed to labor. Now, however, the women are glad to have the men do the hauling, and even other work, and go so far as to ride in the wagons with their husbands on the journeys between the agencies and the base of supplies. The prosecution of this industry compels the men to wear citizens' clothing, and in that particular rapid advance in civilization has been made. Another advantage, and perhaps the greatest one, is the opportunity thus afforded Indians to earn money honestly, and by constant application, in considerable amounts. Hauling is far more profitable than hunting ever was, even when game was abundant. Then the traders, in the purchase of peltries, for which they made payment in tokens, took the lion's share of all the Indians could earn; now their wages are paid in cash, and the Indians are rapidly learning to make a good use of their money. What is not expended for necessaries and comforts is given to the women to keep for future wants.

It is now the settled policy of the government to give all wagon transportation to Indians, and to make them useful in every capacity in which Indian labor can be employed.

STOCK CATTLE

For several years past the experiment of furnishing Indians with cattle for stock-raising has been made from time to time, and it has been found that the Indians have almost invariably herded their cattle well, and have raised young stock in considerable numbers. During the current year, as the following figures will show, very much more has been done in the distribution of stock among the Indians than at any time heretofore. The government has contracted for 11,311 head of stock cattle, which have been delivered in part; the remainder of the deliveries will be made as soon as spring is fairly opened. These cattle are distributed as follows: 1,100 to the San Carlos Agency, 100 to Siletz, 1,522 to Pine Ridge, 1,622 to Rosebud, 900 to Cheyenne and Arapaho, 600 to Kiowa, Comanche, and Wichita; 817 to Osage, 400 to Pawnee, 850 to the Shoshone and Bannack; 100 each to the Sac and Fox, and Kaw Agencies; 200 each to the Western Shoshone, Flathead, and Fort Hall Agencies; 300 each to Crow Creek, and Ponca; and 500 each to Yankton, Standing Rock, Lower Brulé, and Blackfeet Agencies. These cattle have been and will be distributed only to such Indians as, in the opinion of the respective agents, will take the best care of them. Properly cared for, the increase of this stock, in four years, will, with the original herd, amount to nearly 50,000 head, from which it will be seen that the success of the Indians in stock-raising and their ability to profit by it can be demonstrated in a very brief time. These advantages, taken in connection with the issue of agricultural implements and wagons in number to correspond with the issue of cattle, will require but one more act on the part of the government to complete the conditions necessary for Indian self-support. The only thing needful is to provide them with an absolute title to lands in severalty, covered by a patent from the government, with protection against taxation and alienation.

GRANARIES AND ROOT HOUSES

Indians in their natural state are exceedingly improvident, and while for one year, if left to themselves, they might procure seed and raise a large crop, the probability is that before the next planting season their supply of seed would be entirely exhausted. It is necessary, therefore, to exercise some forethought in their behalf, and during the current year the office has directed agents to construct granaries and root houses, and to call upon each Indian who has been engaged in farming to deliver at the agency a sufficient amount of seed for the next crop. In return, the agent gives a receipt for its safe-keeping. This of course renders it necessary for the agent to have a place of storage where the seeds or roots will be safe from destruction or frost.

It is not unusual for Indian traders to give Indians credit to an amount not only sufficient to absorb their whole year's crop, but also to demand, in payment for debt, even the amount left over for seed. For this reason traders have been enjoined not to give Indians credit, but to let them pay in cash and products as far as they may go.

These granaries and root houses, which are necessary to make sure that the Indians do not part with their seed to satisfy passing wants, have been completed or are in course of construction for the following agencies: Cheyenne River, Lower Brulé, Crow Creek, Yankton, Fort Berthold, Sisseton, Blackfeet, Crow, Flathead, Shoshone, Yakama, Tulalip, Neah Bay, S'Kokomish, Siletz, Umatilla, Round Valley, Cheyenne and Arapaho, Pawnee, Osage, Sac and Fox, Santee, Omaha, Winnebago, Great Nemaha, and White Earth.

INDIAN POLICE

It is about two years since the general establishment of an Indian police force, which has proved to be exceedingly beneficial to the service. The policemen have shown the utmost fidelity to the government, and, when necessary, have arrested even friends and relatives with absolute impartiality. At the Pine Ridge Agency, on the 8th of September last, a runner was dispatched from the camp of Young-Man-Afraid-of-His-Horses to notify the agent of the escape during the night of eleven Cheyennes who had taken with them twenty-two head of horses and ponies belonging to the Sioux. Police Captain Sword, with nine of his men, was sent in pursuit, and the next day overtook the Cheyennes—who had twelve hours the start of the police—on Osage Creek west of the Black Hills, about 125 miles distant from the agency. Sword and his party immediately surrounded the fugitives and demanded their surrender. Spotted Wolf, the leader of the runaways, refused, and threw off his blanket, which among Indians signifies a challenge to mortal combat. The police immediately opened fire on the party, killing Spotted Wolf. The remainder then surrendered, and after a two-day march were brought back to the agency. Many other equally noteworthy instances of fidelity have occurred, and as a whole, where agents have entered into the spirit of the system, the results have been of the best possible character.

There is but one drawback, which should be removed by Congress. The pay of policemen which is fixed by law at $5 per month should be increased to $15. The men enlisted in the police service are usually heads of families, and $5 per month is the merest pittance. Indians engaged in other avocations at the various agencies are paid $15, and teamsters, with their ponies, often earn $30 per month. Especially at larger agencies, where there is considerable police work to be done, the payment of the police should be increased as above proposed. At present considerable dissatisfaction is felt among the Indians on account of the scanty pay, and agents report great difficulty in keeping a full quota of suitable men. This should not be the case, as our police system is necessary for the maintenance of order and good government at the several agencies, and is of the highest importance in teaching Indians habits of civilized life and eventual self-government.

MARRIAGES

In my last annual report I recommended the enactment of a law to prevent polygamy, which prevails in almost every Indian tribe, and to provide for legal marriages among Indians. I can do no better than to repeat that recommendation here:

> An act of Congress should provide wholesome and proper marriage laws for Indian tribes. The agent should be required to marry all the Indians cohabiting together upon the various reservations, giving them a certificate of such marriage; and after the beginning of the next year no Indian should be permitted to marry more than one wife. White men cohabiting with Indian women should be compelled either to marry them or to quit the reservation.

* * *

THE OUTBREAK OF THE UTES

By the treaty of March 2, 1868, two agencies were established on the Ute Reservation in Colorado, the Los Pinos Agency in the south for the Tabequache and Muache bands, and the White River Agency in the north for the Yampa, Grand River, and Uintah bands. Abundance of game on and near the reservation with which to supplement the half rations provided under treaty enabled the Utes to postpone indefinitely the time when they should be compelled to adopt civilized habits and means of subsistence. Owing to their proverbial friendliness to the whites and loyalty to the government, their frequent excursions outside the reservation gave comparatively little uneasiness, and was often encouraged by those who wished to gain possession of the large quantities of peltries which the Utes annually secured. By this means the Indians had no difficulty in obtaining in abundance the arms, ammunition, and whiskey which were denied them on their reservation.

The Los Pinos Utes, under the personal influence and example of Ouray, have yielded more readily to agency control and seemed more inclined to make a small beginning in civilized habits than those at White River. The latter, moreover, for a few years past have been divided into two factions, under rival chiefs, between whom a bitter animosity has existed, and any measure proposed by the agent needed only to be supported by one party to be opposed by the other.

The geographical position of the White River Agency is of a very peculiar character, and the query forcibly presents itself why such a location was chosen at all. It can be reached only from the north by but one road, which during some seasons is passable for the transportation of freight but little over two months in the year, and is open on an average only from four to six months in a year. The surrounding country is broken; is out of the line of ordinary emigration westward; and, abounding in game, is in most respects a paradise for wild Indians. Under these circumstances it is not strange that Agent Meeker found the White River Utes to be a thoroughly wild and barbarous people, upon whom civilization had had scarcely any perceptible effect.

Soon after his appointment, Agent Meeker advised the removal of the agency from its old site to a point fifteen miles south, where a milder climate and more arable land was to be found, and where there was a better opportunity for putting the Indians at work. The agency was accordingly removed, new buildings were erected, and quite an extensive irrigating ditch was dug with Indian labor, and for a while the Indians, especially those of Douglas's band, seemed contented with their agent. The rival chief Jack, however, was opposed to the change of the agency, still remained with his people at the old location, and resisted all attempts to interest him in any improvements.

During last winter and spring frequent complaints were made by the agent, both to this office and to the military, relative to the absence of his Indians from their reservation, two of which are as follows:

WHITE RIVER AGENCY, COLORADO,
March 17, 1879.

HON E. A. HAYT,
Commissioner of Indian Affairs, Washington, D.C.

SIR: I am informed that some thirty White River Utes are about to start for the north, having heard of the fighting in the Upper Missouri country. Their object probably is to supply ammunition to the hostiles, and they get full supplies at the stores on Snake and Bear Rivers. These belong to the adverse faction, *who will not work*, and, having no fixed homes nor interest, they can start off at any time. I have sent this information to the commandant at Fort Steele, and I have repeatedly reported to you of the sale of ammunition at these stores, and also reported the same to the commandant at Fort Steele.

Something like a dozen Indians are honestly at work in building and preparing land to plant, and I am doing all that possibly can be done to expedite such interest, which on new land does not grow rapidly, but we are making good progress. By another year I hope the fruits of industry will be such as to keep all the Indians on the reservation.

Respectfully,

N. C. MEEKER,
Indian Agent.

WAR DEPARTMENT,
WASHINGTON CITY, *April 8, 1879.*

THE HON. SECRETARY OF THE INTERIOR.

SIR: I have the honor to transmit for your information copy of a communication from Mr. N. C. Meeker, Indian Agent at White River Agency, stating that a large part of White River Utes are about to start north, probably for the scene of Indian troubles, and requesting that all White River Utes be held or sent back to the reserve if found going north.

General Sherman, in submitting the above letter, remarks that he understands that the White River Utes have agreed to go south to the reservation; and that if they go north they simply complicate matters, and force on the military the most unpleasant duty of capturing them and compelling them to go to their new reservation.

Very respectfully, your obedient servant,

GEO. W. McCRARY,
Secretary of War.

UNITED STATES INDIAN SERVICE,
WHITE RIVER AGENCY, COLORADO,
March 17, 1879.

TO THE COMMANDANT AT FORT STEELE, WYO.

SIR: It is my duty to inform you that quite a large party of White River Utes are about to start for the north, perhaps for the scene of Indian troubles. Whether they intend to mix in is doubtful, but I think it entirely certain they will carry considerable supplies of ammunition for sale to their allies.

I have before reported to you that there are several stores on Snake and Bear Rivers which keep full supplies of ammunition. I would hereby request you to arrest all White River Utes bound north and either hold them or send them back to the reservation. They deserve a lesson. I wish also the sale of ammunition as above kept be put an end to, agreeably to orders in such cases.

Respectfully, yours,

N. C. MEEKER
Indian Agent.

In another communication, dated December 9, 1878, the agent states:

> There are four stores on the northern border of the reservation which sell
> ammunition. As a consequence the Indians all go to those stores to sell
> buckskins and expend what money they can get hold of, so that with the trade
> of the few settlers these establishments are doing a thriving business. Thus it
> is that with abundant supplies at this agency half the Indians are off their
> reservation. This condition of things leads to continued demoralization of the
> Indians; for first, the traders tell them they ought to hunt and not to work;
> and, second, the Indians interfere with the cattle of stockmen by keeping their
> horses on their range, eating what they call their grass. One complaint, from
> George Baggs, a heavy stockman, was of so serious a nature, including the
> stampeding of cattle, that I have sent an interpreter to order the Indians back
> to their reservation. But you must see that the traders will use their influence
> to keep the Indians on those rivers that they may have their trade. I wish
> some steps could be taken to suppress the sale of ammunition. I do not
> suppose I can exercise any authority outside the reservation.

For thus intruding upon white settlements the Indians could easily find
justification by pointing to the numerous mining camps which have been
located on their reservation in direct violation of treaty provisions, viz:

> The United States now solemnly agrees that no persons except those herein
> authorized so to do, and except such officers, agents, and employés of the
> government as may be authorized to enter upon Indian reservations in
> discharge of duties enjoined by law, shall ever be permitted to pass over,
> settle upon, or reside in the territory described in this article, except as herein
> otherwise provided.

This was also expressly reaffirmed in what is known as the Brunot
agreement of 1873. This infraction of the treaty greatly irritated the Utes,
and was undoubtedly one of the causes which eventually led to active
hostilities.

On the 5th of July Governor Pitkin, of Colorado, send the following
telegram to this office:

> Sir: Reports reach me daily that a band of White River Utes are off their
> reservation, destroying forests and game near North and Middle Parks. They
> have already burned millions of dollars of timber, and are intimidating
> settlers and miners. Have written Indian Agent Meeker, but fear letters have
> not reached him. I respectfully request you to have telegraphic order sent
> troops at nearest post to remove Indians to their reservation. If general
> government does not act promptly the State must. Immense forests are
> burning throughout Western Colorado, supposed to have been fired by In-
> dians. I am satisfied there is an organized effort on the part of Indians to de-
> stroy the timber of Colorado. The loss will be irreplaceable. These savages
> should be removed to the Indian Territory, where they can no longer destroy
> the finest forests in this State.

Immediately upon its receipt the following telegraphic instructions were sent Agent Meeker July 7th:

> Governor of Colorado reports your Indians depredating near North and Middle Parks. If correct take active steps to secure their return to reservation. The Secretary directs that if necessary you will call upon nearest military post for assistance. Report facts immediately.

And on the 9th instant the office telegraphed Governor Pitkin that the War Department had been requested to send troops to bring the Indians back to their reservation.

On the 7th of July, before the above instructions were received by him, Agent Meeker also reported to the office that he had been informed that bands of his Indians on Snake and Bear Rivers and in Middle and North Parks were destroying game for the skins and burning the timber, and that he had sent Chief Douglas with an employé to order their return to their reservation and had requested the commandant at Fort Steele to cause them to return.

These papers on the 17th of July were referred to the War Department, and the following reply was made thereto:

War Department,
Washington City, *August 13, 1879.*

The Hon. Secretary of the Interior.

Sir: Referring to your letter of the 18th ultimo, relative to affairs at White River Agency, Colorado, and depredations committed by Indians belonging thereto, I have the honor to state that the complaints therein alluded to have been duly investigated, and I would invite your attention to the inclosed copies of reports in regard to them from Army officers and others.

Very respectfully, your obedient servant,

G. W. McCRARY,
Secretary of War.

Headquarters Department of the Platte,
Fort Omaha, Nebr., *August 4, 1879.*

Respectfully returned to the assistant adjutant-general U.S.A., headquarters Military Division of the Missouri, inviting attention to the report of Maj. T. T. Thornburgh, Fourth Infantry, commanding Fort Fred Steele, Wyo., and the accompanying statements of parties who were in the vicinity, and who were cognizant of all the facts.

Major Thornburgh's report with these statements are forwarded herewith.

From these statements it will be seen:

1. That besides killing the game the Indians committed no depredations.

2. That the post commander of Fort Steele, Wyo., did not receive timely information of the presence of the Indians referred to.

I ask attention to the fact that it is impossible for the military, placed as they are at such great distance from the agencies, to prevent Indians from leaving without authority, unless warning in due time by the Indian authorities is given. Nor can a post commander force them to return without running the risk of bringing on a war, for which he would be held accountable.

For this reason the post commander is required to refer the matter to higher military authority, which also involves delay. Unless troops are stationed at the agencies they cannot know in time when Indians are absent by authority; nor can they prevent the occurrence of troubles, for which they are frequently and most unjustly held responsible.

GEORGE CROOK,
Brigadier General, Commanding.

HEADQUARTERS FORT FRED STEELE, WYO.,
July 27, 1879.

THE ASSISTANT ADJUTANT-GENERAL,
Headquarters Department of the Platte, Fort Omaha, Nebr.

SIR: I have the honor to submit the following report of the recent visit of the Ute Indians from the White River Agency to this vicinity:

About the 25th of June a band of some 100 Indians from the White River Agency made their appearance at a mining camp on the divide near the head of Jack and Savoy Creeks, some 60 miles south of this post and engaged in hunting and trading in this vicinity for about one week, when they departed (as they said) for their agency.

I did not learn of the presence of these Indians until after their departure, nor was I notified by the agent at White River that they had left their agency until June 11, when I received a communication from him dated June 7, stating that a considerable number of the Indians had left their reservation and were burning timber and wantonly destroying game along Bear and Snake Rivers, also warning all miners and ranchmen, and requesting me to cause them to return to their reservation. Upon receiving this letter I made inquiries and could not find such a state of affairs to exist but did find that the Indians had killed a great deal of game and used the skins for trade. The miners they visited in this section were not molested, but on the contrary were presented with an abundance of game. No stock was molested, and so far as I can learn no one attributes the burning of timber to these Indians.

Since I have been in command of this post (one year) Agent Meeker, of the White River agency, has written me two letters, dated November 11, 1878, and June 7, 1879. These letters have usually come to me after the Indians had paid a flying but peaceable visit to this country and departed (as they always say) to their agency. The White River Agency is situated some 200 miles from this post, and there are very few settlers in the country between Fort Fred Steele and the agency, consequently I am not informed as soon as I should be of the movements of these Indians. Bear and Snake Rivers are about 100 miles from this post, and to reach them by traveling this distance would require the trip to be made through a very rough country, impracticable for wagons, the only transportation available.

I have never received any orders from my superior to cause these Indians to remain on their reservation at the request of the agent, but am ready to attempt anything required of me. I have been able to communicate with nearly every ranchman residing within 100 miles of this post in reference to the late visit of these Indians, and forward herewith letters received from them. Both the letters mentioned above as having been received from Agent Meeker were forwarded to higher authority, and instructions have been asked to guide me in this matter.

I am, very respectfully, your obedient servant,

T. T. THORNBURGH,
Major Fourth Infantry, Commanding Post.

[Indorsement on above report.]

HEADQUARTERS DEPARTMENT OF THE PLATTE
FORT OMAHA, NEBR., *August 11, 1879.*

Respectfully forwarded to the assistant adjutant-general, U. S. A., headquarters Military Division of the Missouri for the information of the Lieutenant-General in connection with telegram of 8th ultimo from the Adjutant-General's Office, transmitted for my information and guidance and action, from your office, July 9, 1879. Attention is invited to the report of the commanding officer Fort Fred Steele, Wyo., on the subject, and to the accompanying statements.

GEORGE CROOK,
Brigadier-General, Commanding.

[Inclosures to above report.]

UPPER NORTH PLATTE
BRUSH CREEK, *July 6, 1879.*

MAJOR THORNBURGH,
Commanding Officer, Fort Fred Steele.

DEAR SIR: In regard to your inquiries of the Ute Indians on the Upper North Platte, would say that there was about 65 or 70 lodges, as near as I can ascertain; they camped on Jack Creek, about the middle of June; they were evidently a hunting party, doing no damage and seeming perfectly friendly. They had caught some elk calves which they wanted to trade for cartridges, but the ranchmen would not trade. They traded them some butter for furs and skins, and killed enough game for their own immediate use.

Yours, respectfully,

TAYLOR PENNOCK.

P. S.—They went south towards North Park between the 3rd and 5th of July, but done no damage nor made no threats.

WARM SPRINGS, WYO., *July 23, 1879.*

MAJOR THORNBURGH
Post Commander, Fort Steele, Wyo.

DEAR SIR: In response to your inquiries regarding the Ute Indians who were recently in this part of the country, I submit the following:

The Indians committed no depredations in this settlement beyond slaughtering game by the wholesale. No hostility was manifested toward any of the settlers, the Indians conducting themselves peaceably and quietly. No cattle was killed and no fires set.

Rumors of trouble in the North Park have reached here from time to time, but I cannot vouch for their truthfulness. The Indians left this country for the North Park about the 3d of this month—at least not later than that time.

We have no one to blame for the Indians being in this country but ourselves, for we were aware of the fact that if you had been notified of their presence that you would have at once taken steps to remove them.

J. T. CRAWFORD.

LAKE CREEK, CARBON COUNTY, WYOMING, *July 24, 1879.*

MAJOR THORNBURGH,
Post Commander, Fort Steele, Wyo.

SIR: In compliance with your request, I take pleasure in giving you all the information in my possession, in reference to the late visit of the Ute Indians from the White River Agency to this part of the country. I reside, as you know, about 25 miles south of Fort Steele, on the Platte River, and about the last of June I had occasion to go to Spring Creek, some 12 miles farther south, and I found that a band of some 100 Indians had just left Wagner's Ranch, having remained there only two days, which time they used for trading horses, skins, &c.

These Indians are very friendly, and tried in every way not to get into trouble with any one. They killed considerable game, more than they could use, but that is not an uncommon thing in this country. I heard of no acts of hostility, and in fact I know that none was committed, as I have seen nearly all the ranchmen in 100 miles of me since their departure. I have seen Mr. Jones, a miner, from North Park, who told me that a good many miners when they learned of the approach of the Indians, left and returned home.

No depredations were committed at the Park that I have ever heard of.

WM. BRANER.

NORTH PLATTE RIVER, WYOMING,
July 26, 1879.

MAJOR THORNBURGH,
Commanding Fort Fred Steele, Wyo.

SIR: In reply to your inquiries I would respectfully state that the band of Indians who were lately here left this country on the 1st instant, going south into Colorado. I don't think they set out any fires or interfered with the settlers in any way whilst here, and I have had a good chance to know. They killed considerable game while here.

Yours, respectfully,

B. T. BRYAN.

FRED STEELE, WYO.,
July 26, 1879.

MAJ. T. T. THORNBURGH,
Fort Steele, Wyo.

DEAR SIR: In answer to your inquiry, I have just returned from a seven days' journey through the country which the Ute Indians have been traveling and hunting. Being well acquainted with settlers of the country, have met and conversed with most of them, and have heard no complaint except the great slaughter of game. I traveled 30 or 40 miles along the base of the mountains on their trail and did not see where any prairie or timber fire had originated from their camps, or where there had been any recent fire. I learn from the ranchmen that the Indians left the North Park about July 1, and have heard nothing further of their movements.

Very respectfully,

NEWTON MAJIR.

WARM SPRINGS, WYO., *July 25, 1879.*

MAJ. T. T. THORNBURGH,
Commanding Fort Steele.

SIR: In answer to your inquiry regarding the Ute Indians, I do not think they set any of the fires in this part of the country, as the tie-men admitted to me that the fires on Brush and French Creeks caught from their camp fires. They crossed on Beaver Creek fifty miles south of Steele on June last or July 1, going north.

Very respectfully,

W. B. HUGUS.

GRAND ENCAMPMENT CREEK. *July 26, 1879.*

MAJ. T. T. THORNBURGH,
Fourth Infantry, Fort Fred Steele, Wyo.

SIR: In reply to your inquiries concerning the Ute Indians who lately visited this region, I can inform you that I saw and traded with these Indians on or about the 8th of July, when they were on their way south toward their agency by way of North Park. These Indians—about 50 in number—were very peaceable and polite, and did not commit any depredations, or show any hostility towards any of the settlers in this country. There were fires set about this time in the timber, but it is not known how they originated. I have, since their departure, learned from Mr. John Le Fevre, of North Park, that another band of these Indians were in North Park in June, and that some of the miners talked of driving them off, but on conversing with White Antelope, their chief, they learned that the Indians did not wish trouble, and they immediately left. This is all I know or have heard of this subject.

GREY NICHOLS.

FORT STEELE, WYO., *July 26, 1879.*

MAJ. T. T. THORNBURGH,
Commanding Officer, Fort Fred Steele, Wyo.

SIR: Referring to your inquiries as to the doings of the Utes, who were lately in the Platte Valley, south of this post, I would respectfully state that a party of White River Ute Indians camped on Beaver Creek, June 30, they being then on their way south, and that they crossed the Colorado line July 1. During their stay on the Platte, they killed considerable game, but offered no violence to settlers, nor did they, so far I have been able to learn by diligent inquiry, set fire to any grass or timber in this country.

I have traveled all through the country referred to since the 1st of July, and am satisfied that had any violence been committed by the Indians, I should have heard of it.

Very respectfully,

J. M. HUGUS.

[Fourth indorsement.]

HEADQUARTERS MILITARY DIVISION OF THE MISSOURI,
CHICAGO, *August 6, 1879.*

Respectfully forwarded to the Adjutant-General of the Army, inviting attention to the indorsement of General Crook, and report of Major Thornburgh.

P. H. SHERIDAN,
Lieutenant-General Commanding.

On the 15th of July, in reply to office telegram of the 7th, the agent reported that the mission of Chief Douglass and the employé had been successful; that Middle Park had been vacated by the Indians; and that they were returning to the agency. He also stated that the Indians had no appreciation of the value of forests, and in order to obtain dry fuel for winter use, or to drive the deer to one place where they might be easily killed, fires were lighted, by which large tracts of valuable timber were burned over, to the great exasperation of settlers. To this communication the office replied as follows:

DEPARTMENT OF THE INTERIOR,
OFFICE INDIAN AFFAIRS,
WASHINGTON, *August 15, 1879.*

N. C. MEEKER, ESQ.,
United States Indian Agent,
White River Agency, Col.,
via Rawlins Station, Wyoming.

SIR: I am in receipt of your letter, dated 15th ultimo, relative to the departure of the Indians from the Middle Park, their destruction of grass, timber, &c., and referring to my telegram to you of the 23rd ultimo, directing you to "take a decided stand with your Indians to prevent further depredations," have to state in addition that complaints of a serious character have been made to the office in regard to the fires which have been set by the Indians, as you have been advised by office letter of the 12th instant, and these heedless and lawless acts, unless checked, will lead to collisions between the whites and the Indians. You will, therefore, if possible, ascertain what Indians committed the depredations to which you refer, and have them arrested and subjected to some adequate punishment. Examples must be made of some of them in order to deter others from similar outrages.

In closing your letter you state incidentally that after the Indians have received their yearly distribution of annuity goods "they will depart and roam over a country as large as New England, where settlers are struggling to make new homes, and the Indians think it all right because they are, as they boast, peaceable Indians."

In reply, you are directed to adopt, without delay, decisive measures to put a stop to these roaming habits of your Indians. Office instructions embraced in the circular of December 23, 1878, in regard to their being treated as hostile Indians and liable to arrest, if they are found outside of their reservation without passes, should be enforced, and you should also give them to understand that their annuities will be withheld from them if they do not comply with the requirements of the office.

Very respectfully,

E. A. HAYT,
Commissioner.

On the 11th of August, the agent again complained of the bad conduct of his Indians, as follows:

WHITE RIVER AGENCY, COLO., *August 11, 1879.*

HON. E. A. HAYT,
Commissioner Indian Affairs, Washington, D. C.

SIR: In a letter of this date (A) are several things connected with the subject of this letter. I have a strong belief that a raid is to be made on our herd through the connivance of the Indians, and what I want is sufficient military force to be sent hither to awe these savages, so that they will stay at home. When this shall be done the Indians will be in a condition to improve, but now it is simply impossible; indeed, I fear they are already so demoralized that years upon years will be required to make anything out of them. A few, say twenty or thirty, I have under my control, and I have great hopes of them; but the rest, fully 700, will not stay here. It is useless for anybody to tell me to keep them at home while there is no obstacle to their going away, and even while they are welcomed by white men who teach them all kinds of iniquities.

I had a conversation the other day on the cars with Major Thornburgh, commandant at Fort Steele. He said he had always sent my requests forward and that he had received no orders, and he added that if you should request the Secretary of War to command him to keep the tribes on their reservation he could start a company of 50 cavalry at a day's notice, but without orders he could not go ten miles from the fort.

Another trouble lies in the stores on Snake and Bear Rivers, or even nearer by, which sell ammunition for goods, playing-cards being in large supply. Let me ask you what is the use of my warning these traders when they know I have no power to back me? It is only a farce. I once wrote to the governor of this State about the violation of the law, and he told me if I could apply to the deputy United States marshal for the district he would move. I did not apply to him, because said deputy kept an Indian store himself.

The things to be done are three: Have the military break up the selling of ammunition (and liquor), and the buying of annuity goods at these stores. Then, as the Indians could not hunt they would work to get money, perhaps trap some, and a store would be established here. Of course the military must keep them on their reservation, and white men off. When these things shall be done the Indians will begin to consider the question of sending their children to school, and they will open farms. Now they will not. Already they are making their plans for going north, after they get their annuity goods, to hunt buffalo. If anything can be done I would like to have a hand in it.

Respectfully,

N. C. MEEKER,
Indian Agent.

Upon that letter the following report was made by this office to the Secretary of the Interior September 1st, and was by him referred to the War Department September 2d:

THE HONORABLE SECRETARY OF THE INTERIOR.

SIR: I have the honor to transmit herewith copy of a letter dated 11th ultimo, from United States Indian Agent Meeker, of the White River Agency, respecting depredations committed by Indians of his agency, and difficulties in his way in keeping them upon the reservation without military aid.

The agent states that the large majority of them are "constantly off the reservation and intimately associated with the ruffians, renegades, and cattle thieves of the frontier," and he is opinion that these outlaws, aided by the Indians, will make raids on the herds of government cattle during the coming winter.

The agent also calls attention to the evils resulting to the Indians from the unlawful traffic in ammunition and liquor by traders, whose stores are on Snake and Bear Rivers, and the necessity of military aid to break up this traffic. For the past eighteen months or more frequent complaints have been made to the office on account of the traffic carried on with the Indians by the traders in the locations indicated, at whose stores the renegade Utes of Northern Colorado and hostile Bannocks in Southern Idaho and Wyoming Territories, with other lawless bands, have procured ample supplies of ammunition. Two years since, Capt. Charles Parker, U.S.A., stationed at Fort Steele, was directed on the recommendation of this office, to make an investigation of affairs on the Bear River, with a view to the establishment of a military post there to protect the settlers and break up the lawless traffic with the Indians and keep them upon their reservations. After a thorough investigation of the matter that officer, together with the agent of the White River Agency, reported strongly in favor of the measure, and on the 19th of September, 1877, copies of the papers were transmitted to the department, with a view to securing the necessary action on the part of the War Department; but the views of the General of the Army were then adverse to the recommendation of the officer, and the evils complained of have since become more widespread and serious in their character.

The agent urges the necessity of the employment of a military force to overawe and restrain the Indians, and to break up the traffic referred to on Snake and Bear Rivers; and it is respectfully recommended that his communication be referred to the honorable the Secretary of War, with the request that he cause the necessary orders to issue to the commandant at Fort Steele to detail the requisite number of troops for the purposes indicated.

Very respectfully,

E. J. BROOKS,
Acting Commissioner.

About the 25th of August, the sheriff of Grand County went to the White River Agency with warrants for the arrest of two Indians charged with burning a house on Bear River, belonging to a man by the name of Thompson. In regard to this the agent states: "I attempted to get Chief Douglas to assist, so that these culprits might be found, but he refused, saying he knew nothing about them and he would do nothing. And yet he has been extremely friendly; he sends his boy to school and has worked all summer. The Indians were not found and the sheriff and posse of four returned."

Early in September a difficulty occurred between the agent and the Indians on a matter of plowing, of which the agent made the following report:

UNITED STATES INDIAN SERVICE,
WHITE RIVER AGENCY, COLORADO,
September 8, 1879.

HON E. A. HAYT,
Commissioner of Indian Affairs, Washington, D. C.

SIR: We had recently finished plowing an 80-acre field, all inclosed; then we irrigated a piece of adjoining land, and upon which the agency buildings stand at a corner. This parcel lies between the river and the street coming to the agency, and embraces probably 200 acres, and the plan was to devote 50 acres next the street and agency to tilled crops and the remainder to grass land, and to inclose the whole with one common fence. First, it is necessary to have fields contiguous, that fences may be watched and depredators kept in check, and also to make the work of irrigation as inexpensive as possible, since to carry water far involves heavy outlays, besides being attended with the greatest difficulties by reason of uneven ground. In short, the described parcel was every way fitted for the object stated, and the new location of the agency was made with a view of utilizing and improving this particular land.

When we commenced plowing last week, three or four Indians objected. They had set their tents down towards the river, and corrals had been built, though I had previously told them the ground would be plowed. I offered to move their corrals by employeés' labor, and showed them other places, of which there are many equally good, but they refused to consider. This land is good, and being close to the agency, their horses are protected; in short, they simply need the ground for their horses. Now, since it was evident that if I could have moved the agency buildings two or three miles below they would come and claim equal squatters' rights there also, and I told them so, to which they replied, that I had land enough plowed, and they wanted all the rest for their horses. Still they did indicate that I might plow a piece farther away, covered with sage and grease wood, intersected by slues and badly developing alkali, while at the best it would take three months to clear the surface. They would listen to nothing I could say, and seeing no help for it, since if they could drive me from one place they would quickly drive me from another, I ordered the plows to run as I had proposed. The first bed had been laid out and watered, 100 feet wide and half a mile long, and when the plowman got to the upper end two Indians came out with guns and ordered him not to plow any more. This was reported to me, and I directed the plowing to proceed. When the plowman had made a few runs around the bed he was fired upon from a small cluster of sage-brush, and the ball passed close to his person.

Of course, I ordered the plowing to stop. I went to Douglas, the chief, but he only repeated that they who claimed the land wanted it, and that I ought to plow somewhere else. Then I sent a messenger to Jack, a rival chieftain, ten miles up the river, who has a larger following than Douglas, and he and his friends came down speedily, and the whole subject was discussed at great length. The conclusion was, that Jack and his men did not care anything about it, but I might go on and plow that bed (100 feet wide and one-half mile long). I said that was of no use; that I wanted to plow 50 acres at least, and I wanted the rest for hay, as we had to go from 4 to 7 miles to do our haying, and even there the Indian horses eat much of the grass. Then they said I might go on and plow as I proposed. This was either not understood or not assented to by the claimants, for when the plow started next morning they came out and threatened vengeance if any more than that bed was plowed. Immediately I sent again for Jack and his men, and the plow ran most of the forenoon, when I ordered it stopped, for by this time the employés were becoming scared.

Another long council was held, and I understood scarcely anything that was said, though I was present for hours, smothered with heat and smoke, and finally it was agreed that I might have the whole land and plow half of it and inclose the rest, providing I would remove the corral, dig a well, help build a log house, and give a stove, to which I assented, for substantially the same had been promised before.

Altogether there were not more than four Indian men engaged in this outbreak; properly, there was only one family, the wife of which speaks good English, having been brought up in a white family; the remainder were relatives, and besides were several sympathizers, but by no means active. During all this time I had a team in readiness to go to the railroad to ask instructions from you by telegraph, but the necessity for this seemed for the present averted. My impression is decided that it was the wish of all the Indians that plowing might be stopped and that no more plowing at all shall be done, but that the conclusion which they reached was based upon the danger they ran in opposing the government of the United States.

Plowing will proceed, but whether unmolested I cannot say. This is a bad lot of Indians. They have had free rations so long and have been flattered and petted so much, that they think themselves lords of all.

Respectfully,

N. C. MEEKER,
Indian Agent.

Before the receipt of the above report by this office the following telegram came from the agent, announcing that the opposition to the plowing had been carried to the extent of making a personal assault on himself:

WHITE RIVER AGENCY, COLORADO,
September 10, 1879.

E. A. HAYT,
Commissioner, &c., Washington, D.C.:

SIR: I have been assaulted by a leading chief, Johnson, forced out of my own house, and injured badly, but was rescued by employés. It is now revealed that Johnson originated all the trouble stated in letter September 8. His son shot at the plowman, and the opposition to plowing is wide. Plowing stops; life of self, family, and employés not safe; want protection immediately; have asked Governor Pitkin to confer with General Pope.

N. C. MEEKER,
Indian Agent.

The telegram was received late Saturday evening, and on Monday morning, September 15, at the request of this office, the War Department ordered by telegraph that "the nearest military commander to the agency detail a sufficient number of troops to arrest such Indian chiefs as are insubordinate, and enforce obedience to the requirements of the agent, and afford him such protection as the exigency of the case requires; also, that the ringleaders be held as prisoners until an investigation can be had."

On the same day the office telegraphed Agent Meeker:

War Department has been requested to send troops for your protection. On their arrival cause arrest of leaders in late disturbance and have them held until further orders from this office.

Report full particulars as soon as possible.

To which he repliec on the 22d:

Governor Pitkin writes, cavalry on the way. Dispatch of 15th will be obeyed.

On the 22d of September the office received the following telegram from the honorable Secretary of the Interior, relative to the arrest of two Indians against whom warrants had been issued:

DENVER, COLO., *September 21, 1879.*

Hon. COMMISSIONER OF INDIAN AFFAIRS:

SIR: Two Indian Utes, Bennet and Chinaman, have been identified as having burned down citizen' houses outside of reservation; warrants are out against them. Agent Meeker should be instructed to have them arrested and turned over to civil authorities; efforts should also be made to identify Indians having set fire to forests outside of reservation. On consultation with governor and others, I am advised that settlement of Utes in severalty will be possible, on or near location now occupied by them, if properly managed. Steps to that end should be initiated as fast as possible.

C. SCHURZ.

On the 23d Agent Meeker was instructed by this office as follows:

Secretary telegraphs from Denver that two Ute Indians, Bennett and Chinaman, have been identified as having burned down citizens' houses outside of reservation. Warrants are out against them. Agent Meeker should be instructed to arrest and turn them over to civil authorities; also, to identify and arrest Indians having set fires to forests. You will act on Secretary's suggestion, calling on military for assistance if necessary.

To this the agent replied by telegraph dated September 26:

Would say to yours 23d September, if soldiers arrest Indians and go away, I must go with them. Soldiers must stay. Large bodies of Indians leaving for the north to hunt. They insisted I should give out blankets now. I refused. Trade in guns and ammunition on Bear and Snake Rivers brisk. Company D, Ninth Cavalry, at Steamboat Springs, waiting instructions, which came to-day from General Hatch, and are forwarded to-day by employé.

The employé who carried to Captain Dodge the dispatches referred to was thus absent from the agency at the time of the massacre, and is the only male employé who escaped death.

On the 25th of September, Major Thornburgh, who was *en route* to the agent, sent the following to Agent Meeker:

HEADQUARTERS WHITE RIVER EXPEDITION
CAMP ON FORTIFICATION CREEK,
September 25, 1879.

MR. MEEKER,
Indian Agent, White River Agency, Colo.:

SIR: In obedience to the instructions from the General of the Army, I am *en route* to your agency, and expect to arrive there on the 29th instant, for the purpose of affording you any assistance in my power in regulating your affairs, and to make arrests at your suggestion, and to hold as prisoners such of your Indians as you desire, until investigations are made by your department.

I have heard nothing definite from your agency for ten days, and do not know what state of affairs exists—whether the Indians will leave at my approach or show hostilities. I send this letter by Mr. Lowry, one of my guides, and desire you to communicate with me as soon as possible, giving me all the information in your power, in order that I may know what course I am to pursue.

If practicable, meet me on the road at the earliest moment.

        Very respectfully, your obedient servant,

                        T. T. THORNBURGH.

To this Agent Meeker replies, under date of September 27, 1879, as follows:

SIR: Understanding that you are on the way hither with United States troops, I send a messenger, Mr. Eskridge, and two Indians, Henry (interpreter) and John Ayersley, to inform you that the Indians are greatly excited, and wish you to stop at some convenient camping-place, and that you and five soldiers of your command come into the agency, when a talk and a better understanding can be had. This I agree to, but I do not propose to order your movements, but it seems for the best. The Indians seem to consider the advance of troops as a declaration of real war. In this I am laboring to undeceive them, and at the same time to convince them they cannot do whatever they please. The first object now is to allay apprehension.

        Respectfully,

                        N. C. MEEKER,
                        Indian Agent.

On the 26th of September Major Thornburgh telegraphed to his department commander from Bear River:

Have met some Ute chiefs here. They seem friendly and promise to go with me to agency. Say Utes don't understand why we have come. Have tried to explain satisfactorily. Do not anticipate trouble.

On the 28th of September Major Thornburgh wrote the agent as follows:

SIR: I shall move with my entire command to some convenient camp near and within striking distance of your agency, reaching such point during the 29th. I shall then halt and encamp the troops and proceed to the agency with my guide and five soldiers, as communicated in my letter of the 27th instant.

Then and there I will be ready to have a conference with you and the Indians, so that an understanding may be arrived at and my course of action determined. I have carefully considered whether or not it would be advisable to have my command at a point as distant as that desired by the Indians who were in my camp last night, and have reached the conclusion that under my orders, which require me to march this command to the agency. I am not at liberty to leave it at a point where it would not be available in case of trouble. You are authorized to say for me to the Indians that my course of conduct is entirely dependent on them. Our desire is to avoid trouble, and we have not come for war.

I requested you in my letter of the 26th to meet me on the road before I reached the agency. I renew my request that you do so, and further desire that you bring such chiefs as may wish to accompany you.

To this Agent Meeker replied under date of September 29, 1 p.m.:

> DEAR SIR: I expect to leave in the morning with Douglas and Serrick to meet you; things are peaceable, and Douglas flies the United States flag. If you have trouble in getting through the cañon to-day, let me know in what force. We have been on guard three nights and shall be to-night, not because we know there is danger, but because there may be. I like your last programme; it is based on true military principles.

On the same day, and probably before the receipt of Major Thornburgh's letter of the 28th, the agent telegraphed this office:

> SIR: Major Thornburgh, Fourth Infantry, leaves his command 50 miles distant, and comes to-day with five men. Indians propose to fight if troops advance. A talk will be had to-morrow. Captain Dodge, Ninth Cavalry, is at Steamboat Springs, with orders to break up Indian stores and keep Indians on reservation. Sales of ammunition and guns brisk for ten days past. Store nearest sent back 16,000 rounds and 13 guns. When Captain Dodge commences to enforce law, no living here without troops. Have sent for him to confer.

The employe who was bearer of the dispatches to Captain Dodge relative to breaking up the sale of ammunition to Indians reports that the Indians whom Major Thornburgh met on the 26th were a band of ten Indians under Jack, who camped with the soldiers on the night of the 26th, Friday. The next day he met Jack and his ten men at 11 a.m. on the trail between Bear River and Williams's Fork, and was informed by Jack that 190 soldiers had just passed *en route* to the reservation, and was asked for what purpose they had come. This seems to have been Jack's first intimation that soldiers had been sent for, and from a telegram sent by the agent to Governor Pitkin, it appears that the agent considered it important that the call for troops should be kept concealed from the Indians.

As will appear from the above dispatches, the Indians again visited Major Thornburgh's camp on the 27th instant, with a proposition that he leave his troops 50 miles distant and come with five men to the agency for consultation. The proposition being refused, the Indians evidently considered his advance with all his troops as an act of war, and when he crossed the reservation line at Milk Creek—a point about 25 miles distant from the agency—and was about to enter a cañon, a body of not less than 100 Indians were discovered, who opened upon the soldiers a deadly fire. Fighting as they went, the command fell back on the wagon train which was coming up in the rear. In this retreat Major Thornburgh and several others were killed. Horses, wagons, and everything available were immediately used for breastworks, while the Indians from the surrounding bluffs kept up a galling fire. In this desperate position the command under Captain Payne held its own until the morning of the 2d of October, when it was re-enforced by Company D, of the Ninth Cavalry, under Captain Dodge. This single company of colored troops, hearing of the fight, made forced marches, without orders, through the enemy's country, to the relief of the survivors.

Meantime, as soon as the news of the battle reached headquarters, several large bodies of troops were ordered to Milk Creek, and on the morning of October 5 Colonel Merritt arrived there with 600 men. He found the total losses to be 12 killed and 43 wounded. The combined forces then proceeded to the agency, where they found only dead bodies and burned buildings.

The news of the fight with Major Thornburgh was conveyed by runners to the Indian camp near the agency, and the agent's letter of the 29th to Major Thornburgh had hardly been dispatched when the massacre of the agency employés began. All the men, eight in number, were shot; the wife and daughter of the agent and the wife of one of the employés, with her two children, took refuge in an adobe building and remained there for four hours until the buildings were fired. They then took the opportunity, while the Indians were busily engaged in helping themselves to the annuity goods, to escape to the sage-bush, but during their flight were discovered and fired upon by the Indians, Mrs. Meeker receiving a flesh wound. They were then taken captive and conveyed by the Indians, after a toilsome journey of several hours, to the camp to which three or four days previous the Indian women and children had been removed. Two teamsters who were coming up with Indian goods at the time of the massacre were also killed. The Indians report their loss in the first day of their attack on the troops as 23, and afterwards in their struggle with the employés and the freighters as 14.

While these events were transpiring among the White River Utes, Chief Ouray and his band had started out on a two months' hunt; but, as soon as he learned from an Indian runner of the massacre and the capture of the women, he hastened back to his agency in great anxiety and alarm, and immediately issued the following order:

LOS PINOS INDIAN AGENCY,
October 2, 1879.
To the Chief Captains, Headmen, and Utes at the White River Agency:

You are hereby requested and commanded to cease hostilities against the whites, injuring no innocent persons or any others farther than to protect your own lives and property from unlawful and unauthorized combinations of horse-thieves and desperadoes, as anything farther will ultimately end in disaster to all parties.

OURAY.

At the same time the following message was sent to the agent of the Southern Utes.

SIR: Ouray requests that I should say to you, and through you to the whites and Indians, that they need not fear any danger from the trouble at White River; that he wants his people—the Utes—to stay at home and lend no hand or encouragement to the White River Utes; that the troubles there will be over in a few days; that he has sent Sopenevaro and others to White River to stop the trouble; and that outside interference will only tend to aggravate and do no good.

Very respectfully,

WM. M. STANLEY,
United States Indian Agent.

Upon this the Southern Utes held formal council and expressed their determination to take no part in the hostilities of the northern bands. On the 9th of October, Ouray's courier returned with the report that the White River Utes had listened to the order, had stopped fighting, and had moved with all their effects to Grand River.

This information was conveyed to the office in the following telegram of the same date:

Employé Brady and escort of Indians arrived from White River, reports Utes recognized and obeyed Ouray's order, withdrew, and will fight no more unless forced to do so. If soldiers are now stopped trouble can be settled by peace commission to investigate facts, and let blame rest where it may. This will save life, expense, and distress if it can be accomplished.

I concur and indorse the above.

STANLEY, *Agent.*

OURAY,
Head Chief Ute Nation.

In reply thereto the department telegraphed Agent Stanley, October 13, as follows:

Your dispatch received. Tell Ouray that his efforts are highly appreciated by the government. In view of the attack made upon the troops and massacre of agent and employés the troops will have to proceed to White River Agency. Ouray should endeavor to prevent any resistance to this movement. The troops are now in great force, and resistance would result only in great disaster to the Indians. The hostiles will have to surrender and throw themselves upon the mercy of the government. The guilty parties must be identified and delivered up. We shall see that no injustice is done any one. Peaceable Indians will be protected. Ouray's recommendations for mercy in individual cases will be respected as far as the general interest may permit.

Special agents are being dispatched to Los Pinos with further instructions.

C. SCHURZ, *Secretary.*

These terms were in accordance with article 6 of the Ute treaty of 1868, which provides that:

If bad men among the Indians shall commit a wrong or depredation upon the person or property of any one, white, black, or Indian, subject to the authority of the United States and at peace therewith, the tribes herein named solemnly agree that they will, on proof made to their agent and notice to him, deliver up the wrong-doer to the United States, to be tried and punished according to its laws.

An inspector was despatched to the Los Pinos Agency, and General Charles Adams, former agent for the White River Utes, was detailed as special agent to visit the hostile camp with an escort furnished by Ouray, to demand the surrender of the captive women and children, the murderers of the employés, and those engaged in the attack on Major Thornburgh. During these negotiations the troops were instructed by the War Department to proceed no farther than the White River Agency and to remain there until further orders. General Adams was well treated by the hostiles, and after a long and stormy council the captives were delivered to him without conditions, and on the 21st of October they arrived at Ouray's house, where every possible arrangement for their comfort had been made by himself and wife. On his return from General Merritt's camp two more visits were made by General Adams to the hostile camp to demand the surrender of the guilty parties, and on the 29th of October he reported that the Indians appeared willing to have the guilty punished, and recommended that a commission be appointed to make an investigation, Ouray being in favor of the plan and agreeing to have the White River Utes in attendance.

Meantime the department had already sent to General Adams the ultimatum which was to be offered the White River Utes, viz: that they remove their camp temporarily to the neighborhood of Los Pinos; that a commission consisting of Brevet Major-General Hatch, General Adams, and Ouray meet at Los Pinos as soon as possible, to take testimony to ascertain the guilty parties—the guilty parties so ascertained to be dealt with as white men would be under like circumstances; and that the mischievous element in the White River band be disarmed.

This was accepted by the White River Utes, and on the 10th of November twenty of their chiefs and headmen, in obedience to Ouray's order, came to his house to meet General Adams. The others, whose camp was located 50 miles distant on the Gunnison River, were expected soon. Latest advices are that the commission is now organized, and that Johnson, Douglas, and Sawawick are giving testimony. The testimony of officers who were engaged in the battle at Milk Creek, and the testimony of the captive women will also be given before this commission. Every effort to arrive at all the facts and to mete out exact justice will be made. Troops are stationed at Fort Garland in the south as well as at White River Agency in the north, ready for prompt action in the event of the possible failure of the commission.

The atrocity of the crimes committed should not prevent those individuals who are innocent from being treated as such, according to article 17 of the treaty, viz:

> *Provided,* That if any chief of either of the confederated bands make war against the people of the United States, or in any manner violate this treaty

in any essential part, said chief shall forfeit his position as chief and all rights to any of the benefits of this treaty: *But, provided further*: Any Indian of either of these confederated bands who shall remain at peace and abide by the terms of this treaty in all its essentials, shall be entitled to its benefits and provisions, notwithstanding his particular chief and band have forfeited their rights thereto.

The services thus far rendered by Ouray have been of inestimable value, and while the White River Utes have shown the very worst aspect of savage life, Ouray has shown courage and humanity and virtues of the better type, which should somewhat relieve the name of Ute from the odium cast upon it by the northern bands, for whose brutal and barbarous acts, whatever the provocation, no justification can be found.

In my annual report for 1877 I made the following statement of the case:

I recommend the removal of all the Indians in Colorado and Arizona to the Indian Territory. In Colorado, gold and silver mines are scattered over a wide extent of territory, and are to be found in every conceivable direction, running into Indian reservations. Of course miners will follow the various leads and prospect new ones without regard to the barriers set up by an Indian reservation. Hence the sojourn of Indians in this State will be sure to lead to strife, contention, and war, besides entailing an enormous expense to feed and provide for them. Again, there is no hope of civilizing these Indians while they reside in Colorado, as all the arable land in the State is required for its white settlers. A mining population needs in its immediate vicinity abundant facilities for agriculture to feed it. The question of feeding the white population of the State is one of paramount importance, and will certainly force itself on the attention of the government.

In the Indian Office report for 1878 the following extract will be found which has a bearing on the present issue:

The Ute reservation covers nearly 12,000,000 of acres, and fully one-third of the best arable land in the State; and it is situated in the heart of one of the richest mining regions in the United States. The mining population naturally want the arable land to raise food for their support; and as the white population is rapidly augmenting, their encroachments upon the Indians will be constantly on the increase; besides, their lands, if put in the market, will readily sell at a fair price. These remarks have reference mainly to the two southern agencies. The location of the Northern Utes is not desirable, unless the land shall be found to contain minerals. But all the Ute Indians should be removed at once to the Indian Territory, where there is fertile soil and abundance of wood and water, and where there need be no white encroachments.

The "irrepressible conflict" between the white man and the aborigine may be turned to good account for both parties in the accomplishment of desirable results. Let it be fully understood that the Ute Indians have a good and sufficient title to 12,000,000 acres of land in Colorado, and that these Indians did not thrust themselves in the way of the white people, but that they were originally and rightfully possessors of the soil, and that the land they occupy has been acknowledged to be theirs by solemn treaties made with them by the United States, and that the white people, well knowing these facts, took all the responsibility of making their settlements contiguous to the home of the red man.

It will not do to say that a treaty with an Indian means nothing. It means even more than the pledge of the government to pay a bond. It is the most solemn declaration that any government of any people ever enters into. Neither will it do to say that treaties never ought to have been made with Indians. That question is not now in order, as these treaties have been made and must be lived up to, whether convenient or otherwise.

By beginning at the outset with the full acknowledgment of the absolute and indefeasible right of these Indians to 12,000,000 of acres in Colorado, we can properly consider what is the best method of extinguishing the Indian title thereto without injustice to the Indians and without violating the plighted faith of the Government of the United States. The first step in that direction will be to provide by law for a commission to visit the Utes and obtain their consent to remove from the State to some other location—say to the Indian Territory—on condition of their receiving pay for the value of their lands in Colorado, the same to be obtained by appraisement and sale, in the same manner in which certain Kansas and Nebraska lands have been disposed of for the benefit of Indians who formerly resided within their limits. If a proposition of this kind should be fairly presented to the Utes, I have no doubt they would give their consent, as scores of other Indian tribes, both the wildest and the most civilized, have consented under similar circumstances.

There are other considerations in the case of the Ute Indians which might be considered in connection with the proposed removal. The Ute country at present abounds in game, and as long as that shall be the case the Indians will not work. Moreover, their location is admirably adapted to both defensive and aggressive Indian warfare. Its geographical position is also an advantage by which in time of war the Utes can draw largely on the neighboring Indians for assistance either in men or food.

The advantages to be obtained by removing them to the Indian Territory are (1) an abundant supply of arable land for cultivation; (2) immunity from white encroachment; and (3) better security for keeping the Indians peaceful, as the country is not adapted to Indian fighting and everywhere offers open fields for the use of artillery and all the appliances of civilized warfare, so that whatever be the disposition of the Indians, if resort to force should be necessary, it could be made effective in the interests of peace.

THE UTE COMMISSION OF 1878

As was stated in the report of last year, the Ute commission appointed May 24, 1878, obtained from the Capote, Muache, and Weeminuche Utes, who occupied the southern strip of the Ute Reservation, an agreement to relinquish all that part of the reserve lying south of parallel 38° 10′, and to remove to a reservation on the headwaters of the Piedra, San Juan, Blanco, Navajo, and Chama Rivers, in Southern Colorado, as soon as the agency could be removed thither and buildings erected. The cession was concurred in by all the other bands of Utes. The area proposed to be ceded embraces about 1,894,400 acres, an excess of 728,320 acres over the proposed new reserve of 1,166,080 acres.

The report of the Commissioners, together with the agreement, which will be found on pages 170 of this report, was forwarded to the President, February 3d, 1879, for submission to Congress, with the recommendation that the agreement be ratified, and that Congress provide for the appraisement and sale of the lands ceded; the proceeds thereof, after deducting expense of such sale, to be invested for the benefit of the Indians. No action on the matter was taken by Congress.

The Commission also endeavored to obtain the cession of the tract four miles square which contains a part of the Uncompahgre Park; but the Utes refused to have anything to say on the subject unless a delegation could be sent to Washington for that purpose. Permission for the visit was therefore given, and a delegation visited this city in January last. They agreed to part with that portion of their reservation for the sum of $10,000. The matter was submitted to Congress, with request that the necessary sum for the purchase be appropriated; but no action was taken. The tract referred to is for the most part fine agricultural land, which is greatly needed by the people of Colorado, and upon which white settlers have already gone in considerable numbers. It will be a matter of difficulty, if not impossibility, to remove these settlers, and to prevent others from going in and occupying the land; and so long as it is not paid for the Indians will justly consider such settlements as encroachments. The Indians most interested in the cession are the Los Pinos Utes, and in view of their good conduct during the hostilities of their friends and relatives, it is important that their loyalty should not be subjected to unnecessary tests. I, therefore, hope that the matter will not fail to receive the early and favorable consideration of Congress at its next session.

* * *

Invasion of the Indian Territory

In the early part of last winter an extensive scheme was organized to take forcible possession of certain lands in the Indian Territory which had been ceded to the government for Indian purposes. Letters were published and circulated in the States surrounding the Territory by parties interested in the project, declaring that these were public lands, and were open to settlement by citizens of the United States. In a short time a large number of persons from Missouri, Kansas, and Texas were discovered in the act of entering the Territory, carrying their household goods and farming implements, with the evident purpose of making permanent settlement.

This unlawful conspiracy was ascertained to be so extensive as to necessitate the adoption of speedy and vigorous measures, in order to prevent serious complications and trouble with the Indians. The attention of the President having been called to the matter by this department, on the 26th of April last, he issued a proclamation . . . warning all persons who were intending or preparing to remove to the Indian Territory without permission of the proper authorities against attempting to settle upon any lands in said Territory, and notifying those who had already so offended, that they would be speedily removed therefrom by Indian agents, and that, if necessary, the aid and assistance of the military would be invoked to enforce the laws in relation to such intrusion.

Accordingly, upon the recommendation of the department, troops were posted at available points along the lines between the Indian Territory and Missouri, Kansas, and Texas, to prevent unauthorized parties from entering the Territory, and detachments and scouts were detailed to arrest and remove such intruders as could be found within its borders. By the diligent co-operation of the military authorities with the Indian Bureau, the intruders were speedily removed, and the unlawful invasion was checked.

INTRUSION ON INDIAN LANDS

Intruders have been equally troublesome on other Indian lands. In fact, there is hardly an Indian reservation within the limits of the United States which has not been subject to their encroachments. They resort to all kinds of devices and schemes to obtain a foothold on Indian soil, and offer ready and varied excuses for their continued unlawful occupancy of the same.

The great influx upon the different reservations of squaw-men, or white men married to Indian women, according to the lax custom of the tribes, may be adverted to in this connection. In most instances the man is penniless and dependent for subsistence on the rations which his wife draws from the government, but it is not long before he has a herd of cattle ranging over the reservation. On the Crow and other reserves, there are numerous instances of squaw-men who hold from 50 to 1,000 head of cattle, and the rapid manner in which their herds increase presents a very suspicious aspect. Within the last three years cases have been reported where government cattle have been stolen and the government brand altered by these men, and the cattle resold to the government. During the last two years this has been stopped by the most active vigilance.

The squaw-men assume that by marriage they have all the rights of full-blooded Indians, and they endeavor to exercise these rights not only in the possession of cattle themselves, but also in ranging and pasturing upon

Indian reservations large herds belonging to other white men; and when the removal of such cattle is attempted by the agent, the squaw-men claim property in them under fictitious bills of sale.

The case of certain intruders on the Sioux Reserve in Dakota illustrates another method by which white men enter the Indian country and claim possessory rights. A few years since, when that reserve included both banks of the Missouri, it became necessary to allow white men to go upon the reservation for the purpose of cutting timber to supply fuel for steamboats carrying government freight on the Missouri River. A few white men went on the reserve for that purpose, while a larger number went, professedly for that object, but really with the design of permanently locating on the land, and cutting timber therefrom for the purpose of sale and speculation. The agents, however, now report the Indians as able and willing to supply the steamboats with such wood as they may need. A large tract of country extending along the east bank of the Missouri River, which was added by executive order to the Sioux Reservation, has recently been restored to the public domain; and, if the Indians should hereafter decline or be unable to furnish the necessary fuel, it can be supplied from this tract of land. The necessity, therefore, for the presence of white woodchoppers on the Sioux Reservation no longer exists.

Another class of intruders on the Sioux Reserve, on the pretense that it is necessary for the accommodation of the traveling public, have erected eating-houses, feed-stables, etc., at points on the roads, which were authorized by the treaties, with said Indians to be built through their reservation.

Reservations containing rich and available grazing lands, such as the Crow, Malheur, Uintah, and several others, are often encroached upon by cattle-men, who drive their large herds on the most valuable grazing lands, and once there, the greatest difficulty is experienced in getting rid of them. Both cattle and intruders are often removed, but the herders return, or new herders are employed in their stead, and the cattle are again pastured on Indian lands. The herders are, in almost every instance, irresponsible persons, against whom the penalty fixed by sections 2147 and 2148 of the United States Revised Statutes is ineffectual.

A strong effort was made in March last, by the Montana legislature, to obtain the consent of the department to open up a cattle trail from Helena to the eastern markets through the Crow Reservation, and a variety of specious arguments were advanced in favor of the plan; but, on the ground of its being a direct violation of treaty provisions which would justly endanger the present peaceful relations existing between the government and the Crow Indians, the application was of course promptly refused. The owners of the cattle which have thus been driven through that reserve, so far as they could be ascertained, have been prosecuted under section 2117 of the Revised Statutes.

The attention of this office has often been called to the encroachments of miners and other intruders on the Ute Reservation in Colorado and the San

Carlos Reservation in Arizona. Numerous and extensive mines have been opened on both reservations, especially the latter, and every effort of this office to remove the miners has thus far proved ineffectual. The question of intrusion on the San Carlos Reservation must remain unsettled until the western boundary of the same is resurveyed, and an appropriation to cover the expense of such survey should be made without delay.

Extensive depredations have been committed on timber standing on Indian reservations in Michigan, Wisconsin, and Minnesota, but these depredations have been checked to a considerable extent by the arrest and prosecution of the parties engaged or interested in such timber speculations.

LAW FOR INDIAN RESERVATIONS

In the last three annual reports of this office urgent appeals have been made for the enactment of laws for Indian reservations. The following bill was introduced at the last Congress and received the approbation of the Judiciary Committees in both Houses, and was favorably reported on:

> *Be it enacted by the Senate and House of Representatives of the United States of America in Congress assembled,* That the President may prescribe suitable police regulations for the government of the various Indian reservations, and provide for the enforcement thereof.
>
> SEC. 2. That the provisions of the laws of the respective States and Territories in which are located Indian reservations, relating to the crimes of murder, manslaughter, arson, rape, burglary, and robbery shall be deemed and taken to be the law, and in force within such reservations; and the district courts of the United States within and for the respective districts in which such reservations may be located in any State, and the Territorial courts of the respective Territories in which such reservations may be located, shall have original jurisdiction over all such offenses which may be committed within such reservations.
>
> In respect to all that portion of Indian Territory not set apart and occupied by the Cherokee, Creek, Choctaw, Chickasaw, and Seminole Indian tribes, the provisions of the laws of the State of Arkansas relating to the crimes of murder, manslaughter, arson, rape, burglary, and robbery shall be deemed and taken to be the law, and in force therein; and the United States district court for the western district of the State of Arkansas shall have exclusive original jurisdiction over all such offenses arising in said portion of the Indian Territory.
>
> The place of punishment of any and all of said offenses shall be the same as for other like offenses arising within the jurisdictions of said respective courts.

It is a matter of vital importance that action should be taken to secure the passage of the above bill, or of some measure of equal efficiency to provide law for Indians, to the end that order may be secured. A civilized community could not exist as such without law, and a semi-civilized and barbarous people are in a hopeless state of anarchy without its protection and sanctions. It is true the various tribes have regulations and customs of their own, which, however, are founded on superstition and ignorance of the usages of civilized communities, and generally tend to perpetuate feuds and keep alive animosities. To supply their place it is the bounden duty of the government to provide laws suited to the dependent condition of the Indians. The most intelligent among them ask for the laws of the white man to enable them to show that Indians can understand and respect law; and the wonder is that such a code was not enacted years ago.

DEPREDATIONS ON INDIAN TIMBER

The laws of the United States relative to intrusion and depredation on Indian lands have proved ineffectual to prevent citizens of the United States from cutting and destroying timber standing thereon. Sections 2147 and 2148 of the United States Revised Statutes provide merely for the removal of intruders from the Indian country, and for the imposition of a penalty of $1000 in the event of the return of any party after having been removed therefrom. The intruders, as a general rule, have no property subject to execution, and as the penalty can only be collected by an action of debt, the offenders escape without punishment.

Section 2118 is insufficient, for the same reason, to prevent unlawful settlement on lands belonging to Indians.

Section 5388 makes it a penal offense for any person to unlawfully cut, or aid in cutting, or to wantonly destroy timber standing upon lands of the United States which in pursuance of law may be reserved for military or other purposes. This section and the act of March 3d, 1875 (18 Stat., p. 481), which is somewhat similar in its provisions, were evidently adopted, the former for the single purpose of protecting timber on land which had been or might thereafter be purchased or reserved for the use of the military, or any other branch of the government, and the latter to prohibit the destruction of trees on land which had been purchased or reserved for public use. Neither the provisions of the section referred to nor the act are sufficiently comprehensive (especially in view of the rule of law which requires criminal statutes to be construed strictly) to extend to or include parties who have cut or destroyed timber on land within a large portion of the Indian reservations. The United States district court for the western district of Arkansas, at the last May term thereof, decided that the lands within the Cherokee Reservation in the Indian Territory were not lands of the United States in the sense of the language used in section 5388, and that there was no law to punish parties for committing depredations thereon. The reasoning of the court will apply with equal force to the lands of the Choctaws, Chickasaws, Creeks, Seminoles, and certain other Indians.

Most of the Indian reservations are now completely surrounded by a progressive and adventurous white population, which, only by stringent laws, can be restrained from taking possession of Indian lands, and hauling off or destroying the little timber left thereon. I deem it, therefore, of great importance that such a law be enacted as will prevent parties settling upon or cutting or wantonly destroying timber on the following classes of reservations, viz: Lands to which the original Indian title has never been extinguished, but which have not been specially reserved by treaty, act of Congress, or otherwise for the use of the Indians, or for other purposes, although the Indians' right of occupancy thereof has been tacitly recognized by the government; lands expressly reserved by treaty or act of Congress, or set apart for the use of the Indians by Executive order of the President; lands allotted or patented to individual Indians who are not under the laws of any State or Territory; lands patented to Indian tribes; and lands which have been purchased by, or ceded to the United States for the purpose of settling Indians thereon, but which are as yet unoccupied.

Report of Acting Commissioner of Indian Affairs E. M. Marble November 1, 1880

(Excerpt from *Report for 1880*, pp. 85-92, 98-103)

Commissioner Marble's report provided a follow-up to the report of Commissioner Hayt in areas both of accomplishment and failure. The accomplishments that can be cited for this period are the educational work of men like Lieutenant Pratt at the Carlisle Indian School, the success of the Indian police (though primarily in terms of providing the white authorities with an indispensable coercive arm), and the success of Indian freighting and stock raising. On the debit side, the spoliation of the Indians of the Southwest, particularly of the Mission Indians of southern California, was recorded, as were the consequences of the Meeker massacre.

INDIAN EDUCATION

REPORTS FROM THE schools on the various reservations are full of encouragement, showing an increased and more regular attendance of pupils and a growing interest in education on the part of parents. Persistent calls for the opening of new schools, or the enlargement of those already established, come to the office from every quarter. During the year sixty boarding and one hundred and ten day schools have been in operation among the different Indian tribes (exclusive of the five civilized tribes in the Indian Territory), which have been attended by over 7,000 children, and taught by 338 teachers. In the education of the Indian youth it is the policy of the office to have farm and domestic work occupy as prominent a place as study in the school-room, and the development of character and training of the pupils in the manners and habits of civilized life is held to be quite as important as acquiring a knowledge of books. But the opportunity for teaching Indian children how to live, as well as how to read and think, is found only in the boarding school, and for that reason the effort of the office during the past year has been directed mainly toward increasing boarding-school accommodations at the various agencies. Only three new schools, however, have actually been put in operation, and four new buildings erected.

The educational work of the bureau could have been enlarged to a much greater extent but for the inadequate appropriations made by Congress for the support of schools. Fifty thousand Indians at seventeen agencies have no treaty school funds whatever, and for educational facilities must depend entirely on the general appropriation for Indian education. Among those tribes there are at least seven thousand children of school age. Exclusive of rations, the cost of clothing, books, and instruction in an agency boarding-school cannot possibly fall below $60 per capita per annum. The whole appropriation of $75,000 would therefore enable the office to keep twelve hundred and fifty out of seven thousand children in boarding-schools for the year, or would keep about twice that number in day-schools. But this appropriation must also be used to supplement insufficient treaty school funds at various other agencies. The following extract from the act making appropriations to fulfill the treaty with the Flatheads of Montana shows the inadequacy of many of the treaty provisions for schools:

> For the support of an agricultural and industrial school, keeping in repair the buildings, and providing suitable furniture, books, and stationery, per fifth article of treaty of July 16, 1855, *three hundred dollars.* For providing suitable instructors therefor, per same article of same treaty, one thousand eight hundred dollars.

The sum of four thousand dollars per annum is required for the support of the Flathead boarding-school, of which nearly half must be taken from the general appropriation for schools.

This appropriation must also be used for the erection and furnishing of new school buildings, and the enlargement of those which are already overcrowded.

In compliance with the appeals from neglected agencies, the office has made arrangements for erecting eleven boarding-school buildings during the coming season, and for the establishment of thirteen new boarding-schools. These will be the first schools of any kind ever provided for the eight thousand San Carlos Apaches and Western Shoshones, and the first boarding-schools opened for twenty-five thousand Indians of nine other agencies, where small and irregularly attended day-schools have hitherto met with indifferent success, and made little impression upon the tribes among which they were located. But few of these schools will be fairly in operation till toward the close of the current fiscal year, and the expense of their maintenance will not be burdensome until the following year. In-creased provision for the support of schools will then be absolutely neces-sary, and I trust that not less than $150,000 will be appropriated for that object by Congress at its next session.

The importance of having at least one good boarding-school at each agency need not be argued. After the thirteen boarding-schools above referred to have been opened, thirteen more agencies will still remain unprovided for. At not more than fifteen out of sixty-six agencies can the government be said to have made adequate provision for the education of the children of the tribes belonging thereto; and at very few of the remaining fifty-one agencies will the schools, both boarding and day, accommodate 50 per cent of the school population. The necessity for increased and increasing appropriations to enable the office to keep pace with the demands of the Indians for educational facilities is manifest and urgent.

An Indian boarding-school similar to that at Carlisle has been established during the year at Forest Grove, Oreg., for the benefit of Indians on the Pacific coast. It is under the immediate charge of Lieut. M. C. Wilkinson, U.S.A., and has been in operation since February last. Two buildings, which will accommodate 150 pupils, and another which it is proposed to subdivide into workshops, in which various trades will be taught, have been erected—the latter building entirely by the labor of Indian boys under the direction of one of the teachers, who is a practical mechanic. Forty pupils are now in attendance, representing six different tribes. For Indians like those on the Pacific, who are already in close contact with the whites, and who have adopted to a large extent the dress and habits of their white neighbors, the training which such a school gives is especially needed, in order to prepare them for the competition with white civilization, which must soon be inevitable. The number of pupils in the school will be increased during the year as far as funds at the disposal of the office will allow, but unless some special and generous appropriation is made for the benefit of the school the number in attendance must be kept far below the number of applicants for admission.

The attention of Congress has been repeatedly called to the necessity of making some provision for the education of the Alaska Indians; but thus far no action has been taken on the matter. An appropriation of a few thousand dollars for that object would enable the office to educate some Alaska youth at Forest Grove, who, after a few years' training, would be fitted to become teachers among their own people. A comparatively small expenditure in that direction could, in this slow but sure way, be made of incalculable ultimate benefit to the Alaska Indians.

The Hampton and Carlisle schools now number sixty-six and one hundred and ninety-six pupils respectively. Since November, 1878, one hundred and three pupils, representing thirteen different agencies, have been in attendance at Hampton. The report of S. C. Armstrong, principal of Hampton Institute, which will be found herewith on page 304, testifies to the general good conduct of the pupils, to the gratifying progress made by them in acquiring a knowledge of the English language and of elementary English studies, and to the interest and aptness with which they have taken hold of farm work, and received practical instruction in domestic work and various trades.

The first company of sixty boys and twenty-four girls from the Rosebud and Pine Ridge Agencies reached Carlisle in October, 1879. Since that date two hundred and thirty-nine children have been in attendance, representing the Sioux, Cheyennes, Arapahoes, Kiowas, Comanches, Pawnees, Sissetons, Menomonees, Iowas, Sac and Fox, Lipans, Poncas, Nez Percés, Wichitas, Apaches, and Pueblos. Ten per cent of the number have been mixed bloods, and two-thirds of them children of chiefs and headmen.

Industrial work occupies a prominent place in the school, and fifty apprentices are learning the trades of carpenter, blacksmith, wagon-maker, saddler, tinner, shoemaker, tailor, printer, and baker. A statement of the work accomplished by them will be found in the report of Lieutenant Pratt, page 300, to which attention is invited. Specimens of articles manufactured by the Carlisle pupils exhibited at the county fair attracted much favorable attention from visitors, and the small premiums awarded the Indian boys and girls for excellence of workmanship gave them great satisfaction and encouragement.

Aside from the benefit accruing to the children educated therein, the establishment of these schools has aroused a strong interest in Indian civilization on the part of benevolent people in the East, which has resulted in generous donations to aid in the support and to add to the comfort and happiness of pupils at both Hampton and Carlisle. Moreover, during the summer vacation, forty-eight boys and girls from these two schools were received into various families in Massachusetts and Pennsylvania, where they were given an individual home-training which no institution can afford, and where they gained a practical idea of civilized home-life. The interest thus awakened in the welfare of the Indian race is widespread and increasing, and cannot fail to affect powerfully and beneficially the whole subject of Indian education and civilization.

The rumor which last spring prevailed to some extent, that Indian children were taken to and held at Hampton and Carlisle against the wishes of their parents, was wholly unfounded. On the contrary, Indian parents have urged upon the bureau more children than it was ready to receive, and the office has repeatedly been obliged to deny the earnest request of parents that their children might be educated in the East. If the funds at the disposal of the office justified it, the number in attendance at Carlisle and Hampton could be doubled immediately.

In June last, in fulfillment of a promise made when their children were surrendered to Lieutenant Pratt, a "school committee" of chiefs and headmen, representing nine Missouri River agencies, visited Carlisle and Hampton. They were highly pleased with the comforts their children enjoyed and the care bestowed upon them, and proud of the manifest improvement which they had made. The schools have also been visited during the year by delegations from the Lake Superior Chippewas, the Crows, the Shoshones and Bannacks of Idaho, and the Cheyennes and Arapahoes. Upon them, as upon the Sioux, the most favorable impression was made as to the advantages which the schools offered; and their interest in the education of their children, either at home or at a distance, received a powerful impulse, which will be productive of good to their respective tribes.

Of the eighteen Florida prisoners, with whom the experiment at Hampton was first inaugurated, thirteen have returned to their homes in the Indian Territory, partly to make room for younger pupils and partly because they had become sufficiently advanced to render valuable service at their respective agencies. Of these, eleven were transferred from Hampton to Carlisle, where they remained for a time to form a nucleus for the new school, and where, Lieutenant Pratt reports, they rendered him most valuable assistance in the care and management of the new scholars who came directly from the camps.

Some sickness and several deaths have occurred among the pupils at Carlisle and Hampton. When the first company of scholars was selected for the latter school, it was impossible to secure as thorough an examination of the children and to insist as strenuously upon the requirement of perfect health as was desirable, and in almost every instance the deaths have resulted from diseases contracted before the pupils left their homes. The most careful physical examination is now made of every applicant for admission to the Hampton and Carlisle schools, and only those who are certified to by a physician as being absolutely healthy are accepted.

During the year thirty-six children have been selected from the tribe of Eastern Cherokees and placed in boarding schools in North Carolina—twelve girls at Asheville, and twelve boys each at Weaversville and Trinity College. They are to receive training in industrial pursuits, as well as in the school-room, and it is hoped that they will thus become fitted to elevate their own people and lead them in the right direction.

But the number who can be educated in Eastern schools is and always must be a small fraction of the Indian youth who are entitled to receive an education at the hands of the government, and the necessity for agency schools is not done away with, but increases yearly. The expense of educating Indians away from their homes will preclude the possibility of more than a limited number ever receiving the advantages which those schools afford. The largest results for the expenditure made will, therefore, be obtained by selecting from the agency schools the best material to be found therein; at the same time the hope of being thus chosen to receive such special training, as a recognition of merit, will operate upon the pupils attending agency schools as a powerful stimulus to earnest and persistent study and work.

INDIAN POLICE

The practicability of employing an Indian police to maintain order upon an Indian reservation is no longer a matter of question. In less than three years the system has been put in operation at 40 agencies, and the total force now numbers 162 officers and 653 privates. Special reports as to the character and efficiency of the services rendered by the police have recently been called for from its agents by this bureau, and those reports bear uniform testimony to the value and reliability of the police service, and to the fact that its maintenance, which was at first undertaken as an experiment, is now looked upon as a necessity.

The duties performed by the police are as varied as they are important.

In the Indian Territory they have done effective work in arresting or turning back unauthorized intruders, in removing squatters' stakes, and in driving out cattle, horse, and timber thieves, and other outlaws who infest the country. One of the Osage policemen lost his life at the hands of a supposed horse thief whom he had arrested and was bringing into the agency. Another horse thief, however, was successfully captured and was turned over to the State authorities of Kansas for punishment. In Dakota, surveying parties have required no other escort than that furnished by detachments of police from the different agencies. In Arizona, the San Carlos police for six years past have rendered invaluable service as scouts; and, in general, at all agencies Indian policemen act as guards at annuity payments; render assistance and preserve order during ration issues; protect agency buildings and property; return truant pupils to school; search for and return lost or stolen property, whether belonging to Indians or white men; prevent depredations on timber, and the introduction of whisky on the reservation; bring whisky sellers to trial; make arrests for disorderly conduct, drunkenness, wife-beating, theft, and other offenses; serve as couriers and messengers; keep the agent informed as to births and deaths in the tribe, and notify him promptly as to the coming on the reserve of any strangers, white or Indian. Vigilant and observant by nature, and familiar with every foot-path on the reservation, no arrivals or departures, or clandestine councils can escape their notice, and with a well disciplined police-force an agent can keep himself informed as to every noteworthy occurrence taking place within the entire limit of his jurisdiction.

Violations of the laws and regulations governing Indian reservations are punished by fine or imprisonment.

The diminished influence of squaw men, the curtailment of prerogatives formerly claimed by tribal chiefs, and the development of self-respecting manhood in the police themselves, are among the incidental benefits to the service arising from the police system. It brings into an agency a new element—a party which grasps the idea of the supremacy of law, and which by precept and example inculcates that idea in the minds of others of the tribe. The lessons of self-control, of respect for the rights of others in person and property, of the maintenance of social order by law administered by the community instead of revenge obtained by the individual, when once learned, mark an important advance in the scale of civilization, and rudimentary lessons of this sort are daily taught by the Indian police system, which calls upon one Indian to arrest and pronounce deliberate judgment upon another for offenses, many of which hitherto have not only gone unpunished, but have been unrecognized as meriting punishment.

It is necessary to again call attention to the chief obstacle in the way of perfecting the system, viz, the inadequate pay allowed members of the police force. At two agencies during the year the force has been disbanded, after a successful trial, because suitable men could not be found who would serve longer for the $8 and $5 per month which is the limit of salary fixed by law for officers and privates respectively. The very best men in the tribe should be enlisted in this service; but they cannot be expected to enter it at personal sacrifice. Among the wild tribes there is as yet but little difficulty on this score, through the difference between the wages of Indian policemen and those of Indian scouts, and the earnings of teamsters and laborers, gives just cause for dissatisfaction. But among the more civilized tribes a progressive Indian farmer, mechanic, or teamster can ill afford to relinquish the comfortable living and the opportunity to accumulate property which his own industry brings to him, for the bare support which is offered in return for his responsible and often arduous and unpopular services as policeman.

I must, therefore, renew the recommendations made in previous reports, that Congress be requested to allow the department discretionary power as to salaries to be paid the police at different agencies. The efficiency of the service would thereby be materially increased, even though no increase were made in the amount appropriated. The good already accomplished by the police, even with imperfect organization and inadequate pay, should be all the argument necessary to insure such legislation as will enable the office to establish it at every agency on a permanent basis.

The practical workings of the system are clearly set forth in the following extract from a report of Agent McGillycuddy, of the Pine Ridge Agency, Dakota:

> On assuming charge of the agency in March, 1879, I found that no force had been organized, the failure to do so being out of deference to the feelings of Chief Red Cloud and some of his coadjutors, both red and white. After several months of the most emphatic refusal on the part of the chiefs to allow the enlisting of their young men, and varied opposition on the part of half-breeds and "squaw-men," I succeeded in organizing the force in the month of August. The "squaw-men" have in the past exercised a very powerful control over the Sioux Indians, and it can therefore be easily understood why they so strongly opposed the introduction of the Indian police system, as it placed in the hands of the government a detective and controlling agency that can easily thwart them in any plans they may form. The chiefs' opposition was partly from the instructions of these "squaw-men;" also because they naturally dislike any innovation, and because it put a power in the hands of the government and agent, independent of themselves, and over which they could not exercise the slightest control.
>
> The Indian police force at this agency consists of fifty members, all Indians: one captain, two lieutenants, ten sergeants and corporals, and the balance privates. The force is in charge of one of the white employés, who also acts as deputy United States marshal. There is also attached to the force one special detective and one special interpreter. The members are all armed with the Springfield and Sharp's Army carbine, kindly loaned the agency by General Sheridan, U.S.A.
>
> The discipline of the force is excellent, failure to obey an order being followed by immediate dismissal. It is made up of the best young men of the tribe, many of them being members of the native soldier organization. There are also enlisted two chiefs, White Bird and Little Big Man, the latter being a Northern Indian, and having taken a prominent part with Sitting Bull in the Big Horn campaign of 1878, afterwards surrendering at the agency with Crazy

Horse. A member of the force is on duty all night at the guard-house, making the rounds of the government buildings at intervals of fifteen or thirty minutes, which precludes the possibility of government supplies being surreptitiously made way with.

The police force have rendered varied and very valuable and important service during the past year. Over thirty white men have been arrested by them; some renegades from justice from other States and Territories, and who have been turned over to the proper officials on their arrival for them; some for stealing Indian horses, introducing liquors on the reservation, trading for annuity-goods, larceny, &c., crimes against the United States statutes, and who after a hearing before Chief Clerk Alder, who is a United States commissioner, have been committed, and have answered for their offenses before the United States court at Deadwood, Dak. Still others have been arrested for intoxication and minor offenses, infractions of agency regulations, and having been convicted before an improvised police court, have been fined or imprisoned temporaily in the agency guard-house.

In addition the police have rendered valuable general service in caring for government property, Indian stock, preventing introduction of liquor, &c., and arresting returning "Sitting Bull" Indians, and preventing the departure north of ambitious young bucks from the agency, should they feel so inclined.

Situated as the agency is, in close proximity to the ever-increasing white settlements, it would be impracticable and almost impossible to conduct this agency without this organization. It represents law and order, and the members, uniformed and disciplined, and far advanced in civilization, offer the best and most practical example for the other Indians of the tribe to copy after, which they are rapidly doing in the way of adopting civilized clothing, &c.

In closing, I would request that, in consideration of the valuable services rendered by members of the police, they having aided the government and white men, as against their own people, an effort be made to induce Congress to allow something more than the somewhat ridiculous compensation of $5 per month for service. These men have been led to expect more, and it should be given them, for if ever laborers were worthy of their hire, these certainly are.

TRANSPORTATION BY INDIANS

The experiment of intrusting wild Indians with the transportation of their own supplies and annuity-goods from the railroad terminus to the agency was undertaken first at the Cheyenne and Arapaho Agency in the summer and fall of 1877. Wagons and harness were supplied by the government, and ponies were furnished by the Indians. For the whole distance, 165 miles, they were paid $1.50 per 100 pounds, in cash, or were credited at the rate of $1.75 per 100 pounds on the purchase of the wagons, harness, &c., which they had undertaken to earn. In this way 105 wagons have become the property of the Cheyennes and Arapahoes. Three hundred thousand pounds were transported the first year, five hundred thousand the second, and during the past year over one million pounds of supplies have been hauled by their teams. During the present year the flour and corn, which last season was delivered at the agency by the contractor, will also be taken by the Indians from the railroad, and will add nearly a million more pounds to the quantity to be freighted by them, thus enabling the agent to give employment to others of the tribe who are now eager to engage in the enterprise.

In the fall of 1875 substantially the same plan was carried out at the Kiowa and Comanche agency, in the Indian Territory, and the Sioux Agencies at Pine Ridge and Rosebud, and with the same success. During the past year not less than eight million pounds of supplies were hauled by the Indians of the four agencies above named, over distances of 165, 160, 200, and 92 miles respectively, and in compensation therefor they have received the sum of $115,900. So popular has this branch of industry become that the demands of these Indians for freighting are largely in excess of the quantity of government freight required to be transported, and the letting of a transportation contract for Indian goods to a white man would be deemed an infringement on their rights and privileges.

At the Devil's Lake, Sisseton, Fort Hall, Osage, Kaw, Pawnee, Ponca, Oakland, Sac and Fox, Pottawatomie, White Earth, Great Nemaha, Western Shoshone, Grand Ronde, Siletz, Warm Springs, Green Bay, and Shoshone Agencies, freighting is monopolized by Indian teamsters. Even the Utes have fallen into line, and will this fall undertake to transport the goods and supplies purchased for the Uintah Valley Agency.

By this method not only is the amount paid them for transportation so much really saved to the Indians themselves, but the difference between the rates paid Indians and those charged by white transportation contractors results in an actual annual saving to the government of several thousand dollars. Skill and care in the management of their teams, dispatch in the handling and for warding of the freight, and absolute *honesty* and *trustworthiness* in the care of the goods *in transitu,* have characterized the Indian transportation service. Not a package has been lost; not a case or bale broken open or tampered with. The success of the enterprise has made it a permanent feature in the policy of Indian civilization.

Wagons for Farming and Freighting

Up to a very recent period, but few wagons were furnished for the Indian service, and then generally only for the use of the agents and their employés at the headquarters of the agencies, to enable them to perform the necessary work of hauling fuel for agency buildings and fodder for the government stock. Within the past five years it has been found advisable to furnish the Indians with wagons for farming purposes, and for freighting their own supplies, which latter pursuit, as has already been shown, has become one of considerable magnitude.

The following statement of the number of wagons provided for the purposes above stated, since the 1st of July, 1879, will indicate more clearly than it could be done in any other manner the growing interest of the Indians in the cultivation of the soil, and the transportation of their subsistence supplies, goods, &c.:—For the Blackfeet Agency, 15; Cheyenne and Arapaho, 57; Cheyenne River, 67; Crow, 14; Crow Creek, 38; Devil's Lake, 36; Flandreau, 30; Fort Berthold, 35; Fort Belknap, 14; Fort Hall, 10; Fort Peck, 10; Green Bay, 43; Great Nemaha, 2; Kiowa, Comanche, and Wichita, 27; Klamath, 18; Lenhi, 19; La Pointe, 52; Leech Lake, 15; Los Pinos, 2; Lower Brulé, 44; Mackinac, 25; Malheur, 4; Moquis Pueblo, 2; Navajo, 11; Nevada, 25; Omaha, 50; Osage, 95; Pawnee, 68; Pine Ridge, 51; Ponca, 42; Pottawatomie, 10; Quapaw, 12; Rosebud, 50; Sac and Fox, 4; Santee, 105; Shoshone and Bannack, 123; Sisseton, 135; Standing Rock, 51; Tule River, 22; Uintah, 32; Umatilla, 20; White Earth, 38; Winnebago, 10; Warm Springs, 5; Yakama, 10; and Yankton, 7—a total of 1,555 wagons. Harness was also furnished with the wagons—a double set with each one required for farming, and two sets for each one to be used in freighting.

Nearly three thousand wagons, with the necessary harness therefor, have been furnished the Indians since 1875, and the flattering prospects of the future, evidenced by the manifest interest of the Indians in farming pursuits, make it almost certain that still larger quantities will be needed by them in the next two years.

STOCK CATTLE

The experiment inaugurated a few years since of furnishing Indians with stock cattle has been so fully developed that the question of their ability and willingness to properly care for and protect the same, when issued to them, is no longer an unsolved problem. The reports from all agencies where issues of stock cattle have been made attest the faithfulness with which the Indians have guarded their trust, and demonstrate the wisdom of the project of instructing Indians in pastoral pursuits, for which a large majority of them are eminently fitted.

Since the 1st of July, 1879, stock cattle have been issued as follows, viz: To the Indians of the Blackfeet Agency, 50; Cheyenne and Arapaho, 500; Crow, 82; Crow Creek, 300; Flathead, 706; Fort Hall, 200; Kiowa, Comanche, and Wichita, 1,089; Lower Brulé, 500; Osage, 900; Pawnee, 400; Pine Ridge, 907; Ponca, 300; Rosebud, 1,000; Sac and Fox, 212; San Carlos, 1,125; Shoshone and Bannack, 765; Standing Rock, 500; White Earth, 52; Western Shoshone, 200; and Yankton, 495,—a total of 10,283 head. These, together with stock purchased by the Indians themselves, and with the "agency herds," which had been accumulated from time to time, (in some instances by the voluntary act of the Indians in accepting a smaller beef ration than they were entitled to, and in other cases by natural increase,) and which herds, with one or two exceptions, have been issued to the Indians during the past year, aggregate a total of 78,812 head of stock cattle now owned by the various Indian tribes. With these cattle as a nucleus, with judicious management and care on their part, but a few years can elapse before the Indians at many of the agencies will be the possessors of large herds of cattle, thus placing within their command the ready means of self-support, and rendering them, to a large degree, independent of the care of the government.

Applications for stock cattle have been made by Indians at agencies not already supplied, and in a few cases by Indians at agencies where only a limited number have yet been provided. They will be furnished as soon as the necessary funds for the purpose can be procured.

* * *

SAN CARLOS AGENCY

The reduction of a wild, roving, defiant, and hostile tribe to a condition of obedience to, and dependence on, the United States Government, and the organization from its own members of an Indian police force, which, for six years, has rendered remarkably efficient service, is the work which has been accomplished in the case of the San Carlos Apaches. That they are inclined to agriculture is shown by the perserving efforts made to construct irrigating ditches and raise small fields of grain, and that they are also ready to have their children educated is shown by their repeated requests that a school might be furnished them. A boarding school building is now in course of erection, for which the Indians are manufacturing the adobes, and steps have been taken to have a substantial dam built and suitable ditches laid out by a competent engineer, which will afford these Indians an opportunity to make some progress toward self-support.

They are becoming discouraged with the slight success which has followed their own undirected and unskillful attempts to open ditches; but with the help of a brush-dam, built during the year, under the supervision of Captain Chaffee, temporarily in charge as agent, they have managed to cultivate about 100 acres and to raise 4,000 bushels of wheat, corn, and barley.

In order to become owners of stock-cattle, several families allowed their beef tickets to accumulate until they were entitled to one or more cows, and in that way obtained the nucleus of a herd. This interest in stock-raising has been fostered and stimulated by the issue to them, within a year, of 1,100 head of stock-cattle, which have been highly prized and well cared for by their Indians owners, especially such as have learned to milk the cows, and are beginning to appreciate the value of milk as an article of diet.

There seems to be no foundation for the charge that the San Carlos Indians have aided or abetted Victoria in his lawless raids. On the contrary, the San Carlos Apaches suffered by the depredations of Victoria on their sheep and cattle, and by his attack on a party of Coyoteros at Eagle Creek, in which 11 Coyotero Apaches were killed. Two women were also killed by white soldiers, who mistook them for a part of Victoria's band. The readiness with which groundless rumors of depredations on the part of these

Indians can be started is shown in the following extract from the agent's report:

> On the 19th of May a report came from General Caw, an operator of the telegraph at Tres Alamos, that Indians had committed serious depredations at Bunker Hill Mining Camp; also, that reservation Indians had gone on the war path in that vicinity. The chief of scouts was sent immediately to ascertain the truth, and returned on the 23d, reporting not a word of truth to exist in the case. No Indians had been seen there for two weeks, save peaceable Indians farming at the San Pedro River—Es-kim-i-zines' and Sagul-ly's band. Two miners, in a drunken quarrel, had killed each other, and on finding the bodies it had been attributed to Indians.

The subject of a water supply, which is an all-important one throughout Arizona, becomes a grave one whenever it concerns an Indian reservation, the prevailing opinion being that Indians have no water rights which white men are bound to respect. Although the San Carlos Reserve is comparatively well supplied with streams, and although scarcely a beginning in farming has been made, the water question is already assuming serious proportions. The agent reports:

> The water in Gila is being rapidly depleted by large quantities being taken out by ditches in the vicinity of Pueblo Viejo, twenty miles above Camp Thomas, and a fifteen-foot ditch now being dug by the Mormons in that vicinity will, in low-water, seriously damage the water privileges on this reservation. If there is any law in regard to this it should be enforced, so that the Indians can be protected in their water rights, a matter of vital importance to their advancement and civilization, as work and education are the foundations for their moral elevation.

Unless obstructions of this character are placed in the way, there is no doubt that the "intractable Apache" can, in a few years, be taught to raise the greater part of his own subsistence, provided he is given a reasonable amount of assistance and instruction, instead of being left to become disheartened by failures resulting from his own ignorance.

MISSION INDIANS

The condition of the Mission Indians of California becomes, yearly, more deplorable. These Indians are composed of the following tribes, viz: Seranos, Digenes, San Luis Rey, Coahuillas, and Owangos. They are estimated to number about 3,000, and their settlements are scattered over portions of San Bernardino and San Diego Counties, and chiefly in the mountain and desert districts embraced in a range hundreds of miles in extent.

In the last annual report of this office these Indians were made the subject of special mention. Attention was drawn to the fact that many of

them were occupying, by sufferance, lands which their ancestors had cultivated from time immemorial, and to which they supposed they had an
indisputable right; but that such lands had been found to be within the
limits of private land claims confirmed by the courts to grantees under the
Mexican Government, before the acquisition of California by the United
States; and that the owners thereof were threatening the Indians with
summary ejectment.

Legislation, to provide them with suitable and permanent homes, was
urgently recommended, but beyond the introduction by Representative
Page, of California, of a bill (H. R. 3728, 46th Congress, 2d session),
appropriating the sum of $100,000 for the purchase of San Ysabel Rancho,
in San Diego County, which, it may be remarked, is wholly unfitted for the
purposes of a reservation, no action was taken in Congress.

By executive order, dated the 17th of January last, a prior executive
order, dated December 27, 1875, was canceled (so far as it related to the
Aqua Caliente Reservation and a portion of the Santa Ysabel Reservation)
as being in conflict with certain prior land grants, severally known as the
"San Jose del Valle" and "Valle de San Jose." Referring to this order, Agent
Lawson, in his report for the current year, says:

> In conversation a few days ago with the present owner of the rancho (San
> Jose del Valle), he informed me he was about to sell it, and before he could
> give possession the Indians must be removed. What these people will do in
> this event, or where they can be placed, so as to find subsistence in this sterile
> region of country, are questions that I am not able to answer. This is the
> situation of an equally large body of Indians now occupying the Rancho San
> Jacinto, their ejectment being liable to occur at any time. This, in short, is
> the situation all around; and there being no unoccupied public lands, except
> such as are uninhabitable, the only alternative left to these hitherto peaceable
> and thrifty communities is to wander about singly or by families to swell the
> vagabond class that already infests the villages and towns, to become a prey to
> vices to which, as yet, they are comparative strangers.

The agent also reports that about fifteen families under similar circumstances were a few months ago forced to remove from the Cucco Ranch, in
San Diego County.

In the season of 1879 the supply of water for irrigating purposes on the
desert, some 50 to 80 miles distant from the agency, where hundreds of these
Indians live, entirely failed, and they were compelled to depend for subsistence upon a wild bean which grows in the desert. Never having received
any aid from government, and being accustomed to the miserable destitution enforced by their helplessness, they endured hunger and want without
seeking or expecting aid. Then, for the first time in their history, their
agent, learning of their condition, applied for assistance, and the department promptly responded by ordering a sum of $500 to be expended in
supplies to relieve their wants.

The Mission Indians as a class are reported to be industrious, sustaining themselves by cultivating their little fields or in laboring for ranchmen in the vicinity of their villages. During the sheep-shearing season their services are greatly in demand, as they are especially skilled in this kind of labor. In the interest of common humanity something should be done for this uncomplaining people towards providing them with a home. They do not ask for supplies. All they ask for is a reservation upon which they can earn a subsistence for themselves and families.

Their educational and religious interests have hitherto been entirely unprovided for. Recently the department has authorized the building of two school-houses in two of the larger settlements. But little, however, can be effected in this direction until the tribe is consolidated upon suitable lands and brought under the controlling influence of the agent, and to this end I earnestly recommend the passage of appropriate legislation in their behalf.

UTES

In the last annual report of this office it was recommended that legislative authority be invoked for the appointment of a commission who should visit the Utes and obtain their consent to remove from the State of Colorado to some other location, on condition of their receiving pay for the value of their lands in Colorado. Subsequent to the date of that report a delegation of the Utes, composed of chiefs and principal men from the bands located on the White River, Los Pinos, and Southern Ute Reservation, visited Washington to confer as to the best course to be pursued in regard to a settlement of their affairs.

The result of the negotiations was the agreement dated March 6 and the act of Congress approved June 15 last, which will be found on page 315 of this report. Under the second section of this act, the President appointed Hon. George W. Manypenny, Alfred B. Meacham, John B. Bowman, John J. Russell, and Otto Mears commissioners to secure the ratification of the agreement and to execute the provisions of the same.

The period within which the agreement was to be ratified by three-fourths of the adult male Indians of the Ute tribe was limited in the act to four months from the date of its approval, or until October 15, 1880. The requisite number of Indians signed the agreement between the 29th of July and 11th of September, both days inclusive. The ratification of the agreement by the Utes was certified to the Secretary of the Treasury by the Secretary of the Interior on the 24th of September last, and steps were immediately taken to cause the money appropriated under the 4th clause of section 9 of the act, to be paid to the Indians.

Under the provisions of the first clause of the above-named agreement, no payment will be made to the White River Utes until the surrender or apprehension of those members of their nation, not yet in the custody of the United States, who were implicated in the murder of Agent Meeker, and the murder of, and outrages upon, the employés of the White River Agency, on the 29th of September, 1879; or until the President shall be satisfied that the guilty parties are no longer living, or have fled beyond the limits of the United States.

A portion of the surveys contemplated by the act and necessary for the location of the Indians has been made, but, in consequence of the delay in the passage of the bill and the consequent lateness of the season when the agreement was ratified, comparatively little could be done towards locating the Utes in the localities designated for them, and operations in this direction have been suspended until next spring.

The killing of the son of Chief Shavanaux

Just before the Ute commission had suspended its work, the Indians of the Los Pinos Agency were thrown into a feverish state of excitement by the murder, by a white freighter, of Johnson, son of the Chief Shavanaux. The difficulty occurred on the evening of the 29th of September last, at what is known as Cline's Ranch, about thirty miles distant from the agency, on the Cimmaron. Early the next morning some thirty Indians, headed by Chief Shavanaux, and all well armed, came to the agency, and made known their errand. They were very much excited, and fully determined upon revenge. The agent, after much effort, succeeded in quieting them, and taking with him a military officer and a file of fifteen soldiers, furnished by the commandant of the post at the agency, proceeded with them to the scene of the outrage for the purpose of arresting the murderer. On arriving at the ranch he found that the criminal had been arrested, and was in charge of a number of citizens of Colorado. After due consideration, it was deemed best to place the prisoner in charge of three well-known Colorado citizens, in whose custody the agent found him, to be taken by them to Gunnison City (the nearest court having jurisdiction of the crime), and there turned over to the proper law officers of the State. The Indians and all others seemed apparently well satisfied with this arrangement, and the agent advised the Indians to return to their homes, whereupon, as was supposed, they all left, taking the trail across the mountains leading to the agency. The agent, the military, Colonel Meacham, and others left for their respective stations soon after.

The Indians, however, instigated by certain lawless white men, returned to the ranch the next morning, accompanied by these white outlaws, and finding that the citizens had left with their prisoner for Gunnison, went in pursuit, overtook and overpowered them, took possession of the prisoner, and in all probability speedily killed him.

A warrant was soon after issued by a justice of the peace at Gunnison for the arrest of Agent Berry on a charge of murder, but, not deeming it safe to submit to such a proceeding, and believing that the clamor raised in that vicinity would result in an application of lynch law to himself and others, he kept himself aloof from the jurisdiction of said justice and other State officers until due process was issued by a higher tribunal, when he voluntarily gave himself up to the custody of the United States marshal, and was taken by him to Denver, where he awaits his trial on a charge which, it is believed, has no foundation in fact. The statement made by the agent is fully sustained by Maj. R. H. Offley, the military officer who had charge of the troops and accompanied him to Cline's Ranch. In his report of the matter to the War Department he says: "The Indians seemed to be acting with the utmost forbearance and calmness, desiring nothing but the punishment of the individual who had committed the outrage upon them. . . . . The man who shot and killed the Indian was a stranger in this part of the country, and this was his first trip over the road, and it was stated by parties who saw the men connected with this train that they were under the influence of liquor."

It seems that the Indians applied to the freighters for food, and from their own statements and the evidence of others they were somewhat roughly repulsed. Major Offley says that the testimony of the Indians themselves seems to be straightforward and trustworthy; that they disclaim firing upon the white men or quarreling with them; that they were mounted, and when food was denied them turned their horses to leave, and that Johnson was shot "and fell dead from his horse after going about a hundred feet." That officer adds: "With the light before me I cannot look upon this matter otherwise than as a wanton and unprovoked murder of the Indian by a reckless, half-drunken teamster, and that the fate of the murderer was a clear case of lynching, which, as much as it is to be deplored, is not an uncommon occurrence throughout the country in the midst of civilization and enlightenment." In regard to the recapture and lynching of the prisoner, Major Offley says that white men were with the Indians when they committed the offense, and that "they encouraged and assisted them to lynch him." In regard to the freighter, he also makes the following statement:

> The man Jackson, who was in charge of the train, has told different stories about the affair; he told me that the Indians did not fire at his party; to others he has said they shot twice. He has claimed relationship of nearly every kind to the man who was killed; he told me he was one of his men or boys. He has also said that the party who had charge of the prisoner followed the cavalry to near the Blue; the cavalry did not get to Cline's until the evening of October 1; the prisoner was taken about 11 o'clock in the morning of that day; he also states that Cline [one of the citizens who started with the prisoner to Gunnison] was home in about an hour after starting, whereas he did not get back until next day. The Indian, Johnson, has been employed by Col. Mackenzie during the summer, and was considered a quiet and peaceable man.

THE SIOUX

Among the 32,286 Sioux who are gathered at 11 agencies—9 in Dakota, 1 in Montana, and 1 in Nebraska—peace and good order have prevailed throughout the year. At Santee, Sisseton, and Devil's Lake Agencies self-support is nearly reached, the proportion of the subsistence for those Indians which is derived from the issue of government rations being 35, 20, and 25 per cent., respectively. They are located in severalty, live in houses, wear citizen's dress, send their children to school, own farming implements and stock, and their crops during the past year will average ten bushels of wheat, five bushels of corn, and sixteen bushels of vegetables to each member of the tribe. With such crops, which would furnish ample support for a white man, even a partial issue of rations would seem to be unnecessary, but allowance must be made for Indian appetite and Indian improvidence, and also for what the Indians would consider unjust discrimination on the part of the government, should their Great Father, while issuing rations to his wild and indolent children, entirely withhold them from those who are industriously endeavoring, in every way, to comply with his wishes. Moreover, their surplus crops are largely invested in the purchase of farming implements, cattle, and other appliances of civilized life which directly advance their own civilization, and which would otherwise have to be furnished by the government.

About three-fourths of the Sioux of the Yankton Agency have made equal progress in adopting the customs of civilized life.

At Cheyenne River, Crow Creek, Standing Rock, and Lower Brulé Agencies progress was seriously retarded by the Sioux war, three years ago; but the erection of 718 houses, the selection of individual farms, the breaking of nearly 600 acres (in addition to 1,800 acres previously under cultivation) and the raising of 41,000 bushels of wheat and corn, and 12,000 bushels of vegetables by these Indians during the past year, shows them to be again under the influence of the advance movement which prevails throughout the entire Sioux nation. They remain quietly at their agencies and depend for subsistence, principally, on the issue of government rations. At the Lower Brulé Agency a boarding-school building is in course of erection, and at the others three good boarding and four day schools have been attended by 300 pupils.

The 4,713 Yanktonnais Sioux at Fort Peck, with the 1,116 of the Northern Sioux who have deserted Sitting Bull's camp, and, after surrendering arms and ponies, have attached themselves to the Fort Peck Agency, are the only Sioux who now engage in hunting to any extent.

Report of Commissioner
of Indian Affairs Hiram Price
October 24, 1881

(Excerpt from *Report for 1881*, pp. 1-7, 13-19)

Commissioner Price's report emphasized two themes: the necessity to break up Indian tribal relations and the need to force the Indian to labor for himself. One reads incredulously Price's assertion that "the desire to take lands in severalty is almost universal among the Indians." No better illustration of the adage that the wish is the father of the thought can be found. Price's aversion to feeding and clothing the Indian was patent. It was for the Indian's own good, he asserted, that he be taught to labor for his own support. The commissioner's comments on the Indian police as a power independent of the chiefs, and one that "weakens, and will finally destroy the power of tribes and bands," reveal one of the underlying reasons why Indian police, once established, were so thoroughly supported by the white authorities.

I HAVE THE HONOR to submit herewith the annual report of the Indian Bureau for the year 1881.

In the outset, I desire to urge with earnestness the absolute necessity for a thorough and radical change of the Indian policy in some respects, and in so doing I shall touch upon points which will be referred to more at length hereafter under special headings.

It is claimed and admitted by all that the great object of the government is to civilize the Indians and render them such assistance in kind and degree as will make them self-supporting, and yet I think no one will deny that one part of our policy is calculated to produce the very opposite result. It must be apparent to the most casual observer that the system of gathering the Indians in bands or tribes on reservations and carrying to them victuals and clothes, thus relieving them of the necessity of labor, never will and never can civilize them. Labor is an essential element in producing civilization. If white men were treated as we treat the Indians the result would certainly be a race of worthless vagabonds. The greatest kindness the government can bestow upon the Indian is to teach him to labor for his own support, thus developing his true manhood, and, as a consequence, making him self-relying and self-supporting.

We are expending annually over one million dollars in feeding and clothing Indians where no treaty obligation exists for so doing. This is simply a gratuity, and it is presumed no one will question the expediency or the right of the government, if it bestows gratuities upon Indians, to make labor of some useful sort a condition precedent to such gift, especially when all of the products of such labor go to the Indian. To domesticate and civilize wild Indians is a noble work, the accomplishment of which should be a crown of glory to any nation. But to allow them to drag along year after year, and generation after generation, in their old superstitions, laziness, and filth, when we have the power to elevate them in the scale of humanity, would be a lasting disgrace to our government. The past experience of this government with its Indians has clearly established some points which ought to be useful as guides in the future.

There is no one who has been a close observer of Indian history and the effect of contact of Indians with civilization, who is not well satisfied that one of two things must eventually take place, to wit, either civilization or extermination of the Indian. Savage and civilized life cannot live and prosper on the same ground. One of the two must die. If the Indians are to be civilized and become a happy and prosperous people, which is certainly the object and intention of our government, they must learn our language and adopt our modes of life. We are fifty millions of people, and they are only one-fourth of one million. The few must yield to the many. We cannot reasonably expect them to abandon their habits of life and modes of living, and adopt ours, with any hope of speedy success as long as we feed and clothe them without any effort on their part.

In this connection I wish to call attention to the fact that in almost every case it is only the non-laboring tribes that go upon the war-path, and the stubborn facts of history compel me to say that the government is largely to blame for this.

The peaceable and industrious Indian has had less consideration than the turbulent and vicious. One instance in proof of this can be found at this moment in the case of the White River Utes (the murderers of Meeker) and the Utes on the Uintah Reservation. The White River Utes have just been moved to the Uintah Reservation alongside of the peaceable Uintah Utes. We feed the White River murderers and compel the peaceable Uintahs to largely care for themselves. This course induces the Indians to believe that if they are to get favors from the government they must refuse to work, refuse to be orderly and peaceable, and must commit some depredations or murder, and then a commission will be appointed to treat with them, and pay them in goods, provisions, and money to behave themselves. This looks to an Indian very much like rewarding enemies and punishing friends, and gives him a singular idea of our Christian civilization and our manner of administering justice, which has so much the appearance of rewarding vice and punishing virtue.

Another cause of the unsatisfactory condition of our Indian affairs is the failure of the government to give the Indian land in severalty, and to give it to him in such a way that he will know that it is his. He has learned by painful experience that a small piece of paper called scrip is not good for much as a title to land. He has again and again earnestly solicited the government to give him a title to a piece of land, that he might make for himself a home. These requests have, in a great many instances, been neglected or refused, and this is true even in cases where, by treaty stipulations, the government agreed to give the Indian a patent for his land. Under this state of facts, it is not to be wondered at that the Indian is slow to cultivate the soil. He says, when urged to do so, that he has no heart to do it, when in a month or a year he may be moved, and some white man be allowed to enjoy the fruit of his labor. That is the way the Indian talks, and that is the way a white man would talk under similar circumstances.

Another just cause of complaint which the Indians have is that in our treaties with them, in some instances, we agree to give them so many pounds of beef, flour, coffee, sugar, &c., and then a certain sum of money is appropriated for the purpose of fulfilling the promise, which sum so appropriated (as is the case the present year, because of the increased price of beef, &c.) will not buy the *pounds*; consequently, the Indians do not get what was promised them. This they construe as bad faith on the part of the government, and use it as an excuse for doing something wrong themselves; and thus troubles of a serious and extensive nature frequently arise. This would all be avoided if appropriations were sufficiently large to cover all contingencies, and such appropriations would not interfere with or violate the rules of strict economy; for any surplus (if there should be any) would be turned into the Treasury, as is always done, at the end of the fiscal year, when an unexpended balance remains of any particular appropriation. This would be keeping our contracts to the letter, and would inspire confidence and respect on the part of the Indian for our government, and give him no excuse for wrong-doing.

But I am very decidedly of opinion that ultimate and final success never can be reached without adding to all other means and appliances the location of each family, or adult Indian who has no family, on a certain number of acres of land which they may call their own and hold by a title as good and strong as a United States patent can make it. Let it be inalienable for, say, twenty years; give the Indian teams, implements, and tools amply sufficient for farming purposes; give him seed, food, and clothes for at least one year; in short, give him every facility for making a comfortable living, and then *compel* him to depend upon his own exertions for a livelihood. Let the laws that govern a white man govern the Indian. The Indian must be made to understand that if he expects to live and prosper in this country he must learn the English language, and learn to *work*. The language will enable him to transact his business understandingly with his white neighbors, and his labor will enable him to provide the necessaries and comforts of life for himself and family. The policy thus indicated will in a few years rid the government of this vexed "Indian question," making the Indian a blessing instead of a curse to himself and country, which, judging the future by the past, will never be done by the present policy.

REMOVAL OF THE MESCALERO APACHES

I wish to call attention to the fact that some Indians in Arizona and New Mexico have always been troublesome and difficult to manage. Lawless Indians, belonging to no particular reservation, and desperate white men compose bands of marauders who commit depredations and when pursued fly to the mountains of Chihuahua and Sonora. My opinion is that the most effectual remedy for all this is to remove the Mescalero Apaches, and eventually all other Indians, north of the center line of New Mexico and Arizona, so as to keep them at a distance from Chihuahua and Sonora. The removal of the Mescaleros would not seem to be difficult of accomplishment, inasmuch as a special Indian agent, who was recently dispatched to their agency for the purpose of ascertaining their views upon the subject of removal, reports them as expressing a willingness to remove to the Jicarilla Reservation on the north line of New Mexico.

For the past five years the office has been importuned to take measures for the removal of the Mescaleros from their present reservation and settle them permanently on some other reserve, where they can be more easily guarded and will be far less liable to commit depredations. The citizens of New Mexico and Texas have urged this, and the military authorities have regarded such a movement as indispensable to the protection of the citizens and the welfare and good conduct of the Indians. The county of Lincoln, in which this reservation is situated, has for a population the very worst elements that can be found in the Territory or upon the borders of Mexico—Spanish and Mexican refugees from justice, outlaws from the States, &c. In brief, as stated by Inspector Watkins, who made a thorough investigation of affairs in that section and that reservation in 1878, "the whole county of Lincoln is under the control of cut-throats and thieves." He was also of the opinion, concurred in by many others who have been personally cognizant of affairs there, that a large share of the crimes committed by this class of settlers are charged to the Indians. There is abundant evidence before the office to show that these outlaws have for years been in the habit of enticing the Indians to go out upon their raids, &c., and are the recipients of their plunder. Indians under such circumstances and with such surroundings will not progress very far in civilization. The result has been that over one-half of these Indians within the past five years have been scattered and exterminated; depredations have been committed by them, and large sums of money have been expended by the government in military operations against them.

Two inspectors and one special agent within the past six or eight months have visited this reserve, and all concur in the opinion that the Indians should be removed. The reservation is not adapted to agricultural purposes. It is overrun with prospectors for mining purposes, &c., and numerous claims have been taken, many of them antedating the establishment of the reservation, and it will be impossible to remove the claimants without much litigation and large expenditure of money for their improvements.

To guard these 400 Indians and prevent them from going into Southern New Mexico, Texas, and Old Mexico three companies of cavalry and one of infantry are stationed some 40 miles north of the agency, at Fort Stanton, where large expenditures have been made for barracks, buildings, &c. If the Indians are removed these troops will not be needed there, and thus a large amount of money would be saved to the government annually. Because of the contemplated removal no improvements have been made upon the reservation to any extent for some time; but if the Indians remain there for any considerable time longer, buildings will have to be erected at an expense of $3,000 to $4,000 (the agent estimates their cost at $6,000) which must ultimately be abandoned, for no one believes that this reservation can be a permanent home for these Indians. If removed to the Jicarilla Reservation, one agent can take charge of the two bands, Mescaleros and Jicarillas (the former affiliate well with most of the latter and have intermarried), and the cost of removal will be less than the proposed expenditure for buildings and for troops to guard the Indians where they are.

The agent of the Mescaleros and our special agent advised the office, when the removal to the Jicarilla Reservation was first contemplated, that the military at Fort Stanton and certain persons who have large contracts with that branch of the service would prevent such removal if possible; and, as predicted, these influences are now busily at work to prolong the disastrous state of affairs which for the past ten years have existed in Southern New Mexico, to continue the large expenditures resulting therefrom, and to prevent the government from settling the question now and permanently.

The Indian problem is at best difficult of solution; but by removing the Indians from unfavorable surroundings and bad men, as far as possible, a long step will have been taken in the direction of success.

INDIAN DISTURBANCES IN NEW MEXICO AND ARIZONA

In this connection I wish to call attention briefly to recent Indian disturbances in New Mexico and Arizona, which are the only Indian disturbances of any magnitude that have occurred during the year and which have been greatly exaggerated in the accounts published in the newspapers.

For a few months after the destruction of Victoria and his band in Old Mexico, in October, 1880, Indian raids in New Mexico ceased; but last summer depredations and murders again began, chiefly in Socorro County, which were charged to the "remnant of Victoria's band." It was known that a portion of that band, by their temporary absence from the main body at the time of the fight with Victoria, saved themselves from destruction or capture. This "remnant," under Chief Nana, naturally became a nucleus for renegade Indians in that part of the country, and their number, which General Terrasas reported as 30, has been reported this last summer as about seventy. They have been again followed up by troops and chased toward Sonora.

The following extract from report of Agent Llewellyn, dated July 28, 1881, would show that the return of these Indians to a marauding life was not wholly without excuse:

> As to who these Indians are, I can assure the Department that they are not from this agency, at least have not been here for over one year; it is certain, however, that they belong here, and had it not been for the San Carlos scouts and the soldiers, they would have come into the agency at least two weeks ago.
>
> It seems that some few months since a Lieutenant of the United States Army, then stationed here, gave a written permit to three Indians at this agency to go to Old Mexico and bring back here a party of their friends whom they claimed had left at the time of the Victoria troubles. This party were due here three weeks ago, and at that time attempted to come in, but were chased and driven into the mountains thirty miles from the agency to the south. Since that time they have made, according to the statement of one of the packers for the scouts, who is now at this agency badly wounded, three ineffectual efforts to get into the agency, being prevented each time by the scouts and soldiers; finding that they could not return to the agency, as they had been led to believe they could, they commenced to go on the war-path. I learn on good authority that there are about seventy Indians in this party.

In June and July reports that these "hostiles" were being driven by General Hatch towards Arizona caused some anxiety on the part of the San Carlos agent and the military in the vicinity of that reservation, lest the hostiles might cause disaffection among a few of the Indians there who were related to the renegades, and various precautions were taken and preparations made to resist any attack. These fears, however, were not realized, and, reports to the contrary notwithstanding, the San Carlos Indians seem to have had no part whatever in the Indian raids in New Mexico; on the contrary, at different times they have had no small share in the scouting carried on against them.

In 1875 the Camp Apache Agency, located in the northern part of the San Carlos reserve, was abolished, and the White Mountain Apaches belonging thereto, about 1,800 in number, were turned over to the San Carlos agent. Most of them were removed to the southern part of the reserve and located on the Gila (where a sub-agency was established), and regularly rationed; but some, preferring to take the chance of self-support on their old hunting grounds, remained behind, and were gradually rejoined by others until they numbered between 600 and 700, whose headquarters were on Cibicu Creek, in the northwestern part of the reserve, about 40 miles from the agency and 30 from Camp Apache. In June last, considerable excitement was occasioned among these Indians by the proposition of a medicine-man named Nock a de klenny, at the expense of large gifts of horses, blankets, &c., to bring to life again some chiefs who had died a few months previous. The agent remonstrated with the Indians on the ground of the folly of the thing and the waste of their goods, but they decided to wait till the time specified, and in case the "resurrection" failed, to demand the restoration of their property. Whether he desired only to appease the Indians for his failure, or whether he intended to bring about a revolt, cannot be known; but when Nock a de klenny announced that the spirits had notified him that the dead warriors could not return to the country until the whites had left it, and fixed the date of their leaving at the time of the corn harvest, it was feared both by the agent and the military authorities at Camp Apache that the medicine man was working upon the superstitions of the Indians to bring about an outbreak, or would bring them into such a condition that they could easily be induced to join in any demonstration made by hostiles from New Mexico.

It was accordingly decided that the military should arrest the man at a "medicine-dance" which he proposed to hold at Camp Apache on August 20th. The dance having failed to come off, Colonel Carr, commanding post, sent a messenger to tell Nock a de klenny that he wanted to see him on the following Sunday. Only an evasive reply being received, he started on Monday, August 29th, with 6 officers, 79 soldiers, and 23 Indian scouts for the Indian village, reached there the following day, and arrested Nock a de klenny, who surrendered quietly, professing no desire or intention of attempting escape. But as the troops were making camp for the night, their own Indian scouts and many other Indians opened fire on them. A sharp fight ensued, the medicine-man killed, the Indians repulsed, and the command reached the post the next day, to be again attacked by the Indians, who had already killed eight men on the road to Camp Thomas and run off some stock. The loss in the two fights was 11 killed and 3 wounded. The mutinous scouts were themselves White Mountain Apaches, and though a few of them are exonerated from complicity in the treachery, it is believed that most of them left the post with no intention of aiding in the arrest of the medicine man.

Re-enforcements were sent to Camp Apache and troops were stationed at the agency, and preparations made for an attack at either point. The White Mountain Indians, however, were not long in discovering the folly of their action, and came into the agency and sub agency in small parties, where they were required to surrender to military officers unconditionally, except that they asked and were promised a fair trial for their individual crimes. Six days' notice was given throughout the reserve that a "peace line" would be declared on the reserve September 21st, outside of whose limits all Indians found would be considered hostile, with the exception of Pedro's band near Camp Apache. On the 20th of September the five chiefs who had been leaders in the affair surrendered, and during the ensuing week 60 of their principal men followed their example. Several of the mutinous scouts had been arrested and brought in by the agency Indian police force and delivered up to the military, and by the close of the month nearly all were in or accounted for, and little remained to be done but to proceed with the trials.

It appears, however, that chiefs George and Bonito, who had come in to the subagency, and had gone with Issue Clerk Hoag to Camp Thomas, and there surrendered to Gen. Wilcox, September 25, had been paroled by that officer and allowed to return to the subagency. September 30, Colonel Biddle, with some troops, was sent to the subagency to take them and their bands back to Thomas. Unfortunately this was issue day, and a large number of Indians were assembled. They agreed to go as soon as the issue of beef (which was then in progress) had been made, but later in the afternoon sent word that the troops need not wait for them as they would follow soon with Issue Clerk Hoag. Colonel Biddle replied that they must go at once, and started his command towards George's camp, whereupon he and Bonito fled to the Chiricahuas and so alarmed them that during the night 74 Chiricahuas, including women and children, fled from the reserve, leaving much of their stock behind. The troops followed and are reported to have overtaken and attacked them. In their flight the Indians have captured 8 teams and killed 6 teamsters. Bonito went with them. These are some of the very Indians who under chief "Juh" were induced by Captain Haskell, to come in from Old Mexico in January last. The following, from Agent Tiffany, shows that these Indians were not concerned in the White Mountain troubles, and that their flight was occasioned by fear, not hostility:

> These bands have been perfectly quiet during the whole White Mountain trouble. They have been reported out on the war-path in New Mexico and committing depredations all over the country, but every time inquiry has been made the chiefs and men have always been found in their camps, and on two occasions they were in the agency office talking to me when telegrams arrived as to their whereabouts; and on one of these occasions, R. S. Gardner, Indian inspector, was present. Ten days or thereabouts before the present outbreak they came to me to hear what was going on, and what so many troops meant about the agencies. I explained it to them and told them to have no fear, that none of the Indians who had been peaceable would be molested in any way. They said they had been out on the war-path and had come in in good faith and were contented, that they did not want war or to fight. The only place they would fight was if the White Mountains would come to the agency or subagency they would fight them there.
>
> They inquired if the movements of troops had anything to do with what they had done in Mexico. I assured them it had not. They shook hands, much delighted, and went back. Then the military move was made on the subagency to arrest Chiefs George and Bonito, of White Mountain Indians, and Issue Clerk Hoag at subagency, who has been very efficient and judicious in all this trouble, tells me that they were literally scared away by this movement of troops.

I desire to call attention to the loyalty shown by five-sixths of the Indians on the San Carlos reserve. They have rendered invaluable and hazardous service as police and scouts, in finding, arresting, and guarding the guilty ones, and as messengers for both agent and military when communication was interrupted by the cutting of the telegraph wires.

* * *

INDIAN POLICE

The organization of a United States Indian police force is no longer an experiment. The system is now in operation at forty-nine agencies; the total force employed being eighty-four commissioned officers, and seven hundred and eighty-six non-commissioned officers and privates. In answer to circular letter from this office, dated August 19, 1881, special reports have been received from nearly all agencies as to the value, reliability, and efficiency of this service. These reports are uniformly gratifying in their testimony as to the zeal, courage, and fidelity of the members of the force, and their almost invaluable service to the agents. The Indian police are fully recognized as an important agency in the civilization of their brethren.

The immediate work of this force is to preserve order, prohibit illegal traffic in liquor, and arrest offenders. In the line of these duties, they act as guards at ration issues and annuity payments; take charge of and protect, at all times, government property; restore lost or stolen property to its rightful owners; drive out timber thieves and other trespassers; return truant pupils to school; make arrests for disorderly conduct and other offenses, and especially protect the reservations from the traffic in liquor, which, in the language of one of the agents, is "the root and cause of nine-tenths of all crimes committed." These varied and important duties are performed with a fidelity and thoroughness that is fully appreciated by this office, and its agents.

The indirect results and ultimate influence of this system are even more important than its direct advantages. Well trained and disciplined, the police force is a perpetual educator. It is a power entirely independent of the chiefs. It weakens, and will finally destroy, the power of tribes and bands. It fosters a spirit of personal responsibility. It makes the Indian himself the representative of the power and majesty of the Government of the United States. These latter features constitute its main strength for permanent good. It is true that the Indians need to be taught the supremacy of law, and the necessity for strict obedience thereto; it is also true that where the Indians themselves are the recognized agents for the enforcement of law, they will the more readily learn to be obedient to its requirements.

The force is, at present, limited by law to one hundred officers and eight hundred privates. This limit should be extended so as to allow the appointment of one hundred and twenty officers and twelve hundred privates. There are requests now on file for an increase of force, at points where such increase is absolutely necessary. The requests can not be granted without violating the above law. There are also nineteen agencies without police, a majority of whom would be benefited by its introduction.

A very important matter in connection with the police service is the amount of the annual appropriation therefor. The compensation of eight dollars per month for officers, and five dollars per month for privates, is properly characterized by some of the agents as simply ridiculous. In some cases, members of the force spent fully that sum for traveling expenses in the discharge of their duties; they also furnish their own ponies and feed them. The pay of commissioned officers should be not less than fifteen dollars per month, and privates should have at least ten dollars monthly. The best men of the tribes can be had, if the compensation is commensurate with the value and importance of the work. The appropriation should be such that rations can be furnished at non-ration agencies, and that uniforms, arms, and accouterments, may be of the best quality as a matter of mere economy. A large increase in the annual appropriation is necessary to secure the best men, and to promote the highest interests of the service.

Some selections from recent reports of agents will give intelligent information as to the value, reliability, and efficiency of this service.

Agent McGillycuddy, of Pine Ridge agency, Dakota, says:

> The force, to a man, are prompt to obey orders in making an arrest. It is immaterial to them whether the offender be a white man or an Indian, a head chief or a young brave, the arrest is always made. The white men in this region recognize the fact that to resist an Indian policeman would be to resist a United States official in discharge of his duty. The Indians generally recognize the police authority, for from time immemorial there has existed among the Sioux and other tribes native soldier organizations, systematically governed by laws and regulations. Some of the strongest opposition encountered in endeavoring to organize the police force in the spring of 1879 was from these native soldier organizations, for they at once recognized something in it strongly antagonistic to their ancient customs, namely, a force at the command of the white man opposed to their own. The police were threatened in various ways, but as time passed on we secured the requisite number of members, and among them many of the *head soldiers,* so that to-day the United States Indian police have, to a great extent, supplanted the soldier bands and exercise their ancient powers.
>
> Up to the present time nothing has occurred to cause doubt as to their trustworthiness and efficiency. The Indian freighters and employés at this agency are paid in standard silver dollars to avoid disputes and trouble in cashing their checks by traders. It is expressed through from the Philadelphia mint in quantities of $10,000 to Fort Robinson, Neb., our nearest express office, sixty-three miles away. It is my custom to proceed to that point with ten of the police as an escort, receipt for the money, and *turn it over to the police;* they then transport the same to the agency, camping out *en route.* The money remains in wooden boxes in their charge until wanted, and so far this trust has not been violated, and I feel assured will not be.
>
> In former years this agency was the rendezvous and asylum for the hardest class of white men in the West, such as horse-thieves, road-agents, and escaped convicts. Safely concealed in the camps of the Indians, with whom they affiliated, they successfully defied all efforts to arrest them. Now, with a United States court commissioner and deputy United States marshal stationed at the agency, efficiently backed by the police, things have changed, and a

man—white or Indian—is guaranteed better protection for his life and property on this portion of the Sioux reserve than in any of the bordering States or Territories, as the intervening country between the villages, which are located at various distances up to forty miles from the agency, is continually patrolled by the police, so that no depredation could be committed without soon coming to their knowledge.

In this connection the question might be pertinently asked, "Why is it that the Ogalallas, a people numbering over 7,000, have just passed three of the quietest and to the government and themselves most gratifying years of their existence, and the first that they have passed without the presence of military at their agency?" For this condition of affairs much is due to the police system. The majority of the Indians appreciate the fact that, sooner or later, a regularly organized armed force has to be introduced and play a part in agency affairs. Heretofore that force has been the Army, against which it is but natural there should be a feeling of antagonism among the Indians, and the very presence of which at an agency is a constant reminder that the white man cannot and will not trust the Indian. Recognizing this fact, these Indians have chosen the lesser of (to them) two evils, the Indian police in preference to the white soldier. Here the old adage that "confidence begets confidence" comes into play. Placing, as has been done at this agency, the entire control of the people, the care of their supplies, and the enforcing of the law in their own hands, has certainly given them confidence in themselves, and put them on their good behavior.

Agent Tufts, at Union Agency, Indian Territory, says:

The police system is good, and if well paid and properly managed would be valuable to the Indian service, and the means of saving much money to the government. It would be valuable to the service at this agency, because, while there are fifteen thousand persons in this agency not amenable to the laws of these nations, there is no officer who can make an arrest without obtaining a warrant from the United States court at Fort Smith, Ark., except the Indian police. Crime in this Territory is almost always the result of whisky, and takes place at Indian gatherings. If a United States officer is present with authority to keep order, there will be little trouble. I am certainly of opinion that while it costs the Indian Department something to keep the police on duty, the government has saved much more than their cost to the Departments of War and Justice.

Agent Dyer, of Quapaw Agency, Indian Territory, says:

We now have a force of reliable and efficient men, and as proof of this I would simply call attention to the fact that the eight men in garrison at Camp Quapaw perform the same duties as did the company of troops recently removed. Upon a large reserve, they are invaluable as messengers. As an escort in making annuity payments to the tribes distant from the agency, their worth cannot be estimated except by the amount of treasure in charge. Ready for duty at any time and in any emergency, I consider it the right arm of an agent in the successful conduct of his reservation. Ever alert to the detection of the introduction of liquor, they are a factor that cannot be dispensed with.

Agent Wilbur, of Yakama Agency, Washington Territory, says:

All the members are faithful, prompt, and efficient in the discharge of their duties, though of course there are degrees of merit. Their usefulness in the detection and punishment of crime and preservation of order can hardly be overestimated. Their discipline is good; their general appearance and demeanor among the people is such as to command the respect and confidence of all. They are prompt and obedient, never hesitating to obey an order though it may involve great personal danger to themselves.

Agent Andrus, of Yankton Agency, Dakota, says:

The knowledge that there is a body of organized police upon a reservation serves as a powerful restraint upon both whites and Indians, and checks the inception as well as the commission of much crime. The police have proved prompt and efficient in the performance of the various duties assigned, steadily breaking down and overcoming the strong opposition at first manifested toward them. The chiefs have, I think, withdrawn all opposition because they perceived its futility.

These selections fairly represent the many reports received by this office from all parts of the Indian country. Originally introduced as an experiment, an organized police force has become a necessity. One of the principal duties of the Indian policemen, as specified in the law creating the force, is to prevent the introduction of liquor into these Indian communities. This duty is faithfully performed. At Navajo Agency, New Mexico, the Indians refuse to have a police force because of the small compensation offered, yet the necessity for such a force is well shown in a report from Captain Bennett, acting agent, under date of October 14, 1880. He says:

The evil that has the most damaging effect upon this people is whisky. There are several traders at many points ranging from forty to one hundred miles from the reservation where whisky of the vilest description is dealt out to these people in open violation of law, being an incentive to crime, and greatly improverishing many of them. Decisive and prompt measures should be adopted by the government to put a stop to this nefarious traffic; otherwise results of the most deplorable character may be expected. At several councils, the sensible chiefs and headmen universally deprecated this liquor traffic, and said, "We have no rivers, streams, or lakes of whisky; why does not the Great Father at Washington, who can do anything he pleases, put a stop to this trade and keep white men from bringing or selling whisky to us?" I again urge that the most decisive measures should be adopted to stop this whisky trade.

The civilization, Christianization, and general well-being of the Indian tribes depends in great measure upon the arrest and punishment of these criminals, who not only destroy the happiness and lives of the Indians, but continually jeopardize the peace and quiet of our Western frontier life. The most powerful and efficient agency for the destruction of this traffic that has yet been proposed is a thoroughly organized and well-equipped United States Indian police force.

* * *

ALLOTMENT OF LAND IN SEVERALTY AND A PERMANENT LAND TITLE

No question which enters into the present and future welfare and permanent advancement of the Indians is of so much importance as the question of allotment to them of lands in severalty, with a perfect and permanent title. On the 24th of January, 1879, a report was submitted to the department upon this subject, in which the views of this office were fully set out, accompanied by a draft of a bill the enactment of which it was believed would bring about the desired end. The subject was treated at length in the annual report of this office for the year 1878, and was touched upon in the reports of 1879 and 1880. A bill to carry out this beneficial object was introduced into the Forty-fifth Congress, and was favorably reported upon by the committees of both Houses, but failed to receive final action. A bill similar in its provisions was submitted to the extra session of the Forty-sixth Congress. (H. R. No. 354). At the second session of the Forty-sixth Congress, House bill No. 5038 was reported by the House committee as a substitute for House bill No. 354, but it also failed to become a law. A bill with the same objects in view was also introduced in the Senate at the third session of the Forty-sixth Congress (S. No. 1773), and was discussed at some length by the Senate, but no final action was reached.

Much has been said in Congress, in the public press of the country, in public meetings, and otherwise, and various plans suggested with reference to solving the "Indian question," but no definite and practical solution of the question has been reached. In my judgment, the first step to be taken in this direction is the enactment of a law providing for the allotment of land in severalty, similar in its provisions to the bills above referred to.

The system of allotment now in force under the various treaties and acts of Congress is crude and imperfect, with no provisions for a title which affords sufficient protection to the Indians. In some of the treaties which authorize the allotment of land in severalty, provision is made for the issuance of patents, with restricted power of alienation, (with the consent of the President of the Secretary of the Interior). In others allotments are authorized with no provision for issuance of patent, but simply authorizing the issuance of a certificate of allotment, which carries with it no title at all. This system of allotment, so far as carried into effect, has been fraught with much success and encouraging improvement. The fact, however, that the Indians are not guaranteed a title affording them perfect security from molestation, and the fear that their lands may be taken from them, has created apprehension in the minds of many, and has been a bar to progress in this direction.

The allotment system tends to break up tribal relations. It has the effect of creating individuality, responsibility, and a desire to accumulate property. It teaches the Indians habits of industry and frugality, and stimulates them to look forward to a better and more useful life, and, in the end, it will relieve the government of large annual appropriations. As stated in the annual report of this office for the year 1880, the desire to take lands in severalty is almost universal among the Indians. They see that in the near future the settlement of the country by whites, and the consequent disappearance of game, the expiration of the annuity provisions of their treaties, and other causes will necessitate the adoption of some measures on their part providing for the future support and welfare of themselves and their children. As illustrating the desire on the part of the Indian to take land in severalty, to adopt the habits and pursuits of civilization, to provide a home for himself and family, and to guard against future want, I invite attention to the following extracts from a report made by C. A. Maxwell, United States special agent, dated September 23, 1881, upon a council held with the Crow Indians at their agency, in Montana, on the 22nd of August last, viz:

It will be observed by reference to the minutes of the council that the main point of conversation on the part of the Indians was the subject of more cattle, houses to live in, farming, and a general desire to live like the white man and to adopt the habits and pursuits of civilized life. The Indians are very anxious in regard to the manner of payment for the right of way of the Northern Pacific Railroad through their reservation, an agreement for which they signed on the 22d of August last, and also the money which they believe is due them for the western portion of the reservation, an agreement for the cession of which they signed June 12, 1880. It appears to be almost the unanimous wish of the tribe that the money due or to become due them under both agreements should be invested in cattle for the heads of families and individual members of the tribe, the erection of houses, and the purchase of agricultural implements, which certainly shows a commendable spirit on the part of such wild and untutored savages, and tends to demonstrate the fact that, no matter how wild and nomadic Indians are, they can be taught to follow the pursuits of the white man and to enter upon a more useful life, and, in time, become self supporting. It is but a question of short time when the rapid settlement of the country and the disappearance of the buffalo will necessitate the confinement of the Crows to their reservation, in which event they will, for the greater portion of each year, be in a destitute condition unless some measures are adopted to render them self-supporting.

From what I observed while at the agency, the Crows are very willing to be instructed in and learn of the white man the ways of civilization. It appears that as late as the spring of 1879 not one of the Crows was engaged, or had attempted to engage, in agriculture, while at the present time quite a number of the leading chiefs are occupying comfortable log cabins and cultivating small parcels of ground, some of them having their land inclosed. The Indians manifest great interest and considerable pride in this step toward civilization and the self-support of themselves and families, and the example has had a good effect upon the other chiefs of the tribe. Not a day passed while I was at the agency but what some of the leading chiefs asked Agent Keller for houses to live in, and for tracts of land to cultivate for themselves and their followers. In fact, this subject appears to be uppermost in their minds, and considerable jealousy appears to exist as to whom provision shall be first made for. About one hundred Indians have selected locations for farms, and the agent will erect houses at the points selected as rapidly as possible. While at the agency authority was received for the erection of twenty houses and the breaking of five hundred acres of land, by contract. The

Indians received this information with many manifestations of joy and expressions of satisfaction. As stated by them, it made their hearts feel good.

The disposition manifested upon this subject by such a wild, untutored, and uncivilized tribe as the Crows is certainly very encouraging, and is one of the strongest recommendations in favor of the allotment system. As a further illustration of this desire on the part of the Indians, and of its practical and beneficial results, attention is also invited to the following extracts from some of the annual reports of agents. James McLaughlin, agent at the Devil's Lake Agency, Dakota, in speaking upon the subject of the advancement of the Indians at his agency, says:

Nearly all of them are located on individual claims, living in log cabins, some having shingle roofs and pine floors, cultivating farms in severalty, and none are now ashamed to labor in civilized pursuits. A majority of the heads of families have ox-teams, wagons, plows, harrows, &c., and a desire to accumulate property and excel each other is becoming more general. One thousand acres are under cultivation. Four hundred and five acres of new land were broken this year preparatory to sowing wheat next spring. This breaking was done entirely by Indians on 110 different claims adjoining their old fields.

Capt. W. E. Dougherty, acting agent at the Crow Creek Agency, Dakota, says:

Last summer one band of the tribe was located on land in severalty, each family taking 320 acres, upon which it began some kind of improvement. Last spring the demand of the Indians for the subdivision of the land and the allotment of it in severalty became general. A surveyor was accordingly employed for the purpose, and up to the present time the following-named persons have been allotted land, and are living on their allotments or are preparing to move upon them. [Here follows a list of 173 allotments, with the quantity of land allotted to each.] All the improvements made during the year have been made on these allotments, and consist of the erection of houses, stables, fences, corrals, &c., and the breaking of new land. The latter was done by the government, the other by the Indians. During the past year every family on the reservation has contributed more or less to the advancement of its condition and welfare, while some, with the assistance obtained from the agency, have made themselves very comfortable, and are the possessors of considerable personal property. Forty-five houses have been erected, and about twenty-five moved from the common lands and re-erected on land taken in severalty, by the Indians, unaided.

Isaiah Lightner, agent for the Santees, in Nebraska, says:

Just here I feel that I should speak again of the land title, as it is a subject I have been writing about for the last four years, and nothing special accomplished. I must confess I feel somewhat discouraged. But as I have told the Santee Indians, with my hands uplifted, that I would stand by them until they received a more lasting title to their homes, I must repeat here, to you and all who may read what I have formerly said, that the Santees should have this land given to them by a law that could not be changed, so that the white man could not take their homes from them. At present they have but little assurance that they can remain here, and I know it has been a drawback to them in the way of self-support, for they have repeatedly informed me that they do not wish to open up a farm for a white man to take from them when the whites may feel like doing so. They want a lasting title to their homes the same as a white man, and I think it wicked in the first degree for us, as a nation, to withold any longer such a sacred right—that of liberty and a free home for these people, who eventually will be recognized as a part of our nation, exercising the rights of citizenship as we do. In the name of the power that rules, cannot we bring force to bear that will make right prevail, and produce such a law as will allow the Santee Indians, and those similarly situated, to select their land and hold it as a permanent home.

The reports of nearly all the agents show a similar state of facts existing among the Indians at their respective agencies. The Indian wants his land allotted to him. He wants a perfect and secure title that will protect him against the rapacity of the white man. He is not only willing but anxious to learn the ways of civilization. He is desirous of being taught to work and to accumulate property. His mind is imbued with these ideas, and some decisive steps should be taken by the law-making branch of the government to encourage him in his laudable and praiseworthy desires and efforts towards civilization, self-support, and a better and more useful life.

An approximate estimate shows that 5,972 allotments have been made on the various reservations in the United States, and that 2,793 of this number have been patented to the allottees; also that 1,353 allotments have been made for which certificates have been issued. As before stated these certificates carry no title with them. They are only evidence of the right of one Indian as against another to occupy the tract of land which they describe. It should be stated in explanation of the difference betwen the number of allotments and number of patents issued, that under the provision of some of the treaties the lands allotted to the several members of a family are embraced in one patent issued to the head of the family.

Report of Commissioner of Indian Affairs Hiram Price
October 10, 1882

(Excerpt from *Report for 1882*, pp. 1-8, 10-15, 25-29, 34-36, 38-40, 51-52)

There is in the following report a strong trace of the Iowa bank president and railroad president that Hiram Price was prior to becoming Commissioner of Indian Affairs. Price was quite positive in his knowledge of how best to run the Indian Department internally, and equally secure in knowing what was best for the Indians. Price, in urging the advantages of allotment, even cited Malthus on the evils of common property. Excerpts from Price's report, such as that on Chief Joseph's band of Nez Percés, showed that the businessman also had a heart.

IN COMPLIANCE with the law requiring the Commissioner of Indian Affairs to make an annual report of the condition of affairs connected with his bureau, I have the honor to submit herewith my report for the year 1882. Evidently this law contemplates that the report thus required should show not only operations of the past year and the present condition of affairs, but also make such suggestions and recommendations, based upon the year's experience, as would be beneficial to the service.

The operations and results of the last year in the different agencies, which will be more fully described and explained under their appropriate heads, will, I think, compare favorably with any one of the preceding years. Land has been opened to cultivation; houses for Indian residences have been built; schools opened and operated; and in many cases, and in various ways, the cause of civilization generally advanced; and I might, with this general statement of facts, proceed to give a separate chapter of each reservation and agency; and follow these with the tabulated statements required by section 468 of the Revised Statutes. But such a report would not, in my opinion, be discharging my whole duty, nor would it be such a report as the framers of the law contemplated. When the rules and regulations under the law governing the operations of the Indian Department become perfect, and the machinery less multiform and complicated, such a report might answer the purpose; but until such is the case, a report should not only state what has been done, but also what changes would be advantageous to the service.

DELAY IN SETTLEMENT OF ACCOUNTS

Too much machinery is often worse than too little, and, in my judgment, there is now too much machinery in use in the settlement of accounts, connected with this bureau. I say this with a full knowledge gained by an experience of many years of the absolute necessity of proper checks and balances in the manner of keeping and settling accounts. But after an individual has complied with his contract and produces his vouchers certified and signed by the legally appointed officers, showing that he has performed his undertaking in letter and spirit, he is in all fairness entitled to the prompt payment of the compensation stipulated. But such, I am compelled by personal knowledge to say, is not the case as the law now stands. After all has been done as above indicated, honest claimants have in very many instances been compelled to chase their accounts through twelve or fifteen departments of the government, consuming weeks and even months, and in some instances years of time, until hope has sickened into despair, and men have grown gray waiting for the tardy footsteps of the messenger from whose hands they should long before have received their just dues.

It is no answer to this to say that the system now practiced has been long in use and therefore ought not to be changed. This is no argument for its continuance unless it can be shown that age sanctifies error. I make this statement in the interest not only of fair and honorable dealing, but also and particularly in the interest of economy for the government. A prompt paymaster gets more for his money than one who is not prompt; and when it is understood that delay may be expected in receiving payment for labor or material furnished, those who furnish the labor or material make their calculations accordingly, and charge enough to pay them for waiting. The system of purchasing the annual supplies for the Indian service by inviting and receiving sealed proposals is productive of a healthy competition, and the opening of these bids and awarding the contracts in the presence of the bidders leaves no just ground for charges of unfairness or favoritism, and, in my opinion, there is not much room for improvement in that respect; but I desire to repeat and emphasize it, that the law in reference to settling the accounts ought to be changed.

INDIAN AGENTS

Among the many causes which exist tending to retard the improvement of the Indians, one very important one is the difficulty of procuring men of the right stamp to act as agents. We have over a quarter of a million of Indians scattered over many thousands of miles of territory, many of the points at which they are located being difficult of access. Many of these Indians, outside of the five civilized tribes, are wild roving nomads, preferring savage to civilized life. These are an untutored and untractable people, who are naturally indolent, improvident, and shiftless, and very impatient of restraint or discipline. The object of the government is to transform these uncivilized people into peaceable, industrious, and law-abiding citizens, and for this purpose a system has been devised, good in many respects; but when we come to operate that system we make a fatal mistake, and a mistake which, if not corrected, will, in my opinion, prevent for generations the accomplishment of good, which might otherwise be reached in one decade. I refer, of course, to the present system of appointing and paying the men who have the immediate charge of the Indians, and who are known as Indian agents. When the fact is once clearly established that an agent is utterly unfit from any cause for his place, he ought, on any theory of sound business principles, to be removed *at once,* and a more suitable man put in his place; but it requires as much machinery now, and frequently more time, to get a new agent appointed than it does to appoint a minister to the Court of St. James. Within the last year seven entire months were consumed in making such a change at one of the agencies, where any correct business man transacting his own business would have made the change in less than seven days. This is the fault of the law, and ought to be changed.

These Indian agents furnish the precept and example to which we must look more than to any other cause or influence as a means of changing the habits, manners, and customs of the Indians. If the agent is an *honest, industrious,* and *intelligent Christian* man, with the *physical* ability and disposition to endure hardship and courageously encounter difficulty and disappointment, or, in other words, if he is morally, mentally, and physically above the average of what are considered good men, he will work wonders among these wards of the nation. And I but state what every thinking man must know, that, as a *rule,* this class of men cannot be procured to cut themselves off from civilization and deprive themselves and families of the comforts and advantages of civilized society for the pittance which is now paid to Indian agents. Occasionally men have been found who, for the good which they hoped to accomplish, have voluntarily exiled themselves and labored for the good of these people, but they generally found more trouble from their surroundings and less moral support from the government than was expected, and, becoming discouraged and disheartened, have retired from the service, leaving their places to be filled by less competent men. One agent, in tendering his resignation a few weeks since, uses the following language:

> I have labored faithfully for the good of the Indians, dealing honorably with all men, but I have at last become disheartened, and feel that life is too short to waste any more of it here.

One great cause of embarrassment and discouragement to Indian agents is the trouble and annoyance they find in keeping their accounts so as to comply technically with all the regulations and rulings in reference to the final settlement of their accounts. As the matter now stands, an agent may execute to the letter an order given him by the Secretary of the Interior for the payment of money, and yet that item in his account may be suspended against him, and he and his sureties be compelled by law to pay the money again. The result is, if he refuses to obey the orders of his superior he loses his position, and if he obeys he loses his money.

I give it as my honest conviction as a business man, after one year and a half of close observation, in a position where the chances for a correct knowledge of this question are better than in any other, that the true policy of the government is to pay Indian agents such compensation and place them under such regulations of law as will insure the services of first class men. It is not enough that a man is honest; he must, in addition to this, be capable. He must be up to standard physically as well as morally and mentally. Men of this class are comparatively scarce, and as a rule cannot be had unless the compensation is equal to the service required. Low-priced men are not always the cheapest. A bad article is dear at any price. Paying a man as Indian agent $1,200 or $1,500, and expecting him to perform $3,000 or $4,000 worth of labor, is not economy, and in a large number of cases has proven to be the worst kind of extravagance. The wholesale, sweeping charge of dishonesty sometimes made against Indian agents is not true. Some of them are good and true men, doing the very best they can under the embarrassing circumstances by which they are surrounded; and some of them are capable; but I repeat, the inducements for such men to remain are insufficient, and the difficulties and discouragements which they meet, crowd them out of the service, and until all Indian agents are selected and paid as a good business man selects and pays his employés (which is not the case now), it need not be wondered at if many of them are incompetent, and a few of them dishonest.

CO-OPERATION OF RELIGIOUS SOCIETIES

One very important auxiliary in transforming men from savage to civilized life is the influence brought to bear upon them through the labors of Christian men and women as educators and missionaries. This I think has been forcibly illustrated and clearly demonstrated among the different Indian tribes by the missionary labors of the various religious societies in the last few years. Civilization is a plant of exceeding slow growth, unless supplemented by Christian teaching and influences. I am decidedly of the opinion that a liberal encouragement by the government to all religious denominations to extend their educational and missionary operations among the Indians would be of immense benefit. I find that during the year there has been expended in cash by the different religious societies for regular educational and missionary purposes among the Indians the sum of $216,680, and doubtless much more which was not reported through the regular channels. This is just so much money saved to the government, which is an item of some importance, but insignificant in comparison with the healthy influences created by the men and women who have gone among the Indians, not for personal pecuniary benefit, but for the higher and nobler purpose of helping these untutored and uncivilized people to a higher plane of existence. In no other manner and by no other means, in my judgment, can our Indian population be so speedily and permanently reclaimed from barbarism, idolatry, and savage life, as by the educational and missionary operations of the Christian people of our country. This kind of teaching will educate them to be sober, industrious, self-reliant, and to respect the rights of others; and my deliberate opinion is, that it is not only the interest but the duty of the government to aid and encourage these efforts in the most liberal manner. No money spent for the civilization of the Indian will return a better dividend than that spent in this way. In urging this point I do not wish to be understood as claiming that all the good people are inside the churches and all the bad ones outside; but a little observation, I think, will convince any one that a very large proportion of those who sacrifice time and money for the good of others is found inside of some Christian organization. If we expect to stop sun dances, snake worship, and other debasing forms of superstition and idolatry among Indians, we must teach them some better way. This, with liberal appropriations by the government for the establishment of industrial schools, where the thousands of Indian children now roaming wild shall be taught to speak the English language and earn their own living, will accomplish what is so much desired, to wit, the conversion of the wild, roving Indian into an industrious, peaceable, and law-abiding citizen.

Need of More Liberal Appropriations

This result, however, cannot be reached in any reasonable time unless the means are commensurate with the end to be attained. The conditions which now surround the case are very different from those that existed in the years of the past. The game upon which the Indian subsisted is fast disappearing, and he must of necessity look for subsistence from some other source. The vast domain which he once called his own, and over which he roamed at will, is rapidly being absorbed by the white people, who insist that these fertile valleys and mountains rich in mineral deposits shall no longer remain locked up and shut out from the enterprise and industry of the white race. The commercial interests of the country seem to demand that the means of communication between one section of the country and another shall not be obstructed by denying the right way for trade and traffic; and as a consequence railroads are penetrating these reservations once set apart for the home of the Indian, and in which he had a right to suppose he would not be disturbed.

I do not stop now to canvass the question of right or justice. I only point to the inevitable, and claim that it is unquestionably the imperative duty of the government, as well as the soundest and safest policy, to provide the safest, surest, and most equitable means to induce the Indian to abandon the manners, customs, and traditions of his fathers, and accommodate himself to the new and better way. This can only be done by appropriations much more liberal than those made in the past. If one million of dollars for educational purposes given *now* will save several millions in the future, it is wise economy to give that million at once, and not dole it out in small sums that do but little good. The more thoughtful and intelligent of the Indians comprehend and appreciate the situation, and are anxious to put themselves in condition to meet the new order of things which they see is certain to come, and which will either elevate them in the scale of being, or exterminate them. Chief Keokuk, son of the celebrated chief of that name, said to one of our special agents only a few days ago, "We want schools, churches, and laws, to make our people abandon the wild, roving life of Indians, and become a settled, industrious, and peaceable people."

Within the last few months the Pottawatomie Indians have prepared and submitted to the department for approval, a code of laws for their own government, thus clearly indicating that the thoughts of the Indians are being turned in the right direction.

Unjust Discrimination Between Indian Tribes

I called attention in my last report to the fact that the Indians who obey law and try to conform to our customs, and to cultivate habits of industry and sobriety, are not encouraged as they should be; while Indians who are lazy, turbulent, and insubordinate, get what they demand. If the Indians are in fact the wards of the nation, it is the imperative duty of the government to treat them as a prudent and kind guardian should treat a ward, and this can only be done by rewarding the good and punishing the bad. Rewards should be liberal and promptly given, and punishments should be sharp, quick, and positive. No delay in either case; let the effect follow the cause with certainty and rapidity. Delay in either case lessens the effect intended to be produced.

I feel that I cannot too strongly urge this, because unless a different policy in this respect is pursued in the future from that practiced in the past, bad Indians will increase and good ones decrease. They must be made to know that vice will not be rewarded, nor will virtue be punished. We are to-day feeding with a liberal hand, and at a cost of hundreds of thousands of dollars, a tribe of Indians who have made insolent demands, and defiantly threatened war unless their demands were complied with, while at the same time we are allowing quiet and peaceable Indians to struggle with adverse circumstances on the verge of starvation. The Indians see this and the effect must necessarily be bad.

Surveys of Indian Reservations

One fruitful source of trouble and conflict between Indians and white people arises from the fact that in very many cases it is impossible to tell where the reservation lines are. The Indians claim the line to be in one place and the white man, who is a farmer, a miner, or a herder, claims it to be in another. The only remedy for this is by surveying and plainly marking the boundary lines; this would save much trouble and many lives. I made an earnest request for an appropriation of $100,000 for this purpose at the last session of Congress, but only $5,000 was given. In 1880 it was estimated that there were not less than 6,000 miles of unsurveyed reservation boundaries. But little change has occurred since. Were it not for the aid generously extended by the War Department during the year past the office would have extremely embarrassed in several cases where surveys were absolutely required to prevent threatened conflicts between Indians and whites. Agents at the different agencies are urging the necessity of having the boundaries fixed, and it is to be hoped that this matter will not be neglected at the approaching session of Congress. Where it has not already been done arable lands within the reservations should be subdivided, to enable the agents to allot lands in severalty to Indians as fast as required.

APPROPRIATIONS COVERED INTO THE TREASURY

In reference to the amount of appropriations for the Indian service, I wish to call attention to the fact that many thousands of dollars are annually appropriated, which, on account of the peculiar character of the law governing these appropriations, cannot be and never are used; and this fact ought to be considered in making the appropriations. The books in this bureau show that $228,170.22 have been returned to the Treasury for the last year, for which the accounts are made up. And connected with this fact is another kindred one, to wit; supplies amounting in some instances to many thousands of dollars are purchased and paid for out of money appropriated for the Indian service, but before these supplies are consumed the Indians are removed to some distant locality, the supplies are sold, and every dollar realized from the sale goes back into the Treasury; but all the expense of care and sale must be paid from the contingent fund, for which no calculation was made when the contingent fund was appropriated. The law should be so amended as to allow all expenses of this kind to be paid from proceeds of the sale of the property. For proof and illustration of this condition of affairs I refer to the recent operations on the Malheur Reservation.

CONSOLIDATION OF AGENCIES

There are at present fifty-nine Indian agencies, fifty-eight of them in charge of agents whose salary is provided for by Congress, and one in charge of a military officer acting as Indian agent. A reduction of eight agencies has been made during the fiscal year. Reduction in the number of agencies has been the aim of this office for several years past, and has been frequently recommended by my predecessors. The objects sought have been, (1) reduction in the cost of maintaining agencies; (2) the consolidation of the Indians upon reservations where they may be best protected in their personal and property rights, and (3) the sale of the lands vacated by the consolidation and the use of such portion of the funds arising therefrom as may be necessary in the settlement of the Indians upon the reservations to which they may be removed, the balance of the money to be funded for their use, and the interest thereon to be expended in lieu of direct appropriations for their benefit. This plan is still urged and believed to be for the best interests of all concerned.

But the consolidation of agencies (so called) made at the last session of Congress has not been productive of the good results hoped for by those who advocated the measure. The Indians and all the property and machinery of an agency have been left just where they were and as they were, except that the person in charge is not called an agent, nor can he receive or disburse money. The one man, who is the agent for all of the points attempted to be consolidated, is alone responsible for all the property, and must necessarily travel from one to another; this involves much expense of time and money; and inasmuch as all the accounts have to be examined and reviewed at the point where the agent is located, it requires additional clerical force, and I have found some difficulty, even at this early period of the fiscal year, in finding funds for the payment of the agent's traveling expenses and the additional clerical force required. As a rule it is safe to say that any attempt at consolidation that does not consolidate the Indians by placing them on the same reservation must result in failure to accomplish any good and be almost certain to give much trouble.

The last Indian appropriation act simply legislated agents out of office on June 30, 1882, made no provisions for their salaries or expenses until such consolidation should be completed, and provided no funds by which the Indians could be brought together. A special appropriation should be made to enable this office to carry into effect the provisions of section 6 of the act above referred to, or a sufficient sum for the purpose should be added to the appropriation for contingencies of the Indian service.

ISSUES OF RATIONS

In accordance with suggestions made by some members of the Committee on Appropriations at the last session of Congress, I decided at the commencement of the present fiscal year to have the supplies purchased for Indians under existing appropriations divided into fifty-two parts, and instructed agents to issue one fifty-second part each week, so that the amount appropriated for should last to the end of the fiscal year.

The following is the text of the instructions issued:

> In purchasing these supplies the funds appropriated by Congress for the fiscal year 1883 have been exhausted, reserving only sufficient for the purchase of annuity and other goods estimated for by you, pay of employés, and such

incidental expenditures as may arise during the year. You are therefore directed to divide the above-named supplies by the number of weeks (52), and issue only one fifty-second part of the same per week. Under no circumstances will you be allowed to incur any deficiency, and you will be held responsible for the execution of this order.

This has caused much dissatisfaction among many of the tribes, and a threatened outbreak in some instances; but the system will be adhered to, unless Congress orders otherwise.

Evil of Cash Annuities

In many cases the law now requires money to be paid to certain tribes of Indians. In a majority of these cases, if the law left it in the discretion of the department to pay in cattle or sheep, instead of cash, the result would be much more beneficial to the Indian. This is eminently true in the case of the Uintah and other Utes. The country occupied by them is a good grazing country, but not well adapted for agricultural purposes. If, instead of compelling payment to them in money, as the law now stands, they could be paid in cattle, they could in a few years become self-supporting. The money paid to them does them but little good. In one day, immediately after a cash payment was made to the Utes, two thousand dollars were spent for firearms, ammunition, and whiskey in Salt Lake City, and in a very short time nine-tenths of the payment went in the same direction. If they are the wards of the nation, we should see to it that they get only such things as are beneficial, and not such as are injurious.

While upon this subject I wish to call attention to the fact that there is no law to punish any one for selling firearms to Indians, and the consequence is that the worst and most troublesome Indians are armed with the best breech-loaders that can be found in the market. It is hoped a stringent law may be passed to prevent, as far as possible, this cause of trouble and loss of life.

* * *

Liquor in the Indian Country

The sale and use of liquor has been brought before the public so long as the chief cause of poverty and crime, that when it is stated that nearly all the serious crimes committed in the Indian country are traceable directly to the selling and drinking of whisky, the statement is accepted as truth, as a matter of course. It provokes no comment, and appears to have little effect on legislation. Yet, to-day, whisky is the one great curse of the Indian country, the prolific source of disorder, tumult, crime, and disease, and if its sale could be utterly prohibited, peace and quiet would almost uniformly exist among the Indians from the Mississippi to the Pacific. Whisky is furnished the Indians by disreputable white men, who would sell themselves and their country for so many pieces of silver. Leniency to such men is a *crime*. Their homes should be behind iron bars, with never a human face to look upon, and never a sight of the green earth or the skies above, until, in solitary confinement for months and years, they had been taught the lesson that "the way of transgressors is hard." Most Indians will drink whisky whenever and wherever they can get it. Under its influence they are savages in deed as well as in name.

The agent Quapaw says:

> A quart of whisky will do more to demoralize Indians than a month of patient labor will accomplish to civilize them.

The agent at Sac and Fox, Indian Territory, says:

> The whisky business has been the cause of more difficulty and more crime than all other causes combined.

At Great Nemaha the agent testifies that:

> Strong drink is the greatest curse that besets the red man. Unprincipled whites in the settlements, knowing this weakness, and regardless of the consequences that may follow, will barter their own souls that they may fill their coffers with their unlawful and ill-gotten gains.

At Navajo Agency, one of the chiefs says:

> We do not make whisky—it is the Americans that do it—and we earnestly plead that the Great Father will take it away from us and not let it be brought near us, for our young men drink it like water.

The agent at Tulalip reports that:

> No crimes of a serious character were committed on the reservation, and if it were not for the nefarious trade carried on in selling liquor to Indians by degraded white men, the Indians would be a happy and prosperous race of people.

Page after page might be filled with similar testimonies.

The destruction of the liquor traffic among Indians is necessary, alike for their welfare and for the protection and safety of the lives and property of thousands of good citizens who have their homes near these Indian reservations. The result desired can be accomplished by the passage and enforcement of rigid laws, with severe penalties for the violation thereof. If the guilty ones are surely and sufficiently punished, it will soon be almost impossible for the Indians to get liquor. The present law is defective. It provides that the penalty for giving or selling liquor to an Indian shall be imprisonment for not *more* than two years and a fine of not *more* than $300. This law should be so amended as to specify a *minimum* penalty.

A few selections from reports of agents will show the necessity for such an amendment.

The agent at Grande Ronde says:

> The greatest obstacle . . . is the constant watchfulness required to prevent them from obtaining whisky from a disreputable class of whites who hover around the borders of the agency, or in the small towns, ever ready to furnish Indians liquor and to take advantage of them as soon as they have become intoxicated. I have succeeded in having from forty to fifty of this class of offenders arrested during the past year, nearly every one of whom has been convicted, but the fines imposed are not sufficient to give them a proper respect for law and order. Could our courts be induced to make the sentence imprisonment instead of a small fine, I am confident there would be fewer transgressors.

The agent at Green Bay says:

> During the past year five young men have been killed while intoxicated. Drunkenness will continue among the Indians, in spite of the strongest efforts of agents and Indian police, until Congress amends the law by adding, not less than three months' imprisonment and not less than $50 fine.

The agent of the Mission Indians says:

> But for the leniency of the courts in dealing with offenders who have been detected and arrested for carrying on this traffic among them, better results might be reported.

In view of these statements, and others on file in this office, I recommend that section 2139 of the Revised Statutes be so amended that the punishment for the first offense shall be imprisonment for not *less* than one year, and a fine of not *less* than $100; and that for the second and subsequent violations of law the penalty shall be imprisonment for three years. I deem this amendment absolutely essential, as under the present law fixing a maximum, but not a minimum penalty, the law is practically of little value, the punishment, in some cases, being a fine of ten dollars and imprisonment for one day, and this, too, after the payment of many dollars in witness fees. The penalty should be commensurate with the crime.

Section 2139 provides that "Every person [*except an Indian in the Indian country*]" shall be liable to punishment for sale of liquor to Indians, &c. A bill (H. R. 3942) introduced by Representative Haskell at the last session of Congress proposes to amend the section by striking out the words "except an Indian in the Indian country." I hope this legislation also will be secured.

One other amendment is, in my judgment, necessary. The War Department is authorized to introduce liquor into the Indian country. This should not be. Fire should not be permitted near a powder-magazine, nor whisky near an Indian reservation. Army whisky is no better than other whisky; it does not appear that its effects are any more desirable. An Indian will as surely get drunk on army liquors as on those obtained from less highly favored citizens of the country. I recommend, therefore, that such portions of sections 2139 and 2140 as authorize the War Department, or Army officers, to introduce liquor into the Indian country be repealed.

Notwithstanding the disadvantages under which agents labor on account of inadequate and defective law, and the leniency and indifference with which it is administered, they have made strenuous efforts during the year to repress the sale of liquor to Indians by the prosecution of whisky sellers, and have been fairly successful. Through the efforts of 30 different agents, 136 cases have been prosecuted; 16 failed of conviction, 36 are still pending, one forfeited his bail bond, 19 were punished by fine, 30 by imprisonment, and 34 by imprisonment and fine. The fines varied from $1 to $125, and the terms of imprisonment in jails, houses of correction, and penitentiaries, from one day to 3 years and a half. Only 7 were imprisoned for a year or over, and the average term of the others was 58 days. The average fine was $32.

The tendency of the law to bear the hardest on the weakest party was well exemplified among the Indians of the State of New York, where 3 white men were fined $20, $50, and $75, respectively, for selling liquor to Indians; and for the same offense an Indian was sentenced to 30 days in prison and a fine of $100. A table showing prosecutions and penalties in detail, will be found on page 375, herewith.

Much larger results could have been secured if the office had funds at its command to cover the expense of detecting liquor selling, making arrests, sending witnesses to court, &c. For this purpose I urged last year an appropriation of $5,000, which was granted in the House but failed in the Senate. Whatever difference of opinion may exist as to the use of whisky by white men, there is but one opinion as to the mischief and danger of its use by Indians, and I can see no reason why the small amount asked should not have been granted. I trust that Congress at its next session will show some interest in the matter, and some readiness to assist the office in its single-handed fight against this evil.

LEGISLATION REQUIRED

Intruders on Indian lands.—In my last annual report I drew attention to the insufficiency of existing laws on this subject. On the 29th of March last, the draught of a bill for the more adequate prevention of trespasses on Indian lands, previously prepared in this office, was transmitted by the President to Congress for consideration (House Ex. Doc. No. 145, 47th Cong., 1st sess.)

This bill reads as follows:

> *Be it enacted by the Senate and House of Representatives of the United States of America in Congress assembled,* That section twenty-one hundred and forty-eight of the Revised Statutes of the United States be amended to read as follows, namely:
>
> "Every person who without authority of law enters and shall be found upon any Indian lands, tribal reservation, or lands specially set apart for Indian purposes, shall for the first offense, upon conviction thereof, pay a fine of not more than five hundred dollars, and be imprisoned at hard labor for not more than one year; and for every subsequent offense, shall, upon conviction thereof, pay a fine of not more than one thousand dollars, and not less than five hundred dollars, and be imprisoned at hard labor for not more than two years, nor less than one year; and the wagons, teams and outfit of such person or persons so offending shall be seized and delivered to the proper United States officer, and be proceeded against by libel in the proper court and forfeited, one-half to the informer and the other half to the United States, and in all cases arising under this act, Indians shall be competent witnesses: *Provided, however,* That the provisions of this section shall not apply to emigrants or travelers peaceably passing through such Indian lands, tribal reservations, or lands especially set apart for Indian purposes, without committing any willful trespass or injury to person or property."

I greatly regret that Congress took no action in this matter. The urgent necessity for an amendment of the law is again apparent in the attempted settlement in the Indian Territory by the so-called "Oklahoma Colony," under the leadership of D. L. Payne, which has twice been repeated during the past year; first in May last, when Payne with a party of followers was arrested in the Indian Territory by the military, and afterwards released on the Kansas border; and more recently, in the latter part of August, when, with a party consisting of seven men and two women, and an outfit of wagons, horses, &c., he was again captured by the troops whilst endeavoring to effect a settlement at Oklahoma. Upon this last occasion, refusing to go out of the Territory peacefully, the party were disarmed and taken to Fort Reno as prisoners. Upon the recommendation of this department, they were turned over by the military to the United States civil authorities at Fort Smith, Ark., by whom, it is reported, they have since been released to appear at the November term of the United States court for the western district of Arkansas, to answer to civil suits for the recovery of the prescribed penalty of $1,000, which is the only redress the existing law provides. The result will probably be judgments against them by default, which will be and remain uncollectible.

It is surely time that this farce which has now been going on for three years or more, should cease. If Congress will give us a law (such as has been laid before it) providing for *imprisonment* in addition to fine, for each offense, these periodical invasions will be less frequent, if not altogether stopped, and probably much distress will be avoided to innocent parties who have been deluded by vague promises held out to them.

Timber depredations on Indian lands.—The necessity for legislation to protect the timber on Indian lands has been repeatedly and forcibly urged in prior annual reports of this office. In my last report I adverted to the wholesale destruction of timber in the Indian Territory, and the disastrous climatic effects which it is apprehended will ensue unless the evil is arrested.

At the last session of Congress a bill (S. 1646), prepared in this office, extending the provisions of section 5388 of the Revised Statutes of the United States for the protection and preservation of timber to Indian lands, passed in the Senate, but was never reached in the House. It is hoped that Congress will take up this bill at an early date.

Laws for Indians.—For years past urgent appeals have been made by this office for such legislation as will insure a proper government of the Indians, by providing that the criminal laws of the United States shall be in force on Indian reservations, and shall apply to all offenses, including those of Indians against Indians; and by extending the jurisdiction of the United States courts to enforce the same; in short to make an Indian as amenable to law as any other subject of the United States. From time to time various measures looking to this end have been introduced in Congress; but from some cause or other—lack of time or of proper appreciation of the importance of the subject—they have invariably fallen through, so that to-day the only statutes under which Indians are managed and controlled are substantially those created in 1834, known as the trade and intercourse laws, whose main purpose was to regulate traffic in furs and prevent sale of ammunition and intoxicating drinks and intrusion upon an Indian reservation. As civilization advances and the Indian is thrown into contact with white settlers the authority of the chiefs proportionately decreases. It is manifest that some provision of law should be made to supply this deficiency and protect Indians in their individual rights of person and property. At the same time, the Indian should be given to understand that no ancient custom, or tribal regulation, will shield him from just punishment for crime.

The importance of this subject has been so frequently enlarged upon in the annual reports of this office for years past that it seems almost superfluous to add more; but at the risk of being considered prolix I herewith append an extract from a letter on file in this office from Agent Wilbur, of the Yakima Agency, Washington Territory, an officer of over sixteen years' experience with the Indians. Under date of March 10 last, he says:

> Another, and at this agency, perhaps, equally important matter, is the extension of the United States law over the reservation. Possibly the situation here has brought this matter more forcibly to my attention than to most agents. Just off the reservation, on one side, is Yakima City, and on the other Goldendale, and our Indians are often there for purposes of trade. When there they find themselves subject to a law different from that on the reservation; a law prompt and swift to punish, but powerless to protect them. They witness its administration, and place a far higher value on it than on the

decisions of their councils, and cases have occurred where Indians, thinking themselves aggrieved by the adverse decision of their councils, have watched their opportunity, and, when their adversary happened in town, have procured a retrial of the case before the justice of the peace. It does not affect the case that the original decision was affirmed. The fact illustrates the higher value placed on the United States law, and the desire of the Indians to be judged by it. Some of the more unworthy Indians claim to have taken out "citizen papers," pay taxes, work the county roads, and, boasting that they are no longer under the jurisdiction of the agent or council, give themselves up to all manner of license, and before the police can reach and arrest them are across the line, and defy all reservation authority. It is plain that these things must be utterly destructive of all authority of the agent or council, and equally plain that such a state of affairs cannot much longer continue.

Either all Indians should be placed under the sole jurisdiction of the agent and the council, or all should be brought equally under the operation of United States law. On this point, officers of the law, citizens, agent, and Indians are agreed, and it is strange that so obviously proper and necessary a measure has not long since been adopted.

Criminals and paupers have always existed, and I know no reason why the Indian should not be expected to furnish his proportion of these classes; but I do claim that when satisfied that equally with the white man he is secure in the possession of his home, and that the same law that judges and protects the white man throws its broad shield over him also, he will furnish no more than his proportion.

At the last session of Congress, Hon. E. Willits introduced a bill (H. R. 755) "to extend the jurisdiction of the district and circuit courts of the United States, for the punishment of crimes on Indian reservations within the limits of any State or organized Territory, and for other purposes," which was referred to the Committee on the Judiciary; but no further action appears to have been taken.

I again respectfully recommend that the attention of Congress be called to the subject, with a view to such legislation as it may deem expedient.

In regard to the Indian Territory proper, a bill (S. 181) to transfer the jurisdiction from the western district of Arkansas and to establish a United States court in the Territory at Muscogee, Creek Nation, is now pending before Congress.

* * *

EDUCATION

Exclusive of the five civilized tribes, the whole number of Indian pupils attending school the past year has been 8,412. Of these 476 were in attendance at the Carlisle, Hampton, and Forest Grove training schools. Of the remainder 3,937 attended reservation boarding schools and 3,999 reservation day schools. The average attendance for the year has been 5,126. A table giving the schools in detail, with the attendance and condition of each, will be found on page 376. The following table shows the gradual progress which has taken place in Indian education during the last six years:

	Number of pupils	Average attendance
1877	6,019	3,598
1878	6,229	4,142
1879	7,193	4,488
1880	7,240	4,651
1881	8,109	4,976
1882	8,412	5,126

Boarding-schools.—Six new boarding schools have been opened during the past year at the Round Valley, Lower Brulé, Fort Peck, Western Shoshone, Navajo, and Yankton Agencies, making the whole number now in operation 74, including the training-schools at Carlisle, Hampton, and Forest Grove. In each of the reservation boarding-schools instruction is given the girls in all branches of household industry as well as the making and repair of garments. The work of the kitchen, laundry, dining-room, dormitory, and sewing-room is performed by them under the supervision of the employés of the school, and it is expected that they will receive as thorough and constant instruction in the art of homemaking as in reading and writing the English language. It is in this department that the want of suitable buildings and appliances has been most severely felt, and thereby progress has been most seriously retarded. Want of funds has compelled the refusal to many schools of wells, cisterns, suitable furniture, and clothing materials, and the many articles of convenience which are considered essential to the proper management of a private family, and which are even more sorely needed for the smooth working of a large household. The Indian is an apprentice to civilization, and he cannot be expected to make rapid advancement in his trade if the tools furnished him are poor in quality and insufficient in number and variety. Too often the ingenuity of teachers has been taxed to see how they could manage to do without, instead of how they could teach pupils to use, the appliances of civilized life.

Industrial training for boys is also carried on at reservation boarding schools, and is receiving more and more attention with each year. In connection with 57 schools, 1,245 acres are under cultivation, and the crops the past year have amounted to 8,370 bushels corn, 3,698 bushels oats, 11,683 bushels vegetables, 1,248 bushels wheat, 154 tons hay, 1,250 melons, 1,575 pumpkins, and 2,890 heads of cabbage. In addition to farming and gardening, the preparing of fuel and carrying of water gives many hours of labor to the boys, and the teaching of trades is rapidly being introduced. Blacksmithing, tailoring, and harness-making are taught at four schools; seven teach shoemaking, ten carpentering, and fifteen the raising and care of stock. Training in these branches has been greatly stimulated by the success of the experiments at Carlisle, Hampton, and Forest Grove. Agents are taking these schoools as models of what an Indian school should be, and pupils at home are interested to learn the branches which are being taught their more favored relatives.

In industrial education Indian boarding-schools are doing pioneer work. There are neither precedents nor text-books to follow. In very few schools in the United States can the white child, unless he is a criminal, learn how to work as well as how to read; how to use his hands as well as his head. This need is receiving the attention of educators and philanthropists, and the success of the experiment among Indians is being watched with interest by the friends of the lower classes, both white and black. One of the first obstacles encountered is the outlay of funds required. To fairly equip each reservation school with stock, wagons, farming implements and mechanical tools, and have these articles used not only by children, but by children who have no inherited inclination or aptitude for civilized pursuits, must very largely increase the annual expense of the schools; and though for such expenditure the return in the next generation will be large, the immediate returns will be meager. Nevertheless it ought to be done, and appropriations increased accordingly. Even if Carlisle, Hampton, and Forest Grove could turn out, as they cannot, all the skilled mechanics and agriculturists needed among Indians, yet the value to the Indian boy of mere rudimentary training in some one of the various handicrafts will be worth to his own manhood and the civilization of his race immeasurably more than it will cost, and the *morale* of the school which furnishes such employment and diversion to its restless pupils will be vastly improved.

Too much importance cannot be attached to the agency industrial boarding-school. It is the center of Indian civilization, and will be until parents are willing to send their children away from home to be educated, and the government is willing to assume the enormous expense of that sort of schooling. Until then the reservation schools will be worth as much to the distant training-schools as the training-schools are to the reservation. They awaken the interest in education which first leads the parent to surrender his child, and they so mold public opinion as to make it possible for the returned student to persevere in the habits learned at the East. Unless a strong purifying influence is exerted on the reservation atmosphere while the students are absent, they will return to a fire-damp of heathenism, ignorance, and superstition that will extinguish all the flames of intelligence and virtue that have been kindled by contact with civilization. In this way only can the government hope to escape the humiliating relapses which many years ago discouraged missionary societies from any further attempts at educating Indian pupils away from their tribes. An appropriation of not less than $50,000 should be made by Congress at its next session to properly equip existing reservation schools for industrial work.

Day schools.—Eleven new day schools have been opened this year, but four day schools have become boarding-schools, and twelve have been discontinued, so that the whole number now in operation is 101, five less than last year. Most of those discontinued were small schools, maintained in the Indian camps by religious societies. It is as common a belief that the boarding should supersede the day school as it is that training-schools remote from the Indian country ought to be substituted for those located in the midst of the Indians. But I trust that the time is not far distant when a system of district schools will be established in Indian settlements, which will serve not only as centers of enlightenment for those neighborhoods, but will give suitable employment to returned students, especially the young women for whom it is specially difficult to provide. As General Armstrong has well said in his annual report:

> There is absolutely no position of dignity to which an Indian girl after three years' training can look forward with any reasonable confidence. There is nothing for her but to enjoy or suffer in the present state as best she may. Schools in the Indian camps, under judicious and vigorous supervision (such as are in a few cases already established by the missionaries), would give honorable work, full of inspiration, to our best Indian girls.

Referring to reports from returned students, he also says:

> The local press of the country notes the fact that without the help of the boys of the Indian school some of the farmers of this section would have had great trouble in harvesting their crops. One paper has raised its warning cry for the protection of white labor as against Indian. The boys have worked side by side with the white man, earned the same wages, and this in a section of country where it has always been claimed the Indian would not work.

To erect necessary buildings and pay teachers for such district schools will require another increase in appropriations, which I hope will not be wanting.

When such schools are established, compulsory education can be resorted to. This has already been partially tried at two agencies with considerable success, although the compulsion could not be made universal for the reason that school facilities fell far short of accommodating the school population. Two other agents have signified their intention of adopting such measures, and, with the help of their Indian police, will undoubtedly succeed. At other agencies, however, where there is greater disproportion between the number of children and the size and number of the school buildings, pupils have to be turned away from instead of forced to school.

I desire, in this connection, to renew my suggestion of last year, that the example of New York in extending her common school system over her

Indian reservations and employing educated Indians as teachers, is a most sensible one for other States to follow. The results thereof would be no less valuable to the State than to the general government.

Carlisle, Forest Grove, and Hampton training schools.—By reference to the reports of Lieutenants Pratt and Wilkinson, and of S. C. Armstrong, herewith, pages 237, 247, and 241, respectively, it will be seen that good work has been accomplished during the year at the Carlisle, Forest Grove, and Hampton training schools. They have been attended by 284,91, and 101 pupils, respectively. The Carlisle pupils represent 33 tribes and 18 agencies; the Forest Grove pupils, 10 tribes and 5 agencies.

At Carlisle and Hampton the apprentices in the various shops have not only attended to the large amount of repairing, building, and furnishing required at the schools, but have manufactured for use at the various Indian agencies 253 sets double harness, 13 wagons and 1 buggy, 2,000 pairs shoes, and 14,124 articles of tinware, and the schools have been credited with the value of these articles at the contract prices paid therefor by the Indian Office. The apprentices to the trades of blacksmith, carpenter, printer, shoemaker, tinsmith, wheelwright, painter, butcher, tailor, saddler, and baker have numbered 183. The energies of the rest of the boys were devoted to farm work.

Only eight deaths have occurred at the two schools during the year, the improved health conditions being due partly to acclimatization, but more to greater watchfulness and a better understanding on the part of both instructors and pupils of the requirements of the Indian physique.

The practice of placing pupils in private families during the summer vacation has been continued with most satisfactory results. More homes were opened to them in Massachusetts and Pennsylvania than there were pupils to send; 106 boys and girls have thus been given the best possible individual training. Removed from the rules and restraints which make up the machinery of a large institution and render the life of its inmates more or less mechanical, they are thrown upon their own resources and responsibility, and learn the self-imposed restraints and amenities and tasks which characterize home life. The appreciation of the advantages shown by the children, and their usual readiness to do their share of the work of the farm or the house, has enabled Lieutenant Pratt to secure wages for all the pupils sent out by him this summer. These wages, varying from one to fifteen dollars per month, have been paid direct to the pupils and added to the womanliness and manliness of the recipients. The good record made by the Indian youth in their temporary homes is reported in detail by Lieutenant Pratt. Forty-eight of the Carlisle pupils will remain with their new friends during the winter, doing "chores" and attending public school. The size of the buildings and the appropriation allow for the education at Carlisle of about 300 pupils, but by placing children in private families Lieutenant Pratt proposes to reduce expenses and enlarge accommodations so that he can care for 380 pupils. He will also depend on the continued liberality of friends of the Indian, who have given substantial proof of their interest in the work at Carlisle by the contribution during the year of $7,243.

The first "graduates" from Carlisle, consisting of 37 Sioux from Dakota and 35 representatives of tribes in the Indian Territory, returned to their homes in July last. These were the pupils with whom the school was started in October, 1879. It is expected that the majority of them will return to Carlisle this fall for further instruction. For this the most worthy and promising will be selected, and especially those whose moral stamina has stood the test of the temporary return to the old associations and degradations. Though the record of the students who returned last year from Hampton has been in the main satisfactory, yet it is apparent that to return immature youth to heathen homes after only three years of training under specially favorable conditions is a hazardous experiment. Justice to the child as well as economy in the service require a supplemental course of at least two years, during which the seed sown may have opportunity to take deeper root. Hereafter parents will be expected to surrender their children for five instead of three years.

Industrial work at Forest Grove has met with unusual success. The blacksmith and shoe shops have netted $772 to the school. The apprentices to the carpenter have put up two 2-story additions to the dormitories, 32 by 32 feet, and two smaller additions, 25 by 36 and 14 by 28, besides making furniture for the school and attending to necessary repairs. The renting of 45 acres furnishes an opportunity for practical lessons in farming, while several of the boys have been employed in the harvest field by farmers in that section. Lieutenant Wilkinson reports:

> The local press of the country notes the fact that without the help of the boys of the Indian school some of the farmers of this section would have had great trouble in harvesting their crops. One paper has raised its warning cry for the protection of white labor as against Indian. The boys have worked side by side with the white man, earned the same wages, and this in a section of country where it has always been claimed the Indian would not work.

As stated last year the great need at Forest Grove is the purchase of land which shall be the property of the school.

Injustice has been done this school by the wording of the appropriation for its support, which limits the amount to be paid for the care and support of the pupils to $200 per capita per annum. Expenditures can be reduced to this figure, but it will be at the expense of the best interests of the pupils in attendance.

* * *

ALLOTMENT OF LAND IN SEVERALTY AND A PERMANENT TITLE

In the last annual report of this office this subject was treated at some length. Nothing in the experience of the past year has occurred to demonstrate the inadvisability of the plan, or to cause me to change my views upon the subject. I still believe that in a great measure the future welfare and prosperity of the Indians depends upon giving them a several interest in their lands, with such a title as will protect them and their children in the peaceful and quiet possession and enjoyment thereof. In my opinion this plan is one of the keys to the solution of the Indian question. As stated in my report of last year, "The allotment system tends to break up tribal relations. It has the effect of creating individuality, responsibility, and a desire to accumulate property. It teaches the Indians habits of industry and frugality, and stimulates them to look forward to a better and more useful life, and in the end, it will relieve the government of large annual appropriations." All Indians may not at present be prepared to use to advantage lands allotted to them individually. But many of them are, and where prepared for it, the Indian should have a home of his own, as the white man has.

In many of the treaties with these people no provision is made for the allotment of their lands. In others, which contain such provisions, the amount is entirely inadequate to the wants and necessities of the Indians, being in some instances as low as twenty acres. A great many tribes occupy reservations created by the President. There is no authority of law for the allotment of the lands within this class of reservations. Many of the reservations upon which there is authority for a division of the lands in severalty have never been surveyed and subdivided and in numerous cases where this has been done the monuments, stakes, and other marks of the survey have been destroyed and obliterated by the elements or otherwise, so that even where treaty stipulations authorize allotments they cannot be made from this cause. The correspondence on the files of this office show that very many of the Indian tribes are clamorous for the allotment of their lands in severalty. Why not, then, encourage them in this advanced step towards civilization? Give the Indians his land in severalty. Let him feel his individuality and responsibility, and a sense of proprietorship. Encourage him to go to work and earn his living and provide for the future wants and necessities of himself and family, and abandon his shiftless, do-nothing, dependent life.

Upon the subject of property, Malthus says:

> According to all past experience and the best observations which can be made on the motives which operate upon the human mind, there can be no well-founded hope of obtaining a large produce from the soil but under a system of private property. It seems perfectly visionary to suppose that any stimulus short of that which is excited in man by the desire for providing for himself and family, and of bettering his condition in life, should operate on the mass of society with sufficient force and constancy to overcome the natural indolence of mankind. All the attempts which have been made since the commencement of authentic history to proceed upon a principle of common property have either been so insignificant that no inference can be drawn from them or have been marked by the most signal failures; and the changes which have been effected in modern times by education do not seem to

advance a single step toward making such a state of things more probable in future. We may therefore more safely conclude that while man retains the same physical and moral constitution which he is observed to possess at present, no other than a system of private property stands the least chance of providing for such a large and increasing population as that which is to be found in many countries at present.

These principles apply as well to the Indian as to the white man. So long as the government continues to feed the Indian and encourages him in his lazy, indolent, vagabond life, just so long will large annual appropriations have to be made out of the public treasury for that purpose. The government has before it the alternative of perpetually supporting them as idlers and drones, or of adopting some measure looking to their education in manual labor and other industrial pursuits, and their ultimate self-support and civilization. Bills providing for allotments of land in severalty were introduced in the Forty-fifth, Forty-sixth, and Forty-seventh Congresses, but no final action has been reached. It is to be hoped that Congress at its coming session will take some final and definite action upon a subject that involves so much and which is of such vital importance, not only to the Indian in his advancement and civilization, but to the general government.

Indian Homestead Entries

I again invite attention to the necessity of legislation by Congress to enable Indians to enter lands under the fifteenth and sixteenth sections of the act of Congress approved March 3, 1875, extending to Indians the benefits of the homestead act of May 20, 1862 (now embodied in sections 2290, 2291, 2292, and 2295 to 2302 Revised Statutes), without the payment of the fees and commissions now prescribed by law in such cases.

In my report for last year attention was called to the fact that, until a change is made in the law as therein recommended, it is of great importance that the department should have at its disposal a fund that can be used for the payment of entry fees and commissions, and that an estimate for the sum of $5,000 had been submitted with that end in view. No appropriation for that purpose was made. I have again submitted an estimate for the sum of $5,000 and trust that Congress will either amend the law so as to allow Indians to enter homesteads without cost to them, or will make appropriation of the sum estimated for.

United States Indian Police

Four years have now elapsed since the establishment of the United States Indian police service. Tried as an experiment, it has proved a decided success. It has accomplished all that was claimed for it, and at many agencies has become an absolute necessity. The police force was organized in the summer of 1878, in accordance with an act of Congress approved May

27, 1878, for the purpose simply of maintaining order on the reservations and of preventing the sale of liquor to Indians. Their actual duties take a much wider range. They not only take pride in keeping good order and in breaking up immoral practices, and in preventing the introduction of liquor, but they assist the agents in the discharge of many other important duties. They are proud of being considered United States soldiers, and are uniformly faithful and true to the government. Wearing the uniform of officers of the law, they have an educational influence over their associates the value of which cannot be estimated.

The system is now in operation at forty agencies, the total force employed being eighty-four commissioned officers and seven hundred and sixty-four non-commissioned officers and privates.

I would again invite attention to the small compensation allowed the officers and members of the police force. The character and requirements of the service are such as to demand the very best men at the various agencies, but these cannot often be induced to serve for the small pay offered. I would recommend that commissioned officers be paid fifteen dollars per month, sergeants ten dollars per month, and privates eight dollars per month. A much more satisfactory arrangement would be to invest the Commissioner of Indian Affairs with discretionary power as to salaries, the service at some agencies being of vastly more importance than at others.

* * *

SANITARY CONDITION OF THE INDIANS

The sanitary status of the Indians, compared with preceding years, shows improvement. The number of cases treated during the year ending June 30, 1882, were, males, 41,124; females, 32,409; total, 73,533. Number of cases remaining under treatment last annual report, 1,545; aggregate under treatment during the year, 75,078; recovered, males, 40,099; females, 31,433; total recovered, 71,532.

Died, aged over five years, males 417
Died, aged over five years, females 386
Died, aged under five years, males 202
Died, aged under five years, females 220

Total deaths 1,225

Remaining under treatment June 30, 1882, 2,321. A tabulated statement will be found facing page 426 showing the number of patients treated and respective diseases. The most formidable of the diseases noted are consumption and scrofula, the *sequela* in most of these cases noted being syphilitic infection. The greatest morbific agents have been, in the Southwest, of a malarious character, and in the Northwest, rheumatic and pulmonary. The number of births reported by the agency physicians were, males, 606; females, 553; total births, 1,159; of this number 1,046 are Indians, 99 half-breeds, and 11 are whites. The limited number of births reported is accounted for by the peculiar social custom in vogue among the Indians, which causes them to regard the mention of a birth as an indelicacy, and which precludes the physicians from ascertaining and reporting any except those which come under their immediate observation. The same remarks apply also to the deaths. The number vaccinated successfully was 6,951; unsuccessfully, 2,029; total vaccinated, 8,980.

The medical corps consists of 64 physicians, and the inference is that they have faithfully performed the duty assigned them. The physicians are steadily gaining the confidence of the Indians, and the power of the native "medicine man" is surely and gradually waning. The marked contrast between the civilized method of caring for the sick, compared with the barbarous method of the native "medicine man," has accomplished and is accomplishing much to induct the Indians into the methods and customs of Christian and civilized mankind. To the untutored mind of the Indians every action, to be effective, must have a practical bearing; every endeavor to advance them in the scale of civilization must present a phase looking to their individual temporal well-being. This is strictly true and demonstrable as to the physician's skill and surgeon's art.

When the length of time (three or four years) which is required for the physician to familiarize himself with the language, habits, and mental peculiarities of Indians is taken into consideration, and also the diplomacy which is required to obtain and maintain their confidence, it is obvious that it is specially desirable to procure efficient and, if possible, permanent medical officers of pronounced moral and temperate habits, of great will power, capable of making good and enduring impressions on the Indians. It is detrimental to the service to be continually changing medical officers.

In connection with permanent medical officers, a system should be inaugurated of caring for the blind, insane, and destitute aged Indians.

COAL DISCOVERIES ON THE WHITE MOUNTAIN INDIAN RESERVATION, ARIZONA

In the early part of last year valuable deposits of coal were discovered within the limits of what is generally known as the San Carlos division of the White Mountain Indian Reservation in Arizona Territory. Owing to the scarcity of wood or other fuel in that section of Arizona, the news of the discoveries created intense excitement, and speculators, miners, and prospectors poured in upon the reservation, thereby greatly endangering the peace of the Territory. No serious trouble occurred, however, and by the exercise of prompt and vigorous measures the reservation was finally cleared of intruders and tranquillity restored.

Various expedients were then resorted to in order to obtain lawful possession of the discoveries. Appeals were made for the segregation of the coal-bearing lands from the reservation; requests for leases were presented, and proposals submitted for an exchange of the coal lands for lands adjacent to the reservation elsewhere. A bill was introduced in Congress (H. R. 4146) having for its object the restoration of the lands embracing the coal beds to the public domain, as well as a strip extending along the entire western boundary of the reservation. Another bill, having a similar object (H. R. 5378), provides for an exchange of the coal-bearing lands for grazing and arable lands to be added to the reservation on the north and west. The practicability of removing the Indians to the Indian Territory was discussed, and a proposition of that kind was presented to the Indians themselves; but it was found that they were decidedly and unalterably opposed to any such measure.

This office has been in sympathy with the general desire to have these valuable deposits made available to the public use, but how to accomplish that end without working injustice to the Indians has been a question requiring serious consideration. General Sherman, when on a recent visit to the San Carlos reserve, expressed the opinion that the Indians could never be prevailed upon to remove again, and it is exceedingly doubtful if they would be satisfied with any further reduction of their reservation, it having already been cut down no less than five times within the last ten years. The government cannot undertake to work the mines, nor are the Indians sufficiently advanced as artisans or in ordinary manual labor pursuits to do so advantageously, had they the necessary authority to enable them to dispose of the coal as a means of profit to themselves. Moreover, under existing law there is no authority for permitting the severance and removal from an Indian reservation, for purposes of sale or speculation, of any material attached to or forming a part of the realty, such as timber, coal, or other minerals.

After carefully considering the questions involved, this office became convinced that the most practicable solution of the matter would be the adoption of a system of leasing upon a royalty plan; and accordingly a draft of a joint resolution was prepared in this office and submitted to the department in April last with a view to securing the needful legislation therefor. It was believed that by this means a very large part of the annual expenditure for the support and care of the Indians of Arizona and New Mexico might be reimbursed to the government from the profit of the mines without hardship to consumers, and that the Indians themselves would be greatly benefited, not only by the example of industry set, but through the opportunity that would be afforded them to earn wages by their own labor. The draft of resolution as prepared was transmitted to Congress by the President on April 17, following, but no final action had been taken thereon at the date of adjournment.

The following is the language of the resolution:

JOINT RESOLUTION AUTHORIZING THE SECRETARY OF THE INTERIOR TO LEASE CERTAIN COAL LANDS EMBRACED WITHIN THE LIMITS OF THE WHITE MOUNTAIN INDIAN RESERVATION IN THE TERRITORY OF ARIZONA.

Whereas it has been discovered that large and valuable deposits of coal exist within the limits of the White Mountain Reservation, in the Territory of Arizona, a reservation set apart by sundry executive orders; and

Whereas it would be contrary to the practice, if not beyond the lawful power of the executive department of the government having the management and control of the Indians and the Indian country, to remove the coal there known to exist, or to permit its removal for the purpose of profit, or for any purpose other than to meet the necessary wants of the Indians or the agency or military service in the care and oversight of the Indians, without the express authority of Congress therefor; and

Whereas the government is expending annually not less than three hundred thousand dollars for the support of the Apache and other Indians in Arizona and New Mexico, which amount, it is suggested by the executive department aforesaid, might be largely if not wholly reimbursed to the government without hardship to those who would be the natural purchasers and consumers thereof, if said coal were made available as an article of commerce, by leasing the coal-bearing lands to persons who would mine the same if permitted to do so: Therefore,

Be it resolved by the Senate and House of Representatives of the United States of America in Congress assembled, That the Secretary of the Interior be, and he is hereby, authorized and empowered to lease, after due public advertisement in not less than three newspapers having the largest regular circulation in the Territory of Arizona, for a period of not less than thirty days, to the highest responsible bidder for cash, on a system or basis of royalty, under such terms, restrictions, and limitations as in his best judgment he may see fit to require, and in such tracts or parcels as he may deem proper and necessary for the public good, any or all of the coal beds now known to exist, or that may hereafter be discovered into the Treasury of the United States to reimbursement of any moneys that may hereafter be appropriated for the support and care of the said Apache and other Indians in Arizona and New Mexico: Provided, That if any amount in excess of the sum required annually to maintain and care for said Indians shall be realized from the lease or leases that may be executed under the authority of this act, such amount shall be used to reimburse the government for any moneys that may hereafter be appropriated for the support and care of any of the other bands of tribes of Indians in the Southwest.

I respectfully renew my recommendations in respect of the foregoing.

* * *

THE NEZ PERCÉ INDIANS OF JOSEPH'S BAND

The question as to the final settlement and permanent location of the Nez Percé Indians who surrendered under Chief Joseph to General Miles, in the year 1877, has been a subject of much concern and annoyance both to the department and the Indians themselves. The facts in connection with their surrender and subsequent location in the Indian Territory, are matters of public notoriety, and have been alluded to in former annual reports. At the time of the surrender it was stated, and the information before this office corroborated the statement, that such cruel and unprovoked murders had been committed by Joseph and his band in Idaho as to create an almost insuperable barrier against their return to their old home, and to banish all expectation of peace or safety for Joseph and his followers on that reservation, or in its vicinity, at least until the resentment awakened by these offenses should be somewhat modified by the lapse of time. With a desire to solve the problem in such a way as to maintain and enforce a proper and due regard for the laws and authority of the government, and at the same time avoid doing any injustice to a brave but misguided captive, this office and the department acquiesced in the various recommendations of the distinguished military officials who had been actively engaged in accomplishing the surrender, and who had also taken a very prominent part in endeavoring to secure an amicable settlement of the difficulties, and consented to the removal of Joseph and his band to the Indian Territory.

By the Indian appropriation act of May 27, 1878 (20 Stat., p. 74), an appropriation was made to enable the Secretary of the Interior to remove these Nez Percés, then held prisoners of war at Fort Leavenworth, Kansas, to a suitable location in the Indian Territory, and for their settlement thereon. On the 21st of July, 1878, these Indians were turned over to Inspector McNeil and Agent Jones, and placed upon the Quapaw Reservation. On the 15th of October, 1878, Commissioner Hayt visited them, and took chiefs Young Joseph and Husescruyt (Bald-Head) to the west of the Arkansas River for the purpose of selecting a permanent home for the band. They selected a tract a few miles west of the Ponca Reserve, where the Sha-kaskia empties into Salt Creek, viz, townships 25 and 26 N., ranges 1 and 2 west, containing 90,710.89 acres.

On the 31st of January, 1879, Young Joseph and Yellow Bull, first and second chiefs, acting for the band, made an agreement whereby they proposed to relinquish all claim to their lands in Idaho or elsewhere and settle permanently in the Indian Territory upon four townships of land to be selected and purchased by the government for their use and occupancy, which agreement was submitted to the department February 1, 1879, for ratification by Congress, and was accompanied by a draft of bill for that purpose. The bill did not become a law, yet the Indians have been located on the four townships above named, and Congress for three years has made annual appropriations for their maintenance and support thereon.

It has been hoped that the advantages of the location selected for this band of Nez Percés in the Indian Territory would be such as to engender in them a spirit of enterprise and emulation, which after a few years would make them comparatively contented with their new home. This hope, however, has not been realized, and although, since the time of their surrender, these people have exhibited a quiet and unmurmuring submission to the inevitable, and have manifested a conscientious desire to obey all laws and regulations provided for their government, yet as each year passes numerous petitions and urgent requests come from them praying to be returned to their old home and relatives. Their quiet and peaceable conduct since the surrender, and their efforts to be law-abiding and self-supporting are commendable, and under the circumstances remarkable.

The larger proportion of the Nez Percé tribe is located on the reservation in Idaho, and as a rule this tribe has been a strict observer of all treaty convenants with the government. They were active in their efforts to subdue the outbreak of Chief Joseph and his band, and in the battle with their kindred some of them were killed and others wounded. Joseph and his band appear to be the only ones of the tribe who have ever engaged in hostility against the whites. Not in the least excusing or attempting to palliate the crimes alleged to have been committed by them, it is but fair to say that their warfare was conducted with a noticeable absence of savage barbarity on their part, and that they persistently claim that when they surrendered to General Miles it was with the express stipulation that they should be sent back to Idaho. Whether this alleged stipulation be true or not, it is a fact that their unfortunate location near Fort Leavenworth, when in charge of the military, and the influences of the climate where they are now located in the Indian Territory, have caused much sickness among them; their ranks have been sadly depleted, and it is claimed that if they are much longer compelled to remain in their present situation, the entire band will become virtually extinct.

It is now about five years since the surrender, and a sufficient time has probably elapsed to justify the belief that no concerted effort will be taken to avenge wrongs alleged to have been perpetrated by these people so many years ago. The band now numbers only about 322 souls, and the reservation in Idaho is ample to accommodate them comfortably, in addition to those who are already there, who are substantially self-supporting and who have enough to spare a portion for their less fortunate brethren, and, as I understand, are willing to give them such aid.

The deep-rooted love for the "old home," which is so conspicuous among them, and their longing desire to leave the warm, debilitating climate of the Indian Territory for the more healthy and invigorating air of the Idaho Mountains, can never be eradicated, and any longer delay, with the hope of a final contentment on their part with their present situation, is, in my judgment, futile and unnecessary. In view of all the facts, I am constrained to believe that the remnant of this tribe should be returned to Idaho, if possible, early next spring, and I respectfully suggest that this matter be submitted to Congress at its next session, with a recommendation that an appropriation be made sufficient to meet the necessary expenses of removal thither. But if Congress should decide that the best interests of all concerned will be best subserved by retaining these Indians where they now are, it will be necessary to have such legislation as will perfect the title to the lands which have been selected for them and upon which they now reside.

Report of Commissioner of Indian Affairs Hiram Price, October 10, 1883

(Excerpt from *Report for 1883*, pp. 7-11, 17-20, 48-49)

Commissioner Price's report was concerned basically with the inability of white law to reach the Indian in the Indian country. He cited a particular instance of the lack of jurisdiction over crimes committed by Indians on Indian territory. Price's contempt for Indian justice was patent and it did not occur to him that Indian law might be equally valid or possibly superior to white law in achieving justice and domestic tranquillity. Price also noted the establishment of courts of Indian offenses which the Secretary had authorized to be established among many of the tribes. The success of such experiments, in which Indians themselves took over some of the burden of law and order on the reservation, would soon be confirmed. While complaining about the quality of Indian law, Commissioner Price recounted the story of how illegal intruders were flooding into the Indian Territory, a movement which the white judicial system seemed incapable of stopping. Commissioner Price's comments on the condition of the Indians in Montana provide an example of what happened to an Indian tribe when its traditional sources of food were exhausted.

LAWS FOR THE GOVERNMENT OF INDIANS

IN THE ANNUAL REPORTS of this office for several years past, attention has been invited to the urgent necessity for the enactment of some suitable code of laws for Indian reservations. Indians in the Indian country are not punishable for crimes or offenses committed against the persons or property of each other. Such offenses are generally left to the penalties of tribal usage, involving personal vengeance or pecuniary satisfaction, or the offenders are subjected to a few weeks or months arbitrary confinement in an agency guardhouse or military fort. The Indian is not a citizen of the United States. He cannot sue or be sued under the judiciary act of 1789, and only gets into Federal courts as a civil litigant, in occasional instances, by favor of special law, and in many of the States and Territories he has no standing at all in court.

The evils resulting from this state of affairs are forcibly described by Bishop Hare in his annual report, dated September 11, 1877. He says:

> Civilization has loosened, in some places broken, the bonds which regulate and holds together Indian society in its wild state, and has failed to give the people law and officers of justice in their place. This evil still continues

344

unabated. Women are brutally beaten and outraged; men are murdered in cold blood; the Indians who are friendly to schools and churches are intimidated and preyed upon by the evil-disposed; children are molested on their way to school, and schools are dispersed by bands of vagabonds; but there is no redress. This accursed condition of things is an outrage upon the One Lawgiver. It is a disgrace to our land. It should make every man who sits in the national halls of legislation blush. And, wish well to the Indians as we may, and do for them what we will, the efforts of civil agents, teachers, and missionaries are like the struggles of drowning men weighted with lead, as long as by the absence of law Indian society is left without a base.

No action has been taken by Congress on repeated recommendations from this office and numberless petitions from Government officials, institutions, religious societies, missionaries, and other philanthropists asking for the enactment of a general statute putting Indians under the restraints and protection of law. It has occurred to me that, pending the long delay in the enactment of a general law on the subject, a considerable body of Indians might soon be brought within the jurisdiction of courts in another way. In Dakota and New Mexico are nearly 60,000 Indians. If, when those Territories become States, it shall be provided that the respective State courts shall have jurisdiction over Indian reservations within the boundaries of those States, the condition of the Indians residing therein will be vastly improved. And I would particularly recommend that hereafter, whenever a State is admitted into the Union, the act of admission shall contain a provision giving to Indians within its limits all the rights, privileges, and immunities enjoyed by the citizens thereof, and subjecting them to like penalties, liabilities, restrictions, &c., except in cases specially otherwise provided for by treaty or act of Congress.

In my opinion, Congress should confer both civil and criminal jurisdiction on the several States and Territories over all Indian reservations within their respective limits, and make the person and property of the Indian amenable to the laws of the State or Territory in which he may reside (except in cases where such property is expressly exempted by treaty or act of Congress), and give him all the rights in the courts enjoyed by other persons.

As demonstrating the incongruity of existing statutes in relation to crimes committed by Indians, and the urgent necessity for a radical amendment thereof, I desire to invite special attention to an occurence which has been brought prominently before this office during the current year. On the 18th September, 1882, Robert Poisal, a half-breed Arapaho belonging to the Cheyenne and Arapaho Reservation in the Indian Territory, while driving home with his niece, Mrs. Meagher, from the Sacred Heart Mission, in the Pottawatomie country in that Territory, whither they had been to place some of their children at school, was shot down and killed by Johnson Foster, a Creek Indian. This occurred at a point about 45 miles east of the agency, on the Shawneetown road, about 20 miles from Kickapoo Village, on the Pottawatomie Reservation, a tract of country specially set apart by act of Congress for the Pottawatomies and Shawnees. There was no apparent motive for the murder other than plunder. The murderer was arrested by the Seminole Light Horse and brought into the Cheyenne and Arapaho Agency, whence, in order to escape the summary vengeance threatened by the Arapahoes, he was turned over to the military authorities at Fort Reno for safe keeping.

The facts being reported to this Department, and an examination of the treaties with the Cheyenne and Arapaho Indians seemingly favoring the view that the United States court had jurisdiction of the crime committed, the honorable Attorney-General, upon the recommendation of the Department, instructed the United States attorney for the western district of Arkansas to arrange for the immediate removal of the prisoner to Fort Smith, and for his trial there before the United States court. Section 2145 of the Revised Statutes provides—

> Except as to crimes the punishment of which is expressly provided for in this title the general laws of the United States as to the punishment of crimes committed in any place within the sole and exclusive jurisdiction of the United States, except the District of Columbia, shall extend to the Indian country.

Section 2146 enacts—

> The preceding section shall not be construed to extend to *crimes committed by one Indian against the person or property of another Indian, nor to* any Indian committing any offense in the Indian country who has been punished by the local law of the tribe, or to any case where by treaty stipulations the exclusive jurisdiction over such offenses is or may be secured to the Indian tribes respectively. (See "An act to correct errors and supply omissions in the Revised Statutes of the United States," approved February 18, 1875; 18 Stat., p. 316.)

The United States attorney for the western district of Arkansas, having expressed the opinion that under section 2146, above quoted, the United States court was without jurisdiction in the premises, and that the trial and punishment of the offender was a matter properly belonging to the Indians themselves, the honorable Attorney-General was inclined to think it would be a useless expense to transport the prisoner to Fort Smith, but invited a further expression of the views of this Department before issuing definite instructions to the district attorney. On the 4th November last this office replied through the Department, and referred to the second clause of the treaties with the Cheyenne and Arapaho Indians (15 Stat., 593; *Id.*, 655), reading as follows—

> If bad men among the whites, or among other people subject to the authority of the United States, shall commit any wrong upon the person or property of the Indians, the United States will, upon proof made to the agent and forwarded to the Commissioner of Indian Affairs at Washington city, proceed at once to cause the offender to be arrested and punished according to the laws of the United States, and also reimburse the injured person for the loss sustained.

and took the position that the murder having been committed within the Pottawatomie country, the prisoner came within the meaning of the term "other people subject to the authority of the United States," and was excepted from the general law as expressed in section 2146, and therefore that the United States court could take jurisdiction of the case; citing the case of Crow Dog, a Sioux Indian recently tried and convicted by the United States court in Dakota, for the murder of Spotted Tail, an Indian of the same tribe. On the 7th November last the honorable Attorney-General replied to the effect that, while admitting there was some ground for the argument, he considered the question of jurisdiction by the United States court over the case as so doubtful as to render it inexpedient to incur the expense of the prisoner's removal and trial at Fort Smith.

The military authorities at Fort Reno, having applied through the War Department to be relieved of the custody of the prisoner, this office, in view of the opinion of the Attorney-General, by letter of the 11th June last, inquired of the Department what disposition should be made of the prisoner. Attention was called to the fact that the courts of the Creek Nation, to which nation the prisoner belonged, were without jurisdiction, the murder having been committed outside the limits of their country; that the Absentee Shawnees and Pottawatomies, within whose boundaries the crime was committed, had no laws applicable to the case, and that neither the Cheyennes and Arapahoes nor the Absentee Shawnees and Pottawatomies were parties to the reciprocity compact entered into between the Cherokee, Muscogee, Seminole, Osage and other nations, on the 4th June, 1870 (see Laws of Muscogee, or Creek Nation, edition 1880, p. 85); and it was suggested that in view of the many complications attendant on the case the Attorney-General be requested to reconsider his decision, to the end that the question of jurisdiction might be passed upon by the United States court, or that the Department be pleased to indicate what action should be taken upon the request of the War Department, in order that full justice might be done all parties concerned. Said letter having been duly referred to the Department of Justice, the honorable Attorney-General on the 27th June last replied at considerable length, setting forth his views on the legal aspect of the case and adhering to his opinion already expressed that there was but little ground to hope that the United States court had jurisdiction of the offense. Recognizing, however, the embarrassments prevailing, he stated that if it occurred to the Department as a matter of importance that the opinion of the courts should be taken in the course of a vigorous prosecution of the crime he would cheerfully execute whatever suggestion might be made, adding that such prosecution, whatever its issue, might more effectually call the attention of Congress to the general subject, which indeed seemed to require further legislative consideration. Thereupon the Department, upon the recommendation of this office, availed itself of the Attorney-General's suggestion, and, under date of the 24th July last, requested that the United States attorney for the district of Kansas be directed to take the necessary steps for the trial of the prisoner before the United States district court at Wichita, Kans., to which, by act of Congress of January 6, 1883, is committed jurisdiction over all that part of the Indian Territory lying north of the Canadian River and east of Texas and the one hundredth meridian, not set apart and occupied by the Cherokee, Creek, and Seminole tribes (22 Stat., 400).

In the mean time the prisoner, Johnson Foster, had been removed from the guard-house at Fort Reno by a United States deputy marshal *en route* to Fort Smith, Arkansas, there to be tried for horse-stealing and other minor offenses previously pending against him. The deputy secured a strong guard of troops to assist in escorting the prisoner beyond the limits of the agency, notwithstanding which a small party of young Arapahoes made a bold dash when about 15 miles out from the agency, and came very near getting their man, but finally abandoned the attempt. I am since officially informed by the agent that while on the road to Fort Smith and near the Osage Agency, Foster succeeded in brutally murdering McWeir, the marshal's assistant, and in making his escape. At last accounts he was at large.

Of course, in the event of his recapture, having now murdered a white man, there can be no failure of justice for want of jurisdiction in the United States court, but I have purposely referred to this case in detail as a glaring instance of the injustice of a law which, by remitting the trial and punishment of a murderer of one of their own race to the Indians themselves, recognizes the forfeiture of a few ponies or other property to the murdered man's relatives as a sufficient atonement for the crime. I do not undertake to say that the position contended for by this office in the Johnson case would have been wholly tenable before the United States court. In that respect I am bound to defer to the opinion of the honorable Attorney-General, although he admitted that the question was one by no means free from doubt; but I do venture to maintain that this case pre-eminently shows that it is high time that crimes among Indians should be defined by United States laws, and the Department be relieved from all possible chance of future embarrassment by reason of the exception contained in the statute referred to. What is required is a law for the punishment of crimes and offenses among the Indians themselves, one which shall make the Indian equally secure with the white man in his individual rights of person and property, and equally amenable for any violation of the rights of others.

COURT OF INDIAN OFFENSES

On the 10th of April last you gave your official approval to certain rules governing the "court of Indian offenses," prepared in this office in accordance with instructions contained in your letter of December 2 last. These rules prohibit the sun-dance, scalp-dance and war-dance, polygamy, theft, &c., and provide for the organization at each agency of a tribunal composed of Indians empowered to try all cases of infraction of the rules. Printed copies of the rules have been sent to the various United States Indian agencies (except the agency for the five civilized tribes), with instructions to agents to nominate the judges provided for therein. Many of the agents have as yet been unable to organize the court; some asking for further time, others reporting their inability to secure the services of proper men to fill the positions, the larger proportion, however, assigning as a reason for the delay that their Indians positively refuse to accept a position as judge unless their services in that capacity are paid for by the Government. If this latter objection were removed, and an appropriation made for the payment of a stated salary for the judges, say $20 per month, I am of the opinion that the "court of Indian offenses," with some few modifications, could be placed in successful operation at the various agencies, and thereby many of the barbarous customs now existing among the Indians would be entirely abolished.

There is no good reason why an Indian should be permitted to indulge in practices which are alike repugnant to common decency and morality; and the preservation of good order on the reservations demands that some active measures should be taken to discourage and, if possible, put a stop to the demoralizing influence of heathenish rites. With this end in view the several courts are to be organized; but if it is desired to carry this plan into successful operation, it is absolutely necessary that some arrangement be made to pay a reasonable compensation to those who are to be called upon to preside as judges. I therefore recommend that the matter be submitted to Congress, asking an appropriation of $50,000 to be used in paying the salaries of the judges, at the rate of $20 each per month, the surplus to be used in paying other expenses incident to the organization of the court and the employment of such officers as may be found necessary to carry out and execute the various orders and decrees of the court.

In my opinion the appropriation for this purpose would be in the line of economy, in that it would avoid much of the expense heretofore incurred by the Government in its efforts to suppress offenses which now come under the rules referred to.

* * *

INTRUDERS ON INDIAN LANDS

As stated in the previous reports, an amendment to the law in reference to intruders so as to punish by imprisonment as well as fine is absolutely necessary. An intruder without property has very little fear of a fine. Some intruders have already been removed several times by the Indian police or the military, and as often have returned. The present law, imposing a fine *only*, has no terrors for this class of men. All that can at present be done is to remove the intruder, and if he reappears to bring a civil suit against him in the nature of an action of debt to recover the statutory penalty of $1,000.

I have yet to hear of a single instance in which the penalty has been recovered. The result is expense to the Government for no purpose. Notwithstanding his repeated expulsion from the Indian Territory, Payne and his party of "Oklahoma colonists" have twice during the present year made attempts at settlement in that country, requiring the aid of the military, at great expense to the Government, to effect their removal.

In addition to the urgent recommendations which have repeatedly been made by this office and the Department on the subject, the Secretary of War deemed this frequent furnishing of troops for the removal of trespassers, at great expense to the Government, without any practical results, as a matter of such serious importance in the interests of the military service and of public economy that on the 2d February last he addressed a special communication to the President urging the amendment of section 2148, Revised Statutes, by providing a term of imprisonment for unlawfully entering upon Indian lands. This communication was transmitted by the President to Congress on the 5th February last, and on the 3d of the same month Dr. Dawes introduced in the Senate a bill (S. 2450), some time previously prepared in this office, reading as follows:

> *Be it enacted by the Senate and House of Representatives of the United States of America in Congress assembled,* That section twenty-one hundred and forty-eight of the Revised Statutes of the United States be amended to read as follows, namely:
> "Every person who without authority of law enters and shall be found upon any Indian lands, tribal reservation, or lands specially set apart for Indian purposes, shall, for the first offense, upon conviction thereof, pay a fine of not more than five hundred dollars, and be imprisoned at hard labor for not more than one year; and for every subsequent offense, shall, upon conviction thereof, pay a fine of not more than one thousand dollars, and not less than five hundred dollars, and be imprisoned at hard labor for not more than two years, nor less than one year; and the wagons, teams and outfit of such person or persons so offending shall be seized and delivered to the proper United States officer, and be proceeded against by libel in the proper court and forfeited, one-half to the informer and the other half to the United States, and in all cases arising under this act, Indians shall be competent witnesses: *Provided, however,* That the provisions of this section shall not apply to emigrants or travelers peaceably passing through such Indian lands, tribal reservations, or lands especially set apart for Indian purposes, without committing any willful trespass or injury to person or property."

On the 10th February last the bill as read and referred was reported back by the Senate Committee on Indian Affairs without amendment, but Congress again adjourned without taking action in the matter.

While on this subject I desire to say a few words in regard to the repeated attempts which have been made by United States citizens during the past four years to unlawfully appropriate certain lands of the Indian Territory reserved under treaty by the Government for Indian purposes, under the pretext that such lands are open to the public for settlement. Full accounts of these raids and of the measures taken by the Government to expel the intruders will be found in the successive annual reports of this office for the years 1879, 1880, 1881, and 1882. During the period referred to, D. L. Payne, the recognized leader of the movement, had been repeatedly arrested only to be released by the military authorities on the Kansas border, or held to answer to a civil suit in the United States court at Fort Smith to recover the penalty imposed by the statute, a suit invariably terminating without any practical result. With each repetition the movement appears to acquire additional strength. From official reports made to the War Department and on file in this office, I learn that in the expedition which left Arkansas City for the Oklahoma lands on the 1st February last there were about 250 persons, principally from Kansas and Missouri, including some 20 women and children, with from 80 to 100 wagons filled with provisions and forage sufficient to last them 30 or 40 days, and with tents, furniture, agricultural implements, &c. They appeared in the main to be a well-to-do, quiet set of farmers, and a different class of people from those who had been engaged in previous similar enterprises, but they were all well armed, mostly with Winchester rifles and carbines, and among them it was reported there was one man from Wichita, Kans., who had with him a full wagon-load of whiskey and cigars, intending to open a saloon on arriving at their destination.

Besides this party, there were other and smaller outfits which were discovered and heard of *en route* from Caldwell and Coffeyville, Kans., to join the main body. Those from Caldwell are stated to have been with one or two exceptions persons without visible means of support, whom the citizens, though deprecating the movement, were glad to get rid of at any price.

Payne with his secretary, one W. H. Osburn, traveled with the Arkansas City party, and at a meeting held there the night before starting he is said to have roundly abused the Government and the Army. From the same official sources I learn that every member who joins the Oklahoma colony pays $2.50 for a certificate of membership therein, of which 50 cents are retained by the secretary and the remainder goes into Payne's pockets. The form of certificate is as follows:

This certifies that ——— ———, having paid the fee of two dollars, is a member of Payne's Oklahoma Colony, is entitled to all the benefits and protection of said colony and an equal voice in all matters pertaining to and the formation of its local government.

In testimony whereof the official signatures of the president and secretary are hereto subscribed, and the seal of the colony attached.

——— ———,
President.

——— ———,
Secretary.

I also learn that Payne issues "land certificates" to persons who do not desire to go down themselves by which he guarantees them 160 acres of land in the "Oklahoma Colony" in consideration of $25, which it is also stated he appropriates to his own use. I have no copy of this last mentioned certificate; but, even if there are no other controlling influences at work, it is manifestly a profitable speculation for Payne himself, who is not likely to desist from starting these expeditions so long as he can find persons credulous enough to part with their money on such worthless assurances, or so long as the law in relation to trespassers on Indian lands remains in its present unsatisfactory condition.

From a letter dated June 26 last, addressed to the Department by the honorable Secretary of War, I am advised that Payne has now applied to the United States circuit court at Topeka, Kans., for an injunction restraining military interference with his entrance into and occupation of the Oklahoma district of the Indian Territory, thus bringing up for judicial decision the whole question affecting the status of said district; and that the matter has been referred by the War Department to the Attorney-General to take such measures as may be deemed necessary to protect the interests of the United States in the premises.

I respectfully recommend that the attention of Congress be specially drawn to these aggressive movements on the Indian Territory lands, as illustrating the urgent necessity for speedy and effective legislation in regard to trespassers.

TIMBER DEPREDATIONS ON INDIAN LANDS

Notwithstanding the repeated recommendations made by this office for legislation to protect the timber on Indian lands, no definite action has been taken by Congress, and depredations upon valuable timber, especially in the Indian Territory, are of constant occurrence. At the first session of the Forty-seventh Congress a bill (S. 1646), prepared in this office, extending to Indian lands the provisions of section 5388 of the Revised Statutes of the United States for the protection and preservation of timber, passed the Senate with a slight amendment, but failed to receive action in the House, either at that or the concluding session. The urgent necessity for this measure is shown in the correspondence set out in the report of the Senate committee, to which I beg to refer.

* * *

DEPLORABLE CONDITION OF INDIANS IN MONTANA

The reduction by Congress of appropriations for subsistence of the Blackfeet, Blood, and Piegan Indians, and of the Indians at Fort Peck and Fort Belknap agencies, has already caused a great deal of suffering among these Indians, and is a source of constant and increasing anxiety and embarrassment to this office. It is true that the Indians show a willingness to add to the supplies furnished by the Government by taking advantage of such facilities for procuring subsistence as their reservations naturally afford or can be made to yield by cultivation; still it is clear that, from causes beyond their control or that of this Bureau, they have lately needed more assistance from the Government than formerly, as the game upon which they have depended principally for food and clothing has been gradually diminishing, until it is now nearly extinct, while repeated trials have shown that successful farming on these reservations would be impossible, even to whites, without the necessary irrigating ditches, fences, stock, &c., and for such purposes no funds have been supplied.

Speaking of the Blackfeet, Blood, and Piegan Indians in a report dated July 26 last, an Indian inspector says:

> There can be no doubt but many of the young children died from lack of food during last winter and spring. Never before have I been called upon to listen in an Indian council to such tales of suffering. Three or four years ago this reservation abounded in game and these Indians were, practically, independent of the Government; now, nowhere else have I ever seen a country so destitute of it as this, and there is, practically, nothing for the people to live upon but what is furnished by the Government. I cannot believe that Congress was fully aware of the change in the surroundings of these Indians when the annual appropriation was diminished.

In reference to the same Indians a special agent reports, under date of August 21 last:

> Last week 3,200 persons presented themselves as actually in need of subsistence, to furnish which, in the established quantities (which are found to be merely sufficient to sustain life) for the balance of the fiscal year, would require at least four times the quantity of flour supplied, and although but half a ration is issued, it will all be exhausted about midwinter, and all the beef available will be gone about the same time, although but one-fifth the established ration is being issued. I am fearful that unless additional supplies are furnished depredations must be expected to prevent starvation, and early action is necessary, as the severe winter here renders transportation of supplies at that time impossible in this country.
>
> This reservation cannot be farmed without irrigation, no preparation for which has been made; therefore but little can be expected from Indian cultivation, and as illustrative of the seasons here, this morning, August 21, the ground around the agency is covered with snow.

Under date of the 14th untimo, an Indian inspector speaks of the Indians at the Fort Peck Agency, whose reservation adjoins that of the Blackfeet, &c., as follows:

> During my visit all the Indians were in camp, having returned hungry from a hunt which was unsuccessful. They farm about 700 acres, nearly every field

of which I visited. Their crops, which are principally corn, are a total failure, although well tended; the squaws, in many instances, still hoeing and working in the fields, although it is evident they cannot possibly raise anything. Last year, also, their crops were almost a total failure. As it is, some extra provision must be made for this people during the winter, or trouble will come. It will require at least 1,000,000 pounds of beef to keep them from suffering. Unless this is furnished, or they find plenty of buffalo (the latter even hardly to be look for), they cannot be prevented from committing depredations on stock wherever they can find it.

Their crops must be watered during the growing season, or farming might as well be abandoned here. A field of 1,000 acres on the river bottom near the agency can be throughly irrigated by a ditch which could be dug by the Indians for pay in provisions, to cost about three or four thousand dollars. From this field enough vegetables and breadstuffs could be raised every year to supply all their wants in that line. This outlay would be great economy, as otherwise, if these Indians are to remain where they are they will have to be fed entirely by the Government, as they cannot be expected to succeed in farming where a white man would starve.

The agent in charge of Fort Belknap Agency, the home of the Gros Ventres and Assinaboines, also adjoining the Blackfeet, writes under date of 21st ultimo:

Game on this reservation is practically exhausted. My Indians, many of whom have lately returned to the agency from hunting, all concur in this statement, the truth of which is established by my own observation and by a report of an officer of the United States Army who has lately made an extended expedition over the reserve.

My Indians are already coming in every day complaining of hunger, but I can feed them very little as the winter will soon be here when they must be fed or they will starve and commit depredations. To divide the supplies of flour and beef furnished for the year, viz, 100,000 pounds of the former and 180,000 pounds of the latter, into fifty-two parts would allow but about one pound of flour and two pounds of beef, gross, *per week* to each person. While there was plenty of game this could be made to do, but now I am confronted with a problem which it is almost impossible for me to solve; and unless some assistance is rendered in time, I fear the question of whether it is cheaper to feed or to fight Indians will have another test. If the Government expects ever to make this people self-sustaining, it must furnish means to start them in the right way, viz: by supplying their wants for the present, and assisting them, by irrigation, &c., to live by farming in the near future.

Efforts have been made to establish agency herds for these Indians, but with very poor success, as they cannot be prevented from killing the cattle when driven to do so by hunger.

In view of the foregoing, I would recommend that the early attention of Congress be called to the condition of the Indians at the three agencies mentioned, that such steps as may be considered proper and necessary towards assisting them may be taken at as early a day as practicable.

Report of Commissioner of Indian Affairs J. D. C. Atkins October 5, 1885

(Excerpt from *Report for 1885*, pp. 3-13, 21-24, 51-53, 58-60, 67-69)

Commissioner Atkins began his annual report with a rosy picture of the time when every Indian would own a homestead in severalty. "What a heritage!" he exclaimed. Atkins could not imagine that "there should be an Indian of any tribe in the whole country" who would refuse such an offer within five years from the inauguration of the policy. Atkins would not have long to test the validity of his proposition. He did have the pleasure of reporting the success of Indian police and courts of Indian offenses run by Indians. Although conceived to eradicate Indian customs, they achieved success because they let the Indians do the work of apprehending and judging those of their number. Other portions of Atkins' report detailed the ever-present problem of white encroachment upon Indian land.

IN COMPLIANCE with the requirements of law, I have the honor to submit my annual report of the operations of the Indian Bureau for the year 1885; prefacing the same with some observations which will indicate the policy which I think should be adopted in the management of the affairs of the Indians.

This Bureau will be fortunate if it should, amid the many conflicting interests with which the rights of the Indians are confronted, be able to secure to them full and complete justice; while, on the other hand, it will fall very short of its duty should it waver in its determination to require from them a substantial compliance with its regulations and an obedience to the laws.

FARMS AND HOMES

It requires no seer to foretell or foresee the civilization of the Indian race as a result naturally deducible from a knowledge and practice upon their part of the art of agriculture; for the history of agriculture among all people and in all countries intimately connects it with the highest intellectual and moral development of man. Historians, philosophers, and statesmen freely admit that civilization as naturally follows the improved arts of agriculture as vegetation follows the genial sunshine and the shower, and that those races who are in ignorance of agriculture are also ignorant of almost everything else. The Indian constitutes no exception to this political

355

maxim. Steeped as his progenitors were, and as more than half of the race now are, in blind ignorance, the devotees of abominable superstitions, and the victims of idleness and thriftlessness, the absorbing query which the hopelessness of his situation, if left to his own guidance, suggests to the philanthropist, and particularly to a great Christian people like ours, is to know how to relieve him from this state of dependence and barbarism, and to direct him in paths that will eventually lead him to the light and liberty of American citizenship.

There are in the United States, exclusive of Alaska, about 260,000 Indian souls. Of that number there are in the five civilized tribes in the Indian Territory 64,000. There are in New York, 4,970, in North Carolina, 3,000, and there are some in Dakota, Nebraska, Kansas, Wisconsin, and Minnesota, and a few in California and the Northwest, who are civilized; and still others who can lay some claim to civilization. Many others on the reservations have cast off the blanket and are adopting the fashions and dress of white people. But among all these, except among the Indians of New York and North Carolina, a few in some of the Northwestern States, and a part of the five civilized tribes in the Indian Territory, is a very large number who do not till the soil. Nearly all who are called "blanket Indians" have never tilled the soil to any extent, and fully half of the Indians of the United States, exclusive of Alaska, as yet have declined to commit themselves to the life of the farmer.

Exclusive of the lands cultivated by the five civilized tribes, the number of acres in cultivation by Indians during the present year is 248,241, an increase of 18,473 acres over last year's figures. The acreage of cultivated land has steadily increased for several years past, the amount in cultivation for the last three years being—1883, 210,272; 1884, 229,768; 1885, 248,241 acres. The increased interest in agriculture manifested since the opening of last spring, and the preparations on several reservations for still larger increase of acreage in farming, are among the hopeful signs of Indian progress and development.

This brings me directly to the consideration of the practical policy which I believe should be adopted by Congress and the Government in the management of the Indians. It should be industriously and gravely impressed upon them that they must abandon their tribal relations and take lands in severalty, as the corner-stone of their complete success in agriculture, which means self-support, personal independence, and material thrift. The Government should, however, in order to protect them, retain the right to their lands in trust for twenty-five years or longer, but issue trust patents at once to such Indians as have taken individual holdings. When the Indians have taken their lands in severalty in sufficient quantities (and the number of acres in each holding may and should vary in different localities according to fertility, productiveness, climatic, and other advantages), then having due regard to the immediate and early future needs of the Indians, the remaining lands of their reservations should be purchased by the

Government and opened to homestead entry at 50 or 75 cents per acre. The money paid by the Government for their lands should be held in trust in 5 per cent. bonds, to be invested as Congress may provide, for the education, civilization, and material development and advancement of the red race, reserving for each tribe its own money. This is all the Indians need to place them beyond the oppression and greed of white men who seek, as Mr. Barbour said in 1825 in his report as Secretary of War, "to bereave the Indians of their lands."

The advantages to the Indians of taking their lands in severalty are so important and far-reaching in their effects that I fear to dwell upon them in this report lest I be accused of drawing a roseate picture born of an enthusiastic imagination. Every Indian may own a homestead! For it will be his homestead if he takes land in severalty and dissolves the tribal relation. Contrast his situation with that of millions of white families in the country, to say nothing of the larger number of homeless people in the Old World, and of the negroes of the Southern States. What a heritage! A homestead his own, with assistance by the Government to build houses and fences and open farms; with a fund preserved and guarded by the Government for years to assist in teaching him and his children the arts of civilization; with the title to the homestead held in trust for a generation, if need be, so as to protect him from the selfish greed and relentless grasp of the white man; with the means not only for material development and progress, but also for the liberal education of his children. If this policy were adopted systematically by the Government it would be strange if in five years from its inauguration and establishment there should be an Indian of any tribe in the whole country who would refuse to accept so favorable and advantageous a measure.

Every step taken, every move made, every suggestion offered, every thing done with reference to the Indians should be with a view of impressing upon them that this is the policy which has been permanently decided upon by the Government in reference to their management. They must abandon tribal relations; they must give up their superstitions; they must forsake their savage habits and learn the arts of civilization; they must learn to labor, and must learn to rear their families as white people do, and to know more of their obligations to the Government and to society. In a word, they must learn to work for a living, and they must understand that it is their interest and duty to send their children to school. Industry and education are the two powerful co-operating forces which, together, will elevate the Indian, and plant him upon the basis of material independence. They will awaken the spirit of personal independence and manhood, create a desire for possessing property, and a knowledge of its advantages and rights. An Indian who has gone upon land, opened a farm, built houses and fences, gathered around him some stock, and become self-sustaining, is prepared to understand the advantages of educating his children. Agriculture and education go hand in hand. The labor of the adults and the education of the children will drive away the gaunt specters of want and poverty, which for generations have haunted the humble tent of the Indian, and in their stead will bring to his doors plenty, comfort, and home life.

In proof of the soundness of this position that the Indians can easily be made self-sustaining by agriculture, I refer to the progress made this year by the Apaches on the San Carlos Reservation, in Arizona, showing a most rapid improvement among them in learning and adopting the improved methods of agriculture. At the rate of improvement made this year by these Indians it will be only a year or two until they (the Apaches), the wildest tribe on the continent, will be self-sustaining and independent. I can also cite the advance made in the last few months by the Cheyennes and Arapahoes of the Indian Territory. Since the cattle have been moved from their lands, and they see that the Government intends that they shall abandon their indolent, thriftless habits and go to work, a marked improvement has begun. More than fifty have recently taken up lands for the purpose of farming them, and a general disposition to work is manifested. The same is true of many other tribes, as the records of this office for many years will attest.

Another idea connected with all this is that as you throw responsibility upon the Indians, it teaches them self-respect and individuality, and develops in them higher manhood. The success of the experiments that have been made of establishing Indian police, and courts of Indian offenses, to regulate internal and domestic affairs on reservations, is referred to more particularly in another part of this report. This throwing responsibility upon the Indians who are selected to decide among themselves upon the rights of their fellow Indians, has had an elevating and restraining influence upon them and has made them more law-abiding.

INDIANS CITIZENSHIP

When the farm and the school have become familiar institutions among the Indians, and reasonable time has intervened for the transition from barbarism or a semi-civilized state to one of civilization, then will the Indian be prepared to take upon himself the higher and more responsible duties and privileges which appertain to American citizenship. A wider and better knowledge of the English language among them is essential to their comprehension of the duties and obligations of citizenship. At this time but few of the adult population can speak a word of English, but with the efforts now being made by the Government and by religious and philanthropic associations and individuals, especially in the Eastern States, with the missionary and the schoolmaster industriously in the field everywhere among the tribes, it is to be hoped, and it is confidently believed, that among the next generation of Indians the English language will be sufficiently spoken and used to enable them to become acquainted with the laws, customs, and institutions of our country, and to regulate their conduct in obedience to its authority.

When this point in their upward progress has been attained they will be a part and parcel of the great brotherhood of American citizens, and the last chapter in the solution of the Indian problem will be written. After that we shall hear no more of the Indian as a separate and distinct race; we shall hear no more of him as a "ward of the nation"; but like the alien and the negro, who by our laws are admitted to the great family of American citizens, each individual must stand upon his own bottom, enjoying equal rights and bearing equal responsibilities.

It is confidently believed that the present policy of the Government toward the Indian is fast bringing the younger class of Indians up to the point where they can see the advantage of citizenship. This is strikingly illustrated by the attitude of some of the youth now being educated at the Carlisle Training School, one of whom, writing upon the subject, says:

> I want to be admitted into citizenship, but I would like to know what real rights I will have, what benefits I may enjoy, or under what punishment must I suffer.

Speaking of losing his rights as an Indian if he should become a citizen, the same writer says:

> Lose my rights as an Indian! What are the rights that an Indian has? Is it the drawing of rations and beef every week? No, the Indians have no rights. Then how is it that I shall lose my Indian rights? Is it not the Government policy to abandon all this? Some of the good people do not want Indians to become citizens of the United States, because they want to treat them as separate nations. The negroes became citizens while they were just as ignorant as can be, even now. Why cannot the Indians be allowed citizenship? Free us from the rights of support and ignorance, and give us the rights of civilized citizenship. We are bound to be citizens, and why not now?

While such sentiments are very natural to a young Indian whose aspirations have been awakened by a liberal education, and which would be common to the Indian race if they had equal advantages and a like education, such a new departure to the vast mass of the Indians would now be inopportune, and instead of bringing blessings, would entail disaster. Take, for instance, some of the quiet and peaceable Pueblo Indians of New Mexico. Under the treaty of Guadaloupe-Hidalgo, and the decisions of the courts, they are held to be entitled to the rights of citizenship; but a personal acquaintance with their "governors," as they style themselves, reveals an incapacity which, for the present, must wholly unfit them to exercise the rights of an American citizen. They are rather objects of sympathy and governmental guardianship.

In a recent case (Elk *vs.* Wilkins, 112 U. S. Reps., 94) the Supreme Court of the United States decided that an Indian born a member of one of the Indian tribes within the United States, which still exists and is recognized as a tribe by the Government of the United States, who has voluntarily separated himself from his tribe and taken up his residence among the white citizens of a State, does not thereby become a citizen of the United States, and cannot make himself a citizen without the consent and co-operation of the Government. In view of this decision a bill was introduced in the last Congress by Senator Dawes declaring every Indian born within the territorial limits of the United States, who has voluntarily taken up, within said limits, his residence separate and apart from any tribe of Indians therein, and who has adopted the habits of civilized life, to be a citizen of the United States, and entitled to all the rights, privileges, and immunities of such citizens.

While I consider desirable the enactment of some law whereby the Indians who have dissolved their tribal relations and are sufficiently prudent and intelligent to manage their own affairs, can become citizens of the United States by some process similar to that provided for the naturalization of aliens, still it seems to me this bill is too broad in its operations, and would make citizens of those who are totally unfitted for such responsibilities. Any action taken in this direction must be gradual. The Indian must be educated up to a point where citizenship would be an advantage and not a disadvantage to him. He must be brought up to that standard where he can understand the white man's law, its benefits to him if he obeys it, and its penalties if he violates it.

The treaty of the United States with the Kickapoo Indians provided a mode by which aspiring Indians could become citizens of the United States, which was to accept or receive their part of the reservation lands in severalty in fee-simple, with power of alienation, they being first required to appear in open court and take the oath of allegiance (as in the case of the naturalization of foreigners), and also by proof to satisfy the court that they were able to manage their own affairs, had adopted the habits of civilized life, and had been able for five years to support themselves and families. (13 Stat., p. 624, Art. III.) I do not believe that the above entire legislation was wise or salutary. The power of alienating their lands should not be given to the Indians for many years after they are allowed to exercise the rights of American citizens in all other respects. The history of the Kickapoos and some of the Shawnees and Pottawatomies, and some tribes in Michigan and Wisconsin, who had taken lands in severalty without a restrictive power of alienation, and who have disposed of them, and are now for the most part pensioners upon the bounty of the Government, or are without visible means of support, is sufficient to demonstrate the fact that the Indians in general are not sufficiently advanced in education and civilization to make it safe, and to their best interest, to give them citizenship and title to their lands with unrestricted power of alienation. What I would impress is the fact that there are but few Indians outside of the civilized tribes, who are prepared to own lands in severalty without the Government retaining a lien upon the same as trustee for twenty-five or thirty years, allowing no power of alienation by them either to white men or to their own race.

CONCENTRATION OF INDIANS

Many theories have been advanced by as many theorists as to what policy it is proper to pursue with the Indian. I rejoice to know that one theory has been exploded which had its advocates, if not numerous, at least very noisy for a while, to wit, the theory that "the best Indian is a dead one." The enlightened Christian sentiment of this country—East, North, South, and West—has frowned down any such inhuman and unchristian sentiment.

The friends of the Indians have differed among themselves as to the best mode of promoting their true welfare, one view being to concentrate them upon the Indian Territory, which, under the provisions of the act of May 28, 1830, and various treaties, was set apart for the use and occupancy of the Cherokees, Creeks, Seminoles, Choctaws, Chickasaws, and other tribes; a portion of which has by subsequent treaties been ceded to the United States for the purpose of locating friendly Indians and freedmen thereon, and upon another portion of which the Government is, by treaty stipulations, permitted to settle friendly Indians. From time to time several tribes and fragmentary tribes have been removed there upon these terms, and are now permanently settled and most favorably located.

The Indian Territory has an area of about 64,222 square miles, or about 41,102,280 acres. It is situated between the Arkansas River and the thirty-seventh degree of north latitude, and nearly in the center of the United States, east and west. Its climate is delightful, and its resources almost unbounded. While there are some poor lands within its limits, yet, taken as a whole, it is hardly excelled in its natural resources by any other portion of the United States of the same extent. Its soil is adapted to the raising of all the cereals, and cotton is cultivated with profit in some portions of the Territory, and its grazing resources and adaptability to raising stock are unexcelled. It has an abundance of water, with timber in different portions in limited quantities, while an abundance of coal of good quality is found.

The advantages of this country for the location, advancement, and civilization of the Indian is strikingly illustrated by the progress of the five civilized tribes. These tribes will compare favorably in wealth and prosperity with almost any agricultural or pastoral community of the same number of persons in any of the States or Territories, and rank fairly in education, intelligence, and progress. Each tribe has an organized government, divided into three branches, the legislative, executive, and judicial. They publish newspapers, carry on manufacturing and merchandising; they have their churches and ministers of the Gospel; they have their courts and judges, and lawyers, and stock-raisers, and farmers, and mechanics; they have their schools, seminaries, and other institutions of learning, built and supported by the tribal funds of the Indians, without other aid from the General Government, and in fact there is nothing in any civilized and enlightened community which they do not have.

Now, there is land enough in the Indian Territory, if all the Indians in the United States, excepting those in Alaska, were removed there, to give to each person—man, woman, and child—160 acres. There are, according to the latest statistics of this office, 79,380 Indians in the Indian Territory, and if the lands there were equally divided among them each person would have about 500 acres. Of the 79,380 Indians in the Territory, 67,493 wear citizens' dress wholly and 6,679 in part. Nearly the whole number wearing citizens' dress are either civilized or in an advanced state of civilization.

I have referred thus particularly to the advantages of this Territory in order that the argument of those advocating the "concentration" policy may be fairly understood. On the other hand, the opponents of this plan advocate the idea of the general diffusion of the Indian tribes over as large a space as practicable, with the view of bringing the Indians more directly in contact with a higher type of civilization, so that they can, as they allege, be the more easily absorbed or assimilated and become the more easily citizenized. They also urge that the Indians have strong local attachments to the homes of their ancestors, and to the haunts of their childhood; that their consent to sell their ancestral homes and move to a strange land among strangers, although of their own race, could not be obtained, and that hence it is idle to expect that they will voluntarily concentrate in the Indian Territory, however inviting its beautiful rivers, fertile prairies, and healthful climate.

But a stronger and more potent objection to concentration in the Indian Territory exists than any yet given, and that is the fierce and uncompromising opposition which this proposition meets in the almost unanimous sentiment of the white citizens of the four great States of Missouri, Kansas, Texas, and Arkansas, which surround this Territory. Such an array of political power and influence, speaking as one man, is entitled to respect and grave consideration. In a country like ours, where public opinion crystalizes into law, where it makes presidents, and Congress, and courts, and commands armies, it cannot safely be disregarded. And although the representatives of the other States of the Union might believe that the concentration of the savage Indian tribes of this country in the Indian Territory would be best for the Indians and greatly relieve the treasury of the United States, as it would, nevertheless I would not advise such a step, even if it should be agreeable to the Indians now scattered over a vast area of country against the earnest protestations of the people of the four great States referred to.

That they have any fear that the red man will demoralize or debauch their civilization, I cannot believe; that they could have any just apprehension of danger from the Indians, if the whole 260,000 were settled upon the soil of the Territory, since they would not constitute one-tenth of the population of the four States, is not for a moment to be entertained; besides, it is more likely that small bands of predatory Indians would depredate and go on the war-path, as they style their marauding parties, than if larger bodies were massed with more stringent internal police regulations in force. Furthermore, if all the Indian tribes were concentrated upon the soil of the Indian Territory, it is reasonable to suppose that the United States Army, of which detachments are now stationed at numerous posts all over the country, near the Indian reservations, for the purpose of protecting white settlers and preserving the peace, would no longer be needed at these remote posts, and could be more conveniently massed near the Territory, where it could prevent any disturbances between the Indians in the Indian Territory and the people of adjacent States. Therefore, so far as the peace of the country is concerned, and so far as the army is potent to preserve it, there would be less danger to be apprehended were the entire Indian population settled within the Indian Territory than there is at this time, when only a small portion of the army can be stationed near it. Moreover, any apprehension of danger on the part of white citizens of those States seems less reasonable and well founded, when we take into consideration the additional safeguard afforded for the protection of their communities by the extension, in almost every direction, of railroads and telegraphic lines.

And yet it is said that this sentiment of opposition exists universally among the good people of these four States against the settlement of any more Indians of the wild tribes in that Territory, and some say, of any more Indians at all, friendly or unfriendly, civilized or semi-civilized, or savage. Of course, with the vast unimproved acreage of valuable and fertile lands within the borders of each of those four States, it cannot be that the lands of the Indian Territory have tempted any of their citizens. Still the prejudice exists so strongly as to satisfy me that for Congress to adopt legislation looking toward obtaining the consent of the scattered Indian tribes to give up their present localities and remove to the Indian Territory would be impolitic and would disturb the political and social tranquility of a very large, respectable, and powerful section of the country. If I should mistake the public sentiment of the people and the representatives of these States should be willing to have removed thither the Indians who may be willing to emigrate to the Indian Territory, then, in that event, the subject becomes important to be considered by Congress.

Assuming, however, that I have correctly divined the almost unanimous wish of the States mentioned, and that Congress would feel disposed to respect their wishes, then the further question of purchasing from the Indians all of the lands of the Indian Territory, and of other Indian reservations, which the Indians do not need now, or will not need in the early future, and of opening them to homestead settlement, presents itself for consideration. After allotting to each head of a family and to each child whatever quantity of land Congress, in its wisdom and humane guardianship of this helpless race, shall consider and determine as just and necessary, the purchase of the balance of their lands at a fair price would seem to be wise and expedient, as the proceeds of the sale would subserve a far more valuable end in contributing to their education and material advancement in agriculture and the mechanical arts (as before suggested in this report) than would be subserved by permitting the lands to remain permanently in idle and unproductive waste.

It might be that a prudent economy and a wise administrative policy in dealing with the Indians would suggest another view which is, to remove, with the exception of those who have taken lands in severalty and who desire to continue to remain on their respective allotments, all of the Indians in the States of Minnesota, Wisconsin, and Michigan, to the Red Lake and White Earth Reservations; those in Montana, Idaho, Wyoming, and Dakota, to the Flathead and Great Sioux Reservations; and those in Nevada, Upper California, Oregon, and Washington Territory, to the Yakama Reservation, or some suitable one in that vicinity, selected for that purpose; while the southwestern Indians might be advantageously concentrated upon one or two existing reservations in that locality. Of course this policy could only be adopted by first obtaining the consent of the Indians already on the reservations upon which concentration is suggested, and the consent of those whom it is suggested to remove, all of which would be dependent upon action by Congress.

The money received from the sale of the lands thrown open to settlement under this policy would make the Indians thus consolidated wealthy, and if properly invested the income therefrom would be ample to start them in agricultural and pastoral pursuits, leaving a fund sufficient for educational purposes and the care of the old and infirm. This plan would not only be advantageous to the Indians, but likewise to the Government. The concentration of the various Indians upon suitable and convenient reservations would relieve the Government of a large annual expense in its management of the Indians. It would result in the doing away with a number of agencies, and necessarily dispense with the services of an equal number of agents and many other employés, and save the incidental expenses connected with such agencies.

The INDIAN TERRITORY

I desire to add a few words more in regard to the tribes and lands of the Indian Territory, by way of suggestion rather than definite recommendation. If certain areas of that Territory are not to be held in trust by the United States for the future settlement of friendly Indians, then the policy of removing eastward the Cheyennes and Arapahoes, the Wichitas and the Kiowas and Comanches, is presented for consideration. It is well known that the reservation now occupied by the Cheyennes and Arapahoes is not as well adapted to agricultural purposes as the lands further east—the Oklahoma strip, for instance. The lands occupied by the Kiowas and Comanches are but little better fitted for agricultural uses than those of the Cheyennes and Arapahoes, the great difficulty or drawback in both reservations being the long annual droughts, which make irrigation necessary in order to insure good crops. If any part of the Indian Territory is to be opened to homestead entry and settlement, it should be the western part, running a line north and south through the Territory, and removing all Indians west of that line to lands lying east of said line. Thus the Indians would be upon lands better adapted to their support, and they would also be adjacent to each other and in a more compact form.

What political development lies before the Indians of the Indian Territory it is impossible to foresee; but one thing is evident, the idea of maintaining permanently an *imperium in imperio,* such as now exists, must, in some respects, be abandoned. The idea of Indian nationality is fast melting away, and the more intelligent Indians are themselves awaking to that fact. In a word, the Indians in the Indian Territory must sooner or later break up their tribal relations, take their lands in severalty, and to all intents and purposes become citizens of the United States, and be amenable to its laws, as well as enjoy all of its high and distinguished privileges. When that is done they will be prepared to dispose of the surplus lands they may own to the best advantage to themselves, and in a spirit *pro bon publico.*

* * *

COURT OF INDIAN OFFENSES

Under date of April 10, 1883, the then Secretary of the Interior gave his official approval to certain rules prepared in this office for the establishment of a court of Indian offenses at each of the Indian agencies, except the agency for the five civilized tribes in the Indian Territory. It was found that the longer continuance of certain old heathen and barbarous customs, such as the sun-dance, scalp-dance, war-dance, polygamy, &c., were operating as a serious hindrance to the efforts of the Government for the civilization of the Indians. It was believed that in all the tribes many Indians would be found who could be relied upon to aid the Government in its efforts to abolish rites and customs so injurious and so contrary to civilization; hence these rules were formulated, looking towards the ultimate abolishment of the pernicious practices mentioned.

There is no special law authorizing the establishment of such a court, but authority is exercised under the general provisions of law giving this Department supervision of the Indians. The policy of the Government for many years past has been to destroy the tribal relations as fast as possible, and to use every endeavor to bring the Indians under the influence of law. To do this the agents have been accustomed to punish for minor offenses, by imprisonment in the guard-house and by withholding rations; but by the present system the Indians themselves, through their judges, decide who are guilty of offenses under the rules, and pass judgment in accordance with the provisions thereof. Neither the section in the last Indian appropriation bill above quoted nor any other enactment of Congress reaches any of the crimes or offenses provided for in the Department rules, and without such a court many Indian reservations would be without law or order, and the laws of civilized life would be utterly disregarded.

At each agency, where it has been found practicable to establish it, the reports of the Indian agents show that the court has been entirely successful, and in many cases eminently useful in abolishing the old heathenish customs that have been for many years resorted to, by the worst elements on the reservation, to retard the progress and advancement of the Indians to a higher standard of civilization and education.

The agent of the Nez Percé Agency, Idaho, says:

> The court and police force have worked wonders among this tribe. Friend and foe alike of the Indians in this vicinity acknowledge the same.

The agent of the Western Shoshone Agency, Nevada, says:

> Its existence has been a preventive to the commitment of any serious offenses coming under its purposes.

The agent of the Standing Rock Agency, Dakota, says:

> It is growing to be an important factor in the administration of affairs at this agency. Regular semi-monthly sessions of the court are held, where all offenders are brought by the police for trial, and cases impartially decided by the court. A number of cases for violation of office rules have been tried during the year past, and the offenders punished either by fines or imprisonment in the agency guard-house, and the decisions of the judges have, in every instance, been sustained by the better class of Indians, and usually accepted by the transgressor as just and proper. The present judges are members of the police force, but the judges of this court should be independent of that body, as it places the police officers in an embarrassing position when obliged to arrest, try, and punish offenders. If there were salaries of $20 per month attached to the office of judge the best men among the Indians would be willing to serve in that capacity, as the service is now becoming quite popular, and having these two branches independent of each other would add to the usefulness of both.

The agent of the Siletz Agency, Oregon, says:

> I am well pleased with its workings. I have not had to reverse a decision made. The judges try in every case to do the right thing, tempering justice with mercy. I have every confidence in them. They solve questions oftentimes that are knotty for me.

The agent of the Klamath Agency, Oregon, says:

> The court of Indian offenses has been well conducted, and much improvement in its working has been manifest. It has been of much benefit to the

Indians, and an important factor in their advancement in civilization. Offenses against morality are becoming less frequent, and a due respect for law has been carefully enforced. The judges have become more efficient with practice, and try the cases appearing before them with deliberation and prudence.

The agent of the Cheyenne River Agency, Dakota, says:

Since the organization of the court dancing has been discontinued and plural marriages are unknown. Misdemeanors are of rare occurrence.

The agent of the Santee Agency, Nebraska, says:

I think the court has a good influence and is quite a help to the quiet government of the Indians.

The fines assessed and collected at one of the agencies during the past year have reached as high as $395, and out of this money the agent has been authorized to pay his judges $10 each per month. Although it has worked satisfactorily at the Nez Percé Agency, and has had no apparently bad effect on the decisions of the judges, I am well satisfied that it is not a wise or safe policy to have the salary of an officer contingent on his own decisions, and instead of having the fines collected used for this purpose, it would be much better to use the money for the benefit of the tribe generally, building bridges, improving roads, or for general educational purposes.

In most cases the judges are also members of the police force. This should not be so; the court should be entirely independent of the police, and its members should receive a salary from the Government sufficient to induce the best and most intelligent of the Indians to serve in that capacity. In this connection I beg to say that I fully agree with my predecessor that the judges should have at least $20 per month for the services required of them, and as the court is no longer an experiment, but a success, I trust that Congress will appropriate an amount sufficient to pay this salary to each of the judges, and to defray other necessary court expenses.

INDIAN POLICE

The rapidity with which the entire area of the western part of the country is being opened up and settled, brings settlers to the very doors of the Indian reservations, oftentimes introducing a class of men none too scrupulous regarding the rights of others; men who regard the property of the Indian as lawful prey, and the life of the Indian as no obstacle to the possession of it; men who are without many of the necessaries of life, needing fuel, needing horses or ponies, needing beef, needing grazing ground, and a thousand other things, many of which are possessed by the Indians through issues made by the United States. This has made some kind of a constabulary force on Indian reservations an actual necessity, and the necessity has been increasing every year in a ratio far exceeding the relief granted. Agencies, which a year ago few white men had ever crossed, may be almost surrounded this year with settlers and invaders. Mines, real or prospective, have tempted thousands of men into localities heretofore occupied only by Indians. Without regard to the rights of the Indians, they are constantly trespassing, harassing the Indians, provoking quarrels, thieving, and making the life of the agent one of constant anxiety and vigilance. Agency employés are very few, and cannot be spared for police duty.

Under these circumstances, relief has come through and by the Indians themselves; for, fully realizing the situation, Congress has, for the past few years, provided for the appointment and equipment of Indian police. To a great extent they have met the necessities of the situation, and have proved valuable aids to the Indian agents in preventing trespassing and robbery by lawless whites, and in suppressing disorder, violence, and incipient revolt among the more restless of their own people. Many instances of surprising fidelity to the trust imposed upon them, under circumstances which would swerve many a white man from his duty, might be related of these Indian policemen.

Commencing with the present fiscal year, the salary was increased for the officers from $8 to $10 per month, and for the privates from $5 to $8 per month. This has enabled the agents to select a better class of men for the service, and will tend to make the force more stable, most of the resignations heretofore having been caused by meager salaries. I also confidently expect that the better class of men will render the force still more efficient, so that notwithstanding the increasing necessity for this class of employés their greater efficiency will enable me to lessen their number, and I have therefore estimated for only seven hundred privates and seventy officers for the fiscal year ending June 30, 1887.

* * *

The Old Winnebago and Crow Creek Reservations in Dakota

By an Executive order, dated February 27, 1885, all that tract of country in the Territory of Dakota lying on the east bank of the Missouri River and commonly known as the Old Winnebago and Crow Creek Reservations, except certain portions thereof particularly described in said order, was restored to the mass of the public domain. By public proclamation of the President, dated April 17, 1885, said order is declared to be inoperative and of no effect. The lands intended to be embraced therein are proclaimed to be existing Indian reservations, and as such available for Indian purposes alone, and subject to the Indian intercourse laws of the United States. Following is the full text of the proclamation:

> Whereas by an Executive order bearing date the 27th day of February, 1885, it was ordered that "all that tract of country in the Territory of Dakota

known as the Old Winnebago Reservation and the Sioux or Crow Creek Reservation, and lying on the east bank of the Missouri River, set apart and reserved by Executive order dated January 11, 1875, and which is not covered by the Executive order dated August 9, 1879, restoring certain of the lands reserved by the order of January 11, 1875, except the following-described tracts: Township No. 108 north, range 71 west, 108 north, range 72 west, fractional township 108 north, range 73 west, the west half of section 4, sections 5, 6, 7, 8, 9, 16, 17, 18, 19, 20, 21, 28, 29, 30, 31, 32, and 33 of township 107 north, range 70 west, fractional townships 107 north, range 71 west, 107 north, range 72 west, 107 north, range 73 west, the west half of township 106 north, range 70 west, and fractional township 106 north, range 71 west; and except also all tracts within the limits of the aforesaid Old Winnebago Reservation and the Sioux or Crow Creek Reservation, which are outside of the limits of the above-described tracts, and which may have heretofore been allotted to the Indians residing upon said reservation, or which may have heretofore been selected or occupied by the said Indians under and in accordance with the provisions of article 6 of the treaty with the Sioux Indians, of April 29, 1868, and the same is hereby restored to the public domain"; and

Whereas upon the claim being made that said order is illegal and in violation of the plighted faith and obligations of the United States contained in sundry treaties heretofore entered into with the Indian tribes or bands, occupants of said reservation, and that the further execution of said order will not only occasion much distress and suffering to peaceable Indians but retard the work of their civilization and engender amongst them a distrust of the National Government, I have determined, after a careful examination of the several treaties, acts of Congress, and other official data bearing on the subject, aided and assisted therein by the advice and opinion of the Attorney-General of the United States duly rendered in that behalf, that the lands so proposed to be restored to the public domain by said Executive order of February 27, 1885, are included as existing Indian reservations on the east bank of the Missouri River by the terms of the second article of the treaty with the Sioux Indians concluded April 29, 1868, and that consequently being treaty reservations the Executive was without lawful power to restore them to the public domain by said Executive order, which is therefore deemed and considered to be wholly inoperative and void; and

Whereas the laws of the United States provide for the removal of all persons residing or being found upon Indian lands and territory without permission expressly and legally obtained of the Interior Department:

Now, therefore, in order to maintain inviolate the solemn pledges and plighted faith of the Government as given in the treaties in question, and for the purpose of properly protecting the interests of the Indian tribes as well as of the United States in the premises, and to the end that no person or persons may be induced to enter upon said lands where they will not be allowed to remain without the permission of the authority aforesaid, I, Grover Cleveland, President of the United States, do hereby declare and proclaim the said Executive order of February 27, 1885, to be in contravention of the treaty obligations of the United States with the Sioux tribe of Indians, and therefore to be inoperative and of no effect; and I further declare that the lands intended to be embraced therein are existing Indian reservations and as such available for Indian purposes alone and subject to the Indian intercourse acts of the United States.

I do further warn and admonish all and every person or persons now in the occupation of said lands under color of said executive order, and all such person or persons as are intending or preparing to enter and settle upon the same thereunder, that they will neither be permitted to remain or enter upon said lands; and such persons as are already there are hereby required to vacate and remove therefrom with their effects within sixty days from the date hereof; and in case a due regard for and voluntary obedience to the laws and treaties of the United States, and this admonition and warning, be not sufficient to effect the purpose and intentions as herein declared, all the power of the Government will be employed to carry into proper execution the treaties and laws of the United States herein referred to.

In testimony thereof I hereunto set my hand and cause the seal of the United States to be affixed.

Done at the city of Washington, this seventeenth day of April, one thousand eight hundred and eighty-five, and of the Independence of the United States of America the one hundred and ninth.

GROVER CLEVELAND.

The requirements of the President's proclamation are now being carried out in a manner to cause as little hardship and loss to the settlers as is possible under the circumstances. This office has steadfastly maintained the position that the reservations in question were "existing reservations" at the date of the Sioux treaty of April 29, 1868, and as such were made a part of the reservation thereby set apart (article 2) for the different bands of Sioux Indians parties to said treaty.

The right of the Indians to occupy said reservations under said treaty has been fully recognized since the date thereof, and many of them were residing on the lands when the treaty was negotiated. Extensive surveys have been made on both reservations and paid for out of moneys appropriated by Congress for the survey of Indian reservations, and allotments to the number of two hundred and thirty-seven have been made to the Indians under the provisions of the aforesaid treaty. The agent's residence, agent's office, boarding-school building, large warehouse, issue-house, dispensary, employés' quarters, saw mill, storehouse, corral, slaughter-house, agency farm, &c., are all situated within the tract formerly occupied by the Winnebagoes.

The correspondence shows that the Indian Office has invariably refused to lend its aid or approval to any movement looking to the restoration of any of the lands embraced within these reservations to the mass of the public domain, by Executive order, with a view to their being opened to white settlement. It has always held that the Executive was without lawful power to do so, and that to effect such purpose would require the consent of the Indians and the sanction of Congress.

* * *

ATTEMPTED SETTLEMENTS IN THE INDIAN TERRITORY

At the date of the last annual report of this office the Oklahoma colonists had just been ejected by the military from the Cherokee Outlet lands, south of the Kansas line. Payne, with a number of old offenders, was arrested and sent to Fort Smith, Ark., where they were turned over to the United States marshal September 8, 1884. There, it is understood, Payne was released upon his own recognizance of $1,000 and turned loose, and the commanding general reported that he was back at Hunnewell, organizing another expedition for the Indian Territory, before the troops who took him to Fort Smith could return. Subsequent to this the sudden death of Payne, who for years had been the acknowledged leader of the Oklahoma movement, was announced.

He was succeeded by one W. L. Couch, under whose leadership in the latter part of December, 1884, a large body of armed men again entered the Territory with the avowed object of effecting a permanent settlement, encamping at Stillwater, on the Cimarron River, whence they defied the military to remove them. Couch, the leader, was reported as willing to risk a collision with the troops, as likely to arouse public sympathy, and compel favorable action by Congress in opening the coveted lands to settlement. After maintaining a determined show of resistance for some weeks, their provisions giving out, and the troops gradually closing in on them, the intruders, on the 27th January, 1885, finally surrendered to General Hatch, commanding the military district of Oklahoma, and under escort of the troops were marched back to the Kansas line, and recrossed to Arkansas City. Here Couch and some of the more prominent men were arrested on Federal warrants issued under section 5334 of the Revised Statutes, and taken to Wichita, Kans., where, on March 5, they were placed under heavy bonds to appear in the United States court (which subsequently adjourned to September) to answer to a charge of unlawfully engaging in rebellion or insurrection against the authority of the United States.

In the mean time the subject had largely engaged the attention of Congress, and by section 8 of the Indian appropriation act, approved March 3, 1885 (23 Stats. at Large, p. 384), the President was "authorized to open negotiations with the Creeks, Seminoles, and Cherokees for the purpose of opening to settlement under the homestead laws the unassigned lands in said Indian Territory ceded by them respectively to the United States by the several treaties of August eleventh, eighteen hundred and sixty-six, March twenty-first, eighteen hundred and sixty-six, and July nineteenth, eighteen hundred and sixty-six; and for that purpose the sum of five thousand dollars, or so much thereof as may be necessary, be, and the same is hereby, appropriated out of any money in the Treasury not otherwise appropriated; his action hereunder to be reported to Congress."

Notwithstanding this legislation the colonists still maintained a defiant attitude in camp at Arkansas City, and threatened to re-enter the Territory in largely increased numbers at an early date. An impression seemed to prevail amongst them that the proclamation issued by President Arthur, July 1st, and his subsequent order of July 31, 1884, directing the employment of the military in enforcing the same, had become inoperative with the close of his administration. To counteract this idea, the President, on the 13th March last, issued a proclamation (which will be found herewith, page 283), substantially to the same effect as those of his predecessors, declaring the determination of the Government to maintain the integrity of the treaties entered into with the Indian tribes, and to enforce obedience to the laws of the United States.

The immediate effect of this proclamation, as reported by the commanding general, was to reduce the numbers of the Couch colony, many of whom quietly dispersed and returned to their homes. A large number, however, estimated at from six to eight hundred men, all well armed, still remained in camp, who openly avowed their intention to disregard the proclamation and force their way into the Territory. Meetings of the colonists were held, and resolutions passed expressive of their surprise and dissatisfaction at the course taken by the Government, and demanding of the President an explanation of the laws and treaties governing the Oklahoma lands under which it was claimed they were still Indian lands. A delegation in behalf of the colonists waited on the President and Secretary of the Interior, with a view to securing some modification of the proclamation whereby they might be permitted temporarily to enter the Territory pending the negotiations authorized by Congress, but they were informed that under no circumstances would any settlements be permitted in the Indian Territory until the negotiations with the Indian tribes had been had and authority from Congress obtained.

Upon the return of the delegation to Arkansas City the colonists (April 23) passed resolutions agreeing to await the result of negotiations, and adjourned to meet at the call of their leader. Those having homes returned to them, about two hundred and fifty remaining in camp, near Caldwell, on the Kansas border, where they appear to have since conducted themselves in an orderly manner. Recent advices received in this Department indicating an intention on the part of the colonists to disband and peacefully await further official action in reference to the lands in question, the United States district attorney has been instructed by the Department of Justice to dismiss the suits before referred to, if he is satisfied they have broken camp and retired from the border and relinquished their project of invasion.

* * *

Attempted Appropriation by White Settlers of Lands Belonging to the Zuñi Indians

Under date of June 12 last, Yacqui Pie, governor of Zuñi, addressed a communication to the President complaining that certain white men had made entries and filings, under the general land laws of the United States, covering lands embraced within the reservation set apart for his people; lands which had been occupied, watered, and in part cultivated by them and their ancestors for more than a hundred years. The letter was referred by the Department to this office. I at once examined into the matter, and made it the subject of a special report to the Department, dated July 13, 1885.

It appears that for many years prior to 1877, the Zuñi Indians, who are a poor but very peaceable and industrious people, had been gaining a livelihood by cultivating small patches of arable land found along the Zuñi River and its tributaries, the Rio Los Nutrias and Rio Pescado, the most valuable of which were in the neighborhood of the Nutrias, Pescado, and Ojo Caliente Springs. They owned a tract two leagues square, near the Arizona line, granted to them by the Spanish Government in 1689, but the land being almost worthless, and altogether inadequate to their support, they were forced to find other land to cultivate, and so for centuries they had been in peaceful and undisturbed occupation of small tracts and patches, outside the limits of their grant, wherever water, which is very scarce in that country, could be found. As the country began to settle up it was found that these people would require some protection to prevent their being crowded out, and accordingly it was decided to set aside a tract of country for their exclusive occupation and use, which should embrace their settlements at Nutrias Springs, Pescado Springs, and the Ojo Caliente, and an Executive Order was issued March 16, 1877, defining the boundaries of a reservation for said Indians, as follows:

> Beginning at the one hundred and thirty-sixth milestone on the western boundary line of the Territory of New Mexico, and running thence north 61° 45′ east, 31 miles and eight-tenths of a mile to the crest of the mountain, a short distance above Nutrias Spring; thence due south 12 miles to a point in the hills a short distance southeast of the Ojo Pescado; thence south 61° 45′ west to the one hundred and forty-eighth milestone on the western boundary line of said Territory; thence north with said boundary line to the place of beginning.

There the matter rested, and the Indians continued to reside and culti-vate their lands as usual in conscious security, and, as far as is known, without molestation from any quarter. Finally, however, some one made the discovery that by a strained construction of the terms employed the descrip-tion given in the executive order of March 16, 1877, would not and did not include in the reservation either the Nutrias or the Pescado Springs, and thereupon certain parties immediately set about to enter the lands in the neighborhood of and embracing the Nutrias Springs, which entries the local land officers allowed. As soon as this action became known it was reported to the Department by Inspector Howard, and to this Bureau by Agent Thomas, the agent in charge of the Pueblo Indians in New Mexico, both of whom protested in the strongest terms against the consummation of what they declared to be "a gross outrage upon the Indians."

The matter was immediately looked into, and as a consequence a new Executive order was issued, with a view to describing the reservation with greater definiteness. The parties who had made the entries protested, and a subsequent (third) Executive order was procured (order dated March 3, 1885), excepting their entries from the operation of the order of May 1, 1883, which latter action was, in my opinion, unfortunate and mischievous in its results. If permitted to stand, it would defeat the real object of the original Executive order (March 16, 1877), from the fact that the entries in question cover the Nutrias Springs and adjacent lands, perhaps the most valuable to the Indians of any of the reserved lands.

The object and intention of the Executive order of March 16, 1877, as we have seen, was to secure to the Indians the springs and adjacent lands, the use of which they had so long enjoyed, and which seemed absolutely necessary to their existence, and according to the accepted rules of construction said lands and springs were actually reserved by said order. Courses and distances must give way to natural objects when mentioned in an instrument describing lands and defining boundaries. Applying this principle, the line of the reservation as described in said order would include, as it was intended it should, both the Nutrias and Pescado Springs, and as none of the lands reserved by that order were subject to entry on and after the date of its issuance, I hold that the order of March 3, 1885, the object of which was to protect the entries, clothes them with no shadow of validity whatever. The entries were illegal and ought never to have been recognized. Moreover, the highest judicial tribunal of our country has repeatedly held that a party cannot initiate a pre-emption right under the laws of the United States by intrusion upon lands in the actual possession of another.

In the case of Atherton v. Fowler (6 Otto, 513), the court says:

> The generosity by which Congress gave the settler the right of pre-emption was not intended to give him the benefit of another man's labor, and authorize him to turn that man and his family out of their home. It did not propose to give its bounty to settlements obtained by violence at the expense of others. The right to make a settlement was to be exercised on unsettled land; to make improvements on unimproved land. To erect a dwelling-house did not mean to seize some other man's dwelling. It had reference to vacant land; to unimproved land; and it would have shocked the moral sense of the men who passed these laws if they had supposed that they had extended an invitation to the pioneer population to acquire inchoate rights to the public lands by trespass, by violence, by robbery, by acts leading to homicides and other crimes of less moral turpitude.

Report of Commissioner of Indian Affairs J. D. C. Atkins September 28, 1886

(Excerpt from *Report for 1886*, pp. 79-101, 103-04, 105-07, 115-23, 124-25)

The 1880's marked the high water mark of the Government's attack on "the sentimentality about a separate nationality" and on the "political paradox" of tribal entities within the American union. Although Commissioner Atkins hoped that the Indians would voluntarily change their form of government, "yet it is perfectly plain to my mind that the treaties never contemplated the un-American and absurd idea of a separate nationality in our midst ... These Indians have no right to obstruct civilization and commerce and set up an exclusive claim to self-government...." To Atkins such a notion smacked of accepting a foreign sovereignty on American soil—a theory "utterly repugnant to the spirit and genius of our laws, and wholly unwarranted by the Constitution of the United States." As might be expected, Atkins' report was concerned to a great degree with the effort to reduce the tribal land base. That effort was soon to be expedited by the passage of the General Allotment Act of 1887.

I HAVE THE HONOR herewith to submit the second annual report on Indian affairs under their present management.

It is with pleasure that you, and through you Congress and the American people, are invited to mark the unmistakable evidences of progress made by many of the tribes within the last twelve months. These evidences are apparent from several standpoints. The excellent temper, subordination, and general tranquillity which, with two or three exceptions, have everywhere prevailed among the Red Men under the charge of the Indian Bureau are of themselves a most auspicious omen of progress. The active inquiry among many of the tribes for further knowledge of the arts of agriculture; the growing desire to take lands in severalty; the urgent demand for agricultural implements with modern improvements; the largely increased acreage which the Indians have put to tillage, exceeding that of any preceding year; the unprecedented increase in the number of Indian children who have been enrolled in the schools—these and many other facts fully establish the claim that during the past year the Indian race has taken a firmer step and a grander stride in the great march toward civilization than ever before in the same length of time.

THE "PEACE POLICY" AND ITS ECONOMY

Another year's experience and practical trial of this "humanitarian and peace system" only adds cumulative testimony to the superiority of its methods of Indian civilization over any others ever yet tried. As a further and unerring evidence, I may refer to the fact that the progress above noted has been made without corresponding increase in expenditures. In fact the estimates for carrying on the Indian service are being reduced, as the following statement shows:

Estimate for appropriation:
Fiscal year 1886 .... $7,328,049.64
Fiscal year 1887 .... 6,051,259.84
Fiscal year 1888 .... 5,608,873.64

In the estimates for 1888 an increase of $177,500 is asked for educational work. But for this increase the reduction would have been much greater, and the estimate for 1888 would have fallen below the estimate for 1887 $619,886.20, and below the estimate for 1886 $1,896,676.

A benign policy on the part of the Government toward the Indian race, dictated by a love of humanity, one in which both political parties have fortunately and exceptionally agreed, is a proud national distinction. It speaks well for the great heart of the people which lies back of and behind this Government that they order and command their representatives to foster a policy which alone can save the aborigines from destruction—from being worn away by the attrition of the conflicting elements of Anglo-Saxon civilization. Upon my induction into office I gave to this line of administration mature reflection, critical research, and extensive consultation, and in my last annual report it was briefly summarized, as follows, and its continuance urged:

This brings me directly to the consideration of the practical policy which I believe should be adopted by Congress and the Government in the management of the Indians. It should be industriously and gravely impressed upon them that they must abandon their tribal relations and take lands in severalty, as the corner-stone of their complete success in agriculture, which means self-support, personal independence, and material thrift. The Government should, however, in order to protect them, retain the right to their lands in trust for twenty-five years or longer, but issue trust patents at once to such Indians as have taken individual holdings. When the Indians have taken their lands in severalty in sufficient quantities (and the number of acres in each holding may and should vary in different localities according to fertility, productiveness, climatic and other advantages), then having due regard to the immediate and early future needs of the Indians, the remaining lands of their reservations should be purchased by the Government and opened to homestead entry at 50 or 75 cents per acre. The money paid by the Government for their lands should be held in trust in 5 per cent. bonds, to be invested as Congress may provide, for the education, civilization, and material development and advancement of the red race, reserving for each tribe its own money.

When the farm and the school have become familiar institutions among the Indians, and reasonable time has intervened for the transition from barbarism or a semi-civilized state to one of civilization, then will the Indian be prepared to take upon himself the higher and more responsible duties and privileges which appertain to American citizenship. A wider and better knowledge of the English language among them is essential to their comprehension of the duties and obligations of citizenship. At this time but few of the adult population can speak a word of English, but with the efforts now being made by the Government and by religious and philanthropic associations and individuals, especially in the Eastern States, with the missionary and the schoolmaster industriously in the field everywhere among the tribes, it is to be hoped, and it is confidently believed, that among the next generation of Indians the English language will be sufficiently spoken and used to enable them to become acquainted with the laws, customs, and institutions of our country, and to regulate their conduct in obedience to its authority.

The willing support which the entire people of the United States are giving to this. policy of educating the Indian and placing him upon a homestead with the peaceful implements of agriculture and the mechanic arts in his hands, and the assiduity with which for years the authorities have worked for the accomplishment of this object with varying success among different tribes in all sections of the country in which they are located, and the onward move in this direction now urged and impelled by every agency and instrumentality of the Indian Bureau, as well as by the numerous organizations and societies of various kinds which are all working in harmonious co-operation for the effectuation of this noble purpose, should arrest the attention of these benighted people, and these beneficent endeavors should evoke from their stolid hearts gratitude and kindly appreciation. I am glad to know that in very many instances such appreciation is not wanting.

The "Five Civilized Tribes"

In view of this policy of protection for the Indians, it is reasonable that the Indian Bureau and the country should look to the five civilized tribes of the Indian Territory about whom so much has been said by orators and statesmen, and of whom so much is expected by the friends of the Indian, to set freely and promptly such an example as shall advance the civilization of their savage brethren of other tribes. The influence of their example upon the semi-civilized and savage tribes makes the study of their condition and methods a matter not only of great interest but also of first importance.

The treaties of 1866, and other treaties also, guarantee to the five civilized tribes the possession of their lands; but, without the moral and physical power which is represented by the Army of the United States, what are these treaties worth as a protection against the rapacious greed of the homeless people of the States who seek homesteads within the borders of the Indian Territory? If the protecting power of this Government were withdrawn for thirty days, where would the treaties be, and the laws of the Indians and the Indians themselves? The history of Payne and Couch and their followers, and the determined effort of both Republican and Democratic administrations to resist their unlawful claims and demands, is too recent not to be still fresh in the memory of these Indians. It is not reasonable to expect that the Government will never tire of menacing its own people with its own Army. Therefore it becomes vastly important that these five civilized tribes, who have among them men competent to be Representatives and Senators in Congress, governors of States, and judges on the bench, should cordially and in a spirit of friendly gratitude for what has been done for them, co-operate with the Government in bringing about such a change of affairs in their midst as will bring peace and quiet to their borders, settle existing agitations as to their rights and interests, and dispose of disquieting questions which will surely grow out of the present alarming condition of things in the whole Indian Territory.

At present the rich Indians who cultivate tribal lands pay no rent to the poorer and more unfortunate of their race, although they are equal owners of the soil. The rich men have too large homesteads and control many times more than their share of the land. It will not do to say, as the wealthy and influential leaders of the nations contend, that their system of laws gives to every individual member of the tribe equal facilities to be independent and equal opportunity to possess himself of a homestead. Already the rich and choice lands are appropriated by those most enterprising and self seeking. A considerable number of Indians have in cultivation farms exceeding 1,000 acres in extent, and a still larger number are cultivating between 500 and 1,000 acres. Now, think of one Indian having a farm fenced in of 1,000 acres, with the right, according to their system (as I understand the fact to be), of adding nearly 1,000 acres more by excluding all others from the use or occupancy of a quarter of a mile in width all around the tract fenced. What a baronial estate! In theory the lands are held in common under the tribal relation, and are equally owned by each member of the tribe, but in point of fact they are simply held in the grasping hand of moneyed monopolists and powerful and influential leaders and politicians, who pay no rental to the other members of the tribe, who, under their tribal ownership in common, have equal rights with the occupants.

A case of this sort came under my personal observation on a visit to the Creek Nation in 1885. I was credibly informed that one of the Creeks had under fence over 1,000 acres, and, of course, under their laws and usages, he had the right to exclude all other members of the tribe from claiming any land embraced within the limits of a quarter of a mile in width surrounding the inclosed farm of 1,000 acres, provided he made the first location. This estate was handsomely managed, with many modern methods and improvements. A costly residence stood upon it and large commodious barns, stables, &c., were provided. The owner cultivated this farm with laborers hired among his own race—perhaps his own kith and kin—at $16 per month, and they lived in huts and cabins on the place without a month's provisions ahead for themselves and families. They owned, of course, their tribal interest in the land, but the proceeds of the valuable crops which were raised by their labor swelled the plethoric pockets of the proprietor. In this instance the crops grown, in addition to large quantities of hay, consisted of 25,000 bushels of corn, fattening for market 200 head of beef cattle and 300 head of hogs. The proprietor grows annually richer, while the laborers, his own race, joint owners of the soil, even of the lands that he claims and individually appropriates, grow annually and daily poorer and less able to assert their equal ownership and tribal claim and, shall I say, constitutional privilege and treaty rights.

Now this condition of semi-slavery, shall I call it, exists in each of the five civilized nations, and grows directly out of the holding of lands in common, and is necessarily inherent in this system of tenantry. Agent Owen, in his report, page 375, says:

> The Washita Valley in the Chickasaw Nation is almost a solid farm for 50 miles. It is cultivated by white labor largely, with Chickasaw landlords. I saw one farm there said to contain 8,000 acres, another 4,000, and many other large and handsome places.

I have endeavored to obtain some reliable data as to the number of farms containing 1,000 acres which exist in the five tribes. It did not occur to me that eight times that amount of rich valley land had been appropriated by one proprietor, that another owner had 4,000 acres, and that there were "many other very large and handsome places" in the same valley, each owned by individual proprietors, but all being tribal lands. A system of laws and customs, where tribal relations exist and lands are owned in common, which permits one Indian to own so large a quantity of land, to the exclusion of all other Indians, merely because he was first to occupy it or because he inherited it from his father who occupied it originally, when all other Indians have equal tribal rights with the happy and fortunate possessor, needs radical reformation. Are these the sacred rights secured by treaty, which the United States are pledged to respect and defend? If so, then the United States are pledged to uphold and maintain a stupendous land monopoly and aristocracy that finds no parallel in this country except in two or three localities in the far West; and in these instances it may be said that the titles are clear (having been obtained by purchase from the Government), however questionable may be the policy which makes it possible for one man to own unlimited quantities of land.

How many Indians who have been less provident than these gentlemen who have been shrewd enough to fence up thousands of acres in one farm, and whose claim extends a quarter of a mile in width around the already mammoth estate, are eking out a miserable existence upon some barren homestead, or, worse still, are living by sufferance as day laborers on these large estates, although they own their tribal share of these lands which they are too poor, weak, and powerless to secure or demand! I have no documentary statistics from which I can form an accurate idea of the proportion of the population in the several nations who are hireling day-laborers; but I have been personally informed by very intelligent resident citizens that the ratio of this class in the Cherokee Nation, including those who cultivate less than five acres, is one-sixth of the whole; among the Choctaws, Chickasaws, and Creeks about one-fourth; and that among the Seminoles the ratio is even larger. So it is clear that a large part of the population in each of these nations—held down below the common level of their own race by stress of poverty and the weight of daily necessities, unable by reason of present misfortunes to avail themselves of any opportunity or means to possess themselves of their equal distributive shares of lands, and to so utilize them as to place their families upon a higher social and financial plane—needs some potent influence or power to dispel this system and establish a new order of things—in a word, to raise up the down-trodden people to their proper level.

It is undeniable that the five civilized tribes look to the Indian Office, under the intercourse laws, only for protection from the aggression of white intrusion. In no other particular do they respect or consult the authority of the Government. The United States Army has stood guard over these Indians for fifty years, shielding and protecting them from the grasp of the frontiersman and the settler. Yet they have not seconded the endeavors of the Government to induce among the various tribes a general spirit of taking allotments by setting the example themselves. This does not seem a grateful remembrance of the sacrifices the American people have made for their protection, in submitting to an annual tax of many millions of dollars to support and maintain an Army, without which the Indian Territory would have been reckoned long ago among the things that were.

Allotments.—The following table shows the amount of land held by each of the five civilized tribes in the Indian Territory, and the amount to which each individual would be entitled were the lands of his tribe equally divided and allotted in severalty:

Tribe.	Acres.	Population.	Acres to each individual.
Cherokees*	5,031,351	22,000	228
Creeks	3,040,495	14,000	217
Chickasaws	4,650,935	6,000	775
Choctaws	6,688,000	16,000	417
Seminoles	375,000	3,000	125

*Exclusive of lands west of the Arkansas River.

The foregoing table demonstrates the fact that if in each of the five nations each head of a family and each adult person should be allowed 160 acres, and each minor child 80 acres, there would still remain a large surplus of unalloted land. The practical proposition which it seems to me would be best for these Indians would be to divide their lands in severalty upon the basis I have suggested, or upon some other reasonable basis, and to sell the remainder to actual settlers at a fair and just price. The proceeds of the sales of these surplus lands would enable the very poor of whom I have spoken and for whom I plead—the laborers at $16 per month—to fence and improve their allotments, erect buildings and barns, set out orchards, and prepare themselves to live as they are entitled to live, owning as they do lands sufficient for homesteads for every one. There would also be sufficient funds to put up suitable school buildings and establish good permanent schools in every settlement or district. If this course is pursued it will secure to every Indian a homestead, which he can define and claim absolutely as his own. One which he can improve and adorn; where he can build his house and plant his vines; where his children can be born and reared, and where they may be buried; a homestead which by reasonable labor will secure an ample support for each Indian who now wanders around as a day laborer, with no definite knowledge of where his home is located, and who, although entitled to a home by reason of a common ownership in the lands, is now too poor and weak and ignorant to demand and secure his rights. This class of poor Indians needs to be raised up by the adoption of the policy here foreshadowed.

By the fifteenth article of the Cherokee treaty of 1866 (14 Stat., page 803) it is provided that—

> The United States may settle any civilized Indians, friendly with the Cherokees and adjacent tribes, within the Cherokee country, on unoccupied lands east of 96°, on such terms as may be agreed upon by any such tribe and the Cherokees subject to the approval of the President of the United States.

This treaty further provides that the Indians who may thus be settled among the Cherokees are to have a district of country, set off for their use by metes and bounds, equal to 160 acres for each member of said tribes, at a price to be agreed upon, provided the consent of the Cherokee Nation is first obtained prior to such settlement. Here 160 acres is made the basis of the homestead. I believe that, except in a few cases covered by specific treaty stipulations, such as the Omahas, Sioux, and Yakamas, allotments made to Indians by the Government have not exceeded 160 acres to an Indian. The quarter-section is universally recognized by the Government as the limit of the homestead; 160 acres is the recognized standard number. But I would not confine the members of the five civilized tribes to 160 acres. I only think that all lands in those nations should be divided in severalty equally among the population, so that those members of the tribes who now stand mutely by and see members of their own race occupy and cultivate their lands and pocket the proceeds may be put in actual possession of that which belongs to them.

I shall refer, hereafter, to the untold ills among the five civilized tribes, caused by the want of courts having jurisdiction over all crimes committed by all persons. But before taking up that subject I desire to reiterate that the full and complete remedy for the numerous evils that afflict those people lies deeper than the incomplete system of judicature which prevails within their limits. These people have, in a great measure, passed from a state of barbarism and savagery. Many of them are educated people. They have fine schools and churches. They are engaged in lucrative business of various kinds. In fact, so far as outward appearances go, there would seem to be very little difference between their civilization and that of the States. And yet when we come closely to investigate the laws and customs of their system of government, it is radically different from that of any of our States. Nowhere in the United States, except in polygamous Utah, and a few inconsiderable and widely scattered villages, is there a white community that pretends to hold property, and especially lands, in common. This is the fundamental error from which proceed the troubles which afflict the five nations. The practical operation of this system of holding creates an aristocracy out of a few wealthy and powerful leaders, while the poor, although equal owners, are so impoverished as not to be able to assert their equal rights of property and manhood.

I am not recommending that Congress shall undertake to do anything with reference to these five civilized tribes which is inhibited by the treaties. But I do advise the nations themselves to awake to a true appreciation of their own situation, and to have respect for that public opinion in this country which makes laws and forms States and which has thus far protected them in their treaty rights. I do advise our red brothers, whose interests I desire to see promoted, to advise with each other and to act wisely by passing just and equal laws for the division of lands in severalty, allotting to each member of the tribe his own birthright. The treaties I hope to see observed. But where the continued observance of those treaty obligations works an injury to the Indians by alienating from them the mass of the people of the United States, who are by instinct opposed to all monopoly, or where it does great injury to the Indians themselves, it seems to me it is the duty of the Indians to agree among themselves to a modification of those treaties—to remodel all such laws and customs as give a monopoly to a few (or even to many), and to place themselves abreast the times and in accord with the ideas of free and equal citizenship which prevail in this great country.

Territorial government.—If the Indians of the five civilized tribes would then put away tribal relations, and adopt the institutions common to our Territories or States, they would no longer be subjected to the jealousy, contention, and selfish greed of adventurous land-grabbers who now seem to regard the Indian as a legitimate object of prey and plunder. These adventurers do not attempt to dislodge and drive from their domiciles the peaceful white settlers in their distant homes. Let these Indians once assume all the responsibilities of citizens of the United States, with its laws extended as a protecting aegis over them, and the day of their fear and apprehension of marauding whites will be forever ended. When this is done then will the five civilized tribes, and perhaps other tribes of the Indian Territory, be ready to form a territorial government and pass, as other Territories, under the protection of our Constitution and laws and be represented in Congress by their own delegate.

The great objection that is urged by the Indians to dissolving their tribal relations, allotting their lands, and merging their political form of government into an organized Territory of the United States, arises out of their excessive attachment to Indian tradition and nationality. I have great respect for those sentiments. They are patriotic and noble impulses and principles. But is it now asking too much of the American people to permit a political paradox to exist within their midst—nay, more, to ask and demand that the people of this country shall forever burden themselves with the responsibility and expense of maintaining and extending over these Indians its military arm, simply to gratify this sentimentality about a separate nationality? No such exclusive privilege was granted the Pueblos of New Mexico, nor the inhabitants of California, Utah, and Arizona, or any of the more northern Territories, including Alaska.

It is alleged that Congress has no power, in view of the treaties with those Indians, to do away with their present form of government and institute in its stead a Territorial government similar to those now existing in the eight organized Territories. While I greatly prefer that these people should voluntarily change their form of government, yet it is perfectly plain to my mind that the treaties never contemplated the un-American and absurd idea of a separate nationality in our midst, with power as they may choose to organize a government of their own, or not to organize any government nor allow one to be organized, for the one proposition contains the other. These Indians have no right to obstruct civilization and commerce and set up an exclusive claim to self-government, establishing a government within a government, and then expect and claim that the United States shall protect them from all harm, while insisting that it shall not be the ultimate judge as to what is best to be done for them in a political point of view. I repeat, to maintain any such view is to acknowledge a foreign sovereignty, with the right of eminent domain, upon American soil—a theory utterly repugnant to the spirit and genius of our laws, and wholly unwarranted by the Constitution of the United States.

Congress and the Executive of the United States are the supreme guardians of these mere wards, and can administer their affairs as any other guardian can. Of course it must be done in a just and enlightened way. It must be done in a spirit of protection and not of oppression and robbery. Congress can sell their surplus lands and distribute the proceeds equally among the owners for the purposes of civilization and the education of their children, and the protection of the infirm, and the establishment of the poor upon homesteads with stock and implements of husbandry. Congress cannot consistently or justly or honestly take their lands from them and give or sell them to others except as above referred to, and for those objects alone. The sentiment is rapidly growing among these five nations that all existing forms of Indian government which have produced an unsatisfactory and dangerous condition of things, menacing the peace of the Indians and irritating their white neighbors, should be replaced by a regularly organized Territorial form of government, the territory thus constituted to be admitted at some future time as a State into the Union on an equal footing with other States, thereby securing all the protection, sympathy, and guarantees of this great and beneficent nation. The sooner this sentiment becomes universal the better for all concerned.

SURPLUS LANDS IN INDIAN TERRITORY

The vast surplusage of land in the Indian Territory, much of it, too, not surpassed anywhere for fertility and versatility of production, which can never be utilized by the Indians now within its borders nor by their descendants (for it is not probable that there will be any material increase in numbers of Indian population), must sooner or later be disposed of by Congress some way or other. Were all the Indians of the United States to be uprooted and transplanted to this Territory, all living Indians, including those now resident there, could have 256¾ acres each. This is estimating the whole Indian population of the United States, excluding Alaska, at 260,000. As the Indian Territory has an area of 64,222 square miles, or about 520 acres for each person now in the Territory, of course the problem presents itself for public consideration. What disposition or division of the Indian Territory can be justly, fairly, acceptably, and harmoniously made?

The Kiowas and Comanches, the Wichitas and the Cheyennes and Arapahoes, are the only tribes in the Indian Territory located west of longitude 98°. The reservation of the Cheyennes and Arapahoes is simply set aside by executive order, and the Indians occupying this tract do not hold it by the same tenure with which the Indians in other parts of the Indian Territory possess their reserves. In my last report I suggested that, as Oklahoma is surrounded on three sides by territory now occupied by Indians, its settlement by white people, even were it lawful, would be attended with considerable risk to the peace of both races. Also, that if it should be thought by Congress desirable to open to white settlement any part of the Indian Territory, it would be safer and better for all concerned, and especially the Indians, that the Cheyennes, Arapahoes, Kiowas, Comanches, and Wichitas be removed east, either to Oklahoma or to any other unoccupied land east of longitude 98°, and that all lands west of that line be valued and sold at a fair price, and the proceeds reserved for the civilization of the Indians.

Below is given an interesting table, showing the whole number of acres in the Indian Territory east and the whole number west of longitude 98°, and the distribution of population:

Total number of acres in Indian Territory	41,102,546
Number of acres in Indian Territory west of 98°	13,740,223
Number of acres in Indian Territory east of 98°	27,362,323
Number of acres of *unoccupied* lands in Indian Territory east of 98°	3,683,605
Number of Indians in Indian Territory west of 98°	7,616
Number of Indians in Indian Territory east of 98°	68,183
Total number of Indians now in Indian Territory	75,799
Number of acres each Indian would have if unoccupied lands east of 98° were divided equally among Indians now living west of 98°	483
Number of acres each Indian would have if all lands east of 98° were divided equally among all Indians now in Indian Territory	359

It is apparent that, as there are now only 7,616 Indians west of longitude 98°, if these Indians were placed on the 3,684,305 acres of unoccupied lands east of that meridian, each Indian would have 483 acres, an area of land far in excess of what he would need. But we also see from this table that there are west of 98°, including Greer County, 13,740,229 acres, which would be sufficient to furnish homes of 100 acres each to 137,402 people; and supposing each settler to have five in his family, it would support a population of 687,010 souls. Add to this "No Man's Land," lying immediately west and adjoining, containing 3,672,640 acres, and we see at once that there is territory enough in those two areas to found a State equal in size to many States of this Union. Another advantage of this arrangement would be that the Indians would be altogether in a more compact form, while the whites would be by themselves.

When my last report was made the time and circumstances were auspicious for the adoption of these suggestions, if Congress entertained them at all, for the reason that at that time the Indians west of 98°, especially the Cheyennes and Arapahoes, had been severely admonished by the Government, by a display of military force, that they would no longer be permitted to obstruct those of their tribe who desired to adopt the white man's way. To this admonition almost universal heed was given, and a large number at once began to prepare for settling down and cultivating the soil. In consequence of this recent change in their wishes and habits, very many houses have been erected and a large acreage of sod broken and extensive crops cultivated. A year ago these Indians had less to attach them to their homes than they now have, and therefore their removal east would have been less distasteful then than now. Nevertheless, as the distance is short and the lands to which they might be moved are much superior to those which they now occupy, I doubt not that, by paying them for their improvements or by making similar improvements on their new homes, they would cheerfully obey the wish of Congress should that body conclude to remove them to Oklahoma or to some other fertile unoccupied lands east of 98°. During the last twelve months these Indians have not only made rapid progress in farming, but also in a disposition to have their children educated, more than two thirds of the Cheyenne and nearly all the Arapaho children having been enrolled in school. I am recently and reliably informed by a leading missionary and Indian educator that if sufficient buildings are furnished, all of their children of school age will be at school in the course of another year. Great efforts have been made by these Indians, and far more has been accomplished in the last year in the way of farming than ever before. At this time a general wish prevails among them for the construction of dwelling-houses. All these facts taken into consideration, it become apparent that if it should be the desire of Congress to dispose of this section of the Indian Territory, it will be attended with embarrassment even now, and of course, as the Indians open and improve farms and build houses and prepare to live, they will become more attached to their homes and less disposed to emigrate, even to better lands which are but a short distance away.

My apology, if apology is needed, for presenting these facts and suggestions somewhat earnestly, arises from my deep conviction that the proposition to throw open Oklahoma to white settlement, surrounded as it is by Indians on three sides, would be an experiment dangerous to all concerned, and especially would the Indians west of Oklahoma be abraded and eventually obliterated by the surging waves of white population striking upon them from all directions. This subject is of very great importance; and in view of the persistent efforts which have been made by parties more or less organized to possess themselves of lands within the Indian Territory regardless of law and the rights of these Indians, and in view, too, of the action of a large number of Representatives as expressed by bills presented and speeches made in Congress, I feel it my duty especially to invoke your consideration of the subject, not only as a matter of justice and right and the interest of the Indians, but also as a respectful recognition of the demands of those Representatives whose opinions and views are entitled to the highest respect.

I therefore recommend, as a preliminary step, that Congress authorize the Department to appoint a commission, who shall visit the Cheyennes and Arapahoes, the Wichitas and the Kiowas, Comanches and Apaches, in the Indian Territory, to ascertain their views with reference to the subject of removal to lands in said Territory east of 98°.

If any portion of the Indian Territory is to be opened to white settlement, then I think the suggestions which I have offered are the most practical and would cause the least possible dissatisfaction and injury to the Indians. Those of the Western tribes who would be immediately affected by this action could suffer only temporary inconvenience by removal. The same improvements which they now have could easily be made for them and at little expense in their new home, and the improvements already made on their present location could be sold at their value to purchasers. But until Congress takes definite action upon this subject this office will feel it to be its duty to press forward the settling upon lands or homesteads of all the Indians west of Oklahoma, and to encourage them to open farms, erect houses, and make other improvements as rapidly as possible; for no time ought to be lost in teaching these people to support themselves, and to stop all work and improvement would throw them into a state of idleness which would soon lead to crime and disorder, if not to actual conflict among themselves and with their white neighbors.

U. S. Court in the Indian Territory

The present anomalous condition of legal affairs among the five civilized nations calls for wisest counsel and for the most prudent and thoughtful consideration of the executive and legislative departments of this Government. It is well known that within their borders are many people of foreign or white blood who are intruders, and who are absolutely independent of Indian statutes, and are also independent of the laws and authorities of the several States and almost of the United States Government. Each Indian nation has a form of government, with a system of laws by which malefactors may be punished and litigants may determine their rights, provided they are all Indians. Should a white man violate any of the statutes of these nations he can only be ordered out of the Territory by the Commissioner of Indian Affairs, who seems to be anomalously invested with certain negative and restraining powers, but with no other actual positive authority in such matters. In the event of strife or contention over property or any *civil* cases between white men or between white men and Indians there is no law applicable.

To such an extent has this uncertainty of jurisdiction and authority prevailed that the borders of these nations have become the refuge of thousands of evil-doers who have fled from their homes in the States and made this region a Botany Bay. Murderers, horse thieves, gamblers, and other violators of law have flocked thither by hundreds and are there to-day, and in many instances in open defiance of the United States marshal. Another despicable class of persons have made this country a refuge to shield them and their property from the just claims of legal creditors. They obtain upon credit the property of citizens of adjoining States and then secretly skip across the line into the Indian country, where they are secure from arrest and their property from judicial process. The only remedy is for the agents of the Indian Office with its meager force to hunt out them and their property and drive them across the line again into the States where State law will reach them. During the past year several such cases have been brought to the attention of this office in which judgment having been obtained in the State of Texas against United States citizens the property subject to execution had been fraudulently conveyed to and secreted in the Territory with the deliberate purpose of depriving the creditor of the fruits of his judgment. The State processes not running in the Territory, and there being no law to meet such cases, the Department, on being appealed to, decided that, on broad grounds of public policy, it could not consent to the Indian Territory being made a sanctuary for dishonest debtors or their ill-gotten spoils, and on due proof of the facts alleged in such case directed the removal of the concealed property from the Territory.

A similar state of affairs, though elsewhere it has not yet reached such serious proportions, exists outside the five civilized tribes throughout the whole Indian Territory.

In *criminal* cases in the Indian Territory, where a white man and an Indian are the parties, or where both parties are white, the case can be tried under existing statutes (act of January 6, 1883, 22 Stats., 400) before the United States courts for the district of Kansas, the western district of Arkansas, or the northern district of Texas, according to the *locus* where the crime was committed. The courts at Wichita and Fort Scott, Kans., have exclusive original jurisdiction over all that part of the Territory lying north of the Canadian River and east of Texas and the one hundredth meridian, not set apart to and occupied by the Cherokee, Creek, and Seminole Indian tribes; the court at Graham, Tex., has like jurisdiction over that part of the Territory not so annexed to the district of Kansas, and not set apart to and occupied by the Cherokee, Creek, Choctaw, Chickasaw, and Seminole Indi-' an tribes; whilst the court at Fort Smith, Ark., retains the jurisdiction over all that part of the Territory occupied by the five civilized tribes.

Speaking of this matter the United States Indian agent for the five civilized tribes, in his annual report herewith, page 374, remarks:

> Crimes are gradually decreasing under the very superior management of the United States district court for the western district of Arkansas which has criminal jurisdiction over this agency, the active co-operation of the valuable and efficient Indian police force, and the improving management of the Indian courts. The Indian courts, as a rule, are not well conducted, but are growing more respectable under the strong educational forces at work. The crimes committed are not extraordinary in number when it is remembered that this country, by virtue of its sparse settlement and absence of State law, makes an excellent hiding place for refugees from justice. There has been located at this point (Muscogee) a United States commissioner, Hon. John Q. Tufts, formerly Indian agent, who has been of much service in the administration of the criminal law.
>
> The chief defect in the administration of law at Fort Smith has been the great distances necessary for witnesses to travel who live in the remoter parts of this district. It is as much a punishment on the witness as it is on the accused, almost, for owing to the pressure of business before the court he has probably to make three or four trips, 150 miles each way, across the country, and thus go some 900 or 1,200 miles on horseback to tell what he knows about a horse thief. This is very expensive, and people would rather let crimes go unreported than endure the loss incident to prosecution. It would be an immense saving in mileage for its thousands of witnesses, &c., and other costs to the United States Government, if the court were moved to Muscogee or Fort Gibson. It certainly would secure a better administration of justice, and relieve the Territory people of a heavy expense in attending this court.

Similar representations as to the remoteness of courts of jurisdiction have from time to time been made by other agents located at different points in the Territory; and whilst the condition of things has been somewhat ameliorated by the act of 1883 above referred to, which distributed the jurisdiction over the Territory between three courts instead of one, as theretofore, I have little doubt that many flagrant cases of crime now go unpunished owing to the difficulty and expense of attendance on the courts as now located.

The time-honored maxim, "There is no wrong without a remedy," seems to have no application to the Indian Territory, and some remedy for this unsatisfactory and I may add alarming situation should be wisely considered and promptly applied by Congress. The immediate necessity for the establishment of a United States district court within the heart of the territory of the five civilized nations, at some convenient point accessible by railroad— say Muskogee or Fort Gibson—no longer admits of a doubt. It is the promptest remedy that can be applied to arrest the evils referred to. In this opinion I am sustained by the late Senatorial committee of which Hon. H. L. Dawes was chairman, which last year visited this Territory under a Senate resolution; and Judge Parker, eminent for his learning, efficiency, and patriotism, fully concurs as to the necessity for the immediate establishment of this court.

The treaties made with the civilized tribes in 1866 all contain provisions for the establishment of a United States court in the Territory, with such jurisdiction and organized in such manner as may be prescribed by law; and I understand that there is a general wish among the leading and more intelligent Indians themselves that Congress at once pass the necessary law for its establishment. Measures have been repeatedly introduced, in fact are now pending in Congress, for the establishment of such a court, and I trust that the suggestions made may be deemed worthy of consideration.

In any event, whether Congress decides to establish the United States court in the Territory, or to leave the jurisdiction where it is, provision should be made for extending such jurisdiction to civil cases where an Indian, or person of Indian blood, resident in the Territory, and a citizen of the United States are the parties, and also, if possible, for the enforcement of civil process issuing out of a State court against the property of a United States citizen held or concealed in the Indian Territory. It is due to the commercial industries of the country that they should be protected, and the creditor enabled to get his just dues, without coming as a suppliant to this Department. As has already been stated, in civil cases between Indians and white men in the Territory, the agency is now the only tribunal where they can be adjudicated, and much valuable time, both of the agent and of this office, which should be devoted to other matters, is consumed in hearing and adjusting (so far as possible) such complaints. All this can be remedied by conferring civil jurisdiction upon the United States courts, in which such cases should properly be tried. The power inherent in a judicial tribunal to enforce its decrees would be respected, and the civilized Indian who is capable of making and appreciating a contract would be taught that, whilst his Indian blood would not shield him against the enforcement of his just obligations, his right to a corresponding performance of the contract on the part of the white man would be protected. In regard to this Agent Owen says:

> Owing to the large number of United States citizens in the Territory, there are a large number of civil cases constantly arising between themselves alone, or with Indian citizens, some involving large sums. There is no judicial tribunal to settle such cases, and as they must necessarily increase in number and importance, some provision ought to be made. If the Federal court is clothed with power to try an Indian's right to live, I see no reason why it cannot try his rights to property when disputed by a United States citizen. At all events, this stands as a serious chasm in the law, and it is my duty to report it.

LEASES OF INDIAN LANDS

In my last annual report I gave a history of the troubles on the Cheyenne and Arapaho Reservation, in the Indian Territory, growing out of the grazing leases, and of the measures taken to restore peace and tranquillity amongst the Indians.

Under the President's proclamation, therein referred to, the leases were declared null and void, and the cattle, together with all unauthorized persons, were removed from the reservation as speedily as it was practicable to do so. The removal was peaceably effected, and, I am gratified to say, without conflict between the Indians and the whites.

Contrary to the predictions of interested parties, who foretold all kinds of suffering, disasters, and outbreaks when the lease-money should be stopped, it appears from the report of Captain Lee, of the United States Army (who was placed in charge of the Cheyennes and Arapahoes at the time of the threatened outbreak), that not a single Indian has expressed a desire for a renewal of the leases. On the contrary, all have given pronounced expression of satisfaction that the leases were annulled and the cattle and cattle-men removed. They no longer contemplate the monopoly of nine-tenths of their reservation by outsiders, but in place thereof they view with satisfaction their own fields of corn, and farms inclosed with fences, put up by their own labor, the wire being furnished by the Department. The annual report of Captain Lee, on the condition and progress of the Cheyenne and Arapaho Indians, will be found interesting reading, and great credit is due that officer for the energy and zeal he has put into his work during his comparatively brief tenure of office. His report contains full statistics of farms opened and cultivated, in the face of many obstacles and discouragements, by Indians and persons of Indian blood lawfully resident on the reservation. That the gratifying condition of affairs reported by Captain Lee could ever have come to pass during the existence of the leases is a proposition which needs no argument to controvert.

In my last annual report (supplemented by Senate Ex. Doc. No. 17, made by Indian tribes and bands of lands for grazing purposes, so far as the Forty-eighth Congress, second session) detailed particulars of all leases same had come to the knowledge of this office, were furnished. Of these leases, those made by the Cheyennes and Arapahoes were, as already stated, annulled by Executive proclamation, and the following named have been practically abandoned, viz: the lease from the Quapaw tribe of Indians to H. R. Crowell, the Citizen Band of Pottawatomies to Catherine Grieffenstein, the Prairie Band of Pottawatomies in Kansas to Anderson & Co., and the Crow Indians of Montana to Wilson & Blake. In the absence of any complaints to this office by the Indians, or the several United States Indian agents in charge, none of the other lessees mentioned have been disturbed, pending action by Congress on the general subject.

The decision of the Attorney-General that the system of leasing Indian lands which has hitherto prevailed is illegal without the consent of Congress only adds to the difficulties which beset this office in dealing with this question of leases. In my last report this matter was referred to as follows:

> I cannot too strongly impress upon the Department the importance of an early disposition of this much vexed question. The leasing system should either be legalized, with proper restrictions, or it should be abolished altogether. In its present loose and indefinite shape it is a source of the greatest embarrassment to this office, and a hinderance to the proper and effective administration of Indian affairs.

If Congress would authorize Indians to dispose of their grass, or would take any definite action as to the policy which this office can legally pursue in regard to Indian grazing lands, it would materially lessen the perplexities and confusion which now pertain to the subject. Moreover, if some way could be adopted by which, under proper restrictions, the surplus grass on the several Indian reservations could be utilized with profit to the Indians, the annual appropriations needed to care for the Indians could be correspondingly and materially reduced.

ALLOTMENTS OF LAND SEVERALTY AND PATENTS

During the year 17 certificates of allotments have been issued to the Indians on the Lake Traverse Reservation, under the treaty with the Sisseton and Wahpeton bands of Sioux (15 Stats., 505); 2 to the Indians on the White Earth Reservation, under the treaty with the Chippewas of the Mississippi, concluded March 19, 1867 (16 Stats., 721); 55 to the Sioux Indians at the Rosebud Agency, under the sixth article of the Sioux treaty, concluded April 29, 1868 (15 Stats., 637); and 12 to the Sioux Indians at the Crow Creek Agency, under the same treaty.

Patents have been issued as follows: Two hundred and eighty-one to the Chippewas of Lake Superior, on the Bad River, Lac Court Oreilles, l'Anse and Vieux de Sert, and Fond du Lac Reservations, under the provisions of the third article of the treaty of September 30, 1854 (10 Stats., 1110); 3 to the Sisseton and Wahpeton bands of Sioux, under the fifth article of the treaty of February 19, 1867 (15 Stats., 505); 123 to the Santee Sioux Indians, under the treaty of April 29, 1868 (15 Stats., 637); 68 to the Chippewas of Saginaw, Swan Creek, and Black River, under the treaties of August 2, 1855 (11 Stats., 631), and October 18, 1864 (14 Stats., 657); 167 to the Puyallup Indians, under the treaty of December 26, 1854 (10 Stats., 1132); 46 to the S'Kokomish Indians, under the treaty of January 26, 1855 (12 Stats., 933); 1 to an Omaha Indian, under the act of August 7, 1882 (22 Stats., 341); and 1 to a Winnebago Indian, under the act of February 21, 1863 (12 Stats., 658); making the total number of certificates 86 and of patents 690; grand total, 776.

Two special agents are now engaged in the work of allotting the lands on the Crow Reservation in Montana.

In accordance with your directions, special instructions have been issued to the agents at Yankton, Lower Brulé, and Warm Springs to urge upon the Indians under their charge the importance of taking their lands in severalty, as allowed by their respective treaties, and to press the work of allotting lands with the utmost vigor. Similar instructions will be given other agents as soon as the condition of the surveys will permit such work to be done.

The general allotment bill again passed the Senate at the last session, and was favorably reported in the House of Representatives. As there seems to be no substantial opposition to this bill, it is hoped that it will become a law during the coming winter. Its passage will relieve this office of much embarrassment and enable it to make greater progress in the important work of assisting the Indians to become individual owners of the soil by an indefeasible title.

Nine hundred and fifty-five patents have been delivered to the Omahas during the past year. Reports differ as to the degree of progress attained by the Omahas since they have received allotments and undertaken to manage their own affairs, and it must be expected that some members of the tribe, not so progressive nor so well disposed as others, will take advantage of the newly acquired freedom from agency restraint to enjoy and improve the increased opportunity thus afforded them for shiftlessness or mischief-making. All transition periods have their peculiar difficulties and discouragements. But on the whole the success of the Omahas is such as to impress favorably friends of the Indians and believers in their civilization, and to afford to Indians everywhere the highest encouragement to adopt the same policy. The efforts of a few white friends, among whom the name of Miss Alice Fletcher, of Boston, might receive special mention without injustice to or derogation of the others, have furnished practical demonstration of the disposition and ability of the Indian to support and govern himself. There is something inspiring to the soul and heart of man when he realizes that he is not a slave, or a ward, or a dependent, and that the responsibilities of manhood are thrown upon him and he will be judged according to the way in which he meets and discharges them. I trust the true friends of Indian progress everywhere will unite their voices in this behalf, and will press with zeal, determination, and all practicable dispatch the allotment system among Indian tribes.

FARMING BY INDIANS

According to the intention expressed in my last report, special attention has been paid during the year just past to the encouragement of agricultural pursuits by Indians. A majority of the grown-up Indians on reservations, through want of early training and by reason of repugnance to any kind of manual labor, which their traditions and customs lead them to look upon as degrading, are very poor material out of which to make farmers. Even those who are most willing to work lack the foresight, good husbandry, economy, and persistence necessary to make farming successful. They are easily discouraged; the failure of one crop is almost fatal to their hopes in that direction, and they are inclined to give up further effort. It must be understood, also, that many of them are located on reservations where the soil is poor, or no regular rains fall, or the climate is so severe and the seasons so short that it would be a difficult matter for a first-class white farmer to make a living. These drawbacks to the progress of the Indians must not be lost sight of in considering what results we have, from the expenditures made by the Government to assist them. It cannot be expected that under such circumstances all or even many will at once, or in the course of the next five or ten years, step from the position of ignorant, shiftless, lazy savages to that of successful independent farmers; but this object is being constantly kept in view, and all official action taken by me will tend to that result, for in it, in my opinion, lies the only hope of the survival of any considerable portion of the Indian tribes.

In March last each Indian agent was informed that the permanent establishment of the Indians in agricultural pursuits should be considered the main duty of himself and every agency employé; that all must work for this result; that wherever practicable every able-bodied Indian who had not already done so must commence at once to cultivate a piece of ground, and that those who were already tilling small patches must be induced to go to work on a larger scale; that the farmers at the various agencies must not only advise and counsel with the Indians about farming operations, but must themselves go to work, and by example show them how to select proper land for cultivation, how and when to prepare it, when and what to plant, how to care for the growing crops, to harvest them, to prepare the produce for market, and to market it so as to make farming pay. At the same time they are expected to teach the Indians economy and foresight and patient perseverance, and to show them how to save seed for next year and how to care properly for their work animals and stock and provide food and shelter for winter use.

I considered it my duty to give these specific instructions, and I intend to see to it that they are fully carried out. Unless an Indian can be shown how he himself can farm to advantage, that is, make a comfortable living by farming without help from others, the effort to make him a farmer might as well be abandoned.

Since the beginning of the season good reports have been received from many of the agents, but of course it will be some years yet before it can be definitely ascertained just how far Indian farming has been established on a permanent paying basis. The annual statistical reports of the increased number of acres under cultivation or of the quantity of crops harvested cannot be depended upon to show this; it will only appear in time in the decrease of the amount of supplies to be purchased and the increase in the number of Indian families who have become permanently established in comfortable independence and in their bettered condition generally.

ADDITIONAL FARMERS

By act of Congress, approved July 4, 1884, the sum of $25,000 was appropriated—

> To enable the Secretary of the Interior to employ practical farmers, in addition to the agency farmers now employed, at wages not exceeding $75 per month, to superintend and direct farming among such Indians as are making effort for self-support.

The results of the judicious expenditure of this appropriation were so satisfactory that the same amount was appropriated for like purpose by act of Congress approved March 3, 1885, for the year ending June 30, 1886. The rule was adopted of appointing such additional farmers directly by this office, thus giving an opportunity to investigate each application and ascertain the fitness of the applicant for the position. The results have been eminently satisfactory, and much good has been done by the additional farmers going among the Indians, acquainting themselves with the individual peculiarities and needs of each, and giving the instruction and assistance best suited to each case. Of the $25,000 appropriated, there remains unexpended a very small balance, caused by the fact that the service at a few agencies was not continuous through the year.

The results of the policy of employing additional farmers were of such marked benefit that it could no longer be called an experiment, and by act of Congress approved May 15, 1886, the sum of $40,000 was appropriated for this purpose during the fiscal year ending June 30, 1887. By the expenditure of this increased amount in the employment of active, energetic men who have the best interests of the Indians at heart, there is no doubt that much good will result.

CARE OF AGRICULTURAL IMPLEMENTS AT AGENCIES

Reports of inspectors and special agents have called attention to the fact that at many agencies but little care has been exercised by the agents and employés to see that costly agricultural implements and mechanical tools of all kinds were issued only to the deserving and to those who were prepared to use them and take care of them. Agents seemed to think that they get rid of all responsibility in the matter, which they were desirous to do, by issuing these supplies and paying no further attention to them. Consequently, reapers and mowers, plows, harrows, wagons and harness, and all kinds of costly agricultural implements and mechanical tools were found scattered about on nearly every reservation—perhaps used only a few times, then thrown aside or left where last used, exposed to the weather and going to decay. In some instances fence-wire was given Indians who had no posts to attach it to and knew nothing of erecting a fence, and thrashing-machines and horse-powers, after being used one season, were left to the mercy of the elements until the succeeding year's crop called attention to them, when, in many cases, as might have been anticipated, they would be found to be damaged beyond economical repair, and estimates for new ones would be submitted.

In order to correct this abuse, each agent has been instructed that he must use judgment and discretion in issuing implements; that he must keep every article in a safe and sheltered place until actually needed for immediate use by a deserving Indian, who will agree to take proper care of it when not in use; also that it is the duty of the agent and the employés to see to it that an Indian knows how to use what is given him, and that he has some means of taking proper care of it; and further, that if he neglects to do so, after having been warned and in disregard of the promises which should be required of him and embodied in his receipt for the article, it is the agent's duty to retake possession of such articles as are found lying around neglected, and to issue them to some one more deserving, and thereafter to discriminate against the Indian who disregards his promise and agency instructions. Agents have also been informed that they will be held responsible whenever such agricultural implements and supplies as reapers and mowers, fanning-mills, horse-powers, wagons and harness, plows, &c., and also small mechanical tools, such as augers, axes, hatchets, hammers, &c., are found scattered about a reservation, not in use, but neglected and exposed to the weather. I understand that a great improvement in this respect has already taken place and its continuance will be insisted upon.

EDUCATION

In the extract from my first report, already quoted, I expressed very decidedly the idea that Indians should be taught the English language only. From that position I believe, so far as I am advised, there is no dissent either among the law-makers or the executive agents who are selected under the law to do the work. There is not an Indian pupil whose tuition and maintenance is paid for by the United States Government who is permitted to study any other language than our own vernacular—the language of the greatest, most powerful, and enterprising nationalties beneath the sun. The English language as taught in America is good enough for all her people of all races.

It is yet undetermined what kinds of schools are best adapted to prepare the Indian for self-support and that independence which will enable him to meet and successfully encounter the shrewd competition which henceforth every one will find contesting his path in the social, civic, and business affairs of life. Indian educators themselves differ in opinion as to what kinds of Indian schools are preferable, and the same difference exists among those in both houses of Congress who have charge of Indian matters. That each of the different kinds of schools or methods of education can lay some claims to merit cannot be denied.

The common day school on the reservation of course is the more economic method if limited to the immediate outlay of money for the time employed; but if viewed from the broader standpoint of permanent efficiency and enduring advancement of Indian youth, that plan may justly be challenged, for some years to come, by the friends of other methods as being not only the least efficient and permanent but eventually the most expensive. The greatest difficulty is experienced in freeing the children attending day schools from the language and habits of their untutored and oftentimes savage parents. When they return to their homes at night, and on Saturdays and Sundays, and are among their old surroundings, they relapse more or less into their former moral and mental stupor. This constitutes the strongest objection to this class of schools, and I fear that, in many instances, the objection is too well-founded. But as education and general civilization take deeper hold upon the Indian race, the day school on the reservation will show better results and must eventually become universal, as are our common schools in the States.

At this time, however, after the best examination I can give the subject, I would not advise any diminution of material aid and support to any of the different kinds of schools now fostered by the Government. All are doing most excellent and efficient service in their particular spheres, and all are performing a good part in the grand work of educating and civilizing the hitherto untutored Indians. The honor of this noble work belongs to the great American constituency and their representatives in both the legislative and executive branches of the Government; and I would call upon all officers and agents of the Government who come in immediate contact with our red brothers to impress them with the great benefits that are thus conferred upon them, or which their hearts should swell with grateful emotion.

That the Indians are not lacking in appreciation of their educational advantages is shown by the following statistics, which do not include the schools among the five civilized tribes nor the Indians of New York State, nor boarding and day schools supported by religious societies without expense to the Government.

Schools	1885		1886		Increase in average attend-ance
	No.	Average attend-ance	No.	Average attend-ance	
Boarding schools under agency supervision ..	84	4,066	85	4,817	751
Day schools under agency supervision........	86	1,942	99	2,370	458
Training schools.........................	7	1,425	7	1,582	157
Schools in States.......................	23	710	23	861	151
Total.............................	200	8,143	214	9,630	1,517

Other statistics and statements in regard to Indian education are given in detail in the report of the superintendent of Indian schools. The above figures show that the attendance at all of the schools has been largely increased this year over that of last year, and that the per cent. of increase is larger in the boarding schools and day schools under agency supervision than in the other schools.

This office has used all diligence to introduce school books among the Indian pupils in accordance with the spirit of the late act of Congress requiring the use in the public schools of such text-books as teach the baneful influences of ardent spirits and narcotics on the human system I am thoroughly satisfied of the wisdom of the measure.

As an incentive to make the best use of the educational advantages afforded those pupils of both sexes who attend industrial institutions, I think it would be wise for Congress to make an appropriation from which every Indian youth who shall graduate from school and marry an Indian maiden who has also graduated may be assisted in settling down upon a homestead of 160 acres, in purchasing a team, in breaking and fencing land, and in building a house. If the homestead is not on an Indian reservation the man should also have the privilege of citizenship, including the right of suffrage. Such a law would greatly encourage Indian youths and maidens in their resistance to the evil and savage influences of their untutored friends, and would do much to keep them from a return to savage life.

* * *

Courts of Indian Offenses

Longer experience makes more apparent the value of the courts insti-tuted at various agencies for the punishment of minor offenses committed by the Indians. With one exception, all the agents at whose agencies courts are established speak very highly of the good effect of these courts and of the manner in which the judges perform their duties. As an illustration of the general tenor of the agents' reports, I quote the following from that of Agent McLaughlin, at Standing Rock:

There are regular bi-weekly sessions of the Indian courts held at the agency police headquarters, in a room set apart for that purpose, and the importance of this court is now such that it would seem almost impossible to do without it. Offenses of every character committed at the agency are brought before this court for adjudication, and it has relieved me of much annoyance in trivial matters, and aided materially in the more important cases. The judges, who are the two officers of the Indian police force and John Grass, an intelligent Indian who speaks English, are men of excellent judgment, whose decisions, impartially rendered, have been accepted in all cases the past year without any complaint, except in the instances where an appeal was made, and in two of which a rehearing was ordered upon additional testimony being produced.

These courts are also unquestionably a great assistance to the Indians in learning habits of self-government and in preparing themselves for citizenship. I am of the opinion that they should be placed upon a legal basis by an act of Congress authorizing their establishment, under such rules and regulations as the Secretary of the Interior may prescribe. Their duties and jurisdiction could then be definitely determined and greater good accomplished.

At some of the agencies it has been found impracticable to establish these courts from the fact that good men cannot be found who are willing to serve as judges without compensation. At others the make-shift policy has had to be resorted to of detailing members of the police force to act as judges in court! The payment of a small monthly salary would have a most salutary effect in giving greater dignity to the office and rendering it possible to secure better men for judges. For this purpose I have asked for the next fiscal year an appropriation of $5,000.

JURISDICTION OF CRIMES COMMITTED BY INDIANS

In my last annual report attention was called to certain defects in the ninth section of the act of March 3, 1885 (23 Stats., 385), providing for the punishment of certain crimes committed by Indians. Subsequently a bill was prepared and submitted to Congress relieving the Territories of the expenses incident to the enforcement of the law, and extending its provisions to that portion of the Indian Territory not covered by the laws of the five civilized tribes. I deem the passage of this or a similar bill to be necessary to the proper execution of the act. In Dakota especially the county authorities refuse to prosecute Indians guilty of the most serious offenses, on the ground of the expense incident to such prosecution. As the counties derive no revenue from the reservations within their limits, the injustice of compelling them to assume the burden of these prosecutions is apparent.

* * *

INDIAN POLICE

The greatest number of Indian police in the service at any one time during the fiscal year ending June 30, 1886, was 701. Considering the very meager compensation allowed, viz, $10 per month for commissioned officers and $8 per month for non-commissioned officers and privates, the service has been very satisfactory. The members of the police force are selected on account of their good character and influence among their people; a majority of them have families to support. They have proven themselves to be worthy of confidence, and have rendered valuable assistance to the agents in maintaining order and suppressing crime on the reservations. They are almost without exception courageous, determined men, who will without flinching face any danger in carrying out their instructions.

To bring the police service up to the highest degree of efficiency it is necessary that the entire time and attention of the men be devoted to their work, but it is often difficult to obtain the services of proper men on account of the small compensation. It would tend greatly to increase the efficiency of this branch of the service if a more liberal compensation could be allowed, even though the number of men should be reduced. The police in the discharge of their duties often come in contact with outlaws and men of desperate character, and being thus called upon to face danger and death it is but fair that they should receive a compensation in some degree commensurate with the service rendered. The cost of their support is money well spent, as at most agencies they are the only means which the agent possesses for protecting his Indians against liquor traffic, cattle thieves, the inroads of bad white men, and for the suppression of every kind of vice and lawlessness on the reservation. Without them he would have much less power either to punish the bad or protect the good, and the knowledge that he has this reliable force always at hand has a much greater influence for good than appears on the surface.

Agency Employés

It is well known that the general public has long been impressed with the idea that much corruption prevailed in the employé service at Indian agencies; that many agents having in their own hands the power to employ or dismiss their assistants had surrounded themselves with such material as they could completely control through fear of discharge or by collusion with them in dishonest practices; that this condition of affairs rendered fraud easy and its detection by inspectors, special agents, and this office almost impossible, and that thus the Government and the Indians were plundered with impunity; and that worthless or worse employés were retained in office solely on the ground of their usefulness to the agent or through his fear of the use they might make of their knowledge of his practices in case he incurred their displeasure. It was also claimed that many agents had placed their relatives, or relatives of their bondsmen, in office merely through cupidity or to fulfill promises made, and had kept them there without regard to their fitness for the positions or their endeavors to discharge their duties, and without power to control them.

After giving this matter careful consideration, and becoming convinced that there must be some good grounds for so generally unfavorable an opinion in regard to it, I determined to make such a change as would effectually remove all just cause for doubt as to the honesty and integrity of the service in this particular. Indian agents and school superintendents were therefore notified that the office would select and appoint all clerks as well as physicians and additional farmers. It was believed that this course would meet the approval of all good agents, and of those who considered the good name and best interests of the service paramount to personal preferences, since it promised them competent assistants, and at the same time relieved them of obligation either to their bondsmen or their relatives; and it was thought that thoroughly upright men would prefer to have entirely disinterested proof always at hand that their official acts were without stain.

I am pleased to be able to report that most of the agents were broad enough in their views, and had their own and the best interests of the service sufficiently at heart, cordially to support this move. The reports from various agencies satisfy me that this ruling that agency clerks shall be selected by the Indian Office is a wise one, and it has already been found to tend so directly and plainly to the improvement of the service that I have no doubt as to its necessity for the good of the Indians and the administration of agency affairs generally. A few agents have complained of this change, but they could advance no good reason against it, and I have considered it necessary to make the rule general and to treat all alike.

As I find that but little attention has heretofore been paid by the office to the qualifications for their respective duties of lower-grade employés, the plan has been adopted of plainly laying before all applicants for positions a statement of the duties that will be required of them, and of informing them that if they are found, on trial, to be incompetent, they will not be retained. Clerks must file a sample of their writing and give satisfactory information as to their proficiency, and farmers, blacksmiths, carpenters, &c., must satisfy me that they are experienced and capable in their various callings. Thus, when an appointment is offered to an applicant, he is given fully to understand what will be expected of him, and that if he is not confident that he can discharge the duties of the position it will be only to his disadvantage and loss to accept it. I am determined that, as far as I can ascertain the facts, no improper or incompetent employé shall remain in the service.

Physicians are required to be graduates of some reputable medical institution, and as it has been ascertained that in many cases agency physicians have been in the habit of treating persons not connected with the agency, for pay, to the neglect of their regular duty, they are directed to devote their entire time and professional skill to the Indian service.

Such employés as are directly appointed by this office are told that they are under the immediate control of the agent; that they must work in harmony with him, treating him with due respect and obeying his orders cheerfully; and that, as he is a bonded officer, they must take good care of the property for which he is responsible. On the other hand, while agents are not allowed to suspend or discharge any employé appointed by this office, any statement they wish to make as to the manner in which the employé behaves himself and discharges his duties is carefully considered, and such action taken thereon as is deemed just and for the best interests of the service.

* * *

INDIAN TRADE

The endeavor to regulate and supervise trade among the various Indian tribes has given rise to many perplexing questions. The demand for improvement in the management of this branch of the Indian service, has been emphatic, and careful study has been given the subject, in the belief that changes could be made which would diminish the opportunities afforded unscrupulous traders to take advantage of the Indians.

In accordance with the proposed policy outlined in my last report, Indian agents have been instructed to submit to this office a statement of the annual gross sales of each Indian trader upon their reservations, and the number of trading licenses to be granted at each agency is determined by the amount of trade reported by the agent. Traders are required to forward monthly, through the Indian agents, invoices of all goods received. The maximum amount of profit which may be realized on each article of merchandise is fixed by this office; the average of profits allowed will not exceed 25 per cent. of the original cost of the goods and the freight. A schedule of the prices charged by the trader must be conspicuously posted in each store.

If agents will co-operate conscientiously with this office in executing the above rules and regulations it cannot but effect the desirable end of providing the Indians with such articles as they need at prices which return only a fair profit upon the capital and labor invested by the trader, and of preventing extortion upon the helpless Indian, who, by reason of the remoteness of other stores, is often compelled to deal with the licensed trader.

Some of the traders apparently have failed to understand the restrictions imposed, and thereby have made the office considerable trouble. In some instances non-observance of the restrictions has resulted in a revocation of the license. On the whole, however, the present status of licensed trade among Indians is creditable and gratifying.

But it is earnestly hoped that the necessity for white traders upon the reservations will soon be superseded. Under the law the full-blood Indian is guaranteed the right to trade with the Indians of his tribe, without the restrictions imposed upon half-breeds and white traders. It is the constant aim and effort of the Indian Office to make the Indian self-reliant and self-sustaining, and if this policy is persevered in, with the aid of the educational advantages available at almost every agency, I cannot but believe that the Indians will at an early day acquire sufficient ability to manage the trading posts themselves and supply their people with such goods as they may need.

SANITARY CONDITION OF THE INDIANS

During the year a corps of sixty-seven physicians has been actively engaged in caring for the sick at the different agencies and training schools, and as a rule the men so employed have rendered very efficient service. As has been stated, physicians in the Indian service are appointed directly by the office, upon satisfactory testimonials as to character, ability, and experience. When it is shown that any one so appointed is incompetent or is careless in the discharge of his duties, a change is made at once. They are instructed to use every effort to overcome the influence of the native "medicine men," and to educate and enlighten the Indians in regard to the proper care and treatment of the sick. The good effects of this policy are already quite apparent, for although many of the older Indians cling tenaciously to their time-honored rites and ceremonies, the younger members of the tribes have, to a great extent, abandoned them, and rely upon the agency physicians. The influence which a physician of intelligence and good judgment soon acquires over the Indians under his care enables him to render great assistance in the work of eradicating the superstitions prevailing among them.

* * *

Many of the agency physicians recommend the establishment of hospitals at the agencies, where cases can be taken in and treated successfully, which, if left to the rude care of their friends and relatives and subjected to the exposure incident to living in tepees and rude huts, must, almost of necessity, terminate fatally. Small hospitals could be established at comparatively slight expense to begin with, and could then be added to, from time to time, as necessity might require. An Indian who had been taken into such a hospital and received rational treatment and good nursing would not be slow to communicate his experience to his friends, and thus lead them to trust in the "white man's medicine," rather than in the beating of drums, rattling of bones, and singing and dancing of the medicine men. Nothing convinces an Indian more quickly or thoroughly than ocular demonstration, and when satisfied by his own observation and experience that the methods of the white man are better for him than the customs of his fathers he will soon adopt the former and abandon the latter. Anything that tends to weaken the hold of ancient superstitions and traditions upon the Indians ought to be taken advantage of, and nothing would yield a more prompt or profitable return in this regard than the establishment of agency hospitals. Some provision of this kind is very necessary for Indian schools, so that by isolating pupils affected with contagious disorders it may be possible to prevent the spreading of such diseases, which, in some instances, almost break up schools.

GERONIMO AND THE CHIRICAHUA APACHES

The history of Geronimo and his followers for the past year is too familiar to require repetition here. The Indians have surrendered and are now held as prisoners by the War Department. The whole band of Chiricahua Apaches, numbering between 300 and 400 men, women, and children, have recently, by order of the War Department, been removed to Florida. I trust the effect of this action will be to tranquilize Indian matters in Arizona and to remove henceforth any apprehension of disturbances by Indians in that Territory.

COAL ON THE WHITE MOUNTAIN RESERVATION IN ARIZONA

In referring to this subject in my last annual report, I took the ground that if Congress should decide to segregate the coal-fields from the reservation, it should provide for the sale of the lands thus segregated to the highest bidder, at not less than $20 per acre; the proceeds to be placed in the Treasury to the credit of the Indians, and draw 5 per cent. interest, to be expended under the direction of the Secretary of the Interior in the education and civilization of the Indians of said reservation. I still entertain the same views upon the subject.

PAPAGO RESERVATION IN ARIZONA

I renew the suggestions contained in my report for the year 1885, that an agency should be established on the Papago reservation, and means provided for its maintenance; or that provision should be made to give the Indians land in severalty, with permanent title, inalienable for a term of years. There is continual trouble between the settlers and the Indians upon this reservation, and some steps should be taken to obviate this.

MISSION INDIANS IN CALIFORNIA

I regret to report that the condition of these Indians as regards their land is becoming more unsatisfactory. A case involving the rights of certain Indians residing on the San Jacinto grant has recently been decided adversely to the Indians in the local courts, and other suits are threatened. Instructions have been given to carry this case to the court of last resort. A special attorney has been appointed to defend the rights of these Indians, and he appears to be earnest, faithful, and able in the discharge of his duties; but there are no funds available for his compensation. Provision should be made for the payment of an amount commensurate with the services required of this attorney.

The bill for the relief of the Mission Indians which passed the Senate July 3, 1884, was again passed in that body February 15, 1886, and was favorably reported in the House of Representatives, but received no further consideration.

Round Valley Reservation, in California

The greater part of this reservation (about nine-tenths) is still occupied by ranchmen and others having a title to about 1,080 acres of land, and claims to improvements of more or less value. The matter was fully presented to Congress in office report of December 16, 1885 (see House Ex. Doc. No. 21, Forty-ninth Congress, first session), and a bill, prepared in this office, providing for allotments of lands in severalty to the Indians residing upon this reservation, for the sale of the surplus lands, and for the extinguishment of the claims of settlers, passed the Senate April 27, 1886, but was not acted upon in the House of Representatives. If some such legislation as this is not secured it will eventually become necessary to abandon the reservation and turn the Indians loose upon the surrounding country. In his annual report for this year Agent Willsey says:

> Our lands are still occupied by settlers and trespassers to such an extent that it is almost impossible to increase our stock, or to protect our growing crops from destruction by their stock. Not only do they occupy every part of our range, but that portion of the valley claimed as swamp and overflow lands by Henley Brothers & Corbitt has been completely fenced in, thereby depriving us of the use of a large body of land. I am informed that others contemplate doing the same. The assurance of these people is something incalculable. They seem to think it perfectly right for them to use all of our lands, but we must not trespass upon a foot of land to which they have a shadow of title. It is hard to foretell what will become of this reservation in a very few years if some legislation is not had to protect from these unscrupulous trespassers.
>
> As long as Congress was in session, and there was a possibility that the House would pass the bill allotting land in severalty, and protecting the balance of the reserve, the Indians were quite jubilant, but now that Congress has adjourned without this bill becoming a law, they are much distressed, fearing that the friends of the trespassers are the cause of its defeat.

I trust that the House of Representatives will see the importance of this measure, and take prompt action thereon at the ensuing session.

Klamath River Indians in California

I am informally advised that contract has been entered into to resurvey the Klamath River Reservation. When the survey is completed the work of allotting lands in severalty to the Indians, as directed in Department letter of March 26, 1883, will be resumed. It was suspended on account of errors found in the original survey. When the work of making allotments to these Indians shall have been completed, the matter will be presented to the Department, with a view of obtaining legislation suitable to their wants and necessities. As stated in my report of last year, these Indians do not need all the lands at present reserved for their use, but they should be permanently settled, either individually or in small communities, and their lands secured to them by patent, before any portion of the reservation is restored to the public domain.

Reduction of Great Sioux Reservation in Dakota

In December last a bill was introduced in the Senate by Senator Dawes—

> To divide a portion of the reservation of the Sioux Nation of Indians in Dakota into separate reserves, and to secure the relinquishment of the Indian title to the remainder.

This bill passed the Senate February 1, 1886, and was favorably reported by the Committee on Indian Affairs in the House of Representatives. It was never referred to this office for report, but in its main features meets with my approval. The rights of the Indians appear to be carefully guarded, and their consent, as provided in the treaty of 1868, is necessary before the provisions of the bill can be carried into effect.

The Great Sioux Reservation, including Crow Creek, contains an area of 21,593,128 aces; the area of the separate reservations provided for in the bill is estimated at 12,845,521 acres, a reduction of 8,747,606 acres. This reduced area allows very nearly 500 acres for each Indian. The Indians can never make use of the immense tract of land belonging to them, while the proceeds of the sale of nearly nine million acres would create a fund which, judiciously and honestly managed, would forever supply them with the means of education and self-support.

The Sioux are an intelligent people, and the younger element among them is rapidly become reconciled to a civilized and industrious mode of life. Their advancement is retarded by the older chiefs, who are opposed to any progress that will lessen their own importance. They also desire to live in idleness on their annuities, rather than to receive them as aids to industry and self-support. If these Indians can be brought to accept the provisions of the Dawes bill, with an ample allowance of land in severalty to each Indian, with a large fund for educational purposes, and for the purchase of cattle and agricultural implements, I see no reason why they should not rapidly advance and ultimately become as contented and prosperous as the white communities around them. I earnestly hope that this bill will become a law and that the Indians will cheerfully accept its provisions.

SEMINOLE INDIANS IN FLORIDA

On the 1st of April, 1886, Frank B. Hagan, esq., of Pine Level, Fla., was appointed a special agent of the Department for the purpose of making further efforts to locate these Indians upon homesteads, as contemplated by the Indian appropriation act approved July 4, 1884 (23 Stats., 95). He accepted the appointment on the 27th of June, 1886, but reported that it would be impracticable to visit the Indians before October, that portion of the State occupied by them being covered with water, and inaccessible before that time.

INTRUDERS AND DISPUTED CITIZENSHIP IN INDIAN TERRITORY

For many years, in fact most of the time since the removal to and settlement of the five civilized tribes in the Indian Territory, there has been among them a constant source of disturbance by reason of unsettled disputes as to who are justly entitled to be called citizens of the various tribes. Many adventurous white men have entered the Territory and in time have married Indian women and raised families, while others without such a justification or plea claim citizenship based on long residence and other considerations, so that thousands of persons of white and some of colored blood claim citizenship, which is stoutly disputed by the Indian authorities.

On the 1st of March, 1886, the Supreme Court, in the case of The Eastern Band of the Cherokee Indians *v.* The United States and the Cherokee Nation, rendered the following decision:

> If Indians in that State (North Carolina), or in any other State east of the Mississippi, wish to enjoy the benefits of the common property of the Cherokee Nation, in whatever form it may exist, they must, as held by the Court of Claims, comply with the constitution and laws of the Cherokee Nation and be readmitted to citizenship as there provided.

In view of this decision, and with the approval of the Department, Agent Owen was instructed, under date of August 11, 1886, to issue no further certificates to claimants to citizenship in the Cherokee Nation entitling them to remain in the Cherokee country. Hereafter, all persons who enter that country without the consent of the Cherokee authorities will be deemed intruders and treated accordingly.

So far as relates to the large class of persons denominated "doubtful citizens" already in the Cherokee Nation, no basis of settlement has been determined upon, although a plan was submitted to the Department with report of June 22, 1886. This question of determining who are justly entitled to citizenship and who are not is still under the consideration of the Department and the Indian authorities, and I hope that a just and satisfactory conclusion will be reached, which, without the intervention of Congress, will quiet all apprehension on this subject in future.

KICKAPOO ALLOTTEES

For the last five years attention has been called to the condition of affairs relative to the estates of deceased and female allottees under the provisions of the Kickapoo treaty of June 28, 1862 (13 Stats., 623). I am now able to report that the bill for their relief has finally become a law, and that this subject can now be dropped from the annual reports.

ATTEMPTED SETTLEMENTS BY UNITED STATES CITIZENS IN INDIAN TERRITORY

In the latter part of October and beginning of November, 1885, a large body of intruders, under the leadership of Couch, again entered the Territory, with the avowed object of settlement on the coveted lands, camping on the banks of the Canadian, near Council Grove, whence, upon the representations of the Department, they were again removed across the line by the military, under the President's proclamation of March 13, 1885.

The President having on July 23, 1885, issued a proclamation declaring the leases made by the Cheyenne and Arapaho Indians void, and directing the removal of the alleged lessees, their cattle, and their employés from the reservation within a specified time, thousands of cattle were driven to graze on the Oklahoma lands. Upon the recommendation of the Department (December 3, 1885,) measures were at once taken by the War Department which, according to official reports on file in this office, resulted in the supposed clearance of all cattle and intruders from Oklahoma. Subsequently, however, in the early spring of the present year, it was ascertained that there were still large numbers of cattle on the Oklahoma lands, and these also were removed by the military.

Upon the receipt of a telegram from the commanding officer at Fort Reno, stating that a number of boomers, horse thieves, &c., were congregated in the Chickasaw Nation just over the Oklahoma line, awaiting a chance to enter Oklahoma, and inquiring whether he should arrest them, I recommended to the Department, on the 17th May last, that the Secretary of War be requested to take immediate action, and on the 3d June the necessary orders were issued from the War Department, resulting in the arrest and expulsion from the Indian Territory of the persons referred to.

MOKOHOKO BAND OF SAC AND FOX IN KANSAS

In many instances small bands of Indians leave their reservations and lead wandering, vagabond lives in the neighboring Territories and States. Some of these visit their reservations at the time of annuity payments and receive their annuities, while others remain permanently away, preferring to lose their annuities rather than to return. A notable instance of the latter class is the Mokohoko band of Sac and Fox Indians. These Indians belong to the tribe known as Sac and Fox of the Mississippi, and now number about ninety. In December, 1875, they were removed from Kansas to their reservation in the Indian Territory, but nearly all of them soon returned to Kansas, and have since lived vagrant lives, intruding on the lands of citizens. They are at present on what was an old Indian reservation, which is now owned and occupied by citizens who have complained to this office of the intrusion of the Indians and requested their removal. Repeated efforts have been made to induce them to return to their reservation and remain there, whereby they would receive a large amount of accrued annuities as well as be participants in the future annuity payments and other advantages enjoyed by that portion of the tribe living in the Indian Territory; but they have steadily refused to do so.

It appears from the report of United States Indian Inspector Bannister, who recently visited them, and from other correspondence in the files of this office, that these Indians are of the very lowest grade of humanity, and are steeped in superstition. They have no rights in the State of Kansas, either of citizenship or property, and are simply a roving band of trespassers, naked and starving, without any means of support whatever, and in a most deplorable and pitiable condition. The support, protection, and even the existence of these Indians, and others similarly situated, demand their removal to the reservation to which they belong, where they can be supplied with the necessities of life, and taught to make their living by agriculture, and where their children can be educated.

The principles laid down in the case of "Standing Bear" should not, in my opinion, be applied to a people utterly ignorant and devoid of reason, and mere dependents for existence upon the beauty of the Government. These roving bands are the wards of the Government, and are entirely incompetent to comprehend their situation, and it is the duty of the Government to take such action as may be for their best interest, without applying to them the technical principles upon which the writ of *habeas corpus* is based.

The subject of Indians leaving their reservations is causing the office considerable embarrassment, and I believe the matter should be laid before Congress, with a view to securing such legislation as will enable the Department in all cases, with the aid of the military, if necessary, to send to their reservations all Indians absent therefrom without permission from the Department, and to keep them there.

* * *

Winnebago Reservation in Nebraska

A strong opposition has been recently developed among the Winnebagoes to the passage of the bill now pending before Congress (S. 715) providing for the sale of a portion of the reservation. On February 4 last this office received, by Department reference, a letter from thirty-nine members of the tribe requesting that the influence of the Department be exerted to defeat the passage of the bill, and stating that the tribe had never consented to such sale, but desired that assignments of land in severalty be made to such of its members as had not received any, and further stating that, if all are provided for, there will be no good land to spare, as fully one-half of the reservation is too broken and rough for cultivation. In consequence of the opposition to such sale manifested in the letter referred to, on the 26th of same month I addressed a communication to the Department recommending that the chairman of the Senate Committee on Indian Affairs be requested to see that no final action be taken on the bills in the Senate until the report of the Department should be submitted thereon.

In the latter part of March last I had a conference at this office with a delegation of ten Winnebagoes who had come here for the purpose of discussing the above and other matters of interest to them, from which it appeared that the tribe opposed the proposed sale and desired that allotments be made to all those who had not received any. On March 22 last this office requested the chairmen of the respective Committees on Indian Affairs of the Senate and House of Representatives to allow said delegation of Indians a hearing relative to the provisions of the bill. Since the date of the above-named communications to the chairmen of the committees referred to, no action seems to have been taken on the bill by Congress.

The statement made in my last annual report that the Winnebagoes had expressed a desire to sell a portion of their reservation was based on reports of their agents, who doubtless represented the sentiment of the tribe on the matter, so far as it was then known. I am still of the opinion expressed in said report, that legislation substantially like that recently had for the Omahas (act August 7, 1882,) would be beneficial to the Winnebagoes, who would then have the benefit of and be subject to the laws, both civil and criminal, of the State of Nebraska, and would receive permanent individual titles to their land. It is to be hoped that their consent may yet be given to the sale of a portion of their reservation.

Report of Commissioner of
Indian Affairs John H. Oberly
December 3, 1888

(Excerpt from *Report for 1888*, pp. xl-xlvi, lxx-lxxiii, lxxxvii-lxxxix)

Commissioner Oberly's peroration at the conclusion of his report, in which he insisted that the Indian "must be imbued with the exalting egotism of American civilization, so that he will say 'I' instead of 'We,' and 'This is mine,' instead of 'This is ours,'" adequately summarizes the theory of Indian relations incorporated in his report. However, excerpts from his report dealing with the restrictions placed upon Indians attempting to log on their own lands, and with the inability of the Government to enforce its own regulations against white intruders on Indian lands in California, illustrate some practical implications of the Government's Indian policy.

Logging by Indians

LA POINTE AGENCY, WIS. During the season of 1887–88, under Department authority of September 28, 1882 (full particulars of which will be found in the annual report of this office for 1884), 731 contracts for the cutting, sale, and delivery of pine timber were made by individual patentees of the Lac Court d'Oreille, La Pointe or Bad River, Lac du Flambeau, and Fond du Lac Reservations, severally attached to the La Pointe Agency, Wis. Under these contracts there were cut and banked 190,206,080 feet of timber, which was sold at prices varying from $4.75 to $7 per 1,000 feet, according to quality. The net gain to the Indians, after paying all expenses of cutting and banking, was $428,221.41 (an increase of $154,759.99 over the preceding season), of which sum $149,637.64 was taken out in merchandise and supplies furnished by the contractors.

Of the net gains—

Lac Court d'Oreille Indians received	$218,671.77
La Pointe Indians received	58,491.44
Fond du Lac Indians received	84,582.38
Lac du Flambeau Indians received	66,472.82
	428,221.41

The average net gain per 1,000 feet was $2.25, against $2.12 the preceding season. Some of the contracts have not been completed; but the Indians have all been paid for the timber actually cut.

410

On March 5, 1888, the Senate adopted the following resolution:

> Resolved, That the Select Committee on Indian Traders be directed to inquire into the method of allotting lands in severalty to Indians upon the Court d'Oreille, Lac du Flambeau, Bad River, Fond du Lac, and other Indian reservations in the northern portions of Wisconsin and Minnesota, and into the system under which Indians to whom lands have been allotted are allowed to sell the timber thereon; and especially to inquire whether or not adequate prices are secured to the Indians under such sales; and that for the purposes of this resolution the committee be authorized to exercise all the powers heretofore conferred upon the committee by the Senate.

In view, probably, of the implication of the above-quoted resolution, the following telegram was sent to Agent Gregory on March 13, 1888:

> You will immediately put a stop to the cutting and felling of trees on all reservations under your charge, whether under existing contracts with Indians or otherwise.

On April 21, the following telegram was sent to him:

> By direction of the Secretary you will not permit the driving or removal of any logs until contracts are approved and complete settlement and payment is made to Indians.

On April 23, he was again telegraphed to as follows:

> By direction of the Secretary my order of 21st is modified so that logs may be driven at once to the booms if you are satisfied that payment for them is perfectly secure. Department will not undertake to control the character of the labor to be used in driving the logs.

July 31, the Department instructed this office as follows:

> From the consideration which I have given the matter of sale of pine timber from the lands of Indians, I am satisfied that the regulations under which this important business has been conducted are not such as to secure to the Indians the full value of the timber cut and sold from their lands.
>
> For the purpose of adopting proper regulations and making seasonable arrangements for the cutting of pine timber on Indian allotments you are hereby directed to call upon the agent for the La Pointe Agency, Wisconsin, to ascertain and report to your office, in time for the information to reach you not later than August 25 next, the names of the Indians to whom lands have been allotted and who are in possession of their patents therefor who desire to dispose of the pine timber or a portion thereof from their patented tracts, the character, condition, and probable quantity of the timber upon each of such tracts, and whether it is desirable and for the best interest of the respective Indian patentees that they should be allowed to dispose of their pine timber, and also whether as to any of said patented tracts the contracts made for cutting the timber therefrom last winter have not been completed, and, if so, which of them, and whether it is desirable and proper that the completion of said contracts or arrangements, or any of them, during the coming winter should be permitted.

The agent should exercise care to prevent the Indian patentees from disposing of all of the timber from their allotments. Enough should be reserved for domestic and farm purposes.

No timber will be permitted to be cut and disposed of under any circumstances from any lands except the tracts which have been allotted to Indians in severalty, and for which the respective allottees have received their patents.

On August 1, the office gave directions to Agent Gregory in accordance with the foregoing instructions.

The matter having been further considered by the Department, under its instructions I addressed the following letter, dated October 29, 1888, to Agent Gregory:

You are hereby informed that in cases where contractors were prevented from completing their contracts by reason of office telegram of March 13, 1888, said contractors, who so desire, may be permitted to cut timber sufficient to complete their contracts; but each contractor must file a statement in due form that he was, by reason of said telegram, prevented from completing his contracts, and a further statement of the amount of timber he was authorized to cut by the terms of his contracts and the amount necessary to complete said contracts; this permission to be confined exclusively to tracts which have been allotted and the allotment of which has been approved by the President.

The statements above required, with your approval indorsed thereon, should be forwarded without delay to this Department for consideration and approval.

Before you permit any cutting you must satisfy yourself that proper and full settlement in each case will be made with the Indians; and this must be included in your indorsement of approval of said statements.

As to new contracts for the coming season, I have to say that where an allottee holds a patent for his land, or his allotment has been approved by the President and you are satisfied that the sale of the timber on such allotment would be for the actual benefit of the Indian, you will permit him to contract for its sale, under the restrictions heretofore in force.

The contracts for such cutting should be forwarded to this office, so that they may receive proper consideration and action by December 1,1888, and each contract should be accompanied by your statement showing the reasons why you believe the sale of his timber would result to the advantage of the Indian.

It must be distinctly understood that *no* operations can be commenced until you are notified that the contract has been approved by this office, and that no contract should be made for the sale of timber upon tracts where the allotments have not been approved by the President.

Certain contractors for pine timber on the Lac du Flambeau Reservation having filed their statements in conformity with the above requirements, with request that the allottees be permitted to cut all the merchantable pine timber on their respective allotments, the matter was again submitted for further instructions, and under date of December 3, the Department directed the modification of existing regulations so as to provide that an allottee—

may contract for the cutting, and the contractor may cut all of the pine on an 80-acre allotment which is so situated with reference to the natural opportunities or the constructed roads for hauling and banking logs as that it will be most to the advantage of the Indian to have it entirely cut and no part of it left standing. Indeed, in all such cases, the contractor should be required to cut all the merchantable timber, including every tree which will make a log, the smaller end of which shall be 10 or more inches in diameter, and of which one-third would be merchantable pine. The contractor should, in all cases, be required to cut clean as he proceeds, so that he makes no selection from among the trees to be cut; but if any timber remains uncut, it should be in a compact body and so situated as that in the future it may be advantageously logged.

The Department also expressed the opinion that new contracts—

should be made so as to provide a clean sum to the Indian for the value of his timber standing, and not subject him to the risks of loss in any of the logging or banking operations. The stumpage value of the timber is a thing easily to be ascertained and much more safely to be estimated than the value of it subject to the risks of deduction by the cost of logging and banking.

All such contracts should contain provision that the contractor shall employ Indian labor, on equal terms, in preference to other, whenever suitable.

A form of renewal of uncompleted contracts, providing for the modifications above suggested, has been prepared and transmitted to Agent Gregory, with the statement that all uncompleted contracts, covering lands the allotment of which has been approved by the President, when renewed and modified and accompanied by good and sufficient bonds (the price to be paid as stumpage being satisfactory), will receive the approval of this office.

But few new contracts or logging operations during this season have been presented to this office, and none have been approved. A new form of contract will be prepared at an early day.

Menomonees, Green Bay Agency, Wis. Last season these Indians faithfully adhered to their promise not to cut any growing timber, except such as was necessary to clear land for agricultural purposes, and not to start any fire in the woods. They were, therefore, again allowed to engage in marketing dead-and-down timber from their reservation in Wisconsin; and although they were late in commencing operations their work during the season resulted very satisfactorily, as they succeeded in banking nearly 8,300,000 feet of logs, beside some 575 cedar posts and railway ties, all of which sold for over $86,000. From this amount, according to custom and with their full consent, 10 per cent. was first-deducted and added to their stumpage or poor fund, to be used for the maintenance of their hospital and the support of the old, sick, and otherwise helpless poor of the tribe. The balance, less the expense of scaling, advertising, etc., amount to about $300, and less a further sum of about $1,200, referred to below, was paid by the agent to those properly entitled, in exact proportion to the scale of each man's logs. The payment was entirely satisfactory to all.

The $1,200 still unpaid is the proceeds of a small lot of timber removed from one of the sixteenth sections of the reservation, which section is claimed by a lumber merchant in that vicinity as his, he having purchased it from the State, which assumed the right to dispose of it, for the reason that it had been reserved for school purposes. The question of title in these sixteenth sections on the Menomonee Reserve, of which there are ten, is now before the proper court for decision, and is a matter of much pecuniary interest to the Indians, inasmuch as the timber on these sections is pine of the finest quality.

The Menomonees are making good use of their logging money. The majority of them are industrious, thrifty, and progressive, and fully realize the benefits which they and their descendants may derive from their timber if it is properly handled. They wish to do the work themselves, and from a careful consideration of their work and its results during the past three or four years, and especially during last season, I believe it would be for their best interests to allow them to market all their timber on some such plan as that which has been suggested to Congress.

The Menomonee timber may safely be estimated at from 450,000,000 to 500,000,000 feet. To market this would give the Indians, at a reasonable calculation, twenty-five or thirty years of steady, paying employment during the winter season, when they can not work on their farms.

The matter seems to be of sufficient importance to have the attention of Congress again called thereto.

The authority under which, for the past five or six winters, these Indians have cut and marketed their dead-and-down timber has been granted each year by the Department, on recommendation of this office, said recommendation being based on a decision rendered May 19, 1882, by Hon. H. M. Teller, then Secretary of the Interior, in regard to the right of the Sisseton Agency Indians to market such timber from their reservation in Dakota. The decision was as follows:

> DEPARTMENT OF THE INTERIOR,
> *Washington, May 19, 1882.*

HON. HIRAM PRICE
COMMISSIONER OF INDIAN AFFAIRS

Sir: I have your letter of the 18th ultimo, asking that I approve of the application of Agent Crissey, of the Sisseton Agency, to allow the Indians on that reservations to cut dead and fallen timber and to sell the same. The Indians of the agency hold their reservation by virtue of a treaty made with the United States in 1867. It is recited in the treaty that, in consideration of certain cessions made by the Indians to the United States and the faithful conduct of the Indians, the Government set apart the reservation for the use of said Indians as a permanent home. It is not claimed, however, that these Indians hold by other and different title from other Indians who occupy their reservations by treaty stipulations.

The fee to the reservation is in the Government, and the right of the Indians to the occupation thereof is as unquestioned as the right of the

Government to the fee. In such occupation they can not be disturbed by the Government, save through its legislative department; and it ought not to be supposed that such occupation will be interfered with without the consent of the Indians, unless, by misconduct on their part, the right to occupy should be lost.

It appears that it was the intention of the Government to give the Indians a permanent home on the reservation, reserving to itself the fee, with the right to dispose of it should the Indians abandon it. The Government, then, has no right to complain of the character of the Indians' occupation unless they commit waste. What is waste must always depend upon the character of the holding as well as the acts complained of. It was held by the Supreme Court of the United States in the case of *The United States* vs. *Cook* (19 Wall., 591), that the cutting of pine trees and selling the logs was waste; but the court declared that if the trees had been cut for the improvement of the estate it would not have been waste.

Can it be said to be waste to cut, even for the purpose of sale, then, the dead and fallen timber on Indian reservations? I think not. It is true that it has been repeatedly held that the timber cast down by the winds belonged to the lessor and not to the lessee, yet the relation of lessor and lessee does not exist between the Government and the Indians on the reservation, and it must be held that the Indians have the right to use the entire products of such reservation, so they do not commit waste; and what might be waste if done by a tenant might not be waste if done by an individual Indian or by the tribe. If the Indians will cut, haul, and sell the dead and fallen timber on the reservation it will be a benefit to them, not counting alone the money value to be received from the sale of said dead and fallen timber, but they will thereby acquire some of the habits of industry so essential to their future prosperity, if not to their very existence.

You will therefore instruct the agents of the various agencies where timber is found growing that no live trees are to be cut except for use on the reservation, except on individual allotments; but that dead and fallen timber may be cut, and, if not needed for the use of the Indians on the reservation, may be sold.

Very respectfully,

H. M. TELLER,
Secretary,

The Menomonees having again asked permission to continue the work during the coming winter, I submitted their request to the Department, recommending that it be granted, and suggesting at the same time that, if authority existed for such restriction, none be allowed this privilege whose children, of school age, fail to attend school a reasonable length of time each year.

On November 23, last, the Department replied as follows:

DEPARTMENT OF THE INTERIOR,
Washington, November 23, 1888.
THE COMMISSIONER OF INDIAN AFFAIRS.

SIR: Referring to your letters of October 18 and November 20, 1888, respectively recommending that the Menomonee Indians be authorized to engage in marketing the dead-and-down timber on their reservation during the coming season under certain specified conditions, you are respectfully informed that the subject was presented to the Attorney-General by the Department on October 27, 1888, with request for an opinion on questions stated, with the view to ascertaining to what extent, if at all, this Department was authorized to permit the cutting and sale by the Indians occupying such reservation (the title to which is in the United States) of the dead-and-down timber thereon.

I am now in receipt of the opinion of the Attorney-General, dated 20th instant, on the subject (copy of which is herewith inclosed), wherein it is held that the Indians have no right to cut and sell such timber for their use and benefit, and therefore the authority requested by you can not be granted.

The papers accompanying your letters are herewith returned.

Very respectfully,

WM. F. VILAS,
Secretary.

By the above it will be seen that all the questions involved were presented to the Attorney-General with a request for his opinion. The decision rendered by him is as follows:

DEPARTMENT OF JUSTICE,
Washington, November 20, 1888.

THE SECRETARY OF THE INTERIOR

SIR: By your letter of the 27th of October, 1888, you ask "(1) whether the Indians occupying reservations, the title to which is in the United States, have the right, in view of the opinion of the Supreme Court of the United States in the case of *The United States* vs. *George Cook* (19 Wall., 591), to cut and sell, for their use and benefit, the dead-and-down timber which is found to a greater or less extent on many of the reservations, and which will go to waste if not used.

"(2) If they have such right, whether it is a common right to common property belonging to the tribe or band as a whole, occupying the respective reservations, or whether it is such a right as may be exercised by individual Indians belonging on the reservation, for their individual benefit?

"(3) If they have the right, and it is a common right only, whether the cutting and sale of such dead-and-down timber by the Indians can be regulated by the Indian Bureau under directions of this Department so as to secure to the tribe or band entitled to the proceeds arising therefrom the greatest possible benefits for improving their condition and promoting their civilization and self-support by the methods pursued in the work?"

In the case of the *United States* vs. *Cook* (19 Wall., 593) it is ruled that the right of the Indians on an Indian reservation is one of occupancy only; that that right of occupancy carries with it the right to improvement by clearing land; that the right to clear includes the right to sell or dispose of timber on the land cleared, and to use the timber on the reservation for purposes necessary for improvement or residence; that when cut or severed for sale alone, and not as an incident to the occupancy, the right and title to the timber is absolute in the United States; that "what a tenant for life may do upon lands of a remainder-man the Indians may do upon their reservation, but no more." Dead and wind-fallen timber, as a part of the realty, belongs to the remainder-man, and not to the tenant for life, to the same extent as growing timber does.

In the case of *Bewick* vs. *Whitfield* (3 P. Williams Chancery Rept., 268), in discussing this question, it is ruled, first, that—

"The timber while standing is part of the inheritance, but whenever it is severed, either by the act of God, as by tempest, or by a trespasser, and by wrong, it belongs to him who has the first estate of inheritance, whether in fee or in tail, who may bring trover for it, and this was so decreed upon occasion of the great windfall of timber on the Cavendish estate."

Secondly, "As to the tenant for life, he ought not to have any share of the money arising by the sale of this timber."

The principle thus announced is recognized in *Lewis Bowles' Case* (11 Coke, 81), and in the case of *Shult* v. *Barker* (12 Sergeant & Rawle, 272).

Therefore the dead-and-fallen timber that is not needed or used for improvements, agricultural purposes, or fuel by the Indians is the property of the United States. It is to be preserved and protected as such, and disposed of only as Congress, by law, may provide. This rule will doubtless best preserve the timber on Indian reservations, and avoid much destruction by fires, which would occur as the timber became scarce and valuable, whenever its death might become a source of gain. Your first question is, therefore, answered in the negative, which renders a reply to the remaining inquiries unnecessary.

A. H. GARLAND,
Attorney-General.

On receipt of this opinion, the Menomonees were notified that they would not be allowed to cut or market any timber from their reservation except such as might be necessary to clear land for cultivation, and such as they might require for improvements, agricultural purposes, or fuel. This will be a sad disappointment and great loss to these poor people, as they are in great measure dependent for the necessaries of life on their logging work, and have prepared for it by using what they could spare of the proceeds of last season's sales in equipping themselves with stock, feed, sledges, tools, etc. I hope that Congress will speedily come to their relief by legalizing what has been done, and by granting authority to all Indians similarly situated to cut and market their dead and down timber, thereby benefiting the Indians and at the same time bringing into profitable use timber which, if left alone, will soon become of no value to the Indians, the Government, or any one else.

At an early day I shall take necessary steps to bring this matter to the attention of Congress, and in my opinion its merits should secure for it careful consideration and prompt action by that body, so that if possible logging operations by the Menomonees may be resumed this winter with full legal sanction.

* * *

ROUND VALLEY RESERVATION, IN CALIFORNIA

As stated in the last annual report, orders were given on May 25, 1887, for removal from the Round Valley Reservation of all parties found to be unlawfully thereon. September 30, 1887, Agent Yates telegraphed that while he was proceeding to eject settlers by military force as directed he was served with an order to show cause before the Supreme Court of Sonoma County why he should not be restrained. Immediately upon receipt of this telegram, October 1, 1887, this office recommended to the Department that the matter be referred to the Attorney-General with request that the District Attorney be instructed to represent the interests of the United States in the case, and to use all proper efforts to defeat the contemplated injunction. This request was complied with by the Department of Justice.

On October 27, 1887, General Howard, commanding Department of the Pacific, telegraphed to the War Department as follows:

SAN FRANCISCO, CAL.,
October 27, 1887.

ADJUTANT-GENERAL,
Washington, D. C.:

Acting under instructions (see first indorsement on letter Assistant Secretary Interior to Secretary of War, dated April 5, 1887, and subsequent instructions from the Secretary of War), Captain Shaw's company, First Artillery, was, August 17, sent to evict trespassers upon Round Valley Indian Reservation. On 19th instant he commenced evictions and was thereupon served with injunction, issued by judge superior court of Mendocino County, Cal., by person claiming to be deputy sheriff of same, which Captain Shaw refused to obey and continued to evict. Upon affidavit of said deputy sheriff, judge of said court has issued attachment for Shaw, who declined to surrender.... The action of the local court interrupts the removal of the intruders designated by the Secretary of the Interior. I await instructions.

O. O. HOWARD,
Major-General.

The next day General Howard again telegraphed to the War Department as follows:

Shall I leave Captain Shaw to be arrested and imprisoned, at the call of the trespassers, who have no rights whatever, in obedience to orders of local courts? The United States district attorney has enabled me to file answer and to demand transfer to United States court pending action. Please sustain me, and Captain Shaw, who has not exceeded our orders one whit.

On October 28, 1887, the Secretary of War sent to General Howard the following telegram:

The Department of Justice has advices from District Attorney Caray as to matters on Round Valley Indian Reservation, confirming your telegraphic report of yesterday, and reports that you decline to suspend operations or order your officers to surrender. In view of facts as presented to the Secretary of War, he directs that you desist in declining to obey writ until question of jurisdiction is determined by Federal courts.

To this General Howard replied, on the same date, as follows:

Telegram even date directing suspension of operations at Round Valley received. Captain Shaw has been ordered to obey writ until the question of jurisdiction is determined in Federal courts.

In a communication addressed to the Interior Department, November 29, 1888, the Secretary of War said:

The action of this Department in ordering the military to the Round Valley Indian Reservation to eject trespassers was taken at the request of your Department, and I have the honor to request advice as to what action is now needed to be taken by this Department.

In reply thereto, November 4, 1887, Commissioner Atkins made full report to the Department, and gave the following as his conclusions:

In the present aspect of the case I do not see that any further action on the part of this Department is practicable, at least until the injunction has been dissolved, and I therefore have the honor to recommend that copies of the papers be submitted to the Attorney-General with the request that they be forwarded to the district attorney, with instructions to use every possible legal remedy to arrest these parties and correct the extraordinary state of affairs at Round Valley, which has so long been a reproach upon all who are responsible for its continuance.

On November 19, 1887, the Secretary of War transmitted a telegram from General Howard, stating that injunctions against Captain Shaw and himself had been transferrred to the United States circuit court, and suggesting that as there was likely to be long delay before a decision could be had, it would be well that the troops be withdrawn until the following spring; and, November 29, 1887, this office reported that in view of the fact that the matter was pending in the United States courts, and that the agent had been instructed by the district attorney to stay all proceedings, it was not believed that the military could accomplish any good by remaining on the reservation.

Thus the second attempt to regain possession of the reservation by military force ended in utter failure. Concerning the progress of the matter in the courts I have no information.

On December 14, 1887, Commissioner Atkins submitted to the Department a very full report of the state of affairs then existing and that had existed on the Round Valley Reservation during the past thirty years, and of the various attempts that had been made to rid it of intruders. The report was accompanied by a draught of the bill which, together with the Commissioner's report, was forwarded to Congress by the President on January 5, 1888, with the following message:

> *To the Senate and House of Representatives:*
> I transmit herewith a communication of 23d ultimo from the Secretary of the Interior, submitting a draft of a bill "to provide for the reduction of the Round Valley Indian Reservation, in the State of California, and for other purposes," with accompanying papers relating thereto.
> The documents thus submitted exhibit extensive and entirely unjustifiable encroachments upon lands set apart for Indian occupancy, and disclose a disregard of Indian rights so long continued that the Government can not further temporize without positive dishonor.
> Efforts to dislodge trespassers upon these lands have in some cases been resisted, upon the ground that certain moneys due from the Government for improvements have not been paid. So far as this claim is well founded, the sum necessary to extinguish the same should be at once appropriated and paid.
> In other cases the position of these intruders is one of simple and bare-faced wrong-doing, plainly questioning the inclination of the Government to protect its dependent Indian wards, and its ability to maintain itself in the guaranty of such protection. These intruders should forthwith feel the weight of the Government's power.
> I earnestly commend the situation and the wrongs of the Indians occupying the reservation named to the early attention of the Congress, and ask for the bill herewith transmitted careful and prompt consideration.
>
> GROVER CLEVELAND.
> Executive Mansion,
> *January 5, 1888.*

The bill passed the Senate June ·25, 1888, and I have no hesitation in saying that unless this or a similar bill shall become a law there are apparently no means by which, without great delay, the intruders upon the reservation can be excluded therefrom.

Conclusion

In conclusion I beg leave to say that I have no doubt that under the favorable conditions of an Indian service in which the evils of what is known as the party-spoils system of appointment and dismissal would be minimized, and in which intelligent and zealous action might confidently anticipate the support of the Government; in which, too, devotion and efficiency might labor assured of the applause of the people, and honest administration do its perfect work promptly on all occasions without rebuke or fear of persecution; the Indian question, in all its most perplexing features, might be transmuted from a demoralizing political question into a not dangerous social question. Indeed, it may be declared, without the use of qualifying phrases, that, under the favorable conditions suggested, the Indian would receive our civilization, with all that it implies of social duty and of public obligation. This is said in full knowledge of the many futile efforts that have been made by zealous able men and women, by the churches, and by the Government, to lead the Indian out of barbarism. And to one of such efforts not unprofitable reference may now be made. During the last quarter of the last century an important estate was given to the college of William and Mary, Virginia, for the express purpose of maintaining Indians at that institution of learning, and Indians were maintained accordingly. "But," says [James] Parton, in his *Life of Jefferson,* "Indians can not receive our civilization. If the college had any success with an Indian youth, he was no sooner tamed than he sickened and died. The rest may have assumed the white man's habit while they remained at Williamsburgh, but the very day that they rejoined their tribe they threw off their college clothes, resumed their old costumes and weapons, and ran whooping into the forest, irreclaimable savages."

To this failure, and to other similar failures of more recent times, the disbelievers in the possibility of Indian redemption from barbarism are constantly calling the attention of "those hopeful philanthropists and confident statesmen who refuse to believe that the future experiences of the Indian will be but a repetition of those of his past history. These disbelievers in the possibility of any good resulting from governmental, religious, or humanitarian effort to redeem the Indian from his deplorable condition, overlook the many successful attempts that have been made to lead him into civilization. They disparage into a molehill every mountain of success; they exaggerate into a mountain every molehill of failure.

Since the time when Indian educated youths either died of civilization at William and Mary or ran away from it into the forest and relapsed into savagery, the Five Tribes have been civilized and organized into nations; and of late years the children of nearly all the other tribes have been knocking at the door of the school-house, requesting admittance.

The Indian has indeed begun to change with the changing times. He is commencing to appreciate the fact that he must become civilized—must, as he expresses it, "learn the white man's way"—or perish from the face of the earth. He can not sweep back with a broom the flowing tide. The forests into which he ran whooping from the door of William and Mary have been felled. The game on which he lived has disappeared. The war-path has been obliterated. He is hemmed in on all sides by white population. The railroad refuses to be excluded from his reservation—that hot-bed of barbarism, in which many noxious social and political weeds grow rankly. The Christian missionary is persistently entreating him to abandon paganism. Gradually the paternal hand of the Government is being withdrawn from his support. His environments no longer compel him, or afford to him opportunities, to display the nobler traits of his character. On the warpath and in the chase he was heroic: all activity; patient of hunger; patient of fatigue; cool-headed—a creature of exalted fortitude. "But," says a writer, sketching his character, "when the chase was over, when the war was done, and the peace-pipes smoked out, he abandoned himself to debauchery and idleness. To sleep all day in a wigwam of painted skins, filthy and blackened with smoke, adorned with scalps, and hung with tomahawks and arrows, to dance in the shine of the new moon to music made from the skin of snakes, to tell stories of witches and evil spirits, to gamble, to sing, to jest, to boast of his achievements in war, and to sit with a solemn gravity at the councils of his chiefs constituted his most serious employment. His squaw was his slave. With no more affection than a coyote feels for its mate, he brought her to his wigwam that she might gratify the basest of his passions and minister to his wants. It was Starlight or Cooing Dove that brought the wood for his fire and the water for his drink, that plowed the field and sowed the maize."

These were the conditions of the Indian's existence in the past; but, now, on the war-path and in the chase he can not exalt himself by bravery and endurance, and he should not be permitted to live any longer in idleness and debauchery. He should be brought under the operations of the law, "In the sweat of thy face shalt thou eat bread till thou return unto the ground." He should be educated to labor. He does not need the learning of William and Mary, but he does need the virtue of industry and the ability of the skillful hand. He should, therefore, be taught how to work, and all the schools that are opened for his children should be schools in which they will be instructed in the use of agricultural implements, the carpenter's saw and plane, the stonemason's trowel, the tailor's needle, and the shoemaker's awl. And the Indian should be taught not only how to work, but also that it is his duty to work; for the degrading communism of the tribal reservation system gives to the individual no incentive to labor, but puts a premium upon idleness and makes it fashionable. Under this system, the laziest man owns as much as the most industrious man, and neither can say of all the acres occupied by the tribe, "This is mine." The Indian must, therefore, be taught how to labor; and, that labor may be made necessary to his well-being, he must be taken out of the reservation through the door of the general allotment act. And he must be imbued with the exalting egotism of American civilization, so that he will say "I" instead of "We," and "This is mine," instead of "This is ours." But if he will not learn? If he shall continue to persist in saying, "I am content; let me alone"? Then the Guardian must act for the Ward, and do for him the good service he protests shall not be done—the good service that he denounces as a bad service. The Government must then, in duty to the public, compel the Indian to come out of his isolation into the civilized way that he does not desire to enter—into citizenship—into assimilation with the masses of the Republic—into the path of national duty; and in passing along that path he will find not only pleasure in personal independence and delight in individual effort in his own interest, but also the consummation of that patriotic enjoyment which is always to be found in the exercise of the high privilege of contributing to the general welfare.

Report of Commissioner of
Indian Affairs T. J. Morgan
October 1, 1889

(Excerpt from *Report for 1889*, pp. 3-8, 100-03)

Although new to the job, Commissioner Morgan had little doubt about the proper direction of Indian policy. Congress had recently spoken with a loud voice in enacting the General Allotment Act. The "strongly cherished convictions" with which Commissioner Morgan reported that he entered the job, and which he outlined at the beginning of his report, were in complete harmony with the expressed will of Congress. The reservation system, the tribal organization of Indians, and native cultural traditions were all to become things of the past—hastened on their way to extinction by a stern and unyielding father. In a supplemental report on Indian education attached to his annual report, of which a short excerpt is quoted below, Morgan even planned to deny Indians the right to learn too much about their past, especially about the "wrongs of the Indians," a phrase he carefully put in quotation marks.

I ENTERED UPON the discharge of the duties of this office July 1, 1889. I have had no time as yet to familiarize myself fully with the details of office administration nor to make myself acquainted by personal observation with the practical workings of the Indian field-service. As soon as practicable, I hope to do both.

Unexpectedly called to this responsible position, I entered upon the discharge of its duties with a few simple, well-defined, and strongly-cherished convictions:

First.—The anomalous position heretofore occupied by the Indians in this country can not much longer be maintained. The reservation system belongs to a "vanishing state of things" and must soon cease to exist.

Second.—The logic of events demands the absorption of the Indians into our national life, not as Indians, but as American citizens.

Third.—As soon as a wise conservatism will warrant it, the relations of the Indians to the Government must rest solely upon the full recognition of their individuality. Each Indian must be treated as a man, be allowed a man's rights and privileges, and be held to the performance of a man's obligations. Each Indian is entitled to his proper share of the inherited wealth of the tribe, and to the protection of the courts in his "life, liberty, and pursuit of happiness." He is not entitled to be supported in idleness.

Fourth.—The Indians must conform to "the white man's ways," peaceably if they will, forcibly if they must. They must adjust themselves to their

424

environment, and conform their mode of living substantially to our civilization. This civilization may not be the best possible, but it is the best the Indians can get. They can not escape it, and must either conform to it or be crushed by it.

Fifth.—The paramount duty of the hour is to prepare the rising generation of Indians for the new order of things thus forced upon them. A comprehensive system of education modeled after the American public-school system, but adapted to the special exigencies of the Indian youth, embracing all persons of school age, compulsory in its demands and uniformly administered, should be developed as rapidly as possible.

Sixth.—The tribal relations should be broken up, socialism destroyed, and the family and the autonomy of the individual substituted. The allotment of lands in severalty, the establishment of local courts and police, the development of a personal sense of independence, and the universal adoption of the English language are means to this end.

Seventh.—In the administration of Indian affairs there is need and opportunity for the exercise of the same qualities demanded in any other great administration—integrity, justice, patience, and good sense. Dishonesty, injustice, favoritism, and incompetency have no place here any more than elsewhere in the Government.

Eighth.—The chief thing to be considered in the administration of this office is the character of the men and women employed to carry out the designs of the Government. The best system may be perverted to bad ends by incompetent or dishonest persons employed to carry it into execution, while a very bad system may yield good results if wisely and honestly administered.

Indian Education

The Superintendent of Indian Schools, Daniel Dorchester, D. D., entered upon his duties on the 1st day of May, 1889, and is now engaged in a thorough inspection of the whole school service. By appointment of the Secretary of the Interior, Mrs. Dorchester has been engaged in special inspection of schools.

School Employees

Recognizing the truth of the adage that "as the teacher, so is the school," special pains have been taken to secure the best available talent in the school service. Believing that what is good enough for a white man is good enough for an Indian, the effort is being made to develop for the Indians a non-partisan, non-sectarian public-school system.

As indicative of the efforts put forth to secure good teachers, I submit a copy of a letter that is mailed to those who apply for positions in the school service:

Your application for appointment as teacher has been received. Inclosed please find blanks to be filled out and returned.

It is the purpose of the office to appoint no person as a teacher in the Indian school service who would not be able to secure a similar position in the best schools for white children in the community in which he resides. Indeed, the exigencies of Indian schools are such as to require a higher order of talent to secure success than is required in ordinary teaching.

Emphasis is laid upon the fact that those who are engaged in the Indian school service should be persons of maturity, of vigorous health, with some experience in teaching, and with special fitness for the work. Preference is expressed for those who have had a normal-school training. It is very undesirable that persons should enter the service who, by reason of ill health, age, or other infirmities, are unable to do full, vigorous work.

The blank which is to be filled out by the applicant calls for replies to the following questions:

1 Your Christian name and surname [in full].

2 Date and place of your birth?

3 Your education? [Mention the kind of school at which you were educated; whether common school, high school, business college, academy, college, normal or other professional school.]

How old were you when you finally quitted school?

4 Are you a citizen of the United States?

If a naturalized citizen, when and where were you naturalized?

5 Of what State or Territory are you a legal resident?

How long have you been a legal resident thereof?

Of what town or city and county or parish are you a resident?

How long have you been a resident thereof?

Your present post-office address?

6 Are you married?

Of how many members does your family consist, and what are the ages of your children respectively?

What members of your family will be with you upon the reservation?

7 How long have you been engaged in teaching?

During what years were you so engaged? [Give dates.]

In what grades of schools were you so engaged?

What grade of license to teach, or teacher's certificate, have you held?

Give names of school officers by whom they were granted.

Give names and post-office addresses of two school-officials who have, at some time, had supervision of your schools, and visited them, to whom I may refer for information in regard to your moral character and your proficiency as a teacher. [If you never taught you may omit the questions under "7," and instead give the information asked for under "8."]

8 Give names and post-office addresses of two superintendents or principal teachers of the school or schools where you were last in attendance, to whom I may refer for information in regard to your moral character and your qualifications for teaching and managing an Indian school. [If you are a candidate for a position other than that of teacher, you may leave the blanks opposite "7," "8," and "9" unfilled.]

9 Have you been a subscriber for any educational journal?
If so, what?

What works on teaching have you read?

What subjects are you best qualified to teach?

10 In what places have you resided and what has been your occupation during *each* year for the past five years, and what wages have you received? [Give name and address of your employer or employers, if any, the length of your stay with each, and the reason for leaving their employ.]

11 What has been the state of your health during the past five years?

Are you now physically capable of a full discharge of the duties of the position to which you are seeking appointment?

Have you any defect of sight?

of hearing?

of speech?

of limb?

12. In what institution were you trained or by what experience have you fitted yourself specially for the position for which you are an applicant?

Give the name and address of two responsible persons who are thoroughly acquainted with your qualifications for the position for which you apply, to whom I may refer for further information.

13 Do you use intoxicating liquors as a beverage?

Do you hereby pledge yourself not to use intoxicating liquors as a beverage while you are upon an Indian reservation?

The application must be accompanied by two "statements" filled out by persons who know the applicant, in which replies are given to the following questions:

1 Are you over 25 years of age?

2 What is your legal residence? [Give city or town, county or parish, and State.]

How long have you lived there?

3 Are you well acquainted with the person named above?

4 How long have you known applicant?

5 Are you related to applicant?

What is the relationship?

6 Has applicant been in your employment?

How long was applicant employed by you?

When did applicant leave your employ and for what reason?

7 Would you yourself trust applicant with employment requiring undoubted honesty, and would you recommend him for such to your personal friends?

8 What do you know of applicant's education and qualifications in other respects for the position applied for?

9 What has been the condition of applicant's health since your acquaintance?

10 Does applicant now use or has applicant been in the habit of using intoxicating liquors?

11 Is applicant a person of good moral character?

What moral qualities does applicant possess?

12 Is applicant a person of good repute?

13 Does applicant possess such physical, mental, and moral qualities and have such habits as will in your opinion insure intelligent, faithful, and efficient performance of the duties of the position sought?

14 Are you aware of *any* circumstances tending to *disqualify* applicant for the position applied for?

15 Have you ever, in the performance of your official duty, visited the school taught and managed by applicant?

16 Please give me your estimate of qualifications and proficiency of applicant on the following points:

1. Ability and success in management and control of children.

2. Aptness to teach.

3. Personal appearance and manner, whether pleasing and attractive, or otherwise.

4. Disposition, force of character, dignity, and self-control.

Special stress is laid upon the moral fitness of the candidates, and, though no religious test is applied, those are preferred who are able to exert a positive religious influence over their pupils.

BOARDING-SCHOOLS OFF FROM RESERVATIONS

The system of boarding-schools off from reservations, now in successful operation, is slowly but surely accomplishing revolutionary and desirable results. Children from different tribes are brought together under influences where all tribal differences disappear. They learn to respect each other, and are prepared for association together as fellow-citizens. They hear and use only the English language, are removed from the contaminating influences of camp life, become accustomed to the usages of civilization, and are trained to habits of industry, thrift, and self-reliance.

THE "OUTING SYSTEM"

I quote from the *American Citizen* part of an article written by Mr. H. M. Jenkins, an intelligent and experienced observer of the practical workings of the system:

> The plan of "placing out" the young men and young women from the Indian schools maintained by the Government has now been in operation for more than ten years, and has acquired, both as to the members so placed and as to the measure of success realized, proportions which can not be questioned. The Indian is capable of sustained, systematic labor. He is a good worker. He has traits of his own, but he has the general characteristics of mankind. Where he differs from the white man the points of difference are not all to his discredit or his disadvantage. The inheritance he has of tradition and training includes many things which civilization itself demands and excludes some things which have attached themselves to civilization in spite of its protests.
>
> It was a favorite idea of Captain Pratt, now superintendent of the Indian school at Carlisle, when, in the years from 1867 to 1875, he served on the frontier with his regiment, that the Indian would work, and that the way to teach him practically and easily was to place the young people among the

farmers of the East. While in charge of the Indian prisoners in Florida from 1875 to 1878 Captain Pratt began the work, and in the two years succeeding he helped General Armstrong organize the placing-out system at the Hampton school, securing places for some of the pupils in western Massachusetts in the summer of 1878. Hampton continues the system, and has increased the number sent out. Last year it was about fifty. At Carlisle, however, the plan is more extensively followed. From that school sixteen were sent out in the summer of 1880, and, including that party, there have now been "outings," varying in length from a few weeks to a year or more, for 1,288 boys and 502 girls, counting in these figures the repetitions of those out more than once. This summer there were out at the beginning of July 245 boys and 107 girls, say, in round numbers 350. This is double the average of the ten years, and shows how favorably the system is regarded by the three parties concerned—the Indians themselves, the white families who employ them, and the authorities at Carlisle. The steady increase of the number put out comes about naturally. The pupils desire to go. "During the latter part of winter, and through spring and summer, until they are sent out," says a competent authority on the subject, "Captain Pratt is daily besought by the pupils to give them a chance to go out this year. The opportunity to earn their own way is popular." Last year the number sent out was 225 boys and 101 girls, so that this year shows the usual growth.

These young Indians have been placed in all the counties of southeastern Pennsylvania, and in others of the interior—Cumberland, Columbia, Luzerne, Juniata. Some have gone to New Jersey and Maryland, a few to Ohio and Massachusetts. A larger part of the boys, however, have been placed with the farmers of Bucks County, and many of the girls in Montgomery, Chester, and Delaware. (The two sexes are not sent to the same neighborhood, nor is it usual to place two of the same tribe in one family.) It is a common thing, therefore, to see, at this time, Indian lads and Indian young men at work in the fields of Bucks County, and to find Indian girls cooking and waiting on table in farm-houses of the counties adjoining. Here are the Aboriginal people returned! Here are Cheyennes, whose fathers of the same Algonquin blood as our tribes of the Delaware, kept faith with them centuries ago, and speaking a related dialect of the one language, held the same traditions and the same antipathies. But here, too, are a score of other tribes represented. In the family of the writer there have been, in three years, girls from the Cheyennes, Oneidas, Pueblos, and Pawnees. In neighboring families have been others from the Winnebagoes, Apaches, and Kiowas. And the list beyond these neighborhood examples is extensive.

I recently spent several days with Captain Pratt visiting the pupils from Carlisle Industrial School now scattered among the Pennsylvania farmers, and can fully indorse what Mr. Jenkins says above.

The system admits of large expansion and will be productive of the happiest results. These young Indians are brought into the most vital relationship with the highest type of American rural life. They acquire habits of neatness, industry, thrift, and self-reliance. They acquire a good working knowledge of English, and a practical acquaintance with all kinds of domestic and farm work. They associate with the farmer's children, eat at the same table, attend the same church and Sunday-school, and four months of each year attend the same day school. A better scheme for converting them into intelligent, honest American citizens, self-respectful and self-helpful, could scarcely be devised.

THE HIGHER EDUCATION OF THE INDIANS

Heretofore little has been attempted by the Government towards securing for the Indians anything more than a very rudimentary English and industrial training. The time generally supposed to be required to "educate" a non-English speaking Indian, fresh from the wilds of a reservation, and to fully equip him for life even amid the distressing surroundings of his barbarous home, has been three years. The absurdity of the idea is apparent to any intelligent man who will give ten minutes thought to it. It is no easier to educate an Indian than to educate a white man, and takes no less time. The increased difficulties that confront the young Indian just from school on returning to the reservation is a powerful argument for giving him a longer, more complete education even than is given to the average white child. Very few of the white boys from our grammar schools are prepared to cope with the difficulties of "getting on in the world" amidst the discouragements of reservation life.

RETURNING TO THE RESERVATION

The young Indians should receive a thorough education to fit them for maintaining themselves, and then should be free to seek a home for themselves anywhere they please. There is no more reason for compelling self-reliant Indian boys and girls to return against their will to an Indian reservation than there is of forcibly sending white boys and girls thither. The whole reservation system is an abomination that should cease to exist.

Pupils that prefer to return to their people should be encouraged and helped until they are able to withstand the dreadful influences of camp life and to establish and maintain homes for themselves. But the policy of the Government should be to encourage the Indian pupils educated in the industrial schools to seek homes for themselves wherever they can find the best opportunities to earn an honest living.

*   *   *

GRAMMAR SCHOOLS

As the large mass of Indian youth who are to be educated will never get beyond the grammar grade, special pains should be taken to make these schools as efficient as possible. The studies should be such as are ordinarily pursued in similar white schools, with such modifications as experience may suggest.

Among the points that may properly receive special attention are the following:

(1) The schools should be organized and conducted in such a way as to accustom the pupils to systematic habits. The periods of rising and retiring, the hours for meals, times for study, recitation, work and play should all be fixed and adhered to with great punctiliousness. The irregularities of camp life, which is the type of all tribal life, should give way to the methodical regularity of daily routine.

(2) The routine of the school should tend to develop habits of self-directed toil, either with brain or hand, in profitable labor or useful study. The pupils must be taught the marvelous secret of diligence. The consciousness of power springing from the experience of "bringing things to pass" by their own efforts is often the beginning of a new career of earnest endeavor and worthy attainment. When the Indian children shall have acquired a taste for study and a love for work the day of their redemption will be at hand.

During the grammar period of say five years, from ten to fifteen, much can be accomplished in giving to the girls a fair knowledge of and practical experience in all common household duties, such as cooking, sewing, laundry work, etc., and the boys may acquire an acquaintance with farming, gardening, care of stock, etc. Much can be done to familiarize them with the use of tools, and they can learn something of the practical work of trades, such as tailoring, shoe-making, etc. Labor should cease to be repulsive, and come to be regarded as honorable and attractive. The homely virtue of economy should be emphasized. Pupils should be taught to make the most of everything, and to save whatever can be of use. Waste is wicked. The farm should be made to yield all that it is capable of producing, and the children should be instructed and employed in the care of poultry, bees, etc., and in utilizing to the utmost, whatever is supplied by the benevolence of the Government or furnished by the bounties of nature.

(3) All the appointments and employments of the school should be such as to render the children familiar with the forms and usages of civilized life. Personal cleanliness, care of health, politeness, and a spirit of mutual helpfulness should be inculcated. School-rooms should be supplied with pictures of civilized life, so that all their associations will be agreeable and attractive. The games and sports should be such as white children engage in, and the pupils should be rendered familiar with the songs and music that make our home life so dear. It is during this period particularly that it will be possible to inculcate in the minds of pupils of both sexes that mutual respect that lies at the base of a happy home life, and of social purity. Much can be done to fix the current of their thoughts in right channels by having them memorize choice maxims and literary gems, in which inspiring thoughts and noble sentiments are embodied.

(4) It is of prime importance that a fervent patriotism should be awakened in their minds. The stars and stripes should be a familiar object in

every Indian school, national hymns should be sung, and patriotic selections be read and recited. They should be taught to look upon America as their home and upon the United States Government as their friend and benefactor. They should be made familiar with the lives of great and good men and women in American history, and be taught to feel a pride in all their great achievements. They should hear little or nothing of the "wrongs of the Indians," and of the injustice of the white race. If their unhappy history is alluded to it should be to contrast it with the better future that is within their grasp. The new era that has come to the red men through the munificent scheme of education, devised for and offered to them, should be the means of awakening loyalty to the Government, gratitude to the nation, and hopefulness for themselves.

Everything should be done to arouse the feeling that they are Americans having common rights and privileges with their fellows. It is more profitable to instruct them as to their duties and obligations, than as to their wrongs. One of the prime elements in their education should be a knowledge of the Constitution and Government under which they live. The meaning of elections, the significance of the ballot, the rule of the majority, trial by jury—all should be explained to them in a familiar way.

(5) A simple system of wage-earning, accompanied by a plan of savings, with debit and credit scrupulously kept, will go far towards teaching the true value of money, and the formation of habits of thrift, which are the beginnings of prosperity and wealth. Every pupil should know something of the ordinary forms of business, and be familiar with all the common standards of weights and measures.

(6) No pains should be spared to teach them that their future must depend chiefly upon their own exertions, character, and endeavors. They will be entitled to what they earn. In the sweat of their faces must they eat bread. They must stand or fall as men and women, not as Indians. Society will recognize in them whatever is good and true, and they have no right to ask for more. If they persist in remaining savages the world will treat them as such, and justly so. Their only hope of good treatment is in deserving it. They must win their way in life just as other people do, by hard work, virtuous conduct, and thrift. Nothing can save them from the necessity of toil, and they should be inured to it as at the same time a stern condition of success in life's struggle, and as one of life's privileges that brings with it its own reward.

(7) All this will be of little worth without a higher order of moral training. The whole atmosphere of the school should be of the highest character. Precept and example should combine to mold their characters into right conformity to the highest attainable standards. The school itself should be an illustration of the superiority of the Christian civilization.

The plant required for a grammar school should include suitable dormitories, school buildings, and shops, and a farm with all needed appointments.

The cost of maintaining it will be approximately $175 per capita per annum.

The final number and location of these schools can be ascertained only after a more thorough inspection of the whole field. At present the schools at Chilocco, in the Indian Territory; Albuquerque, N. Mex.; Grand Junction, Colo.; and Genoa, Nebr., might be organized as grammar schools. The completion of the buildings now in course of erection at Pierre, S. Dak.; Carson, Nev.; and Santa Fe, N. Mex., will add three more to the list. It will doubtless be possible at no distant day to organize grammar school departments in not less than twenty-five schools.

PRIMARY SCHOOLS

The foundation work of Indian education must be in the primary schools. They must to a large degree supply, so far as practicable, the lack of home training. Among the special points to be considered in connection with them, are:

(1) Children should be taken at as early an age as possible, before camp life has made an indelible stamp upon them. The earlier they can be brought under the beneficent influences of a home school, the more certain will the current of their young lives set in the right direction.

(2) This will necessitate locating these schools not too far away from the parents, so that they can occasionally visit their little children, and more frequently hear from them and know of their welfare and happiness.

(3) The instruction should be largely oral and objective, and in the highest degree simplified. Those who teach should be from among those who have paid special attention to kindergarten culture and primary methods of instruction. Music should have prominence, and the most tireless attention should be given to training in manners and morals. No pains should be spared to insure accuracy and fluency in the use of idiomatic English.

(4) The care of the children should correspond more to that given in a "Children's Home" than to that of an ordinary school. The games and employments must be adapted to the needs of little children.

The final number and location of these schools can not yet be fixed. Probably fifty will meet the demands of the near future. Many of the reservation boarding schools now in operation can be converted into primary schools.

Report of Commissioner of Indian Affairs T. J. Morgan
September 5, 1890

(Excerpt from *Report for 1890*, pp. iii ff.)

By 1890 the United States Government was confident that it had its Indian policy on a correct course. As the commissioner's annual report phrased it: "It has become the settled policy of the Government to break up reservations, destroy tribal relations, settle Indians upon their own homesteads, incorporate them into the national life, and deal with them not as nations or tribes or bands, but as individual citizens. The American Indian is to become the Indian American." The commissioner's report outlined in exquisite detail the process by which that "Settled Policy" was to be carried out, and even designated that the day on which the Dawes Severalty Act was signed into law, February 8, 1887, was to be a day for celebration and commemoration in the Indian schools. The optimism and good will evident in the anticipation of benevolent change are too obvious to deny. Yet, in a sense, this benevolent change provided an unconscious veneer to the stronger motives which underlay this shift in American Indian policy. Those motives can perhaps best be put in terms of white land hunger and white cultural imperialism.

THE LAW PRESCRIBES that the Commissioner "shall, under the direction of the Secretary of the Interior, and agreeably to such regulations as the President may prescribe, have the management of all Indian affairs, and of all matters arising out of Indian relations." He is charged with the annual disbursement of more than $7,000,000 and with the purchase and distribution of great quantities of subsistence, clothing, agricultural, medical, and other supplies. He gives instructions to more than sixty agents, supervises their work, examines their accounts, decides perplexing questions arising constantly in the course of administration of agency affairs, and through them oversees in detail the various lines of civilization inaugurated among the tribes, farming, stock-raising, building of houses, Indian police and courts, social and sanitary regulations, etc. He determines upon the appointment and removal of over twenty-five hundred agency and school employés, and appoints traders and physicians. Licensed trade among Indians is under his exclusive control.

He considers and determines all questions of law arising in reference to Indian lands; the legal status of Indians with reference to each other and to white people; the conflicts between local or State laws and tribal customs, and between State and Federal laws; also questions of citizenship, guardianship, crimes, misdemeanors; the prosecution of persons for the sale of whisky to Indians; taxation; water rights; right of way of railroads; cattle grazing; conveyances of land; contracts between Indians and whites; sales of timber on Indian reservations; allotment of land, etc. Many of these questions, especially those relating to lands, are of great intricacy, involving interpretations of treaties and laws as far back as colonial times.

He is charged with the duty of organizing a plan of education, with all which that implies; the erecting of school houses, appointing of teachers, and the keeping of a watchful oversight over all Indian school matters.

Bills in Congress relating to Indian affairs are usually referred to the Indian Bureau for information and report, and before an act is signed by the President it is generally referred to the Commissioner for report as to whether there is any reason why it should not receive Executive approval. Original bills and reports are also prepared by the Indian Office for transmission to Congress.

Under the act of March 3, 1885, the Commissioner examines and reports to the Secretary of the Interior on all depredation claims, amounting to many millions of dollars, which have been filed in the Bureau during the last forty years.

The foregoing gives an approximate idea of the responsible duties and the varied character of the work performed under his direction and supervision. The duties and labors of the office are constantly increasing and becoming more arduous and difficult as the progress of Indian civilization makes it necessary to deal with the race, not in their collective capacity as tribes and bands, but with the individuals who are being led to the holding of separate estates, thus multiplying many fold the interests to be considered, developed, and protected.

DIFFICULTIES OF THE SITUATION

I have cited these duties somewhat in detail, because I desire to set forth some of the difficulties which seriously embarrass and limit their satisfactory discharge. The chief one is the lack of sufficient and proper help in the Bureau itself. The nature of the work requires clerical help of a high order. In addition to the force now employed there is needed a chief clerk, who shall be charged with a general oversight of all the correspondence, and who shall follow up important matters from their beginning until the final result is reached.

There should be a solicitor to whom difficult law questions can be referred, and whose special business it shall be to examine and report upon all claims for money presented by Indians. Such an officer might save to the Government thousands of dollars, and at the same time assist the Indians to obtain their just dues. This would obviate the apparent necessity of so many paid attorneys, employed by the Indians at large fees, to prosecute their claims before the office and before Congress.

There is urgently needed at once the following additional clerical help: One clerk of class 4, two of class 3, and three of class 2; also one medical expert, charged with an oversight of the sanitary condition of the Indians. Without sufficient help in the office it is simply impossible to have the work done as it should be. Those now employed are faithful, industrious, and generally competent, but the work is too much for them and must and does suffer. The Commissioner is painfully aware of this fact, but is powerless to help it.

The Indians, with whose welfare and civilization he is charged, are widely scattered, and the territory in what is known as Indian reservations embraces not less than 181,000 square miles. The Navajo Reservation is in extent almost an empire in itself—12,800 square miles. The means of communication between the Bureau and the agents are at best imperfect, and in some instances very unsatisfactory. It is impossible for the Commissioner to visit and inspect all the agencies, he can not always rely upon official reports, and it is often very difficult even for the agents to have a personal knowledge of the territory and the people over whom they are placed.

A great obstacle is found in the strange languages still used by most tribes. They communicate with their agents and with the Bureau through interpreters, who, in some instances, are entirely incompetent for an intelligent transaction of business. Further, the various tribes differ so essentially among themselves in languages, habits, and customs, as well as in environment, as to make it very hard to adapt to their varying necessities any policy which may be adopted.

The entire system of dealing with them is vicious, involving, as it does, the installing of agents, with semi-despotic power over ignorant, superstitious, and helpless subjects; the keeping of thousands of them on reservations practically as prisoners, isolated from civilized life and dominated by fear and force; the issue of rations and annuities, which inevitably tends to breed pauperism; the disbursement of millions of dollars worth of supplies by contract, which invites fraud; the maintenance of a system of licensed trade, which stimulates cupidity and extortion, etc.

The small salaries paid to agents and physicians renders it very difficult to procure the services of thoroughly efficient and honest men who are contented to devote their entire energies to the good of the service without hope of other reward than their meager salaries.

The still all too prevalent public sentiment which looks upon Indians with contempt and regards them as the legitimate spoil of white men, has its influence in lowering the grade of this branch of the public service.

The white people who hang on the borders of the reservations, those who have allied themselves by marriage with the tribes, and even those who have from time to time been in Government employ, have, in many cases certainly, presented to the Indians a type of character and a practical philosophy of life on a par with, if not inferior, to their own.

The natural conservatism of the Indians, which leads them to cling with tenacity to their superstitious and inherited practices, adds to the difficulty of inducing them to abandon their own and accept the white man's ways.

A HOPEFUL OUTLOOK

Notwithstanding all these hindrances, however, there has been for ten or more years real progress in the right direction, and the outlook for the future is encouraging. The following points are especially worthy of consideration, and need to be repeated and emphasized until they are fully recognized by both white and Indians:

It has become the settled policy of the Government to break up reservations, destroy tribal relations, settle Indians upon their own homesteads, incorporate them into the national life, and deal with them not as nations or tribes or bands, but as individual citizens. The American Indian is to become the Indian American. How far this process has advanced during the past year will be shown under the head of the reduction of reservations and allotment of lands.

A public-school system is being rapidly provided, whereby every accessible Indian boy and girl of school age is to be afforded an opportunity of acquiring the rudiments of an English education and the elements of an honorable calling. What progress has been made in this direction during the last year is discussed under the general topic of education.

The Indians themselves are coming to understand the present policy of the Government and are showing an increasing readiness and even desire to adjust themselves to it. During the past year I have had personal interviews with prominent chiefs and representative Indians from Wisconsin, North and South Dakota, Oregon, Arizona, New Mexico, Oklahoma, and Indian Territory, and I have been much gratified with their intelligent apprehension of the situation and with the willingness exhibited, as a general thing, to accept lands in severalty with individual citizenship. Almost without exception they have pleaded with me for more and better schools.

Another fact of significance is the growing recognition on the part of Western people that the Indians of their respective States and Territories are to remain permanently and become absorbed into the population as citizens. While demanding the application of the principle of "home rule" in the selection of agents and other employés from the State or Territory in which the Indians are located, I think they also recognize the obligations which they thereby assume to recommend only suitable persons for appointment. If the Indians of South Dakota, for instance, are to remain forever within the limits of the State, either as a burden and a menace, or as an intelligent, self-supporting, co-operative factor in State life, no others except the Indians themselves can have so deep an interest in their practical status as the people by whom they are surrounded.

There is also a growing popular recognition of the fact that it is the duty of the Government, and of the several States where they are located, to make ample provision for the secular and industrial education of the rising generation, leaving the churches free to prosecute with renewed vigor their legitimate work of establishing and maintaining religious missions. By this harmonious and yet separate activity of the Government and the churches all of the Indians will eventually be brought into right relations with their white neighbors, and be prepared for the privileges and responsibilities of American Christian citizenship.

SUMMARY OF IMPROVEMENTS ATTEMPTED

In addition to the ordinary routine work of the office, the points to which I have given special attention during the year have been the following:

The improvement of the personnel of the service.—Wherever it could be done without too great hardship I have endeavored to remove those who were immoral, incompetent, inefficient, or unfaithful. No one has been discharged on account of politics or religion, and in no single instance except for the improvement of the service. I have steadily refused to remove those who were performing their duties satisfactorily. In making appointments I have, so far as it lay in my power, endeavored to secure persons of good moral character, having special fitness for their work, and where mistakes have been made, I have not been slow to correct them. Allow me, in this connection, to recognize heartily the cordial support given to me in this matter by yourself and the President, and also the painstaking efforts you have both put forth in the selection of Presidential appointees.

The elevation of the schools.—A great deal of thought has been given to this subject, and the schools have been visited and inspected with a care and thoroughness hitherto unattempted. The work accomplished by superintendent Dorchester will appear in his report on page 246. Large and careful expenditures have been made in repairing and enlarging school-houses and providing them with proper equipments, and new ones have been erected where most urgently demanded. A new and carefully revised system of rules, including a course of study, has been drawn up and a series of text-books determined upon. A work of this kind is beset with many difficulties and necessarily proceeds slowly, but when once accomplished is enduring.

The development of industries.—Great improvements have been made at the Government schools in this important direction. Competent instruction is given to boys in blacksmithing, broom-making, carpentering, dairying, farming, fruit culture, harness-making, printing, tailoring, tinsmithing, shoe-making, stock-raising, wagon-making, and wheel-wrighting; to girls, in all the ordinary duties of housekeeping. The work accomplished among the older Indians in teaching them the arts of agriculture are discussed under the head of Indian farming.

The improvement of the sanitary service.—There is a widely prevalent, but very mistaken, notion that the Indians, children of nature, are a healthy, rugged people. Nothing can be further from the truth. They are the sport of disease, are well-nigh helpless in their struggles against the elements, are almost wholly ignorant of the laws of health, are careless of their persons, are dominated by senseless superstitions, are the victims of the crudest kinds of quackery, and perish by hundreds during the prevalence of an epidemic.

The modification of the ration system.—Heretofore Indians receiving rations have been required to go to the agencies to get them, thus involving a great waste of time and strength. The plan of issuing rations at substations, which is now being put into operation, is discussed more at length under the head of Indian farming.

The common method of issuing live beeves to the Indians is a relic of barbarism, cruel and filthy. Stringent orders have been issued for the correction of this great evil and proper facilities for slaughtering are now being provided.

Inculcation of patriotism.—On all Government schools the American flag has been displayed, national holidays have been duly celebrated, the pupils are learning patriotic songs and recitations, and are taught to love the great nation of which they are a part, and to feel that the people of the United States are their friends and not their enemies.

Discouraging the Wild West Show business.—I have refused to grant any more licenses for Indians to leave the reservations or to enter into any other contracts with showmen. I have instituted proceedings against showmen and their bondsmen to compel the fulfillment of former contracts, which required them to treat their employés with humanity and justice.

EDUCATION

In my supplemental report of last year I set forth quite in detail my views regarding Indian education. These views have met with most gratifying acceptance, and have awakened a great deal of interest among all classes of citizens. The plan there outlined has received the indorsement of Dr. W. T. Harris, United States Commissioner of Education, and of General John Eaton, ex-Commissioner of Education, and has been heartily approved by the National Educational Association, the American Institute of Instruction, the New York State Teachers' Association, and other leading educational bodies, besides receiving the warm commendation of distinguished educators and philanthrophic organizations, like the Mohonk Conference, the Indian Rights Association, etc. After a year's practical work in carrying out the ideas there expressed, I see no reason to modify them in any essential particular.

TRAINING SCHOOLS

Under the fostering care of the Government a series of training schools has grown up off reservations where, in addition to the ordinary English education, Indian pupils are trained to habits of industry.

List of training schools with their location, date of opening, and capacity.

Name	Location	Date of opening	Capacity
Carlisle	Pennsylvania	1879	500
Salem	Oregon	1880	256
Genoa	Nebraska	1884	250

Name	Location	Date of opening	Capacity
Haskell Institute.....................	Lawrence, Kans......................	1884	450
Chilocco...........................	Oklahoma..........................	1884	200
Grand Junction.....................	Colorado...........................	1886	60
Albuquerque.......................	New Mexico........................	1886	225
Carson............................	Nevada............................	1890	150
Santa Fé...........................	New Mexico........................	1890	125
Pierre.............................	South Dakota......................	1890	90
Fort Totten........................	North Dakota......................	1890	250

Showing attendance, cost, etc., of training schools during fiscal year ended June 30, 1890.

Name of school	Location	Rate per annum	Ca-pacity	Number of em-ployes	Enroll-ment	Average attend-ance	Cost to Govern-ment
Albuquerque Training...	Albuquerque, N. Mex...	$175.00	225	28	222	164	27,224.36
Carlisle Training........	Carlisle, Pa.............	167.00	500	64	789	702	100,074.34
Chemawa Training.....	Near Salem, Oregon....	175.00	250	33	194	169	30,058.28
Chilocco Training......	Chilocco, Oklahoma....	175.00	200	27	196	154	27,093.21
Genoa Training........	Genoa, Nebr...........	175.00	250	23	203	176	31,851.66
Grand Junction Training	Grand Junction, Colo....	175.00	60	9	48	36	9,428.12
Haskell Institute.......	Lawrence, Kans........	175.00	450	54	460	417	75,961.62
Total.............			1,935	238	2,112	1,818	301,691.59

For the fiscal year ending June 30, 1891, Congress has made liberal appropriations for these schools which will help the Office to put them on a broad basis, and thoroughly equip them for their important work. With the improvements now being made they will be able next year to care for not less than thirty-three hundred students.

In estimating the work done several things should be carefully borne in mind: These institutions are not universities, nor colleges, nor academies nor high schools. In the best of them the work done is not above that of an ordinary grammar school, while in most it is of the primary or intermediate grade.

The pupils come to them for the most part ignorant of the English language, unaccustomed to study, impatient of restraint, and bringing with them many of the vices and degraded habits of camp life. From the very necessities of the case, the length of time which most of them have been kept in school has been very short. The time required for children in the public schools to complete a course of study embraced in the primary, intermediate, grammar, and high school is from fourteen to fifteen years. It has been heretofore commonly supposed that three years was long enough to educate an Indian and fit him to compete with his white neighbor, who has enjoyed so much greater advantages.

The work, embracing as it necessarily does, the supplanting of a foreign language by the English, the destruction of barbarous habits by the substitution of civilized manners, the displacement of heathenish superstitions by the inculcation of moral principles, the awakening of sluggish minds to intellectual activity by wise mental training and the impartation of useful knowledge, has been undertaken by these Indian teachers almost single-handed and alone, unaided by those potent factors outside of school which play so large a part in the education of our own children.

It is a fact not to be forgotten in any discussion of popular education that the most important factors in the development of our American civilization have been in the colleges, universities, and professional schools. Without these there would have been no common schools. If the average of intelligence among the Indians is to be brought up to the level of that of the other peoples which compose our nation, and they are to be prepared to compete in life's struggles on an equal basis, provision must be made whereby those among them who are specially gifted with talent, ambition, and energy may procure a higher education than is offered to them in the reservation and training schools. Already a very considerable number have shown both the desire and ability to pursue higher studies. Several are now successfully teaching, or fitting themselves to teach, others are practicing medicine, some are preaching, and still others are preparing for the practice of law. The desire for these higher studies is steadily increasing and only needs a little fostering to be productive of the best results. A common school, industrial education for all, a liberal and professional education for the worthy few, with a fair field and free competition, is all that is asked for Indians as for others.

The outing system which brings Indian youth into intimate and vital relationship with civilized communities is now steadily developing and is productive of the most hopeful results. During the past year Carlisle has accommodated nearly eight hundred pupils, more than half of whom have had the inestimable advantage of living and working, for periods varying from a few weeks to several months, with Pennsylvania farmers and others, who have paid them a reasonable compensation. Their work has been very satisfactory, and the school has been unable to meet the demand made upon it for help. When the present plans for increasing its capacity are completed, not less than a thousand pupils can be cared for at this one institution, and so far as I can now see it will be entirely feasible to carry perhaps double this number. Every Indian boy or girl who secures a place to work at fair wages has become a producer, and is practically independent and self-supporting.

The superintendent of Haskell Institute writes me that he expects to be able, when the present plans for that school are completed, to care for one thousand students, and to provide homes for a large number of them among Kansas farmers. How far it will be possible to extend the outing system in connection with these training schools I am not prepared to say, but the system seems to have great possibilities, and its development shall receive my constant and careful attention.

These training schools, removed from reservations, offer to the pupils opportunities which can not by any possibility be afforded them in the reservation schools. The atmosphere about them is uplifting, they are surrounded by the object lessons of civilization; they are entirely removed from the dreadful down-pull of the camp. If the entire rising generation could be taken at once and placed in such institutions, kept there long enough to be well educated and then, if such as choose to do so were encouraged to seek homes among civilized people, there would be no Indian problem.

RETURNED STUDENTS

It should be especially remembered that the oldest of these training schools, that at Carlisle, Pa., has been in existence only eleven years, and last year graduated its first class. Very few of the graduates have returned to their homes and none of them as yet had any opportunity to show what they can do. The unfairness of some of the criticisms upon returned students, who are inaccurately denominated "Carlisle graduates," or "graduates of the Carlisle University," is apparent. There has been no time in which to estimate from practical experience the influence which has been exerted upon these pupils. The time has not been too short, however, to show that, notwithstanding all the hindrances under which the work is carried forward, Indian children, under equally favorably conditions, are just as susceptible of education as any other class.

Relatively to the Indian population, a very small proportion of boys and girls have yet been brought under the influence of these schools. The few who have returned home have therefore found themselves in too many cases isolated by their dress and habits, out of sympathy with their surroundings, ostracized by their companions, and too frequently practically helpless. The remedy for this is two-fold. First, the universal education of the rising generation, so that there will be a common bond of sympathy and mutual helpfulness between them. Second, the encouragement of pupils who have finished the course of study in the training schools to seek for themselves homes and employment among civilized people.

Pupils in these schools should be taught that they must depend upon themselves and not expect to be furnished employment by the Government. Ample opportunities are afforded them for acquiring an education, with the expectation that they will prepare themselves to earn their own living. There is no necessity of their returning to the reservations, except as a matter of choice, for all who are intelligent, industrious, honest, and thoroughly capable can secure honorable and remunerative employment among civilized people, which they should be encouraged to seek.

RESERVATION SCHOOLS

Boarding schools.—The following is a list of the sixty-three Government boarding schools on reservations:

Arizona—Colorado River, Fort Mojave, Navajo, Keams Cañon, Pima, San Carlos; California—Fort Yuma; Idaho—Fort Hall, Fort Lapwai, Lemhi; Indian Territory—Quapaw, Seneca; Kansas—Kickapoo, Pottawatomie, Sàc and Fox and Iowa; Minnesota—Leech Lake, Red Lake, White Earth; Montana—Blackfeet, Crow, Fort Peck; Nebraska—Omaha, Santee, Winnebago; Nevada—Pyramid Lake, Western Shoshone; New Mexico—Mescalero;

North Dakota—Fort Stevenson, Standing Rock(2); Oklahoma—Absentee Shawnee, Arapaho, Cheyenne, Kaw, Kiowa, Osage, Otoe, Pawnee, Ponca, Sac and Fox, Wichita; Oregon—Grande Ronde, Klamath, Siletz, Sinemasho, Umatilla, Warm Springs, Yainax; South Dakota—Cheyenne River, Crow Creek, Lower Brulé, Pine Ridge, Sisseton, Yankton; Utah—Uintah; Washington—Chehalis, Neah Bay, Puyallup, Quinaielt, S'Kokomish, Yakima; Wisconsin—Green Bay; Wyoming—Shoshone.

Concerning these schools it may be said: They have been for the most part poorly equipped. The buildings in many cases were small, cheap, inconvenient, often inadequately furnished, frequently very deficient in ventilation, heating, and water supply. Many had been grossly neglected and were sadly out of repair. During the past year, an earnest effort has been made to improve them by repairs, additions, or new buildings, and by supplying water or heating facilities, as needed. There still remains much to be done, however.

If the work is to be made at all adequate to the necessities of the case, there should be a very considerable increase in the number of these schools, and at an early day new schools should be established at the following places:

Arizona—Fort Apache on San Carlos Reservation; Papago Reservation, Navajo Reservation, and among the Moquis; California—Hoopa Valley Agency, Mission Agency, Round Valley Agency; Colorado—Southern Ute and Jicarilla Agency; Montana—Blackfeet Agency, Tongue River Agency; New Mexico—Zuni Reservation; Oklahoma—Cantonment, Jesse Bent's ranch, and Seger Colony on Cheyenne and Arapaho Reservation; South Dakota—Pine Ridge Reservation, Rosebud Reservation; Utah—Ouray Agency; Wisconsin—Oneida Reservation, and four of the reserves of the La Pointe Agency.

The limit heretofore placed by law upon the cost of the buildings—$10,000—has been so low that it has been impossible to provide proper accommodations. To establish a boarding-school involves making provision not only for school rooms proper, but for dormitories, kitchen, laundry, bath-rooms, hospital, and other necessary rooms for pupils, and also of suitable quarters for all the employés, superintendent, teachers, matron, cook, laundress, seamstress, etc. The original cost of the plant is a comparatively small part of the outlay. It is a poor economy to put up inferior buildings and fail to make proper provision for the work expected, which can not be satisfactorily done with such poor facilities. The limit of cost now fixed is $12,000, which is still too low.

These schools are surrounded by influences which necessarily hamper them very seriously in their work. They are far removed from civilization, feel none of the stimulating effects of an intelligent public sentiment, and have little helpful supervision. The parents have ready access to them, and often prove troublesome guests by reason of their clamors for the return of the children to their tepees. It is exceedingly difficult to break up the use of the tribal tongue and to teach them to use the English language. Notwithstanding these difficulties, however, they are doing a good work, directly upon their pupils and indirectly upon the older people of the reservations, and there goes out from them a civilizing force whose strength and value can scarcely be overestimated.

To render them still more efficient they should be increased in number, be better equipped, more closely supervised, and subjected to more rigid discipline. The teachers should be selected with care, have a reasonably secure tenure of office, and have pay equal to that received for a similar grade of work in the public schools of the same State or Territory. These schools should be feeders for the training schools, and deserving, capable pupils should be regularly and systematically promoted.

Day schools.—During the past year there were in operation at the various agencies 106 day schools with an enrollment of 3,967, and an average attendance of 2,367.

Of these schools I wish to say that I found them in existence when I assumed the duties of the office; 11 new ones have been established, and 3 of the old ones have been abandoned. Of the whole number 81 are conducted by the Government and 25 are carried on under contract.

The teachers labor under very great disadvantages. The houses are poor and the furniture scanty. The accommodations for the teachers are very primitive; the isolation and deprivations are hard to bear; the influences of the camps are often wholly antagonistic to those of the schools; it is extremely difficult to break up the use of the tribal language; many of the children are poorly fed, scantily clad, untidy in their habits, and irregular in their attendance.

On the other hand, it must be said that a good day-school well administered is an object lesson of civilization in the midst of barbarism, for the children carry home daily some influence which tends toward a better life. It permits the parents the presence of their children, to which many of them attach great importance, and to whose prolonged absence they could not be induced to consent, and there is gradually being produced, no doubt partly at least through these schools, a public sentiment among the camp Indians more friendly to education and progress in civilization.

I believe it is possible to raise the character of these schools by providing better houses and facilities for work, by introducing some form of elementary industry, and by paying more attention to supervision. The effort to do this is now being made, which, if it is successful, may lead to the establishment of others on a better basis.

INDIANS IN THE PUBLIC SCHOOLS

Believing that the true purpose of the Government in its dealings with the Indians is to develop them into self-supporting, self-reliant, intelligent, and patriotic citizens, and believing that the public schools are the most effective means of Americanizing our foreign population, I am desirous of bringing the Indian school system into relation with that of the public schools. Not only so, but wherever possible I am placing Indian pupils in the public schools. Very few are thus far enjoying these advantages, but in a letter addressed to the superintendents of public instruction in the several States and Territories where there are Indians under the care of the National Government I have invited their co-operation, and have offered to contract with school districts for the tuition of Indian pupils at the rate of $10 per quarter.

I think this will prove a very important feature of the work in hand, and confidently expect within a year to be able to report a great advance in this direction. Indian allottees can be provided with educational facilities for their children in no more satisfactory manner, and the tuition paid by the Government aids the school districts to maintain schools in sections of the country where lands in severalty have been taken by the Indians.

COMPULSORY EDUCATION

My predecessors and many of the agents and superintendents of schools have strongly urged the importance and necessity of a law compelling the attendance of pupils at the schools. I am in favor of compelling every Indian child of suitable age and health, for whom accommodations are provided, to attend school ten months out of twelve. A general law, however, could not now be everywhere applied, for the simple reason that school accommodations are provided by the Government for less than half the children of school age. The question among many tribes is not so much one of filling the schools as it is of finding room for the pupils. With few exceptions every reservation school is crowded, and hundreds of children who are willing to go to school are prevented by want of proper accommodations.

Something in the way of compulsory attendance may be secured through the authority already vested in the agent under direction from this Office, whereby full and regular attendance at school is required upon forfeiture of rations, annuities, or other favors as the penalty for indifference or open opposition. It does not meet the case of the non-reservation schools, however. Under the law children can not be taken from the reservation except by permission of their parents, and although the non-reservation schools are generally better equipped than those at the agencies, at times great difficulty is experienced in inducing pupils and parents to consent to the transfer.

SCHOOL ATTENDANCE

Showing enrollment and average attendance at Indian schools for the fiscal years 1887, 1888, 1889, and 1890.

Kind of school	Enrolled				Average attendance			
	1887	1888	1889	1890	1887	1888	1889	1890
Government schools:								
Training and boarding.......	6,847	6,998	6,797	7,236	5,276	5,533	5,212	5,644

	Enrolled				Average attendance			
Day.............	3,115	3,175	2,863	2,963	1,896	1,929	1,744	1,780
Total.........	9,962	10,173	9,660	10,199	7,172	7,462	6,956	7,424
Contract schools:								
Boarding........	2,763	3,234	4,038	4,186	2,258	2,694	3,213	3,384
Day.............	1,044	1,293	1,307	1,004	604	786	662	587
Industrial boarding, specially appropriated for..........	564	512	779	988	486	478	721	837
Total..........	4,371	5,039	6,124	6,178	3,348	3,958	4,596	4,808
Aggregate......	14,333	15,212	15,784	16,377	10,520	11,420	11,552	12,232*

*The average attendance for 1890 is computed on the attendance during the entire year including summer vacations. The average attendance for the nine months from October 1 to June 30, was 12,462, a gain of 1,021 over the corresponding months of the preceding year.

The total enrollment during the year ended June 30, 1890, is 16,377, while the estimated school population (six to sixteen years of age), exclusive of the Indians of New York State and the Five Civilized Tribes, is 36,000.

Many reasons have combined to cause this comparatively small attendance, of which a few may be mentioned. Very inadequate provision has been made. In some cases, as among the Navajos for instance, where there is a school population of 3,600, with accommodations for only 150 pupils, or at San Carlos Agency, where the conditions are similar, I have no doubt that the attendance could be doubled in one year, simply by making provision for the children who can not go to school because there is no school for them to go to. In many places the Indians are impatient in their demands for the schools which the Government has failed to supply them, though in some cases they have been promised for years.

In many instances the facilities have not only been inadequate, but the school-houses have been unattractive and unhealthy and the children have been neglected or badly treated. Great improvements have been made during the year, and others are under way which will insure for next year a considerable increase in attendance.

In some cases the agents have taken little or no interest in the schools, or have been so occupied with other cares that they have done little or nothing to build them up or make them inviting, while in still others the small attendance is directly chargeable to their ignorance, neglect, or even secret opposition. Where this has seemed to be beyond improvement or remedy, I have not hesitated to suggest it to you as a sufficient cause for removal.

One great hindrance is the poor health so common among the Indian children. Disease is very prevalent, and during the last year the ravages of the grippe were very distressing. There were thousands of cases of it, and where it was not necessary actually to suspend the schools the number of pupils in attendance was very largely decreased. The Indians as a whole suffer especially with pulmonary troubles, sore eyes, and diseases of the skin, and it must be conceded that these conditions offer one of the most serious obstacles to a regular, uniform school attendance.

Another hindrance is, very naturally, the failure of parents and children alike to appreciate the nature and importance of education. They can not see for themselves, and it is difficult to make them understand all it means for them. They either ignore the school entirely or expect it to accomplish wonders in a brief period. Three years they consider a very long time in which a boy or girl should not only fully master the English language, but acquire all the accumulated learning of the white man. Happily, a great change in this respect is taking place, and there is a growing desire among parents as well as among children that the education may be more complete.

If the Government will provide the means to establish and maintain schools in accordance with the system laid down in my supplemental report of last year, it is only a question of time—two or three years I think will suffice—when all Indian youth of school age and of suitable health can be put into school.

The following tables, taken from that report and brought down to date, show the number of Indian pupils who have been attending school since 1882 and the appropriations which have been made for Indian education since 1877.

Showing Indian school attendance from 1882 to 1890, both inclusive.

	Boarding schools		Day schools		Totals	
Year	Number	Average attendance	Number	Average attendance	Number	Average attendance
1882.....	71	2,755	54	1,311	125	4,066
1883.....	75	2,599	64	1,443	139	4,042
1884.....	86	4,358	76	1,757	162	6,115
1885.....	114	6,201	86	1,942	200	8,143
1886.....	115	7,260	99	2,370	214	9,630
1887.....	117	8,020	110	2,500	227	10,520
1888.....	126	8,705	107	2,715	233	11,420
1889.....	136	9,146	103	2,406	239	11,552
1890.....	140	9,865	106	2,367	246	12,232

Annual appropriations made by the Government since the fiscal year 1877 for support of Indian schools.

Year	Appropriation	Per cent of increase	Year	Appropriation	Per cent of increase
1877........	$20,000	....	1885.......	$992,800	47
1878........	30,000	50	1886.......	1,100,065	10

Year	Appro- priation	Per cent of increase	Year	Appro- priation	Per cent of increase
1879........	60,000	100	1887.......	1,211,415	10
1880........	75,000	25	1888.......	1,179,916	02.6
1881........	75,000	....	1889.......	1,348,015	14
1882........	135,000	80	1890.......	1,364,568	01
1883........	487,200	260	1891.......	1,842,770	35
1884........	675,200	38			

In this connection it is worth while to note the allowances made by the Government to other than Government schools for the education of Indians.

Showing amounts set apart for various religious bodies for Indian education for each of the fiscal years 1886 to 1891, inclusive.

	1886	1887	1888	1889	1890	1891
Roman Catholic..............	$118,343	$194,635	$221,169	$347,672	$356,957	$363,349
Presbyterian.................	32,995	37,910	36,500	41,825	47,650	44,850
Congregational...............	16,121	26,696	26,080	29,310	28,459	27,271
Martinsburgh, Pa.............	5,400	10,410	7,500	Dropped	....	....
Alaska Training School........	....	4,175	4,175	....	....	....
Episcopal....................	....	1,890	3,090	18,700	24,876	29,910
Friends.....................	1,960	27,845	14,460	23,383	23,383	24,743
Mennonite...................	....	3,340	2,500	3,125	4,375	4,375
Middletown, Cal..............	....	1,523	Dropped	....	....	....
Unitarian....................	....	1,350	5,400	5,400	5,400	5,400
Lutheran....................	....	....	1,350	4,050	7,560	9,180
Methodist...................	....	....	....	2,725	9,940	6,700
Miss Howard................	....	....	....	275	600	1,000
Appropriation for Lincoln Institution....................	33,400	33,400	33,400	33,400	33,400	33,400
Appropriation for Hampton Institute....................	20,040	20,040	20,040	21,040	20,040	20,040
Total..................	228,259	363,214	376,264	530,905	562,640	570,218

* * *

HOLIDAYS

As a part of their education and a means of preparation and training for civilized home life and American citizenship, it is important that the pupils in these schools should understand the significance of national holidays and be permitted to enjoy them. To this end general instructions have been issued for the appropriate celebration of New Year's Day, Franchise Day (February 8), Washington's birthday, Decoration Day, Fourth of July, Thanksgiving, and Christmas, as well as Arbor Day.

The reports received in reply to these circulars are of unusual interest, showing that both teachers and pupils entered heartily into the spirit of the various occasions. Very creditable programmes of exercises for these different days are on file in the office, in some of which adult Indians took active part, giving good advice to the children, and for the time being, at least, identifying themselves with the new ideas brought forward.

On a few of the reservations Memorial Day could be as fittingly observed as elsewhere, by the decoration of the graves of Indians who enlisted in the United States Army and lost their lives during the war.

Tree planting on Arbor Day was quite extensively engaged in by the schools, and the interest excited led some of the Indians to plant trees around their own houses. The yearly observance of this day can not fail to add greatly to the attractiveness of agency and school premises and to the adornment of Indian homes.

I take pleasure in quoting the interesting account given by Special Agent Alice C. Fletcher of the celebration by the Nez Percés of Idaho of the last Fourth of July:

> The people began to gather a day or two before the Fourth, and to erect their awnings and tents in the pine grove about the church. Over five hundred were present, and the place, otherwise so quiet, resounded with the laughter and chatter of old and young. The day opened with a religious service held at 6 a. m. under a large awning tied to tall trees. At 8 a. m. the children and their parents, all clad in citizens' clothes and decked out in their best, gathered in front of the church, where, on the porch, sat the four elders. Some of the boys carried little flags, and all joined in a song new to me, the words being: "We'll stand, Fourth of July," closing with: "Hurrah! Fourth of July," all the men removing their hats. As I walked about I was greeted with a hand-shake, a nod of the head, and smiles, and "Fourth of July," much as we say "Happy New Year." Soon a procession was formed, the boys leading, and graded as to size; the girls followed, arranged in the same manner down to little tots; then came the men, the women bringing up the rear. The column moved sedately round through the trees, all singing: "We'll stand, Fourth of July," until they returned in front of the church, when all seated themselves, and the native pastor introduced the various speakers—all Indians. These commented on the happiness of an orderly Christian life in contrast to the wild roving life that the people had formerly led, and urged all—both old and young—to be good men and women. One man declared that he did not fully understand what we celebrated, but Fourth of July was to celebrate. Just as a returned student was stepping forth to give the historical data of the day the crier announced that the people must begin to prepare for dinner, and the audience melted at the summons.
>
> The beef and salmon were roasted before large fires, and the meal was served under the awning on table cloths and white china. A blessing was asked, and all fell to with zest. It was a comfortable meal of beef, salmon, canned fruit, bread, cake, and wild potatoes. After dinner the business of adopting certain persons into the tribe was attended to, and in the evening some Indians provided a few fire-works, after which all gathered under the stars for an evening service of prayer, and as happy and peaceful a day as I ever saw came to an end.

The Medical Service

The Government has assumed the medical oversight of the great body of Indians, excepting the five civilized tribes. The Indian "medicine" men are ignorant, superstitious, sometimes cruel, and resort to the most grotesque practices. The only rational medical treatment comes not from among themselves, but is that which is furnished by the Government physicians.

This very important branch of the service is without competent supervision. There is no professional head. The supervision of the medical service should require the entire time of a competent expert. Many of the men now serving as physicians are men of high personal character, of good professional attainment and experience, and are faithful in the performance of their duties; others I have been obliged to discharge for immorality, neglect of duty, incompetency, or unprofessional conduct, and especial care has been taken to fill their places with those who are trustworthy and competent.

With the hope of securing a more satisfactory order of things, I wish to point out some defects inherent to the plan now pursued in supplying the Indians with medical service.

Physicians are appointed without any examination. They are required to produce a diploma from some reputable medical school and to submit testimonials as to moral character and correct habits, and yet their appointments are not guarded with that care which the nature of the services required of them demands. No one should be appointed except upon an examination as to his health, his professional attainments, and his moral qualifications. In addition to his qualifications for general practice, his ability to give instruction on hygienic subjects to school pupils should be tested, and he should possess such scientific and practical knowledge as will prepare him to have an oversight of the entire sanitary conditions of a whole tribe. In short, he should be capable of being a health officer as well as a physician and surgeon.

The work of the physicians is without supervision. The average agent, inspector, and special agent has no expert knowledge of medical practice, and the Indians are ignorant and helpless to make complaint either of neglect or malpractice. The physician at an Indian agency, far removed from civilization, having the care of a barbarous people beset with the formidable difficulties of his anomalous situation, having no professional associations and with no possibility of gaining either increase of income or reputation by devotion to duty, is under a very strong temptation to slight his work. Intelligent, faithful inspection by a medical expert, and official supervision of his labors, with a recognition of good service when performed, would necessarily secure better results than are now reached. The duties devolving upon the physician are very severe. He has the work of a surgeon and physician, with the sanitary oversight of people with whose language he is unfamiliar and who are ignorant, superstitious, and predisposed to a great variety of diseases. He must be his own apothecary; he usually has no hospital and no nurses, and his patients have few of the most ordinary comforts of home, and little, if any, intelligent care in the preparation of their food or the administering of prescribed medicine. He is alone and has to cope with accident and disease without consultation, with few books, and but few surgical instruments.

Without attempting to set forth an ideal system, elaborate and expensive, I wish to emphasize some few changes and improvements which should be made on the score of humanity.

The number of physicians should be increased so as to bring medical aid within the reach of all Indians. That this is not the case at present, a few illustrations will indicate. The Navajo reservation, embracing a territory of 12,000 square miles and a population of 18,000, has but one physician; the Crow reservation, area 7,000 square miles, population 2,500, one. At Pine Ridge Agency one physician is charged with the care of over 5,500 Indians; at Rosebud Agency over 7,000; and at Standing Rock over 4,000, all widely scattered. Thousands of Indians at these agencies and others are utterly unable to have medical care when necessary, and the results are a large degree of needless suffering and hundreds of deaths that might in all probability have been prevented.

Physicians who enter the service through a careful examination should have a fair compensation for their services, political considerations should not influence their appointment, and they should be removed only for cause.

A hospital should be connected with every boarding school, where pupils can receive proper attention when sick, and where Indian nurses and hospital stewards can be trained for service among their own people. There should also be at every large agency a general hospital for the severe cases of illness that require treatment which can not be given at the homes.

Young Indian men and women who are now pursuing courses of study, and show aptitudes for such service, should be encouraged to prepare themselves professionally for work among their own people as physicians and nurses. Drs. Eastman, Montezuma, and Susan La Flesche have already graduated from medical schools and are now in successful practice.

Since it is apparent that Indians are coming into closer relations with civilized society, and that intermarriages are increasing, it is very important that special attention should be given to their health.

REDUCTION OF RESERVATIONS

At the date of the last annual report of this office there were one hundred and thirty-three Indian reservations in the United States (counting the twenty-two small reserves of the Mission Indians of California as one only and the nineteen Pueblo reserves in New Mexico also as one), having an aggregate area of about 116,000,000 acres or 181,250 square miles, which is greater than that of the New England and Middle States combined, greater than the aggregate area of the States of Ohio, Indiana, Illinois, and Kentucky, and nearly equal to the combined area of the two Dakotas and Montana. To carry the comparison further, it is larger by half than the United Kingdom of Great Britain and Ireland, larger than Sweden or Norway, and nearly as large as either France or Spain. The total Indian population of the United States, exclusive of Alaska, was, by the census of 1889, 250,483, and exclusive of the five civilized tribes in Indian Territory, 185,283.

The following table shows the distribution of Indian lands and Indian population in the several States and Territories at the date above referred to:

Showing, by States, population of Indians and areas of Indian reservations.

State or Territory	Area in acres	Square miles	Population
Arizona	6,603,191	10,317½	17,779
California	494,045	772	12,739
Colorado	1,094,400	1,710	1,814
North Dakota	3,188,480	4,982	8,252
South Dakota	22,910,426	35,798⅜	21,461
Idaho	2,611,481	4,080	4,174
Indian Territory	39,199,530	61,249	79,632
Iowa	1,258	2	393
Kansas	102,026	159½	989
Michigan	27,319	42½	7,428
Minnesota	4,747,941	7,419	7,979
Montana	10,591,360	16,549	11,214
Nebraska	136,947	214	3,701
Nevada	954,135	1,490½	8,251
New Mexico	10,002,525	15,629	28,928
New York	87,677	137	5,046
North Carolina	65,211	102	3,000
Oregon	2,075,210	8,242	4,520
Texas			290
Utah	3,972,480	6,207	2,294
Washington	4,045,284	6,321	9,789
Wisconsin	512,061	800	7,543
Wyoming	2,342,400	3,600	1,945
Miscellaneous			1,302

Where it is suitable for agricultural or grazing purposes, it is the present policy of the Government to allot land in severalty to the Indians within their respective reservations—160 acres to heads of families, 80 acres to single persons over eighteen years of age, 80 acres to orphan children under eighteen years of age, and 40 acres to each other single person under eighteen years of age—to patent these individual holdings, with a restriction against alienation for twenty-five years, or longer, in the discretion of the President, and to purchase from the respective tribes any or all of the surplus land remaining after the allotments have been made. The general law for this is the allotment act of February 8, 1887 (24 *Stat.* p. 388), applicable to all reservations, except those of the five civilized tribes and three others in the Indian Territory, those in the State of New York, and one in Nebraska adjoining the Pine Ridge Sioux Reservation, which was set apart by Executive order for the purpose of suppressing liquor traffic with the Indians.

In numerous instances, where clearly desirable, Congress has by special legislation authorized negotiations with the Indians for portions of their reservations without waiting for the slower process of the general allotment act, which involves the survey of the land, the allotment in severalty by special agents appointed by the President for that purpose, and negotiations with the Indians for the cession and relinquishment of their surplus unallotted lands.

It is estimated that under such special legislation about 13,000,000 acres of land have been secured by cession from the Indians during the past year; and there are agreements now pending before Congress, through which, if ratified, the Government will acquire some 4,500,000 acres more; all of which will, under the operation of these laws, be open to white settlement in the near future.

Of the land actually acquired, about 9,000,000 acres are in North and South Dakota, secured from the Sioux (Act of March 2, 1889, 25 *Stat.*, p. 888), and about 4,000,000 acres in Minnesota, acquired from the Chippewas (Act of January 14, 1889, 25 *Stat.*, p. 642). The agreements now pending in Congress will, if ratified, restore to the public domain about 1,600,000 acres in North Dakota, in the Fort Berthold Reservation; about 660,000 acres in South Dakota, in the Lake Traverse (Sisseton,) Reservation; about 185,000 acres in Idaho, in the Coeur d'Aléne Reservation; about 1,095,000 acres in Colorado, being the whole of the southern Ute Reservation; and about 941,000 acres in Oklahoma Territory, now embraced in the Pottawattomie, Iowa, and Sac and Fox Reservations; a grand total of upwards of 17,400,000 acres, or about one-seventh of all the Indian lands in the United States.

This might seem like a somewhat rapid reduction of the landed estate of the Indians, but when it is considered that for the most part the land relinquished was not being used for any purpose whatever, that scarcely any of it was in cultivation, that the Indians did not need it and would not be likely to need it at any future time, and that they were, as is believed, reasonably well paid for it, the matter assumes quite a different aspect. The sooner the tribal relations are broken up and the reservation system done away with the better it will be for all concerned. If there were no other reason for this change, the fact that individual ownership of property is the universal custom among the civilized people of this country would be a sufficient reason for urging the handful of Indians to adopt it.

As a general rule, I would not advise the purchase of the surplus lands until the Indians have been located upon and absolutely secured in their individual holdings. Give them their patents and see that they are fairly started in the paths of civilization, with their children in school, and then it will be time enough to negotiate with them for the sale of the surplus. There is always a clamor for Indian lands, but there is no such pressing need for more land for white settlement as to justify undue haste in acquiring it. It is true the general allotment act authorizes the Secretary of the Interior to enter into negotiations with Indians for the purchase of their surplus unallotted lands in advance of the completion of the individual allotments, if, in the opinion of the President, it shall be for their best interests to do so. In some cases, this may be desirable, but as a rule, I think it better that they should take their allotments first. Their lands are becoming more valuable every year, so that they can lose nothing, in a pecuniary sense, by withholding the sale of so much as they may have to dispose of until after this has been done.

Nor is it good policy to remove Indian tribes from one place to another, especially from one State or Territory to another, merely to satisfy the selfish ends or to suit the convenience of the whites. It creates discontent, destroys the natural attachment for the soil, disturbs whatever progress in localization and settlement may have been made, and retards progress in every way. I fully agree with the late distinguished General of the Army (General Sheridan) that "every section of country should control the bad elements of its own population—not endeavor to foist them upon other more fortunate districts—and this is especially true of the Indians, who should, as far as possible, be controlled where they now are."

There was a time when in the rapid settlement of the Western country it became necessary to remove some of the tribes that were subsisting mainly by the chase and yet occupying vast areas from which the game had practically disappeared. But the conditions are changed. Game can no longer be depended upon as a food supply, and there is nothing left to the Indian but to attach himself to the soil and follow the pursuits of civilized life. In this he should be encouraged and assisted in every possible way, and nothing can be farther from the purpose than to keep moving him from one place to another.

Leaving out the five civilized tribes and the Alaska Indians, it would take about 30,000,000 acres of land to give to every Indian in the United States—man, woman, and child—160 acres each. There would still remain, in round numbers, 66,000,000 acres of Indian land, (exclusive of the reservations of the five civilized tribes), which, at $1 per acre, probably a fair average, would yield $66,000,000, the annual interest on which, at five per cent, would be $3,300,000—a sum sufficient to pay the entire cost of educating all the Indian children in the United States. At the end of a few years, the principal sum might properly be distributed per capita among the rightful owners to assist them in improving their homes, when they could be left like other citizens to care for themselves.

Here we have an immense landed estate belonging to the Indians, which, if judiciously managed by the Government, ought to place them on the high road to prosperity, and relieve the Government of a great financial burden. It is not essential to their prosperity that they should have a great fund in the Treasury to draw upon for their support; on the contrary, it would be a positive evil. But I would sell their surplus lands, place the money in the Treasury, and expend the interest in assisting them to break and fence their lands, to build comfortable houses, to provide themselves with agricultural implements, seeds and stock, and, most important of all, to educate their children.

It will not do to say that they do not hold their land by such a title as to render it obligatory upon the Government to give them the proceeds of the sale of their surplus. All of which I have spoken is held by them either by virtue of sacred treaty stipulation, by act of Congress, or by executive order, and with possibly a few exceptions, even those who occupy reservations established by authority of Congress, or by executive order, have as good a claim, in equity, to absolute ownership as those who hold them by virtue of treaties with the Government.

As already stated, the general allotment act of February 8, 1887, confirms the Indian title in all existing reservations. It provides that in all cases where any tribe or band of Indians has been or shall hereafter be located upon any reservation created for their use, "either by treaty stipulation or by virtue of an act of Congress, or by executive order, setting apart the same for their use," the President of the United States may, whenever in his opinion any reservation or any part thereof is suitable for the purpose, allot the lands of said reservation in severalty to the Indians located thereon, in quantities as specified; and that after lands shall have been so allotted, or sooner, if in the opinion of the President it shall be for the best interests of the Indians, it shall be lawful for the Secretary of the Interior to negotiate with such Indian tribe for the purchase and release by said tribe, in conformity with the treaty or statute under which such reservation is held, of such portions of its reservation not allotted as such tribe shall from time to time consent to sell, "upon such terms and conditions as shall be considered just and equitable between the United States and said tribe of Indians."

I desire to ask special attention to the great importance of the early ratification of agreements made with Indians for the cession of portions of their reservations. Delay in such matters is not understood by them, often works hardships, creates unrest, begets distrust, and greatly retards their progress. It should be remembered that while these agreements often involve the appropriation of large sums of money, the amount is almost wholly reimbursable from the sale of the land.

* * *

SOUTHERN UTE AGREEMENTS

The agreement made with the Southern Ute Indians, of Colorado, in the fall of 1888, which has excited great popular interest throughout the country, is still pending in Congress. Friends of the Indians are loth to believe that it will be for the best interests of the Indians to take them from the fertile valleys of their present reservation and settle them upon the barren, unproductive lands of the proposed reservation in Utah. They believe that they should have lands allotted to them in severalty on their present reservation, where it would be reasonable to expect they would eventually become self-supporting, law-abiding citizens. My own views upon this subject were fully set out in a report to the Department, dated March 1, 1890.

As I see no reason to recede from the position then taken, and as the conclusions reached and the grounds of my objections to the ratification of the agreement were specifically stated in said report, I will repeat them here:

First. From an examination of the records of the various councils held with the Indians by the Commissioners, it does not seem to me that the agreement reached fairly represents the wishes of the Utes; that their consent was reluctantly given, and, under stress of such considerations as appealed strongly to their fears and very largely to their prejudices against a civilized life.

Second. The progress already made by these Indians in civilization will be rudely interrupted by the removal, and they will be placed amid surroundings much more hostile to their progress in learning the white man's ways than those amidst which they are now situated.

Third. It will be exceedingly difficult, if not possible, for the Government to carry out the agreement made with these Indians to protect them from the intrusions of white men on the new reservation.

Fourth. The proposed removal under the stipulated conditions is at variance with the general policy which the Government is now applying to the solution of the Indian problem. Instead of allotting to these Indians their land, and teaching them how to utilize their allotments, the proposed plan would place them upon a reservation three times as large as the present one and encourage them in the idea that they may continue for an indefinite period in that uneducated, uncivilized, semi-savage state in which they now are.

Fifth. The difficulties of administration, if anything is to be accomplished in the way of civilization of this little band, will be vastly greater on the proposed reservation than they are on the present.

Sixth. No proper effort has ever been made by the Government looking towards their civilization. It is my firm conviction that under proper efforts these Indians can, at no distant day, become self-supporting, intelligent citizens of the State of Colorado.

Seventh. This little band constitutes the last remnant of Indians in the Great State of Colorado, and in comparison with the number of Indians in other States—South Dakota, Montana, Nebraska, California, etc.—is very small indeed. Removal merely shifts the burden of their presence from Colorado to Utah and delays their final civilization.

As above stated, the Southern Utes are the only Indians now remaining in Colorado, and they number less than two thousand. Minnesota, Michigan, and Wisconsin each have over three times as many, Montana five, and California six times as many, North Dakota and South Dakota four and ten times as many, respectively, and the State of Washington five times as many; so that in the distribution of our Indian population, to those who regard their presence as a detriment, Colorado seems to have been much more fortunate than many of her sister States.

* * *

WILD WEST SHOWS AND SIMILAR EXHIBITIONS

The practice which has prevailed for many years of occasionally permitting Indians to travel with "Wild West" and similar shows throughout the country and abroad, for the purpose of giving exhibitions of frontier life and savage customs, has been very harmful in its results. I have from the beginning steadily refused to sanction any permits, and I heartily welcome your letter dated August 4, 1890, directing that no more be granted.

In all cases where these engagements have been authorized their employers have been required to enter into written contracts with the Indians, obligating themselves to pay them fair, stipulated salaries for their services, to supply them with proper food and raiment, to meet their traveling and needful incidental expenses, including medical attendance, etc., to protect them from immoral influences and surroundings, and to employ a white man of good character to look after their welfare, etc. They have also been required to execute bonds with good and sufficient securities, payable to the Secretary of the Interior, conditioned upon the faithful fulfillment of their contracts.

While these contracts have been complied with in some instances, in others well-grounded complaints have been made of the abandonment of the Indians and the failure of their employers to pay them their salaries. These complaints will be investigated and steps will be taken to recover the amounts due by instituting suit on the bonds given by the employers.

November 1, 1889, I addressed a circular letter to the agents of agencies from which the Indians have been taken for exhibition purposes, calling for the fullest information upon the subject, with a view to suggesting such modifications in the policy of the Department as the facts might warrant. The replies of the agents fully confirmed my previous impressions that the practice is a most pernicious one, fraught with dangerous results, economically, physically, and morally. It is not only injurious to the Indians who engage in the business, but also to those who remain at home, who, from their peculiar status and isolation, are influenced in a large degree by those who have been absent on such enterprises.

The policy of granting permission for Indians to engage in shows of this character has doubtless rested upon the idea that in addition to readily earning money, they would, by extensive travel through the States, and possibly in Europe, become familiar with the manners and customs of civilized life. But travel is not necessarily elevating or profitable. While they may earn a little money and see something of civilized life, their employment is, from the very nature of the case, temporary, and they are frequently brought into association with some of the worst elements of society. Their representations of feats of savage daring, showing border life as it formerly existed, vividly depicting scenes of rapine, murder, and robbery, for which they are enthusiastically applauded, is demoralizing in an extreme degree. They become self-important and strongly imbued with the idea that the deeds of blood, etc., which they portray in their most realistic aspects, are especially pleasing to the white people, whom they have been taught to regard as examples of civilization.

Their surroundings in these tours are generally of the worst, and they pick up most degrading vices. Instead of being favorably impressed with the religion of the white man, it is more than likely that they come to distrust it through what they unavoidably see, hear, and experience. Traveling about the country on these expeditions fosters the roving spirit already so common among them, encourages idleness and a distaste for steady occupation, and during their absence their families often suffer for want of their care and assistance. They frequently return home bankrupt in purse, wrecked morally and physically, and, in such cases, their influence and example among the other Indians is the worst possible.

The influence of these shows is antagonistic to that of the schools. The schools elevate, the shows degrade. The schools teach industry and thrift, the shows encourage idleness and waste. The schools inculcate morality, the shows lead almost inevitably to vice. The schools encourage Indians to abandon their paint, blankets, feathers, and savage customs, while the retention and exhibition of these is the chief attraction of the shows. Owing to the steady growth of public opinion with reference to the possibility of civilizing the Indians through the education of their children, Congress appropriated this year nearly $2,000,000 for Indian education. The popular impression of the Indians obtained from Wild West Show exhibits is that they are incapable of civilization, and this impression works directly and powerfully against the Government in its beneficent work.

I have endeavored through the various agents to impress upon the minds of the Indians the evil resulting from connecting themselves with such shows and the importance of their remaining at home and devoting their time and energies to building houses, establishing permanent homes, cultivating farms, and acquiring thrifty, industrious habits thus placing themselves in fit position for absorption into our political and civil life.

TRADE

The system of restricting trade with Indians on reservations to persons who hold a license issued by the Commissioner of Indian Affairs is a relic of the old system of considering an Indian as a ward, a reservation as a corral, and a tradership as a golden opportunity for plunder and profit. Reserves were then remote from white settlements, robes and pelts were abundant and were bartered for articles of trifling value, competition was almost unknown, and close supervision of Indian trade was well-nigh impracticable. Now most reservations have towns in their immediate vicinity; hunting has virtually ceased; the Indian wants staple articles and can offer in exchange only other staples of his own raising, trinkets of his own manufacture, money of his own earning, or his fast diminishing "cash annuity"; he can buy and sell in towns or on the reservation as he chooses; and as his time, at his own valuation of it, counts for little, he will go where he can get the best rates or the most credit, without regard to a few miles of distance.

Recent inspection reports from many agencies have represented prices charged by licensed traders as being naturally regulated by the competition of neighboring towns, rather than by the fixed scale prescribed by the Indian Bureau; consequently, in such instances, the supervision of Indian trade now required relates mainly to the personal character of the trader and his employés, their influence among the Indians with whom they are allowed to live, their observance of rules prescribed by this Bureau, and their abstaining from dealing in intoxicating liquors or other contraband articles. Licensed Indian trade is losing its distinctive characteristics.

It is the policy of the office to treat it as a mere matter of business and to allow changes in traderships to take place as they do in other branches of business. Licenses are granted for one year only as hitherto; but if a trader has honestly observed the rules of the office his license is renewed, unless he voluntarily surrenders it or sells out to some one else. In the latter case the office is ready to license the person to whom the sale is to be made, provided he can furnish a good bond and satisfactory testimonials. This policy, which gives to the trade an element of stability, is believed to be for the best interests of the Indians. It is unreasonable to expect men of character and financial standing to put up buildings, make improvements, and invest capital in a business whose legitimate profits can no longer average more than those in other mercantile pursuits, unless they can have a fair prospect of continuing the business provided they properly conduct it.

Competition within the reservation, in addition to that growing up outside, is fostered by licensing on each reserve as many traders as practicable. The office strives to put at least two on every reservation, and fails to do so only in cases where the trade is so small that only one trader can make a fair and honest living out of it.

The office also encourages Indians to engage in trade on their own account, as one of the "civilized pursuits" which they are to adopt as a means of livelihood. Under the law Indians of full blood may trade without license restriction, but those of mixed blood must obtain a license, which the office is ready to grant if the applicants are worthy.

Among the five civilized tribes restriction and supervision of trade by this office has for a long time been mainly nominal, as it is virtually regulated by the respective tribes. Licenses have been issued, on the recommendation of the agent of the Union agency, to all applicants (non-citizens of the tribes) who have presented trade "permits" granted to them by the tribal authorities, and who have furnished the required bond. These annual tribal permits require the holders thereof to pay to the tribe granting the permit an annual tax, as prescribed by the laws of the tribe, the amount of tax varying according to the nature and extent of the business. It has been found, however, that injustice pervades this entire system. The tribal authorities have required some firms to trade with and allowed others to trade without license or permit. In some cases taxes are collected and in others they are remitted. The taxes themselves are not properly graded, nor are they consistently levied according to the tribal laws. Once in a while the office is called upon by the tribes to revoke a license and "remove" some trader who has failed to comply with their requirements, while of others, equally culpable, no complaint is made. Rank discrimination and favoritism prevail to such an extent that the Government must either step in and regulate matters or leave the whole subject to the administration or maladministration of the tribes.

Under the law the former course seems to be the duty of the office. The laws on the subject read as follows:

Section 2129, Revised Statutes: No person shall be permitted to trade with any of the Indians in the Indian country without a license therefor from a superintendent of Indian Affairs, or Indian agent, or sub-agent, which license shall be issued for a term not exceeding two years for the tribes east of the Mississippi, and not exceeding three years for the tribes west of that river.

Section 2133, Revised Statutes: Any person other than an Indian who shall attempt to reside in the Indian country as a trader, or to introduce goods, or to trade therein without such license, shall forfeit all merchandise offered for sale to the Indians, or found in his possession, and shall moreover be liable to a penalty of five hundred dollars.

Act of August 15, 1876 (19 Stats., p. 200): And hereafter the Commissioner of Indian Affairs shall have the sole power and authority to appoint traders to the Indian tribes and to make such rules and regulations as he may deem just and proper, specifying the kind and quantity of goods and the prices at which such goods shall be sold to the Indians.

Act of July 31, 1882 (22 Stats., p. 179): That section twenty-one hundred and thirty-three of the Revised Statutes of the United States be, and the same is hereby, amended so that it shall read:

"Any person other than an Indian of the full blood who shall attempt to reside in the Indian country, or on any Indian reservation, as a trader, or to introduce goods, or to trade therein, without such license, shall forfeit all merchandise offered for sale to the Indians or found in his possession, and shall moreover be liable to a penalty of five hundred dollars: *Provided*, That this section shall not apply to any person residing among or trading with the Choctaws, Cherokees, Chickasaws, Creeks, or Seminoles, commonly called the five civilized tribes, residing in said Indian country, and belonging to the Union agency therein."

Under an opinion of the Assistant Attorney-General dated January 26, 1889, the proviso of the act of July 31, 1882, repeals section 2133 of the

Revised Statutes so far as it relates to the five civilized tribes, thereby relieving licensed traders in those tribes from being subject to the $500 penalty and to confiscation of goods. But it does not relieve them from the operation of section 2139, which forbids any one to trade with Indians in the Indian country without a license, nor from the operation of the act of August 15, 1876, which gives to the Commissioner of Indian Affairs "sole power and authority to appoint traders to the Indian tribes," etc. The Attorney-General adds:

> And it seems to me that the power to appoint "Indian traders," and to prescribe rules and regulations to govern their intercourse with the Indians, necessarily carries with it the power to revoke such appointments for a violation of the rules thus prescribed.
>
> Another question, however, is presented in this connection, to wit: Has the Department authority under section 2149, or under any other law or treaty, to remove a trader from the territory of said civilized tribes for a violation of its lawful regulations? Section 2149 Revised Statutes provides that—
>
> "The Commissioner of Indian Affairs is authorized and required, with the approval of the Secretary of the Interior, to remove from any tribal reservation any person being therein without authority of law, or whose presence within the limits of the reservation may, in the judgment of the Commissioner, be detrimental to the peace and welfare of the Indians."
>
> The question here presents itself as to whether or not the several territories of the civilized tribes are *"tribal reservations"* within the meaning of said section, inasmuch as most, if not all, of said tribes own the fee-simple title to their lands . . .
>
> In view of . . . treaty stipulations with the . . . civilized tribes, whereby our Government has stipulated to keep white people off of their territory; and in view of the fact that no other Department of Government seems to be clothed with the necessary authority to carry into effect these treaty stipulations, I think it fair to conclude that said section 2149, Revised Statues, was intended to give to the Commissioner of Indian Affairs, under the approval of the Secretary, the same authority to remove white persons from the territory of these civilized tribes that he would have if they held their lands by a different and inferior title.

In view of the above the following instructions were issued to Agent Bennett on the 21st of July last:

> First. Under the law, as interpreted by the Assistant Attorney-General, under date of January 26, 1889, traders among the five civilized tribes who have no original nor acquired right of residence therein are under the same necessity for procuring licenses from the Indian Bureau as are traders among other tribes. Also the Indian Office has the authority to revoke such licenses as the penalty for the violation of prescribed rules, and, with the approval of the Secretary, to remove the persons whose licenses have been thus revoked.
>
> Second. In view of the above I deem it the duty of the Indian Office to see to it that no persons who have not otherwise a right to reside among the five civilized tribes shall reside and carry on trade there without a license from this Bureau. You are therefore hereby authorized to notify all persons trading among the five civilized tribes without license from this Bureau (provided such persons have no citizenship in those tribes, original or

acquired) that they must obtain from this bureau a license to trade or their stores must be closed and their business cease.

Third. The above includes all persons who carry on business among the five civilized tribes, merchants, hotel-keepers, peddlers, lawyers, physicians, etc. Every kind of business carried on in the tribes by persons who have no right of residence therein is to be classified by the Government as trading.

Fourth. If, however, in the interest of justice and fair dealing, the office undertakes to insist that all persons having no rights amont the five civilized tribes who go among them for the purpose of trading shall obtain license for such trade from the United States, it must be with the understanding that the several tribal authorities shall be strict and just in their issuance of their own permits for such trade. In other words, that they shall have certain fixed rates of permit taxes which they shall levy upon and collect from all alike, without discrimination and without favoritism.

I may be allowed to express the hope that the day is not far distant when the present anomalous condition of things in the Indian Territory, by which that great region is regarded as an Indian reservation and its inhabitants as wards under the control of the Government, and all questions of trade among themselves and between them and the outside world are regulated from this office, will give way to a settled order of society, and when these communities, already so far advanced in civilization, shall take their places in the sisterhood of States as a free and independent people.

Railroads Over Reservations

Incident to the growing population and material advancement of the Western States and Territories, especially those bordering on the Indian Territory, increasing demands are made upon Congress for legislation authorizing the construction and extension of lines of railway across the Indian lands. Bills introduced in Congress are generally referred to this Bureau for opinion and report as to whether such construction should be authorized.

While it is not believed that Indian reservations should be allowed to stand as barriers to the development of the country surrounding them, it is the opinion of this office that legislation authorizing the building of railroads through reservations should be framed with a due regard to existing treaty stipulations, and, whenever practicable, it should require the consent of the Indians.

In all cases where this office can exercise discretion, the maps of definite location filed by railway companies are transmitted to the agents for investigation and report, particularly as to whether such location is along the line authorized by right of way act, and also with regard to the individual holdings or allotments likely to be invaded or damaged by the construction of the proposed road.

Much unnecessary delay can be avoided if railway companies will systematically comply with the conditions imposed by the acts granting them right of way.

Each company should file in this office

(1) A copy of its articles of incorporation duly certified to by the proper officers under its corporate seal.

(2) Maps representing the definite location of the line. In the absence of any special provisions with regard to the length of line to be represented upon the maps of definite location, they should be so prepared as to represent sections of 25 miles each. If the line passes through surveyed land, they should show its location accurately according to the sectional subdivisions of the survey, and if through unsurveyed land it should be carefully indicated with regard to its general direction and the natural objects, farms, etc., along the route. Each of these maps should bear the affidavit of the chief engineer, setting forth that the survey of the route of the company's road from —— to —— a distance of —— miles (giving termini and distance), was made by him (or under his direction) as chief engineer under authority of the company, on or between certain dates (giving the same) and that such survey is accurately represented on the map. The affidavit of the chief engineer must be signed by him officially, and verified by the certificates of the president of the company, attested by its secretary under its corporate seal, setting forth that the person signing the affidavit was either the chief engineer or was employed for the purpose of making such survey, which was done under the authority of the company. Further that the line of route so surveyed and represented by the map was adopted by the company by resolution of its board of directors of a certain date (giving the date) as the definite location of the line of road from —— to ——, a distance of — miles (giving termini and distance), and that the map has been prepared to be filed for the approval of the Secretary of the Interior in order that the company may obtain the benefits of the act of Congress approved —— (giving date).

(3) Separate plats of ground desired for station purposes, in addition to right of way, should be filed, and such grounds should not be represented upon the maps of definite location, but should be marked by station numbers or otherwise, so that their exact location can be determined upon the maps. Plats of station grounds should bear the same affidavits and certificates as maps of definite location.

All maps presented for approval should be drawn on tracing-linen, the scale not less than 2,000 feet to the inch, and should be filed in duplicate.

These requirements follow, as far as practicable, the published regulations governing the practice of the General Land Office with regard to railways over the public lands, and they are, of course, subject to modification by any special provisions in a right-of-way act.

* * *

STATUS AND RIGHTS IN INDIAN TRIBES OF MIXED BLOODS AND PERSONS ADOPTED

When Indian reservations were remote from white settlements and practically valueless for the purposes of those engaged in civilized pursuits, questions concerning the rights of persons of mixed blood to tribal benefits were rarely presented, and were deemed of little moment. But since the steady march of civilization has brought the red man into close contact with the dominant race, and the real value of tribal lands has consequently increased, and since the Government has inaugurated the system of allotment to Indians of lands in severalty, many persons claiming to be mixed bloods have urged this bureau to enroll them as members of Indian tribes. The subject has thus become one of decided importance, each application requiring careful investigation and consideration.

A striking illustration of the great pecuniary interests involved in some of these applications is furnished by the claims of a number of families to citizenship in the Osage Nation, Oklahoma Territory. If all the securities and credits of the Osages were converted into cash, and distributed equally to the members of the tribe, each man, woman, and child would receive over $5,000; and if the tribal lands should be allotted to them in severalty, each would secure over 300 acres. Hence claimants to citizenship would obtain, if successful, what is considered by many as fortunes.

Some of the applicants for tribal rights have but the slightest trace, if any, of Indian blood; and, in some instances, they have lived among and affiliated exclusively with white people. Indeed, applications have been made to this office for participation in tribal benefits by United States citizens whose sole title thereto rested upon their claim of having aboriginal blood in their veins by descent from Powhatan, through Pocahontas.

While, in some cases the consent of the tribe is readily obtained, in others they strongly protest against the admission of such claimants.

Attorney-General Cushing, in opinion rendered July 5, 1856 (7 Opinions, 746), held that half-breed Indians were to be treated as Indians in all respects, so long as they retained their tribal relations; that when the question of mixed blood arose there was no intrinsic precision in the expression "a white man," and he referred to the fact that there were men of indubitable citizenship in various parts of the country who had Indian blood in their veins. He concluded that the incapacity of race attached to an Indian, as such, may and must be susceptible of being determined by intermarriage with persons of the dominant race, but declined to lay down a rule as to the period or stage of descent at which this occurs.

It was subsequently decided, in the case of ex parte Reynolds (5 Dillons Circuit Court Reports), which was upon a writ of habeas corpus applied for by Reynolds who had been committed for a murder in the Indian country, that whether an individual of partial Indian descent is independent of jurisdiction of our courts as an Indian or is amenable to it as a subject of the national or State government, is to be determined (if the question depends on race, not on residence) not upon the quantum of Indian blood, but upon the condition of his father, under the rule of the civil law *partus sequiter patrem,* which governs in this class of cases. The court quotes in this case from Vattel, in his Law of Nations, page 102, as follows: "By the law of nature alone children follow the condition of their fathers and enter into all their rights;" and adds that this law of nature, so far as it has become a part of the common law, in the absence of any positive enactment on the subject, must be the rule in the case before it.

Nearly all questions which might arise, under the principles to be deduced from the above opinion and decision, as to the loss of tribal rights by residing away from the tribe and assuming United States citizenship, are set at rest by the general allotment act approved February 8, 1887 (24 *Stats.,* 388). Section 4 of that act authorizes allotments upon the public domain to Indians not residing upon a reservation or for whose tribe no reservation has been provided; and section 6 declares that every Indian to whom allotment shall have been so made who has voluntarily taken up his residence separate and apart from any tribe in the United States and adopted the habits of civilized life, is a citizen of the United States and entitled to all rights, etc., as such citizen, without in any manner impairing or otherwise affecting his right to tribal or other property.

But the question still remains, where the point as to residence is not involved, as to the extent to which the principles laid down in the case of Reynolds should be applied to the applications for tribal relations of persons of mixed blood. Should the rule that nationality or citizenship follows the father's condition be construed to determine property rights in Indian tribes, or should it be confined only to questions of citizenship and nationality to which it in term applies?

The Indians living in tribal relations have been declared by the courts to be "distinct political communities" and "domestic dependent nations;" also to be "under the pupilage of the Government." The peculiarity of their status, as thus defined, appears still more anomalous when we consider the fact that each Indian is entitled to and will obtain his individual estate by division of the tribal property, and is thus virtually in the attitude of a tenant, in common with his brethren of the domain of his tribe. The political status and nationality of the Indian tribes is thus interwoven with the property rights of the Indians individually.

Another consideration of importance in the matter is the helpless and dependent condition of the tribes and the resulting necessity for the Government, in adjusting their rights and interests, to pursue a liberal policy, without reference to technical rules.

After careful consideration of the question, I incline to the opinion that the rule laid down in the Reynolds case should not be held conclusive as against the application of mixed bloods for tribal benefits where the claimants in other respects clearly prove their rights thereto.

There is no doubt that there is a stage at which, by the admixture of white blood and non-affiliation with the Indian tribes, persons would be debarred from participating in tribal benefits. The admixture of blood, however, must be considered in connection with all the circumstances of each case; consequently a fixed rule equally applicable to all cases can not well be adopted. Every application for tribal rights by mixed bloods should, as a matter of justice to the Indians, be closely scrutinized.

The adoption by different tribes of members of other tribes or of white persons, and the consequent results, is a subject which has been frequently before this Bureau for consideration. The general rule acted upon is that these adoptions are not valid unless approved by the Department, and that they will be sanctioned only where some peculiar circumstances seem to justify it, especially when the applicant for adoption is a white person or one having but a slight admixture of Indian blood.

As a general thing adopted persons secure no right thereby to lands or annuities and obtain merely the right of residing among the Indians and such minor privileges as the tribes may concede to them, although the practice of this Bureau has not been at all uniform on the subject. In no case, however, has a person been allowed an annuity with two tribes. If he has equal rights in each he must elect with which he will draw annuities.

In a recent application of a tribe to be permitted to adopt an Indian of another tribe, and give him full rights as to property, etc., and where the candidate for adoption filed a written relinquishment of all his rights in his own tribe, the Department declined to sanction the adoption. It simply authorized the enrollment of the applicant as a member of his own tribe upon the rolls of the tribe in which he was seeking adoption, with the privilege of residing with the tribe until otherwise ordered. This course was deemed advisable in view of the fact that some tribes are much richer in lands and annuities than others, and hence that Indians fully adopted by other tribes might materially injure their own interests, or to put it more strongly, give away their birthrights, without fully comprehending it. In addition, the approving of the full adoption of Indians by other tribes would have a decided tendency to encourage restlessness and a roving spirit among them, thus taking their attention from the building up of permanent homes for themselves and families.

Since, under existing conditions, tribal organizations are now rapidly passing away, almost every question of importance depending upon the tribal system will be solved. After this is accomplished, however, questions will arise concerning tribal funds and credits, in deciding which it will be necessary to regard the Indians in the same attitude as if they maintained their tribal status.

INTRUDERS IN THE INDIAN TERRITORY

For many years the respective authorities of the five civilized tribes in the Indian Territory, and especially of the Cherokee and Chickasaw Nations, have alleged the presence there, in violation of law, of large numbers of citizens of the United States, and have requested their removal as intruders, in accordance with provisions of the several treaties. In the Cherokee Nation the number is variously estimated at from thirteen to forty thousand, and with his letter of February 5, 1890, to the President, Hon. J. B. Mayes, principal chief, transmitted a list of over five thousand alleged intruders and requested their removal.

A large proportion of the intruders in the Cherokee Nation is composed of persons who claim that they are of Cherokee blood and entitled to remain, and their continued presence is due to the disagreement between the Department and the Cherokee authorities as to the exclusive right of those authorities to determine the claims of such persons, or the right of the Department to determine for itself according to the general law of the land whether or not the alleged intruders are so in fact and liable to removal; also as to the manner of investigation by which such determination shall be reached.

In accordance with the views of the Department that the Cherokee authorities have no right to exercise jurisdiction over the person or property of intruders in the Cherokee country, and that rejected claimants who entered the nation prior to August 11, 1886, in good faith, should be allowed a reasonable time and opportunity to dispose of their improvements and remove from the nation, all such claimants were notified by the Indian agent about August or September, 1888, to sell their property not of a movable character, and to prepare to remove within six months from the date of said notification. These notices were subsequently suspended or rather indefinitely extended. Two years have elapsed, and so far as this office is advised not one of them has disposed of his property or left the Cherokee country, notwithstanding all know that they are regarded as intruders and that their removal at some time or another is inevitable. This circumstance impresses me as an evidence of bad faith on the part of these claimants, and of an intention to remain in the nation and reap the benefits of the free use of the Cherokee lands (they pay no taxes) until compelled by force to remove. The Department is not called upon to give this class of intruders any more consideration than is due to other persons unlawfully within the Cherokee country, and I would recommend their removal as well as that of all others who are there without authority of law.

While the question of the removal of intruders from the Chickasaw country is not complicated by the question of citizenship, as in the case of the Cherokees, still in view of the large number of those intruders and the desperate character of some of them, it promises to be one almost as difficult of solution. For a time the threatened interference by the officers of the United States district court for the eastern district of Texas with the removal of intruders by the agent caused some embarrassment and uneasiness, but an understanding has been reached by which his jurisdiction will be recognized and upheld in the future. There seems to be no reason to fear now that any serious trouble will result from their removal which should be effected this fall.

Although there are said to be more than twenty thousand non-citizens in the Choctaw Nation, less than five hundred are regarded as intruders, and most of these are Glenn, Tucker, *et al.*, whose claims to citizenship are now being considered by the Department. This perhaps is due to the liberal and hospitable laws of the nation relating to permits, and to the fact that intruders find it easier to comply with them than to seek to evade them.

The insufficiency of the present laws of the United States to prevent intruders who are removed from returning to the Indian country has given some concern, and may to a great extent operate to make the efforts of the Government in that direction a useless expenditure of time and money. The law (sec. 2148 Revised Statutes) provides that—

> If any person who has been removed from the Indian country shall thereafter at any time return or be found within the Indian country, he shall be liable to a penalty of one thousand dollars.

This law, Agent Bennett says, in a letter of June 19, 1890, is rendered inoperative by reason of the financial irresponsibility of the persons who comprise the great army of intruders, and who very often after their removal return to the reservation in advance of the officer who removed them. If the law were amended so as to impose a punishment of imprisonment or fine, or both, it would be more effective in accomplishing the object desired, and in my report of July 20, 1890, I had the honor to transmit the following draught of a bill, which I hope will be adopted:

> That section 2148 of the Revised Statutes be, and the same is hereby, amended so as to read as follows, namely:
> "If any person who has been removed from the Indian country shall thereafter at any time return or be found within the Indian country, he shall be punishable by imprisonment for not less than thirty days nor more than ninety days, or by a fine of not less than one hundred dollars nor more than five hundred dollars, or both, in the discretion of the court: *Provided,* That upon default of payment of fine the same shall be served out in imprisonment at the rate of one dollar per day until paid: *And provided further,* That if any person who shall have been fined or imprisoned as provided in this act shall be found within the Indian country after the expiration of twenty days from the date of his release from imprisonment, or the date of his payment of fine in cases where the penalty of imprisonment is not imposed by the court, such person shall be liable to the same fines and penalties as herein provided for the punishment of persons returning to the Indian country after their removal."

Notwithstanding the deficiency in the law, I am of the opinion that, in view of the positive and definite promises which the United States has made in its treaties with the several tribes in the Indian Territory to keep their country free from intrusions by unauthorized persons, the Department should take such prompt and unequivocal action that the intruders will accept the situation and abandon all effort to continue their unlawful residence therein. I have therefore the honor to renew my recommendations that this office be authorized to take action looking to the removal of all persons who are in the Indian Territory in violation of or without authority of law, and that the Secretary of War be requested to cause a sufficient force of troops to be detailed for the assistance of the agent of this office in the execution of that authority.

* * *

COURTS OF INDIAN OFFENSES

During the past two years the reservation tribunals known as "Courts of Indian Offenses" have been placed upon a quasi-legal basis by an appropriation made by Congress for the pay of the judges of such courts.

These courts, as has been already set forth in the reports of this Bureau, had their origin in a communication of December 2, 1882, from the Department to this office, suggesting that rules be formulated whereby certain specified barbarous and demoralizing practices among the Indians should be restricted and ultimately abolished. Thereupon the office organized a system of Indian courts, and prepared a code of rules which enumerated the crimes and offenses of which the courts should take cognizance, and in several instances named the penalties which should be prescribed.

Each court consists of three judges who are appointed by the Indian Office, upon the nomination of the respective Indian agents, for a term of one year, but are subject to removal at any time. The court holds regular sessions twice a month. The crimes and offenses named in the rules are Indian dances, plural marriages, practices of medicine men, theft, destruction of property belonging to another, payments or offers of payment for living or cohabiting with Indian women, drunkenness and the introduction, sale, gift, or barter of intoxicating liquors.

The court also has jurisdiction over misdemeanors committed by Indians belonging to the reservations, over civil suits to which Indians are parties, and over any other matters which may be brought before it by the agent or with his approval.

The penalties prescribed are fine, imprisonment, hard labor, and forfeiture of rations. In civil cases the court has the jurisdiction of a justice of the peace, and conforms, so far as practicable, to the practices of a justice of the peace in the State or Territory in which the court is located.

Without money, legislative authority, or precedent, these courts have been established and maintained for eight years, and in spite of their crudities, anomalies, and disadvantages, have reached a degree of dignity, influence, and usefulness which could hardly have been expected.

Prior to the fiscal year preceding July 1, 1888, owing to want of funds, the judges gave voluntary service or were selected from the police or paid themselves out of the fines imposed and collected—incongruities which the Indians themselves were not slow to recognize. During that year the $5,000 appropriated for the pay of the judges by act of June 29, 1888 (25 *Stats.,* 233), gave to the courts legislative recognition, and to the judges small salaries, ranging from $3 to $8 per month, during seven months of the year. During the fiscal year just closed a similar appropriation of $5,000 has been carefully husbanded and distributed; and by closing the court for one-third of the time, thus restricting its sessions to eight months in the year, and by paying the ninety-three judges not exceeding $8 per month, and in several instances reducing the pay to $5 and even $3 per month, the office has been able to maintain the court at twenty-five agencies.

For the current fiscal year an appropriation of $10,000 has been made, which will enable the office to maintain these courts during twelve months at twenty-six agencies and to pay the judges' salaries as follows: Fifty-five judges at $10 per month, ten at $8 per month, twenty-three at $5 per month, and ten at $3 per month.

This information is given in detail in the following table:

Showing the agencies at which Indian judges were employed; the number of Indians at such agencies; the number of judges allowed, and for what time, and at what salary, during the fiscal year ended June 30, 1890.

Agencies	Indians	Judges	Period employed	Salary per month	Agencies	Indians	Judges	Period employed	Salary per month
			Mos.					*Mos.*	
Blackfeet, Mont..........	2,293	3	8	$8.00	Pawnee, Oklahoma........	851	3	7	$5.00
Cheyenne and Arapaho,					Pima, Ariz.................11,518		3	8	8.00
Oklahoma.............	3,598	3	8	8.00	Pine Ridge, S. Dak........	5,611	1	8	8.00
Cheyenne River, S. Dak....	2,816	3	8	8.00	Ponca, Oklahoma.........	533	3	7	5.00
Crow Creek, S. Dak.......	1,104	3	8	8.00					
Devil's Lake, N. Dak......	2,356	3	8	8.00	Puyallup, Wash...........	1,814 { 6		8	5.00
Flathead, Mont..........	2,018	4	8	8.00		10		8	3.00
Fort Hall, Idaho..........	1,600	3	8	8.00					
Green Bay, Wis...........	3,320	3	8	4.17	Santee, Nebr.............	1,354	3	8	8.00
Kiowa, Oklahoma.........	4,088	3	8	8.00	Shoshone, Wyo...........	1,945	4	8	8.00
Klamath, Oregon.........	904	3	8	8.00	Siletz, Oregon............	606	1	8	5.00
Lower Brulé, S. Dak.......	1,067	3	8	8.00	Standing Rock, N. Dak....	4,110	3	8	8.00
Mescalero, N. Mex.......	474	2	8	5.00	Tongue River, Mont.......	867	3	8	8.00
Nevada, Nev.............	736	3	8	8.00	Umatilla, Oregon.........	983	2	8	8.00
Nez Percés, Idaho........	1,450	3	8	8.00	Yakama, Wash...........	1,675	3	8	4.17
Otoe, Oklahoma..........	396	3	7	5.00	Yankton, S. Dak..........	1,760	3	8	8.00
					Total.....................		93		

The importance, dignity, and in many cases unpopularity of the position of an Indian judge is such that it should command a salary of at least $10 per month; and the services rendered by the court are of such value in promoting good order and good morals in the community, as well as in familiarizing Indians with the customs, practices, and ideas which they will hereafter meet in white communities, that courts ought to be established for nearly every agency. To enable the office to do this the full amount asked for this year, viz, $15,000, will be required, and I trust that Congress at its next session will recognize the wisdom of appropriating that sum.

The efficiency and helpfulness of these courts when properly organized and conducted is shown in the accompanying extracts from reports of Indian agents. Other testimony to the same effect will be found in the annual reports of agents herewith:

Devil's Lake Agency, N. Dak.—The method of procedure before the court is in accordance with the rules prescribed in "Rules governing the Court of Indian Offenses" as nearly as may be, the officer making the charge, the judge weighing the evidence submitted on both sides and rendering the decision in accordance with the rules and the facts developed in evidence. The agent reviews the proceedings of the court and rarely sees fit to disapprove of them. Records of the court are now being kept, but have not been heretofore, so far as I can learn.

The general influence of the court on the reservation is exceedingly salutary. Our present court exercises very good judgment in the trial of causes and do the very best they can, I think.

Standing Rock Agency, N. Dak.—The Court of Indian Offenses was organized at this agency in October, 1883, by the appointment of the captain, lieutenant, and a private of the Indian police as judges, the private being succeeded in 1885 by John Grass, sr., who, with the two officers of the Indian police, served as judges up to December 31, 1888, at which time the police officers were relieved of this duty and regular appointees under office authority succeeded them, the court being constituted as follows:

John Grass, sr., age forty-eight (present age), appointed January 1, 1889. Served as judge from 1885 to March 31, 1890, but was not carried on the rolls as such until January 1, 1889, there being no pay attached to the office before that time. John Grass is a very intelligent, full-blooded Indian, a man of excellent judgement, impartial in decision, and of general good character. He is the head chief of the Blackfeet Sioux, speaks and understands English, wears citizen's dress, and conforms to the white man's ways. He will use his influence in favor of the allotment of lands, is in favor of education of Indian children, and a progressive Indian to all intents and purposes. Gall, age fifty-two (present age), was appointed judge January 1, 1889, and served from that time to March 31, 1890. Gall is an intelligent, full-blooded Indian, and a chief of the Hunkpapa band; he bears a good, general character, does not speak or understand English, wears citizen's dress, and conforms to the white man's ways. He is at present non-committal on the subject of allotments, but I believe when the time arrives he will declare in favor of them. I know him to be in favor of education of Indian children, and a progressive Indian in all respects, with the above doubtful exception.

Standing Soldier, age forty-three (present age), appointed judge January 1, 1889, served from that time to March 31, 1890. Standing Soldier is a full-blooded Indian belonging to the Lower Yanktonais band, and like the other two is a man of good character. He does not speak English; wears citizen's dress, and conforms to the white man's ways. He will use his influence in favor of allotments in severalty, and I know him to be in favor of education, and a progressive Indian. All the three judges are popular among and respected by their people.

The above is the personnel of the court as constituted prior to March 31, 1890, at which time the compensation ceased and these judges ceased to serve. Since then the duties have been performed by members of the police force. I consider it, however, objectionable to have members of the police force act as judges, as frequently, or rather in a majority of cases, it happens that the police are the prosecutors; in addition to this, there are many other objectionable reasons against the system.

There were 91 cases brought before the court during the year of a criminal nature, besides the settlement of disputes involving ownership of property, damages caused by cattle trespass, dividing lines, hay meadows, etc. The following is a synopsis of the criminal cases:

Adultery, 8; assault, 9; attempt at rape, 10; taking second wife, 3; taking second husband, 2; elopement with another man's wife, 3; desertion of wife and family by husband, 7; desertion of husband and family by wife, 3; seduction, 1; resisting arrest by police, 6; abusive language, 2; maiming cattle, 3; malicious lying, 1; evil speaking, 1; wife beating, 1; offering insult to married women, 4; selling rations, 2; drunkenness, 2; larceny, 4; family quarrels, incompatibility, etc., 19. The punishments imposed by the court were chiefly imprisonment in the agency guard-house, at hard labor during the day, from 10 to 90 days, according to the nature of the offense. In 11 cases guns were forfeited by the offender, others were required to make good property destroyed, and cash fines aggregating $87 the past year were imposed.

The method of procedure before the court is copied, as far as practicable, from the procedure in the white man's court, witnesses being produced in support of prosecution and defense and the decision of the majority of judges rules. The head farmer, who was a mixed blood, attended the court in most cases in the character of clerk and took a pencil memoranda of the proceedings, but no regular record is kept. The general influence of the court tends to reduce crime amongst Indians, and is a means of settling many vexatious differences between members of the tribe; it promotes good government and civilization and prepares the Indians for the inevitable trial by judge and jury when they shall become citizens of the United States. I recommend that the court at this agency be reorganized and constituted of three disinterested and influential men, having good reputations amongst their people, and whose judgment and opinions are respected, and that an adequate compensation be paid them for their services of not less than $10 per month, and that the office and pay be continuous.

Mescalero Agency, New Mexico.—The court of Indian offenses is composed of three intelligent Indians, who preside with becoming dignity and render impartial judgment. The salutary effect produced by the existence of this court is best evidenced by the infrequency of offenses. After a few trials of offenders and their judicious punishment by order of the court there was a sudden decline in the number of cases for trial, and the repugnance to appearing in court as a culprit is so general that it is seldom necessary to convene it. An efficient police is ever ready to enforce its mandates and the substantial jail hard by is a silent terror to would-be evil-doers. It is apparent the simple existence of the court exerts a powerful restraining influence.

Ponca, Pawnee, and Otoe Agency, Oklahoma.—When I took charge of this agency there was no court of Indian offenses, although they had asked the former agent to have it established. When I informed them of the establishment of said court they were highly pleased. The court is composed of the following persons, viz: Brave Chief, Sun Chief, and Eagle Chief. The first two named were appointed December 1, 1889, and have been in continuous service. Eagle Chief was appointed May 1, 1890, to fill vacancy. Brave Chief wears citizens' dress in whole, the other two in part only. They do not speak English, use their influence for the education of the children, live in comfortable log-houses, and are of good character. The number of individuals tried since the organization of the court is 24. Settlement of estates, 4; adjustment of debts, 10; burning other people's property, 3; drinking liquor and being drunk on the reservation, 4; separation of marriages, 3.

The court meets the 3d and 23rd of each month. At the opening of the court the clerk of the court reads the different cases on file and interprets them to the judges. The first case is then tried, all witnesses being sworn before giving the evidence in the case. When the case has been heard each of the judges gives his decision, which two of the same decision carries. The proceedings of the court are carefully taken down by the clerk and are written in a book. When there are no cases to be tried the court frames and makes laws to govern the reservation. The influence of the court is good, and court day always finds the room crowded with Indians. They see how white men try their criminals, and they think it is a better way than to settle with clubs and butcher-knives. They are glad to have a court among them, as it is doing good. The returned school boys are also glad, for it gives them a chance to practice law among their own people. The court of Indian offenses appointed a clerk of their court and two sheriffs to execute the law. The judges should be uniformed and a higher salary paid to make their position more honorable.

Siletz Agency, Oregon.—During the last fiscal year we have only had one judge, Charley Depoe, age fifty-six, appointed October 1, 1889, for nine months at $5 per month. He has given very general satisfaction, is an honest, upright man.

There have been 76 cases in all come up in our court during the last year, of which 48 are civil and 28 criminal, and have been disposed of as follows:

In the civil cases, 7 were dismissed, 7 were compromised, 26 were decided for plaintiff, and 8 for defendant. The amounts involved vary from one dollar up to $100.

The criminal cases were disposed of as follows: Two for indecent behavior, found guilty and sentenced to jail at hard labor, one for 5 days, and one for 20 days; 2 for fornication, one acquitted and one found guilty and sent to jail at hard labor 5 days; 2 for stealing, one acquitted and one found guilty and sent to jail at hard labor 40 days; 1 using profane language in court, sent to jail at hard labor 3 days; 3 adultery, all found guilty and sentenced, one 15 days, one 45 days, and one 50 days in jail at hard labor; 4 wife-beating, one acquitted, one sent to jail 5 days, one 20 days at hard labor, and in the other case both the husband and wife were locked up in different cells for one day each; 1 abuse of sick, found guilty and sent to jail 10 days; 2 attempted rape, acquitted; 2 destroying property, acquitted; 1 abusing stock, acquitted; 5 fighting, convicted, sent from 1 to 7 days in jail; 3 drunk and bringing whisky on the reservation, found guilty, and one sentenced 5 days and two days each in jail at hard labor.

Our court is more like a board of arbitration. We select two policemen in no way related to the litigants and place them on the case with the judge. The chief of police (who has always been my clerk) is clerk of the court; he calls the case, when the police in attendance brings in the plaintiff, who takes the witness stand, is sworn and presents his case, then his witnesses in turn, after when the defendant and witnesses are heard. The court then retires to a room, and after a sufficient time to go all over the evidence they return to the court-room and in the presence of plaintiff and defendant announce the verdict, which is recorded by the clerk under the title of the case in a book kept for that purpose. These people look upon the court as the final arbitrator of all their difficulties, and when the verdicts are strictly enforced by the agent it exerts a healthy and beneficial influence in all their business relations, and as now organized is devoid of all technicality and easily understood by the masses. I do not wish any change made in the court except that we be allowed one judge through the entire year.

Umatilla Agency, Oregon.—I have the honor to hand you herewith the information you require in regard to the court of Indian offenses on this reservation, viz: Names of judges, Pu-pu-tow-yash and Cash Cash; aged respectively forty-six and fifty-three years; appointed July 1, 1883, length of service, seven years. They are held in high esteem by both Indians and whites, speak enough English to make themselves understood, wear citizen's clothes, live in good frame houses, and have been a great help to me in suppressing lawlessness on the reservation, and have always used their influence in inducing children to attend school. Both are strongly in favor of the allotment system.

About 25 cases have been disposed of during the fiscal year just ended. Some were tried for drunkenness, some for plural marriages, and a great many minor cases were tried, such as settling trivial disputes, etc., of which no record is kept.

The fines range from $5 to $10, and when the criminals do not have money to pay their fines they are incarcerated in the agency prison, and serve a day for every dollar fine imposed until the fine is liquidated. The judges usually sit in session together, and the accused is brought before them and given a fair and impartial trial, and is either convicted or acquitted in accordance with the evidence adduced at the trial. Records are kept of all the important cases, and the findings of the court entered in a regular court docket by the agency clerk, who acts as clerk of the court of Indian offenses.

Colville Agency, Wash.—The court of Indian offenses at this agency consists of two full-blooded Indians belonging to the tribe of Lower Spokane Indians, namely: Whistleposem (Lot), who is seventy years of age, and Skos-jock-in (Cornelius), who is sixty years of age. They were selected as judges by my predecessor some time during the year 1887. They speak but very little English, but they are very intelligent Indians. They wear citizens' dress and conform to the white man's ways. They are in favor of allotments of lands and are strong believers in education and general progress in civilization.

There were 16 cases tried by the court during the past fiscal year, 14 for whisky drinking and fighting and 2 for adultery; 8 were found guilty and sentenced to imprisonment in the agency jail; 4 were sentenced to 90 days, 2 to 60 days, and 2 to 30 days.

The Indian judges try the cases coming before them similar to the way a justice of the peace tries cases in the State. They examine the witnesses very carefully, both for and against the accused, and then sum up the evidence as to the innocence or guilt of the prisoner, and if proven guilty they soon determine upon the severity of the punishment to be administered to the guilty party. They ask my advice in some cases during the progress of the trial. There is a record kept in this office of all cases tried by the court and the disposition of each case. The court has been a decided success, and the general influence of the court is growing to be an important factor in the administration of affairs at this agency. The judges should be paid a small salary, and unless this is done I fear I shall be compelled to dispense with this useful branch of the service. Considerable time is occupied in the cause, to the detriment of their farms, and it is nothing more than just that they should receive some compensation for their services, as they are unquestionably a very good assistance to the Indians in learning habits of civilization.

* * *

INDIAN POLICE

In my annual report for last year I called your attention to the subject of the Indian police, urging that increased compensation be given to these men in order that they might receive something like a fair recompense for their services. I cited the fact that the general allotment act, approved February 8, 1887 (24 *Stats.*, 390), provided that in the employment of Indian police preference should be given to those who had availed themselves of the provisions of said act and had taken allotments. Also the further fact that the Indians who had taken their lands in severalty were generally the most energetic and progressive members of their respective tribes, and that to carry out the requirements of the act and appoint them to positions where they would be compelled to devote themselves to the Government service, to the neglect of their own business, at a pittance of $10 per month, could but work hardship and retard their advancement in agriculture and other civilized pursuits.

In the act making appropriations for the fiscal year ending June 30, 1891, Congress has increased the pay of police officers from $12 to $15 per month, but that of privates remains the same, $10 per month.

I desire again earnestly to recommend that the pay of both officers and privates be increased, the former to $25 and the latter $20 per month, for the importance of this force to the service can not be over-estimated. Experience has demonstrated that its members compare favorably in fidelity, courage, loyalty, and honor with any similar body, even when composed of men of higher civilization.

The question has been asked whether these policemen can be depended upon, especially in the endeavor to suppress the liquor traffic on reservations. The testimony of the various agents is almost universal that they are proving themselves worthy of confidence and that they render valuable service in maintaining order and suppressing crime. Almost without exception they are courageous, faithful, determined men, and hesitate at no danger when carrying out instructions. They are not only of practical assistance to the agents in making arrests, removing intruders, seizing contraband goods, etc., but they also act as a deterrent upon the lawless element of a tribe, as the fact that the agent has at hand a reliable police force prevents crime and disturbance which might otherwise prevail. Further, there are frequent occasions when but for this force the services of the military would have to be called in, often at great expense; and in some instances no doubt loss of both life and property might ensue before their arrival. These contingencies are avoided by the presence at the agency, ready on call, of a reliable body of men, authorized to act for the preservation of the peace.

As an evidence of the esteem in which the Indian police force is held by the agents, and of the faithful manner in which their duties are performed, I append a few extracts taken from some of the reports for 1889, which are a fair sample of all:

[Agent McLaughlin, Standing Rock, N. Dak.]

The police force of this agency consisted of two officers and twenty-eight privates throughout the past year. They have cheerfully and promptly executed every order issued in connection with their calling, and have commanded the respect of all whites familiar with their duties as well as of the Indians. They are each assigned to a certain district, over which they have supervision, which, together with their detail at regular intervals for duty at the agency, and special duty frequently required of them, makes the service rendered very great for the small pay received. From the very nature of their service they are obliged to keep a horse, which they must furnish and feed at their own expense, and a salary of $15 per month would, therefore, be but moderate pay for the privates and $20 per month for the officers.

[Agent McChesney, Cheyenne River, S. Dak.]

The police force of this agency consists of one captain, one lieutenant, and twenty-five privates. This number is barely sufficient to preserve order in the various camps, prevent the introduction of liquor on the reserve, keep out intruders, and properly perform the many other duties required. The force has given several pleasing evidences of efficiency and devotion to duty in the year past, and carried out to the full extent of their ability all the orders given them. This class of employés deserve and should receive an increased compensation for their services.

[Agent Anderson, Crow Creek and Lower Brulé, S. Dak.]

It is difficult to say too much in praise of this efficient though poorly paid arm of the service. Their pay was advanced by the last Congress $2 per month each. They now receive, officers $12 per month and privates $10. For this pittance they are expected to furnish their own horses, preserve order, go on long courier services, and numerous other duties, besides being examples or models for the tribe. Their pay is not commensurate with their work and usefulness, and our Government should be ashamed to deny them fair compensation.

[Agent Gallagher, Pine Ridge, S. Dak.]

The police have maintained throughout the year the high point of efficiency reached by them in years past. They are valuable aids to the agent and all deserve honorable mention for their many sacrifices made in the discharge of duty.

[Agent Spencer, Rosebud, S. Dak.]

The alacrity with which they respond to the calls of duty and a readiness to arrest their own kindred, if necessary, is indicative of the responsibility assumed when donning the clothing prescribed by the Government for their use.

[Agent McKusick, Sisseton, S. Dak.]

The police force consists of one officer and five privates. From my short acquaintance and observation I find the force to be very essential and really indispensable. The Indians have learned to obey the police, and a policeman only has to notify any Indian of what is wanted and he obeys promptly. I really hope their pay will be increased to at least such an amount as will furnish them with the necessaries of life.

[Agent Bennett, Union, Ind. T.]

It is due to the police force of this agency to say that they form one of the most efficient auxiliaries to the enforcement of law and order. In this service the Indian himself is the representative of the power of the United States Government, thereby encouraging a feeling of personal responsibility that is decidedly beneficial. There are three officers and forty privates on the force, each of whom has been selected with special regard for his fitness for the duties required. There are many applications for appointment, so that there is an abundance of material from which to select the best. The majority of the men are vigorous, zealous, and fearless in execution of orders, and they have been of incalculable assistance in maintaining law and order.

During the month of July last over 5,000 gallons of intoxicating liquors were destroyed by the police of this agency. This whisky traffic is the most pernicious of all evils and the most difficult to regulate. The Indians do not manufacture it; they are advised and cautioned continuously against its dangers, and yet they are exposed to its seductive wiles and fall victims to its baneful influences. The extent of the evil may be seen from the report of the grand jury made to the United States court at Fort Smith that 95 per cent. of the criminal cases heard by that body were directly traceable to intoxicants— a terrible record of murders, assaults, robberies, and crimes of various degrees.

In July last it became my duty to report the case of one George Buente, a wholesale merchant of St. Louis, who had for several years been one of the largest whisky shippers doing business in the Territory. Buente was doing a regular wholesale business, and hardly a package of merchandise that came from his establishment was allowed to escape the vigilance of the police, and few there were that did not contain a liberal allowance of whisky. I recall a certain hogshead or cask of "queensware," which was captured at Atoka and contained a regular saloon outfit of whiskies, wines, etc. When Buente was arraigned he claimed ignorance of the law, but pleaded guilty and was fined $500 and costs. It is impossible to give you statistics showing the devastation and ruin and death caused in this agency by intoxicating drinks. The fact that at least one life a day is taken in this country as the direct result of whisky, appears not to change the desire and determination of others to die the same way.

Since I have been in charge of the agency the police have served effectively in removing intruders, suppressing crimes, preserving peace, arresting criminals, guarding Government funds, and in many other ways performing arduous and ofttimes dangerous duties. The salary of these men is entirely too meager. They were receiving $8 per month until last July, when the amount was increased to $10. They ought by every right to receive not less than $50 per month. The Government is able to and should pay its servants what they justly earn, and not require them to labor for the lowest pittance.

[Agent Wyman, Crow, Mont.]

The agency police force, composed of one captain, one lieutenant, and fourteen privates, is an excellent body of men, efficient and faithful. They have been employed for several years, and are as devoted to their duty as any body of men in the service. The increase—so richly deserved—in their salary during the current year gave them great satisfaction. I hope to be able to keep them all in the service during my administration.

[Agent Hill, Santee, Nebr.]

The Indian police and court of Indian offenses have been important factors in the administration of affairs at this agency during the past year. The police have been faithful in the discharge of the duties assigned them, quick to report to the calls and demands of the agent, and ever ready to perform the work pointed out to them. They have been valuable co-workers with the Indian court in the suppression of drunkenness and vice and prompt to report to the proper authorities any crime or misdemeanor committed upon the reservation.

* * *

INDIAN FARMING

That the Indians may as soon as possible become self-supporting and have the advantages and comforts of civilization is, of course, the wish of all those who are interested in their welfare, many of whom believe that this end is most likely to be attained by educating, encouraging, and assisting them to become farmers or to engage in stock-raising. There is, in fact, no other form of labor for a large majority of them.

That this should be a difficult undertaking may appear strange to those unfamiliar with existing conditions, conditions which seriously interfere with rapid progress or successful results. Indians who have lived to be, say, forty, without ever having done manual labor, do not offer very promising material for enterprising farmers, and a great number of the present generation are of this class. On the other hand, many are too young to understand the necessity of thinking and working for themselves, and, with no stimulating example before them, they naturally take little or no interest in work of any kind. The necessary labor and care connected with farming are irksome to them, and their half-hearted and often injudiciously directed efforts, bringing little return, are soon relaxed or altogether abandoned.

The act of March 3, 1875 (18 *Stats.*, 449), requires that all able-bodied Indians between the ages of eighteen and forty-five must labor for the benefit of themselves or of the tribe, in order to be entitled to rations. But it is obvious from experience, that the limits of twenty and forty years include all that can be expected to succeed in learning to farm for the first time, and this leaves but a limited number of the entire Indian population available.

It must also be borne in mind that great portions of some of the reservations (actually much the greater part of several of the largest reserves) are, owing to various causes, totally unfit for agricultural purposes. Whatever science or irrigation may accomplish in the future, this condition of the land at the present time makes it necessary to scatter the Indians singly or in small communities on the fertile spots of their reservations, wherever found; owing to this fact many of these small farming settlements are 60, 65, and some even 100 miles from the agency headquarters. Under these circumstances it is impossible for the agent to give the Indians the attention they require, or for the farmers employed to properly instruct and assist them, to be with them as much as they should be, or to give sufficient time to any one point.

Another drawback has been the holding of lands in common, leaving the Indian uncertain whether or not a piece of land which he had improved was actually his own property. This difficulty, however, is being removed by the allotments of lands in severalty.

Knowing the difficulties to be surmounted, I have instructed agents to require from every farmer employed by the Government a monthly statement as to his work. For this purpose blanks have been prepared which contain, among others, the following points upon which the farmer must report:

> Number of days occupied in the field during the month.
> Number of days at headquarters.
> Number of Indians assisted and instructed.
> Number of Indians who have been induced to begin farming.
> Number of acres plowed.
> Number of acres planted.
> The condition of stock.
> The condition of agricultural implements.

He is also directed to state the most pressing needs of the Indians under his charge for such articles as lumber, seeds, agricultural implements, and stock.

These reports indorsed by the agents have been prepared by many of the farmers and, as a general thing, indicate that they are qualified for the work intrusted to them.

From these reports, some of them covering only nine months, from October, 1889, to June, 1890, it is ascertained that during that time in 35,000 cases Indians have been personally assisted and instructed in farming; that 46,000 acres have been plowed, and that at nearly every agency the need of a greater supply of lumber, seeds, and agricultural implements is very pressing. It is also reported that 1,136 Indians who never farmed before have been induced to commence farming.

According to last year's census the entire Indian population on the reservations where farmers were allowed during the year was but 107,283. A close estimate as to the number of those who can be expected to work on a farm would be one-seventh of this number—15,326. This for the nine months in question gives 8 per cent. as those who have been induced for the first time to commence farming. Had these reports been for the year, from all farmers employed, and exhaustive instead of partial, these figures would have been largely increased. On the whole, I consider these reports encouraging.

In my last annual report I called attention to an appropriation made for the year ending June 30, 1889, to increase the number of instructors in farming among Indians. The appropriation provided for the employment of farmers to superintend and direct the work of Indians making effort toward self-support, in addition to the one farmer usually allowed each agency, and a requirement was inserted that these "additional farmers" to their employment in the Indian Service.

The letter addressed by this office to Indian agents in pursuance of this legislation was embodied in my last report. For convenience of reference in connection with remarks on replies thereto part of that letter is again quoted, as follows:

> That I may know exactly the qualifications of each farmer at your agency, and in what respect he is or is not such an employé as the letter and the spirit of the act requires, I desire you to furnish me with the following information:
>
> (1) Give the name of each farmer at your agency.
>
> (2) Date of appointment and when he entered upon duty.
>
> (3) Was he actually engaged for at least five years practically in the occupation of farming previous to his appointment?
>
> (4) In what locality was he engaged in farming previous to his appointment?
>
> (5) Has he a full knowledge of the proper use and care of modern agricultural implements and machinery?
>
> (6) Does it appear by his selection of farm sites, seeds, time and manner of planting, cultivating, reaping, etc., that he thoroughly understands the peculiarities of the soil, seasons, etc., in your locality?
>
> (7) Has he at all times since his appointment faithfully endeavored to discharge his duty by striving to interest the Indians in farm work; in the care of their crops; of stock and their increase, especially brood mares; in the care of their farming implements, both when in use and when not in use; and in that general good management, husbandry, and foresight indispensable to successful farming?
>
> (8) Is he married or single, and is his family with him at the agency?
>
> (9) Admitting that he is an experienced farmer, having all the qualifications above referred to, is he of such a temperament as enables him to impart this knowledge readily to others, particularly Indians?
>
> (10) Is he a man of good moral character, strictly temperate, and disposed to treat the Indians kindly and with patience and consideration for their peculiarities, so that he has secured their confidence and respect?
>
> (11) Cite some of the more prominent of the results of his work among the Indians, such as number of Indians he has induced to begin farming who had never farmed before, giving the names of the Indians who have so commenced, and the number of acres now cultivated by each; increase of stock held by individual Indians, stating the number and description of that owned by each; the number, character, and present condition of the wagons, plows, and all agricultural implements in the possession of each Indian

farmer, stating whether any have failed to provide proper shelter for their stock in winter and for their agricultural implements, wagons, etc., when not in use, and the reason for failure; and give in general your opinion in regard to him personally, and the manner in which he discharges his duties, making such recommendations as you may desire for the best interests of the service and the Indians, and as would, if carried out, result in a more strict compliance with the requirements and purposes of the act. In short, has he succeeded in establishing farming among his Indians on a paying basis, and if not, what is the cause of failure?

It is not the desire of the office to make any unnecessary changes in the force of farmers, nor to unnecessarily disturb those who are competent and faithful. On the other hand, the quality of the service rendered is a paramount consideration, and the good of the Indians must be regarded as outweighing any personal interests in favor of the farmers. With these considerations in view, I wish to know whether, in your opinion, the good of the service would be promoted essentially by any change. If so, state it frankly, and give your reasons for thinking so.

The replies to this letter were in general satisfactory, and called for but few changes among the farmers employed. None were made except for cause. In all cases of employment of farmers since the passage of the act, the requirements of the act have been strictly complied with.

The answers to the questions embodied in paragraph eleven are important, but are too voluminous to be quoted here. I may very briefly refer to some of them, however, as they contain suggestions which are pertinent and of general application to the subject.

One agent (from North Dakota) writes:

I desire to state in regard to the farmers (employés) at this agency that they are men of more than ordinary intelligence and well qualified for the positions they hold; in short, they are practical farmers in every sense of the word . . .

At the time these Indians abandoned their village life (that is, all living close to the agency) they scattered over such an extent of territory that it is now impossible for two farmers (all that can be allowed that agency under existing appropriations) to visit them and give instructions as often as necessary.

One farmer resides permanently in a settlement 25 miles west of the agency. The Indians are scattered along the river for a distance of more than 20 miles on both sides of it. In visiting these Indians he is required to cross and recross the river and to swim his horse at the same time.

Another agent says that his agency—one of the largest in South Dakota—is allowed only an agency farmer and three additional farmers; that all were actually engaged in agricultural pursuits for much longer than five years previous to appointment, and that they are men who endeavor to discharge their duties faithfully, and who try to interest the Indians in farm work, care of stock and its increase, care of farming implements, etc.; that until very recently the Indians made no provision for wintering their stock, but now nearly all have good shelter for their work horses, brood mares, and stock cattle, and understand the necessity of putting up a supply of hay in season.

While this agent asserts that all is being done that four men can do on so large a reservation and that great improvement and progress has been made in the last few years, he gives it as his opinion that the Indians during the last year have not been very successful, although prospering as well as could be expected, considering recent very dry seasons; and he concludes that unless climatic conditions change materially, the Indians, when thrown on their own resources, must depend largely on stock raising, and in view of this he has instructed his farmers to look closely after this branch of practical education.

Another agent in South Dakota reports that his farmers are qualified for the positions they hold; that they take an individual interest in each Indian, and that they have induced a great many to commence farming, while nearly all now have shelter for their stock, wagons, tools, etc., and put up hay in good time. He advises that money should be expended on houses and wells for them, so that they can live on their allotments during the winter, and believes that if they are wisely aided they will eventually be able to farm successfully.

The foregoing are fair samples of the reports of the agents from the Dakotas and Montana. They agree on two points: First, that the Indians must be located in small farming communities on the lands best fitted for agriculture, without regard to distance from agency headquarters, and that a farmer must reside with them, a man of practical ability, experienced in farming, possessed of good judgment, and one who takes a personal interest and pride in his work; and second, that the raising of stock-cattle and good horses must be the leading industry on many of these reservations.

The reports from the agencies of Wyoming and Nebraska show the conditions there to be somewhat similar. The Indians are beginning to comprehend their condition, to recognize the fact that they must strive to make the most of their opportunities, and that by intelligence and industry alone can they succeed. They seem willing to learn, and many of them are ambitious and industrious. The farming Indians are making as good progress as can be expected. As in the Dakotas and Montana, however, stock-raising must in the end be their chief reliance for support, unless the climate changes with the cultivation of the soil, or irrigation is extensively resorted to. In Wyoming the climate and soil are better suited for agriculture than they are in Nevada, and the agent seems to be hopeful about the future of his Indians if they are only properly instructed and assisted for the present. The farmers at these agencies are reported as competent for their positions, but embarrassed by being called on to look after large numbers of Indians living long distances apart.

The reports from Washington, Oregon, and California show that the conditions for farming in these States are much more favorable than in those farther east. Last winter, however, was very severe in all these States, and the Indians, who are largely stock-raisers, suffered greatly. But they are not discouraged, and under the direction of the farmers will put up a good supply of hay for next winter. With a liberal provision for competent instruction and assistance, the outlook for them is encouraging.

The Indians in Colorado, Arizona, and New Mexico depend in a great measure on irrigation, attempting little besides stock-raising. In the selection of farmers for each locality care is taken to obtain men of experience in these particulars. From the reports of the agents it is inferred that the farmers now employed are doing good work, but the Indians will require much more instruction and assistance before they can be independent of help. As they are generally willing, and in many cases anxious, to become entirely self-supporting, the efforts of the Government should not be relaxed, but rather increased.

Reports from Idaho, the Indian Territory, and Oklahoma are also encouraging, indicating that the farmers have done efficient work during the past year, and that the Indians are more than ever interested in agriculture and stock-raising. Though more advanced than many others, they too will require constant attention from the agency farmers for some time to come, and should not be neglected or allowed to become discouraged.

The following table, prepared from the reports of agents, exhibits status of farming, etc., by Indians, exclusive of the five civilized tribes, up to date, crops ungathered being estimated.

Showing number of allotments made, acres cultivated, crops raised, and other results of Indian farming.

Number of allotments made to July 1, 1890, under act of February 7, 1887.	15,166
Number of Indian families engaged in farming	27,328
Number of acres under fence	608,937
Number of acres under cultivation (by Indians)	288,613

CROPS RAISED.

Bushels of wheat	881,419
Bushels of oats and barley	545,032
Bushels of corn	1,139,297
Bushels of vegetables	482,580
Tons of hay cut	130,712
Pounds of butter made	92,968

NUMBER AND KIND OF STOCK OWNED BY INDIANS.

Horses and mules	443,244
Cattle	170,419
Swine	87,477
Sheep and goats	964,759
Domestic fowls (all kinds)	143,056

FARMING STATIONS

One drawback which at ration agencies has greatly hindered progress in farming has been the practice of requiring the whole body of Indians to come to agency headquarters to receive supplies. For example, many of the Indians connected with the various Sioux agencies are located in communities of fifty to one hundred and fifty persons, on lands which they are engaged in cultivating, many miles from agency headquarters. To compel such to come to the agency, 60 or 70 miles each week, or even month, through the storms of winter and the heat of summer, bringing the whole family, as is the custom, leaving crops and cattle to care for themselves, wearing out teams and wagons, and wasting time by being almost constantly on the road, is to inflict hardship on the very best element of this tribe—those who are trying to become self-supporting and are faithfully endeavoring by their own labor to make homes for themselves and to secure their families against want.

This class should be encouraged by every available means in their struggle toward civilization and self-support and they should have all the advantages which a white farmer requires. Their supplies should be convenient, and it should not be necessary for them to drop their farm-work at a critical time and travel a hundred miles to have a plow fixed.

They should have the constant presence of an experienced farmer to teach and encourage them, and it would be well that his wife should be able to teach the women and girls their domestic duties. The example set before them of a well-conducted home would be of great benefit. It might also be that each of the farmers could, with Indian assistants, cultivate a small farm himself, the returns from the farm to go toward reducing the expenses of the station.

There should be a day-school, at least, established in each community.

There should be a blacksmith shop at each station, with a good Indian mechanic in charge, who should also be able to do rough carpenter work, repairing wagons, etc.; and tools of both kinds should be furnished him.

Arrangements should be made by the agents to visit these stations once a month and to take with them, and issue there, a monthly ration of supplies, taking the receipts of the Indians as required by law.

Should this plan be adopted, a considerable amount of transportation will be necessary, and this will give employment to Indian teamsters, who will thus be enabled to earn some money at times when they can spare their horses and wagons from farm-work.

On the 3d of last March I addressed a letter to the Department setting forth the evils of the present system and outlining the plan suggested above, which received your approval. Active measures are now in progress for the carrying out of the new plan at the following agencies: Rosebud, Crow Creek, and Lower Brulé, S. Dak.; Standing Rock, N. Dak.; Crow, Mont.; Shoshone, Wyo.; Uintah and Ouray, Utah; and Cheyenne and Arapaho, and Kiowa, Comanche and Wichita, Oklahoma.

The establishing of these new, independent communities will of necessity increase for a time the number of farmers required for their instruction. The estimates submitted by the various agents for such additional farmers as are required for the year ending June 30, 1891, amount to over $62,000. The sum appropriated by Congress is $60,000. In view of the progress now being made in the allotment of lands, and of the importance that the Indians should be prepared for this step by intelligent instruction in the proper use of their land, and considering that every acre put under cultivation yields a substantial return for the labor and money expended, I recommend that for the fiscal year ending June 30, 1892, the sum of $100,000 be appropriated for the pay of additional farmers.

The Indians should be given distinctly to understand that the employment by the Government of white farmers is a temporary expedient, to be abandoned at an early day. They should be taught that they must very soon depend entirely upon themselves, and that their future prosperity will depend largely upon the use they are now willing to make of the opportunities for learning to farm offered to them by the Government.

IRRIGATION

Large bodies of lands now included in reservations are practically worthless for farming purposes, without irrigation. The spread of the white population over the public domain, the reduction of reservations, the confining of Indians to ever-narrowing borders, makes the problem of their support one of increasing difficulty and urgency. White people are able to combine in the creation of expensive and extensive irrigating plans, which the Indians can not do. From the attention which I have been able to give to the subject, I am led to believe that by the expenditure of moderate sums of money in constructing reservoirs and irrigating ditches, employing Indians to perform most of the labor, and instructing them in the construction, care, and use of these reservoirs and ditches, large numbers of them may be prepared for self-support. It is my purpose during the coming year to pay special attention to this matter, collect suitable data, and lay before you in my next annual report some plan of operation. The matter can not safely be deferred any longer. What has already been done in this direction warrants belief in the advisability of doing much more.

* * *

RULES FOR INDIAN SCHOOLS

IN GENERAL

The importance attached to the subject of Indian education is set forth in the following letter addressed by the honorable the Secretary of the Interior to each newly appointed Indian agent:

In connection with your appointment as agent at the —————— agency, I am directed by the President to inform you that the office to which you are appointed is considered one of far more than ordinary importance, both for the interests of the Government and of the Indians who will be brought under your charge and direction; that sobriety and integrity must mark the conduct of every one connected or associated directly or indirectly with the agency under your charge; that an improved condition in the affairs of the agency will be expected within a reasonable time, both as to methods of doing business and as to the condition of the Indians; that the education and proper training of the Indian children and the agricultural and other industrial pursuits of the adult Indians must receive your constant and careful attention, to the end that they may be advanced in the ways of civilization and to the condition of self-support; and that your commission will be held with the express understanding that you will use your utmost endeavors to further these objects and purposes.

The general purpose of the Government is the preparation of Indian youth for assimilation into the national life by such a course of training as will prepare them for the duties and privileges of American citizenship. This involves the training of the hand in useful industries; the development of the mind in independent and self-directing power of thought; the impartation of useful practical knowledge; the culture of the moral nature, and the formation of character. Skill, intelligence, industry, morality, manhood, and womanhood are the ends aimed at.

Government schools for Indians are divided into five general classes: Reservation day schools, reservation boarding schools of first and second grades, and industrial training schools of first and second grades.

It is the duty and design of the Government to remove, by the shortest method, the ignorance, inability, and fears of the Indians, and to place them on an equality with other races in the United States. In organizing this system of schools, the fact is not overlooked that Indian schools, as such, should be preparatory and temporary; that eventually they will become unnecessary, and a full and free entrance be obtained for Indians into the public school system of the country. To this end all officers and employés of the Indian school service should work.

Superintendent of Indian Schools
Under the law it is the duty of the Superintendent of Indian Schools—

To visit and inspect the schools in which Indians are taught in whole or in part from appropriations from the United States Treasury, and report to the Commissioner from appropriations from the United States Treasury, and report to the Commissioner of Indian Affairs what, in his judgment, are the defects, if any, in any of them in system, in administration, or in the means for the most effective advancement of the pupils therein toward civilization and self-support, and what changes are needed to remedy such defects as may exist; and to perform such other duties as may be imposed upon him by the Commissioner of Indian Affairs subject to the approval of the Secretary of the Interior.

Supervisors of Education

The supervisor of education appointed for a special locality shall visit and inspect the boarding and day schools under his supervision; advise with the teachers, give them instructions in methods of teaching, and report to the Commissioner of Indian Affairs what defects, if any, exist in the schools visited, referring specially to the qualifications and efficiency of each teacher, and the discipline and progress of each school, and shall recommend such measures as in his judgment will improve the condition of the schools and increase the interest of pupils and parents.

RESERVATION BOARDING SCHOOLS

Duties of Officers and Employés

Agent

1. The agent is the highest authority on the reservation in all matters pertaining to the schools, as well as to other interests of the Indians; but he is not authorized to give directions to school employés regarding their school duties, except through the superintendent.

2. The agent shall have general supervision of all school work among the Indians under his charge. He must visit all schools whether Government, contract, or mission, at least four times each year, keep himself thoroughly informed as to their condition and efficiency, and make quarterly reports concerning the same to the Indian Office.

3. It is the duty of the agent to keep the schools filled with Indian pupils, and, so far as practicable, to place every Indian child of school age in school. He should accomplish this by persuasion, if possible, but, when milder methods fail, he may withhold rations or annuities, or use such other proper means as will produce the desired result.

On reservations where there is more than one school and more than one tribe of Indians there should be in each school pupils from each of the tribes. This will facilitate English speaking by the pupils and tend to overcome the race and tribal prejudices of Indians.

4. It is desirable that an equal number of each sex be kept in school. It is likewise advantageous to the children to enroll them at as early an age as possible; but children under five years of age shall not be enrolled except by permission of the Commissioner of Indian Affairs.

5. The agent is expected to see that the pupils have proper moral, mental, and industrial training; that their physical welfare is properly cared for; that abundant wholesome food, suitable clothing, sufficient fuel, and an ample supply of good water are provided the schools; that sanitary laws and regulations are complied with; that the buildings are properly heated, lighted, and ventilated; that the dormitories are not overcrowded, and that proper medical attendance and supervision are afforded.

6. The agent shall exercise merely an advisory supervision over a bonded school within the limits of his agency jurisdiction, or adjacent thereto. He is

required to cooperate with the superintendent in every way practicable for the general well-being of the school. He shall endeavor to keep the school filled with pupils, and when necessary shall assist with his police force in maintaining order, preventing desertions, and returning runaways, and he shall exert his authority whenever necessary to maintain the discipline or efficiency of the school.

School Superintendent

7. The superintendent shall have immediate general control of the school. He is responsible for the discipline, the classification of pupils, and the distribution of duties among the employés. His orders must be carried into effect, both in letter and in spirit. He shall act as principal teacher, unless a principal teacher is provided for the school, and in the absence of an industrial teacher, shall have immediate charge of the duties usually belonging to that employé.

8. The superintendent shall arrange a regular program of school-room exercises and industrial work, and assign teachers and employés to their duties in accordance therewith, clearly defining the duties of each. He shall also decide upon the hours of recitation and industrial work for each pupil in the school.

9. The superintendent shall, as occasion may require, hold meetings with his associate teachers and employés for consultation as to the general welfare of the school; shall treat his subordinates with respect, support them in the exercise of proper authority, and ordinarily shall issue orders to individual pupils through those only who have the special care of them.

10. When the superintendent finds it advisable to correct faults of teachers or employés or to call attention to inefficient service or neglect of duty on their part, it must be done at some other time and place than in the presence of pupils. No public reprimand of an employé is permitted.

11. In cases of controversy or want of harmony which the superintendent is unable to settle amicably, appeal may be made to the agent, who shall give a hearing, in his office if practicable, to all parties concerned, and if he shall be unable to restore cordial relations among the school employés, he shall report all the facts to the Indian Office, suspending offenders if the interests of the service require it, pending definite instructions from the Commissioner of Indian Affairs.

12. The superintendent must give close personal attention to every department of the school. He is expected to visit all employés while in the performance of their duties as frequently as may be necessary to ascertain not only the character of work done by them, but to advise them wherein they fail in fidelity, efficiency, or discipline. The industrial work among the boys must have his special attention. He should so supervise this branch of the service as to leave no excuse for neglect upon the part of teachers or pupils.

13. Once each week regularly at a stated hour the superintendent is required to make a personal inspection of the dormitories and infirmaries,

observing the personal appearance and clothing of the pupils, and the condition of the rooms and everything therein. At such time each pupil must be in his own proper place in the dormitory or infirmary. This personal, vital contact, weekly, with every pupil in the school should enable the superintendent to give such advice and direction as will promote the physical, mental, and moral well-being of those under his charge. It should be made with conscientious fidelity and thoroughness.

14. The superintendent must reside in the school buildings, and where practicable, in the boys' department.

15. The superintendent cooperating with the physician and matron must see that all cases of infectious and contagious diseases are isolated, and that toilet articles used by pupils having inflamed eyes, skin diseases, or other such disorders, are not used by other pupils.

16. In cases not covered by these rules the superintendent is expected to use his discretion and judgment, and he may adopt for the administration of the minor affairs of the school a special code of rules, not inconsistent with those herein.

17. The superintendent shall forward all official communications to the Indian Office through the agent. He is especially advised that absolute union of purpose and effort is essential to the efficiency of his school, and he should therefore strive to cooperate heartily with the agent, upon whose support and friendship much of his success must depend.

18. The superintendent shall submit to the Indian Office, through the agent, at the close of each school year, an annual report giving a full history for the year of the school and of each of its departments. He may require that written reports be made to him at the close of the year by the principal teacher, matron, industrial teacher, and other employés.

19. The superintendent of a bonded school on or adjacent to an Indian reservation is independent of the agent, so far as school management, the duties defined in his bond, and department regulations are concerned, but, as already stated, the agent is expected to exercise an advisory supervision of the school and to report to the Indian Office his observations. The success of the school must depend largely upon the cordial coöperation with the agent, and harmonious relations between the superintendent and agent should be maintained.

Clerk

20. The clerk of a bonded school, if there be one, shall perform such clerical duties as may be required, and may be assigned to other duties by the superintendent. In small bonded schools the clerk will act as teacher or industrial teacher, or in such other capacity as the superintendent may direct.

Physician

21. The school physician shall have oversight of all sanitary matters connected with the school, and in addition to his professional duties shall give the pupils simple, appropriate talks on the elementary principles of physiology and hygiene, explaining the processes of digestion and assimila-

tion of food, the circulation of the blood, the functions of the skin, etc., by which they may understand the necessity for proper habits of eating and drinking, for cleanliness, ventilation, and other hygienic conditions. The correct manner of treating emergency cases, such as hemorrhage, fainting, drowning, prostration from heat, etc., should be explained. Classes composed of the most advanced and intelligent pupils should be formed for instruction by the physician in regard to nursing and care of the sick, administering medicines, preparing food for invalids, and any other points of like character on which it would be proper to give such pupils instruction. In the absence of a school physician, these duties will devolve upon the agency physician so far as practicable. A permanent record must be kept of all cases treated by the physician.

Teachers

22. The principal teacher, under directions from the superintendent, shall have charge of the school-room exercises. He shall arrange classes, define hours of study and recitation, supervise the literary work, teach classes as the superintendent may direct, and perform the duties of any teacher who may be temporarily absent. School-room exercises should occupy about five hours each day, and each pupil should average not less than three hours' work in the school room daily.

23. The duties of each teacher shall be those assigned by the superintendent and principal teacher. Where there is but one teacher he or she shall be secretary of the school and shall keep the school register. Any teacher may be required by the superintendent to assist the clerical work incident to the school.

Matron

24. The matron shall have charge of the dormitories, see that the beds are properly cared for, that the toilet of the girls is carefully made each morning, that the clothing of both girls and boys is kept in proper condition, and also shall have general oversight of the kitchen and dining room, and all the domestic affairs of the school. With the coöperation of the superintendent she shall see to it that the principal part of the work in the kitchen, laundry, dining room, and sewing room is performed by the girls of the school, who shall be regularly detailed for that purpose. She is expected to reside in the girls' building.

Industrial Teacher

25. The industrial teacher, under direction of the superintendent, shall attend to all the outside manual labor connected with the school, cultivating thoroughly the school farm and garden, caring for the stock belonging to the school, keeping a supply of fuel on hand, making repairs on buildings, and seeing that the school property and grounds are kept in good order. All such work must be done, with his assistance and supervision, by the boys of the school regularly detailed for that purpose.

Cook

26. The cook, with the assistance of the pupils, who must be regularly detailed for that purpose, shall prepare all food required for the school,

including such as may be needed by the sick, attend to the setting of the tables, washing of dishes, and cleaning of the lamps each day; see that everything in the kitchen and dining room is kept in proper order, and that the kitchen and dining room are locked at night, and shall be responsible to the superintendent for all the articles in her department.

Seamstress

27. The seamstress, with the assistance of the girls, must perform all kinds of sewing required, including mending, and must teach the girls to make and mend both their own clothing and that of the boys.

Laundress

28. The laundress, with the assistance of the girls, must do all the washing and ironing required for the school. If laundering for employés is done in the school, it shall be paid for by them, the pay for the same to be given to the girls and the laundress who perform the service, upon an agreed basis approved by the superintendent.

Other Employés

29. Mechanics and all other employés not above named shall be assigned their duties by the superintendent, and to the duties usually appertaining to their position the superintendent may add any other duty which the good of the school may require.

30. Some employé must be required by the superintendent, in addition to his regular duties, to have charge of the ringing of bells and keeping time for the school; to see that the boys retire properly; that their clothing and persons are suitably cared for; that they are regularly bathed; that their toilet is neatly made in the morning; and that they are prompt at meals and details; and he shall keep a correct record of absentees.

31. Indians should be employed in preference to whites in positions which they are competent to fill. Every school should have one or more Indians among its employés.

General Rules

32. Employés are expected to reside in the school buildings when quarters there are provided for them; otherwise, as near to the buildings as practicable. Employés must keep their rooms in order at all times.

33. Employés are not allowed to have pupils in their rooms except by permission of the superintendent for specified reasons.

34. No person, other than an attaché of the school, shall be allowed in any school building later than 9.30 p. m. except by special permission of the superintendent.

35. A retiring bell rung at 9 p. m. (or later during warm weather, if advisable) shall be the signal for absolute quiet in all the dormitories and adjacent rooms.

36. Every night, at irregular periods, some person or persons duly assigned to such duty must "make the rounds," visiting every portion of the school buildings and premises, to guard against fire, prevent intrusion of

unauthorized persons, and detect any improper conduct on the part of pupils or others.

37. Social dancing, card playing, gambling, profanity, and smoking are strictly prohibited in the school buildings and on the premises. Pupils are forbidden to carry concealed weapons.

38. There shall be a session of school each evening for reading, study, singing, or other exercises, at the close of which the pupils shall retire in an orderly manner to their dormitories. The employments for Saturday shall be arranged by the superintendent and matron to the best advantage of the school.

39. The Sabbath must be properly observed. There shall be a Sabbath school or some other suitable service every Sunday, which pupils shall be required to attend. The superintendent may require employés to attend and participate in all the above exercises; but any employé declining as a matter of conscience shall be excused from attending and participating in any or all religious exercises.

40. Every school should be carefully graded and pupils should be classified according to their capacity and scholarship and be promoted from grade to grade under such rules as may be prescribed by the superintendent. At the close of each term pupils should be examined in all the studies pursued during the term and promotions should be made on the basis of these examinations. Pupils who have completed the school course should be reported to the Indian Office for promotion to a school of higher grade.

41. All instruction must be in the English language. Pupils must be compelled to converse with each other in English, and should be properly rebuked or punished for persistent violation of this rule. Every effort should be made to encourage them to abandon their tribal language. To facilitate this work it is essential that all school employés be able to speak English fluently, and that they speak English exclusively to the pupils, and also to each other in the presence of pupils.

42. Instruction in music must be given at all schools. Singing should be a part of the exercises of each school session, and wherever practicable instruction in instrumental music should be given.

43. Except in cases of emergency, pupils shall not be removed from school either by their parents or others, nor shall they be transferred from a Government to a private school without special authority from the Indian Office.

44. The school buildings should be furnished throughout with plain, inexpensive, but substantial furniture. Dormitories or lavatories should be so supplied with necessary toilet articles, such as soap, towels, mirrors, combs, hair, shoe, nail, and tooth brushes, and wisp brooms, as to enable the pupils to form exact habits of personal neatness.

45. Good and healthful provisions must be supplied in abundance; and they must be well cooked and properly placed on the table. A regular bill of fare for each day of the week should be prepared and followed. Meals must

be served regularly and neatly. Pains should be taken not only to have the food healthful and the table attractive, but to have the bill of fare varied. The school farm and dairy should furnish an ample supply of vegetables, fruits, milk, butter, cottage cheese, curds, eggs, and poultry. Coffee and tea should be furnished sparingly; milk is preferable to either, and children can be taught to use it. Pupils must be required to attend meals promptly after proper attention to toilet, and at least one employé must be in the dining room during each meal to supervise the table manners of the pupils and to see that all leave the table at the same time and in good order.

46. The superintendent will establish a common mess for the employés and may prescribe rules governing the same. Their meals may be prepared by the school cook, if such work will not interfere with the proper discharge of her regular duties, and she shall receive from the members of the mess a fair allowance for the extra duty thus imposed upon her, such allowance to be divided among them pro rata; or they may hire a cook who is not a school employé. The matron, under the direction of the superintendent, may have immediate charge of the employés' mess.

47. So far as practicable, a uniform style of clothing for the school should be adopted. Two plain, substantial suits, with extra pair of trousers for each boy, and three neat, well-made dresses for each girl, if kept mended, ought to suffice for week-day wear for one year. For Sunday wear each pupil should be furnished a better suit. The pupils should also be supplied with underwear adapted to the climate, with night clothes, and with handkerchiefs, and, if the climate requires it, with overcoats or cloaks and with overshoes.

48. The buildings, outhouses, fences, and walks should at all times be kept in thorough repair. Where practicable, the grounds should be ornamented with trees, grass, and flowers.

49. There should be a flag staff at every school, and the American flag should be hoisted, in suitable weather, in the morning and lowered at sunset daily.

50. Special hours should be allotted for recreation. Provision should be made for outdoor sports, and the pupils should be encouraged in daily healthful exercise under the eye of a school employé; simple games should also be devised for indoor amusement. They should be taught the sports and games enjoyed by white youth, such as baseball, hopscotch, croquet, marbles, bean bags, dominoes, checkers, logomachy, and other word and letter games, and the use of dissected maps, etc. The girls should be instructed in simple fancy work, knitting, netting, crocheting, different kinds of embroidery, etc.

51. Separate play grounds, as well as sitting rooms, must be assigned the boys and the girls. In play and in work, as far as possible, and in all places except the school room and at meals, they must be kept entirely apart. It should be so arranged, however, that at stated times, under suitable supervision, they may enjoy each other's society; and such occasions should be used

to teach them to show each other due respect and consideration, to behave without restraint, but without familiarity, and to acquire habits of politeness, refinement, and self-possession.

52. New Year's Day, Franchise Day (February 8), Washington's Birthday (February 22), Arbor Day, Decoration Day (May 30), Fourth of July, Thanksgiving Day, and Christmas, are to be appropriately observed as holidays.

53. Corporal punishment must be resorted to only in cases of grave violations of rules, and in no instances shall any person inflict it except under the direction of the superintendent, to whom all serious questions of discipline must be referred. Employés may correct pupils for slight misdemeanors only.

54. Any pupil twelve years of age or over, guilty of persistently using profane or obscene language; of lewd conduct; stubborn insubordination; lying; fighting; wanton destruction of property; theft; or similar misbehavior, may be punished by the superintendent either by inflicting corporal punishment or imprisonment in the guardhouse; but in no case shall any unusual or cruel or degrading punishment be permitted.

55. A permanent record should be kept on file at each school showing the history of each pupil, giving name, age, sex, height, weight, chest measurements, state of health, residence, names of parents, and of tribe to which the family belongs, time of entering and leaving school, and the advancement made in education. If an English name is given to the pupil, the Indian name of the father should be retained as a surname.

Industrial Work

56. A regular and efficient system of industrial training must be a part of the work of each school. At least half of the time of each boy and girl should be devoted thereto—the work to be of such character that they may be able to apply the knowledge and experience gained, in the locality where they may be expected to reside after leaving school. In pushing forward the school-room training of these boys and girls, teachers, and especially superintendents, must not lose sight of the great necessity for fitting their charges for the every-day life of their after years.

57. A farm and garden, if practicable an orchard also, must be connected with each school, and especial attention must be given to instruction in farming, gardening, dairying, and fruit growing.

58. Every school should have horses, cattle, swine, and poultry, and when practicable, sheep and bees, which the pupils should be taught to care for properly. The boys should look after the stock and milk the cows, and the girls should see to the poultry and the milk.

59. The farm, garden, stock, dairy, kitchen, and shops should be so managed as to make the school as nearly self-sustaining as practicable, not only because Government resources should be as wisely and carefully utilized as private resources would be, but also because thrift and economy

are among the most valuable lessons which can be taught Indians. Waste in any department must not be tolerated.

60. The blacksmith, wheelwright, carpenter, shoemaker, and harness maker trades, being of the most general application, should be taught to a few pupils at every school. Where such mechanics are not provided for the school pupils should, so far as practicable, receive instruction from the agency mechanics.

61. The girls must be systematically trained in every branch of house-keeping and in dairy work; be taught to cut, make, and mend garments for both men and women; and also be taught to nurse and care for the sick. They must be regularly detailed to assist the cook in preparing the food and the laundress in washing and ironing.

62. Special effort must be made to instruct Indian youth in the use and care of tools and implements. They must learn to keep them in order, protect them properly, and use them carefully.

63. Pupils should be detailed to such work as they will probably have to do after leaving school. Neither girls nor boys must be compelled to perform duties unsuitable to their sex, age, or strength. Therefore, except when necessary, boys should not be assigned to ordinary kitchen duties, though they can be very properly required to keep their own dormitories in perfect order. The work should be so arranged as not to be irksome or discouraging. The details of pupils should be so planned that school-room and other duties will not clash; and so that they will know their duties for each hour in the day. While each one should acquire skill in some special line, his work should be varied enough to give him an acquaintance with other branches.

Removals and Appointments

64. Persons in the Indian school service are engaged with the distinct understanding that character, merit, efficiency, and special qualifications for the work required, are the only considerations upon which they can hope to be retained. Removals will be made for cause, such as immorality, incompetency, indolence, flagrant infirmities of temper, and neglect of or refusal to perform duty, and also for manifest physical disability. An adverse report of any officer of the Department to whom the Indian Office has a right to turn for information regarding the conduct of the schools, shall be sufficient cause for suspension or removal of any school employé. Special investigations will not be ordered at the request of employés dismissed or suspended, but the office will carefully weigh any charges made against employés and take action only after due deliberation.

65. When an agent is of the opinion that the superintendent or any other school employé is not a fit person for the place he holds, or is not adapted to perform its duties, the agent must make written report of the fact to the Commissioner, stating specifically his reasons for his opinion. And when the superintendent of any Government school is of the opinion that any

employé thereof is not efficient, or is not adapted to the work required of him, it shall be the duty of said superintendent to report the fact in writing to the agent, stating specifically his reasons for the opinion. The agent must forward this report to the Commissioner, with such recommendations in relation thereto as he may deem it his duty to make.

65a. The agent shall not suspend any superintendent or other school employé without authority first obtained from the Commissioner, except when the moral welfare or the discipline of the school imperatively demands summary action, in which case he may suspend such employé and select a competent person to perform his duties temporarily, reporting immediately to the Commissioner full and specific reasons for the action taken.

65b. All positions and salaries expire June 30 of each year, and all appointments are made with this understanding. Therefore the Indian Office is not committed to any employé beyond the date named; but the office aims to retain competent and satisfactory employés from year to year, if the positions in which they are employed are continued, and whenever practicable to promote to higher grades those who have distinguished themselves by devotion to duty or special aptitude.

66. Many of the school employés will naturally and properly be nominated by the agent, though the Indian Office reserves the right to appoint or remove all employés. In making selection of school employés the agent should in all cases consult with the superintendent and, if possible, act in harmony with him. Care must be taken to secure persons of proper qualifications, good moral character, special fitness for the duties to be performed, and those who are able to speak the English language fluently and correctly. Personal and political considerations should not enter into the question. For teachers men and women especially trained for their work, with experience in teaching in public schools, who have been educated in American schools, should be given the preference. A certificate to teach in some State or Territorial school, or a normal school diploma, should accompany a recommendation for appointment as teacher or superintendent. In transmitting nominations the agent must forward at the same time evidences of the qualifications of proposed employés.

67. While no test of religious faith or affiliations shall be applied in the appointment of persons in the Indian school service or in their removal therefrom, yet every employé is required to have a decent respect for religion and to be of good moral character. In addition to recognized efficiency and general usefulness, a character which Indian children can imitate to advantage is also essential. Profanity, obscenity, indifference to moral restraints, and infirmities of temper can not be tolerated. Men and women in the Indian-school service are expected to be models of our Christian civilization, and if guilty of conduct which shocks the moral sense of a civilized community they will be summarily discharged.

68. Finally, employés at Government boarding schools must understand

when they accept appointment that hard work is to be performed; that long hours of service are required; that in the nature of things every employé must be willing to work night or day if special emergencies arise; that the duties of an employé do not end arbitrarily at a given hour, but may be continued indefinitely; and it must be understood by any individual entering the service that additional duties, or duties entirely different from those usually attaching to the position to which he or she is regularly assigned, may be required. There is no room for shirks or unwilling workers in the Indian-school service, and the man or woman who is too fastidious to assist in making a camp Indian child or youth tidy in appearance; too indifferent to participate in the general exercises of the school; too obstinate to yield to the judgment of those charged with directing the school work, should not enter it, for efficiency and success can come only to those who are interested in the education of the Indian, physically able for the arduous duties to be performed, and, above all else, willing to do whatever is necessary for the good of all concerned.

TRAINING SCHOOLS

69. Superintendents of industrial training schools report to the Commissioner of Indian Affairs direct. They have entire control of schools under their charge, subject to the regulations of the Indian Office and special instructions of the Commissioner of Indian Affairs. As bonded officers they are responsible for all Government property under their charge. They are authorized to establish such special regulations regarding the details of their school work as circumstances may require; to determine the duties of all employés; to direct the work of the school in all its departments; to administer discipline; to be accountable for money earned by pupils, and to prescribe rules governing its expenditure by pupils, and in general to manage the affairs of the institution; but they shall neither nullify nor modify any order of the Indian Office nor any of the general regulations governing Indian schools, except by permission of the Commissioner of Indian Affairs.

DAY SCHOOLS

70. The day schools on each reservation are under the immediate control of the agent. Where there is no supervisor the agent is required to visit each school at least once in two months. He shall see that proper school furniture and appliances, and an abundance of fuel and good water are provided, and contribute in every way possible to the efficiency of the schools. He will report from time to time with regard to the character of the work done at each school, and the efficiency of each teacher. He will spare no reasonable efforts to keep the schools filled with Indian pupils, and strive to unite

teachers, agency employés, and parents in a common interest in their welfare.

71. The supervisor of day schools upon any reservation shall be constantly in the field visiting schools, teachers, and parents, directing the details of the work, consulting with the teachers, urging parents to send their children to the schools, and performing such other duties in connection with the schools as the Commissioner of Indian Affairs or the agent may direct. He shall report weekly to the agent, and on the last day of each month shall transmit to the Indian Office, through the agent, a report of the work for the month, making recommendations relative thereto.

72. Each teacher will be expected to classify pupils, so far as practicable according to the prescribed course of study.

73. Each teacher must prepare and follow a regular program of exercises, interspersing study and recitations with singing, calisthenics, and intermissions. As most day-school work will be of a primary grade, instructions will be given by slate, blackboard and chart exercises, object lessons and picture talks in English more than by the use of text books. The teacher is expect to stimulate and encourage pupils, and must therefore give to her school intelligent, earnest attention, and use skill and ingenuity in adapting usual methods to the instruction of children who must acquire the language in which they are taught.

74. A session of a day school is five and one-half hours, exclusive of intermissions. A session begins at 9 o'clock and continues until 4 p. m., unless otherwise authorized, with two intermissions of fifteen minutes each, and one of one hour. Sessions must be held on each day of the week, Saturdays, Sundays, and legal holidays excepted.

75. Corporal punishment is allowed only in cases of gravest misconduct, and must never be inflicted by one pupil upon another at the instance or request of the teacher.

76. School rooms are under the control of the teacher, who is authorized to detail pupils to care for the same, but the agent is responsible for the buildings and public property therein. If there be an assistant teacher the assistant shall have supervision of this part of the school work, and shall perform such other school duties as may be assigned by the teacher. The assistant teacher shall not be required to perform personal service for the teacher.

77. So far as practicable a man and wife shall be employed as teacher and assistant teacher, and where they are so employed they shall arrange the school-room work so as to combine industrial training with the study of books, the man teaching industries to the boys and the woman to the girls, the object being to fit each sex for the duties likely to be incumbent upon them in after life. Even where there is but one teacher some industrial training is possible and should be included in the course of instruction.

78. The day-school teacher, being frequently the only white person in an

Indian camp, is expected to be exemplary in conduct and character, and if otherwise can not be continued in service.

79. All the preceding rules relating to boarding schools, the conduct of school employés, and their relations to the agent, shall be in force at day schools so far as applicable.

LEAVES OF ABSENCE

Boarding Schools

1. All positions and salaries in the Indian-school service terminate absolutely June 30 of each year.

2. Should any position not be authorized for the ensuing fiscal year, the incumbent of such position is of course relieved from duty June 30, and has no claim against the Government for remuneration after that period.

3. No employé can claim leave of absence with pay as a matter of right, as there is no law regulating the matter. Such leaves are regulated by the Commissioner of Indian Affairs, under instructions from the Secretary of the Interior, according to the best interests of the service, and they are allowed only for good reasons, not as a matter of course.

4. Leaves of absence are to be taken when the services of employés can be spared with least detriment to the interests of the school.

5. Leaves of absence are, whether from sickness or other causes, during the school year, will be granted upon direction of the Secretary of the Interior by the Commissioner of Indian Affairs only.

6. Leaves of absence during the months when the school is in vacation are authorized in the discretion of the agent or (in the case of a bonded school) the superintendent, such leaves not to exceed three days for each month of service, nor to exceed thirty days in any fiscal year. The time of granting these leaves is left to the agent or superintendent, who will so arrange the same that the necessary work of the schools may be continued through the vacation. If, for instance, the employé entered upon duty October 1 and was in continuous service until June 30 following, his continuous service represents nine months, and consequently he may be granted nine times three days' leave with pay, which is twenty-seven days' leave. Ten or more months' service would give thirty days' leave, the annual limit.

7. Agents and superintendents of bonded schools are cautioned against favoritism in the granting of leaves of absence, and at proper times they must report fully the dates of leaves granted under these regulations. Leaves granted to employés in advance of the receipt of information as to what positions will be authorized during the next fiscal year must be granted with the explicit understanding that should the services of such employés terminate for any cause prior to the expiration of such leaves, the leaves would expire with the termination of service.

Day Schools

8. Beginning July 1, 1891, the school year for day schools will be ten

months and the salary allowed for day-school teachers will be for ten months' service, or pro rata for any period less than ten months. Teachers will be paid for actual service and no vacations with pay will be allowed.

9. In accordance with the above, day-school teachers entering the service at any time during the fiscal year 1891 (July 1, 1890, to June 30, 1891) will not be allowed leaves of absence with pay.

10. Where schools are closed by order of the Indian Office or by reason of fire, flood, disease, or similar cause, for which the teacher is in no way responsible, questions of leaves may be presented to this office for consideration upon their merits.

NOTE.—Pending the time when the above arrangement shall go into effect, the following regulations in regard to granting leaves of absence to day-school teachers who have been in the service during the fiscal year ending June 30, 1890, will be in force.

1. Agents are authorized to grant to day-school teachers who have been in continuous service since September 1, 1889, and who return to duty September 1, 1890, leaves of absence from July 1, to August 31, both inclusive.

2. Agents are authorized to grant to day-school teachers who have not been in continuous service since September 1,1889, but who are to resume their duties September 1, 1890, leaves of absence with pay for such proportion of the vacation period named as their continuous service bears to ten months.

3. Day-school teachers whose resignations have been accepted to take effect at the close of the school year, or whose resignation may be tendered prior to the date of reopening school for the next school year, or who have been notified that they will not be retained in the service, may be granted leave of absence with pay during July, 1890, for a period equal to three days for each month of service since September 1, 1889.

4. Day-school teachers who began service on or since April 1, 1889, and who drew pay for July and August, 1889, will not be allowed pay for any part of July or August, 1890, unless their services are retained for the ensuing year.

5. At agencies, where, under special authority from the office, the vacation period will occur at other times than July and August, the agent will be governed by the spirit of these regulations, and will grant leaves of absence with pay to teachers for periods equivalent to those named herein, reporting his action in each case.

COURSE OF STUDY

Primary Grade

First Year.

English language.—This will be the main study of the first year. By objects, pictures, pantomime, kindergarten helps, conversation games, etc., the names of objects and actions most familiar to the pupils must be acquired by them, and short conversations and phrases in daily use memorized, so that at the end of the year a sufficient vocabulary of nouns, verbs, and modifying words will have been learned to enable them to understand and use English, and to express a large number of ideas, although the sentences may be crude.

Reading and writing.—With the spoken word, so far as practicable, pupils must learn to associate printed and written words. This can be done by reading charts, and by exercises on blackboards and slates, ingeniously devised and varied. Pupils should learn to write and read each word as a whole, and should so understand its meaning as to be able to use it intelligently. By these methods at the end of the year they should be able to read at sight and understandingly the first lessons of the first reader.

Painstaking drill in pronunciation of words and sounds of letters must be given. Such drill must be continued throughout the entire course. Concert exercises are important; but careful and judicious attention must also be given to pupils individually.

Numbers.—By objects and numeral frames, pupils should learn to count in English and read and write figures from 1 to 10, and be given simple oral lessons in mental addition and subtraction.

General exercises.—Singing, calisthenics, marching and action songs, concert exercises, etc., must be introduced to relieve the routine from monotony and to afford opportunity for drill of various sorts. Teach points of the compass and days of the week.

The first year is the hardest and will tax to the utmost the ingenuity, skill, and tact of the teacher. The pupils will be sensitive and diffident. Confidence must be inspired, criticism and ridicule avoided, and all efforts of the teacher must be patient, steady, and persistent.

Second Year.

English language.—With the same use of objects, pictures, and conversations, blackboard and slate exercises as in the previous year, the vocabulary should be largely increased, and skill acquired in the use of verbs and in sentence making, so that the pupil may describe in English what he sees and hears, and make a beginning in letter writing. Every day must see some new words added to the pupil's vocabulary and some new forms of expression familiarized.

Every exercise should be a language lesson. Pupils should not only acquire the habit of expressing themselves in complete sentences, but also of using some variety and discrimination in the choice of words. The thought must precede expression. Hence, in primary work especially, lessons to develop new ideas must come before lessons on word forms and idioms. The end of language teaching is correct and fluent expression. The means are development lessons in which the pupil gains new ideas to express, and drill lessons in which they will have occasion to use frequently the new word idiom taught. The oral expression should precede the written. In both, careful arrangement should be emphasized. In written work the amount should be carefully guarded.

Reading.—Chart reviewed. First reader should be taken up, care being taken that the words and sentences are understood as well as memorized.

Orthography.—Easy words may be spelled orally, and on blackboard and slate.

Form and color.—Systematic instruction should be given in form by use of blocks, clay modeling, paper folding, etc.; also in color.

Penmanship and drawing.—Writing the letters of the alphabet separately as well as combined in words may be taught. Simple lessons in drawing will interest the pupil, cultivate the eye and hand, and give opportunity also for teaching English.

Numbers.—Counting in English to 100. Grube method of numbers from 1 to 20, with continued oral problems in addition and subtraction.

Geography.—Maps of schoolroom and premises and of localities with which the pupils are familiar may be drawn to a scale and all objects of interest located thereon.

General exercises.—Singing, calisthenics, and concert exercises must receive attention, and by whatever method may be most practicable some simple instruction must be given in morals and manners.

Third Year.

The first month should be devoted to reviewing the work of the two preceding years so as to recover thoroughly all ground lost in vacation.

English language.—Sentence making; repeating simple stories about common things; memorizing sentences and short, easy dialogues, and selections from poetry and prose; drill in sounds of letters and in combining sounds; correction of habitual errors of pronunciation and construction. All lessons must be directed to the cultivation of facility of thought and fluency and correctness of expression of ideas in English.

Reading.—Second Reader, with a supplemental reader of same grade, but different series, to increase the vocabulary and prevent parrot-like work.

Orthography.—Spelling orally and on blackboards and slate the words of the reading lesson.

Form and color.—Lessons on form and color continued.

Penmanship and drawing.—Special attention to the writing and to the use of capital letters. Drawing straight and curved lines and making geometrical figures.

Numbers.—Numbers by the Grube method to 50. Oral instruction in mental arithmetic. Simple original problems.

Geography.—Geography of the reservation or county, with map-drawing of the same.

General exercises.—Singing, calisthenics, etc., as heretofore. Simple talks on morals and manners.

Fourth Year.

A month devoted to review of the preceding course will prepare the pupils for formally taking up books; hitherto the instruction has been chiefly oral.

English language.—Language primer begun. Telling and writing the stories of the readers, and everyday occurrences. Memorizing good selections. Sentence building. Drill in idiomatic expressions and the proper use of the different parts of speech.

Reading.—Third Reader. Instructions in the use of capital letters and punctuation marks.

Orthography.—Spelling and defining words from the Reader.

Form and color.—Instruction continued.

Penmanship and drawing.—Special attention should be given to acquiring right positions and good habits of writing, legibility, accuracy, grace, and facility. Drawing geometrical figures.

Arithmetic.—A primary arithmetic may be placed in hands of the pupils.

Geography.—A primary geography may be used, accompanied by easy map work and modeling in sand or clay.

General exercises.—They should be in general as heretofore, but varied so as to meet the increased intelligence and capacity of the pupils. Simple talks on hygiene may be added to those on morals and manners. Interesting short stories may be read to the pupils by the teacher.

For the work in the primary grade, covering four years, little else can be attempted in the way of a course of study than a mere outline. Dependence must be placed mainly upon the ingenuity, faithfulness, patience, and persistence of the teacher. The work of these four years is the most important, and is also the most trying to both teacher and pupil. At the end of the four years every pupil should be able to speak English fluently and correctly; should be able to pronounce and to recognize at sight, whether seen separately or in a printed or written sentence, every word in the First and Second Readers; should be able to spell and write the words of the two readers when pronounced to him; should know at sight figures up to 100; should be able to make change in any sum less than $1, and to combine numbers to include 6x6; and should have a knowledge of the simplest elements of geography. The pupils will have accomplished about what is usually expected of children who have attended the white public schools two years. The difficulty of learning the English language, to them a foreign tongue, and the need of giving the pupils some form of industrial training in addition to school-room studies, necessitates the expenditure of more time in Indian than in white schools for accomplishing the same grade of work.

Advanced Grade

First Year.

Reading.—Third Reader completed, with supplemental readers of same grade.

Orthography.—First spelling book and spelling from reader. Words spelled, defined, and used in simple sentences.

Arithmetic.—Primary arithmetic completed, and oral lessons in written arithmetic, with constant drill in combinations of numbers. Counting to

1,000. Making change to $5. Tables of dry measure and avoirdupois weight explained, illustrated, and memorized. Pupils should be taught to use the common weights and measures.

Form and color.—Instruction continued.

Penmanship and drawing.—Special attention to capital letters and punctuation. Drawing geometrical figures.

Language.—Sentence building; language primer continued. Telling and writing stories. Memorizing.

Geography.—Primary geography and easy map-drawing, with sand and clay modeling. Use of globe. Form and motions of the earth explained.

Observation lessons.—Observation cultivated. The human body. Animals and plants. Nature study. The nature study suggested in the first grade should be continued in all the grades. In spring note the thermometer, the melting of the snows, the forms of water, the first signs of vegetable life. Plant seeds and arouse an interest in the coming of the birds, the leaves, and the flowers. Watch changes in the shadows of the sun. Gather cocoons and study animal life in every way possible by direct observation. In autumn study the fruits, note the changing and falling leaves, the coming of the cold, the changes in the sun's shadows.

General exercises.—Calisthenics, music, singing the scale. Talks on morals and manners, with careful instruction as to how to behave.

Second Year.

Reading.—Fourth Reader, with juvenile papers for supplemental reading.

Orthography.—Constant drill in spelling, both orally and on slates, from reader and spelling-book. Spelling names of groups of familiar objects.

Arithmetic.—Written arithmetic begun and pursued through multiplication, with persistent drill in combining numbers orally.

Penmanship and drawing.—Class should be doing fairly creditable work.

Language.—Language lessons. Elements of English grammar taught in connection with language lessons.

Geography.—Geography of the State or Territory, and general information relative to its resources, occupations, topography, cities, and railways. Map of North America drawn.

Observation lessons.—Talks about physiology and hygiene. Object lessons illustrative of plant and animal life, peoples, ships, cities, and occupations. Instruction in buying, selling, and calculating values of articles. Samples of grains, fruits, etc., should be exhibited. Through the observation lessons the child should gain the habit of accurate observation and definite expression, as well as added knowledge and an intelligent interest in the world about him. These lessons are valuable, not merely for the facts and information acquired, but also as a means of forming right habits of attention, observation, and expression. The teaching should be so directed as to strengthen these habits in the pupils. The instruction should be oral, and should be made interesting and attractive to the children.

General exercises.—General exercises as hitherto, with instructions on morals and manners.

Third Year.

Reading.—Fourth Reader, with supplemental reading.

Orthography.—Constant drill in spelling orally and on slates, from reader and advanced spelling-book. Special attention to sounds of letters and forming syllables.

Arithmetic.—Written arithmetic through decimal or common fractions, but not both, with much practice in mental arithmetic. All the tables of addition, subtraction, multiplication, and division memorized.

Form and color.—Instruction continued.

Penmanship and drawing.—Ordinary forms used in letter-writing. Practice drawing from copies and objects.

Language.—Elements of English grammar taught by oral lessons, in connection with language lessons. Letter-writing encouraged. Pupils writing letters to teacher.

Geography.—The United States. Indian reservations.

United States history.—Simple stories by the teacher from United States history, pupils repeating same at next recitation in their own words.

Physiology and hygiene.—Elementary lessons, including lessons illustrating effects of alcohol and narcotics upon the human system.

Observation lesson.—Oral lessons about plants, animals, places, people, and things.

General exercises.—Morals and manners, calisthenics, music, etc.

Fourth Year.

Reading.—The Fifth Reader.

Orthography.—The Advanced Speller.

Arithmetic.—Written arithmetic, to include percentage, with review of entire book and especial attention to practical application of principles.

Penmanship.—Business letters, notes, receipts, etc.

Drawing.—Individual advancement in this branch to be encouraged. Free-hand drawing. Work with colored crayons.

Language.—A primary work on grammar. Especial attention to habitual errors, and careful drill and encouragement in composition. Lessons mostly written.

Geography.—Geography of North and South America, with instructions in general upon the races, the countries, the climates, and the commerce of the world. Most common phenomena of earth. Map-drawing—the State; the United States; the two Americas.

United States history.—Primary work in United States history.

Physiology and hygiene.—Elementary.

Civil government.—Simple oral lessons in civil government—meaning of terms town, village, county, State, etc.; elections, citizenship, etc.

Observation lessons.—Plants and animals.

Music.—Pupils should be able to read music from the staff.

General exercises.—Music, calisthenics, morals, and manners throughout the year, treating pupils as young ladies and young gentlemen.

The highest efficiency of the school is tested by its results in moral character, and hence its highest duty is effective moral training. These facts are recognized by the present course of study, which makes provision for instruction in morals and manners to supplement the mental training furnished by the regular instruction and discipline of the schools. The course should include lessons on cleanliness and neatness, gentleness, politeness, kindness to others, kindness to animals, love for parents, benefactors, etc., respect and reverence, gratitude, obedience, truthfulness, purity, honesty, courage, honor, reputation, self-control, self-denial, confession of wrong, forgiveness, evil-speaking, profanity, good habits, industry, temperance, frugality; also civil duties, including love of country, obedience to law, respect for civil rulers, fidelity to official trusts, nature and obligations of oaths, the ballot, and other duties involved in good citizenship. A part of this instruction should be given in connection with the opening exercises, and a half hour each week should be devoted to a separate exercise. The general method pursued should be to present the lesson *in the concrete* by means of an appropriate story or incident, to call out the duty or truth thus presented by means of questions, to illustrate and enforce it by a fitting selection of poetry, and finally to set it in the memory in the form of an appropriate maxim. The special aim of this instruction is to give pupils a clear knowledge of duty, to quicken their moral natures, and especially the conscience, and to lead them to the forming of right purposes.

There should be constant review of the preceding course with the special purpose of securely fixing in the child's memory and mental habits the results of the eight years of study above outlined.

Having completed the eight years' course, the Indian boy or girl who has been in health, has ordinary vigor of mind, and has been properly taught, will be able to read, write, and converse in English; to solve any practical problem in written arithmetic, to and through percentage; to locate on the map all the principal rivers, lakes, bays, mountains, and cities of North and South America; to name all the continents; to point out upon the globe or a map of the world the homes of all the great races, and to describe their characteristics; to name the parts of speech and explain their more obvious relations to each other; to know something of physiology and hygiene; to read, understand, and enjoy a newspaper or book; will have acquired a good many facts relative to animal and plant life, and will know how to behave at home, on the street, at church, in the presence of the opposite sex, and in the homes of acquaintances and friends. In short, the training herein proposed is about equal to that obtained in six years at public schools among whites, and fits the pupil either to make his own way alongside the white citizen or to take the advanced course offered in some Indian industrial training school.

INSTRUCTIONS TO AGENTS IN REGARD TO FAMILY NAMES

DEPARTMENT OF THE INTERIOR,
OFFICE OF INDIAN AFFAIRS,
WASHINGTON, D.C.,
March 19, 1890.

To Indian Agents and Superintendents of Schools:

As allotment work progresses it appears that some care must be exercised in regard to preserving among Indians family names. When Indians become citizens of the United States, under the allotment act, the inheritance of property will be governed by the laws of the respective States, and it will cause needless confusion and, doubtless, considerable ultimate loss to the Indians if no attempt is made to have the different members of a family known by the same family name on the records and by general reputation. Among other customs of the white people it is becoming important that Indians adopt that in regard to names.

There seems, however, no good reason for continuing a custom which has prevailed to a considerable extent of substituting English for Indian names, especially when different members of the same family are named with no regard to the family surname. Doubtless in many cases, the Indian name is difficult to pronounce and to remember; but in many other cases the Indian word is as short and as euphonious as the English word that is substituted, while, other things being equal, the fact that it is an Indian name makes it a better one.

For convenience, an English "Christian name" may be given and the Indian name be retained as a surname. If the Indian name is unusually long and difficult, it may perhaps be arbitrarily shortened.

The practice of calling Indians by the English translation of their Indian names also seems to me unadvisable. The names thus obtained are usually awkward and uncouth, and such as the children when they grow older will dislike to retain.

In any event the habit of adopting sobriquets given to Indians such as "Tobacco," "Mogul," "Tom," "Pete," etc., by which they become generally known, is unfortunate, and should be discontinued. It degrades the Indian, and as he or his children gain in education and culture they will be annoyed by a designation which has been fastened upon them and of which they can not rid themselves without difficulty.

Hereafter in submitting to this office, for approval, names of Indian employés to be appointed as policemen, judges, teamsters, laborers, etc., all nicknames must be discarded and effort made to ascertain and adopt the actual names or such as should be permanent designations. The names decided upon must be made well known to the respective Indians and the importance of retaining such names must be fully explained to them. I am aware that this will involve some expenditure of time and trouble but no more than will be warranted by the importance of the matter in the near future.

Of course sudden change can not be made in Indian nomenclature; but if agents and school superintendents will systematically endeavor, so far as practicable, to have children and wives known by the names of the fathers and husbands, very great improvement in this respect will be brought about within a few years.

I have submitted this subject to Hon. J. W. Powell, Director of the Bureau of Ethnology, which gives special attention to Indian linguistics. His reply is appended hereto.

T. J. MORGAN,
Commissioner.

DEPARTMENT OF THE INTERIOR,
UNITED STATES GEOLOGICAL SURVEY,
WASHINGTON, D.C., *April* 4, 1890.

Sir: I beg to acknowledge the receipt of your favor of March 24, with inclosure, relating to the adoption by the Indians of a system of family names.

The old practice in vogue of attaching sobriquets and nicknames to the Indians can not be too severely condemned, and I am pleased that you are about to take steps to substitute another and better method.

The matter is important, not only in its relation to the inheritance of property, but also because it will enable much more accurate census enumeration to be made in the future, and because it will tend strongly toward the breaking up of the Indian tribal system which is perpetuated and ever kept in mind by the Indian's own system of names.

Undoubtedly it will be better, whenever possible, to retain the Indian name as a surname, adding an English Christian-given name. Occasionally, however, it will be found advantageous to make the latter also an Indian name.

In selecting aboriginal names I do not think it will be necessary to limit the choice to such names as Indians already bear. Excellent names may frequently be selected from the Indian's vocabulary of geographic terms, such as the names of rivers, lakes, mountains, etc., and where these are suitable and euphonic, I think they may with advantage be substituted for personal names which are less desirable. Little difficulty, however, will be experienced in shortening Indian names in the interest of brevity and euphony, and the Indian will be found to readily adopt names so changed. I agree with you that in general it is unadvisable to call Indians by the English translation of their Indian names, though in the case of animal names and some others, as deer, hawk, etc., it is not objectionable.

I believe that when the end sought to be obtained by the adoption of family names is thoroughly explained to the Indians they will be willing to coöperate with the several agents in the attempt to select proper names for themselves and families.

J. W. POWELL,
Director.

HON. T. J. MORGAN,
Commissioner of Indian Affairs, Washington, D. C.

LIST OF BOOKS ADOPTED FOR USE IN INDIAN SCHOOLS

Primary Grade

First Year

Reading.—Appleton's Reading Chart. Illustrated Primer, Fuller.

Numbers.—Badlam's Aids to Number, first series (one set for use of teacher).

Second Year

Reading.—McGuffey's Eclectic First Reader, supplemented by Webb's New Word Method.

Numbers.—Badlam's Aids to Number, second series (one set for use of teacher).

Geography.—Topics in Geography, Nichols (one copy for use of teacher).

Third Year

Reading.—McGuffey's Eclectic Second Reader, supplemented by Book of Cats and Dogs, Johonnot.

Numbers.—Grube Method (one copy for use of teacher).

Geography.—Topics in Geography, Nichols (one copy for use of teacher).

Fourth Year

English language.—Hyde's Practical Lessons in the use of English.

Reading.—McGuffey's Eclectic Third Reader, supplemented by Friends in Feathers and Furs, Johonnot.

Arithmetic.—Numbers Illustrated, Rickoff.

Geography.—Barnes' Elementary Geography.

Advanced Grade

First Year

Methods.—De Graff's School-room Guide (one copy for use of teacher).

Reading.—McGuffey's Eclectic Third Reader, supplemented by Robinson Crusoe in words of one syllable and Neighbors with Wings and Fins, Johonnot.

Orthography.—McGuffey's Alternate Spelling Book.

Arithmetic.—Seaver and Walton's Mental Arithmetic.

Language.—Hyde's Practical Lessons in the use of English.

Geography.—Barnes' Elementary Geography (completed).

Observation lessons.—Calkin's Primary Object Lessons (one copy for use of teacher.)

General exercises.—Gow's Primer of Politeness (one copy for use of teacher).

Second Year

Methods.—Prince's Courses and Methods (one copy for use of teacher).

Reading.—McGuffey's Eclectic Fourth Reader, supplemented by Neighbors with Claws and Hoofs, Johonnot, and Swiss Family Robinson, and Harper's Young People, or Chatterbox, or Wide Awake.

Orthography.—Sentence and Word Book, Johonnot.

Arithmetic.—Goff's Elementary Arithmetic.

Language.—Tarbell's Lessons in Language, Book I.

Geography.—Barnes' Complete Geography, supplemented by Our World Reader, No. 1.

Observation lessons.—Hooker's Child's Book of Nature (one copy for use of teacher). White's Physiological Manikin.

General exercises.—Gow's Good Morals and Gentle Manners (one copy for use of teacher).

Third Year

Reading.—McGuffey's Eclectic Fourth Reader, supplemented by Gray's How Plants Grow, and Grandfather's Stories, Johonnot.

Orthography.—The Sentence and Word Book, Johonnot.

Arithmetic.—Goff's Elementary Arithmetic.

Language.—Tarbell's Lessons in Language, Book I.

Geography.—Barnes Complete Geography (finished), supplemented by Our World Reader No. 2.

History.—Higginson's History of United States (one copy for use of teacher).

Physiology and Hygiene.—The House I Live In, Eclectic Series.

Observation lessons.—First Steps in Scientific Knowledge, Paul Bert (one copy for use of teacher).

Fourth Year

Methods.—Lectures on Teaching, Compayré (one copy for use of teacher).

Reading.—McGuffey's Eclectic Fifth Reader, supplemented by American Classics, Swinton, and Stories of Other Lands, Johonnot.

Orthography.—Swinton's Word Analysis.

Arithmetic.—Goff's Practical Arithmetic. The New Arithmetic, Seymour Eaton (one copy for use of teacher).

Language.—Graded Lessons in English, Reed and Kellogg.

Geography.—Monteith's New Physical Geography.

United States History.—Scudder's Short History of United States, supplemented by Stories of Our Country, Johonnot.

Physiology and Hygiene.—Young People's Physiology, New Pathfinder No. 2, Barnes.

Civil Government.—Mowry's Elements of Civil Government; Dawes' How We Are Governed (one copy of each for use of teacher).

Observation lessons.—Calkin's Object Lessons (one copy for use of teacher).

For Use Throughout the Course

Penmanship.—Spencerian or Payson, Dunton & Scribner, or Normal Review system.

Drawing.—Prang's System of Drawing; The Use of Models, Prang (one copy of each for use of teacher).

Music.—Cheerful Echoes, Mrs. Louise Pollock.

Gymnastics.—Strong Bodies for Our Boys and Girls, Blaikie (one copy for use of teacher).

Miscellaneous.—Memory Gems, Pearley; Choice Selections, Northend (one copy for use of teacher).

For Use Where Needed

Kindergarten.—Milton Bradley Co.'s kindergarten materials.

APPLICATION FOR APPOINTMENT IN THE U. S. INDIAN SCHOOL SERVICE

To the COMMISSIONER OF INDIAN AFFAIRS,
Washington, D.C.:

I, —— ——, hereby apply for appointment as —— at ——, and declare upon honor that to the best of my knowledge and belief the answers made by me to the following questions are true, and that they are made in my own handwriting:

1. Your Christian name and surname? [In full.]
2. Date and place of your birth?
3. Present legal residence, city or town, county or parish, and State?
4. How long have you been a resident?
5. Are you a citizen of the United States?
   If naturalized, where and when?
6. (*a*) Married or single?
   (*b*) Number and ages of children?
   (*c*) What members of your family will be with you at the reservation?
7. State your present and your usual occupation, and the experience and degree of success you have had.
8. In what places have you resided, and what has been your occupation during *each* year for the past five years, and what wages have you received? [Give name and address of your employer or employers, if any, the length of your stay with each, and reason for leaving their employ.]
9. What has been the state of your health during the past five years? [Answer explicitly and positively.]

(*a*) Are you now physically capable of a full discharge of the duties of the position to which you are seeking employment?

(*b*) Have you any defect of sight?

(*c*) of hearing?

(*d*) of speech?

(*e*) of limb?

10. Are you subject to any chronic disease, disorder, or infirmity which at any time unfits you for the duties of your present vocation or that for which you are seeking appointment?

11. Do you now habitually use, or have you ever been addicted to the use of, alcoholic liquors, tobacco, morphine, or opium?

12. Do you pledge yourself not to use intoxicating liquors as a beverage, and narcotics, while you are in the Indian Service?

13. Where were you educated, and how old were you when you left school? [State kind of school, scope of studies persued, whether common school, high school, business college, academy, college, university, technical, normal, or other professional school.]

14. Write the Commissioner of Indian Affairs a letter briefly stating your qualifications and training for the place you seek.

15. Have you been trained in the usual household duties, such as cooking, sewing, laundrying, and care of the house generally? If so, when, where, and how?

16. Have you had experience and success in managing, instructing, and caring for the bodily comfort of children? State particulars.

17. Do you understand butter making, care of milk, canning, drying, pickling, and preserving fruits, curing meats, and preparing household delicacies and necessities as usually understood by thrifty, intelligent housewives in farming communities? Answer very fully.

18. Can you cut, fit, and make garments for males and females; crochet, knit, and operate a sewing machine?

Can you patiently and carefully instruct young Indian girls in all the sewing, darning, mending, etc., usual in large families in our best white homes?

19. Can you wash and iron clothing neatly?

20. Can you perform or direct, or both perform and direct the kitchen duties incumbent upon a cook in a boarding school for Indian children?

21. Are you accounted a first-class housekeeper, cook, or seamstress, and could you perform the duties of one or more such positions?

22. What mechanical trades do you understand, and at which have you served a regular apprenticeship?

23. Are you accustomed to the duties of a farmer and stockgrower?

24. Are you familiar with the usual work of a well conducted farm, such as sowing, cultivating, and reaping crops; mowing, curing, and stacking hay, grain, and fodder; planting and cultivating trees, vines, and small fruits; breeding, caring for, and butchering stock; making cheese, storing winter fruits and vegetables, bee keeping, sheep-shearing, etc.?

What experience have you had as a farmer, and when?

Are you acquainted with methods of irrigation?

Do you take an agricultural paper? If so, what one?

25. Are you handy with ordinary farm tools and implements; able to make repairs of buildings, vehicles, harness, fences, and do rough carpenter work?

26. Have you the faculty of winning and retaining the confidence of your associates, employés, and pupils?

27. Have you ever been in the Indian service? If so, where and when?

Why did you leave, and at what time? [Year, month, and day, if possible.]

28. Have you ever taught school?

During what years, and in what grades?

Have you a teacher's certificate? If so, inclose same; it will be returned, if desired.

Give names and post-office addresses of two school officials who have known you in school or at your home, or where you were employed, to whom I can refer for information regarding your moral character, and your proficiency in your studies, and your success as a teacher.

29. Do you sing, and are you able to teach vocal music?

Do you play any instrument? if so, what?

Are you able to teach instrumental music?

30. Have you skill in drawing and painting?

31. Do you understand kindergarten methods, and have you applied them in your teaching?

32. What educational journals do you read?

What works on teaching have you read?

What subjects are you best qualified to teach?

33. In what institution were you trained, or by what experience have you fitted yourself specially for the position for which you are an applicant?

34. Give the names and addresses of two responsible persons who are thoroughly acquainted with your qualifications for the position for which you apply, to whom I may refer for further information.

35. How long do you expect to remain in the Indian school work if appointed, and successful?

36. Why do you wish a position in an Indian school?

In witness whereof I have hereunto subscribed my name this —— day of —— 189—, at —— county of ——, and State of ——.

[Applicant's signature:] ——,

[Post office address:] ——,

—— ——.

To Applicants

Answer *every* question definitely, whether it seems applicable to the position you seek or not.

This blank application is as nearly general as can be made to apply to the qualifications of persons seeking employment in the Indian school service.

There are three general classes of employés, viz: Superintendents, teachers, and industrial instructors. All employés must be competent to teach either in the school room proper, in the household, the field, or the shops. Good health is a prime requisite in all employés.

Superintendents should be teachers of experience, with knowledge of farming, managing business affairs, and possess good executive ability, as well as patience, perseverance, industry, conscience, and skill in directing the details of an extensive institution involving the expenditure of large sums of money and the performance of varied duties by both subordinate employés and pupils. A superintendent should be firm, kind, affable, considerate, and careful. Men wanting in conscience, industry, business acumen, and self-control will not succeed, and should not enter the Indian School Service.

Teachers require all the rare qualifications incident to complete success in teaching white children in the public schools, and in addition, perfect health of body and mind, great patience, tireless perseverance, and above all a conscientious desire back of sustained effort for the physical, moral, and mental development of the Indian pupils committed to their care. They should be resolute, considerate, dignified, even-tempered, above reproach in personal character, discreet, willing to work, and ambitious to succeed.

Industrial instructors include matrons, seamstresses, cooks, laundresses, industrial teachers, farmers, and mechanics. Each of these must have at least a fair English education, and be able to speak and write the English language fluently. Each should be earnest, conscientious, patient, persevering, kindly disposed, and willing. Conduct, associates, and reputation must all be above reproach. Watchful, but not suspicious; attentive to details, but not given to fault-finding; they should also be courteous and polite in all relations with associate employés and pupils.

The female employés are the guardians of the female pupils and must have their confidence and esteem, and so direct their work that they shall not only be well trained in household duties, but elevated in moral character and educated to self-respect, neatness, and industry. The male industrial instructors are charged with the proper development of the character of the boys, and should possess their respect and be examples to them of all that is best in upright manhood, as well as careful to teach them habits of diligence, accuracy, attention to business, the value of time and money, while instructing them in the industries to which they must look for employment after leaving school.

Persons entering the Indian service must understand when they accept appointment that hard work is to be performed; that long hours of service are required; that in the nature of things every employé must be willing to work night or day if special emergencies arise; that the duties of an employé do not end arbitrarily at a given hour, but may be continued indefinitely;

and that additional duties, or duties entirely different from those usually attaching to the position to which he or she is regularly assigned, may be required. There is no room for shirks or unwilling workers in the Indian school service, and the man or woman who is too fastidious to assist in making a camp Indian child or youth tidy in appearance, too indifferent to participate in the general exercises of the school, too obstinate to yield to the judgment of those charged with directing the school work, should not enter it, for efficiency and success can come only to those who are interested in the education of the Indian, physically able for the arduous duties to be performed, and, above all else, willing to do whatever is necessary for the good of all concerned.

I have carefully read the above statements, and agree that if I am appointed it shall be upon the conditions outlined.

———— ————.

[Applicant's signature.]

* * *

INSTRUCTIONS TO INDIAN AGENTS IN REGARD TO WILD WEST SHOWS

OFFICE OF INDIAN AFFAIRS,
WASHINGTON, D.C., October 1, 1890.

———— ————,

United States Indian Agent,————*Agency:*

SIR: This Department is informed that a company is preparing to obtain Indians from some of the reservations to join the "Wild West Shows" in Europe, and will probably apply to this office for the necessary authority therefor.

Should application for the purpose indicated be made the same will be promptly refused, as it is now against policy of this Department to grant permits for such purposes under any circumstances whatsoever, and I am directed by the Secretary of the Interior to adopt immediate measures to prohibit and prevent Indians from being taken for exhibition purposes.

Your attention is invited to office circular of March 8, 1890, advising agents of the ruinous evils generally resulting to Indians who leave their reservations and engage in enterprises of the character indicated, and instructing them to impress upon the Indians the dangers of such practice and to urge them to remain at home and engage in more civilizing avocations.

You are instructed to again lay the matter plainly before your Indians and advise them that if any should hereafter attempt to leave their reservation for exhibition purposes it will be regarded as an open defiance of the authority of the Government and that prompt measures will be adopted to detain them.

You will be on the alert to detect and thwart the designs of any persons seeking, by coming on the reservation or otherwise, to engage Indians for exhibition purposes, and to this end you will instruct all officials and employés at the agency to promptly furnish you any information they may obtain of the intention of Indians to join any shows or exhibitions, and you will report for the action of this office any employé who may give aid or assistance to anyone seeking to secure Indians for exhibition purposes.

Should Indians attempt to leave the reservation for any such purpose in the face of the above warning you will endeavor in every legitimate manner to prevent the same, and if unable to do so, you will immediately report the facts to this office, and appropriate steps will be taken to enforce obedience to these instructions.

R.V. BELT,
Acting Commissioner.

INSTRUCTIONS TO AGENTS IN REGARD TO MANNER OF ISSUING BEEF

OFFICE OF INDIAN AFFAIRS,
WASHINGTON, *July* 21, 1890.

United States Indian Agent,
——— *Agency:*

SIR: As we have entered a new fiscal year, and it is probable that funds to defray the expense of such improvements as may be actually necessary at agencies will soon be available, I wish again to call your attention to the matter of the slaughter of beef-cattle, so that if any improvement in the method you follow can be made it may be done.

It is my wish that the following rules be established and strictly enforced at every agency where cattle are slaughtered:

The killing to be done in a pen, in as private a manner as possible, and by a man who understands the duty, and who uses the most speedy and painless method practicable; and during the killing children and women are specially prohibited from being present.

The butchering to be by *men* in a house or shed fitted with the necessary appliances for suspending the carcasses during the operation, and with a plank or log floor, with water running over or under the floor, or as convenient to the building as possible, so that cleanliness will be insured.

The consumption of the blood and intestines by the Indian is strictly prohibited. This savage and filthy practice which prevails at many agencies must be abolished, as it serves to nourish brutal instincts, and is, as I am well informed, a fruitful source of disease. Some proper means must be taken for the destruction of the offal, so as to prevent foulness and disease.

When the beef is ready to be cut up, this must be done in a clean and neat manner by *men* detailed for this purpose, and with the assistance, or under the immediate supervision of a butcher or other reliable person who understands this branch of the work, and such chopping blocks, cleavers, saws, pulleys, ropes, beams, hooks, benches, etc., as are necessary to secure cleanliness, decency, and order, must be provided and invariably used. The beef will be delivered to men, and not to women, unless in cases of special exigency.

In short, I intend that this branch of the work, which at many agencies has been so conducted as to be a scandal on the service and a stimulus to the brutal instincts of the Indians, shall become an object lesson to them of the difference in this respect between the civilized man and the savage.

It is my desire to afford you every practicable assistance to comply strictly with the foregoing rules, and you may submit an estimate for such material, etc., as may be required to make necessary improvements and additions to your corrals, cattle-pens, slaughter-houses, etc., explaining at the same time in detail how you intend to expend the same, and limiting your estimate to the lowest possible limit.

You will be required to report on this subject as to how far you have carried out these orders, and the attention of inspectors and special agents will be specially directed to this matter.

T. J. MORGAN,
Commissioner.

INSTRUCTIONS TO INDIAN AGENTS IN REGARD TO INCULCATION OF PATRIOTISM IN INDIAN SCHOOLS

OFFICE OF INDIAN AFFAIRS,
WASHINGTON, D.C., *December* 10, 1899.

To Indian Agents and Superintendents of Indian Schools:

The great purpose which the Government has in view in providing an ample system of common school education for all Indian youth of school age, is the preparation of them for American citizenship. The Indians are destined to become absorbed into the national life, not as Indians, but as Americans. They are to share with their fellow-citizens in all the rights and privileges and are likewise to be called upon to bear fully their share of all the duties and responsibilities involved in American citizenship.

It is in the highest degree important, therefore, that special attention should be paid, particularly in the higher grades of the schools, to the instruction of Indian youth in the elements of American history, acquainting them especially with the leading facts in the lives of the most notable and worthy historical characters. While in such study the wrongs of their ancestors can not be ignored, the injustice which their race has suffered can be contrasted with the larger future open to them, and their duties and opportunities rather than their wrongs will most profitably engage their attention.

Pupils should also be made acquainted with the elementary principles of the Government under which they live, and with their duties and privileges as citizens. To this end, regular instructions should be given them in the form of familiar talks, or by means of the use of some elementary text-book in civics. Debating societies should be organized in which may be learned the practical rules of procedure which govern public assemblies. Some simple manual of rules of order should be put into the hands of the more advanced students, and they should be carefully instructed in its use.

On the campus of all the more important schools there should be erected a flagstaff, from which should float constantly, in suitable weather, the American flag. In all schools of whatever size and character, supported wholly or in part by the Government, the "Stars and Stripes" should be a familiar object, and students should be taught to reverence the flag as a symbol of their nation's power and protection.

Patriotic songs should be taught to the pupils, and they sing them frequently until they acquire complete familiarity with them. Patriotic selections should be committed and recited publicly, and should constitute a portion of the reading exercises.

National holidays—Washington's birthday, Decoration Day, Fourth of July, Thanksgiving, and Christmas—should be observed with appropriate exercises in all Indian schools. It will also be well to observe the anniversary of the day upon which the "Dawes bill" for giving to Indians allotments of land in severalty became a law, viz, February 8, 1887, and to use that occasion to impress upon Indian youth the enlarged scope and opportunity given them by this law and the new obligations which it imposes.

In all proper ways, teachers in Indian schools should endeavor to appeal to the highest elements of manhood and womanhood in their pupils, exciting in them an ambition after excellence in character and dignity of surroundings, and they should carefully avoid any unnecessary reference to the fact that they are Indians.

They should point out to their pupils the provisions which the Government has made for their education, and the opportunities which it affords them for earning a livelihood, and for achieving for themselves honorable places in life, and should endeavor to awaken reverence for the nation's power, gratitude for its beneficence, pride in its history, and a laudable ambition to contribute to its prosperity.

Agents and school superintendents are specially charged with the duty of putting these suggestions into practical operation.

T. J. MORGAN,
Commissioner.

INSTRUCTIONS IN REGARD TO CELEBRATION OF FRANCHISE DAY IN INDIAN SCHOOLS

OFFICE OF INDIAN AFFAIRS,
WASHINGTON, *January* 24, 1890.

To United States Indian Agents:

The 8th of February, the day upon which the "Dawes bill" was signed by the President and became a law, is worthy of being observed in all Indian schools as the possible turning point in Indian history, the point at which the Indians may strike out from tribal and reservation life and enter American citizenship and nationality.

This "Franchise Day," as it might be called, can be utilized to give Indian youth in varied and graphic ways clear ideas of what the allotment law does for them, the opportunities which it offers, the privileges it confers, the safeguards it provides, and the duties and obligations which it imposes, and can be made an occasion to inspire them to the best manhood and womanhood of which they are capable.

The observance of this day by appropriate exercises was referred to in my circular letter of December 10 last. In these exercises the pupils should have part, through songs, recitations, tableaux, etc., and in numerous other ways which enthusiasm and ingenuity will devise; and they may be made interesting and profitable, not only to the pupils but also to their parents and friends. The day should not be a mere holiday but a happy, intelligent celebration, by the Indians, of an event of vast importance and benefit to them.

I shall be interested to see programmes of the exercises at the various schools under your charge and will thank you to forward the same to me as soon as practicable after February 8 next, with any remarks descriptive of the exercises and the way in which they were received by Indians.

T. J. MORGAN,
Commissioner.

INSTRUCTIONS IN REGARD TO CELEBRATION OF WASHINGTON'S BIRTHDAY IN INDIAN SCHOOLS

WASHINGTON, *January* 28, 1890.

To Indian Agents and Superintendents of Indian Schools:

Referring to circular letter of the 10th of December last in regard to inculcating patriotism in Indian schools, your attention is called to the suggestion therein made, that Washington's birthday be observed in the various schools with appropriate exercises.

Although the interval between this celebration and that of "Franchise Day," the 8th of February, is short, yet no such opportunity should be lost by which Indian youth may be imbued with ideas distinctively national as distinguished from those that are tribal. Moreover there will be a natural sequence in the exercises of the two days. The Indian heroes of the camp-fire need not be disparaged, but gradually and unobtrusively the heroes of American homes and history may be substituted as models and ideals.

Indian youth can be made acquainted with, interested in, and eventually proud of the great events and persons, the hardships, dangers, and heroisms, by which the country of which they are now to be a part has reached such a position that the highest privilege which it can confer upon an Indian is that of American citizenship. It will be no difficult matter to find in the incidents of Washington's life and times, as well as in his personal character and experiences, abundant material for exercises which will be full of interest to the pupils as well as profitable to them.

I shall be gratified to learn the way in which these suggestions have been carried out in the schools under your charge.

T. J. MORGAN,
Commissioner.

INSTRUCTION IN REGARD TO OBSERVANCE OF ARBOR DAY

OFFICE OF INDIAN AFFAIRS,
WASHINGTON, D. C., *January* 30, 1890.

To Indian Agents and Superintendents of Indian Schools:

It is important that the Indians under your supervision be properly instructed as to the value of forest and fruit tree culture. With this purpose in view, and to stimulate them in this direction, you will designate a day to be known and observed as Arbor Day, the date to be that best suited to the climate of the locality in which your reservation or school is situated. On that day you will encourage every child, so far as practicable, to plant one or more fruit, ornamental, or forest trees. Suitable exercises should be had bearing upon the value and importance of tree culture, and everything should be done to awaken as deep and intelligent an interest as possible in the minds of both parents and pupils with reference to that subject.

You will submit estimates for a sufficient number of trees to accomplish the purpose. If it is not practicable to have each child plant a tree, each class may be interested in one or more trees.

You will advise this office what day has been selected as Arbor Day, and after the day has passed you will report to this office how it was celebrated, inclosing a programme of the exercises and giving such suggestions as may occur to you in regard to the future observance of such occasions.

Interest may be added to these occasions by giving names to the trees planted. When each child plants a tree it may be known as belonging to him. When trees are planted by classes they may be known by the name and year of the class, and when only a few trees are planted they may be given the names of the Indians whom the children would be gratified thus to honor.

After the trees are planted the children must be required to care for them and instructed as to proper methods of tree culture, and it must be made the duty of some one to see that the trees are not neglected, but that they are watered, protected from injury by persons or animals, mulched, wrapped, fastened to supports, etc., as the location and circumstances may demand.

T. J. MORGAN,
Commissioner.

LETTER TO STATE SUPERINTENDENTS OF PUBLIC
INSTRUCTION IN REGARD TO ADMITTING INDIAN YOUTH
INTO THE PUBLIC SCHOOLS, AND REPLIES THERETO.

OFFICE OF INDIAN AFFAIRS,
WASHINGTON, D. C., *August* 15, 1890.

Hon. Superintendent of Public Instruction of the State of——:

SIR: It is the prime purpose of the present administration of Indian Affairs to bring the Indian schools into relation with the public schools of the several States and Territories in which Indian reservations are located as rapidly as practicable. To this end I am modeling the schools under my supervision after the public schools as far as possible.

In most of the States and Territories where there are Indians, some of them are located among the white settlers, and white settlements generally surround the reservations. I deem it extremely desirable that wherever practicable the children of Indians residing on reservations or among the whites be induced to attend the public schools.

They will learn the ways of civilization and acquire the language much more rapidly if associated with white children in the public schools than in any other way.

These Indians pay no taxes, and in many instances are either too poor or too indifferent to place their children in school. Many school districts adjacent to Indian reservations or containing Indian allotted lands are prevented from maintaining schools by the presence of the Indians who do not contribute in any way toward the support of such schools.

In order especially that the Indians who break up their tribal relations and settle upon allotted lands may have opportunities of educating their children, and as an inducement to white settlers to invite Indian children to their schools and assist them to acquire the rudiments of an English education, I would be pleased to have you inform school officers and others interested that the Indian Office is ready to enter into contracts with the school district officers, or other properly qualified representatives of school districts, for the tuition of Indian children at a rate of $10 per quarter, based upon the average attendance of Indian children during the quarter. Out of this $10 per quarter the school districts will be expected to supply necessary text-books to the Indian children. The school district will contract distinctly to give to each Indian child all the opportunities and attention which are given to white children attending the school, and, so far as possible, prevent their white playmates from ridiculing them or in any way discouraging them or preventing their progress.

The Government contributes this $10 per quarter directly for the purpose of benefiting the children of the Indians, its wards, for whose education the national Government is responsible.

The fact that this is likewise a benefit to school districts having Indian citizens or adjacent to Indian reservations must not be lost sight of. I feel that the whites of such localities are as much interested in this plan of educating the Indian children as the Indians are themselves, not only because of the money received, but especially because the Indians thus brought into the public schools and into pleasant relationship with white children will the more readily become fitted for good citizenship.

I trust that you will cooperate with this office in the work of bringing these ignorant little ones into contact with our Christian civilization through the public schools.

T. J. MORGAN,
Commissioner.

Reply of Superintendent of Public Instruction of California

SACRAMENTO, *September* 27, 1890.

DEAR SIR: Your circular of August 15 has been received, and in accordance with your wishes I have given it publicity among school officers and teachers, through the columns of our educational journal.

IRA G. HOITT,
Superintendent of Public Instruction.

Hon. T. J. MORGAN,
Commissioner Indian Affairs, Washington, D. C.

Reply of Superintendent of Public Instruction of Minnesota

August 18, 1890.

DEAR SIR: Replying to yours of the 18th instant referring to "Education No. 2," I take pleasure in saying that I will do what I can to bring it before parties interested. I shall have it published in our educational journal, and bring it to the attention of county superintendents whose counties adjoin the reservations.

D. L. KIEHLE.

Hon. T. J. MORGAN,
Commissioner Indian Affairs

Reply of Superintendent of Public Instruction of North Dakota

BISMARCK, *November* 10, 1890.

DEAR SIR: With reference to your circular letter of August 15, 1890, I have to say that I have been to considerable pains to learn if there are any Indian children who reside in territory contiguous to our public schools who might avail themselves of the opportunity you offer, but have not been able to learn of any such.

I have had no practical experience with Indian children, but so far as I am able to form any opinion, I am heartily in sympathy with the plan which you propose, which I believe is the best plan so far as the Indians' education is concerned, and will at the same time be sufficient remuneration to the public schools to warrant their receiving them.

If there should prove to be any Indian children near any North Dakota free public schools, I will do all I can to further your plan.

W. J. CLAPP.

Commissioner T. J. MORGAN
Department of the Interior, Washington, D.C.

Reply of Superintendent of Public Instruction of South Dakota

PIERRE, *August* 22, 1890.

DEAR SIR: Your favor of the 15th instant, relative to public-school education for Indian children, came duly to hand. In reply we wish to say that we are in sympathy with the movement, and will do anything in our power to advance the work.

If you have any particular plans which you desire to have followed, it will be necessary for us to have some instruction from your office before attempting to assist in the plan.

G. L. PINKHAM.

Hon. T. J. MORGAN,
Commissioner of Indian Affairs, Washington, D. C.

Reply of Superintendent of Public Instruction of Oregon

SALEM, OREGON, *August* 23, 1890.

DEAR SIR: Returning to this office again to-day from a tour in eastern Oregon, where I have been holding teachers' institutes, etc., I find on my table your favor of the 15th instant in reference to the condition of Indian children in the public schools of the several States and Territories in which Indian reservations are located. I shall be glad to write to the agents of the several Indian reservations in this State in reference to the subject matter of your letter. This will be more practicable than any other plan that occurs to me at this time, for, as a rule, the Indian agents are conversant with Indian children that are scattered about in some of the school districts adjacent to the Indian reservations, and also a few children in the more remote parts of the State that are not in the reservation schools and that are subject to public-school education where they live. I could, of course, issue a circular letter relative to this matter to all of the school directors in the State. This, however, is not necessary, as there are not many cases of the kind coming under the province and reach of the work as set forth by you. I shall be pleased, however, to address the several agents above mentioned at the earliest practicable day.

A few instances of Indian children that have been educated in the public schools of this State have come, during the past few years, under my personal observation. Instead of these school children being ridiculed by the white children, my observation was that they were treated as courteously and kindly as any other children in attendance at the schools. This I observed while traveling and visiting schools in one of the counties of our State in which there is located a large Indian reservation. I was so much pleased at the time with the results of these Indian children in the public schools mentioned, that I prevailed on two young Indian boys to attend the State Agricultural College later on, which they did, and from which they graduated with honor. Unfortunately one of these young men took sick and died very soon after his graduation; the other, a brother, still lives and is occupying a useful position in society in this State, and is thoroughly well qualified and educated sufficiently to occupy any ordinary position as a teacher, etc., in this State.

I shall be pleased, of course, to forward the work belonging to your Department so far as this State is concerned, and shall be glad to hear from you at any time.

I beg leave to say here that if, during your administration, your duty should call you to this coast, I should be pleased to have you write me some time prior to your visit, for, as a rule, we are holding institutes and teachers' associations here during all seasons of the year, and it might be convenient for you to lecture for us at some point in the State. Please think about this, and write me relative to the same at your convenience.

E. B. McELROY,
State Superintendent Public Instruction.

Hon. T. J. MORGAN
Commissioner of Indian Affairs, Washington, D. C.

Report of Commissioner of Indian Affairs T. J. Morgan
October 1, 1891

(Excerpt from *Report for 1891*, pp. 1-9, 25-26, 36-47 53-64, 67, 69-72, 123-45)

Commissioner Morgan's 1891 report was, as usual, comprehensive and incisive. It betrayed the commissioner's optimism and firmness, as well as his ignorance. The Indian, he asserted, must be subjected to the law of the survival of the fittest. If they could not adapt, "they must go to the wall." Morgan even predicted that his successor at the end of the century would speak of the "Indian solution" instead of the "Indian problem." Morgan hoped to help along that solution by strictly applying the Government's policies, even if they had to be imposed by force. Morgan's report was spiced by an account of the Messiah craze among the Sioux and the subsequent train of fateful events which led to the "Battle" of Wounded Knee and the shooting of Sitting Bull. Even in the Government's telling of the story, it is possible to observe the enormous gap between cultures—both Indian and white, and military and civilian—which caused misunderstandings and minor injustices to escalate into murder and devastation.

A Settled Indian Policy

A VARIETY OF CAUSES have of late conspired to stimulate public interest in the subject of Indian administration, and to provoke a very widespread discussion of the so-called Indian problem. As was to be expected, there has been a great diversity of views expressed, and many discordant theories advanced as to its proper solution. I think, however, there is coming to be a very general consensus of opinion as to the essential elements that should enter into the settled policy of the Government in all its dealings with these people, and I venture to suggest the most important of them here with a view of furnishing a test of the present administration.

(1) Comprehensiveness.—It is important that any theory shall rest primarily upon a careful induction of all pertinent facts. No two reservations are exactly similar, and no two tribes present the same condition. The Indians, while alike as belonging to one common race and as sustaining to the United States Government the general relation of wards, differ among themselves very widely in language, manners, customs, religion, and environment. They represent a great number of distinct phases of human development.

Some are yet very degraded, living a mere animal life with few of the characteristics of humanity, while others have already become absorbed into

526

our national life and are not distinguishable from their fellow citizens. Some still live by hunting and fishing; others, like the Navajos, are successful herders; many cultivate the soil with an increasing degree of success, and others already participate in manufacturing, mercantile, and professional life. While some, like the White Mountain Apaches, are almost destitute of anything that may be characterized as education, others, like the Poncas and the Pawnees, have almost all their children of suitable age in school. While the great majority of the 250,000 receive absolutely nothing directly from the Government in the way of subsistence or support, others, like the Sioux, Cheyennes, Arapahoes, and Apaches, are dependent largely upon Government rations.

Although many, like those just mentioned, are under the immediate control of the Government and require more or less of vigilant surveillance, multitudes of others, such as the Indians in New York, those in Michigan, and the 65,000 of the five civilized tribes, are only nominally under Government control, while thousands, like the Santee Sioux, the Sissetons and Wahpetons, the Nez Percés, the Puyallups, etc., are, by the operation of the land-in-severalty law, becoming citizens and gradually passing out from under governmental supervision.

Any theory which ignores these essential facts and attempts to deal with them *en masse* must, of necessity, be radically and fatally defective. Any rational scheme, therefore, must rest upon a careful survey of the present condition, needs, and possibilities of each of the tribes, and must also, of necessity, be very general in its character.

(2) Definiteness of aim.—There has hitherto been more or less confusion in the public mind as to precisely what the Government is aiming to accomplish, and so long as this uncertainty exists there can be no considerable progress toward determining the best measures to be adopted. If it were the purpose of the Government to exterminate the Indians by violence, or to leave them to shift for themselves under such circumstances that their destruction would be only a question of time, this purpose would necessarily determine legislation and administration. If the object were to simply guard them as prisoners of war, feeding and supporting them in idleness, as it is sometimes asserted the Government is doing, without regard to the future outcome of this policy, this purpose should be clearly avowed and should have its weight in determining everything pertinent to Indian matters.

If, however, the purpose is to incorporate the Indians into the national life as independent citizens, so that they may take their places as integral elements in our society, not as American Indians but as Americans, or rather as men, enjoying all the privileges and sharing the burdens of American citizenship, then this purpose should be not only clearly and definitely stated, but should be dominant in all matters of legislation and administration. It should be understood not only by our own people but by the Indians themselves, and should be inculcated as a fundamental doctrine in every Indian school.

No pains should be spared to teach the rising generation that the old condition of things is rapidly and forever passing away, and that they must prepare themselves for self-support. This is the inevitable, from which there is no escape. They should be taught that their future lies largely in their own hands, and that if they improve the opportunities for education now so generously offered them by the Government, they may become intelligent, prosperous, strong, and happy; but that if they neglect them they will be swept aside or crushed by the irresistible tide of civilization, which has no place for drones, no sympathy with idleness, and no rations for the improvident.

(3) Clearness of outline.—In the process of elevating a rude and barbarous people to the plane of civilization there is involved a combination of many forces—heredity, tradition, soil, climate, food supply, and the needs of surrounding civilization. There are also involved the great forces of legislation, administration, and institutions—such as industrial schools and missionary agencies—and a failure to comprehend the legitimate work of each of these great factors leads inevitably to gross errors in judgment. We can not gather grapes from thistles nor figs from thorns.

Perhaps one of the most mischievous fallacies is the assumption that because the Anglo-Saxon race has been centuries in developing its present proud civilization it is therefore necessary that the same length of time should be consumed by the Indians in passing through the successive stages of economic and social evolution. Time as an element in human progress is relative, not absolute. Indian children taken from a life which represents Anglo-Saxon barbarism of more than a thousand years ago may, if placed at an early age in proper relations with modern civilization, enter very largely into participation of the best results of nineteenth century life. A good school may thus bridge over for them the dreary chasm of a thousand years of tedious evolution.

(4) Adaptation of means to ends.—If the Indians are expected to thrive by agriculture they should not be thrust aside onto sterile plains or into the mountains, but should be allowed to occupy such portions of the country as are adapted to agricultural pursuits. If the forces of nature are too strong for them to cope with single-handed, than they should have such assistance from the Government as will enable them to succeed. A little timely help would, in many cases, be sufficient to put them upon the road to self-support and independence when withholding would doom them to hopeless struggle. If we expect the rising generation to become intelligent, we should see to it that they have ample opportunities for education. If we design that they should be industrious we should encourage among them all forms of handicraft. If we wish them to become self-reliant we should throw them upon their own responsibility and exact of them strict obedience to law. If we expect them to be just we should set them an example. It is as true in our dealings with them as it is in the natural world that "Whatsoever a man soweth that shall he also reap."

(5) Justice.—The charge most frequently brought against the American people in reference to their dealings with the Indians is that of injustice. This charge is sometimes flippantly made, and oftentimes rests upon no historical basis, and yet it is unfortunately true that the impression widely prevails in the popular mind and is deeply rooted in the mind of the Indians that treaties have been broken and that the Government has failed in numerous instances to perform its most solemn obligations. It certainly cannot be said that this great nation has intended to be unjust, and recent acts of legislation have shown conclusively a desire not only on the part of Congress, but of the people of the country generally, to fulfill to the letter all the obligations, promises, and even expectations of the Indians.

But justice is two-sided. It demands as well as concedes. While it is desirable that we should pay the Indians to the last dollar all that is due them, we should expect of them the fulfillment of their obligations. They should be held to a strict accountability for their deliberate actions, and where, without provocation, they go upon the warpath, commit outrages, destroy property, or otherwise disturb the peace, they should be punished.

It is also worthy of consideration that in the past we have made agreements which later developments have shown to be unwise and undesirable both for them and for us. Such are all those treaties which recognize the autonomy and perpetual independent nationality of the tribes. One great political truth has been made absolutely clear by the march of events, and that is that the people of the United States constitute one nation. There is no place within our borders for independent, alien governments, and the Indians most of necessity surrender their autonomy and become merged in our nationality. In requiring this we do not ask that they concede anything of real value to themselves, but only that for their highest welfare they abandon their tribal organizations, their provincialisms, their isolation, and accept in lieu thereof American citizenship and a full participation in all the riches of our civilization. By this great transformation they are the gainers, rather than we ourselves.

(6) Firmness.—Thousands of them are yet in a stage of childhood; they are living in the twilight of civilization, weak, ignorant, superstitious, and as little prepared to take care of themselves as so many infants. It is therefore unwise, out of excessive regard for their manhood, to defer wholly to their wishes with reference to what is clearly for their good. The allotment of land, the restriction of the power of alienation, the compulsory education of their children, the destruction of the tribal organization, the bestowment of citizenship, the repression of heathenish and hurtful practices, the suppression of outbreaks, and punishment for lawlessness are among the things which belong unmistakably to the prerogatives of the National Government.

Equally evident is it that those who, by the beneficent aid of the Government or otherwise, have been rendered capable of self-support must depend upon themselves and not look to it for help. There is no more reason why the General Government should feed and clothe an Indian who is able to feed and clothe himself by his own industry than there is why it should feed and clothe any other man.

The circumstances that justify and require the establishment and maintenance for a time of industrial schools, in which Indian youth may be trained for self-support, are exceptional and transitory, and in the very nature of the case will pass away. All that can be asked is that a reasonable opportunity be afforded to these people whereby their children can be lifted onto a plane where they will have something like an equal chance in life's struggles along with the more favored races in this country. If, after this reasonable preparation, they are unable or unwilling to sustain themselves, they must go to the wall. It will be a survival of the fittest. It is rightly claimed that thus far they have not had an equal chance with the rest of us, by reason of their isolation, and the present effort of the Government in the establishment of costly Indian schools is for the purpose of removing this inequality and bringing the Indian children into competitive relations with other children. Justice demands this, but it asks no more.

(7) Humanity.—It should be borne in mind, however, that this peculiar people are our brethren, made of the same blood, and as such have claims upon us. This vast country which is now the scene and the support of our greatness once belonged to them. Step by step they have been driven back from the hills and beautiful valleys of New England, the fertile fields of Ohio, the prairies of the West, until to-day, for the most part, they are gathered together on reservations poorly suited for agricultural purposes, and where the conditions of life are the hardest. The buffalo and the deer, which only a few years ago were found in countless thousands and afforded them food, raiment, barter, and occupation, are about gone, and they are, in many cases, driven by stress of circumstances over which they have no control to desperate straits for food. As a people they are poor and weak and well-nigh helpless. The vast and resistless tide of European emigration and the overflow of our aggressive population have despoiled them of their hunting grounds, robbed them of their richest fields, restricted them in their freedom, destroyed thousands of them in battle, and inflicted upon them great suffering.

A large part of this, of course, has been the inevitable consequence of the conflict of a higher, stronger civilization with a lower and weaker one. In this day of our greatness and prosperity we can afford to treat them with the greatest kindness. We can not afford to be cruel. For their own sake, and for ours as well, and for the sake of the history we are making as a Christian nation, we should treat them not only justly and humanely, but with as much generosity as is consistent with their highest welfare. This we are doing.

(8) Radicalness.—"Whatever is worth doing is worth doing well." The course of the Government has not always been self-consistent. Legislation has been tentative and administration fitful. Many things have been attempted, but few have been accomplished. Now that there is coming to be a

pretty well recognized and rational policy, it should be carried into execution with as much vigor as is practicable, to the end that the results anticipated from it may be reached as speedily as possible.

If the policy of allotting lands is conceded to be wise, then it should be applied at an early day to all alike wherever the circumstances will warrant. If we have settled upon the breaking up of the tribal relations, the extinguishment of the Indian titles to surplus lands, and the restoration of the unneeded surplus to the public domain, let it be done thoroughly. If reservations have proven to be inadequate for the purposes for which they were designed, have shown themselves a hindrance to the progress of the Indian as well as an obstruction in the pathway of civilization, let the reservations, as speedily as wisdom dictates, be utterly destroyed and entirely swept away.

If we purpose to educate Indian children let us educate all of them. The reasons that determine us to educate the few apply with increasing force to the education of the many. If we look to the schools as one of the chief factors of the great transformation that is being wrought, why not at once establish enough to embrace the entire body of available Indian youth, and thus not only hasten but render doubly sure their good work. "Make haste slowly" does not seem to apply here. There is now a widespread demand for education among the Indians; it has become comparatively easy to secure the attendance of their children, and the work of education has proceeded so far as to establish beyond question the advisability of educating them to self-support, so that there would seem to be no good reason why the system of education that has been, since 1876, gathering force and strength, should not at once be so far extended as to be entirely adequate for the end in view. If this were done, and there could be gathered by the end of 1893 into well-manned and suitably equipped schools nearly all the Indian children, and they could be kept there for 10 years, the work would be substantially accomplished; for within those 10 years there would grow up a generation of English-speaking Indians, accustomed to the ways of civilized life, and sufficiently intelligent and strong to forever after be the dominant force among them.

(9) Stability.—Having determined upon a policy, we should regard it as permanent until its work is accomplished. Whatever laws are to be passed should be framed with reference to the perfecting and not the essential modification of the plan. All acts of administration should be with reference to its success. Agents should be selected, employés appointed, regulations framed, and orders given with a single eye to the speediest and most complete carrying out of the purpose of the Government as formulated. The day of experiment should be ended. Consistency in legislation, uniformity in administration, permanence of the tenure of office based upon intelligent comprehension of the work to be done, and competence and fidelity in the discharge of duty would very materially hasten the successful accomplishment of the wise ends of the Government.

(10) Time.—The great forces now at work; land in severalty with its

accompanying dissolution of the tribal relation and breaking up of the reservation; the destruction of the agency system; citizenship, and all that belongs thereto of manhood, independence, privilege, and duty; education, which seeks to bring the young Indians into right relationship with the age in which they live, and to put into their hands the tools by which they may gain for themselves food and clothing and build for themselves homes, will, if allowed to continue undisturbed a reasonable length of time, accomplish their beneficent ends. They should be fostered, strengthened, maintained, and allowed to operate.

Other forces scarcely less powerful than these, namely, the progress of our own civilization, which is invading the reservations and surrounding the Indians on every side, the progress of Christianity through the active missionary efforts of the churches, the changed conditions which have forced upon the Indians themselves the necessity of greater efforts towards self-help and improvement, combine and coöperate with the organized efforts of the Government to bring about their uplifting.

How long it will take for the work to be completed depends partly upon the wisdom of Congress when making necessary laws, partly upon the will of the Executive in making appointments and giving direction to Indian affairs, partly upon the fidelity and intelligence of agents and others chosen to superintend the work, partly upon the vigor and efficiency of the schools and those employed to teach industries, partly upon the zeal of Christian churches and humanitarians, and largely upon the spirit of those of our people who find themselves in face-to-face relationship with Indian families and individuals, on the reservations and elsewhere. It is not safe to prophesy, and in view of the past hundred years it may be unwise to predict, yet I will venture to say that it is possible, before the close of the present century, to carry this matter so far towards its final consummation as to put it beyond the range of anxiety. Not everything can be accomplished within that time, but enough can be done so that the Commissioner who writes the seventieth annual report can speak of the Indian solution instead of the Indian problem.

* * *

A Precarious Situation

The Government has now full care of the estates of the Indian tribes as represented by their lands and by their trust funds upon which interest is annually paid to them and for their benefit, and, to a limited extent, it has control over and care of the persons of the Indians themselves. It is in these respects that our relations to the Indian tribes and to the Indians themselves have been said to resemble those of a guardian to his ward. This paternal care and control of their affairs was assumed by the United States by virtue of the necessities of the situation and not by virtue of any power granted the nation in the Constitution. The degraded condition of the

Indians, their thriftless habits, and their ignorance of and inability to adapt themselves to the customs of the whites, as well as to cope with them in commerce, all required that some proper authority should be exercised in protecting the tribes "against further decline and final extinction" and their estates from waste and destruction. As the only power competent under the circumstances to exercise this guardian care it devolved upon the United States.

When the Indians shall have become citizens of the United States this paternal control will cease. They will no longer be subject in any respect to restraint by this office, but will have the right to go where they please and when they please. Their contracts will not be subject to approval by the Commissioner of Indian Affairs or the Secretary of the Interior, but will stand on an equal footing with those of other United States citizens. There will be no restriction of trade with them, and in fact whatever rights may be enjoyed by a citizen of the United States will be theirs, and they will no longer be subject to arrest at the instance of a United States Indian agent or by the Indian police, nor to trial and punishment by the courts of Indian offenses for misdemeanors over which those courts now have jurisdiction.

At the same time, with the exception that their lands received under allotment laws will be exempt from taxation for a period of twenty-five years, and possibly longer, they will be subject to the burdens borne by other citizens, and must manage their own affairs.

Except in a very few cases where the members of a particular tribe have had peculiar advantages over others, in acquiring the habits and customs of our civilization and a knowledge of the laws of our commerce, the Indian naturalized into the United States, under recent laws provided for the purpose, will find himself in a most precarious and dangerous situation. Unaccustomed to the recognition in him of any rights as an individual, and accustomed as he is to regard himself only as an integral part of the unit represented by his tribe, subject to the control and protection of the United States, he will find himself suddenly released from his wardship and ushered upon the threshold of a new life, with new privileges and new responsibilities, the gravity of which his untutored mind is possibly incapable of comprehending. In this new career he will be alone, and alone he must solve the problems of his life. Whether he will be able to successfully conduct his own affairs, cope with his more intelligent and more active white neighbor, and make himself a good citizen, is a problem for the future to solve.

Citizenship Inevitable.

The policy above outlined will eventually make all Indians citizens of the United States, when the Indian reservation will no longer appear on our maps, and the autonomy of the tribes, a fact to us, will be mere history to the generations that will come.

Nearly every year Congress has taken a step toward the full recognition of the individuality of the Indian, the final abolition of tribal organizations, and the total extinction of the tribal sovereignty, and this is what the future has inevitably in store for the race. It may be remote, but the time is surely coming when these alien, quasi-independent nations within our territorial limits will have disappeared, and the individuals composing them will have been absorbed in our population, becoming fully and completely subject to the jurisprudence of the United States, both civil and criminal.

* * *

PRACTICAL CONCLUSIONS

It seems to me that since the Government has assumed the guardianship of the Indian tribes, and has for years, by direct Congressional enactments, controlled their affairs and cared for and protected the Indians themselves, it should now take some steps which will take away from all Indian tribes absolutely their character as nations, and bring them completely and fully under subjection to its laws.

From the foregoing discussion of the political status of the Indians it seems to me the following practical conclusions may be drawn:

First. During the whole course of our history the Indians of this country have been treated as separate communities, sustaining exceptional relations to us. They have been regarded as having relations directly with the General Government alone and not indirectly through the States or to the States.

Second. That the fiction of regarding them as independent peoples has been displaced by the theory of regarding and treating them as wards of the General Government.

Third. That the purpose of the Government, as has been made more evident, is to change their status from that of wardship to that of citizenship.

Fourth. That during the transition period and until the completion of their citizenship they should be regarded as subject to the laws of the General Government and under its care and guardianship.

In this connection I submit that the time has come for establishing laws and courts among the Indians under the authority of the General Government. In doing this it would seem wise that these laws should be assimilated in each case to those of the State or Territory in which the reservation is situated, and that any system of courts should build upon the existing courts of Indian offenses.

Fifth. That the time has come for a declaration by Congress to the effect that hereafter it will not recognize the Indians as competent to make war, but that in our dealings with them they shall be treated not as belligerents, but as subject and dependent people, capable, of course, of insurrection, rioting, or disturbance of the peace, but not of waging war.

Sixth. That the General Government has the right, both for its own protection, for the promotion of the public welfare, and for the good of the Indians, not only to establish schools in which their children may be prepared for citizenship, but also to use whatever force may be necessary to secure to the Indian children the benefit of these institutions. Even in the cases where, by taking their lands in severalty, they are in process of becoming citizens, they are still in a state of quasi-independence, because the General Government withholds from them for twenty-five years the power of alienating their lands, while by exempting them from taxation for the same period it practically excludes their children from the public schools. For these reasons it would seem that the Government has not only the right, but is under obligation to make educational provisions for them, and to secure to their children the benefits of those provisions.

Seventh. I venture also to suggest whether the time may not be near for the passage of an enabling act whereby the five civilized tribes may form either a Territorial or a State government and be represented on the floors of Congress.

Eighth. That the time has come when the Pueblo Indians should be admitted by special act of Congress "to the enjoyment of all the rights of citizens of the United States according to the principles of the Constitution," as contemplated by the treaty of Guadalupe Hidalgo.

Ninth. The definite determination by the highest authority of the actual political status of the Indians is necessary as a basis of wise legislation and to the satisfactory administration of Indian affairs.

Change of Tribal Relations

A matter requiring frequent attention is the desire of Indians to leave the tribes to which they belong and join others. Their nomadic instincts are in a great measure responsible for this, but in some instances, especially among the mixed bloods, business interests or family connections constitute the main reason for the wish to change.

The importance of the subject in the administration of the affairs of the Indian may be readily appreciated when it is remembered that the tribes occupying the various reservations are completely distinct from and independent of each other as to tribal citizenship, property rights, etc., and that some are much richer in lands and annuities than others.

In each case the approval of the office is requisite for a change of tribe, and when the tribe into which incorporation is sought has under treaty or law the exclusive right to its reservation, the request of the applicant is not granted unless he is able to secure a formal adoption by said tribe. It is also essential that he relinquish and renounce all rights, interests, and benefits in the tribe he wishes to leave.

Favorable action upon such applications is not taken as a matter of course upon the adoption of the applicant and his relinquishment of rights elsewhere, but each case is considered in all its bearings upon both parties involved, and is decided entirely on its own merits.

INDIAN SOLDIERS

Indians now form an integral part of the Regular Army. The enlistment of not exceeding 1,000 scouts was authorized by sections 1094 and 1112 of the Revised Statutes—taken from the act of July 28, 1866 (14 *Stats.*, p. 333)—the latter section providing that they should serve in the Territories and Indian country, and should be discharged when the necessity for their service should cease, or at the discretion of the department commander.

On April 1 last, by Department reference, this office received copies of Army orders, directing the enlistment of Indians as soldiers in the regular Army, accompanied by request that the agents in charge of tribes and reservations be instructed to afford every facility and encouragement to the officers of the Army charged with the raising of Indian companies. The office promptly complied with the request.

A later communication from the Secretary of War stated that among the inquiries made by Indians of the recruiting officers was whether those who became soldiers would lose their right to lands, annuities, and other assistance furnished by this bureau in fulfillment of treaties. This office replied in the negative.

Up to the present time quite a number of Indians have been enlisted, and some encouraging reports have been received from those in command of them; but it is of course too early to predict permanent results. The discipline to which they must submit in the military service, and the regular duties involved, will doubtless be of advantage to them, while the feeling that they are United States soldiers, armed to battle by the side of the whites in a common cause, should occasion arise, will awaken patriotic sentiments, and tend to inspire mutual confidence and friendship between the two races. The final outcome of this experiment must, of necessity, depend very largely upon the character of the officers immediately in charge, and upon the kind of discipline and instruction to which the Indians are subjected.

ALLOTMENT OF LANDS

During the past year the work of allotting lands in severalty has been pushed with unusual vigor. The idea of a separate home, with its attendant advantages and incidental disadvantages, has become more or less familiar to the great body of Indians, and has been received by most of them with increasing favor. It is a great change, a radical and far-reaching revolution, for them to abandon their tribal occupancy and to accept of individual holdings.

HINDRANCES TO ALLOTMENT

It is a fact not generally understood, perhaps, that the common possession of land by a tribe is in many cases nominal rather than actual. It occurs among Indians as among others that there are ambitious and powerful men who reach out and lay claim to a larger portion of the common heritage than can be properly claimed by them as individuals. It is not uncommon to find Indians who exercise a sort of ownership over vast bodies of land and who have in their own right extensive herds and flocks. There are among them, as among us, the rich and the poor. When, therefore, it is proposed to divide their land among them individually, giving to each the same amount, the argument for it is, in many cases, very much the same as if it were proposed to take all the real estate of New York City and divide it equally among its several inhabitants. It is not surprising, therefore, that there should be, on the part of the more aggressive, able, and prosperous Indians, very serious objections urged against the policy of an equal distribution of the landed estate of the tribe. It is indeed quite surprising that the general policy of allotting the tribal lands in equal quantities to all individuals has been received with as much favor as it has.

Another hindrance to the successful operation of the land-in-severalty law arises from the fact that there are among the Indians a large number who, for one reason or another, are incapable of managing successfully a landed estate. Many of them know little of farming and care less, and the children, the widows, the diseased, the infirm, are incapable of making any use of the wild, uncultivated lands which are offered them.

Multitudes of them have no true conception of the value of good land, and moreover a large proportion of that which it is proposed to divide up among them is practically worthless. In some instances it consists of vast tracts of sandy plain, absolutely sterile and unfit for cultivation without extensive and costly irrigation; in others, of mountainous tracts fit only for grazing purposes and suitable for this only when fenced and guarded from the encroachments of the cattle of the white man; in other cases it is heavily timbered and valuable only for its lumber, which too frequently the Indians are unable to utilize. In a large number of instances, therefore, giving an Indian 80 acres of land and asking him to make it his home and gain from it a subsistence, when he has no farming implements, no horses or cattle, no house but a tepee, no knowledge of farming, no ability to bring the wild land under cultivation, seems but a mockery.

Another very serious matter to consider in this connection is that when they have received their land in severalty they become thereby citizens of the United States and have thrust upon them the obligations of citizenship for which they are often absolutely unprepared. They are brought under the operation of laws which they do not understand; are taken largely from the care and guardianship of the General Government, upon which they have been accustomed to lean for protection; are thrown upon their own resources and subjected to the fierce competitions of border civilization, for which they have little or no preparation.

Land in severalty has in it "the promise and the potency" of great things, but only the promise and the potency. Very much depends upon the manner of its administration. In many cases it brings unutterable woe, and in all it is liable to leave the Indians worse off then before. It certainly would be a great misfortune to them as a body to thrust severalty and citizenship upon them suddenly; they ought to be prepared for the great change; it should come to them gradually, and certainly should be accompanied with such safeguards as are dictated by common sense and humanity.

Land in severalty without education may prove a bane rather than a blessing.

EARLY ALLOTMENTS

The policy of dividing lands owned or occupied in common by an Indian tribe among its several members was inaugurated by act of March 3, 1839, which authorized division of the lands of the Brothertown Indians (Wisconsin) by a commission of five of their principal head men, and for the issuance of patents in fee simple to the Indians and their heirs and assigns.

The act also provided that upon the filing of the report of this commission, with a map of the allotments, and the transmission of the same to the President, the Brothertown Indians should be deemed citizens of the United States, and be subject to its laws, and to those of the Territory of Wisconsin.

By law or treaty this policy was subsequently applied, with various modifications as to the tenure of the lands allotted, the status of the allottees, the right of alienation, etc., to several other tribes, notably the Ottawas and Chippewas, the Pottawatomies, the Shawnees, and the Wyandottes.

The Brothertown Indians (remnants of the Mohican and other New York tribes) long since passed from the notice of this office, and, so far as the other tribes are concerned, the records show that where their lands were conveyed in fee simple, with no restrictions as to alienation, they soon parted with them without sufficient consideration, and squandered what little they received. The disastrous result of this policy in several cases has led this office to insist that the right of alienation should be limited in some manner, so that Indians can not improvidently dispose of their lands.

PROGRESS IN ALLOTMENTS

In 1887 the first general law was enacted (24 *Stats.*, 388), and by its provisions lands were to be given to the several members of a tribe (except married women), in quantities differing according to the age of the allottee, or status as the head of a family, or otherwise.

Difficulties having arisen in regard to its administration, Congress was asked to amend the act so as to provide for the allotment of the same quantity of land to each member of the tribe. This was done by the act of February 28, 1891 (26 *Stats.*, 794), which secures the only fair and equitable division of tribal property, each member of the tribe having an equal share.

The general allotment act provides that lands, when allotted, shall not be immediately conveyed to the allottees, but shall be held in trust for a period of 25 years (which period may be indefinitely extended by the President), at the end of which it is to be conveyed to the allottee or his heirs, in fee, discharged of the trust and free of all incumbrance. The allottee is thus secured in the possession of his home for at least 25 years, during which time the force of example, education, and contact with white civilization, will, in a great degree, fit him for absolute and unconditioned ownership. Special acts have since been passed or agreements concluded under which allotments have been made or are to be made, but all of them contain substantially the same provision as to the trust period.

The work of making allotments has been carried on since the date of the last annual report, as follows: To the Indians on the Yankton Reservation, 1,484 patents have been issued and will be delivered at an early day. The work of revising allotments made to the Yankton Sioux, rendered necessary by the act of February 28, 1891, was begun about the 1st of June last and will probably be completed by the 1st of January next.

To the Sac and Fox Indians of Oklahoma, 548 patents have been issued and delivered under the agreement ratified by the act of February 13, 1891 (26 *Stats.*, 749), by which 160 acres were allotted to each member of the tribe, 80 acres to be held in trust for 5 years and 80 acres for a period of 25 years.

To the Eastern Shawnees in the Indian Territory, 72 patents have been issued and delivered.

The following allotments have been approved and the issuance of patents directed:

Modocs in the Indian Territory	68
Papagoes in Arizoua	291
Poncas on South Dakota	167
Grande Ronde Indians in Oregon	269
Citizen Pottawatomies in Oklahoma	1,363
Absentee Shawnees in Oklahoma	563
Iowas in Oklahoma	109
Total	2,830

A schedule of 1,530 allotments made to the Oneida Indians in Wisconsin has also been submitted for approval.

The following schedules of allotments have been received in this office, but not yet acted upon:

To Sac and Fox Indians in Kansas and Nebraska	76
To Wyandottes in Indian Territory	238

Work is progressing in the field as follows:

On the Lake Traverse Reservation, in South Dakota, it will probably be completed early in October.

On the Devil's Lake Reservation, in North Dakota, it will doubtless be finished during the present season.

On the Nez Percés Reservation, Idaho, there is fair prospect of completing the work in the field before winter.

Work on the Jicarilla Apache Reservation, in New Mexico, is nearly completed.

Reports from the Siletz Reservation, in Oregon, do not indicate very rapid progress.

Allotments to the Tonkawas, in Oklahoma, are finished.

Allotments are progressing on the Otoe Reservation, though with considerable opposition.

Satisfactory progress is being made on the Crow Creek and Lower Brulé reservations.

Very little has been accomplished among the Kickapoos and Pottawatomies, of Kansas.

Allotments are in progress on the Umatilla Reservation, Oregon.

In April last a corps of five agents was appointed to make allotments on the Cheyenne and Arapaho Reservation, in Oklahoma, as provided in the agreement with these Indians ratified by the act of Congress approved March 3, 1891 (26 *Stats.*, 1022). They proceeded to duty early in May, but owing to the refusal of the Indians to take allotments until they had received the payment stipulated, they were unable to commence work before the middle of July. Subsequently two more agents were added to the corps. On the 13th of September they had made some 1,325 allotments, the total number entitled to allotments being about 3,300. The appropriation of $15,000 available for prosecuting the work became exhausted on the 30th of September, and it was therefore found necessary (on the 26th) to discontinue further work in the field.

Work is in progress on the Sioux ceded lands in South Dakota.

Surveys have been executed on the Wind River Reservation, in Wyoming, with a view to future allotments, and have been contracted for on the Moqui Reservation, in Arizona, and the Rosebud Reservation, in South Dakota.

The present season will close the work on a large number of reservations. Hereafter it will doubtless proceed more slowly, the Indians on many of the unallotted reservations being wholly unprepared for this important change in their condition.

ALLOTMENTS TO NON-RESERVATION INDIANS

Under the 4th section of the general allotment act of 1887, a number of applications for allotments have been presented by Indians off reservations; but owing to the press of other duties during the year and the lack of proper clerical force allotments have not as yet been made.

Prior to March 3, 1891, no appropriation had been made to assist non-reservation Indians in making applications for allotment under said section, and in consequence but little progress could be made in this direction; but whenever and wherever practicable this office has instructed agents and special agents to aid in the preparation of applications and in securing the proof required for an allotment.

October 7, 1890, Special Agent Lewis was instructed to proceed to the vicinity of Redding, Cal., for the purpose of assisting the Wintu and Yana Indians. But soon afterward it became necessary to detail him to ascertain and report the condition of affairs among the Indians around Fort Bidwell, Cal., and subsequently his appointment as United States special attorney for the Mission Indians in that State caused a temporary cessation of the work.

October 13, 1890, Special Agent Litchfield was instructed to allot lands to non-reservation Indians in Washington and Oregon and to assist Indian homesteaders in making final proof and completing title to entries already made.

November 5, 1890, Agent Sears, of the Nevada Agency, was instructed to aid certain Indians in Nevada in securing their allotments, and his successor, Agent Warner, is continuing the work.

By act of March 3, 1891 (26 *Stats.*, 989), the Secretary of the Interior is authorized and directed to apply the balance of the sum carried upon the books of the Treasury Department, under the title of Homesteads for Indians, in the employment of allotting agents, and payment of their necessary expenses, to assist Indians desiring to take homesteads under section four of the general allotment act. Michael Piggott, of Illinois, has been appointed special agent for the prosecution of this work.

Authority has been granted for the agent of the Mission Indians in California to use a portion of the said funds for the purpose of assisting those who desire to take homes in the southern portion of that State.

The office correspondence shows that many Indians, seeing the public lands rapidly disappearing, are manifesting a strong desire and are even making efforts to secure a title to the lands which they have long used and occupied. With the funds on hand and the agents in the field it is expected that the next year will witness much progress in this direction.

PRACTICAL RESULTS OF ALLOTMENTS

I am not in receipt of enough information, nor indeed has sufficient time elapsed, to enable me to judge of the practical results of the allotment policy. I purpose at an early day to institute a series of careful inquiries regarding the status and prospects of individual Indians who have not only taken their lands, but have also endeavored to improve them. The result of such inquiries, if thoroughly prosecuted, ought to be very valuable to this office in administration as well as to Congress in determining future legislation.

I have seen nothing during the year to lead me to change my views as to its ultimate success, although doubtless the change will come with too great suddenness to some of the tribes.

REDUCTION OF RESERVATIONS

The work of reducing the area of the reservations, by extinguishing by purchase from the Indians their title to the land and its restoration to the public domain, has been carried forward rapidly, as is shown in the following detailed statements:

Counting the 22 small reserves of the Mission Indians of California as only one reserve and the 19 Pueblo reserves of New Mexico as one also, the number of reservations as given in the annual report of this office for 1890 was 138, having an aggregate area of about 104,314,349 acres, or 162,991 square miles. This amount is about 12,071,380 acres, or 18,861 square miles, less than the amount reported in 1889, while at the present time there are five more reservations than in 1889, owing to the division of the Great Sioux Reservation, as provided by act of March 2, 1889.

The agreements ratified by act of Congress approved February 13, 1891 (26 *Stats.*, 749), restored to the public domain 391,184.65 acres from the Sac and Fox Reservations, in Oklahoma, including 25,194.61 acres for school purposes; and from the Iowa Reservation, in the same Territory, 219,446.27 acres, including 12,271.75 acres for school purposes. The ratification of agreements by the act of March 3, 1891 (26 *Stats.*, 989), restored to the public domain from the Pottawatomie Reservation, Oklahoma, 309,134.77 acres, including 22,650.44 for school purposes; from the Cheyenne and Arapaho Reservation, Okalahoma, about 3,000,000 acres; from the Coeur d'Alêne Reservation, Idaho, about 185,000 acres; from the Fort Berthold Reservation, North Dakota, about 1,600,000 acres; from the Lake Traverse Reservation, South Dakota, about 660,000 acres, and from the Crow Reservation, Montana, about 1,800,000 acres; a total of about 8,164,765 acres.

The following schedule shows the disposition of the lands embraced within the Pottawatomie, Iowa, and Sac and Fox Reservations above mentioned:

POTTAWATOMIE.

	Acres
Allotted	286,494.33
Opened to settlement	266,241.93
Reserved for school lands	22,650.44
Reserved for (Indian) school, church, and agency purposes	490.63

IOWA.

Allotted	8,685.30
Opened to settlement	207,174.52
Reserved as school lands	12,271.75
Reserved for burying and other tribal uses	20.00

SAC AND FOX.

Allotted 87,683.64
Opened to settlement 365,990.04
Reserved as school lands 25,194.61
Reserved for agency and (Indian) school purposes 800.00

The ceded portion of the Fort Berthold Reservation, North Dakota, consisting of about 1,600,000 acres, has been thrown open to settlement by proclamation of the President.

The ceded lands of the Coeur d'Alêne Reservation, Idaho, were opened to settlement from the date of the approval of the act.

Allotments of land are being made on the Lake Traverse Reservation, South Dakota, and the Cheyenne and Arapaho Reservation, Oklahoma, and surveys are in progress upon the Crow Reservation, Montana, and when they are completed and the terms of the act ratifying the respective agreements with the Indians of the several reservations shall have been fully complied with, the unallotted or vacant lands embraced within the ceded portions will be thrown open to settlement.

The agreement with the Indians of the Southern Ute Reservation, in Colorado, referred to in my last annual report, was not ratified by the last Congress.

NEGOTIATIONS FOR FURTHER REDUCTIONS

The Indian appropriation act for the fiscal year ending June 30, 1892 (26 *Stats.*, 1010), contains the following provisions:

> To enable the Secretary of the Interior in his discretion to negotiate with any Indians for the surrender of portions of their respective reservations, any agreement thus negotiated being subject to subsequent ratification by Congress, $15,000 or so much thereof as may be necessary.

Under the provisions of this act the Secretary of the Interior has appointed three commissioners to negotiate with the Shoshone and Arapaho Indians of the Shoshone or Wind River Reservation, in Wyoming, for the surrender of such portion of their reservation as they choose to dispose of; also three commissioners to treat with the Indians of the Pyramid Lake Reservation, in Nevada, for the same purpose.

For some 2 years or more there has been rumor of the existence of rich gold and silver deposits in the Carrizo Mountains, within the Navajo reservation, in New Mexico and Arizona, and it is the settled belief of the people in that section of the country that there is rich mineral wealth in the mountains referred to.

Prospectors surreptitiously visited this region, and in the spring of 1890, by request of this office, the military removed a party of 15 who were found locating claims.

This reservation embraces an area of about 8,200,000 acres, and, though no accurate census of the tribe has ever been taken, its number has been variously estimated at from 14,000 to 20,000, a large proportion of whom reside outside on the public lands.

The reservation is, for the most part, largely worthless for agricultural purposes, and the Indians depend almost entirely upon their sheep, goats, and horses. They could surrender the northern central portion, where the Carrizo Mountains lie, without disadvantage to themselves. On the contrary, a sale of this land for a reasonable sum and a judicious investment of the same would prove beneficial to them.

It is proposed to negotiate with them at an early date for the cession of this portion of their reservation.

RESERVATIONS SHOULD NOT BE REDUCED TOO RAPIDLY

While perhaps it is possible to push such work too rapidly, I do not hesitate to say that the ultimate destruction of the entire system of reservations is inevitable. There is no place for it in our present condition of life, and it must go. The millions of acres of Indian lands now lying absolutely unused are needed as homes for our rapidly increasing population and must be so utilized. Whatever right and title the Indians have in them is subject to and must yield to the demands of civilization. They should be protected in the permanent possession of all this land necessary for their own support, and whatever is taken from them should be paid for at its full market value. But it can not be expected under any circumstances that these reservations can not remain intact, hindering the progress of civilization, requiring an army to protect them from the encroachments of home-seekers, and maintaining a perpetual abode of savagery and animalism. The Indians themselves are not slow to appreciate the force of the logic of events, and are becoming more and more ready to listen to propositions for the reduction of the reservations and the extinguishment of their title to such portions of the land as are not required for their own use.

The same considerations, however, which suggest the possibility of pushing the allotment of lands too rapidly also suggest the desirability of moving with caution and deliberation in reducing the reservations. If they are broken up too suddenly and violently, the harm resulting to the Indians would not be, by any means, counterbalanced by the benefit conferred upon other people. The ultimate swallowing up of the Indians by our civilization will be to them a decided benefit. Those Indians on reservations who live close to white settlements and come into vital relationship with civilized people make the greatest progress. They learn by contact and observation, and in many cases adopt the better ways of their more intelligent neighbors. There are, of course, exceptions to this, as our civilization bears, unfortunately, many elements of evil as well as of good. The Indians are quite as ready to copy the vices of the white man as his virtues. Gambling, intemperance, impurity, falsehood, larceny, idleness, are not peculiar to the Indians, and oftentimes are intensified by the precepts and examples of those who claim to belong to a superior race. Nevertheless, the fact remains that in general the building of towns, opening of farms, construction of railroads, establishment of schools, building of roads and bridges, etc., which are common incidents of the throwing open of a reservation to white settlement, are beneficial to the Indians who remain in close contact with the incoming tide of population. Among the great disadvantages under which they have lived hitherto have been their isolation, provincialism, and antagonism to civilization. They have looked upon the pale faces as their enemies, with whom they could have no dealings which would be of mutual advantage; but the breaking up of the reservations and the coming of the white men with all their better modes of life necessitate a closer acquaintance with each other and a knowledge of the general superiority of the white man's civilization. Multitudes of Indians are now beginning to understand this, readily accept the situation, and benefit by the change.

* * *

EDUCATION

When I assumed charge of this office I held the opinion that the solution of the Indian question lay chiefly in the line of education, and that consequently one of the most important functions of the Commissioner of Indian Affairs was the perfecting of the scheme for bringing all Indian youth of suitable age under proper instruction. Accordingly I have given to this subject my most earnest attention during the more than two years of my administration. I have considered it in well-nigh every possible phase, and am more and more convinced of the truth of the position which I have stated.

It is not to be expected that any people can be raised suddenly from a plane of barbarism or semicivilization to one of enlightenment and complete civilization. Race prejudices are strong, heredity and environment are hard to overcome, and it is not to be presumed that any single force operating alone can bring about so great a transformation. A scholastic knowledge of books merely will not accomplish it, neither will a knowledge of trades. Even a complete change in the environment will not effect it. There are living to-day in the heart of the city of London people who are as degraded as the North American Indians on the Indian reservations. There are people living in close contact with a superior race, by whom they have been surrounded for centuries, whose language they do not yet understand and whose customs and mode of life differ largely from their own. On the other hand, it is true, and the truth is illustrated in innumerable instances in our own country, that the children of foreigners taken into our public schools, where they learn the English language and associate with our children, imbibe their ideas and grow up to be in all respects Americans in spirit, in habits, and in character.

The process now going on by which nearly 20,000 Indian children are gathered into English-speaking schools, where they are taught by English-speaking people, where they learn the correct use of the English language, and come into relationship with American life and American thought, and have begotten within them new hopes and desires and changed ideas of life, is certain to work a revolution in the Indian character and to lift them on to a higher plane of civilization, if it can be allowed to operate long enough.

That there should be individual exceptions to this statement; that there should be lapses on the part of those who have enjoyed the advantages of these schools; that there should be many instances in which pupils of these schools have gone away without bearing the impress of the school with them, either from one cause or another; that there should be many who succumb to the tribal influences of reservation life to which they often return, is not at all to be wondered at.

All that I contend for, and for that I most strenuously do contend, is that the practical industrial English education now being furnished by the best equipped Government schools is sufficient, if it can be made to reach the great body of Indian youth, to work so complete a change in them that whether on or off the reservation they will enter upon a new career and show themselves in increasing numbers able to fight life's battles successfully. Education in its broad sense has made the American people what they are to-day, and education in the same sense must fit the Indian, if he is ever to become fitted, for participation in our civilization.

GROWTH OF ANNUAL APPROPRIATIONS

The necessity of education for the Indians has grown in the public mind year by year, and has found expression in increasing appropriations for this purpose by Congress. . . .

In fifteen years there has been a very rapid advance in the amount of money appropriated, and this great increase has not only expressed the will of Congress but it has been fully and even enthusiastically indorsed by the people in general. In nothing regarding this Indian question is there a more absolute agreement of public opinion than as to the necessity and desirability of extending the work of education until it shall be adequate for the training of all available Indian youth.

The efforts of the office during my administration have been directed to the study of the defects of the scheme of education which had grown up largely without system, and to the elimination of such evils as had gathered about it and the perfecting and extending of the scheme. The development of the school system has kept pace with the increase of appropriations. Schools already established have been enlarged and better equipped; new schools have been established; the attendance has rapidly increased, and in all respects the system has been greatly improved, and the Government Indian schools are now entering upon a new career of increased efficiency and enlarged usefulness, although much remains yet to be done.

INDUSTRIAL TRAINING SCHOOLS

I found in operation the following nonreservation Government Indian training schools: Carlisle, Pa.; Genoa, Nebr.; Fort Stevenson, N. Dak.; Grand Junction, Colo.; Chemawa, Oregon; Albuquerque, N.Mex.; Chilocco, Ind. T.; and Lawrence, Kans. Additional schools had been authorized by law at Pierre, S. Dak.; Carson, Nev.; and Santa Fé, N. Mex.

It was regarded as important that those already established should be completed and properly equipped. They were subjected to thorough inspection, and much thought and labor have been bestowed upon securing for them as complete an organization as practicable. When the improvements now in progress are finished the schools will rank very high and will do most excellent work. It will be possible next year to take good care of 1,000 students at Carlisle, of 600 at Lawrence, and of from 150 to 400 at each of the other schools named.

New schools.—During the present administration new training schools have been established at Fort Mojave and Phoenix, Ariz., and are now in successful operation.

Similar schools have been authorized and will be established during the coming year in Mt. Pleasant, Mich., Tomah, Wis., Pipestone, Minn., Flandreau, S. Dak., and Perris, Cal.

Attendance.—The following table exhibits the attendance during the year ending June 30, 1891, at the training schools:

Location, attendance, cost, etc., of non-reservation training schools during the fiscal year ended June 30, 1891.

Name of school	Location	Rate per annum	Capacity	Number of employes	Enrollment	Average attendance	Cost to Government
Carlisle School.........	Carlisle, Pa............	$167	*800	72	778	754	$106,393.81
Harrison Institute......	Chemawa, Oregon......	175	250	26	228	164	31,338.15
Howard Institute.......	Fort Stevenson, N. Dak..	....	150	18	112	98	14,420.01
Haworth Institute......	Chilocco, Ind. T........	167	200	31	187	164	24,220.03
Grant Institute........	Genoa, Nebr...........	167	250	33	238	199	41,897.46
Haskell Institute.......	Lawrence, Kans........	167	*500	57	551	487	82,632.17
Fisk Institute..........	Albuquerque, N. Mex....	175	225	40	201	188	29,245.54
Teller Institute........	Grand Junction, Colo....	175	60	12	81	35	....
Dawes Institute........	Sante Fe, N. Mex.......	175	75	17	90	45	10,065.17
Stewart Institute.......	Carson, Nev...........	175	100	16	140	84	13,129.85
Pierre Institute........	Pierre, S. Dak.........	167	150	13	81	49	5,851.21
Fort Mohave..........	Fort Mohave, Ariz.....	....	150	17	101	79	15,546.36

*Not including cost of buildings, repairs, and improvements.

I am constrained to look upon these nonreservation training schools with especial favor as affording facilities for the most useful all-around practical education. In addition to the ordinary elements of an English education, the pupils receive training in the common industries and are brought into close contact with civilized life. They become weaned from the reservation, have aspirations and hopes for a higher life awakened within them, become acquainted with the white man, and gradually learn to adapt themselves to the ways of modern life. I know the criticisms that are made on these schools, but my faith in them is unshaken.

By the "outing system" now in such successful operation at Carlisle and beginning to take root in other places (see Appendix, p. 151), increasing numbers of boys and girls will be enabled to find profitable employment in white communities, and will thus be prepared, as they could not be in any other possible way, for absorption into our national life.

I am fully aware of the objections that may be urged against gathering such large numbers of pupils into one institution, as is done at Carlisle and Haskell. There are, however, compensating advantages in large schools. The per capita cost of maintenance is necessarily greatly reduced; there is an *esprit du corps* awakened by the mere presence of numbers, and it is possible to secure a more perfect organization and distribution of industries in a large school than in a small one.

Heretofore, these schools have been modeled substantially after the same pattern, and all of them have attempted to do much the same kind of work. I am inclined to think that the time is near at hand when there should be some differentiation and when each should have its own specific work. For example, it would be well to devote special attention at Chilocco to the development of farming, including stock-raising and fruit-growing. At Haskell, in addition to shoe, harness, and wagon making, special attention might be paid to normal training. At Perris, Phoenix, and Grand Junction, there are reasons for making a specialty of fruit-growing. Especial attention is invited to the reports of the superintendents of these training schools as showing in detail the improvements that are being made. The record of industrial work is particularly gratifying.

I have recommended the establishment of a school at Fort Lewis for the Southern Utes, but at present I do not see the necessity for the establishment of any more nonreservation training schools unless possibly one should be established for the New York Indians. The nineteen now already in operation or in process of establishment, or recommended, will probably meet all the demands that are likely to be made. It will be desirable to enlarge and more properly equip some of them, but I am of the opinion that it would be better to enlarge those that are already authorized than to establish new ones.

RESERVATION BOARDING SCHOOLS

The following table exhibits the reservation boarding schools now in existence, with the date of their establishment:

Location and capacity and date of opening of Government reservation boarding schools.

	Capacity	Date of opening
Arizona:		
Colorado River	60	Mar., 1879
Navajo Agency	150	Dec., 1881
Keam's Cañon	100	——, 1887

	Capacity	Date of opening
Pima	125	Sept., 1881
San Carlos	75	Oct., 1880
California:		
Fort Yuma	250	Apr., 1884
Idaho:		
Fort Hall	200	——, 1874
Lemhi	25	Sept., 1885
Nez Percé Agency	60	Oct., 1868
Fort Lapwai	150	Sept., 1886
Indian Territory:		
Quapaw	75	Sept., 1872
Seneca, Shawnee, and Wyandotte	75	June, 1872
Kansas:		
Kickapoo	26	Oct., 1871
Pottawatomie	25	——, 1873
Sac and Fox and Iowa	40	——, 1871
		Sept., 1875
Minnesota:		
White Earth	110	——, 1871
Leech Lake	50	Nov., 1867
Red Lake	70	Nov., 1877
Montana:		
Blackfeet	50	Jan., 1883
Crow	50	Oct., 1874
Fort Peck	200	Aug., 1881
Fort Belknap	80	Aug., 1891
Nebraska:		
Omaha	65	——, 1881
Winnebago	75	Oct., 1874
Santee	100	April, 1874
Nevada:		
Pyramid Lake	48	Nov, 1882
New Mexico:		
Mescalero	50	April, 1884
North Carolina:		
Eastern Cherokee	80	Oct., 1884
North Dakota:		
Standing Rock, Agency	100	May, 1877
Standing Rock, Agricultural	100	——, 1878
Fort Totten, Whipple Institute	350	{ ——, 1874 / Jan., 1891
Oklahoma:		
Arapaho	100	Dec., 1875
Cheyenne	100	——, 1879
Riverside (Wichita)	60	Sept., 1871
Washita (Kiowa)	120	Feb., 1871
Fort Sill	45	Aug., 1891
Osage	150	Feb., 1874
Kaw	60	{ Dec., 1869 / Aug., 1874

	Capacity	Date of opening
Pawnee................................	100	{——, 1865 {——, 1878
Ponca................................	100	Jan., 1882
Otoe................................	80	Oct. 1875
Absentee Shawnee...................	60	May, 1872
Sac and Fox........................	40	——, 1868
		April, 1872
Oregon:		
Grand Ronde......................	110	April, 1874
Klamath..........................	110	Feb., 1874
Yainax...........................	90	Nov., 1882
Siletz...........................	70	Oct., 1873
Umatilla.........................	100	Jan., 1883
Warm Springs....................	60	June, 1884
Sinemasho.......................	75	Aug., 1882
South Dakota:		
Cheyenne River...................	60	{Jan., 1874 {——, 1880
Crow Creek......................	85	——, 1874
Lower Brulé......................	70	Oct., 1881
Pine Ridge.......................	250	Dec., 1883
Sisseton.........................	120	——, 1873
Yankton.........................	140	Feb., 1882
Utah:		
Uintah...........................	25	Jan., 1881
Washington:		
Neah Bay........................	56	July, 1868
Chehalis.........................	60	Jan., 1873
Pavallup.........................	125	June, 1871
Quinaielt........................	40	——, 1868
Skokomish.......................	60	Dec., 1866
Tulalip..........................	150	Jan., 1861
Okanagan........................	80	——, 1890
Yakama..........................	150	——. 1860
Wisconsin:		
Menomonee......................	100	——, 1876
Wyoming:		
Shoshone........................	75	April, 1879
Total...........................	6,290	

New schools.—During the present administration new reservation boarding schools have been established at Fort Belknap, Mont., Fort Totten, N. Dak., Fort Sill, Okla., and Okanagan, Wash.

New schools of this character are about to be established at the following places: In the San Juan country, Navajo Reservation; in the southwestern part of the Kiowa reserve; at Seger Colony on the Cheyenne and Arapaho reserve, and on the Round Valley, Rosebud, Ouray, and Oneida Reservations. The Indians of the last three reserves have never had a boarding school, and the Round Valley school has been discontinued since the burning of their buildings in July, 1883.

It is desirable, at as early a day as practicable, to establish additional schools as follows: On Southern Ute, Hoopa Valley, Jicarilla Apache, Western Shoshone, and Spokane Reservations, and possibly in the Zuni pueblo, where no boarding schools have yet been provided, and upon the White Mountain, Navajo, Moqui, Pima, White Earth, and Pine Ridge reserves, where additional schools are required to supply the needs of the school population. Upon many other reservations where new schools are not required existing schools must have their accommodations enlarged to supply the educational needs of the respective reservations.

RESERVATION DAY SCHOOLS

The following table gives a list of the reservation Government day schools:

Location and present capacity of Government day schools.

California:
  Hoopa Valley, 1 school... 60
  Mission, 8 schools.. 231
  Round Valley, 2 schools... 80
  Greenville, 1 school.. 35
Indian Territory:
  Quapaw, 2 schools... 80
Iowa:
  Sac and Fox, 1 school... 30
Michigan:
  Baraga school... 50
  L'Anse school... 40
Montana:
  Fort Belknap, 1 school.. 14
  Tongue River, 1 school.. 30
Nebraska:
  Omaha, Omaha Creek.. 40
  Santee:
    Flandrean... 50
    Ponca... 34
Nevada:
  Nevada:
    Walker River.. 35
    Wadsworth... 24
New Mexico:
  Pueblo:
    Laguna.. 30
    Cochiti... 30
    Santa Clara... 30
    McCarty's... 30
North Carolina:
  Eastern Cherokee, 4 schools... 155
North Dakota:
  Devil's Lake, Turtle Mountain, 3 schools.................................... 150
  Standing Rock, 7 schools.. 280

Ponca, etc., Oakland..	15
South Dakota:	
Cheyenne River, 8 schools..	199
Crow Creek, etc.:	
Driving Hawk's Camp..	30
White River..	40
Pine Ridge, 8 schools...	320
Rosebud, 13 schools..	432
Washington:	
Colville, Nespilem...	50
Neah Bay, Quillehute...	60
Puyallup:	
Jamestown..	30
Port Gamble..	35
Wisconsin:	
Green Bay, 7 schools..	315
La Pointe, 6 schools..	231
Total...	3,295

During this administration very little has been done to multiply day schools. Much attention has been paid to their improvement, old houses have been repaired, new houses have been built, and better apparatus has been provided.

This is especially true of the efforts that are now in progress among the Sioux. Heretofore the limitation of $600 for the cost of a day-school building anywhere has brought the expenditure so low as in many cases to render it impracticable to put up a suitable house. Congress has recently authorized the erection of thirty day schools for the Sioux at a cost of $1,000 each. A residence for the teacher adjoining each day school, with provision for a midday meal for the pupils and for a simple form of industrial training, will equip these institutions for excellent work.

New day schools needed.—I am of opinion that the time has now come for the multiplication of day schools, and during the next year I think a considerable number of new schools should be established and special efforts made to bring into them the younger children. Whenever practicable, kindergarten methods should be adopted and everything possible done, not only to supplement the work of the home, as is done in white communities, but to take the place of systematic home instruction where it does not exist, as is generally the case among the Indians.

EXPENSE OF BOARDING SCHOOL BUILDINGS

One of the most embarrassing things connected with the establishment of Indian boarding schools as well as day schools has been the limitation placed by Congress upon the cost of buildings. Formerly this was fixed at $10,000, including furnishing. This limit was raised in 1890 to $12,000, exclusive of furnishing, but it is still so low as to make it absolutely impossible to do what ought to be done.

The first and absolutely essential condition for establishing an Indian school is the plant, consisting of ground and the necessary buildings. Fortunately in most cases all the land necessary for schools on reservations is readily obtainable without expense to the Government. Everything, however, needed in the way of buildings in most instances has to be created.

As this is a vital matter I have prepared a statement showing the outlay for establishing a new school. In order that there may be a standard of comparison I will assume that the office undertakes to establish on some reservation remote from civilization a boarding school for 100 pupils of both sexes. To afford the needed accommodations and facilities for pupils and employés the following are absolutely essential:

	Square feet
Dormitory for 50 boys (45 square feet each)	2,250
Dormitory for 50 girls (45 square feet each)	2,250
Dining-room for 100 pupils (12 square feet each)	1,200
Kitchen, pantry, and dish closet (20 by 20)	600
Sitting and reading room for boys (30 by 25)	500
Sitting and reading room for girls (20 by 25)	500
Sewing room (16 by 20)	320
Five store rooms for bed linen, clothing, school books, and food supplies (10 by 10 each)	500
Laundry (basement, 20 by 20)	600
Employés' quarters: Mess kitchen (12 by 12), mess dining room (16 by 20), superintendent's office (15 by 16), sitting room (15 by 16), bed room (15 by 16), matron's room (15 by 16), industrial teacher (12 by 15), three teachers (3 rooms each, 12 by 12), cook (12 by 12), laundress (12 by 12), seamstress (12 by 12), reception room (15 by 18) other employés (2 rooms, 10 by 12)	2,978
Infirmaries (2 rooms, 16 by 20 each)	640
Bath room and wash room for boys (5 tubs and 8 basins)	200
Bath room and wash room for girls (5 tubs and 8 basins)	200
Passageways and stairways	2,000
School building:	
First story, stairs, hallways, and three recitation rooms	1,800
Second story, assembly and chapel room for pupils, employés, and visiting parents and friends	1,800
Total superficial area required	18,338
Estimating cost at $1.50 per square foot	$27,507
Barn and cow shed	1,200
Pig sty	75
Hennery	50
Tool and implement shed	400
Root house or cellar	150
Fuel shed	150
Other outbuildings	600
Bath tubs and plumbing	600
Fences for premises and farm	1,000
Shops (one building for the three trades)	1,500
Total	$33,232

In the above showing the estimates are low, and there are no buildings or structures of any kind which are not needed, and the accommodations contemplated can not be called ample. On the contrary, they are meager. But a small amount is allowed for plumbing and no allowance is made for bringing water into the buildings, for heating apparatus, or for sewerage. All the buildings, from the fuel shed to the general assembly room and chapel, are to be constructed in the plainest and most economical manner consistent with good workmanship.

I am forced to admit that I know of no reservation school in the Indian service which possesses the accommodations and facilities above outlined, nor has it been possible to furnish such facilities when the limit of cost of a school building has been fixed at $10,000. The extension of the limit from $10,000 to $12,000 gave some relief, but still necessitates the putting up of buildings too small, too cheap, or ill arranged, thus calling for early and large expenditures for repairs, improvement, remodeling, and enlargement, and meantime seriously crippling the usefulness of the school. By additions made subsequent to the construction of the original structures, fairly good accommodations have been provided in a long course of time for several schools, though at a considerable increase of the expense that would have been incurred had the buildings all been constructed at one time upon one common plan.

The want of suitable school buildings having needed light, ventilation, plumbing and sewerage, and rooms sufficient in number and size and conveniently arranged, is a seriously weak point in the Indian-school service. This lowers the morale and injures the health as well as mars the comfort of the pupils. It also obliges employés to expend, in overcoming the difficulties of inadequacy and bad arrangement, time and strength which to much better purpose might otherwise be devoted to caring for the highest interests of the children and advancing them in school room and industrial pursuits and in home culture.

The cheap, poorly built, poorly planned, rambling, and patched-together buildings which I have found at many agencies, are a discredit to the Government and do not fairly represent its real desire to elevate the Indians by education. The Government can afford to furnish suitable industrial-school buildings when and where they are needed. In the end it does afford them, but under the existing restrictions that no building shall cost over $12,000 the Government ultimately loses money and continuously loses efficiency.

It will be observed that the above estimate contemplates an expenditure on buildings of $332 per pupil. . . .

After two years' embarrassing experience in this office grappling with this problem of cost and after careful study in the field of buildings already erected, I wish to express most earnestly my deep conviction that ordinarily under existing circumstances it is impossible to establish a suitable Indian training school for the accommodation of 100 pupils with the necessary employés for less than $50,000.

COST OF INDIAN EDUCATION

In my annual report for 1889 I submitted the following table of estimates as to the approximate cost of educating the entire body of Indian youth:

Amount required to put and support all Indian children in Government schools.

New buildings and furnishings for 9,410 boarders, at $230 per capita	$2,164,300
New buildings and furnishings for 4,217 day pupils, at $1,500 for every 30 pupils	210,000
Repair and improvement of present buildings	50,000
Additional furniture, apparatus, stock, tools, and implements	50,000
	$2,474,300
Support of an average of 15,000 boarding pupils, at $175	2,625,000
Support of an average of 6,600 day pupils, at $62.50	412,500
Transportation of pupils	40,000
Superintendence	25,000
	$3,102,500

This contemplates an annual expenditure of about $3,000,000 for the work of Indian education after the necessary buildings are erected.

The experience of two years has confirmed me in the belief that this estimate was moderate, and I see no reason for modifying the opinion then expressed as to the desirability of spending the amount of money indicated in the table for the accomplishment of this important work. I regard it as a wise, just, humane, and economical expenditure of the public funds. Money thus used will accomplish its purpose directly, immediately, and permanently. A neglect or failure to so expend it will leave this perplexing question as a legacy for the next when it ought to be solved in the present century. I reiterate my strong conviction that it is wise now to make adequate provision for the education of all Indian youth that can be induced to attend school.

The appropriation made for the fiscal year ending June 30, 1892, is $2,291,650. The sum asked for the year ending June 30, 1893, is $2,917,060, which includes the amount asked for buildings.

* * *

COMPULSORY ATTENDANCE

During the last session of Congress a compulsory law was passed, designed to enforce attendance of Indians at school where compulsion should be found necessary.

The text of the law is as follows:

> And the Commissioner of Indian Affairs, subject to the direction of the Secretary of the Interior, is hereby authorized and directed to make and enforce by proper means such rules and regulations as will secure the attendance of Indian children of suitable age and health at schools established and maintained for their benefit.

The difficulties of executing any compulsory law are many and perplexing. It is an unsettled question how far it is wise or expedient to attempt to compel by force the attendance of children at school. In some instances force has been used, and in others the knowledge of the fact that the Government would use force if necessary has been sufficient. Special pains have been taken to familiarize the Indians with the idea that it is now the settled policy of the Government to educate their children, and they have been told that they are expected to voluntarily avail themselves of the munificent provisions made for this purpose, and that if they do not do this the Government will use such force as is necessary to compel it.

That the Government has a perfect right to insist that the Indians, who are dependent upon it for support and protection, and whose children are liable to grow up in savagery, barbarism, or helpless ignorance, shall allow their children to have the benefit of Government institutions established for their welfare, hardly needs argument. Ordinarily the parent should be regarded as the natural guardian and custodian of his child, and so long as he is willing or able to provide such an education as will fit the child for his position in life as a citizen of the Republic the Government ought not to interfere. When, however, it becomes evident that the parent is unwilling or unable to do this, and that the child, in consequence, is wellnigh certain to grow up idle, vicious, or helpless, a menace or a burden to the public, it becomes not only the right of the Government as a matter of self-protection, but its duty toward the child and toward the community, which is to be blessed or cursed by the child's activities, to see to it that he shall have in his youth that training that shall save him from vice and fit him for citizenship.

If, therefore, the present law is found to be inadequate to secure the purposes designed by its passage, some measure sufficiently comprehensive and stringent should be adopted and put at once into operation, both as a matter of public safety and out of regard for the welfare of the Indian wards of the nation.

CHARACTER AND AIM OF GOVERNMENT SCHOOLS

In Government schools industrial training receives special attention. It is of the highest importance for the interests of all concerned that the Indians should be taught to work, and arrangements have now been completed by which they can receive in the Government schools instruction and training in all ordinary trades and occupations, including farming, gardening, fruit-growing, dairying, stock-raising, the work of the carpenter, wheelwright, wagonmaker, blacksmith, shoemaker, harness-maker, tailor, tinsmith, broom-maker, and printer.

The Government schools have been systematized and now have a carefully graded course of study, a uniform series of text-books, a carefully prepared system of rules and regulations, and are critically supervised.

The teachers in the Government schools are selected with great care, and special stress is laid upon their ability to speak the English language with correctness and fluency in order that Indians shall be trained by them to use the English language with ease.

Special attention is paid in the Government schools to the inculcation of patriotism. The Indian pupils are taught that they are Americans, that the Government is their friend, that the flag is their flag, that the one great duty resting on them is loyalty to the Government, and thus the foundation is laid for perpetual peace between the Indian tribes in this country and the white people. Over every Government schoolhouse floats the American flag, and in every Government school there are appropriate exercises celebrating Washington's birthday, the Fourth of July, and other national holidays.

The utmost pains are taken in the Government schools to inculcate in the minds of the Indian pupils the broadest principles of morality, honesty, integrity, truthfulness, fidelity to duty, respect for the rights of others, etc., in no narrow way, but in such a manner as to lead them to cherish good will towards all, and to be prepared to take their places as American citizens on the plane of good fellowship with all.

In Government schools coeducation prevails. The Indian boys and girls are educated together; they sit at the same tables, recite in the same class, and are thus brought into such relationship as to lead them to respect each other. This is particularly helpful in destroying the false notion which so largely prevails among the Indians as to the inferiority of the women. Indian boys who are educated in the same schools with Indian girls, and who are often surpassed by them in their studies, come to have such a respect for them as will insure to the Indian women in the future a fuller recognition of their rights and a greater respect for their womenhood.

The Government schools are modeled after the public schools, and the Indian pupils who are educated in the Government Indian schools understand their workings, and pass easily into the public white schools, as opportunity offers. Those educated in these schools will be prepared, as they become citizens of the United States, to understand and appreciate the value of the public school, and will seek to establish and maintain such for their own children. The Indians will thus be brought into close sympathetic relationship with one of the greatest American institutions.

In all the large Government training schools there is a blending together of many tribes. There are to-day more than forty tribes represented at Carlisle. By bringing representatives of these various bodies of Indians together they learn to respect and love each other, and there is thus broken down those tribal animosities and jealousies which have been in the past productive of so much harm and a fruitful source of so much trouble both to the Indians and the nation.

Finally, the Government schools all being modeled on the same plan and administered in the same spirit, the thousands of Indian pupils who are educated in them have for each other a fellowship that will in a few years result in bringing about homogeneity among all the various Indian tribes and render future strifes between tribes and wars between the Indians and United States entirely improbable, if not impossible.

MISSIONARY WORK

I would not be understood as wanting in appreciation of the good that may be accomplished for the Indians by the churches through distinctively missionary work. Untold good has already been done; much more can be done, and there perhaps never has been a time in the history of the Indians when they are so susceptible as now to religious influences. There never was a better opportunity for the churches to establish schools or missions and prosecute Christian work among them than at the present; and while it is not the function of the Government to evangelize or to propagate any particular creed, it is desirable that all proper facilities should be afforded to the various religious denominations, without distinction, partiality, or favoritism, for the prosecution of their legitimate missionary work among the Indians. I think, too, that it will be conceded by all friends of the Indians that it is desirable at present, while these people are passing through the transition period from barbarism and heathenism to civilization, that those great fundamental principles of morality, which are recognized by all denominations in common, should be inculcated in the young Indian mind, with the view that they may grow up not simply informed as to their intellect but formed as to their moral character; that they may be not only intelligent, but moral and upright. . . .

INDIANS IN PUBLIC SCHOOLS

Considerable progress has been made during the year in securing the admission of Indians living off reservations into the public schools in their vicinity, and special efforts in this direction will be made during the year to come.

The following table shows the number of pupils for whose instruction in public schools the Government has contracted with public-school districts during the past year. The rate paid by the Government for this schooling, including books, is $10 per pupil per quarter, based on average attendance.

Public schools at which Indian pupils were placed under contract with the Indian Bureau during the fiscal year ended June 30, 1891.

Name and location	Date of contract	Number of Indian pupils
California: Carbon, Shasta County, Albion School District......	June 18, 1891	8
Minnesota: Richwood, Becker County, District No. 4..........	May 1, 1891	10
Nebraska:		
Santee Agency, Knox County, District No. 36..............	Jan. 2, 1891	8
Omaha Agency, Thurston County, District No. 6............	Jan. 9, 1891	10
Oregon: Seaton, Lane County, District No. 32...............	Mar. 20, 1891	5
Utah:		
Cedar City, Iron County, District No. 1....................	Jan. 2, 1891	5
Portage, Box Elder County, District No. 12.................	July 17, 1890	39
Washington: Rockland, Klickitat County, District No. 1.......	Apr. 13, 1891	15

HIGHER EDUCATION

An increasing number of Indian youth of both sexes have evinced a capacity and desire for the prosecution of higher studies to fit them for professional life, some as lawyers, some as physicians, and some as teachers and clergymen. During the past year a number of these who are pursuing their studies in colleges and professional schools received help from the Government.

I have had considerable sympathy with this part of the work, as I believe the higher education of the few who are thus lifted in intelligence and power above the mass is very essential for the highest welfare of the whole. They become leaders and examples and exert a very wide and ordinarily wholesome influence upon their own people and also upon public sentiment by showing the capacity of the Indians for the higher walks of life.

I can not help expressing my regret that it has been deemed wise to suspend this feature of the work.

HEALTH OF INDIAN PUPILS

One of the most perplexing difficulties which the office is called upon to contend with in school work is the health of Indian children. Many of them come to the school already diseased, others with peculiar susceptibilities to disease, and they suffer more or less perhaps from the greatly changed conditions of life to which they are thus subjected.

Some of the diseases with which the superintendents have been called upon most frequently to contend have been scarlet fever, measles, diphtheria, small-pox, sore eyes, and lung troubles.

The difficulties in the way of improving the Indian schools have been so many and so great that at times it has seemed well-nigh impossible to overcome them. It has required all the persistence, patience, ingenuity and hard work that could possibly be summoned in order to make the progress already achieved. The history of the struggle of the past two years will never be written, and is only known to those that have put their lives into it. If the results that issue from these labors, anxieties, and discouragements are at all commensurate with the expectations of those who have endured them, they will constitute their chief reward.

* * *

THE "MESSIAH CRAZE"

During the summer and fall of 1890 reports reaching this office from various sources showed that a growing excitement existed among the Indian tribes over the announcement of the advent of a so-called Indian Messiah or Christ, or Great Medicine Man of the North. The delusion finally became so widespread and well-defined as to be generally known as the "Messiah Craze." Its origin is somewhat obscure and its manifestations have varied slightly among different tribes. A few instances may be cited as representative.

In June, 1890, through the War Department, came the account of a "Cheyenne medicine man, Porcupine," who claimed to have left his reservation in November, 1889, and to have traveled by command and under divine guidance in search of the Messiah to the Shoshone Agency, Salt Lake City, and the Fort Hall Agency, and thence—with others who joined him at Fort Hall—to Walker River Reservation, Nev. There "the Christ," who was scarred on wrist and face, told them of his crucifixion, taught them a certain dance, counseled love and kindness for each other, and foretold that the Indian dead were to be resurrected, the youth of good people to be renewed, the earth enlarged, etc.

From the Tongue River Agency, in Montana, came a report, made by the special agent in charge, dated August 20, 1890, that Porcupine, an Indian of that agency, had declared himself to be the new Messiah, and had found a large following ready to believe in his doctrine. Those who doubted were fearful lest their unbelief should call down upon them the curse of the "Mighty Porcupine." The order went forth that in order to please the Great Spirit a six days and nights' dance must be held every new moon, with the understanding that at the expiration of a certain period the Great Spirit would restore the buffalo, elk, and other game, resurrect all dead Indians, endow his believers with perpetual youth, and perform many other wonders well calculated to inflame Indian superstition. Dances, afterward known as "ghost dances," were enthusiastically attended, and the accompanying feasts were so associated by stockmen with the disappearance of their cattle that very strained relations resulted between the rancher and Indian, which at one time threatened serious trouble.

About the same time the Cheyenne and Arapaho agent in Oklahoma reported that during the autumn of 1889 and the ensuing winter rumors had reached that agency from the Shoshones of Wyoming that an Indian Messiah was located in the mountains about 200 miles north of the Shoshones; that prominent medicine men had seen and held conversation with him, and had been told by him that the whites were to be removed from the country, the buffalo to come back, and the Indians to be restored to their original status. This report excited considerable interest among the Cheyennes and Arapahoes, particularly the Arapahoes, and they raised money to defray the expenses of sending two of their number to Wyoming to investigate the matter. After an absence of about two months these delegates returned, reporting that they had been prevented by snow from making the journey to the mountains to see the "Christ," but that the rumors concerning him were verified by the Indians at Shoshone. Great excitement soon prevailed; all industrial work came to a standstill; meetings were held in which hundreds of Indians would rise from the ground, circle around, and sing and cry until apparently exhausted. At one time they even contemplated leaving their reservation in a body to go and seek the "Christ."

During my absence from the office last fall on a tour of observation among the Indian agencies and schools, which lasted from September 5 to early in December, I had occasion to notice the effect of this craze among several tribes, and it was brought up prominently in a council with the Kiowas, Comanches, etc., of Oklahoma. As I stated in the supplement to my annual report of December 8 last, I found that among the tribes which I visited the excitement was comparatively harmless, and although it had seriously retarded progress in civilization for the time being, it had been readily controlled and had furnished no occasion for alarm; and I added:

> The only danger to be apprehended is that influences from without, emanating from those who in some manner might be benefited by the Indians uprising or the movement of troops, or by the excitement growing out of "wars and rumors of wars," may precipitate a needless conflict and bring on a disastrous and costly war. Of course this is said in regard to the Indians whom I have visited. I have not been among the Sioux of the Dakotas.

Among some of the Sioux the matter became more serious.

In August, 1890, Agent Gallagher stated that many at the Pine Ridge Agency were crediting the report made to them in the preceding spring that a great medicine man had appeared in Wyoming whose mission was to resurrect and rehabilitate all the departed heroes of the tribe, restore to the Indians herds of buffalo which would make them entirely independent of aid from the whites, and bring such confusion upon their enemies, the whites, that they would flee the country, leaving the Indians in possession of the entire Northwest for all time to come. Indians fainted during the performances which attended the recital of the wondrous things soon to come to pass, and one man died from the excitement. The effect of such meetings or dances was so demoralizing that on August 22, 1890, when about 2,000 Indians were gathered on White Clay Creek, about 18 miles from the agency, to hold what they called a religious dance connected with the appearance of this supernatural being, the agent instructed his Indian police to disperse them. This they were unable to do. Accompanied by about 20 police the agent himself visited the place, and on hearing of his approach most of the Indians dispersed. Several men, however, with Winchester rifles in their hands, and a good storing of cartridges belted around their waists, stood stripped for fight, prepared to die in defense of the new faith. They were finally quieted.

But the dances continued, and October 12, 1890, Agent Royer, who had just taken charge of the agency, reported that more than half the Indians had already joined the dancing, and when requested to stop would strip themselves ready for fight; that the police had lost control, and if his endeavors to induce the chiefs to suppress the craze should be unavailing, he hoped for hearty coöperation in invoking military aid to maintain order.

About the same time the Cheyenne River agent reported that Big Foot's band were much excited about the coming of a "Messiah," were holding "ghost dances" and, armed with Winchester rifles and of very threatening temper, were beyond police control.

A similar condition of affairs existed among the Rosebud Sioux.

Agent McLaughlin also reported from Standing Rock October 17, as follows:

> I feel it my duty to report the present craze and nature of the excitement existing among the Sitting Bull faction of Indians over the expected Indian millennium, the annihilation of the white man and supremacy of the Indian, which is looked for in the near future and promised by the Indian medicine men as not later than next spring, when the new grass begins to appear, and is known among the Sioux as the "return of the Ghosts."
>
> They are promised by some members of the Sioux tribe, who have lately developed into medicine men, that the Great Spirit has promised them that their punishment by the dominant race has been sufficient, and that their numbers having now become so decimated will be reinforced by all Indians who are dead; that the dead are all returning to reinhabit this earth, which belongs to the Indians; that they are driving back with them, as they return, immense herds of buffalo, and elegant wild horses to have for the catching; that the Great Spirit promises them that the white man will be unable to make gunpowder in future, and all attempts at such will be a failure, and that the gunpowder now on hand will be useless as against Indians, as it will not throw a bullet with sufficient force to pass through the skin of an Indian; that the Great Spirit had deserted the Indians for a long period, but is now with them and against the whites, and will cover the earth over with thirty feet of additional soil, well sodded and timbered, under which the whites will all be smothered, and any whites who may escape these great phenomena will become small fishes in the rivers of the country, but in order to bring about this happy result the Indians must do their part and become believers and thoroughly organize.
>
> It would seem impossible that any person, no matter how ignorant, could be brought to believe such absurd nonsense, but as a matter of fact a great

many of the Indians of this agency actually believe it, and since this new doctrine has been engrafted here from the more southern Sioux agencies, the infection has been wonderful, and so pernicious that it now includes some of the Indians who were formerly numbered with the progressive and more intelligent, and many of the very best Indians appear dazed and undecided when talking of it, their inherent superstition having been thoroughly aroused.

Sitting Bull is high priest and leading apostle of this latest Indian absurdity; in a word he is the chief mischief-maker at this agency, and if he were not here, this craze, so general among the Sioux, would never have gotten a foothold at this agency. Sitting Bull is a man of low cunning, devoid of a single manly principle in his nature, or an honorable trait of character, but on the contrary is capable of instigating and inciting others (those who believe in his promise) to do any amount of mischief. He is a coward and lacks moral courage; he will never lead where there is danger, but is an adept in influencing his ignorant henchmen and followers, and there is no knowing what he may direct them to attempt. He is bitterly opposed to having any surveys made on the reservation, and is continually agitating and fostering opposition to such surveys among his followers, who are the more worthless, ignorant, obstinate, and non-progressive of the Sioux.

On Thursday, the 9th instant, upon an invitation from Sitting Bull, an Indian named Kicking Bear, belonging to the Cheyenne River Agency, the chief medicine man of the ghost dance among the Sioux, arrived at Sitting Bull's camp on Grand River, 40 miles south of this agency, to inaugurate a ghost dance and initiate the members. Upon learning of his arrival there I sent a detachment of 13 policemen, including the captain and second lieutenant, to arrest and escort him from the reservation, but they returned without executing the order, both officers being in a dazed condition and fearing the powers of Kicking Bear's medicine. Several members of the force tried to induce the officers to permit them to make the arrest but the latter would not allow it, but simply told Sitting Bull that it was the agent's orders that Kicking Bear and his six companies should leave the reservation and return to their agency. Sitting Bull was very insolent to the officers and made some threats against some members of the force, but said that the visitors would leave the following day. Upon return of the detachment to the agency on Tuesday, the 14th, I immediately sent the lieutenant and one man back to see whether the party had left or not, and to notify Sitting Bull that this insolence and bad behavior would not be tolerated longer, and that the ghost dance must not be continued. The lieutenant returned yesterday and reported that the party had not started back to Cheyenne before his arrival there on the morning of the 15th, but left immediately upon his ordering them to do so, and that Sitting Bull told him that he was determined to continue the ghost dance, as the Great Spirit had sent a direct message by Kicking Bear that to live they must do so, but that he would not have any more dancing until after he had come to the agency and talked the matter over with me; but the news comes in this morning that they are dancing again and it is participated in by a great many Indians who become silly and like men intoxicated over the excitement. The dance is demoralizing, indecent, and disgusting.

Desiring to exhaust all reasonable means before resorting to extremes, I have sent a message to Sitting Bull, by his nephew One Bull, that I want to see him at the agency and I feel quite confident that I shall succeed in allaying the present excitement and put a stop to this absurd "craze" for the present at least, but I would respectfully recommend the removal from the reservation and confinement in some military prison, some distance from the

Sioux country, of Sitting Bull and the parties named in my letter of June 18 last, hereinbefore referred to, some time during the coming winter before next spring opens.

At other Sioux agencies the Messiah craze seems to have made little or no impression. At Lower Brulé it was easily checked by the arrest by Indian police of twenty-two dancers, of whom seventeen were imprisoned for eight weeks at Fort Snelling. The Crow Creek, Santee, Yankton, and Sisseton Sioux, through schools, missions, and industrial pursuits, had been brought to give too valuable hostages to civilization to be affected by such a delusion.

This alleged appearance of a Messiah was not an entirely new thing. Some 6 or 8 years ago one of the Puyallup Indians claimed that in a trance he had been to the other world. As a result of his visions a kind of society was formed, churches were built, one of the Indians claimed to be the "Christ," and the band became so infatuated and unmanageable that the agent was obliged to imprison the alleged "Christ," punish his followers, and discharge a number of Indian judges and policemen in order to regain control.

During the past six months ghost dances have almost entirely disappeared, and although the Messiah craze prevailed to an unusual extent among a large number of widely separated tribes, and aroused a general feeling of discontent and unrest, yet it is doubtful if it would have had any history as more than one of many such ephemeral superstitions of an ignorant and excitable people, if it had not been complicated with other disorders among the Sioux in the Dakotas so that it became one of the causes which led to the so-called Sioux war.

TROUBLES AMONG THE SIOUX

As early as June, 1890, a rumor that the Sioux were secretly planning an outbreak and needed close watching led this office to call upon the agents for the Sioux for reports as to the status and temper of the Indians in their charge. The replies indicated that no good grounds for apprehending trouble existed. The Rosebud agent, however, referred to the fact that secret communications had been passing between dissatisfied nonprogressive Indians at the various agencies who had refused to sign the agreement under which a large portion of the Sioux reserve had been opened to settlement by the President's proclamation of February 10, 1890. The Standing Rock agent reported as follows:

So far as the Indians of this agency are concerned there is nothing in either their words or actions that would justify the rumor, and I do not believe that such an imprudent step is seriously meditated by any of the Sioux.

There are, however, a few malcontents here, as at all of the Sioux agencies, who cling tenaciously to the old Indian ways and are slow to accept the better order of things, whose influence is exerted in the wrong direction, and this class of Indians are ever ready to circulate idle rumors and sow dissensions, to discourage the more progressive; but only a few of the Sioux could now possibly be united in attempting any overt act against the Government, and the removal from among them of a few individuals (the leaders of disaffection) such as Sitting Bull, Circling Bear, Black Bird, and Circling Hawk of this agency, Spotted Elk (Big Foot) and his lieutenants of Cheyenne River, Crow Dog and Low Dog of Rosebud, and any of like ilk of Pine Ridge, would end all trouble and uneasiness in the future.

The agent at Cheyenne River reported some little excitement regarding the coming of an Indian "Messiah," as did the agent at Pine Ridge Agency, who also expressed his belief that it would soon die out without causing trouble.

After receiving later reports, already mentioned, which showed that ghost dancing was becoming a serious element of disturbance, the office instructed the agents at Standing Rock, Crow Creek and Lower Brulé, Rosebud, and Pine Ridge Agencies, to exercise great caution in the management of the Indians, with a view to avoiding an outbreak, and, if deemed necessary, to call upon this office to secure military aid to prevent disturbances.

Agent Royer, of the Pine Ridge Agency, was especially advised, October 18, that Major-General Miles, commander of the military division in which the agency was situated, also chairman of the Commission recently appointed to negotiate with the Northern Cheyennes, would shortly visit the agency, and that he would have opportunity to explain the situation to him and ask his advice as to the wisdom of calling for troops.

October 24, 1890, this office recommended that the War Department be requested to cause Sitting Bull, Circling Hawk, Black Bird, and Circling Bear to be confined in some military prison, and to instruct the proper military authorities to be on the alert to discover any suspicious movements of the Indians of the Sioux agencies.

Early in November reports received from the agents at Pine Ridge, Rosebud, and Cheyenne River showed that the Indians of those agencies, especially Pine Ridge, were arming themselves and taking a defiant attitude towards the Government and its representatives, committing depredations, and likely to go to other excesses, and November 13 this office recommended that the matter be submitted to the War Department, with request that such prompt action be taken to avert an outbreak as the emergency might be found by them to demand.

On that day the President of the United States addressed the following communication to the Secretary of the Interior:

Replying to your several communications in regard to the condition of the Indians at the Sioux and Cheyenne agencies, I beg to say that some days ago I directed the War Department to send an officer of high rank to investigate the situation and to report upon it from a military standpoint. General Ruger, I understand, has been assigned to that duty, and is now probably at, or on his way to, these agencies. I have to-day directed the Secretary of War to assume a military responsibility for the suppression of any threatened outbreak, and to take such steps as may be necessary to that end. In the meantime, I suggest that you advise your agents to separate the well-disposed from the ill-disposed Indians, and while maintaining their control and discipline so far as may be possible, to avoid forcing any issue that will result in an outbreak, until suitable military preparations can be made.

November 15 Agent Royer sent to this office the following telegram from Pine Ridge:

Indians are dancing in the snow and are wild and crazy. I have fully informed you that employés and Government property at this agency have no protection and are at the mercy of these dancers. Why delay by further investigation? We need protection, and we need it now. The leaders should be arrested and confined in some military post until the matter is quieted, and this should be done at once.

ARRIVAL OF MILITARY

A military force under Gen. John R. Brooke, consisting of five companies of infantry, three troops of cavalry, and one Hotchkiss and one Gatling gun, arrived at Pine Ridge November 20, 1890. Two troops of cavalry and six companies of infantry were stationed at Rosebud. Troops were ordered to other agencies until finally nearly half the infantry and cavalry of the U. S. Army were concentrated upon the Sioux reservations. When the troops reached Rosebud about 1,800 Indians—men, women, and children— stampeded toward Pine Ridge and the bad lands, destroying their own property before leaving and that of others en route.

On December 1, 1890, in accordance with Department instructions, the following order was sent to the Sioux agents:

During the present Indian troubles you are instructed that while you snall continue all the business and carry into effect the educational and other purposes of your agency, you will, as to all operations intended to suppress any outbreak by force, cooperate with and obey the orders of the military officer commanding on the reservation in your charge.

DEATH OF SITTING BULL

In the latter part of November the military authorized the arrest of Sitting Bull by W. F. Cody ("Buffalo Bill"), but at the request of Agent McLaughlin, who deemed it prudent to postpone the arrest until colder weather, the order was canceled by direction of the President.

Sitting Bull's camp where the dancing had been going on was on Grand River 40 miles from the agency. The number of Indian policemen in that vicinity was increased and he was kept under close surveillance. December 12 the commanding officer at Fort Yates was instructed by General Ruger, commanding the Department of Dakota, to make it his special duty to secure the person of Sitting Bull, and to call on Agent McLaughlin "for such coöperation and assistance as would best promote the object in view." December 14 the police notified the agent that Sitting Bull was preparing to leave the reservation. Accordingly, after consultation with the post commander it was decided that the arrest should be made the following morning by the police under command of Lieutenant Bullhead, with United States troops within supporting distance.

At daybreak, December 15, 39 Indian police and 4 volunteers went to Sitting Bull's cabin and arrested him. He agreed to accompany them to the agency, but while dressing caused considerable delay, and during this time his followers began to congregate to the number of 150, so that when he was brought out of the house they had the police entirely surrounded. Sitting Bull then refused to go and called on his friends, the ghost dancers, to rescue him. At this juncture one of them shot Lieutenant Bullhead. The lieutenant then shot Sitting Bull, who also received another shot and was killed outright. Another shot struck Sergeant Shavehead and then the firing became general. In about two hours the police had secured possession of Sitting Bull's house and driven their assailants into the woods. Shortly after, when 100 United States troops, under command of Capt. Fechet reached the spot the police drew up in line and saluted. Their bravery and discipline received highest praise from Capt. Fechet. The ghost dancers fled from their hiding places to the Cheyenne River Reservation, leaving their families and dead behind them. Their women who had taken part in the fight had been disarmed by the police and placed under guard and were turned over to the troops when they arrived. The losses were six policemen killed (including Bullhead and Shavehead who soon died at the agency hospital) and one wounded. The attacking party lost eight killed and three wounded.

INDIANS CONCENTRATE IN THE BAD LANDS

Groups of Indians from the different reservations had commenced concentrating in the "bad lands," upon or in the vicinity of the Pine Ridge Reservation. Killing of cattle and destruction of other property by these Indians almost entirely within the limits of Pine Ridge and Rosebud reservations occurred, but no signal fires were built, no warlike demonstrations were made, no violence was done to any white settler, nor was there cohesion or organization among the Indians themselves. Many of them were friendly Indians who had never participated in the ghost dance but had fled thither from fear of soldiers, in consequence of the Sitting Bull affair, or through the over-persuasion of friends. The military gradually began to close in around them, and they offered no resistance, and a speedy and quiet capitulation of all was confidently expected.

FIGHT AT WOUNDED KNEE CREEK

Among them was Big Foot's band belonging to the Cheyenne River Agency, numbering with others who had joined him, about 120 men and 230 women and children. They had escaped to the bad lands, after arrest by the military at Cheyenne River, but soon started from the bad lands for the Pine Ridge Agency, and with a flag of truce advanced into the open country and proposed a parley with the troops whom they met. This being refused they surrendered unconditionally, remained in camp at Wounded Knee Creek over night, expecting to proceed next morning under escort of the troops to Pine Ridge, whither most of the quondam bad-land Indians were moving. The next day, December 29, when ordered to turn in their arms, they surrendered very few. By a search in the teepees 60 guns were obtained. When the military—a detachment of the Seventh Cavalry (Custer's old command), with other troops—began to take the arms from their persons a shot was fired and carnage ensued. According to reports of military officers, the Indians attacked the troops as soon as the disarmament commenced. The Indians claim that the first shot was fired by a half crazy, irresponsible Indian. At any rate, a short, sharp, indiscriminate fight immediately followed, and, during the fighting and the subsequent flight and pursuit of the Indians, the troops lost 25 killed and 35 wounded, and of the Indians, 84 men and boys, 44 women, and 18 children were killed and at least 33 were wounded, many of them fatally. Most of the men, including Big Foot, were killed around his tent where he lay sick. The bodies of women and children were scattered along a distance of two miles from the scene of the encounter.

Frightened and exasperated, again the Indians made for the bad lands. Indians en route thence to the agency turned back and others rushed away from Pine Ridge.

AGENCIES PLACED UNDER MILITARY SURVEILLANCE

On January 6, 1891, military officers were assigned to the five Sioux agencies, under the following telegraphic instructions of that date to General Miles from Major-General Schofield:

> You are hereby authorized under existing orders of the President to assign Capt. E. P. Ewers, Capt. J. M. Lee, Capt. C. A. Earnest, and Capt. F. E. Pierce to the charge of the Indians of the several Sioux and Cheyenne agencies, to exercise over those Indians such military supervision and control as in your judgment in necessary, without interfering unnecessarily with the administration of the agents of the Indian Bureau under the regulations and instructions received by them from the Interior Department. It is not deemed advisable to detail two captains from the First Infantry. You will, therefore, please recommend another officer in the place of Captain Dougherty. Also, if you need other officers in addition to those named, recommend such as you think best qualified for that service.

END OF DISTURBANCES

A few skirmishes with the Indians followed the Wounded Knee affair, but by the end of January the Indians had come into the agencies and all serious troubles were practically ended.

Soon afterward a delegation of Sioux representing the different agencies and factions visited this city, had full conference with the Secretary of the Interior and the Commissioner of Indian Affairs relative to their rights and grievances, and were given an audience by the President.

It is worthy of note that the Christian Indians among the Sioux, those who had accepted the teachings of missionaries, were almost universally loyal, and in fact that the large body of the Sioux had no participation in the disturbances except to suffer from the consequences. Undoubtedly the large number among them in the bad lands who had abandoned their homes against their own desire, and were unwilling followers of their leaders, contributed in no small degree to bringing all hostilities to an end. While the damage done to the property of white settlers is slight, many friendly, progressive Indians suffered severely in the destruction of houses, stock, and other property, a loss from which it will take them long to recover.

On several occasions the office has been informed that the Sioux contemplated a renewal of hostilities, and very recently information was received, from a source deemed reliable, that they were endeavoring to induce other tribes to join them in a contemplated outbreak; but these reports prove, upon investigation, to have but little foundation in fact. Although some factions among the Indians are, undoubtedly, sullen and dissatisfied, and idle and vicious Indians have indulged in incendiary utterances, yet good feeling and satisfaction prevail almost universally on the Sioux reservations, and I do not consider that there are reasonable grounds for belief that any portion of the Sioux Nation of sufficient strength to be dangerous contemplates any overt act against the Government or the settlers.

Killing of Lieut. Casey, and Few Tails

It should also be recorded that no attempt was made by the Indians to reach and ravage any white settlements, no white person was killed off the reservation, and except in battle, only two were killed on the reserve.

A government herder, an old man named Miller, was wantonly murdered by a son of No Water. Lieut. E. W. Casey, of the Twenty-second Infantry, was killed by Plenty Horses. The death of this gallant young officer was much lamented. He was deeply interested in the welfare of the Indians, and was zealous in enlisting and drilling them as soldiers. All the facts in the case clearly show that the killing was without provocation, premeditated, and deliberate. Plenty Horses was arrested and tried in the United States court on the charge of murder but was released by the court on the ground that at the time of the killing "a state of war" existed between his tribe and the United States, and that the killing of Lieut. Casey was an incident of the war and not murder under the law.

On the other hand, an unprovoked attack made January 11, 1891, by white citizens upon a hunting party of friendly Sioux Indians, in Mead County, greatly excited the Indians, and had a strong tendency to retard their pacification. Some United States troops, at the instance of the attacking party, joined in pursuit of the Indians and fired upon them. Few Tails was killed and 2 Indian women were wounded. Few Tails was a peaceable Indian, and the attack upon his party was coldblooded and wanton. For the murder of Few Tails 5 white men were indicted in the State court, Sturgis, S. Dak. Their trial, June 22 last, was ended July 2, with a verdict of "not guilty."

CAUSES OF THE TROUBLE

In stating the events which led to this outbreak among the Sioux the endeavor too often has been merely to find some opportunity for locating blame. The causes are complex and many are obscure and remote. Among them may be named the following:

First. A feeling of unrest and apprehension in the mind of the Indians has naturally grown out of the rapid advance in civilization and the great changes which this advance has necessitated in their habits and mode of life.

Second. Prior to the agreement of 1876 buffalo and deer were the main support of the Sioux. Food, tents, bedding, were the direct outcome of hunting, and with furs and pelts as articles of barter or exchange, it was easy for the Sioux to procure whatever constituted for them the necessaries, the comforts, or even the luxuries of life. Within eight years from the agreement of 1876, the buffalo had gone and the Sioux had left to them alkali land and Government rations.

It is hard to overstate the magnitude of the calamity as they viewed it, which happened to these people by the sudden disappearance of the buffalo and the large diminution in the numbers of deer and other wild animals. Suddenly, almost without warning, they were expected at once and without previous training to settle down to the pursuits of agriculture in a land largely unfitted for such use. The freedom of the chase was to be exchanged for the idleness of the camp. The boundless range was to be abandoned for the circumscribed reservation, and abundance of plenty to be supplanted by limited and decreasing Government subsistence and supplies. Under these circumstances, it is not in human nature not to be discontented and restless, even turbulent and violent.

Third. During a long series of years treaties, agreements, cessions of land and privileges, and removals of bands and agencies have kept many of the Sioux, particularly those at Pine Ridge and Rosebud, in an unsettled condition, especially as some of the promises made them were fulfilled tardily or not at all.

Fourth. The very large reduction of the Great Sioux Reservation, brought about by the Sioux Commission through the consent of the large majority of the adult males, was bitterly opposed by a large, influential minority. For various reasons they regarded the cession as unwise, and did all in their power to prevent its consummation and afterward were constant in their expressions of dissatisfaction and in their endeavors to awaken a like feeling in the minds of those who signed the agreement.

Fifth. There was diminution and partial failure of the crops for 1889 by reason of their neglect by the Indians, who were congregated in large numbers at the council with the Sioux Commission, and a further diminution of ordinary crops by the drought of 1890. Also, in 1888 the disease of black-leg appeared among the cattle of the Indians.

Sixth. At this time, by delayed and reduced appropriations, the Sioux rations were temporarily cut down. Rations were not diminished to such an extent as to bring the Indians to starvation or even extreme suffering, as has been often reported; but short rations came just after the Sioux Commission had negotiated the agreement for the cession of lands, and as a condition of securing the signatures of the majority, had assured the Indians that their rations would be continued unchanged. To this matter the Sioux Commission called special attention in their report dated December 24, 1889, as follows:

> During our conference at the different agencies we were repeatedly asked whether the acceptance or rejection of the act of Congress would influence the action of the Government with reference to their rations, and in every instance the Indians were assured that subsistence was furnished in accordance with former treaties, and that signing would not affect their rations, and that they would continue to receive them as provided in former treaties. Without our assurances to this effect it would have been impossible to have secured their consent to the cession of their lands. Since our visit to the agencies it appears that large reductions have been made in the amounts of beef furnished for issues, amounting at Rosebud to 2,000,000 pounds and at Pine Ridge to 1,000,000 pounds, and lesser amounts at the other agencies. This action of the Department, following immediately after the successful issue of our negotiations, can not fail to have an injurious effect. It will be impossible to convince the Indians that the reduction is not due to the fact that the Government having obtained their land has less concern in looking after their material interests than before. It will be looked upon as a breach of faith, and especially as a violation of the express statements of the Commissioners.
>
> Already this action is being used by the Indians opposed to the bill, notably at Pine Ridge, as an argument in support of the wisdom of their opposition.

In forwarding this report to Congress the Department called special attention to the above-quoted statements of the Commission and said:

> The Commission further remarks that as to the quality of rations furnished there seems to be no just cause for complaint, but that it was particularly to be avoided that there should be any diminution of the rations promised under the former treaties *at this time*, as the Indians would attribute it to their assent to the bill. Such diminution certainly should not be allowed, as the Government is bound in good faith to carry into effect the former treaties where not directly and positively affected by the act, and if under the provisions of the treaty itself the ration is at any time reduced, the Commissioners recommend that the Indians should be notified before spring

opens, so that crops may be cultivated. It is desirable that the recent reduction made should be restored, as it is now impossible to convince the Indians that it was not due to the fact that the Government, having obtained their lands, had less concern in looking after their material interests.

Notwithstanding this plea of the Commission and of the Department, the appropriation made for the subsistence and civilization of the Sioux for 1890 was only $950,000, or $50,000 less than the amount estimated and appropriated for 1888 and 1889, and the appropriation not having been made until August 19, rations had to be temporarily purchased and issued in limited quantities pending arrival of new supplies to be secured from that appropriation.

It was not until January, 1891, after the troubles, that an appropriation of $100,000 was made by Congress for additional beef for the Sioux.

Seventh. Other promises made by the Sioux Commission and the agreement were not promptly fulfilled; among them were increase of appropriations for education, for which this office had asked an appropriation of $150,000; the payment of $200,000, in compensation for ponies taken from the Sioux in 1876 and 1877; and the reimbursement of the Crow Creek Indians for a reduction made in their per capita allowance of land as compared with the amount allowed other Sioux, which called for an appropriation of $187,039. The fulfillment of all these promises except the last named, was contained in the act of January 19, 1891.

Eighth. In 1889 and 1890 epidemics of *la grippe,* measles, and whooping cough, followed by many deaths, added to the gloom and misfortune which seemed to surround the Indians.

Ninth. The wording of the agreement changed the boundary line between the Rosebud and Pine Ridge, diminished reservations, and necessitated a removal of a portion of the Rosebud Indians from lands which by the agreement were included in the Pine Ridge Reservation to lands offered them in lieu thereof upon the diminished Rosebud Reserve. This, although involving no great hardship to any considerable number, added to the discontent.

Tenth. Some of the Indians were greatly opposed to the census which Congress ordered should be taken. The census at Rosebud, as reported by Special Agent Lea and confirmed by a special census taken by Agent Wright, revealed the somewhat startling fact that rations had been issued to Indians very largely in excess of the number actually present, and this diminution of numbers as shown by the census necessitated a diminution of the rations, which was based, of course, upon the census.

Eleventh. The Messiah craze, which fostered the belief that "ghost shirts" would be invulnerable to bullets, and that the supremacy of the Indian race was assured, added to discontent the fervor of fanaticism and brought those who accepted the new faith into the attitude of sullen defiance, but defensive rather than aggressive.

Twelfth. The sudden appearance of military upon their reservation gave rise to the wildest rumors among the Indians of danger and disaster, which were eagerly circulated by disaffected Indians and corroborated by exaggerated accounts in the newspapers, and these and other influences connected with and inseparable from military movements frightened many Indians away from their agencies into the bad lands and largely intensified whatever spirit of opposition to the Government existed.

Report of Commissioner of
Indian Affairs T. J. Morgan
August 27, 1892

(Excerpt from *Report for 1892*, pp. 5-31, 37-39, 45-48, 61-62, 93-106, 114-22, 133-40)

Rarely has a Commissioner of Indian Affairs shown the earnestness and dedication of Commissioner Morgan. In his 1892 report he noted his attempts to administer the bureau in a moral but businesslike manner. His efforts were often destructive of Indian values, but they were meant to be, either from an assumption of the superior wisdom of the white man's civilization or by virtue of a mandate from Congress. Morgan, working under the enormously increased workload brought about by the severalty legislation and the increasing educational responsibilities of the bureau, was, nevertheless, not given the additional resources needed. He noted that he had often wondered why the tenure of previous commissioners had been so short, averaging less than two and a half years since 1832. But, having finished his third year and having experienced the multifarious difficulties facing a commissioner, he now wondered why the average term of service had been so long! Morgan's annual reports show an increasing sophistication in his comprehension of the Indian problem and an increasing sympathy for the Indian point of view. Nevertheless, it fell to him to preside over the most comprehensive changes in the Indian's position vis-a-vis his fellow residents of the continent.

POLICY OF CITIZENSHIP

THE GOVERNMENT HAS a well-defined policy of dealing with the Indians. This policy is the outcome of more than a century of experience and of a vast amount of discussion. While it is necessarily open to objections, and while it will fail in many respects to fully meet the expectations of the friends of the Indians, it is the least objectionable plan that has yet presented itself as a solution of the difficulties of the situation. So far as I now see, the only methods that have presented themselves for consideration in competition with the one adopted by the Government are the following:

1. It has been proposed, even seriously, that the whole mass of Indians should be taken and distributed through the Eastern States, only one or two in a place, in order that they might thus come into vital contact with our civilization and be metamorphosed into Americans. The practical difficulties of a scheme like this are so many as to render it absolutely impossible of execution. Indeed a mere statement of it reveals its chimerical character.

2. Of course it is possible to continue the present reservation system and the exercise of guardianship over these people in the future as in the past for an indefinite period to come. The objections to this, however, are many and vital. The agency and reservation system has possibly accomplished some good in the past, and it has, at present, the possibility of benefit during the transition period, but certainly no wise man who understands the situation would venture even to suggest that the system should be made permanent.

3. It is sometimes urged that by one act of law the Indians should be made citizens of the United States, thrown upon their own resources, and relieved of the guardianship of the Government. While this might possibly answer in some cases, it certainly would result in great hardship to those Indians who are not prepared to take care of their own interests, and who, if abandoned now by the Government, would suffer wrong and injustice, and would either be exterminated or would become speedily a burden upon the local communities where they are situated.

The essential element of the policy adopted by the Government is suggested in the one phrase—American citizenship. What is commonly known as the "Dawes bill," or the "land-in-severalty law," which received Executive sanction February 8, 1887, has radically fixed our method of dealing with the Indians. By its operation those who take their land in severalty become citizens of the United States, entitled to the protection of the courts, and all other privileges of citizenship, and are amenable to the laws and under obligations for the performance of the same duties as devolve upon their fellow-citizens.

The progress that has been made in allotting lands, and thus of conferring citizenship, is shown under the head of "allotments."

I have no doubt as to the wisdom of this policy, and believe it ought to be prosecuted vigorously and intelligently until every Indian shall be brought under its operation, so that the relation of all shall be changed from that of wards to that of citizens.

Undoubtedly discretion should be used so as not to allot lands to tribes who are manifestly unfit for citizenship, or who are not soon likely to become so, and it is probable that in some instances mistakes have already been made in this respect. I am convinced that time should be given, so that the Indians to whom allotments are to be made may become familiar with the idea and all that it involves, and may thus be, in some degree, prepared in mind for the great change that must come to them when they are taken from under the protecting care of the agent and the Indian Bureau and are made independent citizens, dependent alone upon their own exertions and subject to the ordinary laws and processes of civilization. The change is a momentous one, and involves a reconstruction in many cases of all their fundamental conceptions of life and a radical change in their relations. It ought not, therefore, to be expected that they will easily and intelligently adapt themselves to the revolution even when they have had time for its consideration.

Citizenship, accompanied by allotment of lands, necessarily looks toward the entire destruction of the tribal relation; the Indians are to be individualized and dealt with one by one and not en masse; they are to stand upon their own personal rights and be freed absolutely from the trammels of the tribe and the limitations of chieftaincy.

Of course this policy carries with it, of necessity, the destruction of the whole agency system and the abolition of the issuance of rations and supplies. After the Indians shall have become citizens it is expected that they will receive from the Government in cash whatever may be due them, and they will then necessarily depend upon their own intelligence for the expenditure of their own receipts.

There are evils and anomalies connected with the agency system which can not, by any possible care in its administration, be entirely obviated, and which will disappear only with its disappearance. The transition period, however, in which the Indians are passing from the agency system out into full-fledged citizenship is one of more or less peril to them, and they should be protected so far as possible from any unnecessary disadvantages which may accrue to them by too great haste in making the change. The agency system is doomed, and must go, and that speedily. The great work of the Indian Bureau at present is to hasten the time when its labors shall be completed, and when it shall cease to exist as a part of the machinery of the Government.

I am strongly of the opinion, and the conviction grows upon me from year to year, that it will be an act of unwisdom bordering upon cruelty to thrust citizenship upon the Indians before they are prepared for it, and to fail to make proper provision for the training of the rising generation for the new duties that must come upon them. The necessity for education for the younger Indians is intensified by the imminence of citizenship. What has been done in this direction and the suggestions which I have to make regarding the subject of education will be considered in a later part of this report.

Citizenship is simply opportunity. To confer upon an uneducated Indian, ignorant of the English language and unaccustomed to American ways, the full privileges of liberty does not necessarily carry with it any advantage to him. It does not change his nature; confers upon him no new faculties; does not increase his intelligence; does not necessarily awaken any new desires, and may be practically a mockery. Where an individual wishes to become a citizen, and is eager for the advantages that citizenship brings with it, and has sufficient intelligence to adapt himself to his changed relations and to avail himself of his new privileges, as well as to perform satisfactorily his new duties, citizenship means very much. There are already among us tens of thousands of foreigners who have been naturalized and made citizens by the operation of the courts, who are in no sense qualified for their important duties, but who, on the contrary, are an element of weakness, if not of peril, to the country. It certainly is not desirable to add to this class of citizens any considerable number of blanket Indians who are made citizens only in name and not in fact.

I appreciate that where an Indian, by virtue of his citizenship, becomes a voter he has a significance in the eye of the vote-getter, and becomes an object of solicitude to all who desire his suffrage in the promotion of their own interests, as well as to those persons generally who know the full meaning and worth of the ballot. Already, in numerous cases that have come under my personal knowledge, Indians, by reason of the fact of their citizenship, have acquired a standing in a community which has been denied them heretofore; and those among whom they live whose interests may be affected for weal or for woe by the ballot which they cast become desirous that they shall be fitted for their new duties. In this respect certainly the mere fact of citizenship becomes immediately helpful to the Indians, or at least may do so.

The fact remains, however, that citizenship is a great privilege and a solemn responsibility, and ought not to be conferred upon the unworthy or the incompetent. I look with extreme solicitude upon the future of some of those who have already become citizens, but who have not had the advantages of education, and who seem indisposed to allow their children to be sent to school.

It is necessary to bear in mind that the condition of the Indian differs essentially from that of the average foreigner who comes among us and becomes naturalized. In the first place, foreigners who come to our shores in most cases have inherited the advantages of old civilization, and while in some instances they are themselves rather poor representatives of the civilization from which they come, they are nevertheless predisposed in favor of the essential elements that enter into American life. It is only necessary to allude to the fact that multitudes of those who come to us from England, Germany, and Scandinavia are persons of liberal culture, and are prepared to enter at once into competition with those whom they meet here in their varied walks of life on terms of equality.

Then, again, our civilization being a composite, transplanted to this continent from different parts of Europe, the foreigners who come to us find at once a point of contact with those who have preceded them from their native country, with whom they almost immediately enter into sympathy, from whom they derive help, and with whom they more or less fully assimilate.

It is entirely different with the Indians. They do not represent civilization. They are not in sympathy with us generally. There are no such points of contact between them and our own people, and it is, consequently, a task of vastly greater proportions to assimilate them than it is an equal number of persons from almost any country in Europe.

Besides this, which is a matter of special importance, the children of foreigners, by virtue of the fact that for the most part they settle in the midst of well-established communities, are admitted at once, and indeed are forced by public opinion, in most cases, into either public or private schools, where they acquire a knowledge of the English language and become associated with American youth, being taught by American teachers, so that they become fitted for the duties that devolve upon them as citizens. It is, however, not so with the Indians. Many of them are gathered in large settlements where there are very few white people and where, as yet, there are no public schools to which their children can go, and where there is no public sentiment in behalf of the education of Indian children. In many cases, indeed, their children are excluded by public sentiment from the public schools, and unless they attend those provided by the Government they can attend none, and consequently will grow up ignorant of their privileges and incapable of performing their duties.

For these reasons, I can not too strongly express my earnest conviction that the work of education should keep far ahead even of that of allotting lands, lest the allotment of lands and the conferring of citizenship prove not only a detriment to the Indians themselves, but, in some cases at least, work harm to the community.

MODIFICATION OF AGENCY SYSTEM

I believe it is entirely feasible and very desirable to modify the agency system and prepare the way for its complete abolition by placing the agency affairs, in certain cases, in the hands of school superintendents.

The act making appropriations for the Indian service for the year ending June 30, 1893, provides for the abolition of the agency for the Eastern Cherokees in North Carolina, and places in the hands of the superintendent of the school, the duties which have heretofore devolved upon the agent, and thus inaugurates a system which, I think, is capable of wide application.

There are several agencies where the Indians have already made great progress; where they have either taken their lands in severalty or are on the point of doing so; where the idea of citizenship has become quite familiar, and where by a little careful oversight, assistance, and advice, such as could be given to them by an intelligent school superintendent, they could soon be thrown entirely upon their own resources. At the same time they would not be left wholly to themselves, and would be thus gradually prepared by experience for the full duties of citizenship and the responsibilities of individual activity.

The power of the agent in cases where land has been allotted—as, for instance, among the Sissetons, the Yanktons, the Nez Percés, and elsewhere— is very limited indeed. Those under him are no longer his subjects, but citizens of the United States. He can not maintain an Indian police force or exercise any of the autocratic power to which he was accustomed when they were still merely wards of the nation. He is agent, therefore, in large part only in name, having the shadow of his office rather than its substance. To entirely discontinue the agency, however, and leave the people who have so long been accustomed to paternal guidance to their own resources would, in many cases, work great hardship.

By placing the superintendent of the school in charge of affairs, transferring to him something of the duties that have devolved hitherto upon the agent, and constituting him their chief counselor, director, and leader, the Indians would be spared many of the evils that might result from too hasty an abolition of the agency system. At the same time there would be the doing away of the agency proper and the saving of the expense connected with it.

The superintendents of the large agency boarding schools are generally men of high personal character and large business capacity. Many of them are under bonds, are fully competent for the discharge of whatever duties would devolve upon them as agents, and in many cases could fulfill them without materially interfering with their work in the schools. This plan would make the school rather than the agency the center of the Indians' thoughts, hopes, and life; would bring them into close relationship with these institutions of learning, and would thus dignify the cause of education and hasten the promotion of intelligence among them.

ARMY OFFICERS AS AGENTS

The Indian bill of July 13, 1892, contains the following proviso regarding the appointment of Indian agents:

> *Provided,* That from and after the passage of this act the President shall detail officers of the United States Army to act as Indian agents at all agencies where vacancies from any cause may hereafter occur, who, while acting as such agents, shall be under the orders and direction of the Secretary of the Interior, except at agencies where, in the opinion of the President, the public service would be better promoted by the appointment of a civilian.

I regard the policy of substituting Army officers for civilians with grave apprehension. It should be borne in mind that the work of an Indian agent is civil rather than military. He is an administrator in civil affairs; has to do with education, with the promotion of civilization, with the adjudication of questions pertaining to the rights of person and property, and his whole business is such as calls for a civilian's training, experience, and ideas, rather than for that of one who has been trained as a soldier.

That there have been Indian agents who have failed to comprehend their duties and who have not discharged them with efficiency, or who have not been men of high character, above suspicion, is doubtless true; but the records of the Army show that such men sometimes wear uniforms. It certainly is a very severe commentary upon our civilization if it can be truthfully said, or if the idea is even prevalent, that there can not be found in the United States fifty-seven men taken from civil life who are well qualified in character, attainments, and executive force to administer affairs at as many agencies.

So far as the substitution of military officers for civilians is an expression of a desire to rid the Indian service of what is popularly known as the "spoils" idea, I am in full sympathy with it, and in so far as it would tend to rescue the Indian service from partisan politics and place it upon the basis of a purely business administration, or to call into service men who are especially qualified for their respective duties and to retain them there during good behavior or until their work shall have been accomplished, it has my heartiest commendation.

I think, however, that these evils can be removed and the ends desired be accomplished in another way, without so great and violent a change as is involved in the substitution of Army officers for civilian agents.

The work of civil administration is not one to which Army officers have been specially trained, nor one for which they have any special aptitude. While it is doubtless true that there are many men in the Army who are capable of doing this kind of work with gratifying success, it is also true that it is wholly foreign to the military idea, and that it is imposing upon the Army a new duty that must, of necessity, work more or less disaster to the *morale* of the Army itself. If the Indian agencies are to be filled by the appointment of the best men that can be found in the Army, this would make a drain upon it that I should suppose would be severely felt; and if by those who are not desirable and whom the Army will be glad to get rid of, it certainly will be a great misfortune to the Indian service.

It should be borne in mind, too, that the officer is enlisted for life; that all his hopes and ambitions are centered in the Army; that he looks to the head of the War Department for an appreciation of his services, for promotion; and that almost of necessity he regards a subordination of himself to the control of any but an army officer as rather an infringement upon his position and rights. So that it would not be at all surprising if there should be on the part of army officers detailed for service as Indian agents, some degree of restlessness under civil control and a possible spirit of insubordination, involving unpleasant consequences both to themselves and to the officer charged with the administration of Indian affairs; and my experience hitherto fully warrants me in expressing such a fear.

This could but lead, at times at least, to a difference of opinion between the War Department and the Department of the Interior, and might result in unpleasant relations, which would be annoying to the heads of those Departments as well as an occasion of anxiety and trouble to the President.

On January 7, 1868, there was submitted to the President the report of the Indian Peace Commission, which is found on pages 26 to 50 of Report of the Commissioner of Indian Affairs, for 1868, and is signed, among others, by W. T. Sherman, lieutenant-general; Wm. S. Harney, brevet major-general; Alfred H. Terry, brevet major-general, and C. C. Augur, brevet major-general, U. S. Army. These men can not be suspected of any hostility to army officers, or of any possible bias in their judgment as to the fitness of military men for the discharge of civil duties involved in Indian administration. I quote from the report the following significant paragraph:

> This brings us to consider the much mooted question whether the bureau should belong to the civil or military department of the Government. To determine this properly we must know what is to be the further treatment of the Indians. If we intend to have war with them the bureau should go to the Secretary of War. If we intend to have peace, it should be in the civil department. In our judgement such wars are wholly unneccessary, and hoping that the Government and the country will agree with us, we can not now advise the change. It is possible, however, that despite our efforts to maintain peace, war may be forced on us by some tribe or tribes of Indians. In the event of such occurrence it may be well to provide, in the revision of the intercourse laws or elsewhere, at what time the civil jurisdiction shall cease and the military jurisdiction begin. If thought advisable, also, Congress may authorize the President to turn over to the military the exclusive control of such tribes as may be continually hostile or unmanageable. Under the plan which we have suggested the chief duties of the bureau will be to educate and instruct in the peaceful arts—in other words, to civilize the Indians. The military arm of the Government is not the most admirably adapted to discharge duties of this character. We have the highest possible appreciation of the officers of the Army, and fully recognize their proverbial integrity and honor; but we are satisfied that not one in a thousand would like to teach Indian children to read and write, or Indian men to sow and reap. These are emphatically civil and not military occupations.

I have carefully considered all the arguments advanced in favor of the change, and have seen no reason to modify my opinion that the change is ill-advised; was not called for by the circumstances of the case; that it will not bring about the advantages which some of its advocates hope for; and that it is liable, at least, to produce unhappy fruits. I sincerely hope that before the policy has become an established rule the law may be changed.

The Evolution of the Indian Agent

As throwing a side light upon this question of who should be employed as Indian agents, as well as upon the general policy of the Government in dealing with Indians, I ask your attention to a brief historical survey of the evolution of the Indian agent during the past hundred years.

In my last annual report, under the head of "The Political Status of the Indians," I outlined the development, by legislation and treaty, of the present Indian policy of the Government. This resumé notes the methods and agencies used by the Government to administer affairs growing out of our relations with Indian tribes.

Prior to the adoption of the "Articles of Confederation and Perpetual Union," each colony or State had independent and separate control of all intercourse between white men and the members of the various Indian tribes within their respective territorial limits. The steps taken by the several States to regulate such matters will not now be discussed.

The ninth article of the "Articles of Confederation and Perpetual Union," provided that—

> The United States in Congress assembled shall also have the sole and exclusive right and power of . . . regulating the trade and managing all affairs with the Indians, not members of any of the States, provided that the legislative right of any State within its own limits be not infringed or violated.

In pursuance of this the congress of the confederation on August 7, 1786, passed an "Ordinance for the regulation of Indian Affairs." After the following preamble:

> Whereas the safety and tranquillity of the frontiers of the United States do, in some measure, depend on the maintaining a good correspondence between their citizens and the several nations of Indians in amity with them,

the ordinance provided that from that date the Indian Department be divided into two districts, viz: The southern, comprehending all the nations of Indians within the United States south of the Ohio River; and the northern, comprehending all other nations of Indians within the United States west of the Hudson River. For each of these districts a superintendent was authorized to be appointed; who was to reside within such district or as near it as might be convenient for the management of its affairs. The superintendent for the northern district was authorized to appoint two deputies "to reside in such places as shall best facilitate the regulation of the Indian trade, and to remove them for misbehavior."

It was further ordained—

> That none but citizens of the United States shall be suffered tc reside among the Indian nations, or be allowed to trade with any nation of Indians within the territory of the United States. That no person, citizen or other, under penalty of five hundred dollars, shall reside among, or trade with any Indian, or Indian nation, within the territory of the United States, without a license for that purpose first obtained from the superintendent of the district, or one of the deputies, who are hereby directed to give such license to every person who shall produce from the supreme executive of any State, a certificate, under the seal of the State, that he is of good character, and suitably qualified and provided for that employment, for which license he shall pay the sum of fifty dollars to said superintendent for the use of the United States.

Also—

> That in all cases where transactions with any nation or tribe of Indians shall become necessary to the purposes of this ordinance, which can not be done without interfering with the legislative rights of a State, the superin-

tendent in whose district the same shall happen shall act in conjunction with the authority of such State.

These superintendents reported to the Secretary of War and were under his direction. They had no jurisdiction over the Indians, and their only duty was to superintend the trade between Indians and those to whom licenses might be issued, to see that the regulations prescribed by the President for the government of such trade were complied with, and that no improper or unauthorized persons engaged in the business. This was all that the congress of the confederation appeared to think necessary to be done by the Government in "regulating the trade and managing all affairs with the Indians."

The framers of the Federal Constitution, which in 1788 superseded the Articles of Confederation, deemed it of importance that the central government should have exclusive power over intercourse with Indians. Therefore, section 8 of article 1 of the Constitution provided that "the Congress shall have power . . . to regulate commerce . . . with the Indian tribes." The limitation on the power of Congress which the Articles of Confederation reserved to the "legislative right" of the States was omitted, and the national Government, through Congress, was given exclusive control of the matter. The Supreme Court of the United States, in Gibbons *v.* Ogden (6 Wheat., 448), decided that "commerce undoubtedly is traffic, but it is something more, it is intercourse;" and in United States *v.* Holiday (3 Wall., 407) it decided that commerce with the Indian tribes means commerce between citizens of the United States and "the individuals composing those tribes." Therefore, it follows that when Congress was given power by the Constitution to regulate commerce with Indian tribes it was also given control of the intercourse between individual citizens of the United States and individual Indians, and that there is nothing that could arise out of our relations with the Indians which is not subject to regulation by Congress.

The first step taken by Congress looking to the regulation of our intercourse with the Indian tribes was the passage of a law August 20, 1789 (1 *Stats.*, 54), appropriating $20,000 to "defray the expenses of negotiating and treating with the Indian tribes," and authorizing the appointment of commissioners to manage such negotiations and treaties. The commissioners thus authorized were sometimes referred to as "agents for treating with the Indians;" but their duties were merely to treat with Indian tribes with a view to securing the cession of some of the land claimed and occupied by them, and to establish peaceful and friendly intercourse between them and our own Government and citizens; their designation as "agents" seems to have been misapplied. In a letter of instructions (dated August 29, 1789, and signed by George Washington) to Messrs. Benjamin Lincoln, Cyrus Griffin, and David Humphrey, those gentlemen were addressed as "commissioners plenipotentiary for negotiating and concluding treaties of peace with the independent tribes or nations of Indians within the limits of the

United States south of the Ohio River." This letter begins with the statement that—

> The United States consider it as an object of high national importance not only to be at peace with the powerful tribes or nations of Indians south of the Ohio, but, if possible, by a just and liberal system of policy to conciliate and attach them to the interests of the Union.

The gentlemen named, under date of November 20, 1789, made a report to the Secretary of War upon their labors as commissioners plenipotentiary, etc., among the southern Indians, especially among the Upper Creeks and the Lower Creeks (the latter now known as the Seminoles), in which they express the belief that—

> In order to preserve the attachment of the several Indian nations bordering upon the United States . . . some adequate means of supplying them with goods and ammunition at moderate prices should immediately be adopted. . . . We respectfully suggest that some uniform plan of granting permits to those who may be employed in the Indian commerce should be established by the supreme authority of the United States.

Out of the suggestions made by this commission grew the licensed-trader system, which in a modified form has continued to this day. By the act of July 22, 1790 (1 *Stats.*, 137), Congress took the second step under the Federal Constitution to regulate commerce with the Indian tribes. This law prohibited all persons from carrying on any "trade or intercourse with the Indian tribes without a license for that purpose under the hand and seal of the superintendent of the department or of such other person as the President of the United States shall appoint for that purpose." The "superintendent of the department" here referred to was probably the officer authorized to be appointed by the ordinance of 1786 to superintend Indian affairs, as no law had been passed under the Constitution authorizing the appointment of any such officer. This law was a continuation of the policy adopted by the Congress of the Confederation and a modification of the ordinance of 1786. In lieu of the certificate of the supreme executive of the State as to the good character of the applicant for license, which the ordinance required, this law provided that any proper person might receive a license upon giving bond in the sum of $1,000 for the faithful observance of such rules, regulations, and restrictions, as should be made by the President for the government of trade and intercourse with Indians.

Except the superintendents and deputies appointed under the authority of the Government of the Confederation, who, like the commissioners appointed under the act of August 10, 1789, were sometimes referred to in state correspondence as Indian agents, no Indian agents seem to have been authorized by law prior to 1796. Meantime, however, apparently upon the authority of the Executive, "temporary agents," or "deputy temporary agents," were appointed to certain Indian tribes or nations. For instance, January 31, 1792, the Secretary of War wrote to Governor Blount, of

Tennessee, who was superintendent of Indian affairs for the southern district, that a delegation of Cherokees, then in Philadelphia, at that time the seat of the General Government, had requested "that a person of reputation should be commissioned in behalf of the General Government to reside in the Cherokee Nation, who should at once be their counsellor and protector." Pursuant to this request Mr. Leonard Shaw, who was described in a letter of February 16, 1792, from the Secretary of War to Governor Blount as an amiable and well-informed young gentleman, and a graduate of Princeton College, was instructed February 17, 1792, as follows:

> The President of the United States is desirous that you should accompany the Cherokee chiefs who are at present in this city to their own nation, for the objects hereinafter particularly stated, as well as for the general purpose of attaching the said Indians, and all the Southern Indians whom you may occasionally see, to the interests of the United States.

Mr. Shaw was designated "temporary agent to the Cherokee Nation."

April 23, 1792, the Secretary of War advised Gen. Israel Chapin of his appointment by the President as "deputy temporary agent" for the Five Nations, and on April 28, following, he was furnished with general "rules and orders" for his government as such deputy temporary agent. Gen. Chapin's instructions were similar to those given Mr. Shaw, and both were to represent the Government among the nations to whom they had been respectively assigned, and to be the channels of communication between those Indians and the United States.

April 18, 1796, Congress adopted a law (1 *Stats.*, 452) authorizing the establishment of trading houses on the "western and southern frontiers or in the Indian country," for the purpose of carrying on a "liberal trade" with the Indians; also the appointment of agents to manage them under the direction of the President. These agents, who occupied the relation to the Government of factors or commercial agents, were the first agents for Indian affairs that Congress authorized. The establishment of the system of trading houses under the control of Government agents was evidently an experiment, for the operation of the act authorizing them was limited to "two years, and to the end of the next session of Congress thereafter, and no longer." The primary object, however, was the protection of the frontiers, as it was hoped that by a "liberal trade with the several Indian nations" a "good correspondence" between them and the citizens of the United States would be maintained. The act was from time to time extended until 1822, when it was permitted to expire, and the system of Government trading houses was abolished. During this period the system was variously modified by Congress. The House of Representatives of the Sixth Congress appointed a committee to "inquire into the operation of the acts making provision for the establishment of trading houses with the Indian tribes, and into the expediency of reviving and continuing said acts in force." This committee reported April 22, 1800, recommending that the capital already engaged in the business be continued therein, "but that it should not be enlarged by

further drafts from the Treasury until the establishment is better understood in its several relations."

The act of May 7, 1800 (2 *Stats.*, 58), provided for the division of the
territory of the United States northwest of the Ohio into two separate governments; also that the "duties and emoluments of superintendent of Indian
affairs" should be united with those of governors of the Territories established by that act, which were the Northwest Territory and the Territory of
Indiana. This act, therefore, created for the portion of country formerly
designated as the Northwest Territory two superintendents of Indian
affairs instead of one, as authorized by the ordinance of 1786, who within
the limits of the Territories of which they might be, respectively, governors,
had full supervision, subject to the direction of the Secretary of War, of
all affairs growing out of our relations with the Indians.

By the act of March 30, 1802 (2 *Stats.*, 139), Congress, "in order to
promote civilization among the friendly Indian tribes, and to secure the
continuance of their friendship," authorized the President to expend annually a sum not exceeding $15,000 in "causing them to be furnished with
useful domestic animals and implements of husbandry, and with goods or
money, as he shall judge proper, and to appoint such persons, from time to
time, as temporary agents, to reside among the Indians, as he shall think
fit."

The functions of the agents to be appointed under this law were broader
than those of the officers of Indian affairs theretofore appointed, whose
duties had been solely to superintend and manage trade and intercourse
with the Indians. "To promote civilization among the friendly Indians and
to secure the continuance of their friendship" required the exercise of a
certain influence over the conduct of the Indians within their own country.
Still, these agents had no power to direct or control the conduct of the
Indians by any other method than advice and counsel. They were temporary agents, to be assigned to any friendly tribe as the President saw fit,
and to be transferred from tribe to tribe, in the discretion of the President.

By an act of April 21, 1806 (2 *Stats.*, 402), Congress authorized the
appointment of an officer to be designated the "Superintendent of Indian
Trade," whose duties were "to purchase and take charge of all goods
intended for trade with the Indian nations aforesaid, and to transmit the
same to such places as he shall be directed by the President." Subsequently,
by the act of March 2, 1811, he was given the additional duty of purchasing
and transmitting to the proper posts and places the supplies, goods, and
moneys promised Indians under treaty stipulations, as well as such other
goods and money as might be required in treating with the Indians and
making presents to them at the seat of Government.

After the passage of the act of 1806 our Indian affairs were administered
by the following officers, viz: First, governors of the various Territories, who
were *ex officio* superintendents of Indian affairs within their respective
Territories (as new Territories were organized, these duties were also

imposed upon their governors); second, agents appointed under the act of 1802, primarily under the control and direction of the superintendents; third, the superintendent of Indian trade; and fourth, the agents or factors in charge of the Indian trading houses, who were under the immediate direction of the superintendent of Indian trade.

An act approved March 3,.1819 (3 *Stats.*, 516), provided—

> That for the purpose of providing against the further decline and final extinction of the Indian tribes adjoining the frontier settlements of the United States, and for introducing among them the habits and arts of civilization, the President of the United States shall be, and he is hereby, authorized in every case where he shall judge improvement in the habits and condition of such Indians practicable, and that the means of instruction can be introduced with their own consent, to employ capable persons of good moral character to instruct them in the modes of agriculture suited to their situation; and for teaching their children in reading, writing, and arithmetic, and performing such other duties as may be enjoined, according to such instructions and rules as the President may give and prescribe for the regulation of their conduct in the discharge of their duties.

It also appropriated an annual sum of $10,000 for the purpose of carrying the provisions of the law into effect.

By this act, what are now known as Government farmers, to instruct the adult Indians in the science of agriculture, and school-teachers, to instruct their children in the primary branches of learning, were added to the list of officers connected with the administration of Indian affairs.

This policy of appointing agents and employés for Indian tribes was so extended and modified by subsequent treaties as to authorize the appointment of agents, sub-agents, farmers, and blacksmiths for nearly all the tribes with which the United States entered into treaty relations, and teachers and other employés for many of them. The language used in the treaties would indicate that the Indians desired to have representatives of the United States reside among them. For example, in the sixth article of the treaty of 1820 with the Choctaws it was provided that—

> The commissioners of the United States further covenant and agree, on the part of said States, than an agent shall be appointed, in due time, for the benefit of the Choctaw Indians who may be permanently settled in the country ceded to them beyond the Mississippi River, and, at a convenient period, a factor shall be sent there with goods to supply their wants. A blacksmith shall also be settled amongst them at a point most convenient to the population, and a faithful person appointed, whose duty it shall be to use every reasonable exertion to collect all the wandering Indians belonging to the Choctaw Nation upon the land hereby provided for their permanent settlement.

The sixth article of the treaty of 1823 with the Florida Indians is as follows, viz:

An agent, sub-agent, and interpreter shall be appointed, to reside within the Indian boundary aforesaid, to watch over the interests of said tribes; and the United States further stipulate, as an evidence of their humane policy towards said tribes, who have appealed to their liberality, to allow for the establishment of a school at the agency, $1,000 per year for twenty years, and $1,000 per year for the same period for the support of a gun and blacksmith, with the expenses incidental to his shop.

In 1822, when the act for the establishment of Indian trading houses was permitted to expire, the offices of superintendent of Indian trade, and the agents and clerks necessary to the conduct of the business, were abolished. Since that time Indian trade has been conducted through the medium of a licensed trader.

In 1824, the Secretary of War organized, without special authority of law, a "Bureau of Indian Affairs," with a chief, termed by courtesy commissioner, a chief clerk and an assistant. The duties of this office, as appears from a letter of March 11, 1824, from the Secretary of War to Thomas L. McKenney, were to have charge of the appropriations for annuities and current expenses; to receive and examine accounts for their expenditure; to administer the fund for the civilization of the Indians; to examine and report to the Secretary of War claims arising out of the laws regulating trade with Indian tribes; and to conduct the ordinary correspondence with the superintendents, agents, and sub-agents.

By act of July 9, 1832 (4 *Stats.*, 564), the President was authorized to appoint a "Commissioner of Indian Affairs, who shall, under the direction of the Secretary of War, and agreeably to such regulations as the President may from time to time prescribe, have the direction and management of all Indian affairs, and of all matters arising out of Indian relations." The Secretary of War was directed to arrange or appoint to "the said office the number of clerks necessary therefor, so as not to increase the number now employed," and, under the direction of the President, to "cause to be discontinued the services of such agents, sub-agents, interpreters, and mechanics, as may from time to time become unnecessary, in consequence of the emigration of the Indians, or other causes." By this law the present Bureau of Indian Affairs was established after the plan upon which it had been operated for eight years.

An act approved June 30, 1834 (4 *Stats.*, 729), "to regulate trade and intercourse with the Indian tribes, and to preserve peace on the frontiers," re-enacted the licensed-trader law of 1790 with modifications, and also greatly enlarged the powers of officers of the Government over the Indian country, and over the Indians themselves. Section 10 authorized superintendents of Indian affairs, Indian agents, and sub-agents to remove from the Indian country persons found therein without authority of law, and section 11 provided that the military power of the United States might be used to expel white settlers from Indian lands. Section 19 is important enough to quote entire.

That it shall be the duty of the superintendents, agents, and subagents to endeavor to procure the arrest and trial of all Indians accused of committing any crime, offense, or misdemeanor, and all other persons who may have committed crimes or offenses within any State or Territory, and have fled into the Indian country, either by demanding the same of the chiefs of the proper tribe or by such other means as the President may authorize; and the President may direct the military force of the United States to be employed in the apprehension of such Indians, and also in preventing or terminating hostilities between any of the Indian tribes.

Section 25 provided—

That so much of the laws of the United States as provide for the punishment of crimes committed within any place within the sole and exclusive jurisdiction of the United States shall be in force in the Indian country: *Provided,* The same shall not extend to crimes committed by one Indian against the person or property of another Indian.

Another act "to provide for the organization of the Department of Indian Affairs," dated June 30, 1834 (4 *Stats.,* 735), provided as follows: For releasing the governors of Florida, Arkansas, and Michigan Territory from obligation to perform the duties of superintendents of Indian affairs, and for the appointment of a superintendent of Indian affairs for all the Indian country not within the bounds of any State or Territory west of the Mississippi River, who should reside at St. Louis.

The duties of the superintendents of Indian affairs were prescribed to be to—

Exercise a general supervision and control over the official conduct and accounts of all officers and persons employed by the Government in the Indian department, under such regulations as shall be established by the President of the United States; and [they] may suspend such officers and persons from their office or employments, for reasons forthwith to be communicated to the Secretary of War.

The President was authorized, by and with the advice and consent of the Senate, to appoint twelve Indian agents, as follows:

Two agents for the western territory; an agent for the Chickasaws; an agent for the eastern Cherokees; an agent for the Florida Indians; an agent for the Indians in the State of Indiana; an agent at Chicago; an agent at Rock Island; an agent at Prairie du Chien; an agent for Michilimackinac and the Sault Sainte Marie; an agent for the Saint Peter's; an agent for the upper Missouri.

Certain agencies named were to be discontinued at a fixed time, and any Indian agency might be discontinued by the President whenever he might judge it expedient, or he might transfer an agent from the place or tribe designated by law to such other place or tribe as the public service might require.

Every Indian agent was required to reside and keep his agency "within or near the territory or tribe" for which he might be agent, and it was made "competent for the President to require any military officer of the United States to execute the duties of Indian agent."

The President was authorized to appoint a competent number of sub-agents to be employed, and to reside wherever he might direct, not, however, within the limits of any agency where an agent was appointed.

The Secretary of War was directed to establish the limits of each Agency and sub-agency either by tribes or by geographical boundaries, and to prescribe the general duties of Indian agents and sub-agents to be—

> To manage and superintend the intercourse with the Indians within their respective agencies agreeably to law; to obey all legal instructions given by the Secretary of War, the Commissioner of Indian Affairs, or the superintendent of Indian Affairs, and to carry into effect such regulations as may be prescribed by the President.

The appointment of interpreters, blacksmiths, farmers, mechanics, and teachers was provided for.

The payment of all annuities or other treaty funds was to be made to the chiefs of the tribes, or to such persons as the tribes might appoint.

The President was authorized to cause friendly Indians west of the Mississippi River and north of the boundary of the western territory, and the region upon Lake Superior and the head of the Mississippi, to be furnished with useful domestic animals and implements of husbandry, and with goods, as he might think proper, not to cost in the aggregate more than $5,-000.

He was also authorized to cause such rations as he might think proper, and could be spared from the army provisions without injury to the service, to be issued to the Indians who might visit the military posts or agencies of the United States on the frontiers, or in their respective nations.

Finally, the President was authorized to prescribe such rules and regulations as he might think fit for carrying into effect the various provisions of the act, and of any other act relating to Indian affairs.

The Constitution did not give nor purport to give Congress power to regulate the conduct of the members of the tribes within the country set apart for their use, or granted to them in perpetual ownership, nor to interfere with the several governments of the tribes. Hence, in the early history of the regulation by the Federal Congress of commerce with the Indian tribes no attempt was made to break down or interfere with the several tribal governments, or to control the conduct of the tribes in their own country; all efforts were directed solely to the regulation of our commercial relations with the tribes, and had in view mainly the interests of our own citizens and the protection and security of our frontiers. But as the population of the United States increased and its settlements pressed hard upon the boundaries of the Indian country a closer and more intimate communication between whites and Indians became inevitable. It was dangerous to both. It became necessary, therefore, in order to prevent the "decline and final extinction of the Indian tribes," to preserve peace on the frontiers, and to protect the lives and property of the white settlers, for the Government to assume a relation to Indian tribes, and in some degree to individual Indians, similar to that of guardian. Thus it came about that by degrees the authority of executive officers over persons and property in the Indian country was enlarged and increased, and naturally and almost necessarily the power of the Indian agent, through whom the laws were usually executed, also grew, and in about the same proportion. The designation of officers of the Army to perform the duties of Indian agents, authorized in the "Indian intercourse act" of 1834, still further tended to increase the agent's power, for the reason that, accustomed to rigid army discipline, army officers expected and required a strict obedience to their orders, and when Indians resisted they were often coerced by military power into submission.

Moreover, the Indians themselves in various treaties acknowledged their dependence on the United States for protection in their rights as tribes and as individuals.

It has been shown how the United States, in the beginning, regarded and treated the Indian tribes as independent nations, taking no step toward governing them or providing them with a form of government; how by degrees, although acknowledging their autonomy, control was taken of their affairs, until, in 1834, the Indian agent was given power to secure the arrest and punishment of Indians even in their own country. After 1834 some years elapsed before Congress deemed it necessary to give the Government further authority over the Indian.

An act of March 3, 1847 (9 *Stats.*, 203), provided that all annuities or other moneys, and all goods stipulated by treaty to be paid or furnished to any Indian tribe, should be paid, not to tribal chiefs according to the law of 1834, but to the heads of families and other individuals entitled thereto. As if to make their dependence on the United States complete, the civil liberties, if indeed they possessed any before, were taken from the Indians by a clause in the act which declared that "all executory contracts made and entered into by any Indian for the payment of money or goods shall be deemed and held to be null and void and of no binding effect whatsoever." Having no power to make a contract, the Indian occupied the position in the eyes of the law similar to that of a minor. His disabilities indeed were even greater than those of a minor, because there was no class of executory contracts that he could make that would not, under the law, be null and void. Thus the Indian by legislation was brought to the condition to which circumstances had already practically reduced him. He looked to his guardian, the national Government, even for his very subsistence. He came to the agent for advice as to matters arising between him and his white neighbors, and later on as to matters arising between him and others of his tribe. He was a child, without rights, except such as his agent allowed him to enjoy.

By act of March 3, 1849 (9 *Stats.*, 395), "to establish the home department," etc., the Department of the Interior was organized and authorized to "exercise the supervisory and appellate powers now exercised by the Secretary of the War Department, in relation to all the acts of the Commissioner of Indian Affairs," etc. Thenceforward the Secretary of the Interior became the head of the Indian department.

The act of 1834 gave no authority to agents or officers of United States courts to take cognizance of offenses committed by Indians on their respective reservations. The act of March 27, 1854 (10 *Stats.,* 270), however, provided for the punishment of Indians for the crimes of arson and assault with intent to kill when said crimes were committed against the property or persons of whites residing upon Indian reservations.

While gradually assuming the guardianship of the persons of the Indians, the Government also acquired, through treaties and laws, the full control and guardianship of their property, and became the holder of large sums of money representing the funds of the various tribes, and these funds, as well as annuities provided for by treaties, have been expended under the direction of Congress for "such objects as will best promote the comfort, civilization, and improvement of the tribe entitled to the same."

By the Indian appropriation act of May 27, 1878 (20 *Stats.,* 86), authority was granted for the appointment of Indian police, to be "employed in maintaining peace and prohibiting illegal traffic in liquor on the reservations." These police are appointed from among the Indians by the Commissioner of Indian Affairs upon the recommendation of the Indian agent, and they are subject to the orders of the agent. Jails or guardhouses have been provided on many reservations in which to confine refractory Indians. The Indian agent was the sole judge of the guilt of Indians charged with offenses on reservations, and the Indian police force executed his judgments without question until April 10, 1883, when this Department promulgated a regulation providing for the establishment of courts on the various Indian reservations, with jurisdiction to try and pass judgment on Indians guilty of certain prescribed offenses, termed "Indian offenses." The judges of these courts were termed "judges of the court of Indian offenses," and, like the Indian police, were appointed by the Commissioner of Indian Affairs from among the Indians upon the recommendations of the agents. While the Indian police force and court of Indian offenses, composed, as they are, of members of Indian tribes, ought to be, and on many reservations are, organizations through which the Indians, in a modified way, govern themselves after the manner of the people of civilized nations, still they may be, and sometimes are, merely instruments in the hands of the agent for the enforcement of his power, which is now almost absolute.

Besides the provisions of statute that have operated to give the Indian agent great power in the Indian country, the regulations of the Indian department that have from time to time prescribed, pursuant to law, and that have the force and effect of law, have further extended and enlarged that power. For example, the agent is authorized in the "Regulations of the Indian Department" to prevent Indians from leaving their reservation without a permit for that purpose, and instructed not to allow the practice of bands of Indians of one reservation making or returning visits to other reservations for the purpose of receiving or giving presents, and he has the power to use his Indian police to prevent the infraction of these rules. The final judgments of the courts of Indian offenses are subject to modification and revocation by the Indian agent, who is given appellate jurisdiction.

The Indian agent, as shown by the foregoing, now has almost absolute power in the Indian country, and so far as the people over whom he rules are concerned, he has none to contest his power. Appointed at first in the capacity of a commercial agent or consul of the United States in the country of an alien people, the Indian agent, under laws enacted and regulations promulgated in pursuance thereof, has developed into an officer with power to direct the affairs of the Indians and to transact their business in all details and in all relations. This is a very curious chapter in our history. There is a striking contrast between "ministers plenipotentiary," appointed by the United States to treat with powerful Indian nations, and an army officer, with troops at his command, installed over a tribe of Indians to maintain among them an absolute military despotism. Yet our policy of dealing with them has swung from one of these extremes to the other in a strangely vacillating way. Indeed, at present, the agent among the Five Civilized Tribes performs rather the functions of a consul in a foreign nation than those of an agent, while the Commission who have recently negotiated with the Cherokees for the cession of the Outlet, commonly called the "Strip," have really treated with them as with an independent nation and have performed the functions of, in one sense, ministers plenipotentiary. On the other hand, the absolute military rule finds its illustration in the present condition of things at San Carlos and in a modified way at Pine Ridge.

The whole tendency of modern legislation in providing for the allotment of lands in severalty and the conferring of citizenship upon Indians has been toward greater freedom for the Indians and a more careful respect for their individual rights. Nothing but the sternest necessity can warrant the Government in deviating from this more humane policy until it shall have accomplished its benign work of the complete enfranchisement of these people.

Law and Courts for Indian Reservations

At its annual meeting in Boston on August 26, 1891, the National Bar Association adopted the following resolution:

> *Resolved,* That it is the sense of this association that the Government should provide at the earliest possible moment for courts and a system of law in and for the Indian reservations.

A committee of three was appointed and instructed on behalf of the association to take steps to "bring to the attention of the President and Congress of the United States the expediency of legislation" such as was contemplated by this resolution. According to their instructions, Messrs. Hitchcock, Thayer, and Hornblower, composing the committee, presented the matter to the President during the early part of October, 1891, in a memorial without date, a copy of which was filed in the Department and referred to this office.

The question to which this resolution relates has for a number of years received the serious consideration of officers of the Government, and I have personally given it much thought, with a view to recommending some action by Congress, if it should appear expedient to do so.

It was for the purpose of relieving the anomalous conditions that existed on Indian reservations by reason of an absence of laws applicable to Indians thereon that the Indian police were established by act of Congress; that later the courts of Indian offenses were organized under the regulations of this Department; and that the Indian appropriation act of March 3, 1885, gave to United States and Territorial courts jurisdiction of crimes committed by Indians on their reservations.

These laws and regulations have operated successfully in the promotion of peace and order on reservations, but they do not afford a jurisdiction within which the Indian can enforce his contract or be required to live up to his own civil obligations. It has therefore seemed desirable that some provision shall be made by which the Indians in the United States who have not become, or are not in process of becoming, citizens might be brought under the influence of some simple system of courts and laws by which they might be instructed in the methods of civil and orderly government, and be more rapidly and suitably prepared for the citizenship in the United States which is surely coming to them under the present policy of the Government. But how this shall be done is the question which always presents itself. The difference in the status of the various Indian reservations, and of the temper and condition of the Indians occupying them, present serious difficulties in the way of formulating a plan which shall be applicable to any considerable number of Indians.

We must begin by determining to what tribes such laws and courts could *not* easily be made to apply by reason of their peculiar conditions or surroundings. These may be divided into four classes, viz:

First. Those Indians who maintain an advanced form of tribal government. Among these are (1) the Five Civilized Tribes, numbering 66,500, who have severally a republican form of government assimilating closely the governments of the several States; (2) the New York Indians, numbering 5,112, whose government is based on a constitution approved and ratified by the legislature of the State of New York; (3) the 1,563 Osage Indians whose government is based on a constitution approved by this Department; (4) the 8,120 Pueblo Indians of New Mexico who live under their ancient form of local town governments, and (5) the 3,000 Eastern Cherokees who have an organized form of tribal government, and also have individually been recognized as citizens of North Carolina.

Second. The Indians who, by taking allotments of land in severalty, have become citizens of the United States and thereby have passed under the jurisdiction and protection of the laws and courts of the States and Territories in which they reside. They number about 30,738. Also those to whom allotments in severalty are about to be made, numbering about 26,691, and about 25,636 more who are now in the act of receiving their allotments.

Third. The scattered bands or tribes of Indians not under the charge of any Indian agent, estimated to number 25,664.

Fourth. The Indians who are not sufficiently enlightened to comprehend the system, or who are so situated as to make it improbable they would be benefited by it. In this class are the Apaches, Yumas, and Colorado River Indians in Arizona, and the Blackfeet and Navajos, aggregating 26,973.

A tabulation gives the following results:

Total Indian population of the United States, exclusive of Alaska. *246,834
Deduct Indians to whom a system of laws can not easily be made to
   apply as above described as follows:
Number in class 1 85,016
Number in class 2 81,344
Number in class 3 25,664
Number in class 4 26,973

                                                      ————218,997

   Leaving total number to whom a system of laws can be applied. .   27,837

These 27,837 Indians occupy many reservations in widely separated parts of the United States. Most of these reservations have a population of less than 1,000 Indians and only two of them have over 2,000. The expense and labor of establishing separate judicial machinery for so many small tribes would hardly be justified by the results.

For this reason I have been unable, after careful attention to the subject, to formulate any plan that appeared to me to really meet the case so as to warrant me in urging upon Congress the adoption of a law to put it into operation. Neither have I been able thus far to indorse plans looking to this end which have been brought to my attention. Therefore, after consideration of the question and consultation with several Senators and others of long experience in Indian affairs and Indian legislation, I have concluded that about all that can at present be done to relieve the situation is the enlargement and extension of the jurisdiction of the Indian courts, so as to place them on a more efficient and effective basis.

Therefore, with this end in view I have revised and modified the regulations under which the courts were established and have been operated. Some of the important changes proposed in the new regulations are: (1) The reservations are divided into districts, with a judge in each district; (2)

*From Annual Report Indian Bureau, 1891.

a court in banc, with a clerk who is required to keep a record, is provided for, and given jurisdiction over appeals from the several district judges, and exclusive jurisdiction over all civil matters arising between Indians on the reservation, and over matters pertaining to administration upon the estates of deceased Indians; (3) the several judges are authorized to perform the marriage ceremony between Indians; and (4) vagrancy is declared to be an offense punishable by the court.

The new regulations to which I refer are as follows:

The attention of Indian agents is specially directed to the fact that Indians are subject under law to the jurisdiction of the State, Federal, or Territorial courts, according to the location of their reservations and to their status as to citizenship in the United States as follows, viz:

Where the Indians of any tribe located upon a reservation within a State or Territory have had lands allotted and patented to them under any law or treaty of the United States, they thereby become citizens and pass under the protection of the Constitution of the United States, and are therefore entitled to the benefits of and subject to the laws, both civil and criminal, of the State or Territory in which they reside. When an Indian takes up his residence separate and apart from his tribe and adopts habits of civilized life, he likewise becomes a citizen, entitled to all the privileges and immunities and subject to all the burdens incident upon such citizenship; but his rights and interest in tribal or other property are not in any manner impaired or otherwise affected. (See Sec. 6, act of February 8, 1887; 24 Stats., 388, 390.)

Crimes and misdemeanors committed by Indians within a State and not within an Indian reservation are punishable in the courts of such State and in accordance with State laws, whether the Indian charged with crime or misdemeanor be a citizen of the United States or not.

FEDERAL AND TERRITORIAL COURTS

Indians committing murder, manslaughter, rape, assault with intent to kill, arson, burglary, or larceny against the person or property of another Indian or other person within an Indian reservation in a State are subject to the same laws, triable "in the same courts and in the same manner and subject to the same penalties as are all other persons committing any of the above crimes within the exclusive jurisdiction of the United States."

Indians, whether citizens of the United States or not, committing any of the crimes named in the foregoing regulation against the person or property of another Indian or other person "within any Territory of the United States, and either within or without an Indian reservation," are subject therefor to the laws of such Territory relating to said crimes, and are triable therefor "in the same courts and in the same manner and subject to the same penalties as are all other persons charged with the commission of said crimes respectively."

In the Indian Territory criminal jurisdiction over crimes against the laws of the United States is exercised by the Federal courts for the Indian Territory, the eastern district of Texas, and the western district of Arkansas. Civil jurisdiction over all controversies, except cases over which the tribal courts have exclusive jurisdiction, is exercised by the United States court for the Indian Territory.

In the Territory of Oklahoma the Territorial courts have the same criminal jurisdiction over Indians in that Territory as is exercised by courts of other Territories over Indians residing therein, and in addition have jurisdiction over civil controversies between Indians and citizens of the United States and between Indians of different tribes.

INDIAN COURTS

1. *Districting of reservation.*—Whenever it shall appear to the Commissioner of Indian Affairs that the best interests of the Indians on any Indian reservation will be subserved thereby, such reservation shall be divided into three or more districts, each of which shall be given a name by which it shall thereafter be designated and known. As far as practicable the county lines established by the laws of the State or Territory within which the reservation is located shall be observed in making the division, provided that each district shall include, as nearly as can be, an equal proportion of the total Indian population on the reservation. All mixed bloods and white persons who are actually and lawfully members, whether by birth or adoption, of any tribe residing on the reservation shall be counted as Indians. Where the lands of the reservation have not been surveyed, or where it is not practicable to observe the State or Territory county lines on the reservation, the lines of the district shall be defined by such natural boundaries as will enable the Indians to readily ascertain the district in which they reside.

2. *Appointment of judges.*—There shall be appointed by the Commissioner of Indian Affairs for each district a person from among the Indians of the reservation who shall be styled "judge of the Indian court." The judges must be men of intelligence, integrity, and good moral character, and preference shall be given to Indians who read and write English readily, wear citizens' dress, and engage in civilized pursuits, and no person shall be eligible to such appointment who is a polygamist.

Each judge shall be appointed for the term of one year, subject, however, to earlier removal from office for cause by the Commissioner of Indian Affairs; but no judge shall be removed before the expiration of his term of office until the charges against him, with proofs, shall have been presented in writing to the Commissioner of Indian Affairs, and until he shall have been furnished a copy thereof and given opportunity to reply in his own defense, which reply shall also be in writing and be accompanied by such counter proofs as he may desire to submit.

3. *District courts.*—Each judge shall reside within the district to which he may be assigned and shall keep an office open at some convenient point to be designated by the Commissioner of Indian Affairs; and he shall hold court at least one day in each week for the purpose of investigating and trying any charge of offense or misdemeanor over which the judges of the Indian court have jurisdiction as provided in these regulations: *Provided,* That appeals from his judgment or decision may be taken to the Indian court in general term, at which all the judges on the reservation shall sit together.

4. *Offenses.*—For the purpose of these regulations the following shall be deemed to constitute *offenses,* and the judges of the Indian court shall severally have jurisdiction to try and punish for the same when committed within their respective districts.

(*a*) Dances, etc.—Any Indian who shall engage in the sun dance, scalp dance, or war dance, or any other similar feast, so called, shall be deemed guilty of an offense, and upon conviction thereof shall be punished for the first offense by the withholding of his rations for not exceeding ten days or by imprisonment for not exceeding ten days; and for any subsequent offense under this clause he shall be punished by withholding his rations for not less than ten nor more than thirty days, or by imprisonment for not less than ten nor more than thirty days.

(*b*) Plural or polygamous marriages.—Any Indian under the supervision of a United States Indian agent who shall hereafter contract or enter into any plural or polygamous marriage shall be deemed guilty of an offense, and upon conviction thereof shall pay a fine of not less than twenty nor more than fifty dollars, or work at hard labor for not less than twenty nor more than sixty days, or both, at the discretion of the court; and so long as the person shall continue in such unlawful relation he shall forfeit all right to receive rations from the Government.

(*c*) Practices of medicine men.—Any Indian who shall engage in the practices of so-called medicine men, or who shall resort to any artifice or device to keep the Indians of the reservation from adopting and following civilized habits and pursuits, or shall adopt any means to prevent the attendance of children at school, or shall use any arts of a conjurer to prevent Indians from abandoning their barbarous rites and customs, shall be deemed to be guilty of an offense, and upon conviction thereof, for the first offense shall be imprisoned for not less than ten nor more than thirty days: *Provided,* That for any subsequent conviction for such offense the maximum term of imprisonment shall not exceed six months.

(*d*) Destroying property of other Indians.—Any Indian who shall willfully or wantonly destroy or injure, or, with intent to destroy or injure or appropriate, shall take and carry away any property of any other Indian or Indians, shall, without reference to its value, be deemed guilty of an offense, and upon conviction shall be compelled to return the property to the owner or owners, or, in case the property shall have been lost, injured, or destroyed, the estimated full value of the same; and in addition he shall be imprisoned for not exceeding thirty days; and the plea that the person convicted or the owner of the property in question was at the time a "mourner," and that thereby the taking, destroying, or injuring of the property was justified by the customs or rites of the tribe, shall not be accepted as a sufficient defense.

(e) *Immorality.*—Any Indian who shall pay, or offer to pay, money or other thing of value to any female Indian, or to her friends or relatives, or to any other person, for the purpose of living or cohabiting with any such female Indian not his wife, shall be deemed guilty of an offense, and upon conviction thereof shall forfeit all right to Government rations for not exceeding ninety days, or be imprisoned for not exceeding ninety days, or both, in the discretion of the court. And any Indian who shall receive, or offer to receive, money or other valuable thing in consideration for allowing, consenting to, or practicing such immorality, shall be punished in the same manner as provided for the punishment of the party paying, or offering to pay, said consideration.

(f) *Intoxication and the introduction of intoxicants.*—Any Indian who shall become intoxicated, or who shall sell, exchange, give, barter, or dispose of any spirituous, vinous, fermented, or other intoxicating liquors to any other member of an Indian tribe, or who shall introduce, or attempt to introduce, under any pretense whatever, any spirituous, vinous, fermented, or other intoxicating liquors on an Indian reservation, shall be deemed guilty of an offense, and upon conviction thereof shall be punishable by imprisonment for not less than thirty nor more than ninety days, or by a fine of not less than twenty nor more than one hundred dollars, or both, in the discretion of the court.

5. *Misdemeanors.*—The judges of the Indian courts shall also have jurisdiction within their respective districts to try and punish any Indian belonging upon the reservation for any misdemeanor committed thereon, as defined in the laws of the State or Territory within which the reservation may be located; and the punishment for such misdemeanors shall be such as may be prescribed by such State or Territorial law: *Provided,* That if an Indian who is subject to road duty shall refuse or neglect to work the roads the required number of days each year, or to furnish a proper substitute therefor, he shall be deemed guilty of a misdemeanor, and shall be liable to a fine of one dollar and fifty cents for every day that he fails to perform road duty, or to imprisonment for not more than five days: *And provided further,* That if an Indian refuses or neglects to adopt habits of industry, or to engage in civilized pursuits or employments, but habitually spends his time in idleness and loafing, he shall be deemed a vagrant and guilty of a misdemeanor, and shall, upon the first conviction thereof, be liable to a fine of not more than five dollars, or to imprisonment for not more than ten

days, and for any subsequent conviction thereof to a fine of not more than ten dollars, or to imprisonment for not more than thirty days, in the discretion of the court.

6. *Judges to solemnize marriages.*—The said judges shall have power also to solemnize marriages between Indians. They shall keep a record of all marriages solemnized by them, respectively, and shall issue certificates of marriage in duplicate, one certificate to be delivered to the parties thereto and the duplicate to be forwarded to the clerk of the court in general term, hereinafter provided for, to be kept among the records of that court; and for each marriage solemnized the judge may charge a fee not to exceed one dollar.

7. *Indian court in general term.*—The judges of the Indian court shall sit together at some convenient place on the reservation, to be designated by the Commissioner of Indian Affairs, at least once in every month, at which sitting they shall constitute the Indian court in general term. A majority of the judges appointed for the reservation shall constitute a quorum of the court and shall have power to try and finally determine any suit or charge that may be properly brought before it; but no judgment or decision by said court shall be valid unless it is concurred in by a majority of all the judges appointed for the reservation, and in case of a failure of a majority of the judges to agree in any cause, the same shall be continued, to be again tried at a subsequent term of the court. The court in general term shall be presided over by the senior judge in point of service on the reservation, and in case there be no such senior judge, the Commissioner of Indian Affairs shall designate one of the judges to preside.

8. *Clerk of court.*—The judges of the court at the first general term, and annually thereafter, shall elect from among the Indians on the reservation some person of good moral character who can read and write English readily, wears citizen's dress, and engages in civilized pursuits, to be the clerk of the court in general term. He shall serve for one year, and it shall be his duty to receive and carefully. preserve all papers filed in any case submitted for adjudication by the court, keep a docket of all cases and a proper record of the action taken by the court in each case, receive and preserve the duplicate marriage certificates furnished him by the several judges of the districts of the reservation as heretofore provided, and perform all other duties usually required of clerks of courts of ordinary jurisdiction in the State or Territory within which the reservation may be, except such duties as may require the possession of a seal.

9. *Jurisdiction of court in general term.*—The court in general term, organized as above provided, shall have jurisdiction to try all appeals by persons convicted before any judge of any offense or misdemeanor, as the same are defined and prescribed in these regulations, and to render final judgment therein.

The said court shall have the same probate jurisdiction over the administration and settlement of estates of Indians belonging on the reservation as is exercised at the time by the courts of probate, in the State or Territory within which the reservation may be, over the settlement or administration of estates of citizens of said State or Territory: *Provided,* That the probate jurisdiction of said court shall extend only to the disposition according to law of such property as members of the tribe may have in their possession on the reservation at the time of their deaths, and to the execution of wills affecting such property.

The said court shall have exclusive jurisdiction over all civil controversies arising between Indians belonging on the reservation.

10. *Practice, pleadings, etc.*—The practice, pleadings, and forms of proceedings in probate and civil causes shall conform as near as may be to the practice, pleadings, and forms of proceedings existing at the time in like causes in the probate courts and the courts of justices of the peace in the State or Territory within which the reservation may be; and the plaintiff shall be entitled to like remedies by attachment or other process against the property of the defendant, and for like causes, as may at the time be provided by the laws of said State or Territory.

11. *Agents to compel attendance of witnesses and enforce orders of the court.*—That the orders of the court in general term and of the judges of the several districts may be carried into full effect, the United States Indian agent for the agency under which the reservation may be is hereby authorized, empowered, and required to compel the attendance of witnesses at any session of the court, or before any judge within his proper district, and to enforce all orders that may be passed by said court, or a majority thereof, or by any judge within his proper district; and for this purpose he may use the Indian police of his agency.

EDUCATION

During the past three years the work of education has been pushed with great vigor and with ceaseless vigilance, and I think it safe to say that this has been the best year of the three. Few people can have any just conception of the enormous amount of labor and the perplexities involved in the development of an adequate school service for the Indians; the schools are so far removed from the office, are scattered over such an immense region of country, are surrounded by conditions so wholly different, that it has been well nigh impossible to put into execution any definite plan that should apply equally to all.

RESTRICTED COST OF SCHOOL BUILDINGS

There has been unavoidable delay connected with the building of school-houses and the development of proper plants for schools. I have been met all the time with the very great difficulty of securing enough money to erect suitable buildings. I have had occasion in former reports to show conclusively that the legal limitations fixed by Congress heretofore have rendered it, in some cases, absolutely impossible to do the work that ought to be done. For example, three years ago the law restricted the cost of any school building on an Indian reservation, including furnishing, to $10,000. Last year, after a great deal of persuasion, the limit was raised to $12,000, exclusive of furnishing. Under this restriction I advertised, for instance, for bids for the erection of a modest, cheap school building, on the Navajo Reservation; received no bids, and was obliged to abandon the enterprise; so that to-day, for 3,000 Navajo children of school age there are accommodations on the reservation for only about 100. I have urged raising the limit of the cost of a building to $20,000, but so far my recommendations have not been adopted. The present law fixes it at $15,000, which is still too small for the accomplishment of the purpose. A very good illustration is furnished in the history of the school at Pierre, S. Dak., which was inaugurated by Congress prior to the beginning of my administration, but which has been completed only recently, and is now in successful operation. It has accommodations for about 175 pupils, and the plant has thus far cost $70,000. Some additional improvements are still required in order to make it adequate for the accommodation of that number of pupils. It will be seen from this that when the office is restricted to $15,000 for the erection of a school building on a remote reservation it is sometimes tantamount to a prohibition of the work.

The limit of $600 placed upon the cost of a day-school building also amounts, in many cases, to prohibition. Where I know that a suitable building can not be erected for that sum I make no attempt to build one.

When discussing the question of the cost of Indian school buildings, it has frequently been suggested to me that inasmuch as these school buildings are only temporary they should be plain and cheap. My reply is that at best the buildings erected are plain to barrenness and cheap in some instances to worthlessness. Any school building anywhere should be so built as to resist the elements and to be at least fairly safe. Cheap workmanship means poor workmanship, and a cheap building means, of necessity, almost, a poor building. One large building which I have in mind I found, on my visit to the reservation, unsafe, and it is now rendered habitable only by dint of iron supports. Another that I recall is liable at any time to collapse. Many of these buildings are exposed to very severe winds, and are apt, unless strongly built, to be destroyed by tornadoes and entail great loss of life. Even at Carlisle, Pa., I was greatly distressed myself personally by the furious wind that tested the strength of the school building during the closing exercises. Had it not been well constructed there would have been fearful destruction of life.

Special pains need to be taken in construction to avoid danger from fire. During the past twelve months four school buildings (Fort Peck, Mont., Klamath, Oregon, Winnebago, Nebr., and Fort Yuma, Cal.) have been destroyed by fire, and several others are so poorly constructed and so greatly exposed that I have been in constant dread lest they might be burned, together with their inmates. One school building that I have in mind now is heated by sixty stoves, which are sixty opportunities for fire, and it has a very inadequate water supply.

Then, again, many schools in the extreme north, in the Dakotas, Montana, Wyoming, and Idaho, are in regions where the temperature is oftentimes very low and trying, and where, consequently, it is necessary that the buildings should be well built in order to insure ordinary comfort for the employés and pupils.

But the great desideratum is sufficient room. Where 100 pupils with the required employé force are gathered together in one building, it is absolutely essential, not simply on the ground of comfort but of health and of life, that there should be sufficient sleeping space, in order that the pupils may not be so crowded into sleeping rooms as to endanger their health and their lives.

There ought to be, in connection with every large school, a well arranged hospital where the sick can be properly cared for, and where those affected with contagious disease can be isolated from the others so as to prevent the spread of the same disease.

When these absolute requirements are taken into consideration it will be evident to any person acquainted with the facts that the limit fixed heretofore by the Government for the cost of boarding school buildings is an unreasonable one.

It has been suggested to me that our fathers attended school in a log schoolhouse, and that this is good enough for an Indian. This suggestion, however, is based upon an entire misapprehension of the situation. Our fathers had decent homes and attended the "log schoolhouse" during a few hours of the day. The question here under discussion is not the erection of a day school in the midst of a well settled, intelligent, religious community, but it is the question of the erection of a boarding school, with all the necessary buildings, on an Indian reservation with no civilization.

* * *

COMMENTS ON INDIAN EDUCATION

This summary review of the situation warrants me in saying—

1. That the system of Government schools now in successful operation is every way credible to the Government of the United States. They are, within the measure of their possibilities, doing most excellent work, and every year hastens the time when, by their aid, there will be a new generation of English-speaking Indians, prepared to become Americans.

2. Nothing should be allowed to hinder the development of these schools along the present lines of their activities and growth until they shall be sufficient to furnish full educational facilities for all the Indian children that can be induced to attend them. The expense involved is necessarily large, but it is money well expended.

In the appendix I present a table showing the per capita cost of reform schools in various States. A comparison of this table with the allowances for the expenses of the Government Indian schools will show that this work costs less than the work done in the reform schools, and from my personal knowledge of that work I have no hesitancy in saying that on the whole the Indian work is equal or superior to that done in the State institutions.

3. In view of the rapidity with which Indians are taking their lands and becoming nominally citizens of the United States, the work of education should be hastened with the view of bringing as large a number as possible of prospective citizens under its influence in order to prepare them for the inevitable duties and responsibilities that await them. Any delay at this juncture will be irreparable for the Indians and may be disastrous to the communities in which they reside.

4. Thus far the operation of the civil-service rules has been, on the whole, satisfactory, and I see no reason to doubt the ultimate success of the scheme. It has, however, developed this fact, that it is very difficult to secure competent persons able to pass the requisite civil-service examination who are willing to accept positions offered them, by reason of the small salaries, the numerous hardships, and the severity of the labors involved.

5. One of the most difficult problems connected with the administration of the Indian schools is that of attendance. Congress has reënacted a law for compulsory attendance, but has provided no sufficient force for carrying it into execution. In some cases it has been found impracticable to use the Indian police for this purpose, and there is a reluctance to resort to military force. I am watching with solicitude, as well as interest, the development of the matter, and am not prepared to say at present what the final outcome is to be.

6. Another serious matter connected with this subject is the health of Indian children. As the work progresses and greater care is used in the scrutiny of those who enter school, it is found that there is an alarming amount of disease among the children, and even under the most painstaking care it develops itself, often rendering it impossible for them to be kept in school. The facts already show that the complaints heretofore made against the unhealthiness of eastern schools were unfounded, because the same conditions manifest themselves in the western schools near to or on reservations. Very great care is given to this matter, and undoubtedly experience has led to a better sanitary oversight of the pupils; but there have been epidemics of measles, scarlet fever, diphtheria, sore eyes, and numerous isolated cases of sickness which have sadly interfered with the work of the schools and have largely increased the care, anxiety, and labor of the superintendents and their assistants.

The sad fact, is that there is a vast amount of disease among the Indians living on reservations, exposed as they are to the severities of the climate, almost entirely ignorant of sanitary laws, and having wholly insufficient medical attendance. They are at the mercy of disease, and oftentimes their children are swept away by epidemics in alarming numbers. As there are no health officers among them, and no complete record is kept of disease and death, these matters do not often come to the surface, so that their real condition is known only to those immediately concerned.

When, however, their children are taken into boarding schools, where their names are enrolled and a record kept of their condition, it very speedily becomes known if they are ill, and especially if they die. The death of an Indian child in school is frequently seized upon by Indians who are opposed to education as an excuse for refusing to send their children to school, or as a pretext for demanding their release if already there.

7. I am happy to call attention to the vast change in public sentiment observable during the last three years on the subject of Indian education. I doubt if there is a question before the public in which there is a more general concensus of opinion. Even the Western States and Territories, where the feeling against the Indian has been exceedingly bitter, show a surprising and most gratifying change in public sentiment. Wherever a school is located, as at Pierre, S. Dak., Genoa, Nebr., Lawrence, Kans., Albuquerque, N. Mex., Phoenix, Ariz., and Grand Junction, Colo., there is developed an extraordinary degree of public interest and sympathy in the work. It is now universally conceded by every intelligent observer that the Indians can be educated, that the Government schools are eminently successful, and that it is a wise expenditure of money from the point of view of economy, philanthropy, and justice to provide for them suitable educational facilities.

Among those who have been active in bringing about this improved public sentiment are the Indian Rights Association, the Women's National Indian Association, the Mohonk Conference, the Boston Indian Citizenship Committee, the leading religious and secular newspapers of the country, and a large number of prominent clergymen and other public-spirited men who have taken a deep personal interest in the matter.

It has been suggested to me that this public interest in the Indian question is a "fad," and should be treated as such. I can only say I wish there were more such fads as this. It is participated in by a vast number of the most intelligent, upright, philanthropic, unselfish citizens of the United States, and represents on this great question an advanced state of morality and intelligence which is highly creditable to our Christian civilization, and marks very honorably the closing decade of the century. We must either fight Indians, feed them, or else educate them. To fight them is cruel, to feed them is wasteful, while to educate them is humane, economic, and Christian.

8. The rudimentary education supplied in these Government institutions, which are necessarily, as yet, on a low plane, ought to be supplemented in many cases by an enlarged course of study. Many Indians of both sexes are showing marked capacity for scholarship and are evincing an eager desire to acquire that broader culture which will fit them for leadership

among their people. One young man thoroughly educated is worth, in many respects, more to his people than a considerable number with only a common-school training.

There is an especial call among the Indians for persons of their own race who are competent physicians and lawyers. The Government makes at best a most unsatisfactory provision for the medical care of these people, and I have felt that wherever a young man or woman among them could be found who showed the requisite qualities for the work of physicians or nurses they should be encouraged and assisted, if necessary, by the Government, in the pursuit of that professional training which should prepare them for this important work.

Every year renders it more and more apparent that the Indians, unless they are prepared to defend themselves in the courts, will be robbed of their property and denied their rights. I wish there were to-day a hundred young men of the highest type, such as can be found among them, preparing themselves, by the study of law, for the defense of their people in their rights of person and property.

* * *

The Indian Exhibit at the Columbian Exposition

Arrangements for an Indian exhibit by this Bureau of the World's Columbian Exposition in Chicago are beginning to take definite shape. Insufficiency of appropriation makes it necessary that the office confine its exhibit almost exclusively to a presentation of the educational work now in progress among Indians.

Accordingly a location has been assigned the office near La Rabida, between the lagoon and the lake, upon which is to be erected an Indian industrial boarding school building, sufficiently large to accommodate 30 pupils and half a dozen teachers and employés. This building will be occupied at various periods, ranging from two to four weeks, by delegations from different Indian boarding schools. Several Government schools will be represented, and different religious societies engaged in Indian school work have also been offered the use of the building for specified periods.

Schools represented will exemplify at Chicago the methods which they are accustomed to pursue in the training of Indian youth. Pupils will recite in the school room, boys will work at their trades, girls will be employed in domestic affairs, and, so far as practicable, the usual school routine will be carried out.

The building will be decorated with specimens of Indian manufacture and handiwork and with scenes illustrative of Indian life and surroundings. An attempt will be made as far as practicable to give some presentation of the work accomplished in Indian schools generally throughout the Indian country by specimens of compositions, examination papers, articles made by the pupils, etc. An added attraction will be the occasional presence of an Indian brass band.

Altogether it is expected that the exhibit will give a graphic and impressive showing of what the Government is trying to do for Indians in the way of education and civilization and of the capacity and readiness shown by the Indian to improve the opportunities thus offered him.

This picture of the Indian citizen in embryo ought to be offset by another view of the Indian as he appeared when America was discovered or as he is still found in places where advancing civilization has made little impression upon his primitive manners and customs. This exhibit will be made in close proximity to the Indian school building by the anthropological department of the exposition, under Prof. Putnam. Coöperating cordially with this Bureau, he proposes to have upon the grounds families of Indians taken from different tribes, who, residing in their native habitations, will pursue the avocations and industries peculiar to their respective tribes.

If larger funds were available for the office exhibit, it would be possible to cover more ground and not to be restricted to presenting but one line of Indian advancement, viz. education; but, even with the meager sum allowed, $25,000, I am confident that the Indian Office exhibit, taken in connection with that of the anthropological department, will be one of the attractive, picturesque, and striking features of the exposition, and will very creditably present the progress which the Indians are making and the efforts which the Government is putting forth to prepare its former wards for the honor and privileges of citizenship now held out to them.

In order to bring Indian schools into line with the public schools of the country in the celebration of Columbus day, on October 21, 1892, the following instructions were issued on August 17, 1892, to Indian agents and school superintendents:

> Inclosed herewith you will find printed sheets which will acquaint you quite fully with the arrangements which are being made among the public schools of this country for the appropriate celebration of Columbus day, October 21, 1892.
>
> You will readily see the importance of having some similar celebration take place in Indian schools, not only to give Indian pupils the historical information which the observance of the day will necessarily impart, but also to bring Indian schools into line with the practices and exercises of the public schools of this country.
>
> You will please familiarize yourself with this entire matter and see that all the schools, boarding as well as day schools, prepare some suitable programme for October 21 and carry it out on that day. The interest and enthusiasm of the children in these proceedings should be thoroughly aroused and the day of the celebration made to exert as inspiring an influence over them as possible.
>
> You will also endeavor to interest adult Indians in the celebration, and particular pains should be taken to have returned students take some part which will renew to them the elevating influences of the school life from which they are now separated.

Each school must be furnished with these printed sheets, and on no account must this celebration be neglected or allowed to fail of success, and preparation for it should be begun in all the schools with the opening of the school year.

For similar patriotic occasions, such as Washington's birthday, Fourth of July, etc., very creditable programmes have been prepared and carried out in Indian schools. I have no doubt that on this occasion, also, the exercises in which the Indian youth will participate will be praiseworthy and peculiarly interesting, and will show that although Indian progress is far behind what it should have become after four hundred years of contact with white civilization, yet a large proportion of the Indian tribes have made great advance in the scale of intelligence and civilization since Columbus found them.

* * *

CASH PAYMENTS TO INDIANS

The payments made to Indians during last year in fulfillment of treaty stipulations, for interest on funds held in trust for them, for lands they relinquished to the Government, and for other legitimate indebtedness to them by the United States were much in excess of those for any previous year, and exceeded by $2,000,000 the payments made for the fiscal year 1890. The comparison is as follows:

	1890	1892
Fulfilling treaties, interest, payment for lands, etc.	$774,268	$2,480,716
Labor by Indians and purchases made for them	642,000	930,000
Total	1,416,268	3,410,716

The above figures do not include payments made to the Five Civilized Tribes.

The labor, care, and responsibility entailed on this office and its agents by such payments is great. The amount paid to each person is usually quite small, and the payment is sometimes attended with danger, because the payees are upon reservations more or less difficult of access, and surrounded sometimes by a lawless white population. The official making the payment is held to as strict account as a bank teller for the funds he handles, yet he has limited facilities and few safeguards. I am therefore specially gratified in being able to report that I know of no injustice having been done any Indian, nor has any agent been a defaulter or the Government a loser to the slightest amount. The labor connected with instructing agents how to make payments, explaining matters to the Indians, and examining the accounts rendered for these large payments was attended to by the regular clerical force of this office without extra expense to the Government.

Although many Indians squander in a short time the funds paid them, yet as a rule Indians are learning to make better use of their money than formerly, and, like other people, they value most highly that which comes to them as a result of their own labor and good management. The $930,000 which they received in that way last year, as shown by the above table, was earned by them in the following manner:

Regular Indian employés at agencies	$98,000
Regular Indian employés at schools	63,000
Irregular Indian employés at agencies	40,000
Irregular Indian employés at schools	37,000
Additional farmers	12,000
Interpreters	20,000
Police	118,000
Judges of Indian courts	12,000
Hauling supplies	105,000
Produce, hay, and other supplies purchased from Indians	280,000
Cutting and banking logs	145,000
	——————
	930,000

INDIAN EMPLOYÉS

One of the chief complaints made by and for the Indians has been the lack of profitable employment. Applications for employment in some Government position, especially of those who have returned home after attending nonreservation schools, have been very persistent. A moment's reflection will convince any thoughtful man, in the first place, that it is impossible for the Government to provide employment as blacksmiths, farmers, wagon-makers, shoemakers, etc., to any considerable number of young men. It is not the business of the Government to inaugurate large industrial enterprises simply for the sake of giving employment to people who wish to work. Such a scheme is visionary. There are but few authorized positions in the Government service on reservations, and most of them require the services of men who are intelligent, capable not only of performing the work required but also of giving instructions to the Indians and of organizing and directing their labors. Although constant effort has been made to find competent Indians for all these positions the office has not met with very encouraging success. Many of the young men who have attended the nonreservation schools have sufficient knowledge of farming or of some of the trades to do fairly well under the direction of a skilled workman, but they lack the requisite intelligence, skill, energy, experience, and independence to fit them to fill successfully the places where leadership is required. Doubtless this will correct itself in time, when they have received a more thorough training than has yet been given to them.

I would not have it inferred from what I have just said that no Indians are employed by the Government. A very considerable number are so employed, both at the agencies and at the schools, as is shown by the following tables:

Positions authorized to be filled by Indians at the various agencies during the fiscal year 1892–'93.

74	police officers	$13,320
850	police privates	102,000
63	interpreters	19,460
123	judges	12,300
2	clerks	2,200
2	assistant clerks	1,500
7	issue clerks	4,320
2	copyists	1,020
2	physicians	2,200
2	physician's assistants	360
17	blacksmiths	8,760
22	assistant blacksmiths	4,980
10	carpenters	3,960
19	assistant carpenters	4,390
5	farmers	2,880
33	assistant farmers	7,580
10	additional farmers	3,600
25	district farmers	1,500
5	harness-makers	1,560
3	assistant harness-makers	660
2	millers	1,320
6	assistant millers	2,000
3	sawyers	1,520
1	assistant sawyer	210
3	wheelwrights	1,020
2	assistant wheelwrights	360
6	butchers	2,340
31	herders	12,550
3	tinners	780
1	painter	300
3	wagon-makers	1,100
1	ferryman	100
1	mail-carrier	240
1	janitor	150
1	off bearer	210
3	overseers	1,200
6	ox-drivers	2,520
1	superintendent of work	540
1	toll-keeper	300
17	teamsters	5,310
7	stablemen	1,900
1	waterman	180
2	watchmen	740
1	wood-chopper	240
61	apprentices	8,540
59	laborers	13,720
1,500		257,940

Estimated amount to be expended for irregular Indian labor, based on expenditures during the year 1891–92 40,000

Total 297,940

From the above table, it will be seen that there are 1,500 regular agency positions authorized to be filled by Indians for the next fiscal year and that the aggregate of salaries is over a quarter of a million dollars. If to this be added the number of irregular employés, it will swell the total to be paid agency Indian employés by the Government to $297,940.

School positions filled by and salaries paid to Indians for year ending
June 30, 1892

2	assistant engineers, at $120	$240
1	assistant engineer	240
1	physician and teacher	720
6	cadet sergeants, at $80	480
30	cadet sergeants, at $60	1,800
1	dairy boy	60
1	stable boy	60
1	farmer	300
1	assistant farmer	240
2	assistant farmers, at $180	360
1	assistant farmer	60
1	carpenter	240
1	assistant carpenter	120
1	night watchman	480
1	night watchman	360
3	night watchmen, at $300	900
1	night watchman	216
2	night watchmen, at $240	480
2	night watchmen, at $180	360
1	night watchman	120
1	herder	240
2	herders, at $180	360
1	housekeeper	240
2	assistant teachers, at $120	240
10	assistant teachers, at $60	600
1	teacher	480
1	assistant disciplinarian	360
1	assistant disciplinarian	180
1	assistant printer	240
2	firemen, at $360	720
1	fireman	120
6	assistant cooks, at $240	1,440
5	assistant cooks, at $180	900
1	assistant cook	300
10	assistant cooks, at $120	1,200
1	assistant cook	100
1	assistant cook	160
4	assistant cooks, at $150	600
1	assistant cook	80
1	Indian assistant	480

4 Indian assistants, at $360	1,440
1 Indian assistant	300
10 Indian assistants, at $240	2,400
13 Indian assistants, at $180	2,340
13 Indian assistants, at $150	1,950
4 Indian assistants, at $200	800
49 Indian assistants, at $120	5,880
1 Indian assistant	160
8 Indian assistants, at $100	800
6 Indian assistants, at $96	576
3 Indian assistants, at $80	240
16 Indian assistants, at $60	960
7 Indian assistants, at $36	252
10 Indian assistants, at $48	480
1 assistant seamstress	360
3 assistant seamstresses, at $300	900
1 assistant seamstress	240
6 assistant seamstresses, at $180	1,080
4 assistant seamstresses, at $150	600
10 assistant seamstresses, at $120	1,200
6 assistant seamstresses, at $60	360
2 assistant seamstresses, at $48	96
2 shoemakers, at $300	600
1 shoemaker	180
1 teamster	360
1 teamster	300
1 teamster	150
1 teamster	120
2 bakers, at $300 each	600
1 baker	240
2 bakers, at $150 each	300
2 assistant bakers, at $120	240
3 assistant bakers, at $60	180
1 tailor	300
1 butcher	120
13 Indian apprentices, at $120	1,560
2 Indian apprentices, at $90	180
29 Indian apprentices, at $60	1,740
1 watchman	300
1 watchman	240
3 watchmen, at $96	288
2 watchmen, at $60	120
1 assistant industrial teacher	400
3 assistant industrial teachers, at $300	900
1 assistant industrial teacher	180
1 assistant industrial teacher	120
1 industrial teacher	600
2 industrial teachers, at $180	360
1 laundress	420
2 laundresses, at $400	800
3 laundresses, at $300	900
1 laundress	260
4 laundresses, at $240	960
1 laundress	200

1	laundress	210
4	seamstresses, at $240	960
3	seamstresses, at $300	900
2	seamstresses, at $290	580
1	matron	480
1	matron	360
1	assistant matron at	300
1	cook	300
1	cook	240
9	janitors, at $180	1,620
2	janitors, at $300	600
4	assistant laundresses, at $240	960
4	assistant laundresses, at $180	720
4	assistant laundresses, at $150	600
12	assistant laundresses, at $120	1,440
432		62,878

Average, $145.55 per annum.

Amount expended for irregular Indian labor 37,000

Total 99,878

From a comparison of the two tables herewith cited, it will be seen that nearly 2,000 Indians receive regular stated wages from the Government for services performed, and that, including those employed irregularly, an aggregate sum of $397,818 is paid out for Indian labor.

While, of course, this does not furnish employment for the whole body of Indian young men and young women who would be glad to have it, it certainly makes such an exhibit as to show that there is no justice in a criticism sometimes made against the Government that it has no care for the Indians, and it ought to silence any complaint made by the Indians themselves that they are discriminated against in Government employment.

It should be remembered also, in this connection, that hundreds of Indian pupils at the Carlisle school are, by the outing system in operation there, afforded an opportunity of earning wages by working among the white people. The same system is now beginning to be operative at Haskell, Genoa, Carson, and elsewhere in the western schools, and I think the day is not far distant when the door will thus be open for multitudes of these young people to find not only temporary but permanent employment among civilized communities.

It would be certainly unfortunate for the Indians themselves if the impression should obtain in their minds that they have a right to demand of the Government that it shall employ them at remunerative wages, especially after it has already educated them to such an extent as to prepare them to earn wages for themselves independently. The idea should be inculcated in their minds with great persistency that they must not only depend upon their own labor for a living but that they must find opportunities for work for themselves, and that they must be governed as other people are by the one great law that if they wish work they must go where work is needed.

They must not expect that the Government will bring work to them but they must go into those communities where there is a demand for the kind of labor which they are prepared to furnish.

DEVELOPMENT OF INDUSTRIES

But the great desideratum in this matter is such an entire change of the industrial situation on reservations as will create work and offer compensating employment to all who are willing to labor.

Where the lands have been allotted, the surplus sold, and a white community has been brought into immediate contact with the Indians, as is the case, for instance, among the Omahas and Sissetons and more recently among the Cheyennes and Arapahoes, it is believed that such an entire change in the situation will be brought about in the course of a comparatively short time that every competent Indian, man or woman, who desires employment can have it either at good wages working for white people or in remunerative return when working at their own homes.

This is a matter that must of necessity be determined largely by individual effort, by the gradual development of the knowledge of civilized ways, and a desire for the benefits that grow from steady, continuous, intelligently directed personal effort.

One great result of educating the younger Indians is the creation in their minds of a desire to work. When they are trained in a school, such as Carlisle or Haskell, situated in a civilized community, the pupils have constantly before them an object lesson of a very impressive character, which, quite as much as the school room does, serves to awaken a desire for the comforts and privileges of civilization. They realize the poverty of their reservation life and wish for something better. They become dissatisfied. Discontent is the mother of progress. If the schools can give them a command of English, awaken among them a universal dissatisfaction with their present state, show them something better, inure them to industry, and teach them to use tools and machinery, they will find employment and make for themselves places in life.

The policy of allotting lands and the breaking up of the reservations will, in many cases, solve the problem here presented in perhaps the only satisfactory way in which it can be solved by the Government.

In other cases the solution does not lie, for the present certainly, in allotments, but rather in the development of a system of industry among the Indians themselves which shall facilitate, by judicious help, the growth of their native industries. The Navajos, for instance, estimated to number from 16,000 to 18,000, are almost wholly engaged in pastoral pursuits, owning and successfully caring for large numbers of sheep, goats, horses, and a few cattle. By some judicious help in the development of water through some carefully planned scheme of irrigation, such as is suggested on page 126, it is believed that the reservation can be made abundantly capable of supporting in comfort, if not in affluence, all the Navajo Indians entitled and desiring to reside upon it. In addition to the care of flocks and herds these people have shown a disposition to engage somewhat in agriculture, and, as is well known, they are very skillful in the production of blankets, which not only furnish them with enough for their own use, but provide them with the means of procuring other necessaries of life by exchange or barter.

Among the Sioux, numbering, perhaps, 20,000, special effort has been put forth by the office to stimulate the grazing industry. Most of that vast region is unfit for agriculture, but large sections of it are specially adapted to the grazing of cattle and horses, and during the present year thousands of head of stock cattle have been issued to them. I am of the opinion that much can be done in the way of facilitating this industry by sinking at proper places artesian wells in order to secure an abundant supply of water.

Among the Indians at Fort Hall particular attention is being given by the office to the construction of an irrigating ditch, and efforts are being made to induce them to become farmers. They take to it, however, very slowly, and not enough has been done, nor has a sufficient time elapsed to warrant any very positive opinion as to the final outcome.

The progress now is being made on the Crow Reservation in the development of a system of irrigation. I have reason to believe, so far as my knowledge will warrant an opinion, that the scheme is being worked out intelligently and that the prospects for those people are full of hope.

Much has been accomplished during the year among the Pimas, who have been for a long time self-supporting, raising as good wheat, perhaps, as is raised anywhere in the United States. A considerable amount of work has been done by them under the supervision of the agent in extending their system of irrigation, and special efforts are to be made to induce them to enter more largely than heretofore into fruit growing. This industry is full of promise in that region because of its climate.

One of the most interesting people within the entire limits of the Indian race are the Moquis, in Arizona. They number nearly 2,000, and in many respects are among the most sluggish and backward of the tribes. They live in villages perched upon their mesas, and when I visited them nearly two years ago they were, it seemed to me, retrograding rather than advancing. The attempts at education which had been made by the Government among them had been almost wholly futile, and the school as I found it was a discredit both to them and to the Government. I secured a thoroughly competent Christian man, Mr. R. P. Collins, for superintendent, gave him the immediate oversight of all the affairs pertaining to them, put into his hands the money to be expended for their benefit, went with him personally and investigated the situation, and gave directions for a movement looking to a great improvement in their condition. The result is most gratifying; they are taking their lands in the valleys, building homes, and show a wonderful spirit of progress. Probably more has been done by them in this direction within the past two years than in any twenty years previous, and the school that was so distressingly poor is now one of the best in the service, doing for them a work of incalculable value.

Special pains have been taken to develop water for these interesting people, and to make it possible for them to extend the range of their agriculture. They have been furnished with wagons, harness, and better horses than heretofore, and are now showing for the first time an interest in the matter of transportation and are eager for work of that kind. This is a signal illustration of what can be done with properly directed efforts for even the most conservative of the tribes.

Field Matrons

Considerable attention has been given to the plan of employing field matrons who shall instruct Indian women in the duties of the household; assist and encourage them in bettering their homes, and taking proper care of their children; and incite among Indians generally aspirations for improvement in their life—morally, intellectually, socially, and religiously. The work begun on a small scale in a few tribes by means of a small appropriation has thus far been attended with results fully commensurate with my expectations. It will be further extended during the current fiscal year by reason of a slight increase in the appropriation, bringing it up to $5,000—a sum, however, entirely inadequate if the work is to be prosecuted on any large scale.

There are, of course, some difficulties connected with the successful accomplishment of this work. Selections of field matrons must be made with the greatest care, for they must be women of judgment, character, industry, sound health, free from family and other cares, so as to be able to devote their entire time and strength to the work and ready to subject themselves to the privations which must be borne, if any tangible results are to be secured. Another difficulty is to provide the field matron with the facilities needed for the accomplishment of her work; for instance, a home into which Indian women can be welcomed by her and taught numberless ways of civilization and refinement. She must also have some facilities for visiting Indians in their homes, which are often widely separated. Moreover, there are many places in which the work of a most faithful and competent field matron would meet with very small results owing to the inability of the Indians to carry out the instructions and suggestions given. Very limited application of civilized ways is possible in a tepee and among families who roam from one place to another. Therefore, it is my policy to locate field matrons among tribes who have received, or are about to receive, allotments in severalty, who are putting up houses and surrounding themselves with some of the appliances of civilization, and who are more or less in the vicinity of white settlements, so that the field matrons can come in at the transition period and save from failure and hopeless discouragement the

Indian woman who begins to see that there is a better way but does not know how to reach it. There are many such places from which come urgent requests for field matrons, and I hope that an increase of appropriation for next year will enable me to heed such calls.

The duties of a field matron and the work that is expected of her are set forth in detail in instructions issued to Indian agents by this office on the 6th of July last, as follows:

The position of field matron has been created in order that Indian women may be influenced in their home life and duties, and may have done for them in their sphere what farmers and mechanics are supposed to do for Indian men in their sphere.

The duties of a field matron, therefore, are to visit Indian women in their homes and to give them counsel, encouragement, and help in the following lines:

1. Care of a house, keeping it clean and in order, ventilated, properly warmed (not overheated), and suitably furnished.

2. Cleanliness and hygienic conditions generally, including desposition of all refuse.

3. Preparation and serving of food and regularity in meals.

4. Sewing, including cutting, making, and mending garments.

5. Laundry work.

6. Adorning the home, both inside and out, with pictures, curtains, home-made rugs, flowers, grass plots and trees, construction and repair of walks, fences, and drains.

In this connection there will be opportunity for the matron to give to the male members of the family kindly admonitions as to the "chores" and heavier kinds of work about the house which in civilized communities is generally done by men.

7. Keeping and care of domestic animals, such as cows, poultry, and swine; care and use of milk, making of butter, cheese, and curds and keeping of bees.

8. Care of the sick.

9. Care of little children, and introducing among them the games and sports of white children.

10. Proper observance of the Sabbath; organization of societies for promoting literary, religious, moral, and social improvement, such as "Lend a Hand" clubs, circles of "King's Daughters," or "Sons," Y.M.C.A., Christian Endeavor, and temperance societies, etc.

Of course, it is impracticable to enumerate all the directions in which a field matron can lend her aid in ameliorating the condition of Indian women. Her own tact, skill, and interest will suggest manifold ways of instructing them in civilized home life, stimulating their intelligence, rousing ambition, and cultivating refinement.

Young girls, particularly those who have left school, should find in her a friend and adviser, and her influence should be to them a safeguard against the sore temptations which beset them. She should impress upon families the importance of education and urge upon them to put and keep their children in school.

Besides faithfully visiting Indian homes, the matron should have stated days or parts of days each week when Indian women may come to her home for counsel or for instruction in sewing or other domestic arts which can advantageously be taught to several persons at one time.

The time actually devoted to the above outlined work by the field matron should be not less than eight hours per day of five days in the week, and half a day on Saturday.

The matron shall make reports of her work monthly to the agent, and quarterly, through him, to this office upon blank herewith. On August 15 of each year she shall make an annual report, to be forwarded by the agent to this office for publication.

ISSUE OF RATIONS

Serious complaints have heretofore been made regarding the quality of the beef issued, especially during the winter season. The practice long obtained, grounded on the necessity of economizing to the utmost degree, of purchasing beef on the hoof and receiving in the fall a sufficient supply to last through the winter. No adequate provision, however, was made for sheltering the cattle or for properly feeding them, so that, as a natural result, when they were issued they had deteriorated in weight and very materially in quality; and just complaint was made by the Indians on this account. Now beef is purchased at such times and in such quantities as is most advantageous, and as a result Indians are receiving full weight and good quality. While this necessitates a larger expenditure of money, it insures good faith to the Indians and promotes their contentment.

I hope the day is near at hand when the entire system of issuing rations shall be done away with, but so long as it continues it should be governed by business principles, dominated by strict justice.

The plan has been inaugurated—among the Sioux Indians particularly, to whom the largest amount of supplies is furnished—of making cash payments instead of issuing goods and subsistence. It is believed that the time has come when the issuing of supplies of various kinds should be gradually discontinued, and that at no distant day it should entirely cease. Whatever the Government owes to these people should be paid in cash wherever they have sufficient intelligence to make proper use of it, and then they should be left to the expenditure of this money in whatever way seems to them best. If they make a bad use of it they should be allowed, as other people are, to suffer the consequences.

Another evil which has greatly hindered the progress of the Indians has been the issuance of rations at some single central supply station, necessitating the movement of large numbers of the tribe frequently, and in some instances almost continuously, in order to receive their supplies. Recently by the judicious establishment of subissue stations at convenient places and by issuing from them the supplies needed for those living in their immediate vicinity, this evil has been very largely removed.

The old practice of turning living cattle loose to be chased by the Indians and shot down on the prairie, in imitation of the old savage method of buffalo hunting, has been almost wholly discontinued. Rigid orders have been issued to stop it entirely, and I am happy to say that in most cases these orders are now faithfully carried into execution. . . .

SALE OF LIQUOR TO INDIANS

In my last annual report I invited your attention particularly to the decision of the United States district court for the eastern district of Texas that malt liquors could be introduced into the Indian country and sold to Indians without violating the law, and to the fact that in consequence of this decision many saloons had been opened in the Indian Territory and large quantities of beer had been shipped thereto, where it was freely sold to whites and Indians alike. I also reported that this office and the Department, in order to prevent as far as practicable the evils of unrestricted beer traffic in the Indian Territory, had instructed Agent Bennett to seize all packages of beer shipped into the Indian country and to turn them over to the United States marshal to be libeled, as provided in section 2140, Revised Statutes.

In pursuance of his instructions, Agent Bennett seized a carload of beer at Lehigh, in the Choctaw Nation, Indian Territory, on February 13, 1892, and attempted to turn it over to the United States marshal for said Territory; but the marshal refused to accept it. This refusal was reported to the Department February 15, 1892, with the statement that the Office was at a loss to see on what grounds the marshal for the Indian Territory could refuse to take charge of the car of beer pending an action of libel against it in the proper court, in view of the law on the subject. The case was then laid before the Attorney-General, and February 26, 1892, he advised the Department that inasmuch as his own view coincided with the decision of the court for the eastern district of Texas respecting the introduction of malt liquors into the Indian country, it would be improper for him to "take any steps which might render the marshal responsible on his bond."

On the same date Agent Bennett reported that the carload of beer had been spirited away and taken into Texas and unloaded, and that the empty car had been surrendered and was then in the custody of the marshal for the Indian Territory, acting presumably under directions of the court in which libel proceedings had been instituted.

Meantime, February 18, 1892, I submitted a draft of legislation for the amendment of the law against the sale of liquors to Indians so as to include in the prohibition all intoxicating liquors, of whatever character. This, in modified form, was adopted by Congress, and July 23, 1892, an act was approved amending section 2139 of the Revised Statutes so as to prohibit "ardent spirits, ale, beer, wine, or intoxicating liquor or liquors, of whatever kind," from being introduced into the Indian country under any pretense, and providing for the punishment of persons guilty of introducing beer or other intoxicating drinks into the Indian country or of selling them to Indians, the penalty for each offense being not more than two years' imprisonment and not more than $300 fine.

The troubles and confusion brought about in the Indian Territory through the sale of intoxicants there have been reported by Agent Bennett to be deplorable. In some places drunken carousals have been so frequent as to make it unsafe for women and children to be out alone on the streets. At one town in the Creek Nation a prosecuting attorney citizen of that nation, with others, become intoxicated on beer, and in their drunken brawls killed a worthy citizen of the town, who had given no cause for offense.

It is gratifying, however, to be able to report that this traffic can now be stopped. There is now no doubt as to the character of liquors that are prohibited by law from introduction into the Indian country and sale to Indians, and it is expected that, with the coöperation of the courts having jurisdiction over the Indian Territory, the agents of this department will be able to prevent further trouble from the sale of beer therein.

In other parts of the Indian country there appears to have been less whisky drinking by the Indian than in former years, owing, doubtless, to the activity of the Indian agents in detecting and securing the punishment of offenders against the law.

In this connection, however, I am constrained to note what seems to be an unfortunate tendency in the other direction. While the office is using every means in its power to suppress all liquor traffic among Indians and to inculcate in them habits of total abstinence, those who have been enlisted in the U. S. Army are allowed the same liberty in regard to obtaining liquor from the canteen and elsewhere as is accorded to white soldiers. This is to be regretted on many accounts. It lowers the character of the Indian himself, makes his return home with the habit of drink a source of evil to his tribe, and gives the impression that enlistment in the Army means an opportunity to indulge in a practice which is strictly prohibited on the reservation. This idea has already been disseminated among Indian pupils at school by their correspondence with friends who have enlisted.

INDIAN TRADE

No change has been made during the year in the policy hitherto pursued by me in regard to Indian trade, which has been fully set forth in my previous reports. The recent act of Congress, by which clearer and more stringent provisions have been added to the laws against the introduction of intoxicating liquors into the Indian country, has already been referred to on page 103. This legislation will be felt only by certain traders among the Five Civilized Tribes. The sale of beer as well as other intoxicating compounds by licensed traders on reservations elsewhere has never been allowed.

As I have before stated, the distinguishing characteristics of Indian trade have nearly disappeared, and the system of licensing traders among Indians will cease as reservations are surrounded by white settlements, or as reservation walls are beaten down by allotments. This state of affairs has already been reached among the Omahas and Santee Sioux in Nebraska, the Sac and Fox, Cheyennes, and Arapahoes in Oklahoma, and the Sisseton Sioux in South Dakota. The Omahas have had no licensed trader for two years, and it is my purpose not to renew existing licenses granted to traders among the other tribes named. As such licenses are issued for only one year, those Indians will soon be free from any such suggestion of their former condition of wardship as distinguished from their present status of citizens.

EXHIBITION OF INDIANS

During the past year numerous applications have been received asking for authority to take Indians from reservations for exhibition purposes. I have steadily refused to countenance in any way anything of the "Wild West" character. Further consideration of the question has only confirmed me in the views expressed hitherto, that it is unwise for Indians to be allowed to appear before the public exhibiting their savage characteristics. It tends to create in their minds the idea that what the white man particularly admires is that which really is a mark of their degradation; it tends to foster a roaming spirit; it brings them, almost of necessity, into contact with the low and degraded white man, encourages vice, and begets false ideas of civilized life; it takes them from home, breaks up any habits that may be forming of ordinary industry, and has a tendency to awaken a spirit of restlessness among those that remain behind. The arguments advanced in favor of the scheme, namely, that it enables them to earn money and to see the world, are by no means conclusive to my mind. The truth is, and it may as well be stated in all its baldness, that the reason for taking these people and making an exhibit of their savagery is the money there is in it for their employers. This is all; other pleas are mere pretexts and subterfuges, excuses designed to cover up the real reason.

I have, however, granted permission in several instances for Indians to attend for a few days expositions in cities near by the reservations, where they could see and learn that which would be of profit to them.

* * *

DEPREDATION CLAIMS

Only ten depredation claims have been filed in this office since my last annual report, which makes the total number now on file 7,995, aggregating in amount $25,672,559.82. The papers in 2,029 of these claims during the last fiscal year have been transmitted to the Court of Claims, pursuant to the act of March 3, 1891 (26 *Stats.*, 851). These added to the number so transmitted in the preceding year, 763, make a total of 2,792, which, added to the 1,454 claims which were submitted to Congress for its consideration, pursuant to the act of March 3, 1885 (23 *Stats.*, 376), leaves 3,749 claims in the files of this office and subject to its "care and custody" and the further orders of the court, as provided by the act of March 3, 1891.

On the 30th day of June, 1892, as I am informed by the clerk of the Court of Claims, there had been filed in that court 7,748 petitions or claims on account of Indian depredations. The similarity in number between the claims on file here and in the court would indicate that about all of the claims known to this office had been transferred to the court; but when it is noticed that the papers in but 2,792 have been called for or transmitted thereto, it is apparent that most of the claims filed in the court have never been on file in this office, and it indicates that the total number of claims which will be prosecuted under said act will largely exceed the number previously filed here.

Judgments under that act have been rendered in 240 cases by the court, the aggregate amount of which is $479,068.62. . . .

It is gratifying to know that deserving claimants are at last to be reimbursed for the losses and damages which they have suffered, and that these particular claims are to be paid without injustice to the Indians or in violation of their treaty rights. But inasmuch as the large mass of such claims still remains to be acted upon, I deem it my duty again to invite attention to the provision contained in the act of March 3, 1891, which practically constitutes a lien on the funds of Indian tribes which have or may have money for the payment of such claims. That provision is as follows:

> That the amount of any judgment so rendered against any tribe of Indians shall be charged against the tribe by which, or by members of which, the court shall find that the depredation was committed, and shall be deducted and paid in the following manner: First, from annuities due said tribe from the United States; second, if no annuities are due or available, then from any other funds due said tribe from the United States, arising from the sale of their lands or otherwise; third, if no such funds are due or available, then from any appropriation for the benefit of said tribes other than appropriations for their current and necessary support, subsistence, and education; and, fourth, if no such annuities, fund, or appropriation shall be paid from the Treasury of the United States: *Provided.* That any amount so paid from the Treasury of the United States shall remain a charge against such tribe, and shall be deducted from any annuity, fund, or appropriation hereinbefore designated which may hereafter become due from the United States to such tribe.

When the bill (H. R. 6457) "to provide for the adjudication and payment of claims arising from Indian depredations," which substantially became the law of March 3, 1891, was referred to this office for "consideration and report," I suggested, by letter of February 28, 1890, a number of changes or amendments, among them one proposing that Section vi be amended so as to provide that the amounts of the judgments—

> Shall be paid out of any moneys in the Treasury not otherwise appropriated, unless, in the judgment of the Secretary of the Interior, it should be deducted from any annuities or permanent funds in the hands of the United States belonging to said tribe or tribes when ascertained, in which latter event an account shall be kept against such tribe or tribes, and such payments shall be charged against them and deducted from any funds which may become due them, as the Secretary of the Interior in his discretion shall direct. . . .

The bill became a law without this suggested provision, and when it was again referred to this office for report, prior to its going to the President for his approval, I again, March 3, 1891, invited attention to the omission of any provision lodging a discretion in the Secretary of the Interior as to the payment of these judgments out of the annuities or other funds of the Indians, and I said:

> While I dislike very much to interpose an objection to prevent the consummation of legislation so long urged by this office, nevertheless the omission of the clause in question is a matter of serious importance, and I deem it my duty to call attention to it in order that it may receive consideration as to whether it is not sufficient to warrant withholding approval of the bill.

The act, unamended, was approved on the 3d day of March, 1891, and is the law to-day. . . .

So earnestly do I feel upon this subject and so firmly do I believe that this law should be amended in this respect that I am impelled to again invite your attention to the subject in the hope that legislation may soon be secured on the lines indicated, whereby justice may be done to meritorious claimants without injustice being at the same time done to the various tribes of Indians whose peace, prosperity, and civilization is made a charge in law and good morals upon the Government of the United States. The moral aspects of the question aside, as a matter of public policy alone such legislation should be had, for the reason that the dissatisfaction of the Indians when they find their funds so unexpectedly diverted to the payment of these claims will be so great that turbulence is liable to ensue and destruction of property and loss of life may follow; and the final cost of reëstablishing peace and good order will exceed, in all probability, the amount of the claims whose payment is likely to produce such disturbance. This condition appears more probable from the fact that, as shown by the tables submitted in my last annual report, the greater number of claims are charged against those tribes which are the most impatient of restraint and least likely to submit, without the exercise of force, to anything which may have the appearance to them of oppression or bad faith upon the part of the Government. That the deduction and payment of these claims, upon a judgment rendered in a suit to which they have not been made a party fully, and have not had the opportunity of fully asserting their rights and pleading their defenses, would have that appearance to their "untutored minds" no one will dispute, especially when it is considered that the funds which are now in the hands of the United States belonging to them are by treaty expressly held "in trust" for their benefit, and are the proceeds of their concessions or relinquishments of lands for the benefit of the white people of the United States. Had it been conceived by these Indians that the proceeds of their sales of lands would be confiscated in this manner, I apprehend that Oklahoma would not now exist as a Territory, and the Great Sioux Reservation would still occupy a large part of the Dakotas.

It is true that the original act of Congress approved May 19, 1796 (1 *Stat.*, 472), guaranteeing indemnification to sufferers by Indian depredations, made it lawful or permitted that the amounts of the same should be paid from the "annual stipend" of such Indians; but in the act of July 15, 1870 (16 *Stats.*, 360), the diversion of annuities and other funds to the payment of claims of this character was prohibited, and it was enacted that—

> no claims for Indian depredations shall hereafter be paid until Congress shall make special appropriation thereof.

This was the law until the 3d day of March, 1891, and under it, and in view of the protection it afforded to the funds of the Indians, treaties have been negotiated and lands acquired which could never have been effected, in my opinion, had the law been otherwise, or as it now stands in the statute. For the United States to thus provide that—

> no claims for Indian depredations shall hereafter be paid until Congress shall make special appropriation thereof—

and then incur a debt to the Indians and afterwards divert the money thus due them to the payment of the claims of its own people without Indian consent or even appraisal, would quite naturally appear to an uncivilized mind as a breach of good faith, which would justify hostility to a Government so apparently perfidious.

In view of these considerations, I would again respectfully recommend that you urge upon the attention of Congress the necessity for amending this law so as to divest it of its arbitrary and confiscatory character, by vesting in the Secretary of the Interior such a proper discretion as was lodged in the President of the United States by the act of May 19, 1796, and as is contained in the special legislation of July 28, 1892. . . .

* * *

ADMINISTRATION OF THE INDIAN SERVICE

Something more than three years have now elapsed since I entered upon my duties as Commissioner of Indian Affairs, during which period I have devoted my entire time and strength to the work of the office. I have studied the situation with as much care as it has been possible for me to bestow upon it; have traveled extensively among the reservations; have had numerous and prolonged interviews with all classes and conditions of Indians, and have consulted freely with agents, school superintendents, teachers, and others familiar with the work.

When the President did me the honor to ask me to take the office he placed before me a high ideal of its administration, and in a subsequent conference with you, you expressed the desire that I would "administer the office on strictly business principles." There was thus laid upon me a duty of the highest possible character. The Indian Office has been in a constant state of flux, owing to frequent changes and short terms of the commissioners. Since 1832, a period of sixty years, there have been twenty-five commissioners, with an average term of service of less than two and one-half years. It is simply impossible that a great bureau like this should be most efficiently managed with such frequent changes in its controlling officer. A commissioner can little more than learn his duties in two and a half years.

For many years the office was under the ban of public opinion, and there was a widespread conviction that it was dominated by false ideas and was not managed on business principles nor in such a way as to satisfy a high public sentiment, an opinion which was not wholly without foundation. One of our most distinguished public men said to me that while he was a member of Congress, whenever he had any constituents clamoring for office for whom he could make provision nowhere else he always unloaded them on the Indian Office. He added, however, that he had afterwards come to feel how utterly indefensible such a procedure was. It is no uncommon thing to have men urged upon me for positions who are utterly incompetent and whose only claim for consideration is their own personal necessities or the political services they have rendered. The opportunities and temptations for fraud and dishonesty have necessarily been many, and they have not all gone unimproved. Undoubtedly persons have attempted to find employment in the service from low or bad motives, and many have failed to comprehend the responsibility resting upon them to perform efficient, honest, and faithful work.

From my three years' experience, however, I am fully convinced that the popular opinion regarding the demerits of the Indian service is greatly exaggerated. I have found very many persons who were actuated by the highest motives and who were possessed of large capacity, and who have devoted themselves with great fidelity to the performance of duty. I have striven very earnestly and have done everything in my power to improve the service and to fulfill the trust committed to me by you and the President, and I do not think that I arrogate anything to myself when I say that I have been in a large degree successful, so far as I have had authority and the power to work. I think it can be confidently asserted without fear of contradiction that the Indian service is to-day, on the whole, a very upright one, and that there is little in it which is open to serious criticism.

I have not been entirely satisfied, however, with the results thus far attained. I have met with unexpected obstacles and difficulties, some of which have paralyzed my most earnest efforts; others have hindered the accomplishment of my purposes, and others have made it very trying even to make an attempt at reform or improvement. Many times I have been so utterly disheartened as to feel tempted to abandon the work, and am free to say that I have continued to discharge the duties devolved upon me, under the limitations, restrictions, criticisms, and disappointments which I have encountered, only from a stern sense of duty. The attractions of the office are few, it labors heavy, its limitations very great, and I do not think any man would continue in it for any considerable length of time and really endeavor to discharge the duties conscientiously in accordance with a high standard who was not impelled thereto by a devotion to duty and an earnest desire to fulfill, to the best of his ability, the solemn trust imposed upon him.

There is, perhaps, no bureau in the Government that has a larger number of business questions to deal with—questions of land, of law, of finance, of interpretation of treaties, the maintaining of an extensive school system, etc. It exercises supervision over 250,000 people widely scattered over a vast region of country. There are more than three hundred separate appropriations on its books, and it disburses enormous sums of money. The office in Washington is so well organized that no breath of suspicion ought to attach to the integrity of its methods, and its books and proceedings are always open to anyone who has the right to inquire into its work.

INCREASE IN THE WORK OF THE INDIAN

The work of this office increases both in quantity and in perplexity of details. The quantity is exhibited by the following facts:

From July 1, 1885, to June 30, 1888, the letters received numbered 101,992, while from July 1, 1889, to June 30, 1892, the number of letters received amounted to 130,475, an increase of 28,483 or nearly 28 per cent.

From July 1, 1885, to June 30, 1888, the number of letters sent by the office was 67,151, while from July 1, 1889, to June 30, 1892, the number was 91,705, an increase of 24,554. Many of these letters it should be said are voluminous documents, requiring great research and care in their preparation, and the mere figures fail to represent adequately the increase in the work.

There are several reasons for this increase. One is the rapid and enormous development of the educational system. The appropriation from the public treasury for this purpose for the fiscal year just closed is nearly a million dollars greater than it was three years ago. This has thrown upon the office a vast increase of business. The planning and erecting of schoolhouses, the appointment of teachers, the keeping of records, and the proper administration of this extensive school system, carried on as it is under such perplexing difficulties, involves an amount of labor that few people have any conception of except those actually engaged in it.

An approximate idea of the increase of work in the educational division is shown by the fact that the number of pages of letters sent out by that division for the three years 1886, 1887, and 1888, was 13,059, while the number sent out by the same division for the three years ending June 30, 1892, amounted to 23,050, almost double.

Another reason for the increase of business is the breaking up of reservations and the allotment of lands. During the past three years more than

24,000,000 acres of Indian lands have been restored to the public domain, and the amount of office work involved in preparing instructions for commissions, examining their accounts, and reporting upon their labors, as well as in allotting lands, has been very great. During the first three years of the last administration 4,125 individual allotments of lands were made to Indians, while during the three years of the present administration 12,273 allotments have been made, or nearly three times as many. This work involves the closest attention to details in order that each Indian may receive a patent for the exact piece of land to which he is entitled.

ADDITIONAL CLERICAL FORCE NEEDED

There are other reasons for this increase of business which I need not enumerate. The fact is that the work thrown upon this office at present is greater than it can properly attend to. The time of the Commissioner is unavoidably largely taken up with personal interviews with people who call to see him on business and with the consideration of a multitude of things that completely engross his time, thought, and energies to such an extent that he can not give to the details of the work of the office that careful attention which is in a high degree necessary. Under the present law the Assistant Commissioner performs the duties of a chief clerk. Aside from such work his duties are so numerous and exhausting that he should be relieved entirely of this extra work which now practically devolves upon both him and the Commissioner. The office needs and ought to have a chief clerk who can attend to all this part of the work, thus not only relieving the Commissioner and Assistant Commissioner, which, perhaps, is a minor matter, but also, which is the main thing, facilitating the work of the office and insuring greater accuracy, thoroughness, and efficiency.

There is also needed an addition to the force of clerks. Some of those who are now here are simply overwhelmed with work, and are not only suffering from it but are in danger of permanent disability by reason of the anxiety and burden of their duties.

I asked, and you cordially approved it, that the last Congress should allow this office a chief clerk, and also an additional clerk, and I was strongly in hopes that this reasonable and urgent request might be granted. I was greatly disappointed, therefore, when not only was the request denied, and both the chief clerk and additional clerk withheld, but Congress took away from the office four clerks whom it already had, so that the office is now six clerks short of the force which I had hoped it would have for the ensuing year.

I earnestly ask your attention to this matter, as it is one which involves the efficiency of the service in the Indian Office, and I feel very sure, if the facts as I have here stated them, corroborated and enforced by many other facts which I could adduce, were fully understood by Congress, they would not withhold from the office the clerical force absolutely necessary for the proper performance of the duties devolving upon it.

CRITICISMS ON THE INDIAN BUREAU

It is only fair to the office to ask your attention to the fact that notwithstanding the vast number of cases, many of them matters of the gravest importance, which have been acted upon by this office during the last three years, it has been a rare circumstance indeed when any valid objection or just criticism has been passed upon its action. Most of the business which has been transacted here has passed unchallenged.

Some of the ablest clerks in the office, experts in their various positions, have been there from twelve to twenty years, and if called upon would testify that there has been no violent breaking with the past, but a careful regard for law and regulation and a faithful observance of precedent, except where deviation has been necessitated by new conditions. But meanwhile the office has been aggressive. The amount of business transacted has been largely increased, great progress has been made in many vital directions, and it is safe to say that its efficient activity was never greater than to-day.

That imperfections and abuses should grow up in a great Bureau like this, having to do its work through 3,000 employés so widely scattered, is not to be wondered at. It is worthy of remark, however, that the criticisms most frequently point to abuses that occurred many years ago, to evils that are incident to the very anomalous condition of things, or to circumstances over which the Office has no control.

The most earnest efforts have been put forth to elevate the personnel of the service, to renovate and improve the school system, and to institute reforms of every practicable character. The Commissioner of Indian Affairs has absolutely nothing to do with the appointment of Indian agents, but has not hesitated to ask for the removal of those who have shown themselves unworthy or incompetent for their work. One of the greatest reforms ever introduced into the Indian service was in extending the rules of the civil service over a large portion of it, on his recommendation.

Any Commissioner who tries to administer this office honestly and fearlessly in the interest of the Indians; who attempts to maintain a fair state of discipline among 3,000 employés; to insist that agents shall discharge their duties faithfully; that evil-doers shall be punished and the weak and innocent shall be protected; that incompetent or unfaithful agents and employés shall be discharged; that spoilsmen shall not corrupt the service; that the land-grabber shall loose his clutches on Indian lands; that cattlemen shall not fatten their herds on Indian grass; that traders shall deal honestly; that contractors shall fulfill their contracts; that public moneys shall not be misappropriated; that attorneys shall not despoil the Indians; that gamblers shall not rob them nor whisky sellers debauch them; that they shall not be lured to vagabondage by "wild west" shows; who insists that the Government shall be just and keep its faith, and shall build schoolhouses to educate all Indian children; who tries to defeat the schemes of powerful lobbyists urging hurtful legislation; who demands that the adult Indians shall keep their agreements, give up their savagery, send their children to school, and go to work to earn an honest living—the Commissioner who insists on progress and improvement, will be reminded very frequently of the utopian nature of his ideas. He will stir up opposition on every side. Criticism and abuse are the inevitable results of an honest endeavor to rightly administer the business of the Indian Office. I believe it can be done, however, if a man is willing to pay the price. The work of the present administration ought to make the next administration easier.

When my attention was first directed to the average length of term of the Commissioner of Indian Affairs (two and one-half years), I wondered at its brevity; after a service of three years and two months and an experience of what is involved, I wonder that the average term of service has been so long.

One very encouraging fact in my experience is that I have had the cordial support of the great religious weeklies, of most of the powerful secular dailies of all shades of political opinions, and of hosts of men and women, whose good opinion I value more than gold. This, together with a consciousness of an honest effort to render a helpful service to an abused people, has been a great solace to me amid the cares and criticism incident to my work.

I have taken a great deal of pains to investigate any and all complaints and criticisms coming to my knowledge in regard to the treatment of the Indians. In some cases such criticisms and complaints proved to be entirely without foundation, and in others they were found to be based either upon a misapprehension of the facts or of the law in the case.

Undoubtedly there have been cases in which there has been a tardiness on the part of the Government in fulfilling its obligations, as well as faults of administration, through which the Indians have suffered loss or inconvenience and disappointment. In very many cases, however, the Indians themselves have misunderstood their relations, misinterpreted their rights, and have often themselves been grossly to blame for a failure to perform their part of the stipulated agreement.

So far as possible I have insisted upon the literal fulfillment of all the obligations of the Government to its wards, and during the past three years a number of important agreements which had been long pending have been ratified by Congress, and their conditions have either been complied with or are in process of fulfillment. So far as I know, there is now no matter of any great consequence pending which the Indians have a right to complain of as a failure on the part of the Government to fulfill its obligations.

In the purchase of subsistence and other supplies I have personally taken great care to see to it that only articles of merit were bought, and a great improvement in the quality of the dry goods, hardware, and agricultural implements especially has resulted. I believe it is now generally conceded by all of those cognizant of the facts that the Indian Department aims to buy only articles of excellent merit and at a reasonable price. Very critical oversight is extended to the delivery of these goods, so that the Indians to whom they properly belong shall receive the full quantity and quality of supplies to which they are entitled. There has been during the past year very little complaint in this particular.

CONCLUSION

From this brief summary of the work of the office for the year it will be seen that every branch of the work has received due attention; that the forces at the control of the Commissioner have been used to the utmost to secure the highest possible degree of efficiency; that very considerable progress has been made in many directions, and that the present state of Indian administration is, on the whole, encouraging, and hopeful.

At the same time I am constrained to point out what seem to me dangers connected with the present situation among the Indians, which very properly may be denominated "the Indian crisis:"

First. There is danger that citizenship will be thrust upon the Indians before they are prepared for it, and that they will thus become the prey of evil forces which are now held in check but will then be let loose upon them.

Second. There is danger that the scheme of education which has grown up in the past and has been moulded and brought into shape, energized, and greatly enlarged within the last three years, may be checked in its beneficent work.

Third. There is danger that the efforts to purify the Indian service, lift it out of politics, and place it upon the firm basis of justice and of business methods, will be thwarted by those who are interested in keeping to the old system and of using the Indian service for personal, political and other mercenary ends.

Fourth. There is danger that the Christian people of this country in the present transition stage of the work, will fail to appreciate the importance of distinctively missionary work for these people by virtue of which they may be weaned from their superstitions and gross errors and be led to the practical acceptance of those fundamental truths which all thoughtful Christian men regard as essential to their welfare.

Therefore it behooves the friends of the Indians to consider with great care the Indian question as it presents itself to-day, with the view of correcting whatever defects there may be in the existing system, and then of maintaining the system and carrying into successful execution the present policy of the Government.

In reviewing the past three years and looking forward to the future, I venture to suggest the following as my mature conclusions:

First. The present policy of dealing with the Indians, which is all summed up in the one word citizenship, should be accepted as final, and should be carried into execution as rapidly as practicable. The one great thought which should dominate Indian administration is that the end is in sight, and that everything reasonable should be done to hasten the winding up of the affairs of the Indian Bureau. It ought not, under wise management, to take many years to complete this work.

Second. Whoever is chosen as Commissioner of Indian Affairs should be selected with particular reference to his administrative qualities his ability, and his willingness to assume the responsibilities of the position, with a single eye to the accomplishment of the above result. He should have a salary equal to that paid to other bureau officers in the Interior Department; should have larger discretion in the discharge of his duties and greater authority in the selection of agents, appointments of commissions, and other matters that pertain so largely to the efficiency of his administration. He should, furthermore, have a sufficient force of clerks to enable him to transact the business with promptness and thoroughness.

Third. It should be understood, proclaimed, and acted upon that hereafter the sole test for appointment and continuance in service of any employé shall be that of fitness. No man should be selected for any position who is not competent to discharge its duties; no one should be continued in the service who has proven himself unfit, and no one should be dismissed so long as he is fully competent for the discharge of his duties.

Report of Commissioner of
Indian Affairs D. M. Browning
September 14, 1895

(Excerpt from *Report for 1895*, pp. 60-80)

Commissioner Browning's detailed report of disturbances in the Jackson Hole country of Wyoming is a classic account of the conflict between state game regulations and an Indian treaty, and of the conflicting economic interests of white "sportsmen" desirous of shooting elk for pleasure and Indian families hunting elk for subsistence. The calculated attempt by white citizens of Jackson Hole to expel the Indians from the area despite their treaty rights was fully supported by the governor of the state.

DISTURBANCES IN "JACKSONS HOLE" COUNTRY,
WYOMING

SINCE MY LAST annual report relative to complaints by whites in regard to Indians off their reservations hunting and "wantonly killing" game, serious trouble has occurred between the Bannock Indians and the whites in what is known as the "Jacksons Hole" country, Wyoming. A full report of this entire affair was made to the Department August 17, 1895, the substance of which is as follows, some of it being quoted from my report of last year:

For more than a year past complaints have been made to this office that Indians of the Shoshone Reservation, Wyo., were wantonly slaughtering elk and deer that had been driven down from the Rocky Mountains by the deep snows and severe weather. The agent of the Shoshone Agency was at once instructed to report the facts to this office, and to take such action as would entirely stop any wanton killing of game by those Indians in the future. He replied that, to his knowledge, no elk or deer had been aimlessly slaughtered by the Indians belonging to that agency, but that it was reported that roving parties of other Indians had killed game outside of the reservation; also that the Indians reported that white men were continually going on hunting expeditions through the country adjacent to their reservation, and killing game merely for the pleasure of hunting. Reports from other Indian agents in that country sustained this charge, the whites claiming they had as good right as the Indians to kill game; and the State officers, in some instances, stating that they did not feel justified in prosecuting white men for violating State game laws, while the Indians were allowed to hunt.

Subsequently more complaints were received from Idaho, Wyoming, and Montana that parties of Indians were continually leaving their reservations with passes from their agents to make social and friendly visits to other reservations; that en route they slaughtered game in large quantities merely for the sake of killing and for the hides, particularly in the country adjacent to the Yellowstone National Park and the Shoshone Reservation, Wyo., and that if such depredations were allowed to continue it would probably result in a serious conflict between the white settlers and the Indians.

In view of the above complaints, the office, on May 22, 1894, addressed a letter to the Indian agents in Idaho, Montana, Wyoming, Utah, and the Dakotas, instructing them to call together in council the Indians of their respective agencies and again put before them the instructions contained in office circular of November 1, 1889, and to notify them that the restrictions as to hunting contained in that circular must be strictly complied with; also that should they obtain passes ostensibly for making friendly visits to other reservations and then engage in hunting while en route, their passes would be recalled by this office and they would not be allowed to leave their reservation again.

The circular referred to reads as follows:

> Frequent complaints have been made to this Department that Indians are in the habit of leaving their reservations for the purpose of hunting; that they slaughter game in large quantities in violation of the laws of the State or Territory in which they reside, and that in many instances large numbers of wild animals are killed simply for their hides.
>
> In some cases Indians, by treaty stipulations, have the guaranteed right to hunt, upon specified conditions, outside their existing reservations. The Secretary of the Interior has decided that the privilege of hunting under such treaty provisions is the right to merely kill such game as may be necessary to supply the needs of the Indians, and that the slaughter of wild animals in vast numbers for the hides only and the abandonment of the carcasses without attempting to make use of them, is as much a violation of the treaty as an absolute prohibition on the part of the United States against the exercise of such privilege would be. This fact should be impressed upon the minds of the Indians who have such treaty rights, and they will be given to understand that the wanton destruction of game will not be permitted. And those not having the reserved treaty privileges of hunting outside of their existing reservation should be warned against leaving their reservation for hunting, as they are liable to arrest and prosecution for violation of the laws of the State or Territory in which offenses may be committed.
>
> In view of the settlement of the country and the consequent disappearance of the game, the time has long since gone by when the Indians can live by the chase. They should abandon their idle and nomadic ways and endeavor to cultivate habits of industry, and adopt civilized pursuits to secure the means for self-support.

All the agents addressed reported that they had complied with office instructions, and had taken extra precautions to prevent the Indians under their charge from wantonly killing game or leaving their reservations for such a purpose.

Captain Ray, U. S. A., acting agent of the Shoshone Agency, in his report of May 29, 1894, relative to the above instructions, stated as follows:

I find that article 4 of the treaty with the Eastern Band of the Shoshone Indians, made July 3, 1868, gives the Indians the right to hunt on all the unoccupied lands of the United States, and they have certainly availed themselves of the privilege, but not a single case of wanton destruction of wild animals has ever come to my knowledge, nor will I ever permit such practice.

In connection with this matter I wish to call attention to the fact that the present ration for Indians on this reservation (one-half pound of flour and three-fourths pound beef, net) is not sufficient to ward off the pangs of hunger, and they must supplement this allowance in some way or suffer. In absence of paid employment, which will enable them to purchase food, they will resort to desperate methods before they will go hungry. Unless they receive sufficient food on the reservation, no power can prevent them from killing game or cattle.

Complaints, however, continued to be made by the governor of Wyoming, the prosecuting attorney of Fremont County, and many others from the region south of the Yellowstone National Park. These complaints were referred to the respective Indian agents for their information and with instructions to be especially careful to prevent any wanton destruction of game by Indians in their charge. From some of their reports it is clear that the Indians had not been justly complained of, and that in many instances the charges against them were either altogether false or grossly exaggerated, sometimes willfully so. For instance, Captain Ray, U. S. A., the then acting Indian agent of the Shoshone Agency, reported that hordes of white hunters infested the country (Yellowstone Park region) entirely unmolested.

A full report as to these complaints was made in letter of November 8, 1894, of which the concluding paragraphs were as follows:

It is my intention to write again to the agents of the Fort Hall (Idaho) and Wind River (Wyoming) agencies, directing them to be watchful to the end that their Indians give no cause for complaint in this matter; but I think it would be well if some attention were paid to the foreign and native tourists and others, who go into that country to hunt without let or hindrance.

It is a well-known and admitted fact that the extermination of the buffalo and other large game in the West was the work of the whites, principally, and not the Indians, and even now the well-supplied curio shops and taxidermists obtain their supply of heads, antlers, horns, etc., entirely from the former, or very nearly so, at least.

No further complaints were received until in the latter part of June last, when Governor Richards, of Wyoming, addressed a letter to the Department stating that he was informed that Indians were then hunting and killing large game in the northern part of Uinta County and the western part of Fremont County, Wyo.; that most of these Indians were from Idaho, some, however, being from the Shoshone Reservation, Wyo. He inclosed a copy of the State of Wyoming Fish and Game Laws, 1895, and requested that action be taken which would restrict Indians from leaving their respective reservations for the purpose of hunting in Wyoming.

July 17, 1895, Governor Richards telegraphed the Department as follows:

Have just received the following telegram, dated Marysvale, Wyo., July 15, via Market Lake, Idaho, July 16:

"Nine Indians arrested, one killed, others escaped. Many Indians reported here; threaten lives and property. Settlers are moving families away. Want protection immediately. Action on your part is absolutely necessary.

> FRANK H. RHODES
> *Justice of the Peace.*
>
> WM. MANNING,
> *Constable.*
>
> (And three others.)

I have received other advices by mail representing situation as serious. The Indians are Bannocks from Fort Hall, Idaho. Arrested for the illegal and wanton killing of game. My letter to you dated June 17 relates to the matter. Can you take immediate action for the protection of our settlers?

This office, on July 17, 1895, therefore telegraphed Teter, Indian agent at Fort Hall, Idaho, as follows:

Governor Richards, of Wyoming, telegraphs this date that nine Bannock Indians belonging to Fort Hall Agency were arrested and one killed on or about 15th instant, at Marysvale, Uinta County, Wyo., for wantonly killing game; that many other Indians are there threatening lives and property, and settlers are moving families away. Proceed at once to scene of trouble and do all in your power to prevent further disturbance and to return absent Indians to reservation. If troops are needed to protect settlers or prevent open conflict, advise immediately. If you have any information now telegraph same to me before starting.

The same date the following telegram was sent to the acting Indian agent, Shoshone Agency:

Serious trouble reported in neighborhood of Marysvale, Uinta County, Wyo. Nine Bannock Indians from Fort Hall Agency arrested and one killed for violation of game laws. Settlers said to be fleeing for their lives. If any of your Indians are absent in that region have them returned to reservation at once. Have ordered Fort Hall agent to scene of trouble. Cooperate with him to fullest extent of your ability in every possible way.

The agent of Fort Hall Agency replied by telegraph the next day as follows:

Will state on 13th instant, upon receipt information Indians were killing game unlawfully in Wyoming, I sent the entire police force to Wyoming to bring back Indians belonging to this reservation. Captain Indian police sent back policeman, who arrived this day, stating that one Indian killed by settlers. Other sources: several Indians killed. I leave for scene of trouble at once.

The same day the Shoshone agent also telegraphed:

Police sent days ago to bring absent Indians back to reservation. Only one Indian reported absent now. Reports indicate that none of my Indians were concerned in Marysvale trouble. Will act for Fort Hall agent whenever possible.

Then followed the sensational and alarming newspaper reports of an Indian outbreak in the Jacksons Hole country; the Bannocks on the warpath; the killing of many settlers by the savages; homes burned to the ground; whites fleeing for their lives; and the appeal to the Government that United States troops be hurried to the seat of war to stop the fiendish work of devastation and murder of whites by the redskins.

July 23 the Fort Hall agent telegraphed this office as follows:

Have investigated trouble between Indians and settlers in Wyoming, and will advise troops be sent there immediately to protect law-abiding settlers; lawless element among settlers being determined to come into conflict with Indians. Settlers have killed from four to seven Indians, which has incensed Indians, who have gathered to number of 200 to 300 near Fall River in Uinta County and refuse to return to reservation. I find Bannock Indians have killed game unlawfully according to laws of Wyoming, though not unlawfully according to treaty of Bannock Indians with United States, usurping prerogative of settlers in that respect, which caused the trouble, and nothing but intervention of soldiers will settle difficulty and save lives of innocent persons and prevent destruction of property.

This office replied as follows:

Send word to absent Indians as coming direct from me that I want them to return peaceably to their reservation before the soldiers arrive. Say that I send this message to them as their friend and urge prompt compliance, knowing it is for their best interest and welfare.

Agent Teter carried out the above instructions, and July 28 telegraphed the following:

On 27th instant I met Sheriff Hawley near Rexburg, returning from Jacksons Hole, where he had been sent to ascertain if settlers have been killed by Indians. Hawley states settlers have not been molested by Indians. Indians are supposed to be in camp 40 miles from settlements in practically impregnable position.

The Secretary of War on July 24, 1895, upon Department request for military aid, ordered Brigadier-General Coppinger, commanding Department of the Platte, to proceed at once to the scene of disturbance in

Wyoming and to order such movement of troops as might be necessary to prevent a conflict between the Indians and settlers and to remove the Indians to their proper reservations.

Governor Richards, on July 31, telegraphed the following:

> Reliable information that 200 Indians supposed to be Utes were seen yesterday near South Pass, Fremont County; also 47 Sioux on Bad Water Creek, same county; all were mounted, armed, and without women or children. The people of Fremont County are under arms and wire me for assistance. Can not these and all other Indians in Wyoming be recalled to their reservations?

This office at once telegraphed the agents of Pine Ridge (S. Dak.), Shoshone (Wyoming), Lemhi (Idaho), and Uintah and Ouray (Utah) agencies to have absent Indians returned to their respective reservations. The Shoshone and Uintah and Ouray agents replied that none of their Indians were absent, and that no trouble was feared.

August 2, 1895, Agent Teter reported by telegram as follows:

> I have returned from Jacksons Hole. Eyerything quiet there. I will recommend that you request the Department of Justice to investigate killing of peaceable Indians by lawless settlers in Uinta County, Wyo., with a view to the prosecution of the guilty parties.

On the following day he further telegraphed:

> All Indians absent from reservation have returned. Had big council. Requested me to telegraph you their hearts felt good. Had not harmed a white man, and would start haying, leaving their grievances to the justice of the white man.

To the latter message this office replied August 7 as follows:

> Your telegram August 3 received. Exceedingly gratifying to me and to all friends of the Indians everywhere that they have returned peaceably to their reservation and gone to work, having committed no acts of violence against the persons or property of the whites, which will certainly be to their lasting credit. Tell them so, and that office will do all in its power to have faithful investigation of the killing of the Indians and to see that justice is done. Am looking for full report from you giving details of the whole affair.

I now quote in full the official reports that have reached this office giving details of the trouble, as follows:

Report, dated July 20, 1895, from Capt. R. H. Wilson, U. S. A., acting Indian agent, Shoshone Agency, Wyo.:

> In regard to the recent disturbances near Marysvale, Wyo., resulting from Indians killing game out of season, I have the honor to report that the Indian police sent to that point to bring back absentees have returned without having been able to effect anything of importance. They report that two of my Indians have been found guilty of the offense in question, fined $75

each and costs, and in default of payment of their fines have been taken to Evanston to serve out sentences, of what duration I am not informed.

Their horses and equipments were seized to satisfy costs. No other Indians are now absent from this reservation without authority, and I do not anticipate any further trouble in this respect. The scene of the disturbance is so remote and inaccessible that it is difficult to obtain reliable reports in regard to it, but I am inclined to believe that the whole matter has been greatly exaggerated. I have been trying to instruct my Indians in the provisions of the game laws, of which they have been entirely ignorant. They have hitherto considered that the provisions of their treaty give them the right to hunt on unoccupied lands whenever they please. I shall, however, in future try to make them comply with the law in regard to killing game in Wyoming, without regard to their treaty, as I consider that this course will be less likely to cause a recurrence of similar trouble.

Report, dated July 20, 1895, addressed to Adjutant-General, U. S. A., from Capt. J. T. Van Orsdale, U. S. A., late acting Indian agent, Fort Hall Agency, Idaho:

I have the honor to make the following report bearing upon the account (newspaper) of the arrest and killing of Indians in Jacksons Hole country, Wyoming, by citizens of said State:

In the treaty made with the Bannocks and Shoshones at Fort Bridger in 1867 or 1868 they were granted the privilege of hunting on any unoccupied public land. Being short-rationed and far from self-supporting according to the white man's methods, they simply follow their custom and hunt for the purpose of obtaining sustenance. It would seem that the killing of Indians under the circumstances is nothing more or less than murder. They are not citizens of the State, and are entitled to the protection of the General Government so far as the rights and privileges granted by treaty are concerned.

While acting agent at Fort Hall Agency, Idaho, I had occasion to look into this matter, and while trying to prevent hunting by Indians during the season unauthorized by State law I took the opportunity to let those making complaints know that the Indians were within treaty rights, and I believe the fact is well known and understood. Further, I believe there is no "wanton" slaughter of game by these Indians, while it is a notorious fact that hundreds of animals are killed by white men for nothing more than heads and horns. There are men in that country who make it a business to pilot hunting parties from the East and the Old Country which not only slaughter elk but capture and ship them out of the country. The killing of game by Indians interferes with their business. Another fact about the Jacksons Hole Basin, it is inaccessible in winter on account of deep snow on the mountains, and game can only be got at by outsiders during the summer or early autumn. If it be the desire of the Government to restrain the Indians and cause them to conform to State laws, steps looking to the change or modification of treaty would seem to be in order. Indians can hardly be expected to submit more quietly to the killing of their people while engaged in the occupation which they think they have a right to follow than white men, and a failure by the Government to take proper action is liable to result in serious loss of life and property.

Having obtained knowledge of affairs in the manner indicated, I believe it a duty to make this report.

[First indorsement.]

OFFICE OF THE POST COMMANDER,
FORT LOGAN, COLO., *July 23, 1895.*

Respectfully forwarded.

I have known the Shoshone Indians since 1873, when I was at their agency, and had twenty-five of them for scouts on a trip I made from Camp Brown through the Yellowstone Park. I heartily concur in what Captain Van Orsdale has written. They are among the best of all Indians I have known.

HENRY NOYES,
Lieutenant-Colonel Second Cavalry,
Commanding Post.

[Second indorsement.]

HEADQUARTERS DEPARTMENT OF THE COLORADO,
DENVER, COLO., *July 25, 1895.*

Respectfully forwarded to the Adjutant-General of the Army.

The writer has had exceptional opportunity to familiarize himself with the Bannock and Shoshone Indians.

From my knowledge of these Indians in 1872, and again in 1879, I feel an interest in this matter, and hope that Captain Van Orsdale's recommendations and views may be favorably considered.

FRANK WEATON,
Brigadier-General, Commanding.

Report, dated July 24, 1895, from Thomas B. Teter, United States Indian agent of Fort Hall Agency, Idaho:

I have the honor to inform you that upon receipt of telegraphic instructions of the 17th instant I immediately proceeded to Marysvale, Uinta County, Wyo., and report as follows upon the condition of affairs I found existing between settlers and Indians from this and other reservations hunting in that vicinity:

I ascertained the number of Indians in the vicinity of Marysvale to be from 200 to 300, about 50 of whom were Bannock Indians from this reservation, all encamped in Hobacks Canyon, or near Fall River, at a distance of 35 miles southeast from Marysvale, in the Jackson Hole country.

The Indians have for many years gone to the Jackson Hole country in search of big game, and it is only since the business of guiding tourists in search of big game has become so remunerative that objection has been made to their hunting in Wyoming.

The treaty of the Bannock and Shoshone Indians with the United States gives said Indians the right to hunt on the unoccupied lands of the United States so long as game may be found thereon and so long as peace subsists among the whites and Indians on the borders of the hunting districts, and the simple Indian mind can not grasp the idea that the State of Wyoming can prevent the fulfillment by the United States of the treaty with them.

I ascertained that settlers last year stated that if Indians returned for big game this season they would organize and wipe them out, the settlers looking upon big game as their exclusive property and considering every elk killed by an Indian a source of so much revenue lost to them. From reliable informants I have no hesitation in stating that for every elk killed unlawfully by Indians two are killed unlawfully by settlers (in this connection I will state I was fed upon fresh-killed elk meat during my entire stay in the Jackson Hole country), and were these Indians citizens and voters in Wyoming enjoying similar privileges to settlers, their killing game unlawfully would never be questioned.

There are a few good citizens ranching in the Jackson Hole country, the majority of the citizens being men "who have left their country for their country's good," the Jackson Hole country being recognized in this country as the place of refuge for outlaws of every description from Wyoming, Idaho, and adjacent States.

The Indians killed by these settlers were practically massacred. The Indians, to the number of 16, having been arrested and disarmed, were taken before a justice of the peace, naturally in sympathy with settlers, and fined $75 each. The Indians being unable to pay the fine were herded like sheep and treated in a manner calculated to arouse their resentment, and which would not be tolerated by white men similarly situated. One batch, disarmed, were being driven by a body of armed settlers, and in passing over a trail where the Indians had been accustomed to ride in freedom, made a break for liberty, whereupon the guards opened fire at once and killed from four to seven Indians, going on the principle "a dead Indian is a good Indian."

The men who committed this crime should be prosecuted to the fullest extent of the law and receive the severest penalty the law can give, not only as an example to other lawless settlers, but as a preventive of future disturbances between settlers and Indians, for if justice is not done the Indians in this case the Indians will seek revenge and a continuous border warfare will be the result.

A certain element among settlers in Jackson Hole country seems determined to drive the Indians from that section at whatever cost, not recognizing any law themselves but that which serves their interests; and when I left Marysvale 75 of these men had organized, not for protection, but to attack the Indians. I warned them to desist, and requested all good citizens to use their influence to prevent this attack, stating I would advise the Department immediately of the true situation.

I, upon reaching telegraphic communication, advised you to send troops to scene of trouble at once, considering if lawless settlers carried out their intention of attacking Indians innocent persons would suffer—Indians as well as whites—and much property be destroyed; considering also that the ill feeling existing between settlers and Indians could not be allayed without the presence of troops.

I consider the Jackson Hole affair a preconcerted scheme, on the part of a certain element among the settlers, to adopt measures to induce the Department to prevent Indians from revisiting Jackson Hole country; settlers having informed me, while I was in Marysvale, that Indians visiting Jackson Hole country kept out hunting parties of tourists, which resulted in a loss to them of many dollars; a settler stating to me he had made $800 last season guiding hunting parties, and that the continual hunting by Indians in Jackson Hole country would ruin his occupation.

Report, dated August 7, 1895, from Agent Teter:

I have the honor to respectfully submit the Indian version of the killing of

Indians by settlers in Uinta County, Wyo., on or about the 15th ultimo, and other matter in connection with the affair.

A hunting party of nine Indians, with their families and camp equipage, encamped on the banks of a stream in Uinta County, Wyo., were surrounded by an armed body of settlers, numbering twenty-seven, who demanded of the Indians their arms. The Indians, upon surrendering their arms, were separated into two parties; the males, under a guard, were placed in the advance, while their families, pack animals, etc., also guarded, were placed in the rear about 50 yards.

The Indians, roughly treated, were driven throughout the day they knew not where, and as evening closed in the party approached a dense wood, upon which the leader of the settlers spoke to his men, and they examined their arms, loading all empty chambers. The Indian women and children, observing this action, commenced wailing, thinking the Indian men were to be killed, which idea prevailed among the Indian men, who passed the word one to another to run when the woods were reached.

Upon reaching the woods the Indians, concluding their last hour had come, made a break for liberty; whereupon the settlers without warning opened fire, the Indians seeing two of their number drop from their horses. During the mêlée the Indian women and children scattered in every direction, abandoning their pack animals.

The following morning the Indians, having gathered together, found they were minus two men and two papooses, and revisiting the scene of the shooting, could not find their people or their belongings, upon which they returned to the reservation, very fortunately meeting with other Indians who provided them with food.

One of the two men supposed to have been killed was recently discovered by scouts. He had been shot through the body from the back, the ball lodging in his left forearm, and he had crawled to a point several miles distant from the place of the shooting, subsisting for seventeen days upon the food which he had in his wallet at the time he was shot.

The body of the dead Indian was discovered in the woods near the place of the shooting, and, upon my recent visit to Jacksons Hole, Indian scouts were sent to bury the body. The Indians state of the man killed, an old man, that his horse's bridle was seized by a settler whilst another settler shot him down.

Of the two papooses lost one was found alive and taken to Fort Washakie by some Mormons; the other papoose, being only six months old, has undoubtedly perished.

A man named Smith reports having killed two Indians in Jacksons Hole. The truth of this report I was not able to ascertain, the settlers evincing an intensely bitter feeling toward me, threats of hanging me, etc., being made, and refusing to give me the desired information.

General Coppinger stated he would thoroughly investigate the Smith affair before he left Jacksons Hole, for me.

I have the names of the twenty-seven settlers who were engaged in the killing of the 15th instant, and I will respectfully recommend that this affair be investigated by the Department of Justice with a view to the prosecution of the guilty parties.

I have recently given much thought tending to a permament solution of this vexed Indian question, and can reach no definite conclusion which would not require Congressional action.

The governor of Wyoming assuring settlers that they would be backed by him in their efforts to drive the Indians out and in keeping the Indians out of Wyoming, in my opinion, renders some decisive action imperatively necessary before the troops leave Jacksons Hole. The Indians, considering their treaty rights give to them the privilege of hunting in certain sections of Wyoming, will go hunting after harvest with or without my consent.

No report has yet been received from the authorities of the State of Wyoming as to this matter, but for the purposes of history I deem it proper to quote at length an article in New York Evening Post of August 2, which purports to give a true account of the killing, as follows:

It turns out as we had anticipated. At all events a war correspondent of the World, who has penetrated to the seat of hostilities, so reports. He has interviewed a number of people at Jacksons Hole, including the man who did the shooting or ordered it to be done. From these sources of information it is learned that on the 7th of June a report came in that certain Bannocks were shooting elk in violation of the game laws of Wyoming. A warrant was issued for their arrest and placed in the hands of Constable William Manning, who selected twelve deputies and started out to find the trespassers. They found one Indian, named George, with several green hides in his possession. He was brought in, put on trial, convicted, and fined $15. The fine was paid, and the hides were confiscated.

On the 24th of June news came of further hunting by Indians. Another expedition was fitted out for their arrest, but they were found to be in such large numbers that it was deemed imprudent to attempt to bring them in. The constable and his men, however, moved freely among them and ordered them to desist, but according to the report which they brought back the trespassers were saucy and said they would hunt as much as they pleased.

Another attempt to arrest them was made on the 10th of July, when Manning started out with twenty-five deputies. They surprised an Indian camp at Fall River basin and arrested the male members, ten in number. All the parties, constables and Indians, and also the squaws, were mounted. The Indians were disarmed and placed in such a way that each one was preceded and followed by an armed white man, while armed white men rode alongside at certain intervals. Manning says that he had reason to think that the prisoners would try to escape, and that he gave orders if they did so to shoot their horses. Being asked if he gave orders to shoot the horses but not the Indians, he said "No; I said nothing about the Indians themselves; I simply said to shoot the horses first. The men understood that they had a right to shoot the Indians if there was no other means of preventing an escape." Then the following colloquy took place, which puts the matter in a perfectly clear light:

"Do I understand that the Indians were arrested, charged with an offense the maximum penalty for which is a fine of $10 and three months' imprisonment; that the men had not been tried, and that you consider that, in the event of their attempting to escape from your custody, you had the right to kill them?"

"I would consider that my right, particularly with Indians, they being savages and likely to do harm themselves and to resist with arms. I believe I would have the right, considering this, to order the men to shoot them."

"But I understand you to say you had satisfied yourself that they had no arms upon them?"

"That is correct as near as we could determine as to their having arms."

The sequel is already known. An attempt was made to escape. The Indians were shot, some killed, some wounded, but no horse was hurt; that would have been a wanton waste of property.

This is the white man's side of the case. The Indians have not been heard yet, except that one of them who was wounded tried to conceal the fact lest he should be put to death also. If the facts are correctly reported this was a case of massacre with premeditation. We trust that all the means at the disposal of the Indian Rights Association as well as the means at the disposal of the Government will be employed to bring the assassins to justice. As to the "Bannock war," there is no such thing. The Bannocks are only a handful, and they have lived at peace with the whites for seventeen years. The survivors of them are only anxious to save their own lives, and well they may be, considering how the white man's law is executed in Wyoming.

From unofficial sources it is known that the Indians returned to their reservation before the United States troops reached the "scene of devastation."

As the truth became known, there came a rapid change of public sentiment in favor of the Indians, who were found to be the wronged parties, and against the lawless whites who had done all the killing that occurred at Jacksons Hole. Instead of the Bannocks declaring war, massacring whites, burning homes, with settlers fleeing for their lives etc., they have, in the opinion of this office, been made the victims of a planned Indian outbreak by the lawless whites infesting the Jacksons Hole country with the idea of causing their extermination or their removal from that neighborhood. The Bannocks while peaceably hunting in that country were arrested by whites, who disarmed them and killed or shot several while they were trying to escape. Much to the credit of the incensed Indians, they returned peaceably to their reservation without retaliating in any manner upon the whites. Not a white person was harmed, nor did they indulge in any act of violence toward the settlers.

The newspapers throughout the country and many prominent and philanthropic persons have denounced this killing of Indians by the whites in Jacksons Hole as an outrage and murder which should not be allowed to go unpunished, and they have urged that a searching official investigation be made by the Government of this entire affair, to the end that the guilty whites may be brought to justice.

The Bannocks themselves have repeatedly been promised that their wrongs should be thoroughly investigated and justice done them by the Government, and doubtless these assurances have had much to do in keeping them quiet thus far. There are, however, some of them that are eager for revenge upon the whites for the killing of their people, as is shown by the following telegram of August 14 from Agent Teter:

Certain Indians state they will go to Jacksons Hole for purpose of hunting as soon as haying season is over, claiming they will starve during the coming winter if they do not kill game at this season for winter subsistence, and that they have a right to hunt in Jacksons Hole. In my opinion it is absolutely necessary to keep the Indians on the reservation even if they are justified in going to Jacksons Hole, as they seem determined to have revenge upon settlers. Will go prepared for that purpose, and are discussing plans to that end.

The best solution of this affair I can present is to enter into the contract for the big ditch on the reservation as soon as possible, which will give the Indians employment and an opportunity to earn money with which to provide for themselves through the winter. The Indians must be given employment or increased rations, as they can not subsist without food obtained from hunting until water is put on the reservation, when they will be practically self-supporting.

Will request you to wire me what I can state to the Indians relative to increased rations or employment should they remain on the reservation.

In reply this office telegraphed the agent, August 16, the following:

Tell the Indians I do not want them to go off the reservation hunting this summer or fall, but want them to remain at home and continue their work, and if they will do this, I will increase their rations when needed and called for by you to keep them through the winter.

I also want to have work on Idaho Canal begun before long so that Indians can get employment and be paid for it. The friends of the Indians all over the country are watching the conduct of the Indians with deep interest and are anxious that they comply with my wishes and plans, knowing that I will do what is best for them. If they break away from me and do not permit me to manage for them, they will lose their friends and the mistake will be disastrous to them.

In reply to the above telegram the agent reported, August 20, as follows:

In reply to your telegram of the 16th instant relative to increasing the Indians' rations and giving them employment, I have the honor to respectfully recommend that the Indians of this agency be given increased rations at once and employment as soon as possible.

The Indians at present receive the following rations weekly: 2,880 pounds flour; 4,800 pounds beef, gross, or 2,300 pounds beef, net; 150 pounds sugar; 75 pounds coffee.

According to the census taken for the fiscal year ending June 30, 1895, the Indians on this reservation number 1,440, and I will respectfully recommend the above table of rations be increased as follows, on the basis of weekly issues: 5,040 pounds flour, or 3½ pounds per individual; 14,400 pounds beef, gross, or about 5 pounds net, per individual; 480 pounds sugar, or one-third pound per individual; 240 pounds coffee, or one-sixth pound per individual.

Should the recommended increase in rations meet with your approval, I will respectfully request you to telegraph me authority to issue same.

This office, in reply to the agent's request, sent him the following telegram, August 31:

Issue rations as requested in your letter of 20th. Report how long increase is to continue, how long present supply will last at increased rate. Estimate for what additional supply will be needed.

The agent, as requested, made the desired estimate for the additional supply of rations on September 3, and was advised by this office September 12, 1895, as follows:

You are advised that the superintendent of the New York Indian warehouse has this day been directed to order, under existing contracts, the following articles (called for in your estimate of 3rd instant), and to ship them to your agency (for issue to Indians during current fiscal year) at the earliest practical date, viz: 13,000 pounds sugar; 6,500 pounds coffee; 540 pounds baking powder, in one-quarter pound tins.

The Honorable Secretary of the Interior has also been requested to authorize you to publish an advertisement inviting proposals for furnishing and delivering the gross beef and flour called for in said estimate, and when said authority shall have been granted you, you will be duly notified.

The gross beef and flour contracts will be increased 25 per cent, as requested, and you will be informed when contractors are notified.

The authority above referred to was granted in Department letter of September 14, and the agent duly notified of the same September 17.

To briefly summarize the facts in the case so far as is shown by the official reports that have reached this office: The Bannock and Shoshone Indians have been in the habit for many years past of going to the Jacksons Hole country to hunt game for subsistence. They have been guaranteed by treaty with the United States the right to hunt upon the unoccupied lands of the United States so long as game may be found thereon and so long as peace subsists among the whites and Indians on the borders of the hunting districts. The settlers of the country bordering this game region have looked upon the said hunting grounds as their own exclusive property, and for the past two years have been steadily complaining through official and unofficial sources to this office to the end that the Indians might be kept out. The Indians, through their respective agents, have been repeatedly warned against the wanton killing of game. Further, the settlers have claimed that the Indians hunted and killed game in violation of the game laws of the State of Wyoming; and it would appear that they had at last organized a scheme to drive the Indians from these hunting grounds regardless of consequences.

The first serious affair occurred on or about July 15, 1895, when a hunting party of nine Bannocks with their families, encamped on the banks of a stream in Uinta County, Wyo., were surrounded by an armed body of settlers, numbering twenty-seven, who disarmed all of the Indians and "drove" them all day in single file closely guarded. In the evening the Indians, who had been roughly treated during the day, became frightened, and supposing they were all to be shot, made a dash for their liberty. The settlers without any warning fired upon them, killing one outright and badly wounding another. Two papooses were lost, one of which was afterwards found alive, the other no doubt having perished, or been killed.

The Shoshone and Bannock Indians have the right under their treaty of July 3, 1868 (15 *Stats.*, 673), to hunt on unoccupied lands of the United States, the fourth article of which treaty provides as follows:

The Indians herein named agree, when the agency house and other buildings shall be constructed on their reservations named, they will make said reservations their permanent home and they will make no permanent settlement elsewhere; but they shall have the right to hunt on the unoccupied lands of the United States so long as game may be found thereon and so long as peace subsists among the whites and Indians on the borders of the hunting districts.

The Shoshone and Bannock Indians know nothing about what is known now in the game laws of the various States as a "close season," during which hunting is prohibited by law. Their treaty must be construed therefore as to mean that these Indians should have the right to hunt on unoccupied lands of the United States where game may be found and at any and all times of the year. The laws of the State of Wyoming which prohibit hunting within that State for certain kinds of game during certain months must be construed in the light of the treaty granting rights to these Indians to hunt on the unoccupied lands within the State, so far as they apply to the Shoshone and Bannock Indians. It is not competent for the State to pass any law which would modify, limit, or in any way abridge the right of the Indians to hunt as guaranteed by the treaty. The fact, as shown in the official correspondence above quoted, that the Bannock Indians, against whom complaint was made and against whom the people of Jacksons Hole country have been so threatening in their demonstrations, were encamped 35 or 40 miles from any settlement in a wild and almost impenetrable country would indicate that this section of country was unoccupied lands of the United States, and that the Indians therefore had a perfect right, and violated no law, in being there to hunt game for subsistence.

It is shown by the official reports from Agent Teter and army officers that the Bannock Indians were not engaged in a wanton killing of game, but that they were in that section of country for the purpose of hunting for subsistence and to prepare against the approaching winter. This they had a perfect right to do, and the action of the authorities of Wyoming in arresting some of them under provisions of the laws of that State and imposing fines under said laws was unlawful, as was held by the Supreme Court in Hauenstein v. Lynham: "If the law of a State is contrary to a treaty it is void." Therefore for the purpose to which the laws of Wyoming were applied by the authorities of that State, viz, to prohibit the Bannock Indians from hunting on unoccupied lands of the United States therein and to punish them therefor, the game laws of the State of Wyoming are absolutely null and void, and the authorities of the State took this action on their own responsibility and were trespassers on the rights of the Indians to that extent. (See Poindexter v. Greenhow, Virginia coupon cases, 114 U. S., 270.) The fines imposed upon them, the confiscation of their property, and the imprisonment of some are all illegal, for which the United States would seem to be responsible to the Indians under article 1 of the said treaty of 1868, which provides, among other things, as follows:

> If bad men among the whites, or any other people subject to the authority of the United States, shall commit any wrong upon the person or property of the Indians, the United States will, upon proof made to the agent and

forwarded to the Commissioner of Indian Affairs at Washington City, proceed at once to cause the offenders to be arrested and punished according to the laws of the United States, and also reimburse the injured person for the loss sustained.

If, as seems to me to be the case under the decisions of the Supreme Court, the laws of the State of Wyoming under which these arrests were made, and fines, confiscations, and imprisonments imposed, are void for the purpose, the acts of the authorities of Wyoming in this regard are to be construed in the same light as if they had been the acts of persons not holding any official relation to the government of the State, and as wrongs committed upon the person and property of the Indians by the people subject to the jurisdiction of the United States, and therefore this Government might be held responsible under the treaty.

It appears from reports that the Indians not only suffered arrests, fines, loss of their property, and imprisonment, but that one at least of them lost his life at the hands of these white people, alleged officers of the State of Wyoming; another was wounded and one child was lost, probably perished in the forests. The killing of this Indian can not be held to be anything less than murder, for it appears from the most reliable accounts received in this office that the so-called deputy sheriffs had, in anticipation of an attempt to escape, agreed between them to shoot their prisoners, although they had been arrested and charged with simply a misdemeanor punishable by a small fine under the laws of the State. The Indians say that when they made their break for liberty they were led to believe by the action of their captors that they were preparing to kill them, and it seems from the newspaper clipping above quoted from the New York Evening Post, that the apprehensions of the Indians were not without some ground, for the officer in charge of the deputies stated that he considered that he had a right to kill an Indian who had been arrested for an offense the maximum penalty for which is a fine of $10 and three months' imprisonment if such Indian attempted to escape, even though he had not been tried.

Recommendation was made in my report of August 17, 1895, that the entire matter be referred to the Department of Justice with the request that a thorough and exhaustive investigation be made into the affair with the view to taking such action as might be deemed expedient and lawful for the punishment of the parties guilty of wronging the Indians.

The case was submitted to the Attorney-General of the United States, who stated, August 23 last, that he had telegraphed the United States attorney for Wyoming, directing him to apply for writs of habeas corpus in case any Indians were confined at Evanston by the State authorities; and that he was not aware of any law under which the Department of Justice could assist in obtaining redress for the Indians who had paid their fines, "or in punishing, civilly or criminally, the persons who have done them injury, even the murderers."

August 30, 1895, the Acting Attorney-General stated that he was informed by the United States attorney for the district of Wyoming August 23, 1895, that he had been unable to learn that any Indians were then under confinement for alleged violation of Wyoming game laws, and that the Bannock Indians who had been imprisoned had been allowed to escape by the authorities at Marysvale. In regard to a report concerning the outrages on the Indians made to him by one of the Government employees in Wyoming, whom he regarded as capable, observant, and trustworthy, the district attorney said:

> From the statements made by him, and from other sources of information, I have no doubt whatever that the killing of the Indian Ta ne ga on, on or about the 13th of July, was an atrocious, outrageous, and cold-blooded murder, and that it was a murder perpetrated on the part of the constable, Manning, and his deputies in pursuance of a scheme and conspiracy on their part to prevent the Indians from exercising a right and privilege which is, in my opinion, very clearly guaranteed to them by the treaty before mentioned.

The Acting Attorney-General, in closing, said: "There is, however, unfortunately no statute of the United States under which this Department can afford any assistance." He inclosed a copy of the report in the case forwarded by the United States district attorney, which reads as follows:

> A careful investigation of the whole affair will, I am certain, result in showing the correctness of the following statements, which are made after personally interviewing a number of the leading participants in the trouble, both among the Indians and the Jacksons Hole settlers, and by noting the exact condition of affairs in the region relative to the habits of the Indians, the settlers, etc.
>
> First, I desire to state that the reports made by settlers charging the Indians with wholesale slaughter of game for wantonness or for the purpose of securing the hides of the animals killed have been very much exaggerated. During my stay in Jacksons Hole I visited many portions of the district and saw no evidences of such slaughter. Lieutenants Gardner, Parker, and Jackson, of the Ninth United States Cavalry, who conducted scouting parties of troops through all portions of Jacksons Hole, also found this to be the case. No carcasses or remains of elk were found in quantities to justify such charges. On August 12 I visited a camp of Bannock Indians who had been on a hunting trip in Jacksons Hole until ordered by the troops to return to their reservation. I found the Indian women of the party preparing the meat of seven or eight elk for winter use, drying and "jerking" it. Every particle of flesh had been taken from the bones, even the tough portions of the neck being preserved. The sinews and entrails were saved, the former for making threads for making gloves and clothing, and the latter for casings. The hides were being prepared for tanning; the brains had been eaten; some of the bones had been broken and the marrow taken out and others were being kept to make whip handles and pack-saddle crosstrees. In fact every part of the animal was being utilized either for future food supply or possible source of profit.
>
> Second. In connection with the troubles between the Indians and the whites, I spent some time inquiring into the causes for the unconcealed hostility of the Jacksons Hole people against the Indians. I found little or no complaint among the settlers of offensive manners on the part of the Indians.

Except in rare instances they have kept away from the houses of the settlers and have not been in the habit of begging. In no instance has there ever been a well-authenticated case where a settler has been molested by an Indian.

About twenty-five of the Jacksons Hole settlers are professional guides for tourists and hunting parties visiting the region from other States and from abroad. The business is very profitable, guides sometimes making sufficient money in the short hunting season to keep them through the remainder of the year. These guides, while most of them have small ranches, make stock raising, or the cultivation of their places, a secondary consideration, and make the business of guiding tourists, or "dudes" as they are called in the region, their principal occupation. The killing of game by the Indians and by the increasing number of "dude" hunters threatens to so deplete the region of big game, deer, elk, moose, etc., as to jeopardize the occupation of the guides.

It was decided at the close of last season to keep the Indians out of the region this year, and the events of this summer are the results of carefully prepared plans. Mr. Pettigrew, United States commissioner at Marysvale, said: "At our last election the question of keeping out the Indians was the most important one we had to deal with, and the township officers elected, constable and justice of the peace, were selected because we knew they would take decided steps to help us keep the Indians out." Constable Manning said: "We knew very well when we started in on this thing that we would bring matters to a head. We knew some one was going to be killed, perhaps some on both sides, and we decided the sooner it was done the better, so that we could get the matter before the courts."

Third. If a full investigation of the Jacksons Hole affair should be had the fact will be established that when Constable Manning and his posse of 26 settlers arrested a party of Indians on July 13 and started with them for Marysvale, he and his men did all they could to tempt the Indians to try to escape in order that there might be a basis of justification for killing some of them. On July 4 a party of eight Bannocks was arrested on Rock Creek near the head of Green River and taken to Marysvale, where six of the party were fined $75 each and costs, the total amount of fines and costs being about $1,400. This the Indians were unable to pay, and they were placed under guard to await instructions as to their disposal. The county authorities from whom the information was asked failed to reply to the inquiries of the Jacksons Hole officers, who at once relaxed guard duty over the Indians who escaped from custody.

The next arrest of Indians was made July 13. Constable Manning and 26 deputies surrounded a camp of 10 bucks and 13 squaws at night, and early in the morning with guns leveled at the Indians made the arrest, the Indians offering no resistance. The arrest was made on Fall River, 55 miles from Marysvale. The warrant was for Bannock and Shoshone Indians, the names and number of the Indians to be arrested not being stated. After the arrest was made, the arms, meat, and other articles in the possession of the Indians were taken from them. Constable Manning also took their passes, ration checks, etc. These papers gave the names and residences of most of the Indians. From an interview with Nemits, an Indian boy, who was one of the party of Indians arrested and shot, and from interviews with several of Mr. Manning's posse, I learned that the constable and his men told the Indians some of them would be hung and some would be sent to jail and that this was believed by the Indians. The constable also said in the hearing of the Indians, some of whom understood English, that if the Indians attempted to escape the men should shoot their horses.

If the truth of the matter can be reached it will be found that the captors did not care particularly about getting their prisoners safely to Marysvale, where the same formality of fining them and then having to let them escape would result, as in the previous case, but on the contrary tempted the Indians to try to escape, first, by making them believe if they tried to escape their horses only, and not they, would be shot. The Indians are in many respects like children, and are very credulous. They believed the threats of being sent to jail and of being hung were true, and they saw no trick in Manning's instructions, given in their hearing, to shoot their horses if they tried to get away.

In an interview with Constable Manning he was asked why he did not tie the Indians on their horses and thus effectively prevent their escape. He said in reply: "The trail was a dangerous one and if a horse fell the Indian tied on might get hurt and I would have been censured." Asked why it was necessary to kill the escaping prisoners when he knew their names and addresses and could have subsequently obtained his prisoners by going to the Fort Hall Agency for them, he said: "The agent would probably refuse to give up the Indians if any demand were made for them."

From Mr. Manning I learned that none of the horses of the escaping party of Indians were shot, notwithstanding his order, but that at least six Indians were hit by bullets. Of these, Timeha, an old man, was killed; Nimits, a boy of about 20, was wounded so that he could not escape, and the others got away. Constable Manning said to me: "The old Indian was killed about 200 yards from the trail. He was shot in the back and bled to death. He would have been acquitted had he come in and stood his trial, for he was an old man, almost blind, and his gun was not fit to kill anything."

When the body of this old, sick, blind man was found after lying unburied in the woods for about twenty days it was found he had been shot four times in the back. The boy, Nemits, who was wounded, was shot through the body and arm. He was left on the ground where the shooting occurred, and remained there, living on some dried meat for ten days. He crawled for three nights to reach a ranch of a man friendly to Indians, and was seventeen days without medical attendance.

The whole affair was, I believe, a premeditated and prearranged plan to kill some Indians and thus stir up sufficient trouble to subsequently get United States troops into the region and ultimately have the Indians shut out from Jacksons Hole. The plan was successfully carried out and the desired results obtained. It would, however, be but an act of simple justice to bring the men who murdered the Indian, Timeha, to trial. I would state, however, in this connection that there are no officials in Jacksons Hole—county, State, or national—who would hold any of Manning's posse for trial. Either the anti-Indian proclivities of these officials or the fear of opposing the dominating sentiment of the community on this question would lead them to discharge all of these men should they be brought before them for a hearing.

August 19, 1895, Agent Teter telegraphed this office as follows:

Bannock Indians are very sullen and very much dissatisfied. Have recently had several brawls with whites, and if another Indian is killed an outbreak is liable to occur; and I will advise as a precautionary measure that soldiers be stationed on reservation until Indians quiet down. Signal fires have been burning on the highest points of the reservation for several nights.

Your telegram promising Indians increased rations and employment did not placate them. They still demand privilege of hunting.

The War Department was thereupon advised of this information, which was transmitted to Brigadier-General Coppinger, who stationed a small military force on the reservation, to remain until the Indians become quieted down.

On August 26, 1895, the agent telegraphed:

> Consider it necessary for purpose of allaying discontent among Indians to send party of Indians into Jacksons Hole to obtain their property held by settlers, and will request authority to have an employee accompany them. Answer.

This was also submitted to the War Department for an opinion as to the advisability of allowing these Indians to go to the scene of the late troubles for the purposes indicated. The Secretary of War, September 7, 1895, stated that the matter had been referred to Brig. Gen. J. J. Coppinger, commanding Department of the Platte, who reported as follows:

> These Bannocks have an undoubted right to seek their property illegally held by white men in Jacksons Hole. If the Bannocks go there without proper guard they run risk of being again shot at, or again arrested under cover of warrant, by the rustlers. The commanding officer of the troops now at Fort Hall Agency can furnish the necessary men for guard or escort. If these Bannocks go to Jacksons Hole they should be placed in charge of a discreet and experienced employee of the Indian Bureau; one accustomed to deal with both Indians and rustlers; this in order to guard against further bloodshed and consequent complications.

The Secretary of War concurred in the views expressed by Brigadier-General Coppinger, and this office therefore instructed Agent Teter, on September 14, 1895, that a party of not to exceed eight Bannocks might be permitted to make the proposed trip to recover their property taken by whites, provided they were accompanied by himself or a trusted and competent agency employee, and by a proper escort of soldiers. Recommendation was therefore made that the War Department be requested to issue such orders as might be necessary for the required escort of United States troops.

In view of the provisions contained in Article I of the treaty of the United States with these Indians, this office, August 27, 1895, addressed the following letter to their agent:

> Article 1 of the treaty with the Eastern Band of Shoshones and the Bannock tribe of Indians, concluded July 3, 1868 (15 Stats., 673), provides as follows:
>
> . . . "If bad men among the whites, or among other people subject to the authority of the United States, shall commit any wrong upon the person or property of the Indians, the United States will, upon proof made to the agent and forwarded to the Commissioner of Indian Affairs at Washington City, proceed at once to cause the offender to be arrested and punished according to the laws of the United States, and also reimburse the injured person for the loss sustained." . . .

I desire you to obtain, at the earliest practicable date, such proof as you may be able to procure of the wrongs committed upon the persons and property of the Bannock Indians in the Jacksons Hole country, and forward the same to this office. Affidavits of the Indians against whom the offenses were committed and of eyewitnesses, or persons knowing to the facts, will answer the purpose.

The agent replied September 3, 1895, transmitting two affidavits from certain of the Indians, which read as follows:

COUNTY OF BINGHAM, *State of Idaho, ss:*

Personally before me appeared Ravenel MACBETH, who, being duly sworn, deposeth and says that he is employed as chief clerk at Fort Hall Agency, Idaho, and while on duty in that capacity he accompanied U. S. Indian Agent Thomas B. Teter to Marysvale (Jacksons Hole), Uintah County, Wyoming, to assist in conducting an investigation relative to the killing of certain Bannock Indians by citizens of the State of Wyoming; that in an official conversation with one Frank H. Rhoads, justice of the peace, he (Rhoads) said to me that before issuing warrants for the arrest of the Bannock Indians who were hunting in Wyoming, he (Rhoads) wrote to Governor Richards, of Wyoming, requesting instructions and asking if he (Rhoads) could depend upon him (Governor Richards) to protect him (Rhoads) in the event of trouble with the United States authorities over the arrest of said Bannock Indians; and that said Governor Richards wrote him (Rhoads), "directing him to enforce the laws of Wyoming, to put the Indians out of Jackson's Hole, and to keep them out at all costs, to depend upon him for protection, and that he (Governor Richards) would see him through," whereupon he (Rhoads) acted. Further deponent saith not.

RAVENEL MACBETH

Subscribed and sworn to before me this 3d day of September, 1895.

P. H. RAY
Captain, Eighth Infantry,
Summary Court Officer.

Witness:
DAN'L T. WELLS
Captain, Eighth Infantry.

Fort Hall Agency, Idaho.

COUNTY OF BINGHAM, *State of Idaho, ss:*

Personally appeared before me Ben Senowin, a Bannock Indian, who, being duly sworn, deposeth and says: That he is the head of a clan, and that on or about July 15, 1895, while hunting on unoccupied Government lands east of Jacksons Hole, in the county of Uinta, State of Wyoming, under a pass from the U.S. Indian agent at Fort Hall Agency, and provisions of article 4 of the treaty with the Shoshones (Eastern band) and Bannock Indians, dated July 3, 1868, and ratified February 16, 1869, in company with Nemuts, Wa ha she go, Ya pa ojo, Poo dat, Pah goh zite, Mah mout, Se we a gat, Boo wah go, thirteen women and five children, all Bannock Indians, were, while in camp, feloniously assaulted and by force of arms attacked by a party of twenty-seven white men, and having been made under threat of death to give up all of their arms, consisting of seven rifles and ammunition, were marched thirty miles, more or less, in the direction of the white settlement; that during the afternoon of the aforesaid date, while passing through a belt of timber, the deponent saw several of the white men placing cartridges in their rifles and believing his own life and the lives of the members of his party to be in danger, called upon his people to run and escape, whereupon the white men, without just cause or provocation, commenced to fire with rifles loaded with ball cartridges upon him, the deponent, and his people; that he, the deponent, saw one Indian named Se we a gat fall dead, killed by said fire, and one Nemuts wounded, and that one infant was lost while they were escaping and has not since been found; and deponent further saith himself and his party were by force of arms of said party of white men and by threats of instant death feloniously deprived and robbed of the following articles of personal property, to wit: Seven rifles, twenty saddles, twenty blankets, one horse, nine packs of meat, and nine tepees, more or less; and deponent further saith that neither he or any of his people were told why or by what authority they were assaulted; that he is not aware that either he or any of his party had committed any offense against the laws of any State or the United States; or that he or any of his party ever attempted or offered any violence, or had made any threats against the life or property of any white man; that the white man never gave him or his party any hearing, or asked him or his party any questions through an interpreter or otherwise; that neither he or any of his party were ever called upon to answer or plead in any court of justice or make answer to any charge whatsoever.

BEN (his x mark) SENOWIN.

Sworn and subscribed to before me this 1st day of September, 1895.

P. H. RAY
Captain, Eighth Infantry,
Summary Court Officer.

Witness:
  RAVENEL MACBETH.

Fort Hall Agency, Idaho.

COUNTY OF BINGHAM, *State of Idaho, ss.*

Personally appeared before me Nemuts, Boo wah go, Ya pa ojo, Mah mout, Wa ha she go, Poodat, and Pah goh zite, Bannock Indians, who, being duly sworn, deposeth and say that they have heard the interpreter read to them the foregoing affidavit of Ben Senowin; that they were there present and know of their own knowledge the statement set forth is true to the best of their knowledge and belief.

NEMUTS (his x mark).
BOO WAH GO (his x mark).
YA PA OJO (his x mark).
MAH MOUT (his x mark).
WA HA SHE GO (his x mark).
POO DAT (his x mark).
PAH GOH ZITE (his x mark).

Sworn and subscribed to before me this 1st day of September, 1895.

P. H. RAY
Captain, Eighth Infantry,
Summary Court Officer.

Witnesses:
RAVENEL MACBETH.
TOMMY COSGROVE.
DAN'L T. WELLS,
    Captain, Eighth Infantry.
Fort Hall Agency, Idaho.

Report was thereupon made to the Department September 11, 1895, inclosing a copy of the above affidavits.

As shown by Article I, heretofore quoted, of the treaty of these Indians with the United States, concluded July 3, 1868 (15 *Stats.*, 673), this Government is bound, under the said treaty provisions, to cause the offenders' arrest and punishment according to the laws of the United States, and also to reimburse the injured persons for loss sustained. The proof necessary, as stipulated in the said Article I, is now before the Department, and, in the opinion of this office, no means should be left untried and no efforts be spared by the Department to the end that the treaty provisions with these Indians may be faithfully carried out and good faith kept with them on the part of the Government.

In view of the above, and of the fact that these Indians are still sullen and very much dissatisfied with the action already had in the case, and urge that the guilty whites be punished, it was submitted in my said report of September 11, 1895, whether or not something could be done by the Department of Justice toward punishing the offenders.

Report of Commissioner of
Indian Affairs D. M. Browning
September 15, 1896

(Excerpt from *Report for 1896*, pp. 56-70)

The legal resolution of the Jackson Hole disturbances, described in Commis-
sioner Browning's report for the previous year, was equally disastrous for
the natives. Although the Indians won a test case in the United States
Circuit Court—which declared invalid the Wyoming laws infringing on the
treaty rights of the Indians and which upheld their right to hunt game on the
unoccupied state public lands in and out of season—the decision was
appealed to the Supreme Court and there reversed.

DISTURBANCES IN JACKSONS HOLE COUNTRY, WYOMING

THE KILLING BY white men of three members of a peaceable hunting party
of Bannocks in the Jacksons Hole country, Wyoming, in July, 1895, and the
arrest, fining, imprisonment, and confiscation of property of other Bannocks, all because of their violation of Wyoming game laws, were narrated
at length in my last report. For convenient reference hereafter I have
deemed it wise to add this year a detailed account of what has since
occurred relating to this affair, including the decision of the Supreme Court
in the case. The Indians were hunting for subsistence under their treaty of
July 3, 1868, but in the test case brought before it the Supreme Court
decided that the treaty right of the Shoshones and Bannocks of the Fort
Hall and Wind River reservations to hunt in the Jacksons Hole country was
terminated by the admission of Wyoming Territory into the Union as a
State.

September 11, 1895, this office submitted to the Department evidence,
received from the United States Indian agent of the Fort Hall Agency, of
the wrongs that had been committed upon the persons and property of the
Bannocks in the Jacksons Hole country; and asked, in view of article 1 of
the treaty of July 3, 1868, with these Indians, if something could not be
done by the Department of Justice toward punishing the offenders. September 24, 1895, the Attorney-General informed this Department that he had
"again taken under consideration the question of prosecuting the whites
who committed the outrages upon the Bannock Indians in the Jacksons
Hole country," and that the United States district attorney for Wyoming
had been instructed "to indict the parties and prosecute the case with
vigor."

Meantime this office, September 20, 1895, instructed Mr. Province McCormick, inspector United States Indian service, as follows:

> I am instructed by the honorable Secretary of the Interior to direct you to proceed to the State of Wyoming and to the Fort Hall Agency, in Idaho, as a representative of this Department, for the purpose of conferring with the governor of Wyoming and such other officials of said State, or other persons as may be necessary, relative to certain matters of importance in connection with the recent troubles between the Bannock Indians and the whites in what is known as the Jacksons Hole country, Wyoming.
>
> You will therefore proceed to Omaha, Nebr., so as to meet Brig. Gen. John J. Coppinger, U. S. A., in that city on the 26th instant and accompany him to Wyoming.
>
> In order that you may have full information of the facts relative to the late troubles between the Bannocks and whites, I briefly state the case as follows:

After a résumé of the case, substantially as contained in report of this Bureau for 1895, the letter continued—

> I desire you to confer with the governor of Wyoming with reference to the right of these Indians to hunt off their reservation in the territory in question and ascertain his views upon the subject. The actions of the lawless whites in this region should be clearly laid before him; so also should the treaty rights of these Indians, as held by this Department. You will state to him that this Department does not desire to have any trouble with the settlers; that it is anxious and willing to do everything it can to prevent the Indians under its charge from committing depredations upon the whites or annoying them in any way; but that it will insist on protecting the Indians in their rights guaranteed to them by the United States.
>
> In case the governor is unwilling to concede the rights of the Indians to hunt as above indicated, you will propose to him that there shall be a test case made and a decision arrived at as to the right of the Indians to hunt on public lands under their treaty, either by having an Indian arrested by the State officials for hunting, and an application brought by the United States attorney for Wyoming for a writ of habeas corpus for the release of such prisoner, or in some other way, and that he shall agree that in case it shall be decided that the Indians have a right to hunt, and that the laws of Wyoming are of no effect as against them, then, in that event, he, Governor Richards, shall, by all the means in his power, protect the Indians in such right; and on the other hand, if it shall be decided by the courts that the Indians have no right to hunt, in violation of the State laws, or, in other words, that the State laws operate to abridge or defeat their said treaty rights, then this Department will recommend to Congress that an agreement be made with them for the relinquishment of the rights guaranteed to them by the treaty of 1868, and which they claim and believe are still in full force.
>
> In case Governor Richards agrees to the above proposition and is willing to have such test case made, the Indian's arrest could be secured through proper consultation with the United States Indian agent of the Fort Hall Agency, in which case this office should be notified of such action in order that the United States district attorney for Wyoming might be properly instructed to proceed in the matter in the interest of the Government.
>
> After you shall have concluded your interviews with Governor Richards, and such other officials of the said State of Wyoming as you may deem

necessary, you will then proceed to Fort Hall Agency where you will, without causing too much inconvenience to the Indians, call a council and explain to them the action which this Department has taken in regard to the wrongs which they have suffered at the hands of the whites in the late Jacksons Hole affair. You should also let them know that this Government fully appreciates their case, sympathizes with them in their troubles, and is determined to do everything possible to right their wrongs. It might be well to call their attention also to the fact that this office and the honorable Secretary of the Interior willingly granted them increased rations, in order that they might not be compelled to suffer for want of food during the coming winter, and to save them the necessity of going into the Jacksons Hole country for the purpose of hunting, which the Department did not want them to do just at that time, in view of the excited state of the whites in this region.

Further, it might be well for you to add in your talk with them that they must be entirely willing and contented to let the matter of the punishment of the whites who killed one of their people and seriously wounded another rest in the hands of this Government, and that if they do not and undertake to seek revenge they will certainly lose the good will and support of this Government and their friends throughout the country.

While at the agency you should, for the information of this office, ascertain the feeling that now exists among the Indians in regard to this affair, whether or not they appear to be sullen and discontented, etc., as recently reported. You should also take note, so far as may be convenient, of the attitude of the officials of the State of Wyoming, and also of the settlers concerning this whole matter.

If you think best, and I am inclined to believe it would be, you may visit the United States district attorney for Wyoming and confer with him in regard to the proposed conference with Governor Richards, and ask him to go with you to the governor. From the strong position taken by the said district attorney as to the rights of the Indians, and his vigorous denunciation of the conduct of the whites in their treatment of them, together with his manifest zeal in the investigation made by him under direction of the Department of Justice, I feel sure that his assistance, counsel, and advice would be of very material aid to you in the matter, and that he will willingly cooperate with you in every proper way.

October 6, 1895, Inspector McCormick reported the result of his conference with the governor of Wyoming, as follows:

In company with the United States district attorney of Wyoming, General Coppinger, and several of the United States Army officers, the prearranged interview with Governor Richards took place in his office (September 29), with the results as shown by the correspondence forwarded from Cheyenne to the Department. Governor Richards in this conference was unwilling to concede the Indians any rights under their treaty to hunt in Wyoming, claiming that said treaty rights were abrogated by the laws. After considerable preliminary discussion he readily accepted the proposition to make a test case, strictly in accordance with my instructions, save that two Indians, instead of one, should be arrested. I readily accepted the suggestion after a consultation with the district attorney, Governor Richards, as shown by the correspondence, pledging himself to abide the decision of the courts and use his State machinery to enforce same. This part of my mission being successfully accomplished I proceeded on the following morning, September 30, to Fort Hall, arriving at midnight. Upon the following day, October 1, after consultation with Agent Teter, we made arrangements to secure two Indians, who filled the requirements for the test case. These two Indians, in charge of the agent with an interpreter, left the agency on October 2, arriving in Evanston, Wyo., October 3, where they now are.

In further compliance with my instructions, I called a council of the Bannocks and Shoshones on Saturday, October 5, this being ration day and most convenient to them. I pursued in this council a course as outlined in my instructions; I urged upon them to rely implicitly upon the Department for a redress of all their wrongs and grievances, pledging them that no effort would be spared to restore to them guaranteed rights and also the punishment of their murderers. After a talk lasting over an hour and then listening to their wrongs, I asked the head men individually if they intended to heed my advice and leave this whole matter to the Department. With one accord they all agreed. I think I can safely say that I have discovered no disposition on the part of a single Indian to undertake for himself any revenge, but that he is relying implicitly upon the Government to right him in this matter. There seems to be none of the soreness or sullenness that one would ordinarily expect to see after the perpetration of such a dastardly, cowardly, preconcerted, outrageous crime as was inflicted upon these defenseless persons by the so-called law officers of Wyoming.

My instructions state that I shall make a report of the action taken by me on this mission and the results thereof, etc.

I have given, as concisely as I could, my action and the results. Ordinarily I would stop here, but there is too much involved. I may be trespassing upon forbidden ground to make any recommendations as to the future settlement of this question, but being here upon the ground and foreseeing, as I believe, what will be the result, I can not refrain from making a suggestion, which sooner or later will be taken.

When this test case is decided, and the courts uphold (as I suppose they will) the treaty rights as guaranteed to these Indians, one point will be gained, a principle will be established, and that is all; but establishing the right of these Indians to hunt on public or unoccupied lands does not protect them in that right. . . . Therefore, I would respectfully suggest that means or steps be taken to treat with these Indians for the relinquishment of their treaty rights to hunt upon unoccupied land.

Following out the above instructions given to the inspector, Agent Teter telegraphed this office October 7, 1895, as follows:

Indians are in custody here for purpose of test case. Must have habeas corpus proceedings tried at once to avoid trouble by keeping them in custody. Please instruct United States attorney for Wyoming to proceed without delay. Answer at this point.

This telegram was submitted for Department consideration October 7, 1895, with recommendation that a copy of the same be transmitted to the Attorney-General, with request that the United States attorney for Wyoming be telegraphed to institute habeas corpus proceedings at once for the release of the Indians. October 7, 1895, the Attorney-General replied that he had telegraphed the United States attorney at Cheyenne "forthwith to issue writs of habeas corpus for the two Indians arrested for the test case."

The case was tried in the United States circuit court before Judge Riner, who, November 21, 1895, decided that the laws of Wyoming are invalid against the treaty rights of the Indians, and affirmed their right to hunt game on the unoccupied public lands of Wyoming in and out of season, and discharged Race Horse from custody. The case, however, was at once appealed by the attorney-general of Wyoming to the United States Supreme Court.

October 12, 1895, Agent Teter telegraphed this office: "I will request the withdrawal of troops from the Fort Hall Reservation, and [as] the Indians are quiet and peaceable." This telegram was communicated to the War Department, and November 1 the Secretary of War replied to the Department, as follows:

> I have the honor to acknowledge the receipt of your letter of the 15th ultimo, transmitting, for such action as may be deemed proper, a copy of a communication from the Commissioner of Indian Affairs, who states that, as the Indians of the Fort Hall Agency are quiet and peaceable, the agent requests the withdrawal of the troops from the agency, and to inform you that the commanding general, Department of the Platte, under date of the 21st ultimo, reports that it had been his intention to withdraw these troops prior to the end of the month, and that in view of your communication he has issued orders for their withdrawal without delay.

December 7, 1895, Agent Teter reported that the decision of the United States circuit court in the case of Race Horse was well understood by the Indians of the Fort Hall agency, and that in his opinion it would be absolutely necessary to adopt measures to settle the question of the hunting privilege of the Indians on unoccupied Government land, "in order to prevent a recurrence in the year 1896 of the Jacksons Hole troubles of the past July." He recommended the appointment of a commission to negotiate with the Indians for a relinquishment of their treaty rights to hunt on unoccupied public land. A provision to this effect was incorporated in the Indian appropriation act approved June 10, 1896.

May 25, 1896, the Supreme Court reversed the judgment of the circuit court, and directed the discharge of the writ and the remanding of the prisoner to the custody of the sheriff. . . .

June 17, 1896, the Attorney-General advised the Department that he had received a letter from the United States attorney for Wyoming, saying that Judge Riner desired that Race Horse, the Bannock Indian from Fort Hall Agency, who stood for the rights of his tribe in the test case, be brought before him on July 14, to be turned over to the State sheriff. As this was an agreed case to test the law, the Attorney-General said that it seemed to him that this poor Indian should not be further punished; and that as this Department made the arrangement with the State authorities for making this test case he would be glad if it would arrange with them to let the Indian go without further molestation. . . .

The Department on June 23, 1896, communicated with Governor Richards, of Wyoming, concerning the case, and on July 1, 1896, received his reply, as follows:

> I have the honor to acknowledge the receipt of your letter of June 23, 1896, inclosing letters from the Attorney-General and the Commissioner of Indian Affairs relating to the Bannock Indian, Race Horse. In these letters it is suggested that this Indian should not be further punished, as the case in which he is a defendant was an agreed case to test the law. The State has no intention of inflicting upon Race Horse the punishment to which he is liable under our statutes, but does desire to close up the case in such a way that he and all of the Indians who claimed hunting privileges under their treaty will understand that they have no such rights and are amenable to the authority of the State if they kill game in violation of our statutes.
>
> To accomplish this purpose, I believe it to be best to have Race Horse brought before Judge Riner upon July 14, as he desires, to be turned over to the sheriff of Uinta County, who will take him before Judge Knight, of the district court for that county. Upon this being done, I am assured by County and Prosecuting Attorney Hamm of Uinta County that he will at once move the discharge of the prisoner, and there is no doubt that Judge Knight will so order.
>
> I believe this course to be best both for the Indian Department and the State. Race Horse and the Indians who accompanied him were much pleased with Judge Riner's decision and returned to Fort Hall convinced that the State authorities had no power over them. It will be a difficult matter to get them to understand that the contrary is true while they are allowed to go unmolested and even uncensured for the violation of our laws. If their experience in this matter has taught them anything, it is that they are only amenable to the Federal authority. Upon the other hand, if Race Horse is brought back to the district court of Uinta County and Judge Knight informs him that he has the power to punish him for the offense he has committed, but upon this occasion will deal leniently with him and forgive him on account of his ignorance of the law, the lesson will be one that he and all other Indians will comprehend, and its effect will be to cause them to respect State and county authority, which will save the Department and the State a vast amount of trouble.
>
> I therefore respectfully request that Race Horse be returned to the custody of Sheriff Ward, of Uinta County, in accordance with the mandate of the Supreme Court.

July 27, 1896, Agent Teter reported that his clerk, Mr. Macbeth, had returned Race Horse on the 20th of July to the United States district court, and three days later had delivered him to the custody of Sheriff Ward, of Uinta County, who released the Indian on a $500 bond for his appearance upon September 7, 1896, the date of the next session of the district court of Uinta County; also that the clerk had given his personal check for the bond, from which he asked to be released, as he needed the money. The agent stated further, that he had been assured by County and Prosecuting Attorney Hamm of Uinta County, that owing to the good faith displayed by the Department in the matter, he would enter a nolle prosequi in the case as soon as Race Horse should be brought before Judge Knight, of the district court for Uinta County.

The agent therefore suggested that if I would give Judge Knight my assurance as Commissioner that the Indian would be returned to custody, he might make the bond nominal and thus release Mr. Macbeth from his obligation. August 7 I wrote Judge Knight assuring him that this Department would be responsible for the return to custody of Race Horse when needed, and asked that he make the bond nominal. I also advised County and Prosecuting Attorney Hamm of this action, and expressed the hope that the friendly relations which seem to have been established between the representatives of this Department and the local (Uinta County) authorities might continue, so that in the future harmonious action might forestall the misunderstandings and troubles so likely to occur between Indians and whites.

Report of Commissioner of
Indian Affairs W. A. Jones
September 10, 1897

(Excerpt from *Report for 1897*, pp. 63-65, 68-71, 80-88)

Three Indian-white confrontations are here excerpted from Commissioner Jones' annual report. In the first, peaceful Navajo herders were frightened off their range in the middle of winter by white sheep owners able to enlist the authority of the board of supervisors of Coconino County, Arizona Territory. In the second incident, the governor of Idaho panicked and put the machinery of white repression in motion in response to the complaint of a local settler irritated by the appearance of Indian families digging roots near his ranch. The final episode records the efforts of white agents of justice to bring to the bar of justice a Cheyenne Indian named Stanley whose wish it was to die with his warpaint on rather than subject himself to the humiliating toils of white law.

ASSAULT UPON NAVAJOES, ARIZONA

FROM A REPORT made to the Navajo Agency by Mr. J. C. Tipton, stationed at Tuba City, Ariz., it appears that January 18, 1897, the board of supervisors of Coconino County placed upon the records the following order:

> Ordered that it is hereby authorized to employ not more than 20 men, at a compensation of $2 per day and furnished, for the purpose of assessing the property of Navajo Indians within Coconino County.

On that date there were 16 Navajo families tending their flocks in a grazing district bounded on the east and north by the Little Colorado River, and on the west by the Colorado River, a portion of the tract being within the boundaries of the "Grand Canyon, National Park." On this national reserve most of the Indians were pasturing their stock on a tract of country which they had thus occupied for generations and which has never been surveyed. No copy of the order was served upon the sheriff of the county, who was ex-officio assessor, and the legal time for making assessments was several weeks later than the date of the order. Nevertheless, the very next day, January 19, the sheriff with an armed posse visited each of these 16 families and demanded that $5 for every 100 head of sheep owned by them be paid to him at once; failing to do so they were to move out immediately. The Navajoes had no money; their prayer for time in which to procure money or to ascertain their rights was denied, and in default of the payment of the arbitrary and unlawful sum fixed by the sheriff, the Indians were forced to gather up their belongings and move.

Snow was falling (a deep snow already covered the ground), the weather was bitter cold, and the ewes were lambing. The Indians pleaded for a reasonable time within which to remove, but were denied. Their houses and corrals were burned and they and their flocks were rounded up and pushed north toward the Little Colorado River with relentless haste, the posse keeping women, children, and animals in a fright by an intermittent fire from rifles and revolvers. When the river was reached it was found to be so deep as to require the sheep to swim. The posse surrounded the flocks and pushed them into the water, and nearly all the lambs, with many grown sheep, went down the stream or chilled to death after crossing, and many died afterward from the effects of exposure. The loss to the Indians was equivalent to several thousand dollars.

From the above facts it is apparent that the order for an assessment was a mere pretext, and that the real intention was the expulsion of the Navajoes from a region continuously used by them almost from time immemorial. Mr. Tipton believes this outrage to be the culmination of a scheme concocted by two sheep owners living in that locality (one of whom was a member of the board of supervisors), who desire to secure control of the entire range.

In forwarding the farmer's report the acting agent stated that on the 5th of January last the sheriff of Coconino County had been informed by him that the Indian Office had decided to allow the Navajoes to use the unsettled public lands until the development of the irrigation system should afford them sufficient tillable lands on their reservation. He recommended that suit be instituted for damages, and that the Indians be given permission to repasture their flocks where, for so many years, they have been accustomed to keep them.

June 24 last the matter was reported to the Department with request that it be carefully considered in order to determine whether the parties guilty of this unprovoked and cruel assault might not be held accountable therefor and be compelled to make restitution for the losses sustained by the Indians. A copy of office report was sent by the Department June 25 last to the Attorney-General with a view to instituting suit for damages against the officers of Coconino County. No reply has been received. On the same date a copy of office report was also sent to the governor of Arizona, who replied July 7, 1897, that he had written the sheriff of Coconino County, giving him a full statement of the complaints against him and demanding an explanation of his conduct.

It is hoped that the final result will be the restoration of the Indians to their former homes and restitution for their losses, and at least that there will be no further molestation of this peaceable Indian community.

*   *   *

INDIAN SCARE AT CAMAS PRAIRIE, IDAHO

June 28, 1897, the governor of Idaho telegraphed the Department as follows:

> Three hundred Indians from Fort Hall causing great anxiety among settlers on Camas Prairie. If same are not immediately recalled, trouble will ensue. Answer.

He also telegraphed Hon. Henry Heitfelt, United States Senator from Idaho, to the same effect, adding that his information was "from sheriff and settlers." The following day he telegraphed the Senator further, as follows:

> Complaints continue to-day. Fences are being burned and cattle killed. Indians come from Lemhi, Umatilla, Fort Hall, and Duck Valley reservations. They must disperse or trouble will soon follow. Answer.

On receipt of these alarming reports the Department telegraphed the Indian agents in charge of the reservations named for full reports, and at the same time requested the War Department to order military assistance to be sent the Fort Hall agent "to preserve order and protect lives and property of settlers, and return Indians to reservations if absent therefrom as reported." The governor of Idaho was informed by telegraph of this action.

July 1 the commanding general Department of the Platte telegraphed to the War Department that, on June 30, he had ordered "squadron Ninth Cavalry" to proceed from Fort Robinson to the scene of the alleged disturbance, but had suspended the movement of troops on receipt of information from Lieut. F. G. Irwin, acting Indian agent at Fort Hall, that the Indians at Camas Prairie were entirely peaceable and were there for the purpose of gathering camas root, and that there was absolutely no foundation for an Indian scare.

Lieutenant Irwin visited Camas Prairie, and telegraphed this office the following:

> July 1: Prominent citizens of Hailey (Idaho) and reliable settlers from Camas Prairie state that no Indian troubles exist in that vicinity. About forty Indians, including women and children, are there gathering camas (root), but have committed no violation of law as far as known here. One of these states that no disturbance of any kind has occurred. Only two are from Fort Hall Agency. No necessity for troops. Will report later when Indian police come in. No excitement here.
>
> July 2: Have brought in all Indians from Camas Prairie—forty-two, including women and children, chiefly from Lemhi. One band of twenty Shoshones had left for their homes in Bliss, Idaho, before my arrival. Will send rest to Fort Hall with Indian police. Passed through the Camas prairies and was informed by reliable ranchers in immediate vicinity of Indian camps that no depredations had been committed by Indians. The presence of

Indians in that region, and the fear that they might give trouble, is the only foundation for alarming reports sent out. Will report by letter from Fort Hall.

With his full report were forwarded clippings from the Wood River Times, a newspaper published in Hailey, Idaho, giving, as he stated, a substantially correct account of the "scare." His report is quoted herewith as a matter of record.

FORT HALL AGENCY, IDAHO, *July 5, 1897.*

SIR: I have the honor to submit the following report regarding alleged Indian depredations on the Camas prairies:

On the morning of June 29 the following telegram was received:

"BOISE, IDAHO, *June 28, 1897.*

"INDIAN AGENT,
Ross Fork, Idaho, via Pocatello:

"Three hundred Bannocks on Camas prairie reported dangerous. Recall them at once or trouble likely to follow. My information is from sheriff Blaine County. Answer.

FRANK STEUNENBERG,
Governor.

I at once began an investigation through the Indian police, and learned that some Indians from the Lemhi Agency and some living in the town of Bliss, Idaho, were gathering roots on the Camas prairies, as has been customary for years, and that three Shoshone families from this reservation were visiting them. Knowing these Indians to be inoffensive, and their principal men to be well known to the whites in that region, and also provided with excellent testimonials from the governor and others, I was convinced that the report was grossly exaggerated; however, I sent C. E. Stewart with Indian police to investigate and return any Fort Hall Indians who might be found there.

Telegrams similar to the above having been received from the Department June 30, I went to Hailey, Idaho, a town about 20 miles from Camas prairie, and there learned that all reports of Indian depredations were groundless. I visited their camps and found the Indians engaged in nothing more serious than digging camas roots and chasing ground squirrels, and totally unconscious of the alarm they were supposed to be causing. They told me that the settlers, men, women, and children freely visited their camps and exhibited no signs of fear or uneasiness. I questioned several ranchers in that vicinity, among them G. S. Humphrey, the originator of the alarming telegrams and petitions to the governor. All of them informed me that they knew of no instance of depredation or violation of law, but that such results were feared.

All Indians found on the prairie, 42 in number, including women and children, were brought into Hailey, and from there sent to Fort Hall under charge of Indian police. They could not see the justice of being forced to leave that country without gathering their winter supply of food, as has been their habit heretofore, but they quietly complied with my orders when assured it was the wish of the Department.

Almost the entire party belonged to the Lemhi Agency, only two families coming from this reservation, and not a Bannock among them. In addition to these Indians another band of about 20 Shoshones had been in the Camas prairies, but had gone to their homes in Bliss, Idaho, before my arrival.

I can imagine no motive for sending out such baseless reports other than the desire on the part of settlers to rid themselves of the annual presence of peaceful Indians by ascribing to them hostile qualities.

Very respectfully,

F. G. IRWIN, JR.,
First Lieutenant, Second Cavalry,
Acting Indian Agent.

* * *

DISTURBANCE AMONG INDIANS OF TONGUE RIVER AGENCY, MONTANA

For some time past there has been more or less friction between the Indians of the Northern Cheyenne Reservation, Mont., and the white cattlemen who have ranches near by. The Indians complained that the ranchers allow their stock to range over the reservation, and the cattlemen charged the Indians with killing their cattle while off the reservation. The facts show both parties to have been at fault.

Nothing serious occurred, however, until last May, when the dead body of a white sheep-herder in the employ of one Mr. Harringer, a ranchman, was found about 3 miles north of the reservation. The killing or murder of this man was at once charged to the Indians by the settlers and ranchmen, who became very much excited and armed themselves for the purpose of seeking revenge. Soon reports were current in the newspapers of an outbreak of the Northern Cheyennes.

May 25 Capt. G. W. H. Stouch, U. S. A., acting Indian agent of Tongue River Agency, reported that the man was undoubtedly killed by Indians belonging to the reservation and that he would make a thorough investigation to discover the perpetrators of the crime; that he did not fear an "outbreak" on the part of the Indians unless it were forced upon them by the whites, and that he had requested the commanding officer of Fort Custer to send two troops of cavalry to the agency to prevent trouble between the excited white settlers and the Indians. He recommended that a troop of cavalry be stationed on the reservation in place of the infantry men there, and June 1 this office recommended that the War Department be requested to send there three or four troops of cavalry.

May 31 Captain Stouch telegraphed that he had arrested an Indian known as "Stanley," who had confessed to the murder of the sheep-herder, and that he would turn him over to the civil authorities at any point outside the reservation which the sheriff of Custer County might designate. June 4 Stanley was taken by Captain Read, U. S. A., with one troop of cavalry as an escort, and was delivered to the sheriff at Rosebud Station, to be taken to Miles City, Mont., for incarceration and trial. June 11 Captain Stouch telegraphed that he had delivered to the civil authorities Yellow Hair and Sam Crow, as accomplices of Stanley, and that the Indians on the reservation were quiet, newspaper reports to the contrary notwithstanding.

July 31 this office recommended that, in view of the peaceable state of affairs, the War Department be asked to give the necessary orders for the withdrawal from the reservation of the infantry detachment and of all but one troop of cavalry; it also reported concerning the question of fencing the reservation in order to avoid most of the causes of contention between white cattlemen and the Indians.

The details of the arrest and delivery of Stanley are given in reports from Acting Agent Stouch, as follows:

TONGUE RIVER AGENCY, MONT.
June 5, 1897.

Hon. COMMISSIONER INDIAN AFFAIRS,
Washington, D. C.

SIR: I have the honor to report the condition of affairs at this agency as brought about by the murder of John Hoover, a white man, and by the capture of the murderer, David Stanley, a Cheyenne Indian. Under date of May 25 I made report to you of the finding of the body.

The body of the murdered man was found on the 23d of May, which was reported to me on the 24th. On the 25th I sent orders to White Bull for him and his band to come to the agency at once, as I was positive that this band held the murderer, their homes being in the vicinity of the crime. They arrived at the agency next day, the 26th, and I sent orders to White Bull to come to the office the next morning. He reported at the office the morning of the 27th. I told him what had happened, explained the whole matter of the killing and the finding of the body; that I, as well as everybody else, believed the murder to have been committed by a member or members of his band; that from circumstances it was very certain that three or more were concerned in the murder; that I would hold him responsible, and that he must find the murderers and turn them over to me for delivery to the civil authorities, they to do the punishing. I explained all fully to him and told him to return to his camp, select seven or eight of his head men; among others I told him to select Badger, Spotted Hawk, and Two Bull; that he was to tell them exactly what I had said, and for all to come to the office that evening for further consultation.

About noon the same day (the 27th) Sheriff Gibb, of Custer County, and about 25 armed men rode up to the office and dismounted. I invited them to enter, which they did. They informed me that enough evidence had been secured at the coroner's inquest, which was still in session, to show that Hoover had been murdered by Indians; that they were a committee sent by the settlers, who to the number of 100 or more were now with the coroner. The sheriff stated that it was only by the greatest difficulty he persuaded the entire number to stay back and appoint a committee of 12 to accompany him to the agency. The band of 25 armed men was composed of this committee and others who joined them at the agency. They made a demand for the murderers. I told them I had anticipated their demand, and explained to them what I had already done in the matter, and that I intended to do all I could to bring the perpetrators to justice; that I believed I would be able to apprehend them, but that I must have my own time and not be interfered with; that everything would be done as speedily as possible. They blustered and made all manner of demands, and for a while would not be satisifed with my assurances that everything would be done by me that I possibly could. After consultation among themselves, the sheriff informed me that he had decided to leave here four deputies, and that they should cooperate with me. This was done to satisfy the demands of the settlers. I told him I could see no reason why this should be done; but he insisted and I consented.

Captain Read with two troops of cavalry arrived just before the departure of the sheriff and his party.

At 6 o'clock that evening I met with White Bull, Badger, Spotted Hawk, Two Bull, and other headmen of the band. White Bull told me that he had informed these men all that I had told him in the morning. I again repeated my orders and charge. I also told them that it was believed among white people that when a crime was committed by an Indian the whole tribe was cognizant of it; that I would only hold his band responsible, and that they must find the murderers and turn them over to me; that it would not be right for the whole tribe to suffer for the crime of three or four. When I concluded, Badger, the father of the accused, said he had always given good advice to the young men. He concluded by saying: "I promise the agent if I find out, and I will try to find out, I will tell him even if it is my own son." They all said every effort would be made to discover the criminal, and then left.

At 9 next morning, the 28th, Captain Read started his troops to the scene of the killing, with a view of interviewing the coroner and the citizens, to get as far as possible all the facts pertaining to the case. He left the agency at about 11 o'clock to join his command. At the time of his departure I was with White Bull, who came to tell me that David Stanley had confessed to the murder. He said Stanley said he was the only guilty one, and that he repeatedly reiterated it; that Stanley informed him he would not surrender, but would fight at 3 o'clock; that he was willing to die to save his people, but would not surrender. I told White Bull that that would not do; that no one would be satisfied with this; that all must be turned over to me; that I would not allow a fight to take place. He then went back to his camp.

I immediately started a courier after Captain Read, who returned the answer that he would get here as quickly as possible.

At 1 o'clock the same afternoon I sent a courier to Rosebud with the following telegram to the Assistant Adjutant-General, Department of Dakota:

"The Indians have given me the name of the Indian who acknowledged killing of sheep-herder. Have demanded names of other two who were engaged in the killing. Surrender of Indian refused. Have two troops of cavalry here now, but think it unwise to act with this force, therefore respectfully request that two troops of cavalry and one company of infantry be ordered here immediately."

The Indians became more or less excited, kept moving about in an agitated and restless manner. The squaws and children took to the hills away from the agency, while those immediately to the west and south were occupied by the bucks. They all seemed to be heavily armed and with their horses. I was told by the Indians that they had only assembled to witness the fight that Stanley was to have at 3 o'clock, and that they had understood that it was postponed until 7 o'clock. I noticed that the Indians had not dispersed until they were called out to by Little Chief, at about 8 o'clock.

Captain Read returned to the agency with his command at about 3.30 in the afternoon. At this time Stanley was on a high hill in the rear of the agency and not a great distance from it. He had his horse and squaw with him, was in his war dress and paint, and was heavily armed; he was all ready for the fight. It was the desire of Captain Read to charge and capture or kill him. At this juncture a greatly excited Indian on horseback approached with the information that Stanley did not want to fight the soldiers, but did want to fight the citizens, meaning the deputy sheriffs who were here. I told him to go back and tell Stanley I would not allow anyone to fight him and for him to come in and surrender. Deputy Sheriff Smith told me he would attempt his capture if I would guarantee his safety from the other Indians. I told him I could not so guarantee, and moreover there would be no fight and that Stanley must be captured without any bloodshed. It was my earnest desire to capture Stanley without the firing of a shot, in order to turn him over to the civil authorities for punishment, after trial and conviction under State laws. I wanted this done as an example for those amongst the Indians who contemplate wrongdoing, and I knew perfectly well that if he were permitted to fight and was killed he would be a hero and brave in the eyes of the tribe, whose example should be emulated by the young men. Stanley followed in the footsteps of Head Chief and Crazy Mule, of whose heroic death stories are told around the fires, making every young man anxious for a similar death, so he, too, can become a brave and famous man.

I believe it was in 1891 that these two young men killed a white boy and hid the body in the hills, where it was found after a search of several days. The murderers were discovered through their boasting of the deed; their surrender was demanded, but it was refused, though they were willing to be killed and would die fighting. Their proposal was accepted, and the five troops of cavalry stationed here were ordered to prepare for the affray. At the appointed time the troops took their station in the rear of the agency buildings, and each young man took his position on a hill on either side of the troops. The young men charged down the hills on their horses upon the troops, singing their death songs and firing at the soldiers. They were finally killed, they only shooting a few of the horses of the soldiers. Stones mark the footsteps of the horses on the hillsides, and the bodies of the "braves" were buried in a grave prepared for them beforehand.

The squaws watched the fight from a point apart from the bucks. At its close the squaws sang the death songs and urged the bucks to avenge the death of the young men; the men became very much excited, and notwithstanding the presence of the five troops of cavalry a fight was narrowly averted. Thus these two young men became "heroes," and to prevent the repetition of this incident I forbade any fighting. These people do not fear death, but have a wholesome fear of hanging or even lengthy imprisonment; and if this man Stanley could be convicted and hanged, it would have a most salutary effect upon these Indians. For these reasons I was opposed to the capture of Stanley by force. Besides, I did not think it wise and prudent to make the attempt with but two troops of cavalry here; while I believe the Indians were not disposed to resist the capture of Stanley, still there was no telling what they would do when one of their people was being fired upon; had they made a resistance there is no telling where it would have ended. They can muster almost 500 warriors, and knowing of their disposition to resist in 1891, when much weaker than now, I thought two troops of cavalry would not stand much show of overcoming these warriors, whose fierceness was noted.

About this time, from remarks made to me by the Indians and by their actions, I became convinced that the Indians were afraid of the deputy sheriffs, because they could not understand why they were here, they not knowing the difference between the representatives of the law and the cowboys; this rendered them very close-mouthed, and I was unable to get any information from them that would answer for evidence against Stanley when he was brought to trial. As the presence of the deputy sheriffs interfered with my investigation, and as I was firmly of the opinion I could get no further evidence from the Indians while they were here, I put the case fairly before them and asked them for the cause of justice to withdraw from the reservation. This they refused to do unless they were ordered to do so. Captain Read and Lieutenant Livermore also urged them to leave, but they remained obdurate. After all efforts had proven unavailing, I finally, on the 29th, gave Mr. Smith the following letter:

"Under section 2152, Revised Statutes, United States, it is my duty as Indian agent to 'procure the arrest and trial of all Indians accused of committing any crime, offense, or misdemeanor, and of all other persons who may have committed crimes or offenses within any State or Territory and have fled into the Indian country, either by demanding the same of the chiefs of the proper tribe or by such other means as the President may authorize.'

"Referring to your presence at this time on this reservation for the purpose of awaiting the arrest of the alleged murderers of one John Hoover, in the vicinity of this reservation, at some time between May 3 and the 20th instant. I have the honor to inform you that I have information that one David Stanley, a Cheyenne Indian under my charge, has acknowledge that he (Stanley) committed said murder. Steps are now being taken to procure the arrest of said Stanley, which will be accomplished as speedily as possible. Upon apprehension of said Stanley he will be turned over to you at such point outside of this reservation as you may request, together with any others who may be found to be implicated in the committing said murder.

"Meantime, I consider that your presence on the reservation is a source of irritation to the Indians under my charge, and may incite them to offer violence. As a matter of expediency in procuring the arrest of the alleged murderers, I am of the opinion that you should withdraw from the reservation as soon as practicable, and therefore request that you do so at once."

After they had left, at 1 o'clock p. m., the 29th, I took the interpreter and went to White Bull's camp, with the intention to have Stanley meet me there, if he would, and have a talk with me. I requested Badger and Red Bird, father and uncle of Stanley, to go with me to see Stanley. I wanted to try and persuade him to surrender, as I was fully determined he should be taken alive and as fully resolved that he would not be permitted to make a "hero" of himself. They said they would be glad to go with me and urge him to surrender, but that they did not know where he was, as they had not seen him since the evening before. I thereupon called the headmen together and asked where he was. They all disclaimed any knowledge of his whereabouts. I then ordered that strict search be made for him; that runners go to the hills and search for him, and bring him in if found. They returned without him, saying he must be in hiding. I then gave the most strict orders that he must be found or that White Bull's band must stand the consequences. But still hearing nothing from him, on the morning of May 30 I ordered out the entire tribe in search of him, with instructions that he must be found and brought in without fail.

At 4 o'clock the morning of 31st word was brought to me by two Indians that Stanley had been seen at Black Eagle's camp about 16 miles from the agency; that he was surrounded and could not escape. At 9 o'clock I started for the place, accompanied by my son, the driver, and Badger, together with two interpreters. As we neared the camp, I was informed by a runner that Stanley had been captured. When I arrived there, I found about one hundred armed Indians on horseback. Stanley was in a tepee with some friends eating his dinner; he was still armed; he refused to talk then, wanted to wait until he got to the agency; he also refused to give up his arms, and I thought it unnecessary as well as useless, as the Indians were afraid of him, thinking he was a dangerous man, ready to fight for his life, to attempt to remove them by force. When we arrived near the agency, he said he was ready to talk with me in the presence of his father, Badger, and Black Eagle. I then persuaded him to deliver his rifle to me, but he was quite obstinate at first; he insisted upon retaining his horse, knife, and ammunition. We then had a talk. I asked him why he killed Hoover. He denied that he killed him; he acknowledged that he wanted to fight so as to die. After some more conversation on this subject, and after my insisting upon his surrender, peaceably, if possible, if not, otherwise, he finally gave his horse to his mother and prepared to go with me. He wanted to visit with his people during the night, and promised to talk next day; but I would not let him get out of my sight again, so I soon reached the agency and placed him in the agency jail, and caused a guard of soldiers to be placed over him.

At about noon this day one troop of cavalry from Fort Custer arrived under command of Major Norvell. Sheriff Gibb and four deputies also arrived at the agency while I was away. That evening I made an appointment with the sheriff for the next morning, as he wanted to talk with me. He gave me a letter, saying "This letter is from the county attorney, and you had better read it before morning, as it might enlighten you concerning your duties," etc. On the morning of June 1 we met in the office. I invited Major Norvell and Captain Read to be present during my interview with the sheriff and his deputies. The first thing the sheriff did was to produce a warrant for my arrest for violating a section of the statute of Montana, in resisting officers while attempting to make an arrest, having reference to letter already quoted in this report. I gave my recognizance to appear at such a time to be arranged by the county attorney and myself. He then demanded the person of David Stanley, and produced a warrant for his arrest. I declined to turn him over at that time, for various reasons, as shown in letter to Sheriff Gibb, which appears below. I tried to show him that in all probability to turn him over now would defeat the ends of justice; that I would deliver him up as soon as I could obtain more evidence from him, which would be within two days. Both Major Norvell and Captain Read endeavored to turn the sheriff, but could not do so, so I was finally compelled to give him the following letter:

"Referring to my letter of May 29, addressed to Mr. William D. Smith, your deputy, the contents of which you are cognizant, and referring to your demand for the prisoner, David Stanley, in tendering your warrant for his arrest this day, I have the honor to inform you that I feel constrained by my sense of duty as agent in charge of the Cheyenne Indians, respectfully to decline complying with your demand for the prisoner. The prisoner, Stanley, was secured yesterday through my efforts and influence with his people; he is in safe custody in the hands of the United States troops stationed here. I have not completed my duty in collecting all the evidence in his case, though I think I have it nearly sufficient to secure his conviction for the murder of John Hoover. Measures are now being taken by me to procure the necessary information as speedily as possible for the arrest and trial of any and all other Indians of this tribe who may have been implicated with Stanley in the commission of the crime.

"I will require the presence here of Stanley for a day or two longer at least, to enable me to gather further evidence against him and his supposed accomplices. As soon as my investigation is complete, Stanley and any others found to be implicated with him will be promptly turned over to your custody for trial by the State courts, together with all evidence that can be obtained which will lead to their conviction.

"Meantime, I consider that the presence of yourself or deputies here on this reservation handicaps me in the performance of my plain duty under the Revised Statutes of the United States, to procure the arrest and trial of the guilty parties, and is a source of irritation and excitement among the Indians under my charge and may incite them to offer violence, should any attempt be made by civil authorities to use or display force in attempting to make arrests here at this time. As a matter of duty in carrying out the policy of the General Government in handling these Indians through the agents appointed over them, and as a matter of expediency in procuring the arrest of the murderers in this case, I am still of the opinion that you should withdraw from this reservation as soon as practicable, and I therefore repeat my request that you do so at once.

"I earnestly urge that you comply with this request in order to aid me in securing the apprehension of the Indians supposed to be implicated with Stanley, and thereby aid in securing the ends of law and justice as quickly as possible; I have no desire or intention to prevent the guilty parties from being brought to trial by the State courts, nor to hinder or thwart you in procuring their arrest, and all evidence which may aid in securing their conviction, but, on the contrary, I desire to give you all the assistance in this matter that may lie in my power; but I must not be hampered by imprudent or hasty action on your part, and must insist in maintaining order among the Indians under my charge on this Government reservation, by restraining them and others from any acts of violence or disturbance.

"Stanley's accomplices, if any, have been demanded of his people, and this demand will be insisted upon by me and every effort is being made by me to ferret them out. You shall have them as soon as they are known."

Sheriff Gibb left soon after receiving the letter, but left his four deputies.

On the evening of June 2 one troop of cavalry and one company of infantry arrived from Fort Keogh, under command of Captain Kinzie, Second Infantry.

I continued my investigations during the 2d and 3d, but was unable to obtain much information. I attribute the reticence of the Indians to the fact of the presence of the deputy sheriffs at the agency. I finally informed Major Norwood, on the evening of the 3d, that I was through with Stanley, and requested him to furnish an escort of cavalry to deliver him to the sheriff at Rosebud Station to be taken to Miles City for incarceration and, in due time, trial. They left here at 4 a.m. the 4th instant, with one troop of cavalry, commanded by Captain Read.

On the evening of the 3d I informed Deputy Sheriff Smith that Stanley would be turned over to the civil authorities at Rosebud upon the arrival of the eastbound train on Sunday, the 6th. He replied that he would leave in the morning, but would leave one deputy here. I told him I could see no reason why any should remain, and asked him to take them all with him. This he refused to do unless put off. I then addressed the following letter to him:

"Referring to my communications of May 29 and June 1, addressed to yourself and Sheriff Gibb, respectively, concerning the arrest and proposed delivery of one David Stanley, a Cheyenne Indian under my charge, accused of the murder of John Hoover, I have the honor to inform you that I consider that the presence here of yourself or other sheriffs or deputies at the time pending investigation of the case in question is a source of irritation and disturbance to the Indians under my charge, and to a great extent hampers me in conducting the investigation and in managing the Indians. Under my authority as provided for by section 2058, Revised Statutes United States, to 'manage and superintend the intercourse with the Indians' under my charge, and further referring to my requests to yourself and Sheriff Gibb in the letters above mentioned, that you withdraw from this reservation, I now direct and order that you and all other sheriffs or deputies leave this reservation without delay, and that you remain outside the limits of the same until you can come provided with duly executed warrants of a specific nature. This measure I deem necessary on the grounds of public peace and safety, and in order that I may more speedily accomplish the procuring of evidence against David Stanley and his supposed accomplices. You presence here hampers me in performing my duty in this connection. Stanley will be turned over as per arrangement between myself and Sheriff Gibb.

I have made another demand upon the tribe for the surrender of Stanley's accomplices. I shall use every means within my power to ferret them out. This may not be accomplished at once, but I have no doubt but what they will be discovered in some future time by admissions made by the interested parties.

I must earnestly urge upon you the consideration and favorable action for the stationing of a troop of cavalry at this point permanently. This is very essential for the peace, if not the safety, of the settlers as well as the employees of this agency. Detachments from the troop could patrol the reservation and by their presence restrain the Indians from committing any overt act, such as killing cattle, leaving the reservation without permission, etc. The settlers have been worked up to a fearful pitch, and the presence of cavalry will restore confidence among them.

The Indians are quiet and in good temper. They have been in this condition all the time, except on the day Stanley proposed to fight, when they were excited and restless. The next day they appeared without arms and resumed the habits and pursuits they had been accustomed to. The Indians are all on the reservation, and have been all the time during the troubles. They have shown no signs of being troublesome, except on the day spoken of; they have not been in their war clothes, nor have they had on war paint. No fights and no quarrels have taken place between settlers and Indians or between soldiers and Indians. The roads have all been open for travel, and no one has been stopped and no one prohibited from entering the reservation, except as shown by the letters to the sheriffs. No one has been assaulted or insulted as I can find out. Not a shot has been fired by anyone, and no one has been hurt or killed. There are no renegade Crows here and no Sioux, and there have been none. Everything has been done by me I possibly could do to bring the murderers to justice. I have never considered it unsafe for the settlers to remain at their homes. I am entirely satisfied in my own mind that there was not the slightest danger of an outbreak by the Indians.

The newspaper reports, which I saw to-day for the first time, are all gross exaggerations. If any such things had occurred as given in the papers, I surely would have notified you at once.

This is a full and complete report of affairs at this agency up to date. I will keep you fully informed if anything should transpire. All of which is respectfully submitted.

I am, very respectfully, your obedient servant,

GEO. W. H. STOUCH,
Captain, Third Infantry,
Acting United States Indian Agent.

TONGUE RIVER AGENCY, *June 23, 1897.*

SIR: I have the honor to make a further report on the affairs at this agency growing out of the murder of John Hoover by Stanley. I made report of the capture of Stanley and all conditions of the Indians and of the reservation under date of 5th instant. Since then nothing of great consequence has occurred. On June 9 Sheriff Gibb and three of his deputies arrived at the agency. I informed him that I was entirely willing to turn over to him any and all Indians for whom he had warrants; he presented warrants for Yellow Hair and Sam Crow, whereupon I immediately sent for them and upon their appearance I delivered them to the sheriff. An escort of cavalry was requested in order to assure their safe arrival at the railroad station, and on the morning of the 10th instant they left the agency for Rosebud Station.

Sheriff Gibb informed me that the judge of the State court advised him that the proper mode of procedure would be for the sheriff to present the warrants to the agent, and that the agent would then deliver the parties to be arrested to the sheriff; a different way from that the sheriff formerly insisted upon, that of entering the reservation with as many deputies as he wanted, even to a company of unorganized militia, without the consent of the agent. I told Sheriff Gibb that if he desired to remain to endeavor to obtain evidence I would assist him all I could, but he declined, as he would be unable to be successful in his inquiries. I also told him if he had other Indians to arrest to come up quietly without heralding his intentions in all the papers and to the settlers in this country so as to frighten them and cause them to leave their homes again, thinking that the Indians would resist. Everything is quiet, the same as it has been since the discovery of Hoover's body, with the exception of the day the fight between Stanley and the sheriffs was advertised to take place. The Indians are orderly and at their homes attending to what duties they have devolving upon them. I apprehend nothing further in the way of excitement and alarms.

I have endeavored to obtain evidence to arrest Stanley's accomplices, if any, but have been unsuccessful, and I am almost convinced that there are none.

I must again urge upon you the necessity of buying out the bona fide settlers on the reservation, ejecting the squatters, fencing in the reservation and stocking it with cattle. I can see no other way to make these Indians self-supporting.

I am, very respectfully, your obedient servant,

GEO. W. H. STOUCH,
Captain, Third Infantry,
Acting United States Indian Agent.

THE COMMISSIONER OF INDIAN AFFAIRS,
Washington, D. C.

Report of Commissioner of Indian Affairs W. A. Jones
September 26, 1898

(Excerpt from *Report for 1898*, pp. 71-73, 96-100)

Two incidents from Commissioner Jones' report illustrate the legal and social restraints placed upon the native Americans of the period. In the first, Ute Indians hunting on their old grounds in Colorado by a right guaranteed to them under a treaty with the United States were killed by state game wardens, who claimed to be enforcing the state's game laws. In the other, two Seminole Indians were literally burned at the stake, and others tortured, by an Oklahoma lynch mob blindly seeking the murderer of a local resident.

KILLING OF UTES IN COLORADO

ON THE 24TH of October, 1897, when a party of Ute Indians from the Uintah and Ouray Reservation in Utah were hunting on the north side of Snake River in Colorado, two of them were killed and two were wounded by a squad of game wardens of Colorado. Immediately, the newspapers contained the usual startling accounts of an Indian outbreak; that the Utes were on the warpath, and settlers in southwestern Colorado were fleeing for their lives, etc.

November 1, Capt. W. H. Beck, U. S. A., the acting agent for the Uintah and Ouray Agency, who was then in this city, received the following telegram from the clerk whom he had left in charge of the agency:

> Two White River Utes were killed and squaws wounded in first encounter, as reported; have heard of the second encounter. Dr. Reamer left last evening to attend the wounded squaws. Indians here are much agitated. I respectfully ask that you request troops be stationed at agency at once.

In accordance with Captain Beck's recommendation the War Department was requested to direct such movement of the troops at Fort Duchesne as would assure protection to the agency, and suppress any hostile demonstration which the White River Utes might attempt to make; which request was complied with.

November 3, 1897, this office recommended that an inspector be sent to the Uintah and Ouray Agency to ascertain the facts, and Special Indian Agent E. B. Reynolds was ordered to make such investigation. December 16, 1897, he rendered his report, of which the following is a summary:

On the 23d of November, at the Uintah Agency, he took the statements of the Indians, and, according to the uncontradicted testimony of Ungut sho one Star, four men and three women were in camp 3 miles from what is known as Thompson's ranch, while the rest of their party were out hunting. On the morning of October 26 Star and So on a munche Kent, on their way to Thompson's ranch, met and had a little conversation with two white men, one of whom was armed with a Winchester rifle and pistol. A short distance farther on they saw a squad of men whom they knew to be game wardens, whereupon they turned back to the camp. So on a munche Kent got away, but Star was captured and disarmed by the wardens, who took him with them to the camp. Upon their arrival at the camp, about 10 a. m., they immediately covered Shinaraff and Coo a munche with their rifles, and afterwards told the Indians that they wished them to go to Thompson's, and endeavored to arrest the men, who resisted and got away. In the afternoon, three or four hours after their arrival, the wardens commenced firing on the Indians, and, after killing two men and wounding two of the women, left the camp. The Indians who had escaped or were out hunting returned and buried the dead, and all started that evening for the agency, traveling all night.

Special Agent Reynolds next visited the place where the killing occurred (150 miles from the agency) and took the testimony of all but one of the wardens connected with the affair and also of a few others, examining each one by himself. From their statements it appeared that W. K. Wilcox, game warden of Routt County, had been notified by the chief game warden of Colorado that Indians from Utah were probably killing game in violation of law and should be arrested unless they left the State. Proceeding with a Mr. McCormack toward Bear and Snake River Valley, Mr. Wilcox was informed at Maybell that the Indians numbered probably 100. He therefore sent back for an additional force to assist him. Two days later, October 24, ten wardens, all but Thompson and Armstrong armed, with two others, decided to visit the Indian camp, but before doing so Thompson and a man named Templeton were sent ahead to try if possible to induce the Indian men to come to Thompson's ranch to meet the wardens and talk over matters. On their way thither they met Star and another Indian, had some conversation, and went on. Meantime the wardens had concluded to follow slowly, and soon came in sight of the two Indians which the advance party had met. One of them turned immediately and started in the direction of the camp. The other was overtaken and disarmed and taken to the camp, which the party reached about 10 o'clock in the morning. There they found six Indian men, eight or ten women, and a few children. All the men were armed, and some of the women had arms in their tents. Two deer, still undressed, many deer hides, with some beef hides, and a quantity of deer hair, were found in the camp.

The Indians were notified that they must leave the State, or be arrested. After some time, attempt was made to disarm and arrest them, which the Indians resisted. Then, to quote from the report of the special agent:

In the final attempt to arrest the Indians, an Indian, unexpectedly to all, fired his gun at one of the wardens, Al Shaw, and as he was about to fire, a warden, Mr. Kimberly, standing near Shaw, struck the gun to one side, and the shot missed Shaw and hit a woman. At this moment the firing was commenced by the wardens and Indians, which was participated in by about only five or six of the wardens and lasted but a few minutes, and when it had ceased, it was found that some Indians had been killed and some wounded, and Shaw was lying on the ground in a senseless condition, having been stricken down by the Indian who had fired the first shot. The wardens then went away to Thompson's ranch.

The wardens deny that they fired the first shot or that they drew their rifles on the Indians before the firing commenced, and on the whole the special agent is inclined to accept their version of the affair as against that of the Indians, and to acquit the posse of anything deliberate or malicious in the killing. Some of them have homes on the Bear and Snake rivers and have lived there for years.

The affair created great turmoil in that vicinity, and women and children were taken to Lay, 25 miles distant, and remained there until the excitement subsided.

This was the old hunting ground of the Utes before they were removed from Colorado and they have always depended on game for no small part of their food and clothing. They can not understand why they should be shut out from it during certain seasons of the year by State laws, especially when the right to hunt game in this region was guaranteed to them by a treaty with the Government, which provided that such right should be inviolable and continue so long as game existed there. However, the United States Supreme Court has held, in Ward v. Race Horse (163 U. S., 504), that the admission of a State into the Union annuls such treaty rights. Therefore the Utes could legally be held by the officials of the State of Colorado to be violating the game laws. The testimony shows that the Indians were aware that their hunting was liable to be objected to, and that they had been for some time rather apprehensively on the lookout for the "buckskin police," and had made inquiries as to what they would be likely to do to them.

* * *

Torturing and Burning of Seminoles in Oklahoma

Early in January, 1898, alarming reports appeared in the newspapers of an impending outbreak by the Indians of the Seminole Nation along the borders of Oklahoma on account of outrages perpetrated in that vicinity. After a searching investigation it was found that the threatened disturbance was due to the burning of two Seminole Indian boys at the stake by a mob of white men from Oklahoma in revenge for the killing of one Mrs. Leard, a white woman living in the Seminole Nation. The facts as to the murder of this women and the burning of the Indians are briefly stated by Leo E.

Bennett, United States marshal, in his report to the Attorney-General, as follows:

On the evening of December 30, 1897, Mrs. Leard, or Laird, a white woman, residing on the "McGeisy farm," 20 miles west of Wewoka, Seminole Nation, and probably 5 or 6 miles east of the post-office of Maud, Okla., was visited by an Indian, who asked to borrow a saddle. This was refused him. He tarried a while, and Mrs. L. became uneasy at his presence and ordered him away. He left, but very soon after returned, and entering the house unannounced picked up a gun and attempted to shoot the woman. The gun failed to fire, and Mrs. L. started to run, whereupon he struck her with the gun, breaking the stock from the barrel. He then picked up the barrel of the gun, and as she passed out the door he struck her several times in quick succession, the force of the blows crushing her skull, and from which she died. The Indian then stepped into the house and made a search for money, but did not find any. He then went out of the house, and drawing the woman's infant of a few months from under her dead body he put the child in the house and left the place.

The only persons present were the woman and the Indian and the woman's children, the eldest a lad of 8 years, the next a girl of 4 years, and the infant. It was not possible for the children to get their mother's body into the house, and it lay outside during the night. Upon the coming of daylight of the following morning the little boy hastened away to the neighbors for assistance. Upon his return with some of the neighbors it was found that the hogs had gotten into the yard and had partially devoured the body of the woman. The body was then cared for and decently interred and a messenger dispatched for the husband of the woman, who was several miles away. Mr. Leard was accompanied to his home by a number of persons from Oklahoma, and as soon as the burial services were closed those present organized a posse to hunt down the woman's murderer. This posse was heavily armed, and rode all over the western border of the Seminole Nations, taking into custody nearly every Indian who came across its path. All were taken before the little boy for identification, and many of them he was able to state positively did not do the bloody deed. Others he was doubtful in so clearly stating their innocence, and all such Indians were then tortured in an effort to make them confess that they were the ones or had had something to do with the crime.

Finally a confession of guilt was extorted from Palmer Sampson, an ignorant, full-blood Seminole Indian, who also implicated Lincoln McGeisy. The latter denied the charge and until the very last declared his entire innocence. The mob held these boys (for I am advised they were about 18 or 19 years of age) several days, and on the night of Friday, January 7, carried them over into Oklahoma, and chaining them together by their necks with chains, securely fastened them to a tree and piled hay and brush around them, and about 3 o'clock of the morning of the 8th set fire thereto and burned them alive. They continued to burn for about twelve hours, and when found by a searching party their legs and arms were burned from their trunks. The tree was cut down Saturday (8th) afternoon and their remains taken to the Seminole Nation and buried, still chained together.

The first information received of there being any trouble in that country reached me on Saturday night (8th) in a telegram from Deputy Marshal Buchner, who was at Holdenville, and who wired me that there was a raging mob in the Seminole Nation, and asked for instructions. I immediately endeavored to ascertain the cause of the disturbance, and was advised of the death of the two boys as above related, also that the mob had burned the farmhouses on the McGeisy place. The mob having dispersed before this information reached me, I consulted with United States Judge William M. Springer, and wired my deputies at Holdenville and Wewoka to meet United States Commissioner Fears at Wewoka and obey his orders concerning an investigation. Commissioner Fears went to Wewoka on the 10th and at once issued process for witnesses and a warrant for the interpreter who had served the purposes of the mob. On the 10th I also wired Assistant United States Attorney Parker, then at South McAlester, requesting him to proceed to Wewoka and aid in the investigation. Mr. Parker did so. I would have personally proceeded to the scene, but could not see the necessity for so doing at the time the information reached me. I was also preparing to transport some prisoners from Muscogee to the penitentiary and had all arrangements made to leave with them.

On the night of the 11th telegrams reached me describing scenes of bloodshed and terror because of an alleged uprising of the Indians, it being positively set forth that the town of Maud, Okla., had been burned and that more than twenty-five men, women, and children had been murdered by the Seminole Indians. This information was traced directly to the telegraph operator of the Choctaw, Oklahoma and Gulf Railway at Earlsboro, Okla., who gave them out as facts. About noon I received telegrams from my deputies and other officials then at the scene of the alleged trouble that the reports sent out by the operator at Earlsboro were all fakes and wholly unfounded, but had been circulated for the purpose of creating a sentiment to shield the members of the mob who came from Oklahoma and burned the two Indian boys. Commissioner Fears also wired me that there was no necessity for my going to Wewoka, as all was then being done that was possible to discover the identity of those who composed the mob.

Mr. Fears advised me that he had issued certain subpoenas and warrants and that he had no doubt the facts would be developed. That night (12th) I received a telegram from one of my deputies that he had reached Wewoka with one of the parties, and asked instructions as to disposition of prisoner. I directed him to take the prisoner and subpoena witnesses before Commissioner Fears at Eufaula. That night I left for Boonville, Mo., Columbus, Ohio, and Washington, D.C., with United States prisoners. I am advised, under date of the 16th, that one of my deputies has secured a full list of the names of all persons who were implicated in the burning of the two Indians, together with the names of witnesses to the crime, and that the whole matter has been presented to the grand jury, now in session at Vinita. I have this list of names before me, but for obvious reasons deem it proper to omit giving them in this connection. Three or four of those on the list were residents of the Indian Territory, but the majority of the mob was made up of residents of Oklahoma.

I desire to assure you that every officer connected with the United States courts in the northern district of Indian Territory will use all lawful means at his and their command to bring the guilty party before the bar of justice. In another communication I will present to you certain suggestions which are, in my opinion, proper for your attention.

It may not be out of place for me to advise you at this time of the fact that along the eastern boundary of Oklahoma, within 200 yards, in some cases a mile, from the west line of the Seminole and Creek nations there have been established a great many whisky joints, from which there are daily sold to these Indians many gallons of the vilest of whisky and of alcohol. Such places are located at Maud, Violet Springs, Earlsboro, Keokuk Falls, Stroud, etc. Nearly all the crime along the western portion of my district arises from the presence of these saloons just across the line, and I believe that fully one-half of the whisky introduced in the northern district comes from Oklahoma. The officers of this district hope to secure the cooperation of the official of Oklahoma in putting a stop to this traffic by the prosecution of those who are engaged therein, and steps in this direction were taken several weeks since.

In response to a resolution of the Senate of January 20, 1898, asking that the Attorney-General and the Secretary of the Interior inform the Senate as to what steps had been taken to ascertain the facts in the case and to punish the alleged offenders, information and copies of correspondence were given, which will be found in Senate Docs. Nos. 98 and 99 (parts 1 and 2), Fifty-fifth Congress, second session.

In the latter part of January last Hon. John T. Brown, principal chief of the Seminole Nation, officially advised the Department of the outrages perpetrated upon members of the nation, and requested, "in view of article 18 of the treaty with the Creeks and Seminoles dated August 7, 1856, whereby the Seminole Nation was promised protection and guaranteed indemnity for all injuries resulting from invasion or aggression," that a suitable person be appointed to ascertain and report the facts as to the burning of the two young men and the inhuman torture of other Seminole Indians, and also to ascertain and report upon the amount and value of the property destroyed or stolen by the mob, to the end that indemnity might be made by the United States for injuries sustained.

Article 18 of the Seminole treaty proclaimed August 29, 1856 (11 *Stats.*, p. 704), provides as follows:

> The United States shall protect the Creeks and Seminoles from domestic strife, from hostile invasion, and from aggression by other Indians and white persons not subject to their jurisdiction and laws; and for all injuries resulting from such invasion or aggression full indemnity is hereby guaranteed to the party or parties injured out of the Treasury of the United States, upon the same principle and according to the same rules upon which white persons are entitled to indemnity for injuries or aggressions upon them committed by Indians.

In accordance with Department instructions of January 24, 1898, Dew M. Wisdom, United States Indian agent of the Union Agency, Indian Territory, was directed by this office, January 27, to make the investigation, and was instructed as follows:

> In accordance with the above instructions, you will at once make the desired investigation in the premises. Of course, you will take sufficient time in this work to make it thorough and complete; and, so far as possible, all the evidence obtained should be supported by proper and sufficient proof in the form of affidavits, etc. It is presumed in this case that many claims will be made for damages, and great care should therefore be taken in investigating the same, to the end that none but those justly entitled thereto shall be reported to this Department.
>
> The method of procedure in making this investigation will be left largely to your own judgment and discretion; but it is desired that all parties to this

unfortunate affair should be given a full hearing, and should be allowed to submit such evidence in relation thereto as they may have or wish to offer.

The agent's reply of March 29, 1898, was transmitted to the Department in office letter of April 4 last. In this report the agent stated in effect that Thomas S. McGeisy and Mrs. Sukey Sampson were the only parties who suffered any loss of property or damage to property at the hands of said mob, and that the following parties, Peter Ossanna, Kenda Palmer, Billy Coker, Chippie Coker, Cobley (or Copley) Wolf, George P. Harjo, Samuel P. Harjo, Duffy P. Harjo, Johnson McKaye, Sever Parnoka, John Washington, George Kernells, Thomas Thompson, Johnny Palmer, Sam Ela, Sepa Palmer, Shawnee Barnett, and Billy Thlocco, and Moses and Peter Tiger, were arrested and otherwise maltreated in their persons by said mob of United States citizens; that he was unable to obtain affidavits or statements from the two last named, for the reason that they were in prison at Fort Smith, Ark.; that Palmer Sampson, son of the said Mrs. Sukey Sampson, and Lincoln McGeisey, son of said Thomas F. McGeisey, were the two Seminoles who were chained to a tree and burned to a crisp in the most fiendish manner by the mob; that Mrs. Sukey Sampson lost a horse, bridle, and blanket valued at $80; that Mr. McGeisey lost two houses, a barn, some sheds and other outhouses, a well, some fencing, corn, lot of books, trunks, clothing, and house and kitchen furnishings, all of which he values at $2,515.65, and that with the exception of the valuation of $1,250 placed upon the "frame and hewed log house" by Thomas McGeisey, which he, the agent, thinks is fully double what it is really worth, the valuations are approved.

The act of Congress approved July 1, 1898, making appropriations for sundry civil expenses of the Government for the current fiscal year, contained the following provision:

> To enable the Secretary of the Interior to cause an examination and investigation to be made of outrages and injuries alleged to have been perpetrated on individual Indians belonging to the Seminole tribe by an armed mob or band of lawless persons who invaded the Seminole country during the months of December, eighteen hundred and ninety-seven, and January, eighteen hundred and ninety-eight, and if, upon such examination and investigation, it shall appear that outrages and injuries have been so perpetrated and that the United States is under treaty obligations to pay for such outrages and injuries, he shall ascertain the amount which should be properly paid said Indian or Indians, or their legal heirs or representatives, and pay such sum or sums as he may deem just and reasonable, and for such purpose a sum not exceeding twenty thousand dollars is hereby appropriated.

As all the facts in the case are now before the Department, it is thought that indemnity will soon be paid by the Government to members of the Seminole Nation injured by the mob of lawless whites in this disgraceful occurrence. Further, the whites guilty of the outrages are now being prosecuted by the Department of Justice.

Report of the Commission to the Five Civilized Tribes in the Indian Territory October 3, 1898

(Excerpt from *Report for 1898*, pp. 1051-57)

The progress report of the Commission to the Five Civilized Tribes, of which Senator Henry Dawes was chairman, was included as an adjunct to the 1898 Commissioner of Indian Affairs report. This commission was designed, along with the so-called Curtis Act, to destroy the tribal governments of the Indian Territory and to hasten the process by which "the government of the Indian Territory and its land system may, at an early day, be brought into harmony with those of the United States and of the States by which it is surrounded, assuring it a most encouraging and hopeful future."

THE COMMISSION to the Five Civilized Tribes submits the following report of the progress of the work under their charge since the report made October 11, 1897. At that time the commission had just completed the work required of them by statute of June 10, 1896, "to hear and determine the application of all persons who may apply to them for citizenship in any of the said nations, and after said hearing they shall determine the right of such applicant to be so admitted and enrolled." There had been presented to them some 7,500 different applications under this law, each application, in many cases, embracing others alleged to be of the same family and claiming under the same title, amounting in all to nearly if not quite 75,000 individual cases requiring a separate application of the evidence upon which they rested.

Of these applications there were admitted by the commission as follows, viz:

In the Choctaw Nation	1,212
In the Chickasaw Nation	334
In the Cherokee Nation	274
In the Creek Nation	255
Total	2,075

The large number of failures to obtain admission to citizenship by the commission thus shown is attributable in a great measure to the fact that the commission was required by the statute "in determining such applications to respect all laws of the several nations or tribes not inconsistent with the laws of the United States and all treaties with said nations or tribes, and give full force and effect to the rolls, usages, and customs of said nations and tribes." This was right and proper for the reason that for half a century or more the tribal governments had been permitted to control the matter of citizenship and had, therefore, legislated upon it, and to disregard their laws, usages, and customs at this late hour would be revolutionary and impracticable. The erroneous idea had, however, become prevalent that blood alone constituted a valid claim to citizenship in the several nations, regardless of other qualifications required by treaties and the constitution, laws and usages of the several nations by which the commission was to be governed. A large number of those rejected have appealed, as provided in the law, to the United States court in the Territory. But in a recent statute, the Curtis law, it is enacted that "no person shall be enrolled who has not heretofore removed to and in good faith settled in the nation in which he claims citizenship." An appeal has been allowed by the Indian appropriation bill, approved July 1, 1898, in all these citizenship cases, which were appealed from the decisions of the Dawes Commission to the United States courts in the Indian Territory, directly to the United States Supreme Court. It will be, therefore, impossible for some time to ascertain the precise number which will be ultimately added to the rolls of citizenship of these nations under these provisions. But as the Curtis bill, section 21, has enacted that "No person shall be enrolled who has not heretofore removed to and in good faith settled in the nation in which he claims citizenship," there need be little apprehension that the roll of citizenship ultimately entitled to allotment will be unduly swelled by these appeals.

Under this law the commissioners had no power to interfere with the existing citizenship rolls in the several tribes beyond the addition thereto of such persons as brought themselves, on the evidence, within the requirements of the laws and usages of the nation in which they claimed citizenship. Indeed, the same law expressly confirmed the existing rolls and continued the tribal authority to add new names thereto. There had grown up, however, grave suspicions as to the integrity of these rolls. Many scandals respecting their manipulation under tribal authority had become very generally to be believed by the conservative citizenship of the several nations. The commission had, therefore (in their report of November 18, 1895), felt compelled to call attention to the condition of these rolls. It is not necessary to repeat here the statements then made, which are not believed to have been exaggerated. The work of the commission in adding new names to citizenship had proved so satisfactory to that class of citizens before named that a desire became general among them that the commission be clothed with authority to also review and reform the existing rolls. This resulted subsequently in that power being conferred on them by Congress. Their workings under this provision will be reported in another connection.

There were pending and awaiting ratification at the last report two agreements with this commission, one with the Chowtaws and Chickasaws acting together of date April 23, 1897, and one with the Creeks of date

September 27, 1897. There was afterwards one made with the Seminoles of date September 16, 1897. These agreements were duly reported to and are on file in the Department. The one with the Seminoles has been since duly ratified and is now the law which will hereafter control in that nation both its government and property holdings. It appears to be giving general satisfaction, and the future of this people is very encouraging. As soon as the duties of the commission elsewhere will permit, they will, in conjunction with the acknowledged authorities of the Seminoles, proceed to carry out its provisions.

The agreement with the Choctaws and Chickasaws was ratified by the council of both nations as required by law, but the Chickasaw nation had also required it to be submitted to a popular vote of that nation, which resulted in a small majority against it, believed to be only 112 votes. This agreement thus failed.

The agreement with the Creeks was rejected by the council, the chief, Isparhecher, some of his friends and other persons interested in leases obtained from the nation, opposing the changes contemplated in it.

Pending the ratification of the agreement with the Choctaws and Chickasaws the Senate passed, July 17, 1897, a joint resolution, suspending as to said tribes that provision of law which transferred their judicial jurisdiction to United States courts after January 1, 1898. After the failure of ratification of that agreement this resolution was in December withdrawn from the House by the Senate and indefinitely postponed.

The commission was required by act of June 7, 1897, to "examine and report to Congress whether the Mississippi Choctaws under their treaties are not entitled to all the rights of Choctaw citizenship except an interest in the Choctaw annuities." This is a small and feeble band of Choctaws who declined to remove to the present territory under the treaty of September 27, 1830, and has remained in Mississippi ever since, under certain concessions made to them in that treaty. They claim not only to enjoy these concessions, including a continuance of their residence in Mississippi, but at the same time to share in all the rights of property of the Choctaws in the Territory except their annuities. The commission has attended to that duty and, after a careful examination of the provisions of that treaty and its history and listening to the arguments in support of the claim, they arrived at the conclusion and reported to Congress "that these Mississippi Indians have a right at any time to remove to the Indian Territory and, joining their brethren there, claim participation in all the privileges of a Choctaw citizen save participation in their annuities, but that they could not maintain this claim otherwise than after such removal." They recommended, however, in view of the importance of this claim that provision be made for a judicial determination of the question. A bill containing this provision has passed the Senate and now awaits the action of the House. A copy of our report leading to this conclusion accompanies this report.

In the meanwhile, in contemplation of the condition in which the

Territory would be left by the possible failure to ratify pending agreements, Mr. Curtis, of the Indian committee of the House, addressed himself to the preparation of a bill, the general design of which would be to transfer the control of the property rights in these nations from tribal authority to that of the United States, much the same as their political government had been transferred by the act which was to take effect January 1, 1898. The result of this undertaking of Mr. Curtis, on which he bestowed much time and exhaustive labor, availing himself of all the assistance of others which he could command, has been the act entitled "An act for the protection of the people of the Indian Territory, and for other purposes," known as the "Curtis bill." The knowledge of the preparation of this bill aroused great opposition of those in the Territory opposed to any change in the exclusive use of tribal property by the few controlling the government of the Territory. Accordingly large delegations were sent to Washington, at great expense to their national treasuries, for the purpose of preventing such legislation and procuring, if possible, the repeal of the law taking away so much of their political power, which was to take effect January 1, 1898. It was deemed necessary, therefore, to require the presence of the commission in Washington during the pendency of such legislation to give information to the committees having it in charge as to the real condition of the Territory and the needs and character of the legislation proposed. At the request of these committees, and with the approval of the Department, the commission remained in Washington until final action upon this bill, rendering such assistance as was in its power to the several committees, based upon accurate and reliable information in relation to the many questions involved in the comprehensive scope of the proposed measure, as well as upon their experience and observation while in the Territory. After many changes and modifications, it is believed to have taken the best final shape possible under the circumstances.

Immediately upon the final passage of this bill the commission returned to the Territory to the discharge of the new duties required of it, in connection with those that had heretofore been imposed. In this work the commission is still engaged.

The Curtis bill is designed, in place of the present exclusive holding and use by a few under existing tribal governments prostituted to the perpetuation of such uses, to substitute a new code of United States law for the Territory. It changes these communal holdings from this exclusive use into individual holdings under United States control. It necessarily involved in its preparation very many provisions, some of them of an exceedingly complicated character. It is too much to expect that on its application the modification of some features of so comprehensive a measure may not be found necessary, but its purpose is wise, and so far as can be foreseen its provisions are adequate. The Curtis bill provided, in addition to its general enactments, for the resubmission, with certain specified modifications of the two agreements—that with the Choctaws and Chickasaws and that with the

Creeks—for ratification, to a popular vote in their respective nations, and provided further that if ratified the provisions of these agreements, so far as they differed from that bill, should supersede it. The Choctaw and Chickasaw agreement was accordingly so submitted for ratification on the 24th of August, 1898, and was ratified by a large majority.

Chief Isparhecher has so far failed to call an election, as he was authorized and directed to do by provision of the Curtis bill, but it is believed that if such an election were held it would result in the ratification of the agreement with the Creeks. Therefore, in many of the more difficult details of allotment and other features of that law it will hereafter be enforced only in the Cherokee and Creek nations.

Both this law and the recently ratified treaties have imposed many new, arduous, and responsible duties upon this commission, likely to consume much time before such duties can be completely and finally discharged. In addition to what was heretofore required of them, this act and these agreements, among other things, require them to take a census of all the citizenship of each nation before perfecting a final roll for allotment, and in doing so they are "authorized and required to make correct rolls of the citizens by blood of all the tribes, eliminating from the tribal rolls such names as may have been placed thereon by fraud or without authority of law, enrolling only such as may have lawful right thereto and their descendants born since such rolls were made," etc. This compels the commission to pass judicial judgment upon the right to citizenship of every name upon the citizenship roll of each of the Five Tribes. No clerk or other substitute can do this work. It must be done personally by the commission and upon a hearing of evidence in each case where there is any question.

This law requires also of the commission that it shall make a correct roll of all the freedmen entitled to or claiming any rights under the treaties of 1866 with the respective tribes and of all their descendants born since the date of these treaties. In respect to the freedmen in the Choctaw and Chickasaw tribes this will prove a very difficult task, the latter having never made a roll or registry of those made freedmen by that nation, nor kept any trace of them or their descendants since emancipation. Nor are these tribes able to furnish any considerable assistance in determining what portion, if any, of the present colored population has come into the Territory since that date. In the Chickasaw tribe there is the additional difficulty growing out of the fact that for many years the tribal authorities have disowned and ignored in all their relations these freedmen, and have endeavored to effect their removal from the Territory. It becomes also the duty of this commission to determine and report to the Secretary of the Interior of the identity of the Mississippi Choctaws claiming rights in Choctaw property under the treaty of September 27, 1830. The commission is further required, "before any allotment of land is made in the Cherokee Nation," to "segregate therefrom, in separate allotment or otherwise, the 157,600 acres purchased by the Delaware Indians from the Cherokee Nation under the agreement of

April 8, 1867, subject to the judicial determination" of the Delaware rights therein. The Delawares have commenced a suit for the determination of those rights, which is now pending in the Court of Claims.

It is apparent that the proper discharge of these new duties will require of the commission much labor and great care. They are of such a character as will not permit of the calling in of much assistance of other persons. Personal attention and the exercise of their personal judgment are required at almost every step in it. Much time will necessarily be consumed in the proper discharge of these duties. Yet they must all be completed in each of the nations before any steps toward allotment can be taken in that nation. And upon the care and accuracy with which this preliminary work is done will depend the justice and value of all final allotments.

The commission has been engaged since its return to the Territory in the work of taking a census of the Seminole, Creek, and Chickasaw tribes in conformity with the present law. The commission has very nearly completed a census of the Creek and Chickasaw Indians and freedmen and has fully completed that of the Seminoles, and rolls of the latter are about completed, so that the commission may at any time, when provided with means, begin the work of allotment according to the provisions of the agreement; but in order to do this work an appropriation of at least $50,000 is believed to be necessary for employment of adequate assistance therefor.

In the prosecution of this larger work of taking the census and perfecting the citizenship roll the commission has found it necessary, in order to insure accuracy and dispatch as well as to relieve as much as possible claimants of unnecessary expense, to go themselves into the country and to meet those claiming each enrollment in person, and to determine from their own story under oath and such other evidence deemed necessary the justice of each claim, thereby relieving the applicant as much as possible from the expense and delay attendant upon the employment of counsel to present their claim at particular points and on stated days for hearings. This has made it necessary for the commission to procure tents and camp equipage required in passing from place to place and in maintaining themselves and clerks in the open country much of the time while conducting the work. The result has fully justified this method. In addition, it has enabled the applicants, more clearly than any other method could, to understand the purpose of the Government in these proceedings, thereby creating a better feeling in this class of Indian citizens toward the Government and its officials. Hitherto they have been kept as far as possible in ignorance of the purposes of the Government in seeking the changes proposed by this commission. It has been for the interest of many influential persons among them, to keep them in the belief that the United States in these negotiations is seeking to wrest from them their heritage. This method of working among them is doing much to dispel this delusion and open their eyes to the real purpose.

They have pursued the same method in the Chickasaw country, keeping a separate roll of the freedmen.

They have been gratified by the manifestation on the part of the Chickasaw officials to render all the assistance in their power. The freedmen have also, through leading representatives, been of great aid. This has lessened the work of the commission, and is believed to have resulted largely from the closer contact and the better understanding of the real purpose of the Government.

A brief summary of what has been accomplished during the past year in the work under charge of the commission will show the most gratifying results and a greater advance toward the attainment of the objects aimed at by the Government than in any previous year. Since the last report the Indian laws in force in the Territory and the Indian courts in which they were administered have given place (with a few unimportant exceptions) to laws corresponding to the laws of the State of Arkansas affecting the same subject-matter, and have been made applicable to all persons in the Territory, without distinction of race. These laws are to be administered in United States courts and enforced through United States officers. Every Indian resident claiming to be a citizen can try his title in these courts, and obtain a final decision, if he desire it, in the United States Supreme Court, like any other citizen of the Republic. These courts are now open to every Indian citizen to secure, as against the tribe or anyone claiming under it, the equal use with all other such citizens of the common property of the tribe, or, if he choose, he can have his equal part set off to him by partition for his own exclusive enjoyment. All laws hereafter enacted in the legislative councils of these tribes are to be, before taking effect, submitted to the President of the United States for his approval or disapproval, and all the moneys of these tribes are to be paid to and disbursed by United States officers. The royalties from their coal mines and rentals from their grazing lands are no longer to be paid to individuals, but into the Treasury of the United States, for the equal benefit of every member of the tribe. Provision has also been made during the year for the allotment of all the tribal lands of the Territory equally among all its citizens. And this has been attained as to nearly all of them upon terms to which the tribes themselves have by popular vote agreed. If the agreement with the Creeks be ratified, as is expected, this will be true of all except the Cherokees, and as to them it has been provided by statute. It has been also provided by these agreements and this statute that the white residents in the towns in the Territory, now numbering many thousands, unable heretofore to obtain title to the land upon which they have built their homes and expensive business houses in flourishing towns, can now purchase, at a fair appraisal, the land upon which they have built and on which they have expended large sums in expensive business outlays.

In short, whatever rights, civil or political, are enjoyed by the citizen resident in any of the Territories of the United States, the same rights are now secured to the citizen Indian, and largely to the white resident also, in the Indian Territory.

While much work is still before the commission in the important duty of allotting these lands, as well as in carrying to completion the minor details made necessary by these larger comprehensive measures, yet what has been done is fundamental, embracing the elementary conditions essential to the healthy growth of a prosperous people. By them the government of the Indian Territory and its land system may, at an early day, be brought into harmony with those of the United States and of the States by which it is surrounded, assuring it a most encouraging and hopeful future.

As the Territory, in view of fundamental changes already accomplished and others soon to be effected, seems about to enter upon an entirely new period in its history and development, it becomes of the highest importance that the United States Government should lend all possible aid in giving the right direction and needed support to that development. The relation of this Territory to the General Government is peculiar and unlike that of any other of the Territories. Hardly any analogy will be found in its treatment with that hitherto governing legislation for the Territories. The commission in familiarizing itself, while engaged in its work in almost every part of the country, with its needs, has been so impressed with one great call for Government aid, standing in front of all others and fraught with disastrous consequences if delayed, that it feels compelled to call urgent attention to it. That is the need of some provision by the National Government for the purposes of education in the Territory. While the funds and resources of the several tribes, properly managed, can probably supply sufficient support for the schools of the citizen Indians, yet the white residents can not share in them and must look elsewhere for the means of educating their children. The means resorted to in all the other Territories, and out of which ample school funds have been provided, do not exist in the Indian Territory, in which the United States has not an acre of public land or other property beyond that in public uses. If the white residents are to receive any aid from the United States, it must be from the outside and by direct appropriation. If they are left without any such aid, it will be a harsher treatment than has been meted out to the residents of any other Territory and will be attended with the most disastrous consequences. There are believed to be between 250,000 and 300,000 white residents in the Territory to-day, and well-nigh 30,000 of them children of school age. They are there to stay, making homes for themselves and destined to be a part of the body politic of a State. While some of them, living in the towns, are anxious to educate their children, and may be able to some extent to do so from their private means, yet it is quite different with the poor pioneers in the country, who constitute by far the larger part of this white population. They, however anxious, cannot of themselves command the means or the opportunity to educate their children. Consequently a very large proportion of this 30,000 children of school ages, increasing in number every year, are in danger of growing up in ignorance, to take upon themselves the responsibilities of citizenship. This is not the fault, but the misfortune, of these residents of the Territory. The evils that will come of indifference to this situation can not be measured. They will not admit of delay. The commission has had occasion heretofore to call attention to this pressing need, and greater familiarity with the conditions of the people in the Territory only deepens the conviction that justifies this renewal of it.

Respectfully submitted for the Commission to the Five Civilized Tribes.

Report of Commissioner of
Indian Affairs W. A. Jones
September 30, 1899

(Excerpt from *Report for 1899*, pp. 130-31.)

An indemnity for the lynching of two Seminole Indian boys, described in Commissioner Jones' report for 1898, was made by Congress as reported in this excerpt from his 1899 report.

INDEMNITY FOR LYNCHING OF SEMINOLES, INDIAN TERRITORY

IN THE LAST annual report a full account was given of the torturing and burning of Seminole Indians at the stake, by a mob of white men from Oklahoma, in revenge for the killing of one Mrs. Leard, a white woman living in the Seminole Nation. It was also noted that Congress had appropriated (in act approved July 1, 1898) a sum not exceeding $20,000 as indemnity to be paid other members of the Seminole Nation who had been injured by the mob.

January 4, 1899, the Department transmitted to this office a report dated December 20, 1898, from J. George Wright, United States Indian inspector, giving the names of the Seminoles entitled to "indemnity for injuries or aggressions" committed upon them, and also the amount to which each one was, in his opinion, entitled by reason of personal injury, loss of a relative, or destruction of property. January 19, 1899, after consultation with Inspector Wright, the office submitted to the Department a statement of the injuries sustained by each of the twenty-four persons found to be entitled to remuneration, with recommendation made as to the amount that should be paid in each case, as follows:

1. Thomas McGeisey:
   - (a) For amount of property destroyed $1,113.25
   - (b) For the burning to death of his son Lincoln 5,000.00

   $6,113.25

2. Mrs. Sukey Sampson:
   - (a) For amount of property destroyed 82.50
   - (b) For the burning to death of her son Palmer 5,000.00

   5,082.50

3. John Washington:
   - (a) For severe personal injuries 500.00
   - (b) For property lost 33.00

   533.00

4. George P. Harjo, for severe personal injuries $300.00
5. William Thlocco, for personal injuries 300.00
6. George Kernell, for personal injuries 100.00
7. Sam Ela, for personal injuries 100.00
8. Kenda Palmer (light horseman), for arrest and deprivation
    of liberty 50.00
9. Tul Masey (light horseman), for arrest and deprivation of
    liberty 50.00
10. Peter Osanna (light horseman), for arrest 50.00
11. John Palmer (light horseman), for arrest 50.00
12. Seper Palmer, for arrest 25.00
13. Chippy Coker, for arrest 25.00
14. Duffy P. Harjo, for arrest 25.00
15. Samuel P. Harjo, for arrest 25.00
16. Johnson McKaye, for arrest 25.00
17. Parnoka, for arrest 25.00
18. Cobley Wolf, for arrest 25.00
19. Sever, for arrest 25.00
20. Shawnee Barnett, for arrest 25.00
21. Moses Tiger, for arrest 25.00
22. Peter Tiger, for arrest 25.00
23. Thomas Thompson, for arrest 50.00
24. Billy Coker, for arrest 25.00
                                                                                        ──────────
                 Total 13,078.75

January 21, 1899, the Secretary directed payments to be made as above
through the United States Indian agent for the Union Agency, Indian
Territory, and the agent was so instructed February 2, 1899. Out of the
$13,078.75 to be disbursed, he has paid up to the present time about
$11,000.

Report of Commissioner of Indian Affairs W. A. Jones October 1, 1900

(Excerpt from *Report for 1900*, pp. 5–13, 173–74)

The coercive arm of the Government in Indian affairs became more evident in the first decade of the twentieth century. The ration system, annuity payments, and leasing of allotments came under attack as discouraging Indian self-sufficiency. The Bureau ordered agents "not only to encourage, but also to enforce, regular labor among Indians" by withholding rations unless the Indian worked. In another example of the coercive methods employed at this time, the Bureau, dissatisfied with the way the Osages were conducting their affairs, abolished the Osage tribal government.

OBSTACLES TO SELF-SUPPORT

THE RATION SYSTEM

A matter that occupied the earnest attention of those who are engaged in Indian work and devoted to the cause of elevating the Indian race is the system that prevails and has prevailed for some time of issuing rations regularly to certain of the tribes.

The ration system is the corollary of the reservation system. To confine a people upon reservations where the natural conditions are such that agriculture is more or less a failure and all other means of making a livelihood limited and uncertain, it follows inevitably that they must be fed wholly or in part from outside sources or drop out of existence. This is the situation of some of the Indian tribes to-day. It was not always so. Originally and until a comparatively recent period the red man was self-supporting. Leading somewhat of a nomadic life, he roamed with unrestricted freedom over the country in pursuit of game, which was plentiful, or located upon those spots fitted by nature to make his primitive agriculture productive. All this is changed. The advent of the white man was the beginning of the end. From east to west, from one place to another, like poor Jo in Bleak House, the Indian has been "movin' on" until he can go no further. Surrounded by whites, located upon unproductive reservations often in a rigorous climate, he awaits the destiny which under existing conditions he is powerless to avert. Of the causes that led to this or of the wisdom or unwisdom of the policy pursued it is not necessary now to speak. The purpose of this is to discuss the present and not to criticise the past.

While much has been written about it, the extent of the ration system is probably not generally known. It may contribute to a better understanding of the subject to describe the situation just as it is.

According to the most reliable information the Indian population of the United States is about 267,900. Of this number, about 45,270 receive a daily ration. It is not meant by this that rations are given out daily, but that they are issued periodically, generally twice a month, the quantity issued being based upon a certain daily allowance for each individual. Issues are made to the heads of families, each member of the family being counted, even to the smallest infant, except the children in boarding schools. These are not included in the number receiving daily rations given above.

Except for the Sioux, who will be spoken of later, the kind and quantity of the subsistence issued is not fixed by treaty or agreement with the tribes, but is regulated by the Department according to the means and necessities of each tribe. The principal articles issued are beans, beef (or its equivalent in bacon), flour, coffee, and sugar.

According to Department regulations, the following constitutes the ration of these articles:

> To 100 rations:
> 150 pounds net beef (or bacon in lieu).
> 3 pounds beans.
> 3 pounds coffee.
> 50 pounds flour.
> 7 pounds sugar.

This, however, is the maximum allowance, which of late years has rarely or never been issued, the policy and practice of the office being to reduce rations as far as practicable.

As has been said, the ration issued varies according to the tribe, and its value varies correspondingly. The following will show the tribes that are receiving daily rations and the per capita cost of the ration allowed to each for the current year:

Tribes other than Sioux receiving rations, and cost of ration.

Agency	Tribes	Number requiring rations	Cost per capita
Blackfeet, Mont.	Blackfeet, Blood, and Piegan	1,850	$33.00
Crow, Mont.	Crow	1,850	29.00
Fort Belknap, Mont.	Grosventre and Assiniboin	1,027	42.00
Fort Peck, Mont.	Yanktonai Sioux and Assiniboin	1,654	23.00
Tongue River, Mont.	Northern Cheyenne	1,354	47.00
Shoshoni, Wyo.	Shoshoni and Northern Arapaho	1,400	30.00
Southern Ute, Colo.	Ute	972	13.00
Ouray, Utah	..do..	700	17.00
Uinta, etc., Utah	..do..	770	12.00
Fort Hall, Idaho	Shoshoni and Bannock	1,288	13.00

Agency	Tribes	Number requiring rations	Cost per capita
Lemhi, Idaho................	Shoshoni, Bannock, and Sheepeater....	365	17.00
Fort Berthold, N. Dak........	Arikara, Grosventre, and Mandan.....	1,018	17.00
Yankton, S. Dak.............	Sioux...............................	1,540	13.00
Cheyenne and Arapaho, Okla..	Cheyenne and Arapaho..............	2,500	16.00
Kiowa, Okla.	Apache,Kiowa,Comanche,Wichita,etc..	3,296	9.00
Jicarilla, N. Mex.............	Jicarilla Apache....................	843	23.00
San Carlos, Ariz.............	Apache..........................	2,627	24.00
Fort Apache, Ariz.............	.....do.........................	1,789	9.00
Colorado River, Ariz........	Mohave, etc.....................	550	6.00
Total.................		27,383	....

As the value of the full established ration at current prices is about $51, it will readily be seen to what extent the issue of rations has been reduced.

Of the 45,270 receiving daily rations from the Government, 17,876, or nearly two-fifths, belong to the great Sioux Nation, known as the Sioux of different tribes, located in North and South Dakota. These Indians are not included in the foregoing list, as their case is different from the others in that the rations and the conditions under which they are to be given are specifically named in the agreement of 1876, ratified by the act of February 28, 1877. That agreement, in consideration of the cession of certain territory and rights, obligates the United States to provide the Indians with subsistence consisting of a ration for each individual of:

> 1½ pounds of beef, (or ½ pound bacon in lieu thereof),
> ½ pound flour,
> ½ pound corn; and

For every 100 rations—

> 4 pounds coffee,
> 8 pounds sugar,
> 3 pounds beans,

or in lieu of said articles the equivalent thereof: such rations, or so much thereof as may be necessary, to be continued "until the Indians are able to support themselves."

The value of the full Sioux ration varies somewhat according to the location of the agency to which the Indians belong, but at the average prices paid it is about $50 per capita per annum. The full ration, however, is not now issued, nor has it been for the last few years, it having been gradually reduced in accordance with the policy of the Office.

The following will show the bands of the Sioux Nation that are receiving daily rations, and the per capita cost of the ration allowed for the present year:

Sioux receiving rations, and cost of the ration.

Agency	Band	Number requiring rations	Cost per capita
Standing Rock, N. Dak.......	Yanktonai, Hunkpapa, Blackfeet......	3,215	$34.00
Crow Creek, S. Dak.........	Lower Yanktonai	867	35.00
Cheyenne River, S. Dak.	Blackfeet, Sans Arcs, Miniconjou, and Two Kettle.	2,440	36.00
Lower Brulé, S. Dak........	Lower Brulé.......................	374	33.00
Pine Ridge, S. Dak..........	Oglala............................	6,318	33.00
Rosebud, S. Dak............	Brulé, Loafer, Two Kettle, and Wajiaziah	4,662	36.00
Total.................	....	17,876	....

The average cost per capita for the whole nation is about $35.

It may give a better idea, perhaps, of what these Indians get to take the two principal items of beef and flour and show what is allowed each individual. With the sum named enough has been provided of these two articles to give over 1 pound of net beef and over 5¾ ounces of flour to every man, woman, and child on the reservations (outside of school children) every day in the year. Besides this they get the additional articles named. Improvidence may make the Indians go hungry, but with the rations issued they are certainly in no danger of starvation. Although the Sioux agreement says that rations are to continue only until they are able to support themselves, the Indians protest against any reduction and claim the full ration as a right. If this is conceded, the time when they will be self-supporting lies in the very distant future, if it comes at all, for as long as they are supported by others there is no necessity for supporting themselves, and consequently they make little or no effort.

In addition to those receiving a daily ration, a number of Indians are assisted by occasional issues, and at several agencies the old and indigent are provided for. These, however, are comparatively few in number, aggregating about 12,570. Altogether there are about 57,570 Indians receiving subsistence in some degree or other from the Government out of the total population of 267,900. This, as has been said, is exclusive of children in boarding schools, who are wholly cared for and liberally provided for there.

The total cost of the subsistence purchased for issue to Indians for the current fiscal year is about $1,231,000.

The evils likely to arise from the gratuitous issue of rations were early anticipated by the Government and steps taken looking to their prevention. In 1875, for the purpose of inducing Indians to labor and become self-supporting, Congress passed a law requiring all able-bodied male Indians between the ages of 18 and 45, in return for supplies and annuities issued them, to perform services upon the reservation for the benefit of themselves or the tribe to an amount equal in value to the supplies to be delivered, and that such allowances should be distributed to them upon condition of the performance of such labor. The Secretary of the Interior, however, was authorized to exempt any particular tribe from its operations where he deemed it proper and expedient.

In accordance with the letter and spirit of that law, the Regulations of the Indian Office make it the duty of an agent to distribute supplies and annuities according to labor. These regulations go further than this, and in order to enable agents not only to encourage, but also to enforce, regular labor among Indians, require that sugar, coffee, and tea, except in cases of old age or infirmity, shall be issued to Indians only in payment for labor performed by them for themselves or for the tribe. The regulations also make it the duty of agents to see that each able-bodied male Indian is given an opportunity to labor, and when this is done to judge whether or not the Indian is entitled to a daily ration, determining the matter rather from the spirit and disposition to work manifested than from the value of the work performed. Though agents are required to and do certify upon the issue vouchers that labor has been performed upon the reservations by the Indians to whom the supplies have been issued, it may be doubted if either the letter or spirit of the law and regulations are complied with on some of the reservations.

There has been a decided improvement in the method of issuing rations in late years. The old-fashioned way was for the Indians to assemble at a central supply station on ration day. At a given time the cattle, wild by nature, frightened and desperate by their surroundings, were turned loose to be chased by the Indians, yelling and whooping, and shot down upon the prairie in imitation of the savage method of buffalo hunting of the early days. When the animal was killed a motley assembly of Indians, ponies, and dogs of all sizes and ages gathered around where it lay. The bucks and squaws gorged themselves upon the raw entrails and smoking blood, the hide was taken to the traders, and the squaws divided up the carcass and took it away. To satisfy a morbid curiosity people used to travel sometimes a long distance to visit the agencies on ration day to witness these savage sights. Another evil connected with the old system which hindered the progress of the Indians was the time necessarily consumed by them in going to and from the central issue station. In many instances the distance they had to travel was so great that they were almost continuously on the road. All of that has been done away. Issue stations have been established at convenient places. Beef, with other supplies, is issued to them in a civilized way, and the necessity for so much travel no longer exists.

Notwithstanding all this, it is the consensus of opinion of those who from observation and experience are qualified to speak intelligently on the subject, that the gratuitous issue of rations, except to the old and helpless, is detrimental to the Indian. It encourages idleness and destroys labor; it promotes beggary and suppresses independence; it perpetuates pauperism and stifles industry; it is an effectual barrier to the progress of the Indian toward civilization.

Yet, objectionable as it is, the system must continue as long as the present reservation system continues. Until the Indians are placed in a position where the way is open before them to support themselves they must be assisted. A civilized nation will not permit them to starve. As a method of aiding the deserving while they are learning the art of self-support the ration system is commendable. That is its aim and object. The great evil lies in the gratuitous distribution to all alike. With the necessities of life assured without effort, the incentive to labor disappears and indolence with its baleful influence reigns supreme.

It is difficult to point out a complete remedy for the evils described, but as a beginning the indiscriminate issue of rations should stop at once, a somewhat difficult thing to accomplish as long as tribes are herded on reservations having everything in common. The old and helpless should be provided for, but with respect to the able-bodied the policy of reducing rations and issuing them only for labor should be strictly enforced, while those who have been educated in Indian schools should be made to depend entirely upon their own resources.

ANNUITY PAYMENTS

In intimate connection with the ration system with respect to its effect upon the Indians is the payment to them annually of various sums in cash. During the fiscal year ended June 30, 1900, $1,507,542.68 were sent out to the officers of the Department for distribution among the various Indian tribes. Several of the payments were very large, others were very small, the per capita ranging from $255 down to 50 cents. The money distributed was that appropriated in pursuance of treaty stipulations, or derived from interest on trust funds in the Treasury belonging to the tribes, or was the income from grazing. As the law or treaties provide that these treaty and trust funds shall be paid per capita in cash, the office had no other alternative. . . .

That much, if any, good is derived from these annual payments is doubtful. Many of them are too small to accomplish either good or harm, while others are so large as to be useful for good or powerful for evil. The latter it is to be regretted is the general result. Not having to earn the money distributed, the Indians do not appreciate its value. It either goes to the traders on account of debts contracted in anticipation of the payment or is squandered, often for purposes far remote from civilizing. The larger payments especially are demoralizing in the extreme. They degrade the Indians and corrupt the whites; they induce pauperism and scandal and crime; they nullify all the good effects of years of labor.

Even without any payment the very existence of the money is a constant menace to the welfare of the Indian. The knowledge that he has money coming to him some time leads unscrupulous people to induce him to go into debt; and then, when the debt has accumulated and the Indian's credit is gone, pressure is brought to bear by the creditors upon the Government to pay the Indian so that he can pay his honest (?) debts. If this is done, the same routine is repeated to go on until the money is exhausted. The state of affairs growing out of this around some of the agencies is a scandal and a disgrace.

There is now in the Treasury to the credit of Indian tribes $33,317,-955.09, drawing interest at the rate of 4 and 5 per cent, the annual interest amounting to $1,646,485.96. Besides this several of the tribes have large incomes from leasing and other sources. It is a safe prediction that so long as these funds exist they will be the prey of designing people.

The ultimate disposition of the Indian trust funds is a subject for the most serious consideration. In some cases they are small and in others very large. With respect to the former they can, as a rule, be paid out to the Indians with little, if any, evil consequences. With respect to the latter their proper disposition is more difficult. It is admitted that great wealth is a source of weakness to any Indian tribe and productive of much evil. How to apply it so as to avoid evil consequences and produce only beneficial results is a problem which, though having occupied the earnest attention of the best and wisest friends of the Indians, seems so far not to have been satisfactorily solved.

It has been suggested that the best means of remedying the evils described are—

1. To provide for the gradual extinction of these funds. This is to be done by setting aside a sufficient sum to maintain the reservation schools as they now exist for a definite period of years—say twenty-one—and then dividing the balance per capita and paying to each member of the tribe between certain ages and to each one who shall thereafter arrive at the proper age his or her share thereof, proper provision to be made for the disposition of the shares of the old and incompetent and excepted ages.

2. As a corollary to this, to divide the land belonging to the tribe per capita.

The remedy proposed is a heroic one and is not new. If applied, the immediate result would almost invariably be to relegate the Indians affected, or many of them, to a state of poverty. The remote result might be, and this is the argument used in its favor, that finding their substance gone and themselves in actual want they would realize that they must work or starve, and so from necessity, if not from choice, put forth some effort in their own behalf. The result would be that in time they would become industrious, prosperous members of the community. In the minds of many this is the true solution of this vexed question. Be that as it may, the sooner steps are taken to break up their interests in common and place them upon an individual basis the sooner will they come to a realizing sense of their own responsibility and prepare to find their proper place in the body politic.

LEASING OF ALLOTMENTS

In discussing the ration system in these pages the idea is advanced, or rather the old idea is repeated, that benefits should be bestowed on Indians only in return for labor. At the same time it is admitted that it is difficult, if not impossible, fully to carry out this idea so long as they are herded on reservations and have everything in common. In treating of annuity payments a step further is taken, and it is suggested that this community of interest should be broken up and the Indians brought to understand that upon their individual effort depends their future rise and progress.

It now remains to discuss how this may be brought about. It is more difficult to create than to destroy, and it is easier to point out an evil than to afford a remedy; but it is believed that in the allotment system wisely adapted lies the true solution of the Indian problem. The idea of breaking up tribal relations and making Indians independent was early entertained, and some of the older treaties contain provisions for putting the Indian on land of his own. But like many another thing in Indian treaties it was not always carried out, and it was not until after 1887 that there was any systematic attempt to allot lands. In February of that year the act for the allotment of Indian land was passed. That act has been discussed so much that it is unnecessary for present purposes to quote it here. It is sufficient to say that it provides for the allotment of lands in severalty to Indians on the various reservations. Since then the work of allotting has gone on steadily until now a large number of the tribes are allotted—on paper at least. The operations under this act will be found reported from year to year in these Annual Reports, and the details for the current year are referred to hereafter.

The true idea of allotment is to have the Indian select, or to select for him, what may be called his homestead, land upon which by ordinary industry he can make a living either by tilling the soil or in pastoral pursuits. The essentials for success are water and fuel, but above all the former, for fuel can if necessary be procured and brought from a distance. To put him upon an allotment without water and tell him to make his living is mere mockery. His allotment having been selected he should be required to occupy it and work it himself. In this he must have aid and instruction. If he has no capital to begin on, it must be given him; a house must be built, a supply of water must be assured and the necessaries of life furnished, at least until he can get a start and his labor become productive. The better to assist them the allottees should be divided into small communities, each to be put in charge of persons who by precept and example would teach them how to work and how to live.

This is the theory. The practice is very different. The Indian is allotted and then allowed to turn over his land to the whites and go on his aimless way. This pernicious practice is the direct growth of vicious legislation. The first law on the subject was passed in 1891, when Congress enacted that whenever it should appear that by reason of age or other disability any allottee could not personally and with benefit to himself occupy or improve his allotment or any part thereof, it might be leased under such regulations as the Secretary of the Interior should prescribe for a period not exceeding three years for farming or grazing, or ten years for mining purposes. In 1894 the word "inability" was inserted, and the law made to read, "by reason of age, disability, or inability." The period of the lease was also fixed at five years for farming or grazing and ten years for mining or business purposes. This remained unchanged until 1897, when "inability" was dropped out, age or disability alone made a sufficient reason for leasing, and the periods changed to three and five years, respectively. This law was operative until the current year, when it was again changed, "inability" restored, and leases limited to five years, for farming purposes only.

It is conceded that where an Indian allottee is incapacitated by physical disability or decrepitude of age from occupying and working his allotment, it is proper to permit him to lease it, and it was to meet such cases as this that the law referred to was made. Had leases been confined to such cases there would be little if any room for criticism. But "inability" has opened the door for leasing in general, until on some of the reservations leasing is the rule and not the exception, while on others the practice is growing.

To the thoughtful mind it is apparent that the effect of the general leasing of allotments is bad. Like the gratuitous issue of rations and the periodical distribution of money it fosters indolence with its train of attendant vices. By taking away the incentive to labor it defeats the very object for which the allotment system was devised, which was, by giving the Indian something tangible that he could call his own, to incite him to personal effort in his own behalf.

* * *

ABOLISHMENT OF THE OSAGE TRIBAL GOVERNMENT

A crisis in Osage governmental affairs was reached in the election of tribal officers in 1898. After a bitter factional controversy, and after an investigation had been conducted by Inspector McLaughlin, the Department, on February 21, 1899, decided the contest in favor of Black Dog, representing the full-blood element, as principal chief, and Ma shah ke tah, the candidate of the progressive or mixed-blood party, as assistant principal chief. The Osages, however, became involved in another dispute over the election of members of the national council, which was only settled by the Department order of January 18, 1900, recognizing twelve members as having been duly elected and constituting a quorum of the council, leaving three vacancies to be filled by that body.

These and other considerations impelled the office, on February 21, 1900, to recommend the issuance of a Departmental order abolishing the Osage national government, excepting the national council and the offices of principal chief and assistant principal chief. Such an order was issued March 30. May 19 the office recommended the abolishment of the national council which was ordered by the Department May 21, 1900.

The principal causes that led to the abolition of the Osage tribal government were: (1) Acrimonious disputes between the two factions over elections; (2) entire absence of harmony between the Osage tribal officers and the Indian agent in the administration of tribal affairs; (3) the selection of ignorant men as officeholders, and (4) the profligate use of moneys received from permit taxes.

The tribal government was abolished after the conditions had been fully investigated by a special Indian agent and after the facts developed in his investigation had been carefully considered by this office and the Department. It was determined upon as the wisest step to take, in view of the tangle into which the affairs of the Osage Nation had gotten. It has resulted in the reduction of expenses and consequently a considerable saving to the tribe in the amounts heretofore expended for salaries of a long list of tribal officials.

Report of Commissioner of
Indian Affairs W. A. Jones
October 15, 1901

(Excerpt from *Report for 1901*, pp. 1-7, 39-41, 163-66)

Commissioner Jones' 1901 report added education to his previous list of policies of which he disapproved. There was, he wrote, too much mollycoddling, too much concern with attempting to educate the Indian. What was required, he believed, was to guarantee that the Indian had the opportunity for self-support. Then "he should be thrown entirely upon his own resources to become a useful member of the community in which he lives, or not, according as he exerts himself or fails to make an effort." Also excerpted from Jones' report is his discussion of the Bureau's handling of a revival of the Messiah craze in Montana.

WELL-MEANT MISTAKES

IN THE LAST annual report some attention was given to the obstacles in the way of the Indian toward independence and self-support, and three of the most important were pointed out and made the subject of discussion. It was shown that the indiscriminate issue of rations was an effectual barrier to civilization; that the periodical distribution of large sums of money was demoralizing in the extreme; and that the general leasing of allotments instead of benefiting the Indians, as originally intended, only contributed to their demoralization.

Further observation and reflection leads to the unwelcome conviction that another obstacle may be added to these already named, and that is education. It is to be distinctly understood that it is not meant by this to condemn education in the abstract—far from it; its advantages are too many and too apparent to need any demonstration here. Neither is it meant as a criticism upon the conduct or management of any particular school or schools now in operation. What is meant is that the present Indian educational system, taken as a whole, is not calculated to produce the results so earnestly claimed for it and so hopefully anticipated when it was begun.

No doubt this idea will be received with some surprise, and expressions of dissent will doubtless spring at once to the lips of many of those engaged or interested in Indian work. Nevertheless, a brief view of the plan in vogue will, it is believed, convince the most skeptical that the idea is correct.

There are in operation at the present time 113 boarding schools, with an average attendance of something over 16,000 pupils, ranging from 5 to 21 years old. These pupils are gathered from the cabin, the wickiup, and the

703

tepee. Partly by cajolery and partly by threats; partly by bribery and partly by fraud; partly by persuasion and partly by force, they are induced to leave their homes and their kindred to enter these schools and take upon themselves the outward semblance of civilized life. They are chosen not on account of any particular merit of their own, not by reason of mental fitness, but solely because they have Indian blood in their veins. Without regard to their worldly condition; without any previous training; without any preparation whatever, they are transported to the schools—sometimes thousands of miles away—without the slightest expense or trouble to themselves or their people.

The Indian youth finds himself at once, as if by magic, translated from a state of poverty to one of affluence. He is well fed and clothed and lodged. Books and all the accessories of learning are given him and teachers provided to instruct him. He is educated in the industrial arts on the one hand, and not only in the rudiments but in the liberal arts on the other. Beyond "the three r's" he is instructed in geography, grammar, and history; he is taught drawing, algebra and geometry, music, and astronomy, and receives lessons in physiology, botany, and entomology. Matrons wait on him while he is well and physicians and nurses attend him when he is sick. A steam laundry does his washing and the latest modern appliances do his cooking. A library affords him relaxation for his leisure hours, athletic sports and the gymnasium furnish him exercise and recreation, while music entertains him in the evening. He has hot and cold baths, and steam heat and electric light, and all the modern conveniences. All of the necessities of life are given him and many of the luxuries. All of this without money and without price, or the contribution of a single effort of his own or of his people. His wants are all supplied almost for the wish. The child of the wigwam becomes a modern Aladdin, who has only to rub the Government lamp to gratify his desires.

Here he remains until his education is finished, when he is returned to his home—which by contrast must seem squalid indeed—to the parents whom his education must make it difficult to honor, and left to make his way against the ignorance and bigotry of his tribe. Is it any wonder he fails? Is it surprising if he lapses into barbarism? Not having earned his education, it is not appreciated; having made no sacrifice to obtain it, it is not valued. It is looked upon as a right and not as a privilege; it is accepted as a favor to the Government and not to the recipient, and the almost inevitable tendency is to encourage dependence, foster pride, and create a spirit of arrogance and selfishness. The testimony on this point of those closely connected with the Indian employees of the service would, it is believed, be interesting.

It is not denied that some good flows from this system. It would be singular if there did not after all the effort that has been made and the money that has been lavished. In the last twenty years fully $45,000,000 have been spent by the Government alone for the education of Indian pupils, and it is a liberal estimate to put the number of those so educated at not over 20,000. If the present rate is continued for another twenty years it will take over $70,000,000 more.

But while it is not denied that the system has produced some good results, it is seriously questioned whether it is calculated to accomplish the great end in view, which is not so much the education of the individual as the lifting up of the race.

It is contended, and with reason, that with the same effort and much less expenditure applied locally or to the family circle far greater and much more beneficent results could have been obtained and the tribes would have been in a much more advanced stage of civilization than at present.

On the other hand it is said that the stream of returning pupils carries with it the refining influence of the schools and operates to elevate the people. Doubtless this is true of individual cases and it may have some faint influence on the tribes. But will it ever sufficiently leaven the entire mass? It is doubtful. It may be possible in time to purify a fountain by cleansing its turbid waters as they pour forth and then returning them to their original source. But experience is against it. For centuries pure fresh-water streams have poured their floods into the Great Salt Lake, and its waters are salt still.

What, then, shall be done? And this inquiry brings into prominence at once the whole Indian question.

It may be well first to take a glance at what has been done. For about a generation the Government has been taking a very active interest in the welfare of the Indian. In that time he has been located on reservations and fed and clothed; he has been supplied lavishly with utensils and means to earn his living, with materials for his dwelling and articles to furnish it; his children have been educated and money has been paid him; farmers and mechanics have been supplied him, and he has received aid in a multitude of different ways. In the last thirty-three years over $240,000,000 have been spent upon an Indian population not exceeding 180,000, enough, if equitably divided, to build each one a house suitable to his condition and furnish it throughout; to fence his land and build him a barn; to buy him a wagon and team and harness; to furnish him plows and the other implements necessary to cultivate the ground, and to give him something besides to embellish and beautify his home. It is not pretended that this amount is exact, but it is sufficiently so for the purposes of this discussion.

What is his condition to-day? He is still on his reservation; he is still being fed; his children are still being educated and money is still being paid him; he is still dependent upon the Government for existence; mechanics wait on him and farmers still aid him; he is little, if any, nearer the goal of independence than he was thirty years ago, and if the present policy is continued he will get little, if any, nearer in thirty years to come. It is not denied that under this, as under the school system, there has been some progress, but it has not been commensurate with the money spent and effort made.

Throwing the Indian on His Own Resources

It is easy to point out difficulties, but it is not so easy to overcome them. Nevertheless, an attempt will now be made to indicate a policy which, if steadfastly adhered to, will not only relieve the Government of an enormous burden, but, it is believed, will practically settle the entire Indian question within the space usually allotted to a generation. Certainly it is time to make a move toward terminating the guardianship which has so long been exercised over the Indians and putting them upon equal footing with the white man so far as their relations with the Government are concerned. Under the present system the Indian ward never attains his majority. The guardianship goes on in an unbroken line from father to son, and generation after generation the Indian lives and dies a ward.

To begin at the beginning, then, it is freely admitted that education is essential. But it must be remembered that there is a vital difference between white and Indian education. When a white youth goes away to school or college his moral character and habits are already formed and well defined. In his home, at his mother's knee, from his earliest moments he has imbibed those elements of civilization which developing as he grows up distinguish him from the savage. He goes to school not to acquire a moral character, but to prepare himself for some business or profession by which he can make his way in after life.

With the Indian youth it is quite different. Born a savage and raised in an atmosphere of superstition and ignorance, he lacks at the outset those advantages which are inherited by his white brother and enjoyed from the cradle. His moral character has yet to be formed. If he is to rise from his low estate the germs of a nobler existence must be implanted in him and cultivated. He must be taught to lay aside his savage customs like a garment and take upon himself the habits of civilized life.

In a word, the primary object of a white school is to educate the mind; the primary essential of Indian education is to enlighten the soul. Under our system of government the latter is not the function of the state.

What, then, is the function of the state? Briefly this: To see that the Indian has the opportunity for self-support, and that he is afforded the same protection of his person and property as is given to others. That being done, he should be thrown entirely upon his own resources to become a useful member of the community in which he lives, or not, according as he exerts himself or fails to make an effort. He should be located where the conditions are such that by the exercise of ordinary industry and prudence he can support himself and family. He must be made to realize that in the sweat of his face he shall eat his bread. He must be brought to recognize the dignity of labor and the importance of building and maintaining a home. He must understand that the more useful he is there the more useful he will be to society. It is there he must find the incentive to work, and from it must come the uplifting of his race.

As has been said before, in the beginning of his undertaking he should have aid and instruction. He is entitled to that. Necessaries of life also will doubtless have to be furnished him for a time, at least until his labor becomes productive. More than this, so long as the Indians are wards of the General Government and until they have been absorbed by and become a part of the community in which they live, day schools should be established at convenient places where they may learn enough to transact the ordinary business of life. Beyond this in the way of schools it is not necessary to go—beyond this it is a detriment to go. The key to the whole situation is the home. Improvement must begin there. The first and most important object to be attained is the elevation of the domestic life. Until that is accomplished it is futile to talk of higher education.

This is a mere outline. There are many details to be considered and some difficulties to overcome. Of course it can not all be done at once. Different conditions prevail in different sections of the country. In some places the conditions are already ripe for the surrender of Government control; in others the natural conditions are such and the Indians are so situated that if protected in their rights they should soon be ready for independence. But in other places the question assumes a more serious aspect. Located in an arid region, upon unproductive reservations, often in a rigorous climate, there is no chance for the Indian to make a living, even if he would. The larger and more powerful tribes are so situated. So long as this state of things exists the ration system with all its evils must continue. There can be little or no further reduction in that direction than that already made without violating the dictates of humanity. Already in several quarters there is suffering and want. In these cases something should be done toward placing such Indians in a position where they can support themselves, and that something should be done quickly.

But whatever the condition of the Indian may be, he should be removed from a state of dependence to one of independence. And the only way to do this is to take away those things that encourage him to lead an idle life, and, after giving him a fair start, leave him to take care of himself. To that it must come in the end, and the sooner steps are taken to bring it about the better. That there will be many failures and much suffering is inevitable in the very nature of things, for it is only by sacrifice and suffering that the heights of civilization are reached.

Cutting Off Rations

In pursuance of the policy of the Department to cut off rations from all Indians except those who are incapacitated in some way from earning a support, this office issued an order in June last to the six great Sioux agencies directing the agents to erase from the ration rolls all Indians who had become self-supporting and had therefore complied with the Black Hills treaty of 1877. And further, to issue rations to other Indians only in accord with their actual needs and to inaugurate, wherever it is possible, the policy of giving rations only in return for labor performed, either for themselves or for the benefit of the tribe.

While a sufficient lapse of time has not taken place to determine the great benefit this action will have on the industrial and educational progress of these Indians, the results obtained so far have been very gratifying, as well as surprising. At one agency 870 persons were declared entirely self-supporting and were dropped from the ration rolls; at another, 400, at another, 300. Of course a large number of these were "squaw men" and their families. Some were not only self-supporting, but able to live in comparative affluence; some had grown wealthy through the ration system. At first the order caused considerable dissatisfaction among those it affected, as naturally it would, but it was well received by the majority of the Indians. It would seem rather a sad commentary on the ration system to see Indians driving into the agency regularly in buggies and carriages to receive a gratuitous distribution of supplies from an indulgent Government "to keep them from starving."

Since the issuance of the above order to the Sioux a somewhat similar order has been issued to all other ration agencies. These agencies receive rations under a somewhat different arrangement, as in almost every instance the ration is a gratuity and not stipulated by any treaty, as in the case of the Sioux. Here the order has been better received and the result has been equally surprising. The office feels that a great stride has been taken toward the advancement, civilization, and independence of the race; a step, that if followed up, will lead to the discontinuance of the ration system as far as it applies to above-bodied Indians, the abolition of the reservation, and ultimately to the absorption of the Indian into our body politic.

The application of the present policy to Indian reservations is not by any means entirely new except in the general application. A very few agents had adopted the system already with very marked and gratifying results. On one reservation quite a number of those erased from the ration rolls became earnest advocates for this policy, and were very much elated when another name would fall from the rolls. These became excellent helpers, and rendered the Government much assistance by example and precept. Their influence was very strongly felt and was worth more toward the advancement of the tribe than many times their number of "outside" or white people.

*   *   *

INDIAN EDUCATIONAL RESULTS

The ultimate result of all Indian educational processes should be the preparation of the younger elements of the tribes for the duties and responsibilities of American citizenship. They should leave the schools fitted to cope with men and nature in the struggle for existence. By education they should be made superior to their fellows in the tribes who have not taken advantage of the opportunities presented by the Government. Therefore, unless these processes produce these results, there should be a radical change of methods, so that the end desired may be more quickly and effectually attained.

An analysis of the data obtained by this office indicates that the methods of education which have been pursued for the past generation have not produced the results anticipated. It must not be contended, however, that all the efforts have only produced failures.

On April 15, 1901, a circular was addressed to all "Indian agents and bonded superintendents of reservations," stating:

> In order that this office may form a just estimate of the relative merits of the different methods of educating Indian children and the value of those methods in their relation to after effects upon the character and life of those who have attended the reservation and nonreservation schools, you are directed, immediately upon receipt of this circular, to make a careful canvass of all returned pupils from nonreservation schools now living upon the reservations under your charge, and upon the within blank give their names and the information as indicated on same. You will be careful to give briefly your estimate of their character and conduct with reference to the results of their educational course at the school attended, using the following terms in their arbitrary sense, as follows: "Poor," that the returned pupil has not been, so far as his life and actions are concerned, in any manner benefited by the education which the Government has given him; "fair," that while the results of his education have not been good, they have yet raised him somewhat above the level of Indians in the same environment; "good," that the returned student has made such average use of the advantages and facilities given him at the schools attended that he may be said to compare favorably with white boys and girls under similar circumstances; that his course of life and actions since his return to the reservation indicate that his career is that of the average white man; "excellent," that the results of the educational methods in his particular case have demonstrated that he has taken full advantage of them and he stands out above the average of returned students, and would be classed, if in a white neighborhood, as a man elevated somewhat above those with whom he is brought in contact.

From the data thus obtained statistics relating to returned Indian pupils were collated, from which it appears that the Government officials, who are thrown in immediate contact with this class of Indians, rate 10 per cent as "excellent," the results of the educational methods demonstrating that they have taken full advantage of them, standing out above the average returned pupils, and would be classed, if in a white neighborhood, as men and women elevated somewhat above those with whom they are brought in contact; 76 per cent compare favorably with white boys and girls under similar circumstances, and indicate by their actions, since their return to the reservations, a career similar to that of the average white man; 13 per cent have raised themselves somewhat above the level of the Indians in the same environment, but the results of whose education can not be said to be good; 1 per cent have not been, so far as their lives and actions are concerned, in any way benefited by the education which has been given them.

The first attempt to collate statistics on this subject was made in 1897, and the results were printed in the annual report of this Department for the fiscal year 1898. For the purpose of comparison those figures are again repeated, as follows: "Excellent," 3 per cent; "good," 73 per cent; "poor" and "bad," 24 per cent.

An inspection of these figures will disclose that in about three years the average standard has been materially raised. While these results are extremely gratifying to those interested in the welfare of the Indian, they should not mislead, nor should they indicate the immediate settlement of the questions involved in the final destiny of the tribes. We sometimes forget that the efforts of superior races to elevate inferior ones at a single stroke generally meet with failure, as new conditions are introduced for which the latter have no standard. In order to lift them up to or near the standard of civilization, it must be left to education, extended through several generations, to make them value and appreciate those conditions; then, and only then, can education be permanent in its results. Each generation thus has ample opportunity to adopt some of the conditions imposed, and by heredity transmit a portion to the succeeding one, in time fixing the characteristics of civilization by constant impact, to the exclusion or material modification of hereditary barbarism.

The plan of the Indian Department relative to the civilization of these people is predicated upon the theory outlined. This plan was practically begun about twenty-one years ago, when there were not 5,000 children in all the Indian schools. Taking this into consideration, the results of one generation are conclusive that the time is not far distant when the Indian will have so advanced that his education may safely be turned over to the States, with whose population the adults will be rapidly assimilating.

The data above presented is a complete refutation of the statement that the educated Indian returns to his reservation to take up the blanket and his old customs. That such was the case eight or ten years ago may have been partially true. Then the reservations were wilder, conditions more primitive, and the number of pupils returned quite small. Now conditions have changed, and where then there was one returned student in the tribe, now there are hundreds. Then the boy or girl who had been educated in the white man's ways was compelled alone to battle for his or her new rights, and it is no small wonder that there were many modern martyrs on Indian reservations, where everything combined to wean him or her away from the acquired habits. But the seeds thus implanted have grown an hundredfold, and to-day the returned student is the most prominent factor in the development and upbuilding of his tribe.

The sum of the whole matter is that the average Indian girl or boy is doing as well in his own environment as the same type of the American.

The danger attending the education of the Indian lies in the Government holding out places of profit in official life to those who graduate from the schools. The policy of years has been parental in dealing with the tribes, to pay them annuities and issue rations, until unfortunately there has grown up in the minds of some, not unnaturally, the idea that after their school career is closed the Government will continue to furnish support and maintenance as employees of schools or agencies. The general public is not thus called upon to support either Indians or whites under such circumstances. The schools, therefore, seek persistently to teach them to earn wages for themselves independently, to seek outside opportunities for work, and not wait for gifts of life to be handed to them unsought or not labored for. Hundreds have left the reservations and are mingling with the white people in the eager struggle for existence. It is difficult to obtain more than meager data concerning the results of education upon these brave students, who are putting in active practice the inevitable laws of existence. Abolish rations and annuities, throw the educated Indian on his own resources, and the settlement of the Indian question is the natural sequence.

* * *

The Revival of the Messiah Craze in Montana

May 5, 1900, Agent James C. Clifford reported a serious condition of affairs existing at the Tongue River Agency, Mont., growing out of the prospective revival among the Northern Cheyennes of the "Messiah craze," with its attendant "ghost dancing," which some ten years ago prevailed at widely separated points throughout the Indian country. Porcupine, a Northern Cheyenne, who was the leader of the Messiah craze of a decade ago, had advised the Indians not to obey the orders of the agent or of the Department, but to listen to him, as he was an inspired "medicine man;" and he had made his followers believe that he was endowed with supernatural powers. He assured them that if they did not heed his advice they would certainly die, and that the resurrection was surely coming in the summer, when all the dead Cheyennes would come to life and sweep the whites out of existence.

The agent's report was submitted to the Department May 14, 1900, and was communicated to the Secretary of War, who instructed Brigadier-General Wade, U. S. A., to look into the matter; this he did, reporting May 23, 1900, that he did not anticipate any serious trouble from the Indians concerned.

About a month later (June 8) the agent reported further particulars as to the doings of this troublesome Indian, as follows:

> On April 2 Red Robe, an employee of this agency, reported that a meeting of the Messiah men had been held in the tepee of Little Hawk, on the Rosebud, in which Porcupine, the organizer and chief oracle of the ghost

dancers, took a prominent part. Porcupine told them that he intended to go on a journey to see the Messiah; that they must do as he told them. On April 16 the police reported to me that Porcupine, Crook, White, an old Arapaho Chief, of Rosebud Creek, and Howling Wolf, of Tongue River, were on Upper Tongue River engaged in "making medicine," as they call it. Among the senseless acts performed was the cutting off of small pieces of skin from the wrist and forearm of one of those present who desired to talk with a deceased friend or relative. By simply blowing the breath upon the pieces of skin the spirit called for would appear and lend his assistance in making medicine. Of course the Indians believe this, being so superstitious.

I instructed the police to break up this gathering and to send the participants of this meeting home and to tell them to stay there. The police told me that Crook told them that Porcupine was teaching him to be a "medicine man," endowing him with great power. Shortly after this, Crook was reported as being on Tongue River, engaged in his medicine feasts. He and Porcupine were telling the Indians not to listen to the agent or to the commissioner, and not to obey them; that they should listen to Crook and Porcupine, and that all the Indians should stay together and then all would be well with them. Policeman Little Sun and other Indians heard this talk.

On April 29 I ordered Crook brought to the agency, the police starting after him on the 30th. Instead of coming in quietly, about twenty of the worst element on the Rosebud came in with him. They refused to go into the council room when told to do so, saying that they could talk outside on the prairie. They were then outside in front of the office, and were all armed. A short distance away Roach, a son of Kills Night, fired a revolver, whereupon this armed band charged down upon the agency, with their horses running their fastest. This fact alone showed their evil intentions. The wife of White walked up and down the line, saying that if any of the men ran she would push them back. She was bearing arms supposed to belong to her husband and to Crook, her son. Crook was reported to have said that the Great Father in heaven had directed him to procure the blanket he was then wearing—a bright red one—which was bullet-proof.

There are about forty, probably, of these Indians who are firm believers in Porcupine and his power, and they are, of course, the worst ones to do anything with in the way of advancing them, for they will pay no attention to what they are told after they get out of sight.

I am still of the opinion that the best interests of the Northern Cheyennes and the service would be subserved by the removal of at least Porcupine and Crook from the reserve and their being held in custody until such time as they are thoroughly cured of their dangerous ideas. This man Porcupine is a smooth talker and a cunning Indian. Crook is a younger man and easily led, and he has been in trouble before.

June 27, 1900, Agent Clifford reported that Porcupine had left the reservation without permission, taking with him several of his followers; that it was said he had gone to visit the "Great Messiah," and that the party ought to be arrested and returned to the reservation. About two weeks later he advised the office that the destination of Porcupine was the Fort Hall Reservation, Idaho, where he no doubt intended to inculcate his doctrines. The Fort Hall agent was therefore instructed to keep the office fully advised as to the movements of this fanatic, in order that if he attempted to make trouble among the Bannocks at Fort Hall he could be properly dealt with.

August 1, 1900, the Tongue River agent forwarded to this office the formal proceedings of a council held July 26, 1900, with the Indians under his charge and signed by 328 "headmen and members of the Northern Cheyenne Indians." They condemned the disrespectful language used against Inspector McLaughlin by a few of Porcupine's band, and said: "Porcupine has been for years trying to lead the young men on the road which has made trouble for us, and if he is not stopped we fear trouble will come as soon as he returns." They earnestly requested that Porcupine be taken away from the reservation and put "in prison at some place far away for two or three years, until he learns some sense and quits his Messiah teachings and attempts at ghost dancing."

October 10, 1900, the agent reported that, with the cooperation of the agents of the Fort Hall and Shoshoni agencies, Porcupine and party had been arrested among the Bannocks in Idaho and brought back to the Tongue River Agency under charge of the Indian police, "without seeing the 'Great Messiah' or even securing the 'medicine arrows' he promised to bring back to use on the whites." They arrived at Tongue River on August 27 and were at once confined in the agency guard-house. The agent was convinced that the removal of Porcupine from among the Indians would have the effect of entirely breaking up the bad influence he had among his followers.

October 20, 1900, the office reported to the Department on this matter, as follows:

> The Indian "Porcupine," referred to by Agent Clifford, is doubtless the same "Cheyenne medicine man Porcupine" who started the craze in 1890 and whose operations at that time were first reported through the War Department.
>
> In the annual report of this office for 1891 a history of the "Messiah craze" is given, and it is stated that this Indian "claimed to have left his reservation in November, 1889, and to have traveled by command and under divine guidance in search of the Messiah to the Shoshone Agency, Salt Lake City, and the Fort Hall Agency, and thence—with others who joined them at Fort Hall—to Walker River Reservation, Nev.; and that he by the next summer had returned to his reservation and declared himself to be the new Messiah. The present movements and actions of Porcupine would seem to parallel those of ten years ago, except that his successful return to Tongue River has been prevented by his having been arrested and brought back under guard.
>
> From the agent's reports and the petition of the Northern Cheyennes themselves, it appears that the presence of this Indian on the reservation is a constant source of trouble and danger, and is very detrimental to the peace and welfare of the said Indians. In fact, viewing his recent actions in the light of his record of a decade ago, this office regards his continued presence at the Tongue River Agency as a most dangerous obstacle to the proper government and welfare of not only the Northern Cheyennes but also of the Indians of the other tribes who were once infected and crazed by his pernicious teachings. So long as he is allowed to continue to spread his fanatical religious ideas among the Indians without being properly punished, he will remain a dangerous menace to the service.

It is therefore respectfully recommended, should it meet your approval, that authority be granted for the removal of Porcupine from the Northern Cheyenne Indian Reservation, Mont., in accordance with the provisions of section 2149 of the Revised Statutes, as his presence thereon is detrimental to the peace and welfare of the Indians of the same; and this being done, that he be taken under guard and turned over to the commanding officer of Fort Keogh for confinement at hard labor at that post until such time as he shall be thoroughly disciplined and taught to respect and obey the officers of the Government and otherwise properly demean himself, and give satisfactory assurance to the military officers that in the future he will behave himself and cause no further trouble. The War Department to be reimbursed by this Department for the cost of the rations issued to the prisoner during his confinement.

October 22, 1900, the Department recommended to the Secretary of War that Porcupine be confined and punished at Fort Keogh or elsewhere. Accordingly Porcupine was turned over to the commanding officer at Fort Keogh and confined at hard labor.

February 28, 1901, the commandant of this post reported that Porcupine appeared to be thoroughly disciplined. His conduct had been excellent in every respect since his confinement, and he had promised that in the future he would behave himself and cause no more trouble; he therefore recommended that Porcupine be released. No objection being made thereto by the Tongue River agent, Porcupine was released from custody March 28 and allowed to return to his home on the reservation. Since then nothing further has been heard from him, and it is believed that the punishment has been effective.